MORRIS KIGHT

HUMANIST, LIBERATIONIST, FANTABULIST

THIS PANSY WAS GIVEN TO YOU AS A TRIBUTE TO HOMOSEXUAL FREEDOM

Morris Kight: Humanist, Liberationist, Fantabulist
A Story of Gay Rights & Gay Wrongs

Process Media
1240 W Sims Way #124
Port Townsend WA 98368

ISBN: 9781934170809
Printed in the United States of America
10 9 8 7 6 5 4 3 2 1

MORRIS KIGHT

HUMANIST, LIBERATIONIST, FANTABULIST

A STORY OF GAY RIGHTS & GAY WRONGS

MARY ANN CHERRY

PROCESS

This book is dedicated to:

The Underdog:
The undermined and the underappreciated.
To every eccentric, black sheep, misfit, reject,
and loser, to the odd duck, the quirky, the loner,
the lost, the ignored, and the forgotten—
this is for you.

If one young homo or queer gets one thing out of this book, any little scrap that might inspire or motivate them, then I will have lived a purposeful mission.

The research for this book was made possible
by generous support from:

John E. Donaldson and Dennis J. Perkins Foundation
James C. Hormel, EQUIDEX
Thomas J. Dodd Research Center
AIDS Healthcare Foundation

Introduction

ON A COLD and rainy day in December 2002, I visited the legendary gay activist Morris Kight in his hospital room at Cedars Sinai Medical Center in Los Angeles. He was quite cheerful despite his recent medical prognosis that he was at the end of his life. After a few minutes of pleasantries, in true form he wanted to get down to business. Specifically, he wanted to sign the most recent codicil to his will. I asked a man—a stranger who I saw in the hallway—if he had a moment to act as a witness to this. He kindly agreed and, with his young son in tow, followed me into Morris' room.

Morris was sitting up with his legs and feet dangling over the side of the hospital bed, the sheet covering most of him. He was able to maintain his venerable presence even with a nose tube and an IV. In his usual regal manner, he introduced himself: "Hello, I'm Morris Kight." People who did not know Morris would sometimes mistake him for nobility, or a business mogul. With his controlled air of authority and mysteriously powerful persona, he could also pass for an eccentric underground mob boss.

As he and the stranger wrote their signatures on multiple papers, Morris, exercising his natural curiosity about people, focused his questions to the man's son. He asked the youngster about his studies, his interests, and if he liked what he was learning in school, and Morris concluded with the bonus question: "What are your dreams?" Morris showed genuine interest and encouraged the young boy to go after what he wanted in life. He advised the youngster to "go for it," all goals were achievable; don't let anything interfere with them.

When all the signing formalities were completed, an odd thing happened. The boy's father shook Morris' hand and then he took my hand, held it, and looked me directly in the eye and thanked me with great sincerity. I knew the man was not offering thanks for being randomly asked to do a favor. Instead, it was apparent he was grateful to me for bringing his child into this gentleman's room to spend a brief moment with this stranger of strangers, one who so quickly had touched these good people.

That was the magic of Morris Kight.

I knew Morris personally. For the final ten years of his life, I helped to prepare and fax many of his missives and correspondence. Sometimes he introduced me, in his most imperialistic tone, as "a fahn-tas-tic typist." (I still cringe.) I was familiar with the 6 a.m. phone calls that many people whom I interviewed also had experienced. The phone would ring at 6 a.m., and a chipper Morris Kight would be on the other end of the line—with hardly a courtesy —narrating the day's agenda, all of which would be news to me. He would begin by making a statement about something that needed to happen that day, under his direction, as "a priority," and then give me just enough time to agree or disagree to join his magic carpet ride for the day. And just as quickly, the phone line would die. Where there once was the sound of Morris Kight, there was silence. He hung up as soon as business was completed—nary a goodbye. He was too busy going down a list, written on a yellow legal pad, getting about the day's business of righting wrongs and changing the world.

Later, I became "the ride" who, like so many different people, transported Morris Kight to where he needed to be on a daily basis. Following the list on the yellow legal pad, Morris would direct the day and do his many errands. He liked to hand-deliver certain messages to people—he felt that it made an impact.

Often we had lunch. We talked about everything—politics, men, relationships, family, a little gossip—always peppered with his tales of olden times. He told me many stories, a good number of which are included here. Morris often talked with specificity about his early life in Texas. He felt very affected by it, and yet he never dared a complete analysis of himself. I could almost envision a mini-version of the grown-up Morris Kight moving through the crude, macho world of east Texas in the early 1920s with his perfect posture and elocution. He was, by his own admission, an odd kid.

He once told me about the phony turquoise jewelry that he had learned to make from the natives in New Mexico. (No one ever got the exact arcane recipe from Morris.) For many years, he bought and sold legitimate antiques and artifacts; yet at times, he supported himself selling these faux pieces too. (He assessed my own turquoise jewelry to be of "ehhx-cellent quality and quite auhhh-thentic, my dear.") He could spot a phony gemstone, or person, from across a room. Of course, some people who knew Morris might say, "It takes one to know one."

In the course of researching this book, as expected, I came to know and understand Morris—the man, the liberator, the negotiator, the media genius, and the egomaniac—much better than I had gotten to know him during those lunches.

I always sensed that he was a complex individual, but I had no idea what was in store for me.

It turned out my gut feeling was correct; he had been sitting on a great story. The fact that he was an innate radical was no surprise. Morris was not a weekend liberal who facilitated a grassroots movement once or twice in his life. No, Morris was a lifelong activist dedicated to the bigger, grander cause in the name of good, and none of this was news.

Kight, the grand panjandrum of gay liberation, was indeed a complicated character. In some circles, he was known as an egotist. Meanwhile, right down the street is another group of people who would describe him as a Gandhi-like godfather. Some people I spoke with about him simply needed to vent. Others gushed. A few people refused to speak to me at all. His self-importance is legendary even without this biography. Yet some of his worst and most appalling qualities served a broader purpose and benefited many people—while at the same time serving to beef up the profile of Morris Kight. None of this was new information.

As much as possible I have left Morris' own words intact—including his affected articulation, Edwardian enunciation, and seemingly run-on sentences. His impeccable use of the English language and inflection in his speech is significant; there is not a trace of a small-town Texan drawl—unless he chose to use it for emphasis (and then it was without a doubt an authentic, poor dirt-farm twang). His stories offer not only an amazing accounting of the time (his history is solid) but conjure up a complete picture of the young Morris who showed an awareness of the world around him, while also providing a glimpse of how he viewed himself. Morris' perception of himself is always paramount—vacillating between shades of Oliver Twist and Quentin Crisp. What finally struck me was that Morris never dropped his guard. He never, ever fully revealed himself, even when he was most vulnerable—and he certainly never attempted an honest and humble assessment of himself.

I culled rooms full of files and yellow notepads with Morris' scribbling, and along the way I'd find clues from Morris, a name or a date or a location. That would lead me to yet another fascinating person, place, or commentary, and on it went. Perhaps, in the end, that was Kight's biggest ruse—his story really is as interesting as he was trying to tell us.

Morris told me about files that he had sent in the early '70s to a new archive on the East Coast. He believed they were "lost, gone forever" is how he put it. A few years after Morris died I scoured Morty Manford's papers at the Special Collections Department at New York Public Library and found a blurb in a newsletter announcing that the University of Connecticut had acquired the archive of Foster Gunnison, which included Morris Kight papers. The Thomas J. Dodd Research Center, at the university, graciously invited me to peruse the papers and therein was another treasure of gay history. In Connecticut, there was correspondence linking to letters that I had found on the West Coast in Jim Kepner's papers at ONE and Harry Hay's files at San Francisco Public Library. This book can provide a few missing pieces to the puzzle of the wider gay historical narrative.

Morris did not expect that I would travel to Texas to meet with his former wife, Stanlibeth. On three separate occasions, Stanlibeth told me the story of their marriage and life together in the 1950s (repeat visits were necessary as Stanlibeth suffered a stroke shortly before our first visit). He fully expected that I would interview his youngest daughter, Carol, but he could never have imagined that eventually his eldest daughter would also want this story to be told.

Soon, I discovered that Kight's story fell naturally into the space where academic research meets old-time chin-wagging. Therefore, in some parts of this book I let other people tell the story, much like an oral history. It seemed necessary because there are enough inconsistencies and contradictions and I left much of those intact, partly for entertainment value but also, as it turns out, the many contradictions are in fact an important element of Kight's story and, quite separately, of gay history as well. Areas will remain open to interpretation and subject to perception. This book does not provide all the answers on the history of gay liberation; however, it may pose a few new questions.

No doubt, Morris Kight bruised more than a few personalities and made some serious enemies on the road to gay liberation, but the contradictions and arguments are indicative of the larger gay movement as well. He had secrets and inconsistencies. He was an ironclad iconoclast who operated on a whole lot of blind faith. With a steadfast commitment to nonviolent social change, he tarnished his do-gooder image with endless self-promotion. Everyone who knew Morris will attest that for all his endless hard work and personal sacrifice in the name of a bigger cause, it remained important to him that he receive his kudos. His insatiable appetite for acknowledgment teetered between comical and pitiable. The praise fed a very real need deep inside of him, which later bordered on an obsession with his legacy. Despite all the successes along the way, the accolades and awards, and the aspects of his work that will live on forever, Kight never believed that he received enough recognition.

This biography has not been written in praise of Morris Kight, and yet at times it *will* praise him, simply because the facts, and those interviewed, speak for themselves. His thinking was light-years ahead of his contemporaries. He took calculated risks that no one else would dare to attempt, and held back from taking other actions until he knew it was strategically the right time. For example, in the late 1950s he did not believe gay marriage was a worthwhile pursuit because, at the time, homosexuals did not even have the right to walk down a street holding hands. He assessed, correctly, that the right to marry was a long way off with many necessary steps along the way.

It would take a huge, unstoppable ego to correct the deeply imbedded and steadfast belief systems that made the world so hostile for homosexuals. As it turned out, it required *many* strong egos. The post-Stonewall gay movement tipped the equilibrium of society like no other civil rights movement had or has; it rocked the status quo from the inside out and the world, in my opinion, is a far more interesting and better place as a result.

Of course, Morris Kight's story by no means encompasses the entire history of gay liberation. Despite all his achievements, which will be recounted here, he did not do it alone and the gay rights movement continues. I have purposely included other worthwhile reading that can fill in the historical narrative.

In this telling, however, Kight is central. Whatever the disputes (and there are many), despite how many people his out-of-control ego alienated along the way,

Morris was definitely in the delivery room, if not on the table, for the birth of gay liberation. Kight's contribution to the gay liberation movement and his place in gay history certainly warrant a fair analysis and I have made an honest attempt to do just that.

Several people with whom I spoke wanted to know why I was the one telling the Morris Kight story, and it is a fair question. Any writer worth their salt will attest that a good yarn is gold, and I sensed that Morris Kight had a story that was worth mining. As I delved more deeply into Kight's narrative and true nature it became clear that my sense was correct. It also became somewhat uncomfortably clear that this story is well-served by the fact that I do not have a claim in gay history. I have no stake in purifying or prettying it up. I have enormous respect for the value of gay studies in world—and specifically American—history. My only agenda here is to tell the truth as kindly as possible. Yet the truth is not always kind. Because of the complexities and conflicts that Kight represents for some people, the scar tissue that surrounds his reputation, the utter dislike others have for his "ilk," it became apparent that if I did not tell this story as honestly as possible with an objective perspective, probably no one else would.

Kight's contributions could easily have been marginalized from the bigger account of gay history, which already continues to be at risk because of its *own* marginalization. In my interviews, I came across resistance, an open attempt to separate the contemporary, more respectable gay movement from Kight and his socialist roots. No matter how unlikely it is that an effective gay movement could have been born from an upper middle-class, law-abiding, conservative populace, there are those who do not want gay history to be overly identified with a liberal ideology. There are obtuse efforts to deny the "hippie" element that makes up a huge part of the DNA of gay rights. Kight represents a generation of smart gay men who had to live on the periphery of society simply because they were gay. He also represents a class of activists, a few of whom still exist today, who very purposely, cleverly and successfully live under the radar, financially close to the edge, keeping themselves in a place with nothing to lose—thereby able to risk everything to serve as valuable social activists.

Many people thought they knew Morris, and they did—*at the time* that they knew him. A bit of an enigma, Morris was a loner who believed in the power of community. As much as we want our heroes to be faultless and altruistic—especially the ones who espouse the teachings of Gandhi—Kight's flaws hung out like a stained shirttail at a Sunday social. His insecurities would suddenly slap his most loyal supporters in the face, and yet the gratitude that I felt from most people went deeper than Morris' political activism; it was personal, spiritual and life-affirming. It did not mean *agreeing* with Kight, though most of us will agree with him at some point about something. Personally, I had the opportunity, as many people did, to *disagree* with him and that was nothing to be grateful for either. What was so dynamic about Morris Kight was how he straddled the two points of view—those of agreement and of disagreement—to bring about one profound change that ultimately metamorphosed the entire argument, and he still achieved his goal.

Some will ask, was he magical or manipulative? In return, I must ask, does it really matter when looking at his impact on social reform?

He knew that he was not going to live long enough to witness complete equality for gay persons yet he never stopped working toward that goal. He never wavered from his belief in the inevitability of equal rights for all gay, lesbian, bisexual, and transgender persons.

It was in the final minutes of that hospital visit in 2002 that I told Morris it had been a privilege to be of service to him. It was important to me that I tell him that, and I meant it. He graciously returned the sentiment. That was the last time that I saw Morris Kight, except for one brief visit at Carl Bean Hospice. We spoke on the telephone a few times right up to the day before he passed—he continued working from his deathbed. We talked about this book. We knew there was a ton of material already on him, especially on his work in the '60s and '70s; he told me where much of it was stored and then he gave me his blessing to tell his story. Morris wished for his story be a source of teaching, grounding and reasoning during times of instability and change. Kight's legacy was the most important thing to him and, in my opinion, his legacy stands without him propping it up.

At some point between that last phone call with Morris and where I sit today, I accepted the fact that this book will not please everyone. Morris Kight did not please everyone. I came away with a new understanding that when assessing an individual's life, in the most specific and broadest ways, perhaps it is best that the person not always be judged by their character, but by their actions. In regard to his achievements, Morris Kight stands shoulder-to-shoulder with the greatest activists of any time.

It truly was a privilege to be of service to Morris. It has been an even bigger honor to tell his story. Kight's story is about many people. He positively affected so many lives, people who will never know him, from different walks of life, certainly people I love. His work ultimately affected the entire world in a positive way because it empowered individuals, homosexuals and all the rest of us, to make the world a better place.

My hope is that there is never a need for another revolution like the gay revolution. My wish is that this story will serve as a reminder and perhaps it will offer up a little historical guidance for activists—all the good people who continue to show up and make noise, the brave nonviolent social reformers who know peace in their hearts and courage in their bellies.

Respectfully,
Mary Ann Cherry

No Sad Songs For Him

AL MARTINEZ

MORRIS KIGHT IS dead, but you won't find me crying into my martini. Here was a man, to paraphrase Zola, who lived out loud, filling much of his 83 years with commitment, a fighter and teacher who led every parade he organized and was at the forefront of every battle he fought. Not a bad legacy to leave behind.

Kight was the quintessential gay activist going back to a time when that wasn't a terrific thing to be. He stood in the open like a soldier under fire, calling for the troops to follow, leading the way. I don't have a lot of heroes, but Kight, a funny little man with an affected manner of speech, was one of them.

His life was a monument to high conscience.

I remember him best bustling about and commanding attention, a guy in control of his commitment to elevate and celebrate gays and lesbians everywhere. But I also remember talking to him in the hospital two weeks before he died when his fire was damped to a whisper, thinking the man still had authority in his voice.

Kight had all kinds of firsts to his credit, but you can boil them all down to a belief in human rights and a willingness to stand up for them. He marched for peace and disarmament too, because he knew they were right, but his main cause was to free gay people from the chains of hatred.

He was co-founder of what is now the Gay & Lesbian Center and an organizer in 1970 of the West Coast's first gay parade, which became a declaration of pride and freedom for L.A.'s gay population. It's a model for the nation, if not the entire world.

I met Kight years ago when he put me up for a humanities award given by the L.A. County Human Relations Commission. He'd been a member of the commission then for 20 years and retired just last year. I remember thinking how theatrical he seemed, how his simplest comment was accompanied by a grand flourish, as though he were performing before a crowd.

He telephoned many times after our first meeting, mostly to talk about what was going on in his life, and I began to get the uneasy feeling that he was trying to use me as an instrument to publicize his grandeur. I was right and I was wrong.

Looking back, I think Kight could have been sensing that the end was near and wanted to be certain that he would be remembered not just for his own personal glory but also as a way of perpetuating what he had begun. And I began to understand how theatrics are an element of leadership, the ability to call attention to one's self as a focus of the message that must be heard.

Oddly, Kight seemed uneasy with the praise offered on the day he left the Human Relations Commission, at one point almost cutting off Supervisor Zev Yaroslavsky, his most ardent supporter. He fidgeted and wanted to move on, to use what energy he had left for something better than the ritualization of the work he'd done in that one area of his life. He was thinking ahead.

What I recall most from the last commission meeting Kight attended was a comment by Yaroslavsky that Kight had emerged from an era when it was dangerous to be openly gay but was willing to risk his life for the benefit of a people who had been too long in the shadows. "When the history of civil liberties is written," Yaroslavsky said, "he'll be there."

Kight knew almost from the beginning what it was like to be the victim of hatred. While his father was understanding of his "gayness," his mother remained hostile toward him until she died. After her death, Kight told me in a voice strangely muted, he found notes she had written that burned with hatred toward homosexuals. "She'd have been happier," he said softly, "if she had loved me."

Many will attempt to define Morris Kight as the months and years pass. It won't be easy. Humans are complicated creatures and leaders even more complicated. He was, as we all are, a series of contradictions that eventually merged into a single life's goal. That goal was to galvanize a generation into believing in itself and, in effect, gathering the courage to believe in himself.

Great leaders do what they do partly, I think, to fill an emptiness in their own souls, and we all benefit from that effort.

You'll hear a lot of that at Kight's memorial next month. But what will remain as the years pass is the simple reality that he was a guy who stood in the face of fire, a portly figure in a wide-brimmed hat and with a funny way of speaking, who lived out loud and who died in peace. That legacy is safe. Play taps.

MORRIS KIGHT

HUMANIST, LIBERATIONIST, FANTABULIST

Part I

Before Gay Was Okay

Chapter 1

The End

2003. Program from Morris Kight memorial at Metropolitan Community Church, West Hollywood. Photo: Tony Sears. Courtesy AIDS Healthcare Foundation.

MORRIS KIGHT WOULD have liked to have been remembered as the Moses of gay liberation, as the man who parted the Red Sea and led his people away from heterosexism. He claimed to have founded almost every gay-lesbian-bisexual-transgender organization since the creation of Earth and it was often speculated that he may have created Earth too, for the sheer joy of creating homosexuality.

For weeks after he died, there was a steady stream of praise and gratitude for what he did do to improve the homosexual existence. On February 1, 2003, a standing-room-only crowd gathered inside Metropolitan Community Church (MCC) in West Hollywood, California. The church's founder, Reverend Troy Perry, lovingly began by welcoming the crowd to "Morris' last demonstration."

The altar overflowed with flower arrangements from the offices of every city, county and state representative in Los

Angeles and California, and a choir sang "Let There Be Peace on Earth." A slideshow of about two hundred photos was projected onto the full-screen backdrop behind the speakers: an overdone celebration befitting the memory of a larger-than-life personality.

The program at the memorial listed many of Kight's efforts in the creation of the gay and lesbian movement and broader community. Kight's fingerprints could be found on the founding of the first Gay Pride March; the Christopher Street West organization; the Los Angeles Gay and Lesbian Community Services Center; the Stonewall Democratic Club; and The Morris Kight Collection of gay and lesbian art and artifacts.

The print obituaries had been plentiful and international. Columnist Al Martinez wrote in the *Los Angeles Times* that Kight "was the quintessential gay activist going back to a time when that wasn't a terrific thing to be. He stood out in the open like a soldier under fire, calling for the troops to follow, leading the way. I don't have a lot of heroes," Martinez continued, "but Kight, a funny little man with an affected manner of speech, was one of them."

Dozens of people, upper crust and commoners, wanted to speak at the memorial and had been contacting the event organizers since Kight's passing on January 19. Many were not aware that Kight had already dictated what was to happen at his own memorial.

"I want music, flowers, food, large posters declaring that I have passed on—the whole works," he said. Kight asked for media lawyer Gloria Allred to talk and suggested that "perhaps Ed Asner would come to read." He had chosen award-winning author John Rechy (*City of Night*) and renowned author and psychotherapist Betty Berzon to be keynote speakers.

"The mayor and all of the Los Angeles City Council members should arrive by bus to the corner of Fairfax and Santa Monica Boulevards. They should meet up with the West Hollywood City Council and the Board of Directors of the [Gay and Lesbian] Center and walk two blocks to the Matthew Shepard Triangle. As they walk, they should all be talking about Morris Kight—wasn't he terrific and too bad he's gone."

Certainly no one was there that morning to celebrate Kight's modesty.

The mayors and every single City Council member from both Los Angeles and West Hollywood were in attendance, though none had arrived by bus. This was probably a better attendance than at recent City Council meetings.

Kight's protégé Michael Weinstein [CEO and founder of AIDS Healthcare Foundation] addressed the crowd: "Well, Morris, you packed the house. I can't think of anyone who wanted to attend their own memorial more than Morris."

That Saturday morning in 2003, the crowd that overflowed from MCC Church—onto the front steps and into the streets of West Hollywood—was divided only when another chauffeur-driven car arrived to deliver another dignitary. There was a roster of folks who had come to bid farewell to this "round little fellow with twinkling eyes" as California State Senator Sheila Kuehl described him. She brought news that the Senate had adjourned in Kight's memory and she held a certificate from the State Senate acknowledging Morris Kight as "widely viewed by human rights activists as a key figure in the West Coast fight to end discrimination against gays and

lesbians." After listing ten "whereas's" enumerating Kight's many contributions, the proclamation ended with a resolution by Senators Jack Scott and Sheila James Kuehl, "revering the accomplishments and legacy of a distinguished and caring individual who lived life to the fullest, whose generosity was extended to everyone without hesitation or expectation of reward, and whose spirit will live forever in the hearts and memories of all of his loved ones."

California Governor Gray Davis made a special trip from Sacramento (though unlikely by bus) to speak of his experiences with Morris. He had first met Kight in the '70s when Davis was working with then-Governor Jerry Brown, "and I can't tell you what an impact he had on my life and the lives of all of us then working with Jerry Brown."

State Assemblymen and women, State Senators, County Supervisors, actors, playwrights, novelists, and activists all spoke at the memorial. Some recited poetry. All told anecdotes and sang the praises of Morris Kight. To share a Kight story contained sweet political value—the more grassroots, the more respected.

Reverend Perry told the crowd about his first meeting with Kight: "'I'm going to mentor you, Troy Perry,' Kight told me, 'around justice issues.'

"Morris immediately saw something in me that I didn't see in myself. I gotta tell ya, he was the first person to tell me that I didn't have to be afraid of the police. He said, 'You're doing it all wrong. You don't call them and ask permission. You call them and tell them what you're fixing to do.' And here we are today."

Indeed, the world had come a long way during the 83 years that Kight had walked the planet. He had helped to carry some of those changes across the threshold from yesteryear. In 1919, the year that Morris Kight was born, the nicest thing that could be said about a homosexual was absolutely nothing. Any person unfortunate to be branded a "homosexual" quickly had a reputation as being "sick," "perverted," a "deviant," a "social misfit," and an "outlaw." Shame was automatic.

The pioneer's old-time friend and mentee, Miki Jackson, talked about the "little, bitty, dirt rock hard place in Texas called Comanche County," where Kight was born.

"A more hardscrabble place you can't imagine. There was no television back then. Morris was born in a time and in a state known for racism. Comanche County was known for being especially racist, especially

2002. Morris Kight "The Last Sitting"
Photo: (c) Henning von Berg.

THE END

backwards, and especially hard to live in. And in that bare soil, Morris invented himself. How did he do that? How could anyone do that?"

Jackson thought for a minute and continued: "It was a gritty place and Morris had a lot of grit. And he took the grit from those hard beginnings and he took how much he cared about people and racism and from those hard, hard beginnings, he turned it into something amazing. To think, from where he started to where he arrived."

When Kight was coming of age in that harsh environment, there was no such thing as "coming out." The process was called "getting caught and having your life ruined." Kight remembered that time as "the bad old days."

In pre-gay-rights America, the social stigma of being gay was not only in the eyes of the oppressive straight society. Prejudices and self-destruction within the homosexual circles themselves were at times crippling. Organizing this diverse and marginalized group of people, who often had nothing more in common than their "deviant and perverted" secret, would have been unimaginable in 1919 and thereafter; homosexual life was hushed and shameful, and nice people were sure not to discuss it.

Yet in 2003, the mayor of the nation's second-largest city was publicly singing the praises of one its most influential gay citizens.

Los Angeles City Mayor James Hahn, who didn't want "to make this any longer than it already is," quickly got to the point: "I dearly loved Morris Kight. I appreciated very much when he would call me a 'dear, dear man.' He was a dear, dear man—almost a magical being.

"For over 20 years I considered him a friend and a mentor. There won't be another Morris Kight, but there are a lot of people who have been influenced by Morris, who are inspired by him. Because there are still so many fights that we will continue in his name, this day is a *joy* to remember his life. He was a joyful and joyous person. I certainly will miss him, the city will miss him, the state and the nation will miss him, but no one will ever forget him."

There were no symbolic gestures made just to be polite. People spoke bluntly and from the heart, and a few spoke off the cuff.

Weinstein: "Morris loved me. I knew that because he told me that all the time. And I loved him and he knew that. We shared not only unconditional love but unconditional respect."

Speaking on behalf of John Rechy, who was called away on an unfortunate out-of-town emergency, Michael Kearns read Rechy's prepared remarks: "Among the many reasons that I admire Morris was that he refused to be pushed aside. He continued to fight battles that might've been lost without his energy and vigor. As all good lives finally are, his was a wonderful performance. He was theatrical to the point of exhibitionism, arrogant in his belief that what he championed was right, and a hound for media attention. That is—he had all the characteristics required for a terrific leader."

Appropriately enough, the media was there to report on the story, Morris Kight's favorite topic: Morris Kight. He requested a specific Op Ed reporter from the *Los Angeles Times'* Long Beach office, "to be sure that she writes the story" the way he would want it.

One of the tragedies of "the bad old days" is a disastrous lack of existing history on American gay lives. For the most part, historical records are de-sexed and shaped by what is relevant at the time of writing. Without rethinking of common beliefs and public opinion, the homosexual experience might have been cursed to oblivion.

Longtime friend, political activist and widow of actor Jack Albertson, Wallace Albertson explained one of the ways Kight helped to prevent oblivion from happening again—by leaving behind a well-documented, thoroughly respected legacy. "Morris wished to be remembered, yes, we all know that. He relished his recognition as a role model—and rightly so. But his best legacy will be when an enlightened youth steps forward to pick up the torch and advance our progress in human affairs."

Many speakers at the memorial mentioned how important Kight's legacy was to him. While many accepted that his concern over his legacy was simply part and parcel of his obsession with media attention, all acknowledged that his legacy also had genuine historical value. This was particularly emphasized during a special presentation—before the first break in the three-part event—in which the Trustees of the Morris Kight Collection gave the Collection to the ONE National Gay & Lesbian Archives.

It mattered not that Kight did not believe in heaven; this crowd packed his bags for a penthouse suite behind the pearly gates.

Gray Davis: "God has called him home, because God felt that his mission on Earth is complete. I pray that he enjoys the warm embrace of God. I know that he does and that God will bring the peace that passes all understanding. God bless you, Morris. We love you."

"Don't let them say that I am in a better place or any of that nonsense," one friend quoted Morris as saying, "I will be dead. That's dead, and that's that." However, he never went so far as to declare himself an atheist.

With regards to Morris' religious philosophy, Wallace Albertson said, "Humanism evolved during the late fifteenth century and into the Renaissance as an opposition to the religious theology of the Middle Ages. Humanism dismissed all the supernatural and abstract. It was essentially a revolt against ecclesiastical authority—and boy, could Morris fight authority. Humanism is Man-centered, not God-centered. Although Morris certainly was among one of the most spiritual persons I have ever known, he believed in the essential goodness of mankind, over and above all. So we have in Morris a man who did not adhere to traditional beliefs, but who nonetheless was one of the most spiritual beings, albeit a Spiritual Pragmatist. Morris had no fear of death. But he did have a concern that social evolvement may diminish over the years to come through apathy or worse, a misguided appetite for aggression. Morris is with the angels of our better natures now, and we love him dearly and we will miss him, and he will always be with us to guide us."

Following Kight's specific instructions, a 15-minute break for refreshments and conversation was followed by a "processional from MCC to the Matthew Shepard Memorial Triangle, at the corner of Santa Monica Boulevard and Crescent Heights." It was just less than a mile walk under the midday sun. Many had not worn the appropriate attire or footwear for a trek, but onward they marched. Unlike most of the marches Kight had organized, there were no protest signs, though many were

asked to carry a wreath or a floral arrangement. As the loosely organized procession moved east, passersby stood and watched, not sure exactly why the street was closed off, and their Saturday afternoon was being interrupted. Unlike the old days, no one from the sidelines threw anything at the marchers. No one in the procession shouted political slogans.

Even the police stood by in deference, which seemed odd because Kight had spent years fighting against entrapment and wrongful arrests of gay people by this very police force. It was odd because Kight had been sprayed with mace by Chicago police at the 1968 Democratic National Convention.

The procession passed the notorious Barney's Beanery—locale of the 1970 Gay Liberation Front picket line and boycott that lasted until the restaurant's owner finally surrendered his hateful "Fagots Stay Out" sign to Kight. Yet on this day in 2003, it was very quiet, reflective and respectful.

At last the marchers reached the Matthew Shepard Memorial Triangle where a tent covered seats for a hundred or so people. Kight's instructions had specifically said to "tent the area, bring in a proper podium, and have Doctor Berzon and John [Rechy] have at it. Won't this be lots of fun?"

First, the Gay Men's Chorus began their melodious salute with "Gaelic Blessings." Away from the stage was the socializing area, where food, soft drinks, wine and harder spirits could be found. Guests enjoyed refreshments shaded by a Chinese magnolia tree that had been dedicated to Kight in 2002 to honor him as a founder of the original Christopher Street West parade. Kight never did see the brass plaque that marks his memory there: "Venerable Morris Kight, In Recognition of your Tireless and Peaceful Efforts to Liberate [GLBT] People."

Part Three of the endless memorial became more casual and the anecdotes started to get a little bawdy, continuing well into the evening with an open mike. No one was stopped from saying whatever they had to share—mirroring the code in the early gay movement. But these speeches gushed like an uncapped fire hydrant of gratitude for Kight's life and work. People expressed thanks for having known him, for having been in the same room as him, for breathing the same air as he had; people were grateful for walking the planet at the same time he did. It was just the kind of sappy idol worship that Kight would have loved and would have quietly criticized depending upon which side of the sap he sat.

2002. Morris Kight "The Last Sitting"
Photo: (c) Henning von Berg.

Given the solemn reality behind the occasion, it was fun. The spectacle perfectly fit Kight—theatrical and relentless. His every wish was followed and fulfilled as best as possible: "Three marvelous days of fun, flowers, and dancing."

But he couldn't control every last detail. Earlier in the day, back at MCC, there had been audible gasps of shock when Ivy Bottini introduced Carol Kight-Fyfe, Morris Kight's daughter.

Kight's "other life" was not common knowledge and he had worked hard to keep it that way. Now Kight's hetero-closet was being flung open. People crooked their necks to get a peek at the real-life DNA of this pioneer of a gay revolution. Yes, she resembled the father she barely knew—not as much in physicality as in her speaking style. Her elocution wasn't as affected as his, but her precise, crisp way of speaking and her degree of intelligence was distinctively Kight.

"There are lots of daughters in this room; and lots of sons, and lots of brothers and sisters and heroes. A hero has died, but I see heroes in this room—heroes who I have heard about, read about, people who I equate with Martin Luther King. I am so in awe and so grateful to be here. I thank you very much for sharing my family's sorrow, but I feel truly that we should console you. You stood beside him, you walked his walk, you talked his talk. You lifted his causes up and made them your own."

Carol Kight's humility was all her own. She spoke from the heart of her concerns.

"As a non-gay, I want to say that I still feel that you are in peril—you are in danger. I still do not believe that you are fully enfranchised."

The woman understood better than probably anyone else in the room the oft-ignored collateral damage caused by "the closet." She represented the hetero lives that were left shattered once "the dirty secret" was no longer a secret, though it was still considered dirty. Her tears were genuine.

"Morris was not banished from straight society. He came to you, to live with you, to be your mentor, your father, your mother, your brother, your sister, all of the roles that you can play, familial roles."

She closed by saying: "I thank you very much for your contribution to my father's life, and I love you very much."

In Kight's 83 years, he had witnessed and participated in the creation of many first-time organizations for homosexuals and support groups for parents, friends, and children of gays. Most people sitting in the MCC Church that day didn't know that in 1919 there was no pride for gay people.

Kight had dictated the instructions for his memorial from his deathbed. Included was a note that he had "lowered his voice conspiratorially and said, 'After it is over, smuggle my remains and sprinkle them all around—a little bit here and a little bit there. Can you dig it? Won't this be lots of fun?'"

The memorial program featured a favorite saying of Kight's: "As it began, so shall it end."

Not necessarily so in this story.

THE END

Chapter 2

Proud Southerners

THE KIGHT ANCESTORS were rugged individualists, pioneers: sowed seeds when the soil was right, built whatever needed to be built, and they followed the work.

The Kight name is common enough throughout the South and particularly in the never-common state of Texas. Morris Kight's tribe were English colonists "from very proud but not haughty ancestors." In America, the name extends back at least five generations, the earliest traces appearing in the early 1700s. It is speculated and often argued in Texas barrooms that the name is also spelled "Kite," making Kight and Kite one and the same clan. With hardly an exception, all Kights and Kites are connected to John Kight. Born in a small rural town in England in 1695, John Kight was 16 years old when he first came to what would later be known as the United States as a single man. He built a one-room log house in the territory then known as Virginia (currently North Carolina). John went back to England in 1713 to marry his paternal first cousin, Margaret, returned to the colonies when he was 23 years old, and never looked back.

During the 1730s in Atlanta, Georgia, John Kight's only son, Henry, had two sons, Noah and Shade (Samuel), both born near Look Out Mountain. The family moved to North Carolina where another son, David, was born in 1768. David was Morris Kight's great-great-great grandfather and, like Morris, lived a very full 83 years.

The Kights considered themselves agriculturists and they did quite well. Pre-Civil War Kights were landowners first, then planters (as farmers were then known). They lived life as seasoned Southerners, plantation and slave owners, and described life as being both tranquil and prosperous.

David Kight had one son, also named David, born in 1791. The second David Kight was married four times. John Paty, David's third child from his first wife, Cynthia, born in Georgia in 1833, was Morris' great-grandfather. Morris Kight's most notable physical features were likely inherited from the fair-skinned, golden-haired, blue-eyed boy, John Paty.

This prominent civil rights leader of the twenty-first century was descended from Confederate blood. Twenty-seven Kights served the South during the American Civil War, and almost as many died in the lost cause. Though they proudly wore Confederate coats at the time, the Kights were singing new songs by the early 1900s: "He laid away a suit of gray to wear the union blue."

John Paty Kight was in charge of a commissary wagon in Leesville, Louisiana, during the war, which began a multi-generational family involvement in restaurant and hotel businesses. After the war, John married Mary Ann Smith and they initially lived in Perry County, Arkansas. The couple moved to Yell County, Arkansas, for a period where John Paty began to write poetry that he liked to recite just for the family.

One of ten sisters, Mary Ann's "old maid" sister Betty was a devout Christian Baptist who washed the preacher's feet and sang "What a Friend We Have in Jesus." After living with Mary Ann and John for years, Betty went to live in Sherman, Texas with another sister, Mary Jane, who was married to John's brother, Elijah Kight.

Postwar life was difficult for all Southerners and the Kights were no exception. Most of John Kight's farmland was either commandeered or destroyed so they had to start life all over but they survived as a close-knit clan. Even though they still described themselves as "people of the land," the land that was left was impossible to work without the skill and labor of the slaves. The Kights left their homes in Arkansas, North Carolina, Georgia, and Louisiana, and slowly migrated west and north. Not all survived. In 1861, typhoid fever took David's second son, Marion, and Marion's daughter died soon afterward.

1920. Sister Lucy, baby Morris, brother John Lewis. Morris Kight Papers and Photographs, Coll2010-008, ONE National Gay & Lesbian Archives, Los Angeles, California.

John Paty Kight had a quirky personality. After his second child, Nancy Clementine, survived measles, he subscribed to an old folk remedy and insisted that everyone wear a hunk of asafetida in a packet around their necks to ward off diseases. John and Mary Ann's third child, George Lewis (G.L.), was born in 1860 in Vienna Jackson Parish, Louisiana. Morris' grandfather G.L. was not as talkative as the other Kights but he was agreeable and carried the family sense of humor and hearty laughter.

With their three sons and one daughter, John and Mary Ann moved every couple of months, making difficult pilgrimages by horse and wagon, pursuing seasonal opportunities for work. Following any chance to feed the family and chase down every reasonable prospect for employment, they had their troubles. In Walnut Springs, Texas, in an unsettling foreshadowing, a team of horses threw John Paty from the saddle and dragged him quite a distance. He survived the incident, but was left with a serious neck injury that lasted the rest of his life, often being referred to as "the man with the broken neck."

It was a gradual migration to Texas, first settling in Dallas on Christmas Day in 1875. Later they moved to Ellis, then Falls County, and eventually Walnut Springs. While it took them a while to find footing in the Lone Star State, once they were settled, they were there to stay.

In addition to farming, the Kights sold coal in Avaco, Texas, while others operated rooming houses, before the family eventually bought and sold real estate in Stamford, Texas.

In 1879, G.L. married Minerva Alice Howell, the daughter of an old family friend and Confederate veteran who had served in the war with John. Minerva's father, William Howell, a widower, had married Elijah Kight's widow, Mary Jane Smith.

G.L.'s older brother William was the first to find work in the railroad business in Stephenville. In 1891, G.L. went to Proctor, Texas (Comanche County), to take over the new railroad station. G.L. didn't take to the town in its "swaddling clothes" and did not intend to stay in Proctor. It took almost a year before the patriarch moved his family, the Smiths and the Kights, from Stephenville.

In Proctor, G.L. built a stable life working for the St. Louis-San Francisco Railway (the "Frisco"), a great postwar opportunity, and later became the first Telegraph Operator and eventually, Station Master. A robust man in his adult years, G.L. lived a large, rich life, embracing his home, his family, his trees, and he ultimately came to love the railroad. A romantic at heart, family lore says that he often woke the household early in the morning, playing the violin.

G.L. and Minerva had seven children. Four died in infancy and three survived, a girl, Letha Kight, and two boys: Jesse Kight and William Lee Kight, born in Selfish Springs, Texas in 1888.

G.L. suffered the greatest loss of his life when his beloved Minerva died in 1911.

With good looks and large manly build, William Lee (Willie), Morris' father, was like all the Kights before him: a hard worker, resourceful with a deep love of life and land.

Comanche County, legally formed in 1856 and named for the Comanche Indians, became the perfect fit for the Kight family as they helped shape the burgeoning community located near the geographical center of Texas.

Rich in natural resources—mostly oaks, cedars, and pecan trees—Comanche County eventually exploited its oil and gas resources. Still a trove for fossil and rock enthusiasts, Comanche is one of the leading peanut-producing areas in the U.S.A.

More a widening in the road than it was a town, Proctor, one of a handful of cities in Comanche County, had one thing to boast about: its own railroad station.

Morris Kight described where he grew up: "Everyone in Comanche County was an immigrant from Ireland or England or Germany or the Lowlands, all foreign countries and good ones—established for five thousand years. Yet they came to where there was lots of cheap land. So they used it up, because it was so plentiful.

"Comanche County was mixed. It was on the Edwards plateau, the ocean came up behind it, and for millions of years the soil was three grades, ideal for farming. It let the farmers, including my own father, plow the clay and the clay rolled straight when plowed. They loved to brag about the straight road. We planted that road to go right down the hill—straight like a shotgun.

"Soon [the land] was destroyed. There was a sand dune at the end of the road, next to our farm, nearly seven feet tall. The sand had blown up and the soil did not contain moisture. The wall was fine. However, they ignored geological reality; they just plowed and plowed and exploited the land. It was destroyed by the mid-thirties. That farm had been essentially de-neutered [sic]."

Twenty-two years after Minerva's death, G.L., still full of life at 72 years of age and still living in Proctor, married Nancy Partin, a woman many years his junior. The union titillated the town gossips, with one family historian sternly saying, "We don't talk about her." G.L. and Nancy remained married until his death in 1938.

In 1912, at 24 years of age, Willie Lee married Bessie Mary Grimes from Bell County, Texas, and they also settled in Proctor.

Their third child, Morris, was "born on a cold winter evening [November 19, 1919] at eleven o'clock at night." Morris detailed the events of his birth as if he were sitting right there with them, taking notes. "My mother and father knew that day that I was to be born, as she started passing water. So he got into the wagon, long before there were cars, with my brother John Lewis sitting in the buck ward, and the two went to Comanche County—to bring a well-known midwife. She came and she did all the things that midwives do, and she spent the night caring for my mother and me.

"We had one stove in the house, that heated one room, and the rest of the house was cold. The following morning she cooked a hearty breakfast for everyone and they said, 'We know you get paid for this service, you certainly should. However, we are a little short of money and we have a proposition for you. We want to give you the six dollars that we have on hand and name him for you.' Her name was Miss Virginia Morris and so I wound up with the name Morris, which is English for Moses, one of the greatest biblical creatures."

From the way he describes his own birth, if Morris Kight had not been destined for greatness, he certainly was determined.

Chapter 3

Bessie

"MY FATHER," MORRIS KIGHT would start, "a hardworking man, filled with the work ethic up to here, gets off from working on an oil field in Smackover, Arkansas. There was no telephone anywhere in town; somehow or another, a letter or whatever, my mother knew that he was coming. It was a cold winter night. One room in the front of the house was warm and he came in ten-thirty, eleven o'clock at night, something like that. He bought us gifts. So old-fashioned that he brought gifts feeling that was necessary. And so he bought a kitchen utensil for my mother. It was practical, a dress for my sister, practical. Bought a toy train for my brother who was mad about trains.

"And he bought me an embroidery set with cotton colored thread with the design of a deer and a giraffe. He kissed me. He had a hard beard and I liked it. The kiss felt good and with the gift, I thought that he was saying to me, 'I know something about you that you'll find out for yourself.'"

Kight could recall historical events from his childhood with exactitude, as if he had experienced them as an astute adult. It cannot be known if his awareness of the social condition in which he was raised was a result of being a voracious reader and precocious child, or the reflections of a seasoned adult pontificating on an enlightened childhood. From an early age, Kight exhibited an analytical mind and quickly developed critical thinking. He knew that he was different. He never expressed regret or hurt feelings. He never repressed his proclivities.

From his early childhood in central Texas, Kight described the horrors of the Ku Klux Klan. The Klan was rampant and Kight believed it grew out of the Civil War, specifically from the Republican Congress' response to emancipation: "They passed a whole variety of reforms that went to the opposite extreme" (i.e., to reprove the South). As a very young child, Kight detested racism. Surrounded by racism, he often said that it was "simply horrible what this country has done to people of color," referring to a period in early American history as an "Aryan genocide" of Native Americans and African Americans; we "robbed the life from them."

"In 1925, 25,000 members of the Ku Klux Klan marched in Washington, D.C. from the Capital to the White House. And that affected my thinking of where I was."

As an adult, he realized that his middle name Lee was given in honor of that celebrated Civil War Confederate general, Robert E. Lee. At some point in the mid-1970s, Kight ceased using his middle name. As a much older man, he'd adamantly refuse to discuss his middle name. "My middle name was Lee and I did everything I could to obliterate it everywhere I possibly could. I use no middle name. I'm not proud of Lee."

Anti-Semitism was another thing that affected young Kight's thinking. "I've been horrified by it all during my lifetime. I saw it in Hasse, Texas, in 1929." Kight recalled a time when the school board hired a Jewish couple from the Bedford-Stuyvesant area of New York, as superintendent and principal. As Kight tells the story, he implies that he had clarity and wisdom beyond his ten years of age.

"They followed the Jewish prescription by the book—you read and debate and talk; it's how Jewry is defined, how it's inculcated. They wanted to wish their value system on us and we would do that—I did, but the students were saying that they were bored with school and they didn't like it.

"And so one day, I arrived at campus and here came the parents and the older students—the ninth, tenth, and eleventh grade students. Not me. They conducted a revolt, pretty much like you had in Russia [at that time]. [Bureaucrats] forced that man and woman from their classroom,

Map of the State of Texas featuring Comanche County, almost center of the state, with Fort Worth northeast.
Mapsof.net/texas

calling them Kikes and many hateful expressions. They called them Christ-killers. They never had any due process; there was no meeting of any kind. They drove them to the railroad station and sent them out of town. Drove them out of town, without even getting their possessions.

"As senior students, we had the peculiarity of substituting for the Jewish couple; I was one of the substitute teachers. In the last two months of school I had to conduct class."

Kight was ten years old at the time of this claim.

The unfledged Kight was able to digest the experience and many others like it, always aware of how it affected him. Even as a child he thought a great deal about these situations. His adult analytical mind was always rational, objective, tied to the young self who sorted out these big questions and formulated a more complex view of social dynamics.

"Where did that come from [the hatred of Jews]?" he'd ask. "They used those same words, the same language in Europe during the Inquisition. Exactly the same. It's somewhere in the brain, it's somewhere in the memory bank, that anti-Semitism. It is because our anti-Semitism is so horrible that we can't have discussions with Jews about imperfection? There is some imperfection in the Jewish community. We can't talk about imperfection because we'd be accused of being anti-Semitic."

Another issue that had a powerful impact on Kight's childhood was the theory of evolution. Dr. Charles Darwin wrote a popular best-selling book, *The Origin of Species*, which was subsequently condemned and anyone who advocated it was condemned. Kight demonstrated his intellectual, secular leanings very early. "By the time I was conscious of events, five or six years old, I was conscious of the battle of evolution and had already decided that he was right and that's correct and his was an important intellectual advance. That settles that, our creation is one of many creations and we are ahead of the other vertebrates because of an opposable thumb and an electrified brain." Kight did not inherit this kind of analytical thinking; it did not come from anyone in his life nor was it encouraged, much less understood by anyone in his family.

"I think I was aware of the Scopes Trial—a schoolteacher named John T. Scopes—had taught evolution in school and was arrested for teaching false doctrine. The case became a great battle between William [Jennings] Bryan who was a Fundamentalist Christian [and a three-time Democratic nominee for President of the U.S.] and Clarence Darrow, who had so much style, a brilliant, non-theorist, attorney and analyst. [He was] a terribly decent man. And the two met in court and fought it out."

Darrow represented teacher Scopes, Bryan represented the State of Tennessee. "After eight days of trial, the jury had no choice but to find Scopes guilty. Three weeks after the trial Bryan died, partly because he was dangerously overweight and partly because he had just lived such a poor existence… I didn't talk to anybody about it, I just figured out [evolution]."

Although Scopes was convicted in 1925, the trial did do a lot to discredit the fundamentalist movement of the day. "When I arrived at TCU [many years later], I enrolled in some of the similar class courses. A Dr. Mundhenke, whose first name I have forgotten, was the chairperson of the Department of Philosophy. He opened his class by going to the blackboard and spelling out his name and next to it, 'evolution.' He said, 'In this course the only science that you will be asked to accept without debate is the science of evolution. It's so sane, so realistic, and so wonderful. And during this course, I don't want to deal in class week after week debating evolution. Accept it. If you really don't accept it, that is your business, but I won't argue about evolution because it's an unrealistic [argument].'"

Kight also felt that his childhood was influenced by the Women's Suffrage Movement and he recalled historical events up to and including 1920 in a very personal way. "These militant women marched on the streets all over the country—white women, by the way—to get the right to vote. It was while the troops were in Europe during WWI; they took advantage of that, or the absence of men, to get the vote. It became an amendment to the Constitution... The right to vote is only just a tiny part of feminism. We had to have a new movement, a brand new one; which is not nearly, nearly done."

Kight often told a story about his high school graduating class. There was supposed to have been four graduates but one girl became pregnant and was forced to leave school in her senior year. The unfair treatment of his schoolmate stayed with Kight. He said that it shaped his concern for the "respect of another's sexual being, of not invading another's privacy, or forcing sex upon a woman." He mentioned the girl from his high school when he talked about his passion for woman's rights, including accessible birth control and the right to a safe abortion. Kight considered himself a feminist, another strange notion for a child from Texas. He believed the women's revolution needed to continue and he always saw himself a part of it.

No one could say if Kight always knew, or realized in retrospect, that Comanche County was small and the era in which he was living an ignorant one. Yet Kight always claimed to have recognized, early on, a need for a great many improvements in all areas of social reform and human existence.

Kight talked about the Victorian-era values that lingered from his childhood. "For centuries in the Western world there was a vitriolic prohibition of masturbation. It was considered a mortal sin. There were posters advertising the horror of it."

In 1930, Kight was attending grammar school at the Comanche County Public School. One day the principal, with the faculty, segregated the male and female students. "The girls were off to one section and the boys were off in a classroom conducted by [the principal]. Teaching the horrors of masturbation, he went to the blackboard and made a drawing of various parts of the brain and a tube leading down through the spine to the penis. He had a direct tube going from the medulla oblongata, down through the spine, to the seminal vesicle where there was brain matter. Once that was used up, he instructed, it was gone forever. You were driving yourself crazy. He had statistics to convince all the boys in the room who were masturbating like fury [in their private lives] to feel terribly frightened and inferior. Now [2002], the AIDS prevention organizations hire people to teach the art of masturbation."

Young Kight had an incredibly active mind both in and out of school. One of the first things he remembered figuring out was that he was not like other people. "I also learned that was something you didn't talk about. You didn't advertise that. You didn't say that out loud." He was good at all the subjects in school. "And all the while I was feeling different feelings than other people. I suffered a great deal of ostracism. I was left out of games. There were sex games and sports games and I was left out of both. I accepted that as a fact."

When speaking in the late 1990s, Kight said, "I didn't do what young people now do—turn to drugs or alcohol. Instead I turned to perfecting myself. I started writing and reading poetry."

Kight always claimed that he never internalized the isolation he experienced as a child, and maybe he didn't—at the time.

In 1934, the little school in Hasse, Texas was able to get a federal grant to buy books for their very first school library. They bought 136 books, "with such pap as *Rebecca of Sunnybrook Farm, Black Beauty,* a bit of Mark Twain, mostly just half novels." Kight quickly exhausted the contents of the new library which only whetted his thirst for knowledge. He had an insatiable appetite for books and was desperate for new information.

"I was an aggressive kind of guy and had a way of getting around. I wrote to libraries around the country asking for books. I wrote to a private library that I really didn't know anything about, a library in Chicago. I said that I was isolated in the country and our library doesn't have [many] books. And back came a letter from them saying, 'How did you learn about us? We're a private library, a family-owned library; we are not a lending library, we're not interested in lending. We're not a public institution. However, your letter fascinated us so much so that we decided to take you on as a client. We'll mail you a book and you write back a synopsis or review of the book and we'll decide whether to keep you on as a client.'"

And so Kight commenced to delve into the works of Dostoevsky, Tolstoy, William James, and others. This was rain in a drought, crop to a famine, tinder to ignite a young man's mind. Kight was introduced to many iterations of new thought including one particular influence: the first printing of Dale Carnegie's *How to Win Friends and Influence People,* which he claimed as one of his "bibles." Kight remained a devotee of Carnegie, a descendant of the free thought movement, for his entire life.

"I read the books and wrote back reviews of them. And then would come a letter from them saying 'Wonderful, you understood clearly.' Or, 'You didn't understand the symbolism in *Anna Karenina* at the railroad station. You naughty boy, you've got to think about it.' And so by the time that I graduated from high school in 1936, I had received a classical education." Few would argue that Kight was extremely well-read, quick with literal allusion, and he always, throughout his entire life, was able to quickly process written materials.

Another disagreeable memory of the time and place of Kight's childhood was the abject poverty. It wasn't the poverty in itself that bothered Kight, it was the inevitable outcome of poverty: ignorance and hopelessness. "The lack of self-esteem in the working class, the farmers, or the workers in town was abysmal. Comanche County suffered from low self-esteem. It comes from fundamentalism, a lack of education, a peculiar sense of values and attachment, and the lack of self-esteem reflected often in how people responded to us. They were the most judgmental people I have ever met in my life, my neighbors in Comanche County.

"On intercourse, sexual relations among young women and young men, they insisted that the young women were responsible. 'She led him on, and coaxed and got him and the first thing you know she's pregnant, so she's to blame for the whole thing.' It takes two to tango. It takes a man and a woman together to create a child. Thus, the women were eternally kept in fear. Which, of course, defines the Southern man's life—to keep women in fear."

Where there is poverty, there is ignorance. Where there is ignorance, there will be violence. "The violence in Comanche County was just horrendous, very little shooting because people were too poor to own a pistol, but knifing was very common. One night in 1933 [at 13 years old], I said at a fairly large gathering of people that if the same rate of violence applied in Chicago that applied in Comanche County, they'd call out the National Guard. Every weekend there were at least two knifings. The gossip on Monday and Tuesday was 'he knifed so-and-so and some kind of so-and-so was stabbed. Both dead.' I heard a lot about it.

"Life was so barren in Comanche County. There was so little, there were no books, very little recreation, no park. Fishing and hunting were pretty much the solutions. [And going to the courthouse to watch murder trials] with lunch in their hands, they ran up the courthouse steps to get in, the courtroom was packed. All of them, judging. I was not going to accept the judgment of ignorant people, I fought against it. I hope people can see the note of that."

Kight liked to integrate his life experiences as life lessons for the masses.

Sometime in the early 1980s, Kight was on a road trip along the western coast with Steve Berman and Tony Sullivan to plot the course for an AIDS walk. In 2005, Tony Sullivan described the trip: "We traveled in a little car, up to the Oregon border. Every time we passed [an open] field, Morris would freak! Of course, in his Texas upbringing, and evidently, regardless of what education he got—there had to be some poor dirt farmer [in] there. He told us that he couldn't bear the cotton fields. He hated them! He hated them, because it hit something very profoundly deep within him."

Kight certainly did remember the cottonwood and he also remembered chinaberries, the oaks, the cedars, and the pecan trees as well. Kight grew up "tilling the soil," and next to books, the garden was his best friend.

The youthful Kight continued to counter his environment and personal experiences with every opportunity for new thoughts. He had an insatiable appetite for fresh information and felt an entitlement to knowledge. An unlikely source, as it turned out, was the local newspaper, the *Comanche Chief*, which Kight continued to subscribe to until his death. "Not one thing in the *Comanche Chief* has ever changed in all the years I've been reading, except the names of the dead. They can't repeat the same names in the obituaries.

"In the 1920s, it wasn't practical for the *Comanche Chief* to write their own editorials, so they subscribed to a New York editorial service. And these were liberal, progressive plants. They were creeping in some socialism and some contemporary thinking, and so on, in those columns. Just a little beyond what was the milieu, but not enough to offend."

It was an editorial in the *Comanche Chief* in 1933 where he first read about Mohandas K. Gandhi and two words: "ahimsa" (meaning nonviolent, harm no one) and "satyagraha" (truthfulness, soul force). "And that fascinated me. I wanted to know, who is that? I was 13, but by that time, I had figured out that I would be some kind of social revolutionary. I had figured out that I would be part of the change mechanism."

Through his arrangement with the non-lending library in Chicago, he absorbed everything they would send him on the teachings of Mohandas Gandhi. Kight began to shape his belief in social change through nonviolent protest. "I knew there couldn't be violence, 'cause I was opposed to all violence." Thus began his lifelong commitment to pacifism, nonviolent protest, non-cooperation, and peaceful resistance as powerful forms of activism.

▲

KIGHT SAID THAT HIS ART COLLECTING BEGAN DURING A FAMILY trip to Fort Worth in 1925. "We didn't have much money—we had a roadster, a passenger car with two seats. A seat in front for them and a seat in the back for us, [it] had isinglass windows that you rolled up with a screw. And the four of them [his parents, brother, and sister] went off together, parked on Jennings Avenue in Fort Worth, at the end of town and left me behind. That wasn't considered odd in those days, it was hardly called child abandonment. That's a more modern, fascist creation.

"And two junk stores were there. And I, a five-year-old kid, got out and looked in the two junk stores. And in one was a French steel engraving for a dollar. I don't have any idea where I got [what might have seemed like] a dollar. And I bought it. The next store had an equally interesting, and I use the word with great caution, French engraving of a dancer. You know, this gay kid fantasizing the other world. And that cost a dollar. And they were both mounted, glazed, framed, and they were excellent steel engravings. When my family got back, there I was in the back seat enjoying my prints. They scolded me, saying 'Where did you get a dollar from?' I didn't know. And 'Why did you waste it?' And 'Why didn't you ask us?' and so on. I said, 'Well, I wanted it.'"

Kight developed a lifelong appreciation and a fondness for collecting art. This was key to the person he was to become and he explained it best: "Rather than suffer oppression sickness as others have, become a drunk, or a second-story worker, or violent, I concentrated on art, music, literature, culture, and folklore. I'm an arcane authority on folklore. I am a folklorist of slight consequence."

Memories of his early family life were warm and soothing, modest and humble. His home life was jovial and stable. Kight's father, Willie, was a deeply devoted family man and a hard worker. Like all the Kights before him, Big Willie (as he was fondly known) followed the work. G.L. was able to give him work on the railroad as needed, but it wasn't consistent. Willie was a skilled carpenter and a blacksmith who also worked in the oil fields when he could. In 1919, Willie and Bessie traded a piano and a thousand dollars for a farm in Proctor, Texas, and he worked the land, including the livestock, for the rest of his young life.

Kight's father had the middle name Lee as well. "Everyone named Lee in the South is carrying on a racist tradition—that [General] Lee was the greatest man of them all. My father, who was a good man, said that it was wrong, morally, critically, and socially incorrect—that it was guaranteeing slavery. I think that even now, young men in the South are named Lee and it's just a racist name." Yet, family tradition to use the name Lee took precedence.

Kight did not often talk about his father but when he did, he liked to make it memorable. "My father's mother and father named him Willie, a pretty good name. His nickname was Dick; dick is a word that describes a man's penis, and while I never saw it, he was said to have a simply humongous penis. And all of his brothers, sisters, classmates, everybody called him Dick—a sexist thing to call a man by a physical characteristic.

"One day in 1926, [Mother] said, 'Kids, we're going to have a picnic with your father.' So she went to the kitchen and cooked biscuits, and whatever. John, Lucy Mildred, Mother, and I started out to the back of the farm, where my father was plowing and singing. He had a wonderful singing voice. He pushed the mules along as he was singing: 'I'm going home to my Lord and be free.' So we stood in the woods, peering through the trees and brush to see him, and listened. I had never heard anything so beautiful in my life. Mother said, 'This is your father.' Eventually, we came out, he quit plowing, and we had our picnic."

The song lyrics "Home to My Lord" would stay with Kight for the rest of his life and would serve a significant moment for him in 1969.

"There were two kinds of Protestants in the rural South," Kight said, "Methodists and Baptists. We fell on the Methodists side"—a Protestant family of Methodists. Sometime around 1925, the family moved from the farm in Proctor to a home in Hasse. At that time, the family went to church every Sunday. "And one Sunday morning, I couldn't have been a minute more than five, I came to my mother and father and said, 'I would like not to go with you today. I know that I'm young and you worry about me, but I'm okay. I can take care of myself and I have a lot of gardening to do.'"

Kight said that he stayed home from church every Sunday thereafter and "tilled the soil." "Because," he explained, "they were saying things that I knew were not true." When pressed about the subject of religion in his childhood, Kight couldn't pass up an opportunity to demonstrate a bigger matter than just going to church.

"The marriage of church and state, I have always, all my lifetime, disagreed with the marriage of church and state. The Bill of Rights of the United States, the most powerful legal document in the world, makes us stronger and tougher; it gives things that the government can't do and the citizens can. Congress passed a law. So I really advocated that religion be private. Despite that the schools in Hasse and Comanche (which was seven miles north) and the principal of the Comanche School was a Fundamentalist Christian.

"Every Wednesday we had chapel—that public school conducted a church service, we had Bible study and the class was encouraged to bring a Bible and for an hour we had to recite Bible passages and sang Fundamentalist hymns. After we recited three Bible pages, I said 'I won't do that.' Well, the principal came raging, eyes blazing and waving a Bible in my face, 'If you don't have a Bible we'll buy you one.' I'm ten years old. Ultimately, he hated me so badly that going to chapel was a frightening experience. It was a frightening experience anyway. I believe that any integration of church and state is a pawn."

Kight would only identify Pacifism-Humanism as his 'religion.'

All in all, early family life was idyllic and loving.

"April 7, 1927, my father, my brother, my sister, my mother, and I worked on the family plot which was in downtown Hasse. All around the lot were a row of Chinaberry trees. Chinaberry is the most nuisive [sic], nonsensical tree in the world. It has something dropping all the time. In the spring, it bloomed and the tip of the bloom would fall and make a great mess. Then that bloom was replaced by a seed, a very oily seed, terribly oily. That fell and made an enormous amount of rubbish. We cleaned out the stalls at the barn and put all that rubbish in the wagon.

"My father, a cheerful man, went singing off to the farm, which was two miles west of Hasse, to put the rubbish into the soil, to refurbish the soil. When he returned, the pair of Percheron mares (Percheron mares are big, somewhat like the Clydesdales), passed over a wooden bridge crossing the creek. At that very moment a great burst of lightning struck—big, big, big, straight down, and a heavy rain started. The sound of the wheels hitting the wood on the bridge, the fire of the lightning, and the rain spooked the horses and they started running. They got totally out of control.

"The horses rounded a corner headed toward our house, two or three blocks away. The wagon went off the road and ran into a pole. The pole fell across him and crushed him to death."

Kight was not yet eight years old when his father died.

Life was forever changed for everyone in the family.

Kight talked about his father's death with abject objectivity and even emotions—focusing on how it affected the rest of his family, not him. Bessie was an absolute wreck after her husband died. "She was simply unable to cope. And my brother loved him [Father] desperately." Many years later John Louis wrote, in his own handwriting, "4-7-1927 Wagon turned over. That broke everything."

Kight continued, "It was just maddening. Within two weeks, my brother ran away from home, at 13 years old, and never returned. My mother had the worst climacteric that I have ever known anyone to have. She was grieving a lot. She'd stand in the farm crying after my father. My sister did not receive parental guidance from my mother. I thought she had been abused [by Mother] more than we had." In the labor-hungry, post-suffrage era that valued men over women, Lucy was deemed a burden. She left home at 14 years old and never returned. From that time on, for all practical purposes, Kight was an only child of a traumatized, single mother.

"With a climacteric mother, ignorance, alienation and grief, I became an adult in a hell of a hurry." Kight accepted his lot in life and discovered, by eight years of age, that he was a resourceful child.

"That was when I started working. When I was a kid, I had started a garden. When my father was killed, I intensified the gardening. I planted copper dams, arranged rocks across the stream, and created a dam behind it, to block it, and that was working. Grass was growing, trees were growing, the whole farm became like a jungle."

Bessie was prone to fits of selfishness and isolation. Kight withdrew and learned how to take care of the home, the utilities, and himself. He repaired the family's old Model A, and he learned how to negotiate a contract. They were still making payments on one of the more valuable farms in Hasse so they almost immediately took in a boarder for the extra income. Mother and son were a bit odd, loners, dependent upon each other so that they would not need anyone else. "We did not have a strong church identity, it just wasn't that kind of family—church, yes, but church identity? Not me, certainly." Growing up in Texas he "didn't have a strong political identity because there really was no politics except for the Board of Education.

"And so I had independent time because I was so different—absolutely very different from everybody else. Well, I had some respect from my classmates at Hasse School. At Comanche Schools, I was terrified by the student body who called me 'sister' and they hooted at me. One day, a child on the school ground shot me with a BB gun and the BB hit my left breast and it was really very painful. Not any interference from the faculty, no reprimand, nothing. I realized that I was violated."

Kight consistently claimed that he did not internalize his experiences as a child, and yet he'd say, "I was constantly thinking. When we went back to the farm, for we kept going back there, I was isolated. I was ostracized, literally ostracized. And so I found something to fill up every moment of the time. I had a shovel and I went around the farm making cofferdams, gullies, and I created a brick wall to stop the water and hold back the soil. It cured the erosion, which had eaten our farm nearly alive. In 1932, I planted cottonwood—I actually saw the cotton go into the ground and I chose it."

In 1962, Kight went back to Texas with his mother to visit that same farm.

"When we arrived, that farm that I had tilled with a shovel [as a child], the cottonwood was 60 feet tall, rye grass was level with the shoulder, the gullies had all been cured, and it was just a grower's paradise. I stood down the road and looked upward and I wept. I wept awhile because I had created that. And I knew that I would never see that place again because I was going on."

Kight never forgot the isolation and grief. Perhaps while toiling that soil, trying to imagine his place in the world, as a youth Kight planted many seeds inside his fertile mind. Seeds that would take longer than it took the cottonwood to grow, but would, over time, go on to sow a new and improved life for many people.

"My mother was not a very sentimental person" was one way that Kight described his mother. Another family member described Bessie as a "pernicious influence in Morris' life." No one's candidate for Mother of the Year, she was likely at the root of Kight's ease with the more sinister, dark side of life.

She gave depth to Kight's Southern roots without rancor and her background solidified his pioneering spirit. Grimes, another common surname in Texas, originated in Northern Europe, the Ireland-England region. Bessie Mary Grimes Kight was born sometime around 1890 in Bell County, Moffat, Texas. She was the sixth of eight children born to James Jesse (Jim) and Lucy Grimes. Unlike his father's ancestry, Kight's maternal lineage is steeped in Bible-thumping early American fundamentalism.

Jim Grimes was a Bell County native, born in 1853. His father, James Alexander, Kight's maternal great-grandfather, settled in Maury County, Tennessee in 1821 and became a Methodist minister. The son of William and Mildred Ricketts Grimes, he served as a commissioner in Hampshire, Tennessee. James Alexander first purchased land in Lafayette County, Mississippi, and sold that land in 1846 in order to move to a newly developed region, Smith County, Texas.

James Alexander married Edna Angelina Beene from Marion County, Alabama, in 1847. Always active in the Methodist Church, they had eight children. Eventually settling in Moffat, James Alexander did very well in "land transactions," which would be known as "banking" in today's terms. Kight's grandfather, Jim, was their fourth child.

Jim Grimes married Lucy J. Bland on January 4, 1872, two years after Lucy moved to Bell County from Arkansas with her family. The third of eight children, Lucy was 16 years old when she married Jim Grimes—an unlikely match as Lucy's grandfather was Reverend Jesse 'Old Hardsides' Bland, a famed Baptist minister.

Destined for fame from a very young age, Old Hardsides was an imposing figure with a larger-than-life personality, nicknamed for his hard-boiled preaching style. Hardsides was born in Nelson County, Kentucky, into a family of early settlers in the midst of brutal hostility between Native Americans and the encroaching white men. A particularly brutal raid on Kincheloe Station in 1782 proved to be a massive victory for the multiple tribes, after which the area became known as Burnt Station.

During the raid, the local Indians kidnapped young Jesse Bland, who could not have been more than five years old. Local whites preferred a quick death to the frightful possibility of capture by the Indians but Jesse Bland survived and wandered back to his people many years later to tell the tale. He had grown so much that he was hardly recognizable, but surviving family members eventually identified him from some childhood scars.

Kight never met Old Hardsides as Reverend Jesse Bland died in 1843. Of all of Kight's ancestors, Old Hardsides is the one Kight probably favored most in terms of his drive, ambition, and personal presence. It was not the content of Old Hardsides sermons that Morris would have responded to, but Old Hardsides' style in handling of the crowd.

In later years, Morris woke the neighbors whilst watching fundamentalist preachers on late-night television; he found a secret pleasure as well as an inexplicable comfort in televangelist preachers. It fueled him, inspired him. The louder and more impassioned the better; he would blast them into the night, regardless of the content. It served as background music for the elderly Kight.

Indirectly, Old Hardsides contributed to the modern civil rights movement through the persuasive personality and charisma that he passed on to Morris, his great-great-grandson.

Old Hardsides was married three times. His third wife was Nancy Kilpatrick; the seventh of their eight children, Calvin Bland, was born in Saline County, Arkansas, in 1825 and was Kight's maternal great-grandfather. Calvin married Carolina "Julia" Chennault (born in 1829 in Alabama) and they moved their large family, including Kight's grandmother, Lucy, to Bell County, Texas, in 1870.

It is not known what influence the strong Methodist and Baptist roots had in the James and Lucy Grimes household, but what is known is that it had no constructive effect on their sixth child, Bessie Mary Grimes.

Kight did not talk about his mother or her family often. “They are racist in the South,” he said. “I went to the Alamo with an aunt of mine. ‘Can Morris come with me? I want to show him the list of Grimes people who died at the Alamo.’

“I ran away from her. I was up to here with anyone who would honor that kind of imperialism... We took the land from the Mexicans by guile and force, and force of arms is a form of subversion. We are living on land that once belonged to the Mexicans; it also once belonged to the Spanish Empire; it also belonged to the Native Americans and it belonged to France. It went from one imperialism to another.

“The Alamo, in my world, is not an honor. By the way, saying that in a book will get me tried after my death. They will have a trial for me for besmirching the Alamo while our ancestors died there.”

There was one story about his mother’s side of the family that did come up. “The Ku Klux Klan became our government; it was a government. My mother’s father had a young man working for him who was having sex with a neighborhood woman. That led to her getting pregnant. And so the Ku Klux Klan came at 4:00 in the morning and said, ‘Mister Grimes, have nothing to do with this, this is none of your business.’ They took him [the laborer] out and hung him. You could think of a dozen happier solutions.”

By 1910, James, Lucy, and their four sons had moved to Bronte, a young West Texas town, two hundred miles away in Coke County. Bessie didn’t go with them. At around 16 years of age, she had keen survivor instincts and set out on her own. It is not known what she did during the two years before she found her way to San Angelo, Texas, and into the arms of ‘Big Willie’ Kight. They were married in 1912 and by all accounts, even though it was another seemingly unlikely match, Willie was a good catch for the girl from Moffat.

Settled in Comanche County, she didn’t quite fit in with the lively, tight-knit Kight-Smith-Howell family. The Kight clan were not certain what to make of the stranger who arrived with no family, though they knew of her great-grandfather, Reverend Jesse ‘Old Hardsides’ Bland. They also knew of the financial successes of her other grandfather, James Alexander Grimes. They thought that Bessie “came from money,” and she did nothing to dissuade their assumptions.

While Willie was alive, Bessie didn’t make enemies but she never went out of her way to make close friends. Bessie did fit in as a hard worker, and she and Willie weathered the seasonal and economic changes. There was nothing sensational about Bessie except that she had married Willie. She doused Willie with affection and kept the marriage alive in all ways. Willie shared everything with his children and created a family. From early on, Kight knew that his mother was not a very affectionate person with her children. She was not a nurturing mother; she took good care of her children, but her sentiments were focused on her husband.

After Willie’s death, she was a wretched mess. “She hardly functioned,” Kight said. All of her relationships became contentious. She alienated Kight’s paternal grandfather, G.L., who still lived in Proctor, but Kight never mentioned G.L. as a significant part of his childhood. A few years after Willie’s death, G.L. married Nancy Partine, a much younger woman.

Soon after Willie’s death, when Morris was seven years old, the family unit vanished. John Louis, who was six years older than Morris, left immediately after the funeral and never came back home to visit. Kight made efforts to keep in touch with John Louis and his family, traveling to Odessa from New Mexico for a cousin's wedding in 1951. In later years, Kight was able to establish relationships with John Louis' children as adults and had a marginal relationship with this family.

Kight's sister, Lucy Mildred, four years older, was indifferent toward her little brother and that distance remained for most of their lives. On the tip of Bessie's boot, Lucy left home by age 14, making room in the Proctor house for a paying boarder. Lucy stayed with maternal relatives for a short time, then she was on her own.

Kight grew up "in a hell of a hurry. I became the head of the house before I was ten years old." As time went on, Bessie became an "awfully mean person." Yet Kight remained loyal to her, even through the worst of times that were still yet to come. Willie had died two years before the Depression hit and though they were never affluent, by keeping the farm working, they were financially sound.

In addition to the alienation that young Kight was experiencing, his life became terribly strange and strained. There is no indication of physical abuse, but the psychological twists and turns would have an effect on a young boy, even one who claimed that he "did not internalize."

After Willie's death, while Kight was still quite young, Bessie trained him to become a skilled and cunning thief. She did not tell him to steal food or anything out of need. No. Bessie had a feeling of entitlement and she taught Kight to take personal items from other people's homes or luxury items from stores. She'd say, "Mother wants that lovely lamp" and boost little Morris up to an open window of a home. He'd squirm his way in and either unlatch the inside lock and let Bessie in, or he himself would snatch up the lamp or a vase or a picture frame, whatever his mother wanted. Once out of the house, he'd earn that nod of approval that he so rarely received. They would walk down the road, not very likely hand-in-hand, she with a lump under her coat and no one the wiser.

The cunning thievery provided Kight with a contingency expertise that would later come in handy. For Bessie, it satisfied a deep emotional need. She always felt wronged by the world; grief did not help. Thievery gave her a feeling of importance and control over young Morris. For his part, it was vital that he fulfill her every demand. She was his entire world. Kight needed to keep her satisfied; he accepted that as his mission in life. Her approval gave him purpose and value.

Just as he was unlike the other children in school, Kight's mother was an outsider. He found an identity in her. In 1984, Kight described his mother to Greg Byrd for a *Frontiers* article: "She had some kind of an independent daring that I enjoyed and that I think I benefited from."

Despite Bessie's pathology, Kight was, for the most part, a healthy, curious ten-year-old. "I commenced to find out who I was, to learn more about myself. As a child, I was different from anyone else. I was literate, and I spoke clearly, brilliantly, and thoughtfully. I read poetry and wrote poetry. I started developing a philosophy of social positions." Being a loner did not burden Kight with modesty.

"I left Comanche County June 30, 1936, when I graduated from Hasse High School. There were signs on the road saying, 'This Way Out,' and I thought 'Good grief! They're speaking to me, time to get out of here.' And so I fled." Immediately after Morris' graduation, in the middle of the Great Depression, mother and son packed up the Proctor house, leased out the farm and headed north, with young Morris in the driver's seat.

Texas boasted a year-long, statewide celebration of its centennial victory over the Mexican Army at San Jacinto and the Republic's independence. Just about every community had ongoing festive events honoring the state. Dallas had the first World's Fair ever held below the Mason-Dixon Line, beginning in June of 1936. Mother and son stopped at celebrations along the way and yet, as unsentimental as Bessie was and as unaffected by the Republic's independence as young Morris was, the two travelers showed no interest to stop in Dallas for the World's Fair.

In the middle of the most severe heat wave and drought in modern history of North America, they made their way to Fort Worth—to a region established post-Civil War infamously known as Hell's Half Acre. Hell's Half Acre was a generic name for any red-light district in any of the many frontier towns. The southern end of Fort Worth was the first thing cattle trail drivers, who were making their way north to Kansas, saw as they approached the town from the south. Only those looking for trouble or mischief stopped in The Acre to partake in the usual activities: brawling, gambling, cockfighting, horse racing, and prostitution.

The first thing Bessie and Morris saw when they hit Fort Worth was viewed as a golden opportunity: a collection of one- and two-story saloons, dance halls, bawdy houses, a lot of empty lots, and a handful of legitimate businesses.

Even though there were quite a few years left in the Depression in Texas, they were able to open a roadhouse diner and beer joint at 310 South Jennings Avenue, in the expanded region of Hell's Half Acre. They called the establishment The Worth Inn; "for what it's worth," Kight would joke. They served hamburgers, cheeseburgers, bowls of chili, and beer at ten cents a bottle.

The area attracted gunmen, highway robbers, card sharks, con men, and shady ladies, and The Worth Inn served everyone. Kight described the time: "Bootlegging became a very proper earning for some people, including us. The bootleggers were blamed for everything that ever happened negatively. Real bootlegged booze was really good. I was a beer master and, oh, I approached it scientifically and the beer that I produced was just the best—very, very popular for miles around. No one ever got drunk at our place. They couldn't afford it: beer was ten or fifteen cents per bottle, four bottles and you were broke."

Kight stressed, "We never got drunk, nor did anyone ever become an alcoholic, never. It was handled as a beverage, as a social experience. And yet we were blamed."

Predictably, this was the beginning of Kight's sex life as the area and the business they were in was an entrée for the young gay man who claimed to have had quite a lot of sex with various people at 17 years old. "Talk about pre-NAMBLA!" he'd add.

As an adult, he was very open about having had sex with a lot of men and women. "I never felt guilty about that. I suppose it was a natural kind of experience. Fort Worth was quite gay at the time and it was also very closeted. Of course, [the men] were alcoholics, all of them." Ignoring his contradictions about alcoholism, Kight described his sex partners: "Some of them suffered horribly. They had all kinds of problems."

For all his activity, Kight was discreet. He said that "to proclaim being gay at that time was certain genocide.

"I never believed in our relationships' inferiority. I never thought that we were queer. Queer is oppressive. Queer was considered a really bad thing; it was unpopular. I thought we were of value but we hadn't yet found a method to express that."

Kight never believed in his own inferiority and always possessed a sturdy ego.

Though he had some very powerful romances at the time, with no confidants, he didn't talk about them and later claimed that he never felt badly or traumatized. It was a very dynamic internal world for the young man who claimed that he did not internalize. "Since I didn't have a family of any kind—my mother was not there as a mother—we didn't talk about such things." He figured it out and just accepted himself without anyone's permission.

From the gate, as a rite of passage, Kight engaged in a lot of anonymous sex. These men, many of them strangers passing through town, temporal romances with transients, it all seemed so natural for him: the only affections Kight knew as a burgeoning young man.

Kight wasn't the only one at The Worth Inn who was having a lot of sex. When Bessie finally did emerge from her grief, it was as a full-blown, self-assured madame. With prostitution under her nose in her own establishment, she participated as a prostitute and as a solicitor for prostitutes. She became the "go-to" person in Fort Worth for all things prohibited—mostly alcohol, sex, and gambling.

"My mother was called 'Old Lady Kight.' She was about 40 at that time, but 'old' was added because they hated old people. It was terrible prejudice among the ignorant, against the old—'old this,' 'old that.' It was used as a put-down, as a pejorative. So to have your own mother referred to as 'Old Lady Kight' was really very painful. She had problems but she also had some good points."

Soon, however, the pretty young woman who had swept Big Willie off his feet transformed into a demanding and manipulative monster. Formerly a petite lady, she kept growing in size and sound until she finally dominated anything that she looked at, which was young Morris Kight on a daily basis. She was loud and uncouth. One family member remembers the elders shouting, "Hide the ketchup!" whenever Bessie was on her way to visit because she was known for dousing her food with the red syrup. The antithesis of a Southern belle, she was not cultured or refined, and was quite content that way. It gave her an edge. She was able to charm when it was convenient and she could swipe that sword of a tongue at the drop of a dime. Strangers stayed at arm's length, and the locals knew better than to cross her. Bessie was aware of her notoriety and she made the most of it.

Morris bore the brunt of her brutality. Being nobody's fool, Bessie quickly realized her son's sexual proclivities. She didn't deal with it as a concerned mother; she never spoke directly to him. She used it against him. She'd bribe him with disclosure and tear away at him.

Kight would not allow himself to be as cynical as his mother. Their relationship, especially during this period in Fort Worth, plays like a mental cat-and-mouse game between a conniving, bitter, street-smart old lady and an ambitious, book-smart, self-assured young man. Given the perfect opportunity to apply Dale Carnegie's principles from *How to Win Friends and Influence People*, Kight figured out how to appease her. "Mother" needed to feel like she mattered. By satisfying her needs, he believed that he could get what he needed as well. He could not control her, but he could mitigate her control over him.

Despite their unusual relationship, Kight and Bessie had an innate entrepreneurial spirit and they set out to build a small motel in the back lot of The Worth Inn. It could add value to the property and Bessie's hooker business. Kight said, "We cut every corner in the world to build the motel. It was on a sandy lot and had little drifts of sand around it. I wanted to get that plowed down but we didn't have any money to hire an engineer. So a road crew came down the street, strengthening the road, and I rushed out and said, 'Come and have a six-pack [of beer]' and then I would ask them to scrape the land. So they came around and scraped the land, and we put the motel down."

The motel was built and Kight never discussed what besides beer was bartered for labor. Bessie taught her son not to be afraid to bargain; he learned skillful negotiation on his own. Together they made The Worth Inn a success, with a reputation for taking care of travelers' basic needs and a bit more. Bessie was at the center of everything, politicking and pulling strings to obtain whatever anyone needed.

Kight's leanings toward social services work began to blossom in Fort Worth. He tactfully said, "I soon discovered that we were in a hotbed of prostitutes, woman hookers, many who were with syphilis and most with gonorrhea." He had to have known that these women worked with his mother. The exposure to prostitution shaped Kight's moral detachment; from an early age, he accepted sex as a natural fact of life and primary need, much like hunger and thirst.

Amidst much violence and illegal activities happening in the 1930s, suicide was responsible for more deaths than murder, and the chief victims were prostitutes, not gunmen. "There was no real treatment of any kind for venereal disease in 1936–37. There was definitely no treatment for venereal disease anywhere in Texas. So I discovered the United States Health Service was running a VD Control Project in Hot Springs, Arkansas.

"We had a two-seater sedan, a Ford car with open windows around the side. In the winter, we put up plastic shades of some kind. So I loaded up a gaggle of hookers in my car. I was a 17-year-old kid, alone with the hookers, and we drove all the way across Texas." This 17-year-old kid was accustomed to driving around to deliver hooch to the locals but this was a longer, more adventurous trip. No doubt, the prostitutes appreciated the young man's mission. "We slept in the car on the road. We went to Hot Springs to see the doctors, the epidemiologists who were running the Venereal Disease Control Project." Kight's story typically veers into people's interest in the boy from Texas.

"They said 'How old are you?' I said, 'I'm 17.' 'Where is all this coming from, where are you getting this from? How'd you find out about us? You fascinate us. We'll take your patients.' And so they took them and housed them, and I went back alone in the car. A week later, I brought another load, and a week after that, another." Perhaps overstating his abilities he added, "I cured a pocket of syphilis and gonorrhea and thus [prevented] many people from getting it."

Bottles of hooch paid the doctors for curing Bessie's prostitutes. Seventeen-year-old Kight figured out, and reasoned with his mother, that curing the prostitutes made good business sense, creating a good reputation for The Worth Inn as having "clean" girls, as well as serving a bigger purpose for the larger community.

Without ever admitting that he and his mother ran a brothel, Kight liked to tell this, the story of his early public health service.

Young Kight's response to segregation was unfailing from the beginning. A favorite story that that he liked to tell: "In 1936... at The Worth Inn, an African-American family came by and said, 'We've driven all across this country and nobody would serve us. We're very hungry. Would you serve us?' I said to them, 'Sit down, sit down.'

"I knew mixing the races was a violation of the law but I served them anyway. Another couple came in, saw us and told the sheriff. I was detained." A family member on his father's side (probably his grandfather G.L.) came to Kight's rescue.

Kight was lectured on the dangers and illegalities of mingling the races and was cautioned not to try that again. He'd always say, "I was proud of my first act of civil disobedience."

With Bessie stabilized and set up in business (and probably a few side businesses) in Fort Worth, Kight was able to think about his own future. It is not likely that Bessie knew of Morris' plan to attend university; this was not something she would support. People in their family just didn't go to college, and besides, Bessie believed she and her son worked well together in their crude life of petty crime. As much as she'd hate to admit it, they were a good team. He never had any intention of staying in Fort Worth in servitude to his mother; there were bigger and better things in store for him.

He identified with the emerging American Enlightenment movement, an elite minority who were exposed to learning, "men of science," thinkers for the common man. Kight was an innate intellectual, opposed to everything fundamentalist, and he wanted to catch this new wave of free thinking and individualism.

The common argument against American Enlightenment and higher education was that so much learning could place one citizen above another. Education was meant to train a man to earn a living, and that was that. Thinking as a way to occupy one's time, or thinking in order to create bigger thoughts, was a new and threatening phenomenon.

When Bessie, who had minimal education, learned that her son would leave home to attend college, she berated him. She didn't know about reading or learning. She besmirched him for self-aggrandizement, his high-mindedness "with all his books." She accused him of the worst possible motives and sneered that he thought himself better than others, too good to stay in Fort Worth. She threatened him with disclosure of his sexuality, which could cause the worst possible ending for the young man. She would never verbalize a fear of being left alone and he carefully prepared everything so that she didn't need to.

It did not matter what she said. He had learned to be heroic on his own behalf—it was necessary. He was determined and clever. If serving that African-American family in the diner was his first act of disobedience, leaving Bessie would be his second. This was a big showdown.

To prepare for the face-off with his most contentious foe, his mother, he had figured out everything necessary to relinquish her dependence on him. Armed with Dale Carnegie's fundamental techniques in handling people, he listened intently and was able to convince her that it was in *her* best interest for him to go to college. He successfully "aroused an eager want" in her and made her feel important.

Following his interpretation of the basic teachings of Gandhi, Kight decided that it was for a greater good of the world that he be better educated.

At the time, no one could have said what long-term effects Bessie's close and harsh maternal bond would have on Kight. By today's standards, his mother's behavior would have qualified her for a clinical diagnosis. But in 1936, there were no studies on dysfunctional parenting or its impact on offspring. In Kight's case, the effect of Bessie's parenting would remain obscure for many years and never manifested in the foreseeable depression/anxiety disorder or destructive alcoholism later in his life. Kight's ego simply would not allow his mother's negative parenting or affectionless control to stop him from achieving something brilliant.

He would continue to seek an unconditional maternal love, but he was smart enough not to try to find it from his own mother.

Bessie stayed at 310 South Jennings Avenue for the next 13 years, managing The Worth Inn, the bootlegging and prostitution side businesses, and her little orb of influence in Fort Worth. In the fall of 1938, Morris Kight left home and went away to college to make something of his life.

Chapter 4

The Best Thing to Ever Happen

KIGHT WAS INNATELY ambitious. Through his voracious reading, he determined that his ticket out of the roadside diner in the backwoods of Texas was a university education.

In 1998, Kight recollected: "I was so uppity and so ambitious that I wrote to universities all over the country—Fordham, Notre Dame, Gonzaga, University of New York at Albany. I wrote them for their catalogues. I got maybe 150 catalogues, and I kept them for years. Reading a university catalogue is kind of an education."

Young Kight was as pragmatic as he would be in his adult years. He was never conciliatory about his potential for success. His reality demanded that he cleverly negotiate with Bessie to get what he needed, so he promised her that he'd get home for weekends and the summer break and help her at the diner.

In looking back, Kight offered minimal reflection on his early life, rarely spoke of his mother and when he did it was mostly positive. Privately, and not often, only with people with whom he felt safe—friends and confidants, who had already accepted his own eccentricities, would he more accurately allude to his mother's eccentricities. The public Kight preferred to decorate his recollections with the great many opportunities that he was able to create for himself. He didn't mention the challenges he faced, either—he never mentioned that his mother resented his education and that he had to pay his way through school.

Kight figured out the college path on his own; while he politely took counsel from whoever offered it, ultimately he charted his own course. He entered Texas Christian University in Fort Worth in the fall of 1937 with little more than the first edition of Dale Carnegie's *How to Win Friends and Influence People*, one sack of clothing, a headful of self-learning, and bushels of self-confidence.

He lived on campus and met the academic demands of college life, a huge adjustment for young Morris. He struggled through his first semester with a slightly better than C average. In spring of 1938, he dropped "Geography of North America" and deferred to part-time status. However, he was determined. He stayed on campus through the summer of 1938 to repeat two classes: Freshman Math and General Biology, earning an A and a B, respectively. It was worth the effort, and from then on, he was able to maintain a better than B average until his graduation in 1942.

"So I went to TCU and, being bookish, I got a stack pass to go back in the stacks, and rushed to read books, to find out who I was. So I went to the stack and looked up 'homosexuality' [and] found five books. Two were on the evils of masturbation… In those faraway days, [masturbation] was considered a mortal sin. I found three other books, and one of them was called *Abnormal Psychology*. Nine hundred pages, [and] at least two or three hundred of those pages had to do with homosexuality, casting us in the role of polymorphous perverse, schizophrenic, weak father/strong mother, and so on and so on. So I found nothing of value there. Bear in mind, never ever did I *ever* feel guilty about being a homosexual."

In 1992, he talked about his social life at TCU: "There was a place downtown called the Southern Club, which had a closeted gay clientele, but conversation between us would indicate some level of gay consciousness and some frankness and some class difference." Kight explained the "indications, kind of signals that you sent. There was a language that went with the signals. The language would often go around the 'gay'—'what a gay tie you're wearing,' 'it was a gay experience,' 'we went to the theater and it was so gay,' and so on. If after eight or ten or twelve such references the person didn't respond, then you just assumed he wasn't understanding it; if he did respond, often this led to a social contact and to a sexual liaison. It was tenuous and risky, but often satisfying, if not thrilling."

1942. Kight graduated from Texas Christian University near the top of the class with a major in Political Science and a minor in Economics. Photo provided by Texas Christian University.

He did find other library material that proved helpful in shaping who he was to become. "On a shelf I found a pamphlet about Mahatma Gandhi. I was entranced, an instant convert to pacifism and using nonviolent protest as a tool to gain social justice for the disadvantaged. I wrote the ashram listed in the pamphlet and began a correspondence with Gandhi's aides." Kight's lifelong commitment to pacifism began.

To fund his education, Morris worked in the library, the dorms, and the school cafeteria and personnel department; he stacked books, filed papers, cleaned toilets, and swept stairs. In his more senior years at school, he worked as a dormitory house manager and became a leader on campus. He also worked in the on-campus Employment Bureau where he "had to find jobs for students and capable students for jobs," a service he'd perform for members of the gay community many years later during the early gay movement.

Kight remembered, "I discovered that I could be helpful in counseling at the university, so I got on the staff of Dean of Men. The Dean of Men was Dr. Otto R. Neilson, who was very kind to me and very supportive of me. I wound up as a peer counselor for students in trouble." Morris felt this kind of experience gave him "a vast understanding of human relationships."

Young Morris was beginning to navigate and enjoy the risks involved with leading a double life. In referring to his social life, in 1992, Kight recalled, "I was an employee of the university ... and it was risky to be associated with gay people. There was a lot of gossip, we were gossiped about ... but never, ever, for a moment in my life did I consider going to a psychiatrist. There was no reason to, I didn't feel any guilt feelings, and why pay a psychiatrist? They're not in the business of hearing people who are happy, so why go? Many acquaintances of mine went to psychiatrists and concealed their homosexuality from the psychiatrist. They paid him/her money, good hard-earned money, to conceal the very thing that they went there to deal with in the first place. I never could understand the hypocrisy or cupidity of that. The psychiatrists were often much more sophisticated than their patients or clients. They had to cajole them into it, had to keep setting the stage to try to get you to proclaim your gayness."

In 1992, at 73 years old, Kight remembered his guilty feelings and 'coming of age' in a different way. "The first time I engaged in active anal intercourse with a man I had guilt feelings. I don't know where the conditioning came from, why oral copulation or '69'-ing didn't have a trace of guilt connection with it. Here I was actively intercoursing a man for the first time and I did have guilt feelings about it. But I felt that if you're thrown from a horse, get back on and ride again. It's known as the best cure to try again, so I attempted another active anal intercourse and it was thrilling and wonderful, and I felt, 'Why have I waited so long,' and the rest is sexual history."

TCU provost Dr. Neilson served as Kight's mentor for many years and invited Kight into his family home. Morris also became friendly with Neilson's wife and the whole family. Dr. Neilson generously invited Kight and a small group of select students to Sunday dinners with his family and, oftentimes, to soirées with other invited guests. Many years later, Neilson's daughter, Elizabeth, recalled her father's guests as the "most memorable people."

The young man benefited greatly by being exposed to the Neilson family. This was certainly a more traditional, grounded home life than he had ever experienced, and he absorbed as much as possible. This is where Kight learned to have proper discussions, intellectual conversations, and share differing ideas. The intellectual curiosity and respect expressed around the table was important to his development. They discussed everything from politics to art to new thoughts. These Sunday events nourished Kight's desire for upward mobility, a more refined life, and helped him to discover his natural talents for the art of conversation. He slowed down and softened his speech. He learned to listen.

TCU was known as being at the center of the Stone-Campbell Movement, also known as the Restoration Movement, a theology that claimed to be Christian in nature, nonsectarian in spirit and open-minded intellectually. Around the Neilson dinner table, they discussed varying ethical theories and Kight began to think about the bigger world, the natural order. Soon he solidified his belief in reason and scientific inquiry over the belief in a god and embraced the philosophies expressed through secular humanism.

The non-theistic belief system known as Humanism corresponded to Kight's natural instincts and, like Kight himself, was an anomaly; Humanism serves as a religion of non-religious beliefs. The thinking worked well with Kight's pacifism, and he automatically accepted the basic precept of Humanism: people could do good deeds without religious ties guiding them. He once said, "There is not a conversion to Humanism. You just grow into it." He continued to grow into humanism, and in 1950 he joined the American Humanist Association and stayed connected for the rest of his life.

He injected many of the same social justice principles and personal ethics into his work with the antiwar movement of the 1960s and later the gay rights movement. Though he'd debate the rationality of the need for organized religion, philosophy, and spiritual movements, he remained true to his pacifist and Humanist roots. At times, he claimed to be a believer of Jainism—a sister path of Hinduism that places a special emphasis on *ahimsa* (harm no living beings). He "believed very deeply in Humanism and I believe that it requires extra responsibility. Because if you belong to a theistic religion, you can blame God for the fact that you didn't pay the light bill and they turned off the lights. Humanism requires that you work to pay the light bill. Enforcing a basic belief in the importance of each and every single person in this world; each of us is stunningly important, or has the potential to be." Kight shunned impalpable aspects of religions, explaining "a Humanist needs to be more practical than most humans are. There are responsibilities to keep yourself functioning." In explaining Humanism, Kight always emphasized the importance of personal responsibility as a way toward strong community.

A strong influence on Kight's anti-establishment roots was Professor William Jackson Hammond, an esteemed academic, writer, and local politician. Prominent in Fort Worth's Progressive Democratic Party, Hammond advocated social action and human values, and focused his energies on civic issues such as public housing, jail reform, crime prevention, and empowerment through education.

Kight joined Hammond and a group of self-proclaimed radicals who, in an effort to gain college admittance for blacks in the segregated South, conducted school classes on the streets. Kight later claimed that his participation in such radical movements led to an obligatory appearance before the Dies Committee (the famous precursor to the House Committee Investigating Un-American Activities). Kight's appearance before the Dies Committee is unsubstantiated, though Professor Hammond was a target of investigation and questioning. Before his 20th birthday, Kight's socialist sensibilities were completely and perpetually entrenched into his ideologies.

He also reaped the rewards of a college social life. He liked to tell people that he founded the Oscar Wilde Club, "perhaps the first official and open gay club on any campus." The club was either deeply underground or short-lived, as there is no record of an Oscar Wilde Club at TCU. There were other clubs on other campuses around the same time who met every Thursday night to discuss Wilde's work with nary a mention of sexuality, Wilde's or anyone else's. After the meetings—again, without a mention of sexuality—they would go off quietly in pairs. It was a typical early "gay club": the behavior was so taboo that it had to be a unanimous compartmentalization, not discussed inside a room, behind closed doors, or in private. Never a word uttered in reference to homosexual behavior.

"I never went to a psychiatrist, a psychologist, a counselor, a minister, or anybody. I didn't confess to anybody because I didn't have anything to confess to—I think that's kind of unusual."

It is unusual when considering the myriad other appropriate topics Kight could have brought to a therapist's office, not only his sexuality.

Juvenile Kight accepted the clandestine nature of his sexuality, never "internalized" shame as he discovered who he was, expressed his latent and natural talents and embraced his genuine interests. He satisfied his curiosity for the darker side of campus life and appreciated the virtually buried homosexual culture.

"In 1940, [while I was] staff of Dean of Men and a proctor for the dormitories at the university, a young man conducted a masturbation training class in his room. He gathered together eight other students and scattered them around beds and said, 'Here's how you masturbate—first you take off all your clothes.'

"'Well,' [everyone said], 'I don't know if we're going to do that'—so he got them to take off their clothes. And then—I won't act it all out, I'll just describe what he was doing. Then he said, 'You have an image…' It was Masturbation 101.

"Well, the gossip was so great that by six in the morning the word had spread from one end of the campus to the other, and he was brought up on charges. The Dean of Men convened a hearing board to try him for violation of rules of sanity. I, as a staff member of the Dean of Men, got appointed as the hearing clerk for the board. I was desperate to do it because I wanted to hear what was going on. Because the University was so hard up for money (the Depression was still going on), they couldn't possibly afford to lose a student. So they put him on probation, punished him and kept him on."

In 2000, Kight was invited back to his alma mater to speak to the campus gay and lesbian organization, eQ Alliance. He didn't mention his early academic challenges or how he funded his education. Instead, he stressed to his young audience to "overcome isolation. I am not recommending any young man or woman to go through that isolation. The way to do that is to come out, to say that you are lesbian or gay."

In some instances, while reminiscing about his life story, Kight said that he and Bessie "lost the diner" after he served the African-American family, and at other times, depending upon the situation, he recollected that they "sold the diner" to help him go to college. Neither was true.

Bessie stayed on at Jennings Avenue and ran the diner for many years. Once Morris left for college, he didn't help out as much as he thought he would; he overestimated his abilities to work university jobs, the diner, and carry 15 units at school.

Bessie resented his studies and his being away from the diner. She would appear unannounced at the student housing at inappropriate hours, and stand outside yelling and screaming for Morris. He told a confidant that his mother wanted to move into the men's dorms with him. She'd shout, "You're living in luxury while your poor mother is starving." A large woman, she wasn't starving for anything but his attention. Sometimes she'd bear a gift of moonshine for the college boys, but she was primarily there to scold and embarrass young Morris, threatening to shout out his dirty taboo to the world.

She learned that he was having his first serious love affair with an unnamed TCU professor, igniting an acerbic and dangerous cat-and-rat game between mother and son. She threatened to expose her son's sexuality and began to bribe him for small favors, things he probably would've done for her anyway. She verbally lashed out at him. He withstood her barrages and intrusions and skillfully calmed her down. Bessie was another compartment in Kight's psyche and, like his homosexual behavior, he was able to keep her very neatly in her place. He said that he benefited from her daring. He also benefited from learning to juggle her extremes and maneuver her outrages.

In retrospect, he always saw himself as "this gay kid fantasizing the other world." He focused his attention on the cultured, educated world of TCU and the Neilsons. The fledgling Morris cultivated a style, always impeccably dressed with perfect posture and manners. He continued to refine his way of speaking—slow, eloquent, a bit affected. He was disciplined; he emulated Gandhi and made a commitment to be the change he sought.

At TCU, Kight was active in the International Relations Club and student government. He supported the new labor movement and the Progressive Democratic Party. He was already writing letters to the editors of local and national publications, including the *New York Times,* as an outspoken opponent to World War II, an incredibly unpopular position at the time. Many years later, in more unnecessary exaggerated claims, Kight said that he "denounced Hitler's treatment of gays," when, at the time, few people even knew about or would acknowledge Hitler's mistreatment of Jews, much less gays.

While still at TCU, in September of 1940, he enrolled in pre-law graduate courses at University of Texas in Austin. He was not genuinely interested in becoming a lawyer and did not do well in law school academically. The only class in which he received a grade was Legal Bibliography. He withdrew from UT in May of 1941, though not before picking up enough information in Contracts and Torts and Real Property law classes to serve him well throughout his life.

Academics notwithstanding, University of Texas proved worthwhile for Kight in other ways—he befriended many up-and-coming muckamucks in local and national politics. One particular friend, Walter Jenkins, also a short-term UT student, went on to become a close confidant and aide to President Lyndon Johnson. In 1963, Jenkins suddenly became the *de facto* Chief of Staff for a new President of the United States, and by late 1964 Jenkins was neck-deep in a curious sex scandal.

Often described as a likely and typical case of entrapment, Jenkins was arrested for "indecent acts" at the YMCA on G Street in Washington, D.C. Kight told a friend that Jenkins contacted him at the time for a referral to a lawyer. It has never been confirmed that Jenkins called Kight, but that is exactly the kind of referral service that Kight was providing to gay men in 1964, at the time of Jenkins' arrest in D.C.

Kight received his bachelor's degree from TCU in 1942, graduating near the top of the class with a major in political science and a minor in economics.

With the United States officially embroiled in World War II in Europe and Asia, Kight was not as self-assured and confident as he would have liked to have been. He graduated college at the height of World War II and "faced a dilemma," he explained. "The world was at war, and I was of the age to serve, but how to do so without wielding a gun?"

The U.S. Selective Service Act required that all men aged 18 to 45 were subject to military service, and all men aged 18 to 65 were required to register. Kight, already a member of the nonviolent War Resisters League (WRL), was strongly influenced by the teachings of Mahatma Gandhi. Even though he saw himself as a Conscientious Objector, according to President Roosevelt, CO status was limited to religious resisters. Kight's best hope in the highly charged, nationalistic push to support the war was a "noncombatant service" assignment.

Another hero of Morris Kight's was First Lady Eleanor Roosevelt. He idolized Mrs. Roosevelt. He quoted her every word from the newspapers and radio announcements. If Bessie needed anything else to be jealous of, it would have been Eleanor Roosevelt; Morris had a boyhood crush on the First Lady that bordered on an obsession. Kight would unnecessarily brag that Mrs. Roosevelt attended his TCU graduation, and sometimes he said that she spoke at the commencement; neither version of the story is corroborated. A leader in social reform, Eleanor Roosevelt profoundly affected Morris Kight's life when she created the National Youth Administration (NYA), which provided financial aid to students and training to recent graduates that could fulfill the requirement for military service.

Kight loved to tell the back story: "Mrs. Morgenthau, the wife of the Treasury Secretary, and Mrs. Ickes, the wife of the Interior Secretary, and Mrs. Roosevelt visited England. They had an audience with the King and Queen at Buckingham Palace and observed the British Civil Service while there. Now, whatever you may think of the British as being empire builders, they are very good bureaucrats, and they installed their brand of bureaucracy in countries wherever the British flag flew, [and] they installed the British system of justice and administration. [The three American wives] liked the idea and brought it home and sold it to Mr. Roosevelt.

And thus the U.S. government created the U.S. Career Service Training Academy," that would function as part of the NYA.

In February 1941, Kight carefully printed his application to be a Student Aide with the NYA under the Department of the Interior.

"I didn't know what [the position] was, it hadn't been described. It just said 'aide,' training, and so I enrolled." Kight said that in the competitive tests, he scored in the top three out of 140,000 persons from all over the country.

By June of 1941, Kight still hadn't heard anything from the commission. So he handwrote a letter, in perfect penmanship, and sent it via Western Union to the Department of the Interior, saying, "I am very eager to have this work, but have received no communication from you regarding acceptance… I need to make my plans for the summer soon." On the same day, June 2, unbeknownst to Morris, an internal department memo discusses two other candidates for the aide position—one had declined, and the other was serving in the Army, leaving the position open.

Kight's letter of acceptance to the Career Service Training Program, dated June 14, 1941, made him one of 28, out of 140,000 candidates, selected for the program.

"And we were sent to Albuquerque, New Mexico, for training. There, in the summer of 1941, I was a cadet in the first U.S. Career Services Academy class, and what a marvelous experience that was. I gloat about that. It was the finest thing to ever happen in my life—besides being gay, which is the other good thing that happened.

"We had the days divided into three segments. Four hours of class for Public Administration, four hours a day we worked at a desk—we were assigned to the United Pueblos Agency, an agency of the U.S. Bureau of Indian Affairs—and then we spent evenings working with the people in the field. I worked on a water well, digging and putting pipes together and so on. We were constantly graded and constantly examined."

Kight liked to brag and editorialize that the professors in the Career Services Training "read like a Who's Who of pre-World War II America." More than 50 years after the experience, he could still recall their names, complete with correct spellings.

"The lead professor was a Dr. John Pfiffner, the founder of the Modern Science of Public Administration… [We also had] Dr. Edith V. Mirrielees, closeted… Dr. Virgil K. Whitaker, a closeted Professor of English at Stanford University; Father Flanagan of Boys Town, to teach us how to treat children with special needs.

"Ruth Murray Underhill, a world-famous anthropologist, was there to train us in how to deal with different environments and cultures. She said, 'You'll go to Pine Ridge Indian Reservation and you'll be shocked at the sounds. The sounds will be strange. They are bleeding animals and coyotes while people will be chanting and singing. You'll be shocked at the smells of fecal matter and barnyard smells and garbage; you'll feel alienated.' So I sensitized myself on how to deal with persons in a poverty situation. I can go on with a list of these. There was one distinguished professor per cadet."

Certainly the 22-year-old romanticized the outreach and social services work that he expected to do within the newly formed Bureau of Indian Affairs [BIA] or as it was referred to in internal documents: "Indian."

"The Bureau, being run on socialist lines, had provided a bull and a female cow for the local Indian Pueblo tribe at Zia (north of Albuquerque, going toward Santa Fe) to create livestock, [provide] meat and food for sustenance. And then along came the veterinarians from the Bureau of Indian Affairs who vaccinated the bull and the cow. The vaccine killed the bull and the cow. So the Chief of the Zia came to our office to ask for compensation. Nobody asked him to sit down, [he was] the Chief of the Zia and nobody asked his name. And they said, 'We can't pay you for them. We gave them to you. Why should we pay you?' He left and the director of the economics branch said, 'That Indian's got a lot of nerve, coming in here to ask for money.' I said, 'I can't do this.' I didn't want to work for the government. Instead, I used that training to do other things."

Kight's personnel file from the Department of Interior, formal and cryptic with government-speak, tells its own story.

His probationary appointment officially began on June 20, 1941, with an annual salary of $1,440. He signed the standard oath of loyalty to the U.S. government and was assigned to United Pueblos in Albuquerque. His probationary review was less than satisfactory and the evaluation contains unsatisfactory remarks for "adaptability," "manner," and "tact." In a letter regarding Kight, his general superintendent, S.D. Aberle, wrote to the Commissioner of Indian Affairs in Washington, D.C.:

"We are recommending Mr. Kight's separation rather than a furlough because, although his work was sufficiently satisfactory to continue him throughout the entire period of the Program, we do not believe that he is fitted for permanent appointment in the Service. Although he has the intellectual capacity to perform administrative work, he has personality weaknesses which seriously affect his fitness for the Service."

"Personality weaknesses" was military code for a "homosexual," or more aptly, "blatant homosexual."

The letter continues: "Mr. Kight's separation should be considered in a different light than those who were separated from the [Program] before it was completed. It is believed that the reason for his separation should be that his services are no longer necessary in view of the completion of the Career Service Training Program."

Kight was indeed treated differently. His separation papers included a handwritten note to a personnel clerk with special instructions: "This is a different type case."

He was officially discharged, without prejudice, on September 11, 1941. The official reason given for the termination was "the completion of the Career Service Training Program" and abolishment of his position.

1941. Instead of military service, Kight was chosen to the newly formed Career Services Training in Albuquerque, NM.
Photo provided by U.S. Department of Interior.

In a rare reflection interview in 1994 Kight stated: "Let me say something self-serving. In one branch of sociology there is a word called 'sport.' A sport is a person of a class who escapes the constraints of that class and becomes a sport. Not athletics sport, different. Sport–ing. Hearing a different drummer. I've always thought of myself as a sport.

"All my lifetime, I've heard stuff that I thought was just abominable. 'I don't agree with that,' but rather say, 'There's another way to look at that.' Or, 'Had you considered this?' So I've always felt that I was a sport. I didn't hear the middle-class drummer. I didn't hear the drummer of the Protestant Fundamentalists, the punitive crowd. But I heard a different drummer. I heard a drummer somewhere with a wonderful kodo drum, drumming away. [sings in Native American] And I could see myself dancing around fire—and I did that. And I felt water, Apache Indians Reservation, in the summer of 1941. I danced to a drum, just like I've described, around a fire. Indian women, Native American women, and Native American men, and us from the United States Career Service Training academy, the 28 cadets danced all night around the fire. [sings again in Native American]"

Kight said, "So I graduated from the school and decided that I did not want to work for the government. Bureau of Indian Affairs was just a pocket of racism."

1942. Kight enlisted in the U.S. Marines to finish his service in San Diego, CA.

Photo provided by Military Personnel Records, St. Louis, MO.

Kight always referred to his time in the Career Service Training as "the best thing to happen to me." He used the training he received in every position he held for the rest of his life, especially in the conception and establishment of the Gay Community Services Center.

With an early departure from the NYA program, he was still obligated to fulfill his mandatory service to his country.

In August 1942, Kight reported to the Fort Worth recruiting board, where he enlisted in the U.S. Marine Corps Reserve and was ordered immediately to active duty at Dallas, Texas. He was transferred to serve as a clerk, Private 1st Class, at the recruit depot in San Diego, California. In March 1943, he was promoted to Corporal and in July of that same year he was "examined and found qualified for promotion to the rank of Sergeant." A handsome young man, Kight rarely spoke of his military service and would describe it with a glint in his eye: "I wore myself out providing personnel services to our men in uniform."

With the U.S. in the thick of two simultaneous wars, Kight was justifiably concerned about an assignment in active duty. The war was a year away from ending, and in October 1944 Kight knew the only way he could assure that he didn't serve in combat was to be thrown out of the service. He was recommended for termination of service by reason of medical survey: "Psychoneurosis, Anxiety Neurosis." He never discussed and no one ever knew the details of the unusual arrangement with the U.S. military, but he received an Honorable Discharge as Corporal and took a deep sigh of relief.

He didn't go back to Fort Worth, Bessie and the diner; instead, he floated around New Mexico for the next few years, ambitious but a bit unfocused.

The burgeoning metropolis of Albuquerque seemed to be a good fit for the unusual young man with an odd collection of talents and interests, which included map collecting, architecture, and pre-Columbian, Mexican and Navajo crafts.

Albuquerque welcomed Kight who saw many opportunities to help shape their city—and make a name for himself. He got a hat and hung it up, loosened his tie, sat down, and for the first time in his life thought about making a home for himself.

Part II

Before Gay Rights There Were Gay Wrongs

Chapter 5

Land of Enchantment

NESTLED CLOSE TO the center of the state of New Mexico, the city of Albuquerque is also known as Duke City—the original name given by its early settlers in reference and reverence to the aristocratic Duke of Albuquerque in Spain. The region had been alternately under both Spanish and Portuguese rule and still retains much of its historical Spanish cultural heritage. From its earliest days, the area has maintained a military outpost and many different federal government agencies and research institutions along the Rio Grande. The Atchison, Topeka and Santa Fe Railway arrived in 1880, and, in 1926, the world-famous highway Route 66 came through the city.

When Morris Kight decided to plant roots in Albuquerque, it was predominantly peopled by Anglo merchants and mountain men working hard to create a major mercantile commerce. The influence of the American Indian population was very much present, though their participation in local commerce was restricted by law. While there were still many dirt roads in Albuquerque in the 1940s, the city was entering its most promising phase of development. It was ripe with opportunity and positioned to become a major draw in commerce and culture in the southwestern United States.

Kight was enchanted. Albuquerque reciprocated the young man's advances and by 1947 he called the small city his

1950. Kight as a businessman in New Mexico. From the personal collection of Cori MacNaughton.

home. He set up a tidy real estate office on North Second Street in the middle of town. He mortgaged the Fort Worth diner to become the owner of the Rio Grande Duke City Hotel; later he changed its name to the New Mexican Hotel. He managed the cozy Spanish-style lodging for road-weary travelers and temporary housing for summer stock theatre companies on tour.

Kight's enchantment with Navajo jewelry, particularly rings, began sometime in the early 1940s. He had a particular ring that he wore for the rest of his life that was given to him by the artist who had designed the ring, Andrew Roanhorse. "I've worn it all these years," Kight told Cain in 1994. "It's badly, badly worn. It's a pomegranate blossom… And inspired Andrew Roanhorse to design this ring. We talked about that a lot. And it was from him that I got the expression, 'Folk art is the song we sing in our heart.'"

Early on Kight demonstrated an independent entrepreneurial spirit. He didn't blend in well in most places and quickly realized that he would need to be his own boss. Once he was established in the hotel business, he became involved in real estate and made a little bit of a name for himself by booking road shows and circus acts.

In 1949, Kight opened another real estate office on South Second Street and called the new business Kight and Manzano Land Company. Manzano was not a real person; it was the name of a local mountain range, and also the name of a very exotic fruit called Apple Manzano Banana (which is actually a banana, not an apple). Kight thought the extra name added prestige and made the company image appear to be thriving and more legit. His real estate business mostly entailed buying and selling foreclosed properties.

He became involved in small community efforts. He went from booking traveling vaudeville shows and circus acts to art exhibits, and he had the shows included in the Albuquerque tours. The importance and prestige of the shows he did curate grew and fed Kight's profile in the compact community.

Kight's recollections of his life in New Mexico were always selective and sparse. Though much of the documentation was tightly concealed or long ago destroyed, a few public records and radio recordings demonstrate that he clearly left an impression. The large town that dressed up as a small city has a piece of Morris Kight in its history, even if that piece may be stored in a vault behind a closet somewhere. The entrepreneurial spirit of Kight as a young, ambitious man is indeed thinly woven into the cultural fabric of the southwestern city. In the early 1950s, there was a new mark on the timeline of Albuquerque signifying the transition from "Old Albuquerque" to "New Albuquerque." There could be also be a transition for the city known as "before Morris Kight" and "after Morris Kight."

As a way to participate in radio dramas, in 1949 Kight registered for classes at the University of New Mexico, which introduced him to a whole world of avant-garde people with local influence. One person described him as trying to "ingratiate himself with the university crowd." He befriended speech and English professor Robert Barton Allen, who was also involved with radio broadcasting, and as a specialty service to newspaper and radio announcers, Allen was an expert in correct pronunciation of names of places, which no doubt impressed the younger Kight who later became known for his enunciation. Allen may have also influenced

Kight's interest in folklore; much later Kight began to refer to himself as an "arcane authority of the subject," declaring at one point, "I am in love with folklore."

UNM Professor John Donald Robb, credited with being responsible for the growth of fine arts in the community through the 1940s and '50s, was known as a pioneer composer of electronic music. Kight participated in a few of his field experiments in the desert which incorporated indigenous music along with Western, Spanish, and Mexican folklore. It was all very experimental—equally primitive *and* advanced for the time.

In 1994, Kight recalled for Paul Cain: "In 1950... the tape recorder had just been invented and a professor [Robb] had a recorder. He recorded the oral history of Native Americans and pioneer Americans and Hispanic Americans from New Mexico. He came to me to ask for support of his project. Well, I liked it. I went out and raised a lot of money for that. I [went] with him to Pie Town, New Mexico, to do a demonstration project. We stayed for three days.

"For three days we sat and this stunning history reeled out at us. And so I've always been fascinated by folk art."

Robb's field equipment consisted of a reel of thick copper wire, a tape recorder, and his car battery for electricity. Kight helped to organize some of the field events, where the main focus was to appreciate the inventiveness and originality of the "folk." On one of Robb's field recordings, Kight is heard introducing folklorists from Corrales, New Mexico. He had already perfected his devised and distinctive style of speaking. He spoke carefully and slowly, like a dutiful youngster chosen for an important assignment.

"Our friend from Corrales has brought us some more of her neighbors... who will want to sing."

He could have passed for a slick Ivy Leaguer with his perfect pronunciation of all the English and Spanish proper names.

"Demetrio Rivera, Canuto Rivera, Eloy Gonzales, Miss Anita Chavez, Mr. and Mrs. Moes, and Jack Miller from Corrales." He then handed the microphone to Robb.

Kight enjoyed doing some part-time radio announcing on local shows and he cultivated good relations with all the local media. He became involved with the community-run San Felipe Playhouse and Summerhouse Theatre as a booker and handler of press relations. To feed his acting bug, he was a member of the Old Town Players and in 1953 he was cast in Mark Reed's farce *Petticoat Fever*.

By 1950, Kight had a regular radio program on Tuesday nights at 8 p.m. called *This Enchanted City* on the local ABC AM affiliate, KOAT. In promotional material, Kight was known to be active in "art development ... though not himself an artist"; the radio program allotted time for him to interview local artists and craftsmen and promote activities and exhibitions. Kight participated in a round-table discussion on KOB-TV, with local socialite Dorothea Frick Whitcraft, titled "Can Albuquerque Be an Art Center?"

Kight found his way into the confidence of the local Pueblo Indians, ingratiating himself by becoming their drinking buddy. They shared their crafts, pottery skills, moonshine, local history, folklore, agricultural knowledge, and select indigenous secrets with the curious Texan.

While Kight lived somewhat on the cutting edge, he was never marginalized in Albuquerque. Socially, he was invited to join the city's circle of cultural elites and taste-makers. He was close to the center and was actively participating in making Albuquerque a viable commercial and cultural reality. He was building a fine reputation.

Political ambitions not forgotten, Calvin Horn, ten-year member of the New Mexico legislature and an alternate delegate at the Democratic National Convention, became a close friend. Described as bookish, a little pretentious, and an honorable man, Horn owned a local publishing company, as well as a separate moving company.

Kight had a dynamic nightlife in Albuquerque. It was the "other" life that could never see the light of day. Albuquerque had a very active underground gay world that could be found in small obscure bars with names like Hitch'n Post and Paradise Alley (known as "paradise" to the city's males since no women were allowed inside its doors). These places were often marked by oblique signs such as "Rear Entry Only." Morris knew the right places to go, and he was never alone when he got there. He enjoyed more than a couple of drinks and a few minutes of intimacy, companionship, and conversation. He'd help the new army recruits in town to find housing, often at the New Mexican Hotel, and would direct them where to find male fellowship.

His nightlife did crisscross with many of the same people from his day life, but social protocol of the era demanded that nightlife was never discussed in daylight company. Much like his relationships in college, the two worlds were kept separate and compartmentalized. Kight was confident and comfortable in both worlds.

His FBI file reveals an arrest in 1949 for fighting, though all local records have been purged. More than likely it involved an advance or a pick-up that turned against him. It was not uncommon in those gloomy times for a gay pick-up to turn sour after the sex deed was complete; it was often a skewed way of deflecting guilt and shame. Kight never experienced an ounce of shame and was not a fighter. He didn't know how to physically fight.

He was living a dream life. He grew in stature and ambition and he knew that as a single man in the late 1940s, he was restricted in what society would accept from him.

In October of 1950, Kight was invited to a Sunday afternoon cocktail party thrown by local movers and shakers Dick Wager Smith and his wife Alice. A female colleague from Smith's engineering firm, Ouida [Oh-wee-dah] Peters, engineered an introduction of Mister Kight to her 21-year-old daughter, Stanlibeth. He was not necessarily attracted to her natural beauty and brains, or her cultured nature. She also had a naïveté that was convenient for Kight under the circumstances, but that wasn't necessarily what convinced him that she'd be a good mate for him. Many years later, Stanlibeth remembered that they shared a well-rounded interest in history, archeology, and anthropology. "It's rare," she said, "to meet someone who had those interests if you're a bright young woman." Miss Peters grew up in southern New Mexico, was educated in New England for a few years, and then took a tour of Europe before coming back to New Mexico and getting a job at an Albuquerque advertising agency.

Ouida, a formidable woman on her own, was married to Stanlibeth's loving and adoring stepfather, Lawrence Fyfe Peters. A fighter pilot who settled in Albuquerque after World War II, "Fyfe," as he was fondly known, flew cargo out of Albuquerque airport and had local and far-reaching connections in important places. Stanlibeth was an only child of a very controlling mother whom she described as "a wonderful woman, both positively and negatively," and at times had "a nasty streak." It may have been a joke born out of a bad sense of humor, but the older woman knew that her daughter would react to the charms of the cultured Mister Kight.

Kight worked hard at charming Ouida; he courted her just as much as he courted his intended. Stanlibeth remembered that her mother "didn't like anybody who didn't cater to her." Familiar with such personalities, young Kight stroked her ego, innocuously flirted and made sure that the grand dame received a lot of attention. More than 50 years after the fact, her daughter, Stanlibeth, wondered about Ouida's motive in orchestrating the romance the way she did. Ouida believed that the ambitious young man from Texas was headed toward greatness and prosperity. She also believed that she could control him and thereby control her daughter. Fyfe "didn't think much of [Kight]," but he went along with it for Ouida. Young Kight could not resist the important political ties he could gain through both Ouida and Fyfe. With the benefit of retrospect, Peters recalls her husband's motives: "He had to marry somebody who would have connections in Albuquerque."

Kight had something that any young woman would be attracted to at the time—something that few people had in that era—a car. He drove a big, comfortable automobile which allowed them mobility. Kight liked the prestige of a car. "He had not known that I was pretty enchanted with the whole thing," Stanlibeth remembers.

Despite the ten-year age difference, or perhaps because of it, the courtship was quick: "not long enough," is how Stanlibeth described it. They met in late October. A month later—during the week between Morris' birthday and the Thanksgiving holiday—they became engaged. They were married in a large church wedding on December 18, 1950.

When Morris Kight got married, he had reached the inevitable crossroads in the lives of many gay men of the day. At this defining moment, they had a choice: the choice to act straight and marry or to act straight and stay single. Morris Kight's social aspirations always superseded his sexual identity. In Stanlibeth Peters, the dirt farm kid from Texas struck societal gold. And he knew it.

By the time of his wedding, Kight already knew a lot of homosexuals who were in sham marriages. Not uncommon for his gay friends to be married, some married couples masqueraded as heterosexuals to survive their respective lesbian and gay closets, while other homosexuals needed to create their own alternate reality in order to exist in a hostile world. The role models who showed homosexuals how to live comfortably within societal norms of the day all advocated some form of deception. Intellectually it made sense to Morris Kight. Never one to fully endorse the institution of marriage, he accepted that being married was expedient in a public life. He never openly questioned the value system behind the societal norms that held the proverbial closet door shut. For all the interviews that he gave, Kight never discussed his marriage, and that may have been to protect the other parties.

He never discussed his rationale for entering into a sham marriage or if he ever gave it much thought.

Enchanted and in love, Stanlibeth entered the marriage with all the zeal, sincerity and loyalty that a young woman affixes to her wedding vows. The society pages covered everything, beginning with the engagement announcement, followed by a blurb regarding the requisite champagne party in honor of the bride-elect and her fiancé given by Mr. and Mrs. Bernie May at "their extensive new home on Coors Road." A week later there was an announcement detailing "a dessert-bridge and shower" to honor Miss Peters given by more local big names that was to be attended by additional names. A few days later, the same society section gave a paragraph to a "trousseau tea held in honor of" Miss Stanlibeth Peters given by her mother, Mrs. Laurence Fyfe Peters.

The following Monday, they were married with a full half-page of the daily newspaper dedicated to the wedding that took place "before an altar banked with evergreens and baskets of white gladioli and red poinsettias." The double-ring ceremony at St. John's Episcopal Cathedral had seven attendants, an organist, a soprano singer, followed by a reception at the prestigious Albuquerque Country Club with "a square cake encircled by camellia foliage and white pompoms … silver heirloom candelabras … [and] two champagne punch tables decorated in camellia foliage."

Morris' brother, John Lewis, came from Nome, Texas, and his sister's two daughters, Peggy Joyce and Faye, came from Odessa, Texas, for the wedding. Bessie arrived in a large and loud pickup truck with an unknown man, an artist of some type who wound up selling postcards of his work at the reception. No one from the bride's side had met Bessie before the wedding. Many years later, the bride remembered, "If I had met her before I married Morris, I would not have married him.

"She threw a tizzy fit at the reception. She [Bessie] behaved during the wedding [ceremony]. I don't know who was twisting her arms. But at the reception, there were tears. 'You're stealing my only son, blah, blah, blah.' She was a typical madam…. You could see the sparks" between Ouida and Bessie. The more socially refined Ouida, who had more class currency to lose, made sure to keep a cold distance from Bessie.

Even though the bride had never encountered anyone as "mean and vindictive" as Bessie, before the wedding day was over, she stood up to the older woman and would not be bullied. "She was a dragon," the bride said. Bessie briefly retreated, but this behavior provided a preview of the pattern in Bessie's behavior that would escalate over the next six years. "I don't know how he survived her" is oft repeated by many different people in wonderment at Morris' and Bessie's relationship.

Morris had selected a marquis diamond from a New York wholesale jeweler for his bride. He boasted of the selection, the cut, and the quality of the ring and showed off photos of it to everyone. Stanlibeth believed that he put a deposit down on the diamond ring, but the ring never arrived and she remained too polite to question him. He never mentioned the ring again either, and no one ever queried if the ring ever made its way to her finger. He did gift her with a miniature schnauzer, a prized show dog which quickly became the object of his bride's affection.

On the wedding night, before they left for their honeymoon which was one day and one night in Santa Fe, Kight left his bride for a few hours to meet his mother for a few drinks. Within a few years, the bride realized that this was probably when Bessie began extorting Morris, threatening to reveal his secret until he worked out an arrangement with her.

After the wedding, Bessie never left Albuquerque. Morris found her an adequate upstairs apartment at 114 North 2nd Street in a place called the Lido Hotel that was also referred to as a "whorehouse." Bessie was remembered as always having an oversized pickup truck and a new nameless man to drive her around in it. She was perfectly content at the Lido until 1952, when it became the Golden West Cocktail Lounge, and Morris moved his mother to 52nd Southwest Street. He was devoted to Bessie. Morris would have been loyal to Bessie even without her threats. She was far too mean to adapt to the new town without him. Theirs was a complex and genuinely durable bond.

After the honeymoon, Morris went back to his radio program, committees, and his life as usual. For Stanlibeth, "It was hell from there on." It did not take long for Kight's strange loyalty to his mother to create friction in their marriage. Soon after the honeymoon, there was a police manhunt for an Oklahoma murderer who was on the loose and, it was speculated, was headed toward Albuquerque. The public had been alerted. Morris left Stanlibeth, took the car to check on Bessie and remained gone most of the night. "I was terrified," Stanlibeth remembered.

The marriage didn't go sour immediately. Shortly before the wedding, Kight had purchased a piece of property at 610 12th Northwest Street that had two houses and an eight-unit apartment building. He moved his bride into one house on the property. Without asking for any input, he did all the decorating himself. He chose a "Mexican casual" motif and "treated [Stanlibeth's] antiques like junk." The couple rented out the other house and managed the apartment building.

Stanlibeth shared a particular memory of those days: "One morning we woke up to a lot of noise in the driveway. Morris looked outside and said, 'Don't come.' 'Okay, why?' He said, 'It's our neighbor [a tenant in the house], dodging a skunk, stark naked and he is having a serious loss of civility.'"

The newlyweds had enough in common to build a successful life together, including an exciting social calendar. Stanlibeth remembered, "Morris and I befriended people very early on." They entertained frequently, always with highballs and cocktails; they were not just at the center of the party—they *were* the party. The society page of the *Albuquerque Journal* ran the headline: "Kights Plan Art Party." The brief three-paragraph story details Mr. and Mrs. Morris Kight throwing "a dude party with chuck wagon chow for refreshments and the Duke City Wranglers to play for those into dancing" to honor everyone from the All Albuquerque Art Show. The last paragraph says: "Mr. Kight recently acquired the inn, formerly the Old Town Auction Gallery, and the party will mark its dedication."

Because young Stanlibeth enjoyed Morris' aspirations, the couple mattered in the community. As Stanlibeth put it, "He was always trying to be important." They socialized with the fine arts crowd in Albuquerque and were heavily involved on the advisory committees with community-based theatres and galleries. At one point, Kight was among a group who resurrected the long-dismissed Old

Albuquerque Museum Association to find a permanent museum of art and science in Albuquerque. He befriended local grande dame and impresario Dorothea Fricke Whitcraft, who was head of the University of New Mexico's Art Department and founder of the New Mexico Art League in the 1940s. With Kight and Carmen Espinosa, from a local pioneering family, they put on a series of 71 exhibitions called *Art and Artists of Albuquerque*. They used multiple community spaces simultaneously to create an event, which exhibited community art done by local professional and amateur artists while cultivating local interest in art. It was a novel and ambitious idea, and over time the name evolved to the All Albuquerque Art Show.

Kight helped to conceive the shows; in addition, he picked the artists and art—including some controversial shows that involved nudes. He promoted and hung the shows, found and fostered sponsor support, and co-wrote the catalogues for each exhibition. To generate further excitement and interest, they created an Art Club Awards show to honor local artists. Kight acted as master of ceremonies and, able to air the event over KOAT as a special half-hour radio broadcast, he invited the public to see the show live in the studio.

As early as 1950, he hobnobbed with prominent members of the community and fine arts world. He worked closely with the Albuquerque Historical Society and he was elected president of New Mexico Art League in 1952. A vital and contributing member of the community, his name frequently appeared in the society section, the events page and the art news of the local newspaper.

Kight desperately wanted a membership to the Albuquerque Country Club, founded by Stanlibeth's maternal grandparents. Membership eluded the ambitious Kight as the grandparents were not forthcoming with a recommendation for admittance to the exclusive life.

The young bride realized that "he was not all the male that he pretended to be." Still, they conceived their first child within the first year of marriage. "The night before our first child was born we had a dinner party. I could keep up with my social obligations." Within two years, they had their second daughter. Kight was fully ensconced in an upwardly mobile middle-class life. He was described as "indifferent, irresponsible [as a father]. He'd get the girls up at midnight to show them off to somebody," and that created disharmony at home.

Kight's life in Albuquerque was very good, complicated and not perfect, but it was good. His businesses were successful, by all appearances his home life functioned well, and he was always busy booking or promoting the next cultural event coming to town. He was more active in cultural affairs than local politics and he was thought of as a shaper of the malleable community. His dutiful wife kept a scrapbook of clip files from their many successes. They regularly appeared in the *Albuquerque Journal*'s society page, and her presence and participation in the various receptions and parties were important to his success.

Kight's ambitions grew, his profile grew, his ego grew, and his curiosity for enculturation became voracious. For a period of time, he had become essential to the fine arts in Albuquerque and kept his finger on the proverbial pulse of the community. His hotel business kept him in contact with everyone who passed through town, and he loved the constant flow of new people. The San Felipe Hotel became the venue for many events related to the New Mexico Art League, which

Kight was able to parlay into his many committee assignments and generate good business for himself and others. The hotel was a good business to abet his nightlife activities, which never ceased. He continued to go out on his own and come home late after too many drinks, sometimes having been a little roughed up. There were four minor arrests for various incidents, mostly drunken fighting. The District Attorney was an old college buddy of Fyfe's, so the charges were always quickly dismissed. That was Morris Kight's best attempt at being happily married.

With as much as they were involved as a couple, Stanlibeth was beginning to feel very isolated. In the summer of 1952, Morris was very involved with a summer Art Colony at Cloudcroft, a mountaintop village 225 miles south of where they lived in Albuquerque. Stanlibeth spent most of the summer alone. With the exclusion of luncheons with women friends and occasionally seeing her parents, she had no contact with anyone else. She remembered Morris often told her not to trust anyone.

Yet they continued to build a successful life together. He continued to buy and sell properties, and with their few real estate holdings and multiple sources of income, life worked well for the young couple. Morris took care of all the business, the paperwork, and he took control of all the wedding gifts. He picked the projects they would be involved with, at the galleries, museum, theatre, and the playhouse. By mid-1952, Morris was speaking at various civic engagements, such as the Women's Club, on a variety of topics including the "early days in New Mexico" and had made himself to be a general expert.

He had connections in high places and at times may have exaggerated the overall scope of other people's money. It may have been his own naïveté or it may have been Kight straddling his two worlds, but sometimes things were a little messy. In a damage suit brought against Dorothea Whitcraft, artist Adja Yunkers claimed he had been promised a job as director of a new art school to be called the Rio Grande Workshop. Yunkers claimed in court that Kight was to raise funds, Mrs. Whitcraft was to invest and give the grounds, and Yunkers would take the directorship. After returning from a trip to New York where he resigned from his position as professor at the New School for Social Research, Yunkers contacted Kight about the school and Kight told him that he "should skip it." As it turned out, Whitcraft soured on the project when Yunkers arrived at her house for an appointment and asked her if she had any beer in the refrigerator.

Morris Kight was busy, active, doing interesting things. His was a good life, pretty much everything that a "gay kid fantasizing the other world" must have dreamt it could be.

As good as life was for Morris Kight, his ambitions called for his involvement in larger statewide projects. In 1998, Kight offered a rare description of his life in New Mexico and he chose to emphasize his social services work.

"I created in northern New Mexico a whole variety of special-interest projects. I became a [founding] charter member of the New Mexico Conference on Social Welfare made up of distinguished men and women, psychiatrists, psychologists, professors, and a whole variety of technicians. And we were providing examples of how much better social services could be in New Mexico, particularly for poverty whites, Native Americans, and poverty Hispanics. For example, we found that pinto beans, which grow very naturally in the red clay soil of northern New Mexico, are very high in protein, and protein is necessary to maintain the body chemistry. We were constantly urging more planting of beans and better beans and so on and so on. [I] did social work there and took up many projects including environmental concerns.

"The Bureau of Engineering wanted to reroute the Rio Grande River outside of the Rio Grande riverbed ... to dig a cement trench north from Taos (at the beginning of the Rio Grande River) down across the desert to El Paso and on to Brownsville, Texas. We opposed that, saying that that was fouling up nature. The river serves a unique purpose. It brings refined sand down and creates an alluvial plane. It makes it a better planting field, a better playing field, and a better place for other livestock, game birds, coyotes, rabbits—they grow in the underbrush. You put the river up on the hill and you destroy the environment. So we fought that in court and won. And they kept the Rio Grande in the Rio Grande riverbed."

Also on a state level, Kight volunteered for a venereal disease eradication program in New Mexico. His in-laws had contributed greatly to the creation of a sanitarium in Albuquerque for TB, and Morris did outreach to coordinate nine thousand volunteers in a tuberculosis identification and treatment program.

In addition to his intelligent and compliant wife, Kight's in-laws were completely supportive. Morris did not keep his political aspirations a secret, and soon Ouida and Fyfe were on board to support their son-in-law in a run for governor of New Mexico. Ouida and Fyfe were both old-time Democrats and if they supported anyone for political office, it was automatically assumed that the candidate would be on the Democratic ticket. In retrospect, Kight appears to have been more of a "convenient Democrat." It is worth noting Kight's hubris to begin a political career at the advanced level of governor, and moreso given the obvious challenges to such a campaign. Early on it was communicated to potential gubernatorial candidate Kight that his mother Bessie was a political liability.

A well-connected name in the New Mexico Democratic Party machine was Tingley. Clyde Tingley was governor for two terms in the 1930s. After 1940, he served on and off on the Albuquerque City Commission and in 1950 had been re-elected its chairman—the equivalent to being Mayor. A few introductions were made, and soon enough Mrs. Morris Kight was having regular lunches with Mrs. Clyde Tingley.

"They were really an incredible pair of people," Stanlibeth said of the Tingleys. "As wonderful as you think they were, they were better than that."

The Tingleys had personal interests that were similar to the Kights', mostly centered on the betterment of Albuquerque and on saving the Rio Grande. The Tingleys had a personal dedication to improving children's hospitals. Carrie, Clyde's wife, was a survivor of tuberculosis who demurely served as the dutiful wife working behind the scenes to do good for the community. She was a perfect role model for young Mrs. Kight, and the two women began to frequently update each other over lunch. The Tingleys were part of a much older crowd, so for as much as the Kights entertained, they didn't entertain the Tingleys at the house. Still, the two couples became closely acquainted.

Clyde was older and more experienced in politics and may not have taken Morris Kight's political ambitions too seriously. Tingley was 'Old Albuquerque' and Kight was definitely 'New Albuquerque.' Kight looked to the older man less as a political role model and more as a stepping stone. Except for Bessie, Morris had never known anyone quite like Clyde Tingley. Where Kight was refined, the brash Tingley was known for his sometimes bawdy humor and for making grammatical errors with humorous results. Still, Tingley was greatly admired, and for Kight, he was a quick study. Clyde Tingley was a big man with a large personality who liked a lot of attention from the community. Kight would let him know when to be at the Albuquerque train station to pick up a bit of limelight, greeting visiting Hollywood stars and incoming talent. Tingley was definitely aware of Kight's contributions to the community and knew him not just for his political ambitions.

A little-known fact about Tingley is that he used to drive around Albuquerque at night, alone. Not to speculate how familiar he was with all the nightlife in Albuquerque, in Erma Fergusson's notes on an unpublished biography of Clyde Tingley, she wrote: " … His constant overseeing drives through the town … drives which were really inspection tours of the city … which kept him in touch with what was going on and often resulted in discoveries of real use … sometimes he picked up rather queer leads. One night, driving down Fourteenth Street toward Rio Grande Park, he noticed a man whose manner [was] somehow surreptitious or suspicious. This came to mind the next morning when Shorty Gonzales, the zookeeper, reported that two raccoons and a beaver had been stolen during the night. That was enough. Mayor Tingley alerted the police department who ascertained within hours that a roadside seller of Western regalia had just bought two raccoons and one beaver skin, properly stretched but obviously fresh."

Through hard work and his wife's connections, Morris Kight's stature in the community escalated. At one point, Stanlibeth personally signed a one-million-dollar insurance contract to borrow Pablo Picasso's work from the British Museum to show at the Old Albuquerque Museum. As a result of this deal, Picasso's work toured the entire country. The Kights were becoming known for providing Albuquerque cachet in the fine art world.

But Kight, Stanlibeth remembered, was most fond of the "little theatre people. He was very elated to see them. Theatre people were 'New Albuquerque.'"

"Morris and I hosted the Irish Dublin Players over Christmas," his former wife remembers a fun time. "A busload of 20-plus actors, in a touring production of the Sean O'Casey play *Juno and the Paycock,* made a stop in Albuquerque." In early November 1954, the *Albuquerque Journal* listed "Dec 27 through Dec 30, Morris Kight, director of the Old Albuquerque Museum presents the Dublin Players" in the Approaching Productions section.

Stanlibeth remembers: "After the performances, they had a few days off before they needed to be at their next booking," so the Kights invited them to stay at the San Felipe Hotel and hosted a memorable time. They took their guests through the back alleys of Albuquerque for The Pageant of Christmas then on to Christmas Eve Mass, which was followed by a long night of dancing and drinking on the Plaza. A festive mood prevailed into the late night. The Irish guests showed Morris how to dance correctly. The hosts introduced their guests to hominy, fry bread, chili, local customs, folklore and music unique to the Pueblos. After carrying on all night, "we cooked two huge turkeys … we couldn't [all] eat in my house because it was too small. So we had to haul everything to the [Albuquerque] museum to eat. We had a great time." It was the kind of entertaining that Morris Kight could not have done on his own—he needed Stanlibeth with her local connections and knowledge of the customs because, as she said, "he didn't know a damn soul there."

"We had a very successful year," Stanlibeth remembers. "We did enjoy success on our own." And Morris "took credit for everything."

Stanlibeth knew that Kight needed to feel special and well-connected. He bragged about his connections to the Indians and continued to do so long after he left New Mexico. "He got to go to a couple of weddings and he felt like he was the one Anglo who was being in with the Indians. They invite *tourists* to their weddings." Kight would sometimes say to his wife, "I admire your amazing heritage." She didn't realize until some years later that he assumed that she was from Indian ancestry.

At one point in the early 1950s, Morris, Stanlibeth, and Bessie drove to East Texas for a Grimes family funeral. Stanlibeth remembers Morris' sister as a very stolid woman who "hated him." Stanlibeth never learned exactly why Lucy Mildred hated Morris, though it may have been his close relationship with Bessie. Bessie was wildly unpopular with her own family, and during this visit her older brother told her not to come back to see the family again. John Louis, Morris' brother, also told Stanlibeth to "be very careful. Don't trust Bessie Mary, she's not a good woman. [Even] if you inherit any money, your life will not be worth a dime."

After a few years, Morris wouldn't even pretend that he could control Bessie.

In Albuquerque, Bessie upped her antics. She was "horrible," Stanlibeth recalled. "After we were married, she'd go to stores and demand credit," from shop owners who knew Stanlibeth and her family. "I'd love to buy something here," Bessie would bemoan, "but I can't. My son is married to that [so-and-so] … and she's taken all the money." There were frequent public outbursts in the chatty town; Bessie would sit in the shops and scream, "He married that South First Street whore," which made no sense since Stanlibeth never lived on South First Street. Bessie would go on and on about how poorly she was treated. Another oft-repeated phrase was "I have nothing but carrots to eat." Stanlibeth knew of one storeowner who threw Bessie out of his shop.

Stanlibeth expressed her concern to Morris. Morris responded that he'd "take care of it." He implied that he had consulted an attorney about Bessie who said there was nothing that could be done. According to Stanlibeth, "We couldn't stop her. Morris said lawyers said you can't do anything about it."

Kight confided to his wife that Bessie had syphilis. Since he was 17 years old, Morris had driven dozens of Fort Worth prostitutes to their cure in Arkansas, but not his mother. Through her own obstinacy, Bessie's syphilis remained untreated. While it certainly excused some of her behavior, her reputation for being eccentric and selfish went back to her childhood. There was nothing that Morris could do but to appease his mother. He tried to maintain calm in the highly charged and unstable dynamic. Gandhi himself would have been challenged to keep the peace between his mother and his wife and in-laws.

With the benefit of reflection, many years later Kight's ex-wife appreciated that Morris could not be expected to have "an inner governor, he had no healthy boundaries, no scruples—having been raised by Bessie, he had no place to get it from."

There seemed to be no end to the problems that Bessie could create. Stanlibeth recalls an acrobat dog "that some performers had left at the hotel," that Bessie took into her care. "A nasty little thing," vicious, and did not get along with the show dog that Morris had given to Stanlibeth.

Later in the marriage, Stanlibeth remembers that "Morris gave Bessie a key to [the 12th Street house]. The two kids were asleep and [she came into the house and] tried to kill me. I defended myself with a bronze candlestick.... I told her 'You go. Get the hell out of my house.'"

The house locks were immediately changed. Bessie's daughter-in-law described her as having "the morals of an alley cat and the grace of a buffalo."

Bessie was wreaking havoc and destruction through Morris' life that could not easily be repaired, all of which had to frustrate a man with Kight's ambitions.

By the mid-1950s, Morris Kight's life had become quite complicated.

Chapter 6

The Kight Family Museum

KIGHT BECAME IMPATIENT with his double life. He became more blatant with his sexuality and began making passes in the daytime and letting his guard down. "He really attracted both men and women," his former wife remembered. Drunken late nights were more frequent and more marked. Arrests were piling up. If Morris "had one drink, he was okay. But he had a couple [drinks] and made passes." Stanlibeth said that Morris began offending people: "He patted them on the butt and he was an expert on everything."

Kight had been either very careless or extremely insensitive, or both. Perhaps he purposely wanted to sabotage his happy heterosexual existence, or he had an arrogant fantasy of a way in which things could work out even while he kept his wife in the dark. By mid-1955, his risky behavior basically led to "a silent political suicide" when he made an unwelcome pass at his friend Calvin Horn. Perhaps a drunken misjudgment, Kight knew immediately that he had a made an irreversible error. Horn simply withdrew from Kight. There was no fight, no harsh words. Yet Kight must have known, from that moment, that there would be no political career for him.

In 1998, Kight recalled: "In 1954, two FBI agents came into my house at 610 12th Street Northwest, Albuquerque, on a sunny summer afternoon. They flashed their identification and said, 'Mr. Kight, are you communist and homosexual?' I said, 'Good grief. Wow, what a question! Why ever are you asking about my private life?

Whatever law is there that you're enforcing? There's no law. Oh, there's a law regulating homosexual behavior of military, but not civilians. No law, so why are you asking? What business is this to you?'"

Kight told the story many times, never veering from the same details. "'Well, you have a reputation.' 'So what? It's none of your business.'" Kight realized that being a sexually active homosexual, he was associated with the homosexual crowd, "even though we were all in the closet, but somewhere we had a social life," and that automatically made his reputation vulnerable. "Our parties were raided quite regularly by the police department. So they knew that. And the FBI thought they were going to compromise me, and I wouldn't allow it."

Kight said to the FBI agents, "'And communist… I always made a point of never indicating my party affiliation of any kind, and I don't intend to answer that question. In the meantime [I said], I need to check your identification.' 'We showed you our identification.' 'No, you didn't. You just flashed it by me. Let me see your identification… This photograph, Orville T. Boylinton, is that you?' 'Yeah, that's me.' 'It doesn't look like you. What about you? Gregory T. Banks, is that you? The pictures don't look like you. What makes you think that I won't believe that you are KGB agents and that you are in the secret employ of the Soviet regime? I'll just call up the FBI and check on you.' So I took up the phone, and they said 'No, you can't just call.' And I said, 'You're here *not* at my invitation. You're not welcome here.' I called up the head of the FBI office at the local telephone number. I said, 'There are two agents here in my house, and they seem very suspicious and I'm not sure if they aren't spurious.' They said, 'Let's talk to them.' And they left my house, and I never heard from them again. I suffered a lot of invasion by the FBI."

Kight's FBI file confirms: "Letter to the Director from Morris L. Kight, dated 1/8/54."

1952. Morris and Stanlibeth with their oldest daughter. Albuquerque, NM.
From the personal collection of Angela C. Chandler.

An earlier entry in the FBI report: "Albuquerque letter to the Director captioned [deleted], dated 7/31/53 with three enclosures. The name Morris Kight appears on last page of third enclosure." And thus began Morris Kight's ongoing relationship with the Federal Bureau of Investigation.

Ignoring his error in judgment with Calvin Horn, he pushed to be more involved and prominent in the community. He expressed his desire to see his name on something of significance and permanent, even if it wasn't going to be the governor's door.

The former Mrs. Kight recalls, "The San Felipe Hotel was home of the Gardening Club and they owned the whole building and somehow it had come up for lease. Morris had coveted it for a long time. So he leased it immediately" without consulting anyone, and without a plan to utilize it, it was purely an emotional decision. He borrowed heavily from his in-laws to lease the building and, according to Stanlibeth, knew that "it wouldn't make money for a long time." He decided, before he even signed the lease, to call it "The Kight Family Museum."

Dated back to the early 1700s, the building was originally built as a private residence and later it became a stagecoach stop. During Prohibition, it was used as a gambling house and bar, then it became a Kingdom of God revival house. In the late 1800s it served the Episcopal Church until the Civil War when it was turned into a military post.

Kight began to sell off pieces of silver from Stanlibeth's hope chest in order to make money to purchase indigenous arts and crafts, which were famously considered worthless at the time. He decorated the museum with borrowed antiques from Stanlibeth's collection and found crafts and drapery. In retrospect, Stanlibeth understood much better. "Someone told me the lobby of the hotel [which he decorated] mirrored the lobby of a bordello. But I'd never been in a bordello [so how could I know]."

Kight moved the Summerhouse Theater Company onto the premises and managed the building and museum on his own. The new venture added further strain on the marriage.

By 1955, Kight was consumed with his new self-titled museum, his hotel business, and his demanding mother. Whatever was left of his attention was captured by one particular man. Edwin Steinbrecher was in his early twenties when he met Morris Kight. Kight hired Edwin and his younger brother Michael to work in a makeshift manufacturing shop set up underneath the Kight Family Museum. According to a mutual friend, "Edwin worked in the basement making fake Indian turquoise jewelry."

The local Pueblo tribe taught Morris how to make fake turquoise and manufacture, sometimes custom manufacture, antique jewelry. Kight set up a lucrative side business with East Coast collectors looking for inexpensive Indian jewelry. According to a friend of Kight and Edwin who was somewhat familiar with the process: "The boys did the antiquing. And that involved an elaborate process of various chemicals, burying the [fake silver and rock] in the ground, doing various things to age it, corrode it, and patina it with [more] chemicals and with techniques that only Morris knew, had learned [from the local tribe]."

Morris and Edwin became romantically involved. Nights in the basement were more frequent, and days were spent upstairs at the unprofitable Kight Family Museum. Edwin was an energetic intellectual. He possessed an innately curious mind and a bright open future—qualities that would be attractive to the mid-thirties

Kight, who was soon all but ignoring his family. Other than providing a home and financial support, by the mid-1950s Kight was never active in his children's day-to-day lives and was barely a perfunctory parent.

The distraction and stress of the situation may have contributed to Kight's carelessness, but it could never explain his reckless decisions during this period.

Stanlibeth: "Even though he was a gentle man, a kind man, he was a drunk. I just had enough of it. He got arrested. I got called from the police. I had to call a sitter, go down there at three in the morning." For someone who so desperately wanted to be important and to have societal status, he had become incredibly reckless in his personal life.

Morris always had the family car—Stanlibeth never had transportation of her own. "We had a lot of fights about me being isolated," she recalled. When her friend Charlie stopped by the house to show off his new station wagon, she jumped at the opportunity for a ride. He offered to drive Stanlibeth to Gallup to visit her parents. She had to get a babysitter because "Morris was irresponsible with the kids."

Once at her folks' house in Gallup, Stanlibeth told Fyfe that she needed to talk to him privately. It was unprecedented that Stanlibeth would talk with Fyfe without Ouida orchestrating the conversation. "We had a long talk and I said, 'I cannot take this anymore.' Fyfe kept saying, 'Honey, it's not you.' I finally told him, 'I want a divorce, but I'm afraid.' 'Why are you afraid?' he asked me. I said, 'I'm afraid that I'll lose my children.' He said, 'How are you going to lose your children?' I said, 'Morris won't let me spend any time with them.' He said, 'Honey, he can't do anything about it. He's a fag.' I said, 'A *who*?'

"Then my father explained it to me. I did not know until then. I promptly went down the hall, threw up and came back. I didn't know what it was, but I didn't want anything to do with it. Then Fyfe and I drank shots of whiskey. And then I went to bed. In the morning, I said to Charlie, 'We gotta go back.'

"I had just had enough. Enough, enough, enough. So I moved out. I went straight to Pete McAtee, my attorney, and … I said, 'Pete, I need a divorce.' He said, 'You got it, kid.' We filed that day. [McAtee] was just waiting."

Stanlibeth and the children immediately moved out of the house and rented a duplex on the other side of town on Princeton Drive. Morris and Stanlibeth never spoke again, communicating through lawyers and relatives.

Morris was promptly served with divorce papers and he too moved out of the house and completely settled into the basement of the Kight Family Museum, which was still often referred to as the Old San Felipe Hotel. Stanlibeth remembers that Morris' response was "almost nothing." He never contested the divorce, never questioned why she left him. In fact, he never addressed her at all. She speculated that it was as much of a relief for him as it eventually was for her.

The town wagons quickly circled around their favorite daughter, and the gossips did their duty to fill in some of the details. Over the next few weeks, more information was revealed, and the unspoken questions that the once-young bride had were answered. Calvin Horn's secretary told Stanlibeth about the pass that Morris made toward Calvin a few years earlier. Stanlibeth remembered, "A number of people in town said to me, 'I knew but didn't know how to tell you. I'm ashamed.' I said, 'You should be.' I wanted to smack them. Damn near everyone in the state knew what he was but me." The betrayal struck deep and she was devastated. She felt a stigma had been placed on her children. "It couldn't help but feel like a betrayal. I suppose if Morris had told me, then it might've been different."

At the same time, a second scandal erupted in the small town. Professor Barton Allen and another man were found engaged in homosexual intimacy and they were arrested. This added to the fodder for the town gossips, and Barton Allen's case made the local newspaper. He was forced out of town and, as Stanlibeth remembered, "That was one reason that [my scandal] was given no attention by the newspaper, [Allen's scandal] covered for me, really."

In a 1994 interview, Kight recalled the situation, without naming names, and how it informed his later work in Los Angeles. "An Albuquerque peace officer, a dedicated homophobe—though that word hadn't been invented yet, that's what

1952. Morris being a father with oldest daughter, Angela, and her Great-Grandmother, Abbie McNatt. Albuquerque, NM. From the personal collection of Cori MacNaughton.

he was—spied on the washroom in the basement of City Hall and saw a young Hispanic man and a professor from the University of New Mexico having sex, and went in and arrested them. The professor lost his job in just hours. No public hearing was held, no trial was held, and he was not brought up on charges. He was assumed to be guilty. He fled the city in disgrace. The young man ended up derelict here in Los Angeles in just five years. I just felt that injustice had to stop. So I started intervening in whatever way I could in gay and lesbian cases, and that brought a lot of pressure for me. I was socially ostracized because I was speaking out for a lesbian or gay person."

While Kight slowly began to intervene on others' behalf, he had plenty of his own problems in mid-1950s Albuquerque. Stanlibeth wasn't the only one who wanted him out of town; everyone did. The locals wanted Kight to go away, like Professor Allen had. He was a nasty reminder of nocturnal shenanigans in their simple city. Yet Morris refused to leave.

"Several people offered to kill him," Stanlibeth remembered. A local carpenter contacted Stanlibeth to say "[Morris] should be driven out of town, and we could all practice our marksmanship. And Fyfe got an offer from an Indian."

Morris, however, wanted to stay in Albuquerque, live as a single gay man and continue to build on the life that he had started. He never seemed fazed by his new notoriety. He carried on at his Kight Family Museum, making a living through the hotel and by selling phony turquoise jewelry. He began to barter in items and sold some of the furniture and more of the heirloom silver.

No longer welcome in the Fyfe household, most doors of opportunity were closed to him. The entangled politics of the city's cultural community dictated that Kight be abolished from its inner circle. Shock was followed by hysteric amnesia. His opinion was no longer sought; it mattered not what he thought. The well-placed connections were gone, friends with recognizable names no longer knew him. His mainstay positions on multiple art committees were dissolved, his radio show cancelled, daytime friends at the university were scarce. The underground gay nightlife in Albuquerque became more unsafe and insular. The local shopkeepers were no longer indulgent of Bessie and her antics. When contacted for research for this book in 2005, a 90-something-year-old survivor of the era remembered Kight and when pressed further, harshly withdrew saying, "I told you that I remembered him, not that I wanted to talk about it."

Stanlibeth went back to school and started to work at the offices of McAtee, Toulouse, and Marchiondo, the firm who also became her divorce attorney. The Kight couple had a lien on the property where the Kight Family Museum stood, and this became one of the few issues of contention in the divorce settlement.

When the hearing finally occurred, Morris was represented by a local female attorney who advised him that it was pointless for him to fight for child custody. Pete McAtee had already said that he'd have Kight thrown in jail before he ever got the children. Kight's 'get out of jail free' card was no longer valid now that he lacked the family connections. In regard to child custody and retaining any property, "Morris didn't have a chance in hell," Stanlibeth recalled, "because there were five judges [in New Mexico] that went to college with Fyfe." Kight was granted visitation without a set schedule and would show up intermittently to spend time with the children, though not too much time since the youngest was still in diapers and this was beyond Kight's parenting abilities. It was not an era in which men learned how to change diapers.

Kight planned to get on with his life in Albuquerque. He believed that he could navigate around the more backward ways of thinking and make a life there—eventually as an openly gay man. He continued to deal with local traders and his East Coast connections. He readied the Kight Family Museum for recognition in the art world and set up the Summerhouse Theater. He let everything else go—the New Mexican Hotel, the house, the apartments, and what was left of his real estate business—but he wouldn't abandon his museum. Divorce or not, Morris Kight moved full steam ahead with his own plan. In retrospect, Stanlibeth understood that "he would've been a difficult person to be married to, even if it weren't for him being gay. There was only one person in his world—him."

Kight became willing to leave Albuquerque but not New Mexico. Stanlibeth: "Morris wanted to try anywhere else in the state. My attorney wouldn't allow it. He had thought that my attorney would see his side of things; my attorney did not see his side of things."

September 1956 headline: "Fire Destroys Old San Felipe Hotel and Kight Family Historic Museum."

The Albuquerque fire department fought the blaze in the early Sunday morning hours. The newspaper account reported that "the entire Kight Museum collection was destroyed in the blaze." The collection included "numerous pieces of weaving and other articles," and a sixteenth-century altar that was "split through the middle by the intense heat."

The fire was clearly caused by arson but there was minimal investigation into the exact cause. Due to local opinions, Morris Kight seemed to be the only suspect. Stanlibeth believes that it was unlikely that Kight burned down his own museum; it was his reason for staying in Albuquerque. The property and building

1953. Morris and Angela pose for a studio photograph. Albuquerque, NM. From the personal collection of Angela C. Chandler.

were insured, but the contents were not. Kight had nothing to gain and everything to lose. Life, as he once imagined for himself, was officially over.

Though Morris never described it as such, 1956 commenced the first of some bumpy vagabond years where he risked marginalization and disenfranchisement, living on his wits and some of Bessie's old tricks. His FBI file lists arrests and charges, starting in 1956, for fraud, theft, "obtaining money under false pretenses," and burglary.

He continued working with the local pueblos and supplied some of the phony turquoise jewelry that they liked to sell to tourists. He and Edwin continued their relationship which fueled mostly erroneous speculation about Morris Kight for the rest of his life. One confab summed up the common false assumption that "Morris abandoned his family and ran away with Edwin when Edwin was 17 years old."

According to public record, Edwin Steinbrecher was born in 1930, which would put him in his mid-twenties in 1955 when he and Morris Kight began a relationship.

Kight moved to Los Angeles with Edwin and bounced between Albuquerque, Los Angeles, and Texas for the next few years. He wrote to his children occasionally, always on holidays and birthdays. Stanlibeth remembers: "He wrote a letter about running a hotel in Texas. He wrote a great deal about himself." Bessie stayed in Albuquerque and kept to herself. When he was in Albuquerque, Kight often stayed at the Franciscan Hotel, a "handsome hotel with a lot of political activity." He saw his children sporadically, when it was convenient for him, which was not much different than before the divorce. Uncomfortable with the task of parenting, he wanted to know his children and especially wanted them to know him. Yet he was careless.

Morris picked up his eldest daughter, who was three or four years old at the time, for an afternoon visit. He brought the child over to Bessie's and left her there. Bessie packed the toddler into the car and drove to Odessa, Texas, to visit some of her friends and didn't return until the early hours of the following morning. Later that same morning, Stanlibeth and attorney McAtee went to the Assistant District Attorney Paul Tackitt, and "Morris never took the kids again."

Many years later, after Kight's death, his youngest daughter reflected: "I never asked Morris why he did that to Stanlibeth. Why he betrayed her or deceived her. I wanted him to address it, but during that period of time he never talked about it. Morris never talked about it in all those years, and I never developed the courage to say, 'How could you do that to somebody?'"

For all their differences, Stanlibeth remembered their marriage as a good partnership. She briefly indulged another scenario: "If I had been a little world-wise, we would have been an old Boston marriage. I'd have my affairs on one side and he'd have his affairs on the other. [But] I wasn't that sophisticated. I couldn't cut that. The situation was a compromise of integrity that I couldn't live with."

Stanlibeth said, "I don't mind homosexuals. It's harming a decent woman [that I don't like]." Years later, she recognized that she and her family were casualties of the social codes of the time that created the necessity for a "gay closet." In retrospect, she described her ex-husband as "not Saint Morris and not the devil incarnate either," adding, "Morris used everything and everybody. It led me into a life of pain, a lot of misery. The girls are the only thing that saved my sanity."

Stanlibeth remarried; her new husband adopted the two children, "mostly to protect them from Morris' mother." There was a court hearing, which Morris attended, sitting in the back row as his attorney represented him. Stanlibeth remembered that "it didn't take very long" and Morris Kight had relinquished all parental rights. It is the first memory his youngest daughter, Carol, has of her father. She recalls peering around from the front of the courtroom, "and I knew it was him. No one told me directly, [though] everyone said he was there."

Morris cruised out of Albuquerque that day. He drove to Los Angeles in his large early-model automobile. His dirty secret was out in the open and Bessie had no way to blackmail him. He told her to stay in Albuquerque and do her best to stay out of trouble. He wasn't coming back, certainly not to live. Kight's vanguard vision of himself was unwavering. Yet reality dictated that he was seen as being arrogant or visionary.

Kight preferred to remember it in more flowery ways.

In 1994, he added a slightly different slant when recalling his life in New Mexico:

"Before 1957 ... I was doing all kinds of things, including advocacy for gay and lesbian cases, indirectly, in person, and in the newspapers. That was quite radical. I [already] opposed the manufacture of the atom bomb. I supported the Rosenbergs [Julius and Ethel] in their defense and did so publicly, by name. But I had a [bigger] vision—that the sorry state of lesbian and gay affairs could be changed.

"And so I came to L.A., to create a gay liberation movement."

Part III

Before Gay Rights

Chapter 7

Angels of the City

1950s. The "Fagots Stay Out" sign that hung in a popular West Hollywood café, Barney's Beanery, much like "No Coloreds Allowed" signs that were common in the South.
ONE National Gay & Lesbian Archives, Los Angeles, California.

"AND SO I came to Los Angeles," Kight said, "to start out to create a gay liberation movement," adding, "except that I knew I had to do it in easy stages."

In 2003, while explaining the specific appeal of Los Angeles, Kight said: "Los Angeles has always attracted exotics, crazy people, visionaries.... In the very beginning out on the lecture trail, I said that any community that could create Aimee Semple McPherson—who was really a certified nut, you know, who created a worldwide religion—and J. Paul Getty, who was a billionaire and who was a nut also.... Any city that could create them could certainly create Morris Kight, couldn't it? I mean, it's just one more aberrant person, one more crazy, leaping up on the platform and saying, 'Never again. Never again will you be able to do this to us!'"

Never modest, Kight may have been comparing his achievements or eccentricities to those of McPherson and Getty or, more likely, he equated their notoriety with his goal for renown in Los Angeles.

Kight gave a simpler and yet no less self-serving description of why he chose to move to Los Angeles in a 1994 interview: "1957, I decided that I could not stand, I wouldn't like myself as much as I would like to, if I didn't do more about the sick, sad, and sorry state of affairs for gay and lesbian persons—again, those words were not used, 'homosexual' was the word. I read widely, saw lots of maps, read lots of publications, and so I deliberately moved to Los Angeles. I moved here because I knew this was the seat of the most homosexual activity in the country....

"So I think that the environment contributes to it, the fact that we're all rootless. Nobody in Los Angeles really pays much attention to genealogy, to family history and so on—to hell with it. They lived and then they died. We hope they lived well, we hope they died well, but it doesn't matter. You can't be who we were in the twelfth century. And we don't bring that with us."

In actuality, it took Kight over a decade before he fully warmed up to Los Angeles and stopped eyeing San Francisco and other West Coast cities.

In the mid-1950s, when he was no longer young but not yet old, Kight made the decision that he was not going to try to pass as hetero anymore. He would live true to his genuine, oddball, homo self. He'd had his shot at fame and fortune through conventional means and it hadn't led to happiness. He made a mindful decision to live modestly and create a much simplified and yet purposeful life. He decided that he would deal in cash as often as possible, keep his overhead low and his profile lower. He had a plan.

Kight very purposely told Bessie to "stay in Albuquerque." He didn't want her following him to Los Angeles. She persisted with her threats to out his sexuality, even though the threats held no consequence that he cared about. In a rare raw moment, in 2002 Kight revealed, "I was getting as far away from her as I possibly could. She was in Albuquerque and I was in Los Angeles, and I indicated in every way that she was not welcome to come here because she was a nuisance." He also accepted that his mother was mentally ill and could only be helped, not cured.

When they first came to Los Angeles, Morris and Edwin stayed in Santa Monica with Edwin's Aunt Jo. Soon, Edwin was off in his own direction, following his own passions, which included studying spirituality and Jungian psychology at UCLA. Edwin and Morris parted company soon after moving to Los Angeles, though they would stay in touch for many years. Edwin went on to become "a recognized intellectual" and an expert in the fields of meditation and parapsychology. In April 1973, he founded D.O.M.E. Inner Guide Meditation Center in Santa Fe, New Mexico. Someone who knew Edwin for many years described him as a person who "evolved into a very wise, studied, extraordinarily insightful man." Gay spirituality would not click with Kight. He wasn't religious, but more importantly, he had already, long ago, decided on his belief system and was no longer in search of new answers.

The first stop for any gay man new to Los Angeles in the 1950s and 1960s was Pershing Square—a public park in the middle of downtown that became a common cruising and meeting ground. Kight was there day and night. He quickly became acclimated to the comparatively big city, met new people, and found a little apartment at 143 Fourth Street in the Bunker Hill section of downtown Los Angeles.

"I headquartered on Bunker Hill. I first took a single, paid $45 per month for it. Utilities were included, except for the telephone. I had to get my own phone. The manager, Miss Kennedy, I told her up front who I was and what I was about. I said, 'You need to know that because people will be coming to see me,' and she said, 'So what?'"

What Kight "was about" was the creation of an underground social outreach system for gay men (and ostensibly for gay women as well). This was all very unprecedented at the time and not without some danger. "My number was Madison 8-8610 and I printed cards with my name, address, telephone number. Imagine, in 1957, printing cards with your name, address, and telephone as an upfront homosexual and passing them out in the essential gay and lesbian ghetto—Bunker Hill, downtown Los Angeles, Crown Hill, Westlake Park, Echo Park, and East Hollywood. I passed out my card [so] that I could be of service to people. Nobody else was doing what I was doing. I went into the street, hands-on, not for a fee—nobody was charged a fee. First place, I was not a licensed social worker, and second place I was dealing with a poverty community. My role was not subject to charge. So I went around, going to bars, going to courtrooms and jails and prisons. I visited the homosexual prisoners in Tehachapi Prison, went all over San Francisco and San Diego."

Kight made his services available to gay men who needed help—any kind of help—and what followed was extraordinary. Many people called his number just to talk or cry. Some people needed a meal, a sofa on which to sleep, or someone to call from jail. Applying the knowledge he gained from his work in the Bureau of Indian Affairs, he studied the kind of help that was needed and began to create ways to provide services. He set out—one gay man at a time, one problem at a time—to create a new existence for homosexuals. It was, in effect, the beginning of the end of the introverted, powerless sissy boy and the disenfranchised, depressed, marginalized homosexual. He found what he expected—self-loathing, pauperization, marginalization, shame, and loneliness—issues that were pretty much unique to the population of "sexual deviants" and had never been specifically addressed for them. He also discovered an untapped market of social service needs. Kight met rich men who had health problems and poor men with legal problems—it all added up to a disempowered faction of society that needed help. In time, he created relationships with doctors and lawyers and socialites who were sympathetic to the cause and would provide support and services.

Kight realized that gainful employment was a particular challenge for homosexuals and he learned of a code that employers and employment agencies used to identify the obvious homosexual. "They coded you at the top of the page as a '33'; I never knew where that came from." So Kight purposely developed relationships with gay-friendly (or at least gay-shortsighted) employment agencies to which he referred gay men and women who were competent but otherwise unemployed because of their blatant sexuality.

Longtime friend and Kight associate Jaime Green recalls that Pershing Square was "where all the organizing activities took place, setting up all that [innovative] stuff. There was this group of queens that used to come together. They were kind of like a debate society, and they're the first ones who started organizing rescue for people who got in trouble with the law. That all took place at Morris' office, which was a certain bench under a banana tree [at Pershing Square]. He would be there certain hours. His early morning routine was to go to the police station and see—demand to talk to—all the people who had been arrested for lewd conduct the night before."

Jon Platania explained, "Back in those days, the fun-sport of the vice squad was to bust as many gay men as they could and publish their names in the newspaper—arrest people for putting their hands on somebody's shoulder in a bar, arrest people for even touching on the hands while dancing in a bar. Lives were ruined wholesale. Morris filled this really important role of finding lawyers and doctors, and finding people who could help other people. He really did that more or less single-handed."

Most of the "lewd and lascivious" arrests in those days were trumped-up charges of the equivalent of Jim Crow laws for gays, or else they were cases of blatant entrapment. Kight developed multiple ways to raise funds for bail. He directed men who called him from jail to attorneys who knew how to plea lewd and lascivious behavior charges down to a misdemeanor. He created good relationships with a few select attorneys, specifically Sheldon Andelson and a heterosexual libertarian attorney named Al Gordon. Andelson and Gordon also became patrons of Morris, not just because he was a great source of referrals but because they came to believe in what he was saying and what he was doing. And he was, as many noted, one of the few with nothing to lose.

Kight had his own brushes with the law. He had developed a habit of petty crime and his FBI file lists a series of arrests that had begun in 1956 for "removing and concealing mortgaged property" in Odessa, Texas, a charge which was probably linked to loose ends on the diner he'd owned with Bessie. Besides a few traffic misdemeanors in 1958, in August of that year he was arrested in Las Vegas, New Mexico, for "obtaining money under false pretenses." That arrest might have been for selling phony turquoise jewelry, or it could've been for almost anything. He was ordered to make restitution of $75. In November 1958, he was arrested in Los Angeles for suspicion of burglary.

According to the background information provided in his FBI file, he was arrested in 1960 for grand theft auto and again in October 1962 for shoplifting in the Echo Park area of L.A. He was booked but served no time. His last known arrest was in December 1963, for theft. He served 30 days in L.A. County Jail, released in January 1964. That is the last entry in his arrest record though his FBI report references additional arrests. Their investigation revealed "On January 14, 1963 … Vice-Square, Albuquerque Police Department, advised that Morris Kight was booked on April 15, 1961 … was booked on … for contributing to the delinquency of a minor." These charges were later dismissed. A separate notation says that the "Albuquerque Police Department advised … The records show also that he was arrested … for failure to answer a citation and $45 bond was posted … he was arrested again for the same citation and $20 bond was posted. No disposition was listed."

Separate searches of Albuquerque Police Department records in 2004 and 2005 produced no results. Whatever files there might have been on Morris Kight had been purged.

In 1956, he rented a small apartment at 5738 Carlton Way in Hollywood. In the early '60s, he moved a little further south to 4274 Beverly Boulevard where the first real signs of his new business appeared. At the same address on Beverly Boulevard he also listed "Old Stuff and Things/Antiques." He didn't stay there very long; soon he moved further south, close to MacArthur Park, and set up shop at 716½ South

Bonnie Brae, a small cottage behind a four-unit building. Every time he moved, he remained close to the center of the city and became more enmeshed and familiar.

In the early 1960s, he was still going back and forth between Albuquerque and Los Angeles in a half-hearted attempt to maintain a relationship with his two daughters. He was under an FBI "logical investigation" for suspicion of transporting obscene pictures "between the two cities for commercial purposes." According to Kight's FBI file (in which most of the names are redacted), this particular investigation was "predicated upon information received" by a telephone call and two subsequent letters to the FBI regarding Morris Kight. According to the file, "She stated that this man had a 'wild place' at 716½ South Bonnie Brae, phone number Hubbard 3-0319 in Los Angeles." The FBI investigated everyone in Los Angeles and Albuquerque who knew Kight, including neighbors, his landlady, and the owner of the Satellite, a local tavern that Kight frequented.

According to longtime Kight friend and cohort Gino Vezina, "Bonnie Brae was the beginning of the Gay Community Services Center. There is no way to get away from that. He had a large group of people who stayed there" and would go there when they were in trouble.

A separate informant told the FBI that they "had no knowledge of any obscene literature of pictures or interstate transport," though they did mention that someone (whose name is redacted from the report) "was always attempting to put [Kight] into a mental hospital." (It has been speculated by a number of persons familiar with the situation that it was most likely Bessie who tried to put him in a mental hospital.)

In the latter part of 1963, the FBI raided the Latino Photo Shop at 716½ Bonnie Brae near downtown Los Angeles, expecting to find photographs of underage boys. The raid was fruitless. According to Kight's FBI file, during the raid Kight was temporarily staying at the Franciscan Hotel in Albuquerque using the aliases "Kurth," with no first name, and "Leo Parks."

It's not known what the Latino Photo Shop was, other than a cover for Morris Kight. Kight did, in fact, live at 716½ Bonnie Brae in 1963, and, according to multiple sources, had a small mail-order business that distributed nude, muscle-men types of photographs that he'd mail to "podunk" towns throughout the Midwest and Pacific Northwest—places where homo-curious young men and old men had no access to such material. There is no evidence that Kight was involved in shooting any of the photography, just the distribution. As a number of people commented, "He did what he had to do [to survive]." More than once, Kight said: "I have always lived my life with one hand to the Lord in heaven and one hand in the garbage bin." Borrowing from Oscar Wilde, he'd add: "You can still see the stars even if you are lying in the gutter." Kight didn't use the word "Lord" sanctimoniously as referring to a more refined, existential element of being.

"I was," Kight recalled, "constantly looking for cheaper rent because 45 dollars was high. I know this sounds ridiculous in today's standards.... Gasoline was 30 cents a gallon.... The phone cost a lot of money." The phone was essential to his plan. "Virginia Campbell, a non-gay woman who was a pioneer of our concerns, was out looking for a place for both of us to move to. On South Hope Street, four blocks south of where I was living, she found two cottages—a cottage for her and a cottage for me—for 35 dollars a month each. A sitting room, a dressing room, bathroom, kitchen, a courtyard porch, a little dining room off that, and then a room downstairs which I used for storage."

Kight continued to receive phone calls and he had long talks with his callers. He became more familiar with the most urgent needs. At the time, a state law required that all STD cases be reported to the County Health Department. Doctors knew this puritanical law created a potential public health crisis because most people would not seek treatment; Kight saw it as another bureaucratic means of disempowering consenting adults. One case of gonorrhea could destroy an entire life, including career and family—a fact that was just as true for heterosexuals as it was for homosexuals. Soon, with these brave doctors, Kight was able to offer anonymous treatment for sexually transmitted diseases in the back room of his bungalow. He made arrangements with doctors who would donate their services to treat sexually transmitted diseases, anonymously.

Already unprecedented, this community service was also, as Kight described it, "not-for-fee." While he always welcomed donations, no one was ever turned away. He put the word out on the street by way of his cards with his phone number. He left his card at bars, public phone booths, public restrooms, and on park benches in Pershing Square. Soon his little house and underground operation became known as the "clap shack." Over time, Kight had a huge following of closeted people, and he was always careful to protect secrets. "Madison 8-8610" became the most important phone number to know if you went to prison or you had a venereal disease or you were on the brink of self-destruction. Kight provided the same services throughout the 1960s and into the early 1970s.

By the mid-1960s, the FBI was keenly interested in Kight. His FBI file cites that he was "a member of the 'gay' crowd" during this period. Because Kight accurately suspected the FBI was interested in what he was doing, he kept no records. His place had been broken into a number of times, though nothing of value was ever taken; it was more about riffling through papers and files.

"And that brought the next visit from the FBI, who said, 'Mister Kight, how do you make a living?' I said, 'Why are you asking? What concern is this of yours?' 'Well, we have word that you're engaged in some criminal activity.' 'Me? I'm a law-abiding pacifist.' I didn't tell the FBI, because it wasn't any of their business, that how I supported myself was that I'm an arcane authority on antiques, china, silver, linen, brass, sorting silver, and Native American jewelry. I just had a sense of that [sort of thing]. It is a stereotype, by the way, that is true that some gay men are into antique dealing and interior decorating. I was pretty good at that. And so I gathered stuff and conducted, every six months, what nowadays is called a 'yard sale.' In those days, yard sales hadn't been invented yet. I conducted backyard sales."

Often, these Sunday yard sales fronted for a series of clients being treated in the "Clap Shack" in the back room.

One of Kight's oldest friends in Los Angeles, Gino Vezina, remembers that Kight "had many ways of getting money. He never worked at a regular job; he was very clever at that. There were so many large community gatherings that people would pay to get in [or Kight would pass a hat and], he made money." At times, Kight was also a souvenir vendor at Dodger Stadium.

Before too long his antique business developed valuable repeat customers. He made enough money for "leaflets, the car, the phone, and to keep myself going. Liberace [Valentino Liberace, an American pianist and vocalist] was an antique collector and he was one of my customers," Kight recalled. "He was a swish and a Nelly and he had baroque taste, and I collected some baroque things. I got quite enough money—not to pay myself a salary, of course, but to just eke by. So I did that without having to work."

"In the meantime," Kight continued, "I had accumulated a great many what I call 'befriendees,' people I befriended. I avoided the word 'client,' which creates a relationship that you know everything and they don't know much, or 'patient' because I never considered anybody sick. And so I just called them 'befriendees.' I accumulated a great many of them and I held 'rap groups' in my house on Saturdays and Sundays."

Kight held regular Sunday afternoon soirées that very often spilled into a Sunday night party. Every Sunday, he sat outside with his yard sale and casually hosted an all-day open house and Sunday dinner as a way, Kight described it many years later, of "previewing for a more purposeful life for gays." He was reinventing his own life to be more suitable and fulfilling to the dreams of that gay kid in Texas who fantasized about "the other world."

Lawyers, doctors, all professionals, and borderline derelicts were all welcome on Kight's new merry-go-round, any time of any day. It took years, but eventually, Kight created a network of supporters who could help each other with perhaps a sofa to crash, a day job, or a cooked meal—Kight would coordinate everything with a few phone calls.

Gino Vezina considers the era as "the beginning of the Gay Community Services Center," though that formal institution would not come to fruition for another 15 years. "When he lived on Fourth Street, that was the very beginning of the outreach. Seeds were planted for a services center. There is no way to get away from that; he had around him a large group of people, [some] who lived there, and proceeded from there" to build a community.

In 1992, gay activist Frank Vel recalled for a KCET profile on Kight: "Before there was gay liberation and before the Gay Community Services Center, Morris was a walking gay community center. Wherever he went, he attracted other gay persons. He would put people in contact with each other and his telephone was like a clearinghouse. There were calls coming in at all hours, every day, two, three o'clock in the morning: 'I'm new in town, I just found out about being gay, I've run away from home, what do I do?' Morris would get up, go down to the bus station, wherever it was, get this person and take care of them, bring them into the house. And Morris always had an extended family. When you were at Morris' house, you felt like you were with family, and that was important before gay liberation, because a lot of people could not come out to their own family. Their own families would've shunned them."

Vezina was aware that "some people were bedazzled by all this, but some were not." According to Vezina, Kight was, for the most part, "surrounded by alcoholics or losers who connected with Morris to get a roof over their head. He always managed to have a roof to put over their head."

He considers that Kight "would've been a very successful hetero, had he remained in the South and became a Southern politician," in the vein of Tennessee Williams' *Sweet Bird of Youth*. And yet, many persons who were involved with Morris Kight wanted to *be* him.

For all the transient goings-on in Kight's home and life he was, as Vezina witnessed, "not prone to promiscuous activity. Morris was a one-at-a-time [lover]." A more accurate description would be that Kight was a serial monogamist. Vezina describes him "as more of a passive partner," not to imply that Kight played a passive sexual role. Multiple first-person accounts freely offered that Kight enjoyed the same well-endowed genetics passed down by his father, Big Willie. Kight was not aggressive in his interest to pleasure his partner; he was, for the most part, emotionally unavailable. He kept his true feelings very much in check—he was guarded, detached, and quick to avoid anything that might smack of a feeling. Despite all he did for all the strangers who knocked on his door, he rarely became emotionally involved. In fact, Kight went beyond the emotional detachment necessary for effective social work, often behaving outright listlessly toward those nearest and dearest.

Vezina remembers the fate of a pet dog that Kight had had for a few years: "The dog was hit by a car and was still alive. Morris wouldn't go to the dog in the street. He couldn't. I had to go and deal with it. Morris didn't want to deal with emotion." This behavior might have been due to emotional scar tissue from his life with Bessie, or it could have been a result of what had happened to him in Albuquerque. Or perhaps Kight may have subscribed to a common viewpoint of men of the era that emotions were a character weakness, a flaw. He had never been an overly demonstrative person. Years later, Kight did develop ways of expressing emotion without feeling the burden of having to be overly demonstrative.

As much as Kight enjoyed his new life, Los Angeles in the early 1960s was a challenge for most homosexuals, and Kight was no exception.

"Well, it had been physically pretty rough. In 1960, I left a gay bar down on Main Street, Harold's at 656 South Main Street. I left at two o'clock in the morning and went out to the parking lot where my car was, and I got in the car, and there were three men—two young adults and a younger man, maybe 15 to 16 [years old]—in the car next to me and they grabbed me, jerked me physically into their car, and put me in the back seat, started speeding out of the lot so fast I couldn't even turn. They went south on Santa Fe Avenue, and by the time they got to Willowbrook I knew full well I had been kidnapped and that it was not going to be a good night.

"They robbed me of all my money and my jewelry, my keys, all of my identification, everything. And they took me out to Santa Fe Springs—which is a built-up city now but then it was vacant land—and there was a kind of rice paddy or some kind of place that has water in it. They took me out in the field and beat me mercilessly."

Santa Fe Springs is about 12 miles from downtown Los Angeles.

"And ultimately [they] left me, I think maybe for dead, or maybe that's an exaggeration. I crawled through the mud up to a kind of a country road and got out [of the water]. It was a narrow, paved road in the country. This was part of Los Angeles; [it's] built-up now, but at that time it was country. I went down the road, and I had my hand out, and car after car would speed by. And a young man stopped in a brand-new red car, it was brand-new, it had that wonderful new car smell. He said, 'You're in terrible trouble, aren't you?' I said, 'Yes, I am. And I need to get where I can get help.' He said, 'I know where the sheriff's substation is in Santa Fe Springs. I can't take you where you need to go, because I have an appointment. But at least I'll take you there.' So he brought me up the steps of the sheriff's station in Santa Fe Springs. I went inside and rather than go to the sheriff's desk, I went up to the washroom, to the mirror, to see how badly hurt I was, and I was bruised and [had] contusions everywhere. Skin torn, eyes blackened, and blood everywhere. So I rinsed the blood out of my hair and off my skin, and rinsed out my underwear to get through the worst part of it, and then finally, blood everywhere, I left the washroom and went to the sheriff's desk. A deputy sheriff came to the edge of the desk and said—you'll have to take my word for it, this is strange, strange history—[he said] 'Mister Kight ...' Mind you, I had not mentioned my name.

"He said, 'Mister Kight, have you ever been arrested for a morals charge?' And I said, 'Whatever kind of question is that? Can't you see that I'm badly hurt? That I'm badly bruised? That I may be ready to die? Can't you see that I desperately need medical help? Why is not that your first question, is what to do for me?' He said, 'Well, we're concerned about your morals.' 'I'm concerned about my health. I'm concerned about trying to get out of this.' And they made a lot of fun of me. I was bleeding.

"And so, finally, one of the [sheriffs] came and said, 'Well, we can't take you back to downtown L.A., but we'll take you to the edge of our jurisdiction, where the LAPD will meet us, and take you home.' So that's fine. So they took me in a warm car, it was cold that night, at that hour, but daylight was coming. And they took me to the edge of the county jurisdiction and then the LAPD took me back to my car on Main Street in Los Angeles. Happily for me, I had hidden a set of keys underneath the car, so I had keys to get back to my house at 341 South Hope, where a member of my family was visiting and had a key to get inside."

Indeed, Kight was "in terrible trouble" by the time that he got home. His head and ears were ringing and he knew that he was in bad shape. He went to California Hospital in downtown Los Angeles and they immediately X-rayed and admitted him. He stayed in the hospital for several days and "it was touch-and-go," Kight recalled.

"Oh, a week or so later, when I got strength, I went back to the corner of Sixth and Main Street, and there was their car. I thought, 'Well, I could call the police on them, but it would reverberate against me. They would say, 'Mister Kight, the morals ...' and they would say the kid was there, that I came on to him. So I knew I would lose that. I also thought about going and getting an ice pick and stabbing their tires. But I felt, they know where I live [since they had stolen his wallet] and I live alone. I live on the side of a hill. And they could come and kill me. So I suffered in silence. It was just horrible. Whatever happened to them, where are they now? I don't know. I hope they got well."

Kight was a pacifist through and through. He also knew isolation and he had experiences with fear. This served him well when serving others, not to bond in victimhood but to have genuine empathy. Kight was never simplistic or overly sympathetic with those who came to him needing help. He helped them pragmatically and changed the course of their lives.

By the early 1960s, Kight had quite an assortment of colorful characters around him—some were happy and some disturbed; they were a cluster of disenfranchised nobodies. Despite the obvious adversities and challenges, Kight and his new friends had come together and created a makeshift family who took care of each other and found endless reasons to have parties and galas.

Kight: "Gino Vezina…maintained a house at 613 South Coronado where he also entertained on the weekends. Purely entertainment, he did a [drag] show, he did a shtick, and had dances." There were two Ginos—Gino Vezina and Gino Riddle—who had regular drag shows on Friday nights with the stage personas "Gina and Gina." They became quite famous in the underground scene. Both homes were so popular that, Kight explained, "there was a trail across Westlake Park through the grass, a trail from his house at 613 South Coronado to my house at 716½ South Bonnie Brae.

"613 South Coronado became a very famous address. In Venice, Italy there is a great building named Diocesan Palace. So I renamed his place The Bitch's Palace. And a young flit—a flit is kind of a homophobic language from my other past—came from Chicago to LAX [Los Angeles International Airport], came out to get a cab and said, 'I am visiting and I know the name of the place where I am going, but I don't know the address.' [The cabbie] said, 'What is it?' 'The Bitch's Palace.' The cab driver said 'Get in. I know where it is,' and he took him to 613 South Coronado. For years and years it was a famous place."

Gino Vezina recalled, "I was a person who emptied out the bars for 2 a.m. gatherings. Morris Kight didn't do that. Morris wasn't a druggie either."

Kight, who preferred to use Gino's drag names, frequently recalled the wild parties with the Ginas. He was quite fond of both of them and became lifelong friends with Gino Vezina.

"[Gino's] exploits during that time were and are legendary," Kight wrote in a 1982 "Memorandum for Archives."

"Episodes of the time: Raid on Jerry's 666 [a popular gay hangout], Gina's organizing of the *Alvarado Pigs*, a takeoff on *West Side Story*. It was a morale booster and a sensation in Westlake Park, which was the gay ghetto of the time. Hundreds of us lived there. I entertained on the weekends as did Gina and Co. We always cleared the dates with one another.

"It was in these sessions that some of the format of later radical groups came. Gina's influence on this was enormous. We were upfront, we were out, and we won the support of our neighbors, totally. Absolutely no resistance from the neighbors at 613 [Coronado] or at 716½ [Bonnie Brae], but later at 1822 [West Fourth Street] one group of neighbors were hostile, others friendly."

Kight expressed his love and admiration for Gino, saying his drag shows took "courage." On other occasions he called Vezina a "beautiful brother."

As Vezina said, Kight wasn't a hardcore druggie. He did drink and, it being the hippie era, he partook in the recreational drugs of the time; he did his share of experimentation. He was surrounded by injured psyches, some of the most fragile, beaten-down individuals in society, and even the parties weren't always festive. There were two deaths at Kight's home that Vezina remembered. "The first one in 1962 or 1963, a guy named Don Watson committed suicide with rat poison and aspirin." And a few years after that, "Larry Allen, a 28-year-old drug addict, died on the sofa of Morris' living room from a drug overdose. Morris threw a blanket over him and told people that he was sleeping. They knew that he was dead and went around and took a collection to get booze." Some might have called the party a "wake" for Larry, but Vezina remembers that many had actually expressed relief because "Larry was a burden to Morris." The party continued and everyone became quite inebriated around Larry Allen's dead body.

Kight's circle included a lot of "pixies," Vezina remembers, "people who surrounded him and kowtowed. I never did that. He was a great friend, but I never catered to his ego like that," which, according to multiple sources, was "a bottomless pit." Through all his do-gooding, taking care of others and bringing people in, helping them get back on their feet, directing them to the right lawyer (who would charge on a sliding scale) or to discreet doctors (who would treat STDs without reporting to the Board of Health), Kight made a lot of friends and connections. He received a lot of gratitude and, eventually, a lot of recognition. At the time, his lifestyle was tailored around the needs of others, and in return, Kight received the one thing he had never gotten before: appreciation. For Morris Kight, this could be seen as the psychological equivalent of water to a thirsty horse.

Kight was clever. Survival was fun and games for him and certainly he didn't limit his social circle to his new befriendees. One of his oldest friends in Los Angeles was Reverend Robert Humphries, known as "Bob," who moved to Los Angeles from the San Francisco Bay Area around the same time that Kight relocated from New Mexico. Together, Bob Humphries and Kight enjoyed using their wits to survive and both were equally comfortable living on the periphery of societal norms. Morris said, "We were the outlaws. We had a sense of camaraderie and hanging tough." They automatically eschewed all facets of living within the defined parameters of The Establishment. They sometimes outwitted each other in a bit of friendly competition, and they were good at coming up with schemes to meet their needs.

One scheme they had was a way to "borrow" a car any time they didn't happen to own a running vehicle but needed one. Kight and Humphries each owned parking valet uniforms—velvet jackets with epaulettes and valet caps. They'd put on the jackets and hats and confidently walk up to a hotel curbside valet service, gently take a car from an unsuspecting guest and "borrow" it for a few hours. Later they would return the car to the general area where it had originally been "borrowed." The scheme may have backfired in May of 1960 when Kight was arrested in Los Angeles for "grand theft auto." He was booked, but no charges were ever filed, due to lack of evidence.

His sometime partner-in-crime Bob Humphries had actually come to Los Angeles as a self-ordained minister of a self-created church called the Church of the Androgyny. Humphries preached a self-created philosophy that "God is neither man nor woman." Always described as "non-denominational," Humphries' whole philosophy appealed to Kight as it more resembled a theory Bessie might have subscribed to than it did any Bible teachings. Leaning less toward Judeo-Christianity than it did toward Humanism, it was mostly innocuous barstool preaching.

The Church of the Androgyny was spirited in another sort of way. The annual meetings were cause for boozy evenings dressed in ecclesiastic-drag robes that Kight and Humphries might have picked up at the same secondhand store or costume shop where they'd found the parking valet jackets. Kight never missed an annual board meeting of the church, which was often held in a local tavern or steakhouse.

The church provided a valuable tax-exempt status that allowed Humphries to raise funds as a legitimate nonprofit entity. As a function of the church, in 1962 Bob Humphries founded the United States Mission to help the homeless. It operated under the philosophy "A hand up—not a handout." (The U.S. Mission is not to be confused with the Los Angeles Mission, which has served the homeless living on Skid Row in downtown Los Angeles since 1937.) Jaime Green, who served as a director on the board of the Church, recalled that the Mission also "started in Pershing Square. Bob Humphries recruited homeless boys that had nowhere to go—often they had alcohol or drug problems. They couldn't get social services because there were no programs set up for that kind of stuff until [much later]. As of [2009] the U.S. Mission has never received funding from federal, state or local government programs or from other social service organizations. All funding comes from philanthropic corporations and generous individuals in our local community."

Yet the humble roots of the U.S. Mission were not so clearly benign. Quite a few people close to the situation felt that the U.S. Mission was not a totally legitimate operation. One person went so far as to call it "a front for unsavory things. In many ways I felt that they were, honestly, preying upon some very unintelligent, uneducated people as part of their operation in the Mission." The associate continued, "[About the] U.S. Mission: they used to collect money and [Humphries] would keep like 90 percent of it or something. But he would always give 10 percent to the community. But of course you didn't know that he kept 90 percent. Well, apparently a lot of charities do that. So no, this guy had no guilt whatsoever. He was just something you don't come across every day. He was on a different wavelength, totally different."

Eventually, the group designed a gold seal to use on the incorporation papers and all official documents generated by the U.S. Mission. The gold seal was quite ornate, with an open cross at the center holding the symbol for the U.S. dollar. In a note written in 1971, Kight explained the theory behind the symbology: "Note the cross and the U.S. symbol imposed thereon. Some say this is a dollar mark, and indeed it does look like one. But Bob Humphries, founder of the Mission, says that it's the ancient seal of the U.S. itself, which comes out as a dollar mark. Some people have been critical of the marriage of God and Caesar; others think it's right on."

Another friend quickly described Humphries as a "hedonist. Not on the up and up."

Like Kight, Humphries enjoyed cheap booze and big cars. Unlike Kight, he liked to gamble; he'd bet in card games, on ponies, at casinos on slot machines. Humphries would go to any place that served alcohol and would take a bet.

Someone who knew both men described Humphries as "a very bizarre guy, extraordinarily bizarre. [He was] a guy who was proud to cater to his passions of alcoholism, sex, and gambling … such a colorful character, like something that popped out of a Charles Dickens novel. He was very close to Morris Kight and I remember … this guy was half-drunk all the time and gambling. Actually, he had a sweetness about his character, but as I say, he was obsessive about his passions and quite proud of it. And none of that guilt. No Christian guilt of any kind. He was like a pagan. He was a modern-day pagan and catered to his passions, indiscriminately with no guilt. [Humphries] had no inner turmoil. He wasn't encumbered in any way with social restrictions of any kind."

Miki Jackson, Kight's longtime close friend, described Kight and his associates at the time as "having larceny in their hearts." According to many others, the larceny was not contained to their hearts.

In private with close friends, Kight clarified his feeling about the U.S. Mission operation: "If we did 51 percent good, I didn't feel so bad."

A large chunk of that 51 percent of good happened on Thanksgiving Day.

Sometimes Kight remembered it as starting in 1957; at other times he said it began in 1958, and other times he said it began in 1962 (which is most likely). What began as a gathering of the sick and elderly who lived in Kight's apartment building grew into something more. In a completely novel idea at the time, Kight and Humphries invited indigent and homeless people off the streets (by way of flyers) to the courtyard of the North Hope Street address and served them a homemade Thanksgiving turkey dinner. The first few years, the dinner attracted a few dozen homeless individuals, plus, of course, Kight's and Humphries' associates.

Jaime Green: "Originally that dinner was started in Morris' kitchen, and Aunt Jo [Edwin Steinbrecher's aunt] used to finance it. Morris would buy the turkeys and all the trimmings, and she and her friends would cook. They were cooking for three days before that event. But Thanksgiving was really big and became a very special party."

The popularity of the annual event grew as the homeless population in Los Angeles grew. Soon, they were feeding close to one hundred people, then over a hundred people.

Jaime Green: "[We were] organizing the [Thanksgiving] dinner to the point that [in the 1960s] we started having to have it in De Longpre Park and busing people." Every year for the rest of his life, Kight solicited funds and in-kind donations from individuals and businesses to help feed the homeless on Thanksgiving Day. Eventually, the event received support from the Los Angeles County Board of Supervisors, and many years later moved to a downtown shelter where the cooking was handled by a large kitchen staff.

The U.S. Mission was very generous with allowing Kight to use its 501(c)(3) tax-exempt status for his many causes. Kight could solicit donations as tax deductions, which helped fund the Thanksgiving dinner and various antiwar and civil rights efforts. It might also be said that perhaps some funds were siphoned off for a few bail funds every now and then.

In November 1983, *Frontiers* headlined an article: "Gay Friends to Serve 600 Free Turkey Dinners in Park," citing Kight as "the originator of the open invitational dinner."

Humphries' particular twist on Humanist philosophy was demonstrated by helping runaway teenage boys. Expanding his services from Pershing Square, Humphries drove around in a big car and would come across lost, runaway boys, who had left abusive or intolerant homes in faraway places and had come to Hollywood in search of better options for life or maybe a long shot at fame. He would "rescue" them off the streets of Hollywood or at the Greyhound bus station and offer them a meal and a place to stay. In exchange for keeping them off the streets at night, Humphries expected them to panhandle during the day and pay a stipend for living expenses. Sometimes the relationships became more "involved," in order to satisfy Humphries' basic instincts and the boys' thirst for new experiences.

Rhyming with the word pagan, Kight referred to their little group as the "Fagins," describing his old friend Bob Humphries as being "sort of at the edge of my affairs for [many] years."

Kight, on the other hand, never became intimately involved with his befriendees; he felt it too easily added confusion. However, his close association to Humphries unfortunately put Kight in a vulnerable position to be likewise accused of exploiting the very people he helped.

No matter the source (and there have been many), every discussion of depth about the history of gay rights in America will eventually head down the dark alley of older gay men 'inducing' or 'indoctrinating' younger gay men. Of course, the same has been true at every time in history and from every angle of sexual identity; it is not a 'ritual' unique to homosexuality. The subject has always remained just as consistently opaque as it is present. Yet it is mentioned often enough that it is necessary to acknowledge it here.

For the purposes of Morris Kight's life story, there is no conclusive evidence that he shared his bed with younger men who came to him for help. Multiple first-person accounts clearly state that Kight did not share Humphries' desire for carnal companionship with matured boys who were on the verge of young manhood. The sources who claim Kight never sexually exploited his young befriendees far outnumber the obtuse conjectures that Kight used in-need boys for sex. He definitely used them in other ways—for caretaking and errands. He gave them purpose and they propped up his ego. He always paid them a stipend, but he never used them sexually.

Depending upon the particular individual, there were instances that someone who came to Kight for help ended up at Humphries' home, and a few of the young men whom Humphries picked up off the street, if they were higher-functioning, did better under Kight's guidance. There was a calculated and detached assessment made of each young man. Though Kight didn't share Humphries' craving, he did not judge his friend. Kight remained active and involved with the U.S. Mission and served on the board of directors for the Church of the Androgyny for the rest of his life, participating right up to his last year in the gently debauched semi-annual inauguration called "The Red Wand" ceremony, created to pick a new director.

Kight did not have a monopoly on early efforts toward a gay rights movement in America, and there were a quite a few things happening on the West Coast before Kight arrived. One of the first things Kight did when he came to L.A. was to familiarize himself with the underground gay scene—the "homophile" effort, as it was called.

In 1950, while Kight was still living the hetero life in Albuquerque, Harry Hay, along with a select group of men, came together in the living room of Hay's Los Angeles Silver Lake home and founded the Mattachine Society—the first known effort to organize homosexuals for the purpose of discussion and to "perhaps come up with ideas to make things better" for themselves. All known previous attempts to organize homosexuals as a social movement had been too risky, too radical, and never succeeded. After World War II, however, such efforts were more hopeful. Servicemen had traveled the world and had met others like themselves; the isolation lessened and numbers added might. Still, in 1950, the Mattachine Society needed to be extremely cautious. Secrecy was their predominant concern, and they purposely did not use the word "homosexual," preferring the term "homophile" so as to not call attention to themselves. Some men were so nervous they brought along a female "date" to meetings to act as a beard. The Mattachine Society exercised careful judgment before bringing in new members, and used a secret cell structure to protect its membership, as well as many other strategies Hay had learned from his earlier membership in the American Communist Party.

The Mattachine rank-and-file greatly expanded in early 1952 when founding member Dale Jennings, with the help of the organization, successfully fought an arrest on a morals charge. The group helped find Jennings a competent attorney and held fundraisers to pay his legal expenses. In an unprecedented legal victory against the Los Angeles Vice Squad, Jennings was able to prove that he had been arrested by entrapment. News of Jennings' acquittal spread like wildfire through underground gay communities and greatly buoyed the morale of the underclass citizens.

By the summer of 1953, as the rank-and-file further expanded, the Mattachine Society was losing most of its founding leadership. Homophiles did not want to be associated with Communists. As radical as the idea for Mattachine was, the final outcome of the organization was quite conservative. A loud voice arose from within the organization that wanted to present a respectable front and therefore felt justified in discriminating against transgenders and openly "swishy" men. They wanted to fit in with straight society. Hay, on the other hand, believed that "gays were unique" and he was developing a radical view of homosexuals and their place in the world. Hay was not about assimilating into straight society; rather, his long-range view was that straight society would conform to homophiles or homosexuals would have influence and not be seen as a social ill. Still, the early gay leaders were quite conservative; they wore ties and buttoned shirts. Hay's original Mattachine group held on for as long as possible, but within a few years they were replaced by a new leadership of a significantly more conventional mindset who rewrote the Mattachine mission: "To help professional researchers find the cause of homosexuality and end the problem." The backstory of this organizational infighting is pertinent to the Morris Kight story because it demonstrates that acrimony and dissolution preceded Kight in the leadership of the gay rights movement.

By the late 1950s when Kight came to Los Angeles as an openly gay man, Harry Hay, Jim Kepner, Dorr Legg and the others were seasoned gay radicals. Many of these early gay pioneers of Los Angeles developed a healthy curiosity about the newly arrived Texan from New Mexico. Many of them quite liked Morris and enjoyed his more liberal politics. He was, after all, amicable and intelligent and on the right side of gay—even if on the wrong side of the philosophical discussion.

For his part, Kight put forth an effort also: "I tried to be as friendly with the homophiles as I could." He claimed to have met Jim Kepner and Harry Hay around 1958, though Kepner's and Hay's respective recollections differ with Kight's in different ways at various times. He may have originally met Harry Hay through Edwin's Aunt Jo, who was described by one longtime friend as traveling in the "Aldous Huxley circle." Despite their eventual differences, Hay and Kight maintained an always amicable love-hate relationship for the next 40-plus years.

Kight: "I've known Hay for about the same time I've known Kepner.... He was a thinker, deeply concerned about the welfare of the labor community, deeply concerned about First Amendment rights."

Kight and Hay both had strong personalities and equally strong opinions. A few years older than Kight, Hay had an equally brilliant mind. He had been an aspiring actor and screenwriter at one time. Both men were natural leaders and were easily competitive.

Mina Meyer described a "rivalry between Harry and Morris, they were both competitive. Morris tried to make Harry less than he was, he was not very nice." Meyer explained that in the 1970s, "everyone knew Morris Kight, they didn't really know Harry. Morris could've been kinder to Harry."

In 1974, to Jeanne Cordova, a fairly new acquaintance at the time, Hay wrote about being "bitchy" toward Kight: "I know Morris well. We've tangled ass-holes, and my dearest companion and I are probably more responsible than anyone else in lining him up for the Gay Movement. We love each other dearly although Morris stands for an eventual 'it's alright to do it in the streets' Anarchy, while Johnny and I hold out for a qualitative leap into the GAY Consciousness which will require—among many other things—totally obsoleting all the unexamined assumptions in our Male-derived Male-oriented thinking which underlies more of our present baggage of Western Knowledge. This level of thinking both Morris and Don Kilhefner, to mention only two, find superfluous impedimentum [sic]."

Hay never completely settled with the ideology that Kight used toward gay liberation. He called it a "do-it-first and develop a theoretical framework around it later."

Kight would sometimes quip, "Harry will never forgive me for being right about communism." (It is not likely that communism had anything to do with Hay's sometimes overt contempt of Morris Kight.) In 1994, for a reason only known to the deepest recesses of Morris Kight's mind, he claimed, "Both of us were victims of the McCarthy era. I don't know how bad his [experience] was, because I've never asked him, but I can tell you how bad mine was." And he then changed the subject. (Kight was not a victim of the McCarthy era as much as he was a victim of the backward thinking of the era and his own poor judgment.)

While Kight liked many of the individuals who were involved with Mattachine, he disdained the entire "homophile" notion. According to Kight the Mattachine Society was all about intellectualism. Kight believed they were incredibly bright and brave thinkers, but not people who would actually make a difference. "I knew Chuck Rowland, Dale Jennings, Tony Reyes, Don Slater—a whole variety of people who were involved in the Mattachine ... the pretense that there was a vigorous movement is just that. It was a pretense. Some people, here and there, found surcease in relating to the Mattachine."

In 1994, Kight recalled: "I chose not to associate very publicly with the homophile effort, because I thought it was arch-conservative. I thought it was pretentious, that they were fighting a battle for which the turf had never been designated. I felt that they were pseudo-intellectual. They were doing research on what was called the 'homosexual condition,' which I found to be a stunningly homophobic commentary [even though] that word, 'homophobia,' had not been invented yet." Kight knew the books the homophiles espoused and did not believe that mainstream society would be swayed through such intellectual discussions.

Kight: "I did not publicly utter criticism, did not criticize them, I just thought they were politically and situationally [sic] incorrect." (His aloofness toward the established gay guard would make him vulnerable later to others' snide claims that he was living in the closet through the 1960s.)

Kight enjoyed many long friendships with these men and over the years they became used to his pushiness, often joking about it to each other. Later, though, after years of dealing with Kight and watching his ego grow with his renown, a serious rivalry developed: Kight was subjected to outright jealousy that created an effort to thwart acknowledgement of his place in history.

Both the initial founders and the later obstructionists in the Mattachine Society had one important thing in common: they were all engaged in an intellectual crusade. Kight, on the other hand, believed that a gay revolution would be through social services and on the streets. Kight knew that it would be a long road to affect public thinking.

Kight: "I never, ever doubted that we would do it. I never, ever doubted that the world wasn't ready for it." But while he still believed that it was possible, in 1957 Kight felt such a movement was a long way off. He thought it silly to engage in long philosophical discussions about things like gay marriage before homosexuals could even walk down the street holding hands.

Kight was already closely involved with many left-of-center causes and knew that even within those leftie organizations public thinking was still weighed down by a lot of fear of homosexuality. Kight believed that most of the people who would join a gay movement didn't want to study; they needed help, as much as they needed to *do* something. Like the peace movement and the growing civil rights movement, people wanted action. Kight had a more hands-on, pragmatic and long-range approach for gay liberation.

Many years after the fact, as gay history began to be written and the Mattachine Society took a rightful place in the telling of the gay rights movement in America, Kight was anxious to identify what he himself had done in the late 1950s and throughout the '60s. In the 1990s, he began referring to his earlier effort as the "Gay and Lesbian Resistance." In 2002, Kight, often portraying himself as the outsider, told an interviewer, "I created the Gay and Lesbian Resistance in Los Angeles against the support of the homophile effort. Bill Lambert [a.k.a. Dorr Legg] . . . absolutely disdained what I was doing, absolutely hated what I was doing, which was fine with me because it gave me all the independence in the world to go on and organize a resistance." As the years passed, Kight minced his words less: "I was so disdainful of the homophile effort, because it was so poky and so pretentious that they fantasized that they were thousands of people, when there weren't. I just was horrified at that."

A frequent complaint that Kight had about the telling of his earlier efforts was that there was "not a word about the fact that we [his small band of helpers and followers] were a handful, just a handful and not attracting any members" and the lack of attention given to "planks of that resistance, how I defined them and then how I trained them." Certainly everyone's efforts contributed to what later became gay liberation and then gay rights, but the argument itself reveals the lifelong rivalries between old friends and activists, rising from varying factions within gay culture and sometimes being passed down to the next generation.

Arguably, the best thing to come out of the early Mattachine Society was the offshoot group named ONE, Inc. (from a quote by Victorian-era writer Thomas Carlyle who said, "A mystic bond of brotherhood makes all men one"). ONE was begun soon after the founding of Mattachine. Chuck Rowland, Dale Jennings, Donald Slater, Dorr Legg, and Antonio Reyes were all founders of ONE and contributed to *ONE* magazine, which was the first publication openly aimed at a homosexual readership. Morris Kight had to acknowledge the value of the earlier pioneers' efforts. In a 1996 speech before the Humanists Association, Kight said: "Oh, here in the city there was one homophile organization called ONE Incorporated, which did literature and research and libraries—valuable work." Not content to praise the homophiles completely, he went on to point out, "They didn't work in the street dealing with people who had great needs, who were in desperate need for succor, desperate need of belonging, of being a person."

Our Foreign Policy Must Always Be An Extension. Pandora Productions.

Photo: Irv White ©Connections Offset, 1968. Madison, WI ID. Courtesy of the Center for the Study of Political Graphics. ID 4093

In 1953, *ONE* had an unprecedented cover story on "Homosexual Marriage" which Kight saw as more of a fantasy than a feasible strategic goal. (In the mid-1950s, he disliked the idea of gay marriage, saying it was "so heterosexist." Thirty years later, post-AIDS, he changed his stance, saying that he had "undergone a conversion, and now believe that I was politically incorrect on that, and that joining [sic], couplings, or meetings, or whatever you wish to call it—I don't think we should have to use the word 'marriage' particularly—I think that indicates a new mood of dignity, and a note of concern for self, so I have come to advocate . . . gay couplings.")

ONE had its challenges and victories; the most famous began in 1954 when the U.S. Post Office seized and refused to mail an issue of *ONE*, citing its contents as obscene and lascivious. A protracted legal battle ensued with every court ruling against ONE. In 1958, the U.S. Supreme Court unanimously reversed all lower courts' decisions and created a legal base for gay publications to be distributed through the mail. *ONE* magazine expanded and eventually evolved into ONE National Gay & Lesbian Archives.

Contrary to what its name might imply, from its earliest days, ONE was rife with internal conflicts. "[Jim] Kepner was on staff, and off staff, on staff, off staff, on staff, off staff at ONE, Inc.," Kight explained, referring to the many battles between the ONE organizers. "He would bring in his books and then angrily he would leave with them. I don't know if he knew from day to day if he was going to be there or not." Simplifying the complicated history and relationships among all the founders of ONE (which had become an important archive as well as the publication), Kight explained, "[Kepner] officed [sic] at 2256 Venice Boulevard. They—Dorr [Legg] and others that founded ONE Inc, officed [sic] at South Hill Street downtown in two rooms. Venice Boulevard was spacious quarters. Although I do not wish to be sentimental about the past ... 2256 Venice Boulevard was the most serene place. There were huge windows receding to the floor that opened onto the east, onto a row of marvelous ficus trees. And seeing out that window was so serene. There were Sunday afternoon meetings there—they were arch-conservative, but they were therapeutic. Kepner officed there a lot, and I reached him there when he was on staff, and when he wasn't, I reached him elsewhere. Because he was a figure I would talk with about so-and-so and this and that and the other. I'm not sure how much of this he remembers, or how much he chooses to remember, because he has a very selective memory."

Indeed, in an unpublished 1980 essay that Jim Kepner wrote about his recollections from 1956, he included: "Morris Kight came to Los Angeles in June from Albuquerque and he says he quickly began the prototype for what a dozen years later became the Gay Liberation Front. [Morris] became something of the typical old 'Queen Bee,' the one who can be counted on to raise bail, find a doctor, provide a shoulder to cry on, a spare meal, or a handout. Don Slater had been somewhat involved with Morris' circle and others on Bunker Hill, where Don had lived earlier. Morris often spoke about working with us since the 1950s, but neither Dorr nor I remember him before 1966, and not much after that."

Harry Hay wrote in a 1974 letter to Jim Kepner: "As I understand it, Morris had always been a one-man Midnight Mission for street hustlers who needed to be sprung outta pokey [sic] or who needed bail or a place to crash after they were sprung. I think he'd been doing this in L.A. since about 1960 ... Don Slater would know."

Kight recalled, "The person on staff [at ONE] that I enjoyed the most and related to the most was Don Slater. While he was an arch-conservative Republican [and] had a whole different value system than mine, he was fair and clever, and I sought his counsel. I sometimes ignored it, I sometimes accepted it, but that's what you do with all counsel. So I've known him since 1958."

Kight enjoyed long and drawn-out arguments and stimulating debates with Don Slater (who was also a drinking buddy of his) and Kepner. Harry Hay and Morris would debate in person and often ended up agreeing to disagree; their written correspondence was a little more formal.

Kight regularly visited the offices of ONE and engaged in many ongoing discussions with the people there, but he never contributed as a writer to the publication. Slater often let Kight use a desk and phone at their office to make and receive calls and to meet with befriendees.

Kight once remembered, "I had introduced [Dorr] at the ballroom at the Hilton Hotel in downtown, saying that he was one of the mystical, magical preachers who had warmed and populated our movement—and I really believe that—when at the office on South Hill Street, the FBI were chasing an African-American man down the street and he went into the building, and went upstairs, in the building. Two FBI agents came into the ONE, Inc. office and flashed their badges. Dorr is, despite his Republican [tendencies and] seemingly arch-provincialism, is vigorously as anti-police as I am. And so the two FBI agents came in, and said, 'How do you do, sir? Did an African American come through here?' And Dorr pulled himself to his full five-feet-eleven and said, 'Do I look like a Negro to you? You may leave my office.' I've always remembered that as just a singular act of defiance."

There were a number of homophile organizations and efforts springing up throughout the country. They each did what they could under the circumstances of the era to improve the quality of life for homosexuals. "What they were doing was important," Kight recalled. "It just didn't seem important enough for me to associate with them. I didn't choose to be in direct action with the homophiles. I was doing something else."

Kight was peripherally involved with an early gay rights organization that used the acronym SIR [Society for Individual Rights]. A San Franciscan gentleman named Gay Strait disliked the homophile efforts as much and for the same reasons that Morris Kight disliked them. Kight recalled, "He was just so horrified by their poky ways and their pretentiousness that he organized a meeting [in 1964] at his house on Gough Street [in San Francisco]. He brought together people to talk about founding something, and before that afternoon was out, he mentioned the Society for Individual Rights. A number of people attending the meeting disliked what he was saying. Disliked him, because they thought he was much too liberationist, and so on. And so they went across the street to Bill Plath's house at 832 Gough Street, to continue the meeting without him."

SIR went on to become the first gay rights organization to actively court, and with great success, political candidates. Kight: "I felt that they [the new SIR organizers] were much closer to what I was talking about. Not close enough, but much closer." By 1967, although remaining predominantly regionalized in San Francisco, SIR had become the largest homophile organization in the country.

Kight described himself as being "in and out" of SIR. "I was liked at SIR and so I was there often to speak before them. They had huge crowds."

Members of SIR produced a monthly magazine called *Vector*. The first issues were about ten pages in newsletter format; it progressed to be an easily available, slickly produced glossy magazine covering all sorts of gay issues and concerns—everything from politics to leather trends.

SIR worked very closely with The Tavern Guild, an organization of San Francisco gay bar owners and liquor wholesalers (1962–1995) that came together in response to police harassment. Kight spoke before the Tavern Guild, to "250 people…It was a big bar, and I spoke about yet-to-come gay liberation. The first-ever standing ovation ever granted *by* the organized lesbian and gay community *for* a member of it. Somebody came to me and said, 'Good grief! The Tavern Guild wouldn't give a standing ovation to God!'"

By the mid-'60s, however, because of Kight's unshakable loyalty to the antiwar effort, he was becoming less enthused about the direction of SIR. "I disapproved and disdained the fact that they would not welcome people under 21." Kight was more interested in politicizing young people rather than older people who were already set in their ways. "I also disliked the fact that they stuck to what they called gay issues. I wanted them to come out in opposition to the war in Vietnam, which I thought was a gay issue because I felt that our person-power, our money, our good name, our fortunes, were being wasted in Vietnam. By the way, I think that was correct. I think the country's never been as good since, and never will be again. So I wanted them to oppose the war in Vietnam, and they refused to do so."

In 1965, Frank Kameny and Barbara Gittings, representing the Mattachine Society and the Daughters of Bilitis (respectively) and both significant figures in the pre-Stonewall gay rights movement in America, organized a small group to march with signs at the White House and at Independence Hall in Philadelphia. They protested the federal government's policy on discrimination of homosexuals. Kameny and Gittings began working together to organize an event they called the Annual Reminder for gay rights. In the 1990s Kight said, regarding Kameny's and Gittings' activism in the mid-'60s: "[It] was really a terribly closeted activity. They put out a leaflet that men should wear jackets and ties, and the women should wear dresses and skirts, and that they should do nothing to offend anybody. And so they marched with signs in front of the White House. It would be easy now to belittle that effort. But I would be the last person in the world to do that. The 16 or so people who did it are to be forever honored [for their] unbelievable bravery."

Another early gay effort was PRIDE (Personal Rights In Defense and Education), which, according to Kepner, "was conceived and structured, between April and June of 1966, to develop among Los Angeles homosexuals a well-rounded social program, with a subsidiary militant program aiming to reform laws and public attitude that penalized homosexuals." There were some initial successes and "local repute," but by mid-1967 "an imbalance in its program led some" of the founding members to become "anxious lest PRIDE be carried away by excessive militancy, to support perhaps too hastily, a change of administration." This was according to a letter to remaining officers and members of PRIDE from Jim Kepner dated Feb. 18, 1968. Kight had nothing to do with PRIDE.

With exceptions, before 1969 Morris Kight's efforts for gay rights were less focused on organizations and groups; his work was primarily underground and personal.

He focused on the endless flow of the individuals' needs, the disenfranchised and "generally screwed over," and "the sick, sad, and sorry state of affairs for gay and lesbian persons." He also, very keenly, engaged many gays and lesbians in the tactics of peaceful protest and nonviolent demonstrations. He was, in a way, preening them for their own revolution when the time was right.

Kight helped to parent a new generation of gay men and women. He dealt one-on-one. He gave individual attention and addressed one problem at a time. He nurtured young homosexuals to become self-sufficient and functioning members of society while not having to forsake their sexual identity. Richard Little was one person of many who benefited from Kight's help and was later able to contribute to a larger gay movement.

In July of 1966, Richard Little was a 19-year-old farm boy coming from Ohio to Los Angeles with the hope of finding a better life as a homosexual. By August, he was in jail for petty theft and remembers, "I spent my 20th birthday in Los Angeles County Jail and was released on Christmas Eve 1966." Little had no money, no clothes but "the rags on my back, and no place to stay." He knew enough to find his way to Pershing Square and though it wasn't a "regular habit" for the young man, he went home with a somewhat older gentleman who "cooked a steak dinner and let me take a shower." They had sex and Little enjoyed a good night's sleep. The next morning "the trick" asked Richard what his story was, what he needed, and where he was going. When the 20-year-old spilled out his woes, the older man said, "I know a guy." He made a phone call and then gave Richard Little bus fare, a Cahuenga Boulevard address, and Morris Kight's name.

"I remember taking multiple buses to find Cahuenga Boulevard. I couldn't even pronounce [the street name] correctly." He found his way to a small, cramped office which he thought "was a Christian Science Reading Room." The office was in fact the offices of *Tangents* magazine and the Homosexual Information Center [HIC], where Don Slater allowed Kight the use of a chair, a desk and a phone. Little walked in and "amidst the stacks of books was a little old man with glasses, reading. I asked for Morris Kight and named the gentleman who referred me to him."

Without introducing himself, Kight told the young man to sit and he listened to his whole story—all that he had been through and about his upcoming court date and the fact that his mother could send him a little bit of money but certainly not enough. At some point Richard Little realized that Kight had heard this story—or stories very similar to his—many times before, mostly from men, young and old, who called on the phone in the middle of the night or who had sat in the very same chair that Richard Little sat in that day.

"I was startled," Little recalled, when Kight asked him, "'What are your expectations?' I couldn't remember anyone ever asking me that question."

More than likely, Kight was assessing the young man, figuring out if he had a grasp on reality or if he was floating on dreams of Hollywood stardom and needed to be immediately returned home to his family in Ohio (in which case, Kight had a separate fund and different plan).

Kight then made a few phone calls and "a little while later [Little] was getting into his car and we went to his home near MacArthur Park." Soon after getting to Kight's "small cottage," some other men arrived—"a couple," Little remembers—and they drove him to their house, not far from where Kight lived, where Little slept on their sofa. The following morning he had a lead to "gay-friendly" Jane Arden Employment Agency that "many of them had used."

Richard Little stayed at the men's house for a couple of weeks and he was there on January 6 for the celebration of the Little Christmas, when his hosts "awakened me with a small gift and a big celebration."

Little was able to make his court appearance and eventually cleaned up his record. He got a job as a stock clerk at a wholesale sheet music factory earning $350 per month, and soon he found a single apartment on Rampart Avenue for $66 per month. Over time he pulled his life together. Little did not see Morris Kight again until 1971 at the newly opened Gay Community Services Center on Wilshire Boulevard.

Almost 50 years later, he fondly remembers Kight as "the reason I am alive."

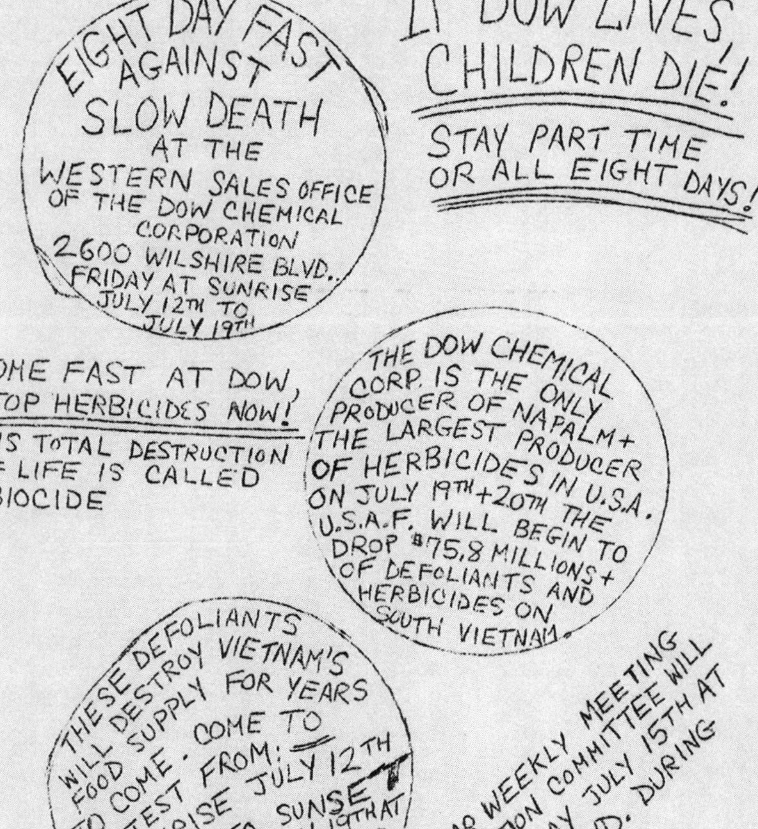
EIGHT DAY FAST
AGAINST
SLOW DEATH
AT THE
WESTERN SALES OFFICE
OF THE DOW CHEMICAL
CORPORATION
2600 WILSHIRE BLVD.,
FRIDAY AT SUNRISE
JULY 12TH TO
JULY 19TH
IF DOW LIVES,
CHILDREN DIE!
STAY PART TIME
OR ALL EIGHT DAYS!
COME FAST AT DOW,
STOP HERBICIDES NOW!
THIS TOTAL DESTRUCTION
OF LIFE IS CALLED
BIOCIDE
THE DOW CHEMICAL
CORP. IS THE ONLY
PRODUCER OF NAPALM+
THE LARGEST PRODUCER
OF HERBICIDES IN U.S.A.
ON JULY 19TH+20TH THE
U.S.A.F. WILL BEGIN TO
DROP $75.8 MILLIONS+
OF DEFOLIANTS AND
HERBICIDES ON
SOUTH VIETNAM.
THESE DEFOLIANTS
WILL DESTROY VIETNAM'S
FOOD SUPPLY FOR YEARS
TO COME. COME TO
PROTEST FROM:
SUNRISE JULY 12TH
FRIDAY TO SUNSET
FRIDAY JULY 19TH AT
2600 WILSHIRE BLVD.
(NR. MACARTHUR PARK)
THE REGULAR WEEKLY MEETING
OF THE DOW ACTION COMMITTEE WILL
TAKE PLACE MONDAY JULY 15TH AT
2600 WILSHIRE BLVD. DURING
THE 8-DAY FAST.
SPONSORED BY:
DOW ACTION COMMITTEE
619 S. BONNIE BRAE
483-9699 LA 90057

Chapter 8

Dow Shalt Not Kill

BESSIE DIED IN Albuquerque in March of 1962.

As Kight told it to Andrew Colville in 1999, "My mother was on the phone battling with somebody over real estate. She was buying a piece of property. It was her act to get them hooked and then to start accusing them of defrauding her, in order to get it cheaper. She said, 'You monster, you're overcharging me,' and she had a heart attack and dropped dead."

More elaborate accounts say that Bessie was on the phone arguing with a local church minister regarding a real estate transaction, and amid her screaming and cursing rampage suddenly the line went quiet. The minister, who was familiar with Bessie's outbursts and mercurial personality, called out her name a few times and eventually hung up the phone and drove over to Bessie's cottage. Through the front window, the minister could see Bessie in her chair, frozen dead, with the telephone clutched in her fist.

"She just died. I think that would be a wonderful way to go," Kight romanticized, "fighting with somebody over justice or liberation or food or clothing or housing and you could drop dead. What a hell of a way to go." As is often the case with

1968. Flyer/informational for an eight-day fast at the Dow Offices on Wilshire Blvd. Kight participated in the fast for the entire eight days. 20th Century Organizational Files, Southern California Library (Los Angeles, California)

deceased loved ones, Kight sometimes glamorized Bessie's eccentricities. In all ways, Bessie remained an influence on Morris.

A larger indication that a new era was upon Morris Kight was Eleanor Roosevelt's death in November 1962. Kight truly grieved Mrs. Roosevelt. He grieved with puppy love and hero worship. She too would remain a role model for Kight, but not in all ways.

In 1965, Kight took an apartment at 1249½ West Sixth Street in the MacArthur Park area and he published his new phone number: Huntley 1-3907.

In early 1967, Kight moved to a cottage on the other side of MacArthur Park (which had become a popular staging area for peace and labor demonstrations). 1822 West Fourth Street was also within walking distance of the Latino Photo Shop and Langer's Deli, a popular and reliable eatery and meeting place. It was in this house, a 1,000-square-foot cottage, one of six single-family homes on a 6,500-square-foot lot, that Kight's underground gay outreach program took root and grew as an essential part of gay life in Los Angeles. His phone number at this time was Huntley 4-8104, which may have been the most valuable phone number to have and to pass on to a friend or acquaintance.

In 1996, Kight recalled the "bad old days": "And [another] source of our [homosexuals'] oppression was ourselves. We were artful liars. We posed as something we weren't. We were good liars, good actors. We pretended to be straight. We memorized a whole language, a whole colloquy. You can't do that, you can't lie about something so very personal without paying a horrible spiritual...is that an okay word? [It is] a hard personal task, of concealing the most important part of your personality. We drank. We drank a lot. We hid out. We didn't prepare résumés, compete for jobs. We accepted an entry-level job as our worthy fate."

Kight focused his efforts toward curing that handicap with one individual at a time, as they showed up, and many not knowing themselves what they needed until Morris Kight spun them around and pointed them in a new direction. And not all were saved.

Kight's political activism never waned. One of his earliest and most consistent political affiliations was with the War Resisters League (WRL). Founded in 1923 by suffragist-lesbian-absolute pacifists Tracy Mygatt and Frances Witherspoon, Kight was required to sign the pledge: "The War Resisters League affirms that war is a crime against humanity. We therefore are determined not to support any kind of war, international or civil, and to strive non-violently for the removal of all causes of war."

Morris Kight embraced every radical idea that came through the WRL. Kight regularly attended WRL meetings in Los Angeles and read their materials and the underground press. As early as the mid-'50s, there were stories about the U.S. sending "military advisors" to a small country in Southeast Asia called Vietnam. At the same time, the seeds of an antiwar movement were taking root. As the government prepared to send troops to a far-off country no one had ever heard of, radical pacifists, and Kight was one, prepared a vigorous antiwar campaign. From the very beginning, opposition to U.S. involvement in the Vietnam War was unprecedented in its strength and organization, but it was not popular right away. Morris Kight was at every nonviolent demonstration in Los Angeles and many in

San Francisco, organized by such groups as Peace Action Council [PAC] or the Southern California Mobilization Committee to End the War in Vietnam.

Very much spawned and nurtured on the West Coast, the antiwar movement first attracted a marginalized mix of beatniks, folk musicians and university scholars. Before too long, the antiwar movement was national and had become a major happening, the original happening from which all other happenings sprung. It morphed into the hippie, anti-establishment and free-love movement. It was a cultural revolution, from civil rights to fashion to drug experimentation. By the mid-'60s, the peace movement and the cultural revolution worked in unison and had the attention of the media. You were either a part of the revolution or you were completely distracted by it. The antiwar movement had the support of celebrity talent, Hollywood royalty and defecting government employees. The movement was social, intellectual, radical, and everything that Morris Kight adored. By 1967, Kight was in his element, living a dream of radical activism, and his life was a better representation of what that gay kid in Texas had fantasized: it was filled with exotics, eccentrics, intellectuals and down-and-outers. Kight sat at the top of his little social mountain and embraced the hippie love movement in all its experimentation and openness. Every left-wing cause of the time easily supported each other. They carried similar themes and the same people could be seen at many different demonstrations. The peace movement snuggled up with the civil rights movement, which sprang out of the poor communities, and that led directly to the migrant farmworkers fighting for labor rights. It was, by all appearances, an ideological and social love-fest, except for some accounts of anti-white sentiments within some civil rights groups. Anti-homosexuality was accepted within most left-wing organizations. An above-ground gay rights movement hadn't yet taken shape, and through all the rhetoric for how to make the world a better place, there was little general discussion about the oppression of homosexuals. A homosexual movement had not yet identified a mainstream side on which to swim.

Many years later, Reverend Troy Perry, who did not personally know Morris Kight during the antiwar demonstrations but knew *of* him, recalled a young woman whom he had met, "a heterosexual woman," Perry described her, "who demonstrated against the war in Vietnam and [she] asked me if I knew Morris Kight and I said 'Absolutely I knew Morris Kight.' And she said a very very strange thing. She remembered going down and marching against the war ... [Kight] was sitting with others and they were all demonstrating. She said the people marching along with them said, 'You know he's a fag' about Morris Kight." Within the antiwar movement, there were some very backward ideas regarding social reform. That did not matter to Morris Kight; he was a devout pacifist and he'd be against the war if he were homo or hetero. Perry: "It underlined everything that Morris had said to me about the peace movement and that [the war] was one of the most important things to stop, and he told me that, but it took a while to understand the significance of what all of that was about."

Kight was supportive and kept abreast of the many different left-wing crusades. Always a voracious reader, instead of reading novels he now read every bulletin and newsletter available. He subscribed to every radical rag and every publication from every organization, including the oppositional propaganda. He truly engaged the dictum that "knowledge is power." Before the 1960s were over, Morris Kight would be very knowledgeable and he'd come to like power very much.

Daily, Kight attended rallies and planning meetings. He organized and participated in demonstrations in MacArthur Park and Pershing Square. In addition to his antiwar and civil rights activities, Kight marched arm in arm with the Farm Workers Union seeking collective bargaining. He idolized and cheered the words of labor leaders Cesar Chavez and Dolores Huerta. From the farmworkers he learned about generating enthusiasm and ways to recruit new support and he took that with him when he demonstrated for low-income housing opportunities.

A distinguished openly gay African-American national activist, Bayard Rustin, organized a historic nationwide demonstration called the March on Washington. It took a year of planning, and Kight, with many others, raised funds for the trip by selling handmade paper poppies with an attached peace message, fashioned after paper poppies sold by the Veterans of Foreign Wars (VFW). They traveled cross-country by bus in November 1963 to attend the March on Washington which culminated with Martin Luther King's celebrated "I Have a Dream" speech. Morris Kight was there.

Kight was inspired by Bayard Rustin as much as he was by Dr. King. Rustin was a leading strategist in the civil rights movement and the antiwar efforts, as well as draft resistance. From Rustin's efforts, Kight learned many of the legal outlines that he employed in his draft-resistance counseling.

Kight needed the influence of the radical activists Rustin, Chavez, and others to strengthen his organizing skills and sharpen his awareness of agitprop (agitation and propaganda). They were mobilized and practical. They always had the required permits and they provided monitors for all demonstrations. They took care of anyone who showed up to a demonstration (arrestees were immediately bailed out). They were creative and outlandish, all for the purpose of getting on the evening news. The Vietnam War was the first war that came to America's dinner table through television. The antiwar movement was in the news as much as the war itself. Kight learned savvy media skills and he had an impressive list of contacts at every major media outlet. He could quickly prepare and deliver a press release. Kight also created and implemented a strong phone tree that effectively communicated to 50 and then a hundred people, and eventually he was able to reach hundreds and hundreds of people to show up at a particular time for a demonstration or rally.

Through the 1960s, a refinement happened to Morris Kight: the activist. His exterior toughened up; he was resilient and knew how to survive living close to the edge. He had always been confident—a bit overconfident, really. But now there was a nuanced change inside of Kight: his self-confidence no longer emanated from his possessions and connections but arose from inside the core of his being. His primary belief was in himself and his abilities.

He continued his other works. He helped strangers who called any time of the day or night, he kept a few scams and cons going with Bob Humphries, and his "antiques and collectibles" business had a steady clientele. But he was happiest with himself when he could oppose or serve a bigger purpose, and there was no shortage of "bigger purposes" in the 1960s. Kight's vocation became radical politics and he was a full-on member of the anti-establishment; he made it his job to actively contribute toward a nonviolent social reform in every way—judicial, militarily, economic, and world peace—lofty goals for even the most optimistic of times.

In addition to being a radical activist, as were many homosexuals of the time, he operated within an underground that had no real boundaries and remained on the economic fringe.

In 1994, Kight explained: "At some time in my life, I've lived in homes I owned. But because I had to de-emphasize money, because I wanted to serve the lesbian and gay community, I couldn't compete in the marketplace for a job. Because I was jealous of the hours, hours that I wanted to serve. This is from 1950s onward, despite the revisionism by my critics. Jealous people, in other words."

Kight made friends with people who were making a difference, people who were shepherding the counterculture, and he became a top deputy in multiple radical left-wing organizations. He worked with the NAACP and ACLU. He did coalition-building for a group of concerned citizens who wanted to preserve the steel rebar sculptures known as the Watts Towers. Kight was very involved with the Battle for Chavez Ravine when a group of homes owned by generations of Mexican-Americans in a canyon just outside downtown Los Angeles were forced to sell to L.A. City to make room for re-development (including what became Dodger Stadium). There was another case of residential eminent domain that Kight opposed and it hit close to home—the coalition to save Bunker Hill.

In March 1965, the United States' involvement in Vietnam escalated and President Lyndon Johnson sent the first ground troops to war. Every pacifist in the country was outraged. An immediate call to action was issued, and Kight was at the frontline of the antiwar movement.

"So, the war in Indochina became very serious," Kight recalled. "I felt that even though it broke my heart, it made me feel just terrible, that I should reduce my commitment to troubled, or in-trouble, homosexual persons and go off to fight the war—or fight against the war. In 1965, I spent half [my] time against the war in Indochina."

The other half of his time was spent on his "antiques business" and helped many befriendees, young and old, rich and poor. While Kight was at rallies, he would leave a person to man the house in case someone came by or called to make an antiques purchase or needed help. He also continued his Sunday socials and yard sales. Sunday was a good day of the week for volunteer doctors to offer a few hours of anonymous treatment in Kight's back room. All kinds of people were treated for various venereal diseases that, if left to standard-of-care practice of the time, would have either remained untreated or ruined entire lives.

Kight was active in the Peace Action Council [PAC] in Los Angeles where they coordinated the various antiwar demonstrations throughout Southern California. He was part of the National Mobilization Committee to End the War in Vietnam [NMC] and his FBI file confirms his participation in the "National Mobilization Committee to End the War in Vietnam demonstration at Washington, D.C. in October 1967." This was a massive demonstration at the Pentagon that became known as a call to "Confront the Warmakers."

Two decades later, Kight described it: "We marched up to the rows of troops in battle attire. They used tear gas to repel us. At 3 a.m., I was asked to join a group of religious protesters commencing a vigil on the Pentagon steps. Locking arms, we knelt in silent witness, faced by soldiers with rifles and bayonets. After some time, one among us fainted, and our line fell forward into the line of troops. There was a moment of alarm. The soldier who had stood for hours in front of me had his bayonet right next to my stomach. With his free hand he braced me, then helped me regain my place. He had taken a firm grip on my hand, and when our line was restored I found in the palm of my hand a single piece of chewing gum he had silently placed there."

At home, his days were filled with ongoing brainstorming sessions, debriefings, and demonstrations. There was also, at times, organizational self-analysis to address "internal problems of the antiwar movement." Such internal conflicts are often artificially manufactured by infiltrators from opposition groups or the FBI in order to upset progress of an organization. Not wanting to get derailed by internal politics, the administrative body of activists chose to form subcommittees to focus their efforts and to be able to weed out any infiltrators and informants.

Recognizing that war is a far-reaching machine, PAC meetings involved ongoing discussions of ways to impair the expanding military-industrial complex. Soon a thorough report and analysis, compiled by members of the PAC think tank, became available of all the U.S. corporations that profiteered from the war in Vietnam. Sometime in 1967, the idea of a widespread corporate boycott took root at PAC. They quickly realized that boycotting *all* the corporations on the list would be impossible, so they had to narrow their focus. Not at the top of the list, but certainly with a wide range of products to boycott, Dow Chemical Company greatly profited by manufacturing for the U.S. government the toxic chemical napalm that was used in Vietnam. There were many chemicals used in Vietnam warfare, but for the purposes of hyping the antiwar effort and launching a media campaign, PAC decided to focus on napalm for its horrifying and dramatic impact. There were two major U.S. manufacturers of napalm, Witco Chemical and Dow Chemical Company. Both corporations profiteered and it would be easy to direct the general public disdain toward these companies.

Kight had an innate need not to follow trends but to create them, and in late 1967 a whole new opportunity presented itself for Morris Kight that fit perfectly with his self-image.

"Along the way I founded the Dow Action Committee," Kight recalled in 1994. "It was the only antiwar group in the country designed to attack a particular company for its criminal activities. We were after the Dow Chemical Company for their manufacturing of napalm—ethyl gasoline that burns at 3500 degrees and burns everybody in its path—and herbicides and defoliants for military use. 245T Agent Orange was so volatile that it was packaged in [hazard] orange packaging and sent to Vietnam, and it was used as a defoliant over the landscape (so you can see through it and shoot through the forests). And as a result, we so poisoned the soil of Vietnam that Vietnam has the highest infant mortality rate of any country, [higher] than anywhere else in the world, because of our herbicide."

Kight often said that he "founded" or "co-founded" DAC and sometimes he claimed his founding was as early as 1965. A note to the archives that Kight wrote in 1994: "[Went] Off to MCC All Saints to hear Reverend Troy. When he found [that]

I was in the audience he availed the opportunity to talk of our work together, it was very pleasing, very humble, very mutually satisfying. He did something no one has done before. He credited me with stopping the manufacture of napalm. I did, you know.... I had founded the Dow Action Committee in 1967 at a meeting in the Gold Room of the Mayfair Hotel over on W. 7th St."

Though pickets against Dow Chemical Company began as early as 1966, the Dow Action Committee (DAC) was 'officially' born at a meeting at the Peace Action Council in late 1967. (Witco had already ceased napalm production by the time the boycott began.) DAC was an offshoot of PAC and was obligated to report to PAC. Internal conflicts within the antiwar movement grew and quickly took root in DAC. Disruptors were always suspected of being infiltrators, and according to the Dow Action Committee FBI file, the FBI did successfully infiltrate DAC.

Kight and Marcia Silverstein worked as committee co-chairs of the Dow Action Committee [DAC]. In the beginning, they shared duties, and missives were signed by both Kight and Silverstein (she was sometimes listed as "secretary" and Kight as "Committeeman"). Kight and Silverstein shared the writing, typing, necessary copying and distribution. Kight was a good typist and always kept his manual typewriter in good working condition on his desk in its carrying case so he could carry it to meetings as needed.

The first official meeting of the Dow Action Committee took place in Los Angeles and is documented by an undated purple mimeographed sheet that was handed to all attendees. With the distinctive heading "Dow Shalt Not Kill," the one-sheet introduced the Dow Action Committee, what it was about, and set forth a challenge, written in Kight's singular tone.

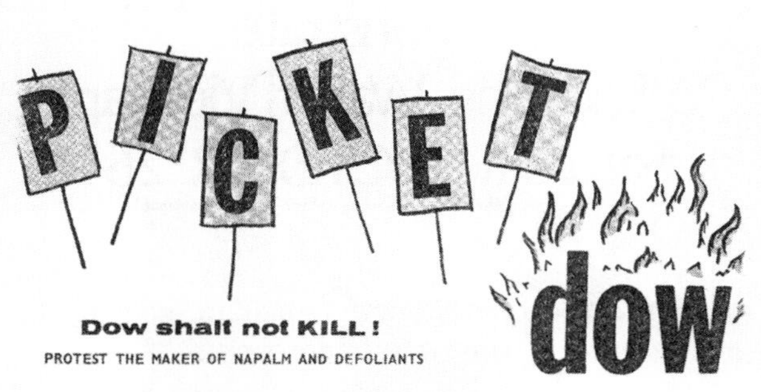

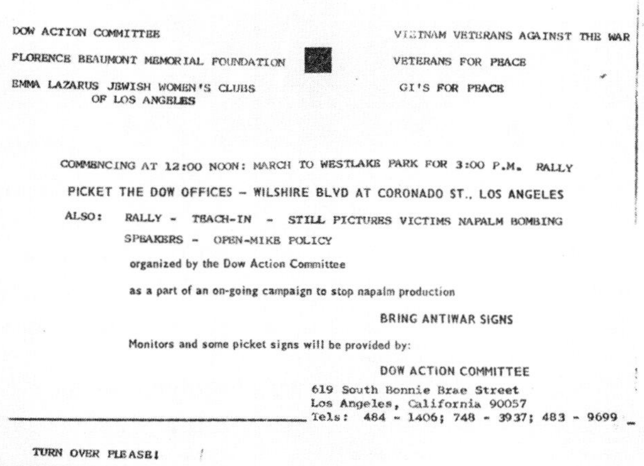

1968. DAC-created flyer for "Dow Shalt Not Kill!" picket and rally outside the Dow Corporate Offices on Wilshire Blvd. 20th Century Organizational Files, Southern California Library (Los Angeles, California)

"You came down here this evening because you feel that an effective program protest against Napalm and its producer, The Dow Chemical Company, is a viable method of protesting the war, and providing a means of educating other Americans to the folly and error of that war.

"It is important to each of us in the Movement to understand that such a program doesn't really exist at this point. The potential for such a program exists here in this room tonight. You must create it if it is to be done; that is why you were invited, because the movement has confidence in your ability, energy, creativity and imagination.

"The people who called this meeting have done so for the purpose of getting you together with other people like yourself, people who hold the same convictions on the war so that you could, with them, create a program against Dow and Napalm.

"So, it is up to you. We must all remember that the lives and futures of millions of people are at stake: Vietnamese, our children, ourselves, the people of the world.

"It is not easy work, and tonight must only be the beginning of a program. You must organize if you are to be successful. Do not leave here tonight with nothing to do; with no participatory role in developing a program. Join with your brothers and sisters here tonight: outline the program, form an organization, plan on getting back together.

"You've been called together, the rest is up to you, there isn't anyone else who will do it."

The missive ends with a typical Kight call to action preceded with a question: "Is Los Angeles capable of building a program against Dow and Napalm? Some would say no, but you know better, right?"

And thus the challenge was set before some of the sharpest antiwar activists in Los Angeles. They promptly picked up the proverbial gauntlet and proceeded to exceed all expectations.

The boycott itself easily bore upon the conscience of the American people. It gave them something to do, to focus on, once they decided the very important and personal question about supporting the war or not supporting the war. If you did not support the war, "Don't buy Dow," said DAC directives, which included a list of all Dow products to avoid purchasing: "Saran Wrap; Handi-Wrap; Dow Oven Cleaner; Dowclene, a washing compound; Dow Latex Paints; Dow Snail Slug N'Bug Killer; Dow General Weed Killer; Dow Crab Grass Killer; Dowpon, and other grass killers; Dow Insecticides; Dowzene, animal wormers; Diryl Flea Power; Steuben (Crystal); All Pitman-Moore Drugs—Novahistine, Neo-Polycin, Jefron and many more; Dow Corning Glassware."

"We committed civil acts of disobedience all over the city," Kight recalled. "We fasted at Coronado and Wilshire for ten days, at the headquarters of Dow Chemical Company. We leafleted and we did demonstrations."

Every day, Kight showed up to demonstrate at the Dow Chemical sales offices on Wilshire Boulevard in Los Angeles, and sometimes he joined the daily pickets at the Dow Chemical manufacturing plant in the city of Torrance in the South Bay. They held signs, leafleted, and handed fact sheets to every employee entering Dow. On the West Coast, there were demonstrations throughout San Francisco as well as in Los Angeles' MacArthur Park and simultaneous demonstrations at Cheviot Hills

Park and the Century Plaza Hotel in Century City. DAC showed up to demonstrate against the war pretty much everywhere and the enthusiasm for demonstrating took off across the country. Demonstrating became a part-time hobby for many and a full-time commitment for others. DAC received the help of ACLU attorney Darby Silverberg to successfully appeal to a higher court when a parade permit was denied. DAC had a huge presence at an antiwar demonstration at the "[Hubert] Humphrey for President" headquarters on Wilshire Boulevard. Kight was a spoke on the inner circle of antiwar activists whose coordinated efforts made all this possible.

Soon, Dow Action Committee was everywhere and boycott information spread across the country. In New York City there were daily pickets at the Rockefeller Center offices of Dow Chemical. By mid-1968, DAC planned and participated in many demonstrations with another group called Vietnam Veterans Against the War (whom the FBI described as "a loose-knit organization theoretically composed of veterans of the war in Vietnam which is opposed to this war"). The two organizations shared many of the same members. DAC shared their meeting rooms with Veterans for Peace and Social Workers for Peace and the Monitors Training School (a group that assisted in keeping all the demonstrations focused and nonviolent).

DAC's stated objective was: "to stop the production of napalm, and at the same time show the imperative need to end the war in Vietnam." The FBI stated the aims and purposes of DAC as "through demonstrations, hopes to dramatize its opposition to United States participation in Vietnam and also its opposition to the

1969. DAC flyer/invite to picket line and rally. In the circle, listing the speakers, "Morris Kight of the universe and other galaxies." The demonstrations stressed having fun. 20th Century Organizational Files, Southern California Library (Los Angeles, California)

NAPALM

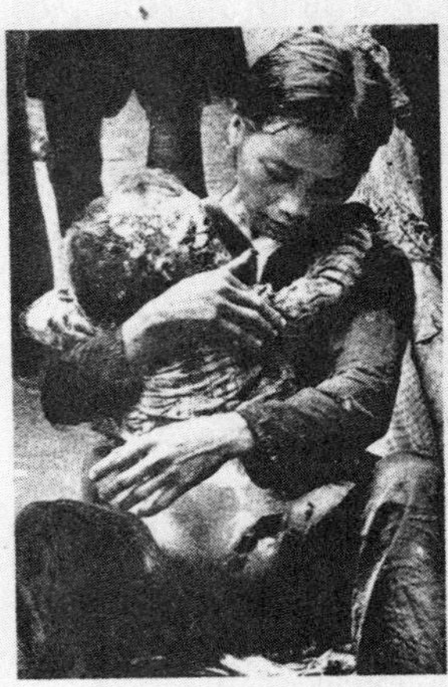

NAPALM IS A FLAMING GASOLINE MADE STICKY WITH SYNTHETIC RUBBER. THE BURNING JELLY CANNOT BE WIPED FROM THE SKIN. A 1000-POUND BOMB MAKES A FIRE 200 FEET ACROSS. PEOPLE ARE ROASTED ALIVE OR SUFFOCATED AS THE FLAMES EXHAUST ALL THE AVAILABLE OXYGEN.

NAPALM KILLS: IT ALSO LEAVES THOUSANDS BURNED BEYOND BELIEF — IN A HELPLESS AGONY OF LIVING DEATH.

NAPALM IS USED EVERY DAY AGAINST RURAL VILLAGES IN SOUTH VIETNAM, BUT BECAUSE OF ITS INACCURACY AS A WEAPON, WE ARE, ON OCCASION, EVEN POURING NAPALM ON OUR OWN SOLDIERS. (NEWS RELEASE 8-26-66)

SO.VIETNAMESE MOTHER CRADLES HER CHILD BURNED BY NAPALM.

CHEMICAL COMPANY, THE MAKER OF SARAN WRAP, ALSO MAKES NAPALM

HOW CAN YOU WRAP FOOD IN SARAN WRAP AND HANDI-WRAP KNOWING THAT AT THE SAME TIME VIETNAMESE PEOPLE ARE BEING WRAPPED IN THE FLAMES OF DOW'S NAPALM—FOR THE SAME PLASTICS THAT MAKE YOUR CONVENIENT WRAPPER ARE USED TO MAKE NAPALM THAT MAIMS AND KILLS.

"ONE DISTRAUGHT WOMAN APPEARED AT A FIELD MEDICAL STATION HOLDING A CHILD IN HER ARMS WHOSE LEGS HAD LITERALLY BEEN COOKED BY NAPALM. THE CHILD IS NOT EXPECTED TO LIVE." (S.F. CHRONICLE, 2-15-66)

THIS HAPPENS EVERY DAY. THIS IS HAPPENING NOW. MORE THAN 30,000 SOUTH VIETNAMESE CHILDREN HAVE BEEN BURNED BY NAPALM.

WOULD YOU POUR A HIGHLY FLAMMABLE STICKY JELLY ON A CHILD? OR HIS MOTHER?

WE CANNOT DISASSOCIATE OURSELVES FROM WHAT OUR GOVERNMENT DOES. OUR ARMED FORCES ACT FOR US. THEREFORE, IN THE EYES OF THE WORLD AND IN REALITY, WE ARE POURING NAPALM ON THE PEOPLE OF VIETNAM.

WHAT CAN YOU DO?

1. DON'T BUY DOW PRODUCTS!

   SARAN WRAP
   HANDI-WRAP
   DOW OVEN CLEANER
   DOWCLENE, A WASHING COMPOUND
   DOW LATEX PAINTS
   DOW SNAIL SLUG N' BUG KILLER
   DOW GENERAL WEED KILLER
   DOW CRAB GRASS KILLER
   DOWPON, AND OTHER GRASS KILLERS
   DOW INSECTICIDES
   DOWZENE, ANIMAL WORMERS
   DIRYL FLEA POWDER
   STEUBEN (Crystal)
   ALL PITMAN-MOORE DRUGS
   NOVAHISTINE
   NEO-POLYCIN
   JEFRON, AND MANY MORE
   DOW - CORNING GLASSWARE

2. Write to President Johnson and your Congressmen, asking that the use of Napalm and the bombing of Vietnam be stopped NOW!

3. Write to DOW Chemical Company, Midland, Michigan, and 2600 WILSHIRE BOULEVARD, LOS ANGELES, CALIFORNIA, 90057, stating that you will not buy their products as long as they produce Napalm.

DISTRIBUTED BY S.F. WOMEN FOR PEACE, P.O. BOX 2364, SAN FRANCISCO, CALIFORNIA.
and by the DOW ACTION COMMITTEE, P.O. BOX 54986, Terminal Annex Los Angeles, California, 90054.

Dow Chemical Company. Through the use of a boycott of products manufactured by Dow Chemical Company, the DAC hopes to cause Dow Chemical Company to cease its production of napalm."

In the beginning, DAC organized around a few central slogans: "Bring the Troops Home Now!" "A Movement of Millions Can End the War," and "Dow Shalt Not Kill."

In their three-month report to "Committee Members, Supporters, Friends of Peace," Marcia Silverstein wrote that they had organized "a large picket line at Dow's West Sales Office ... interviewed its employees on how they feel about working for an outfit like Dow; published 20,000 leaflets educating the public about the nature of Dow Chemical's atrocities ... extensive research into Dow's products, napalm, defoliants, herbicides, and Dow's corporate connections ..." and they organized a phenomenal number of people.

DAC became multilayered. The media campaign featured straightforward graphic images of Vietnamese children with their skin burning off after being sprayed with napalm. Their printed factsheets to educate the public were powerfully pointed: "The United States is the only country currently manufacturing napalm and Dow is the nation's sole contractor for napalm.... DOW makes $6,550,000 a year on the sale of napalm bombs." DAC also exploited the link between Dow Chemical with the West German company Badische Anilin, the maker of Zyklon B, the chemical agent that was used in WWII gas chambers.

The demonstrations were daily and sometimes gimmicky—very similar to what would later become trademark Gay Liberation Front consciousness-raising efforts. The point of all the antics was to gain media attention, and in that they were highly effective.

Dow Action Committee FBI file entry: "On July 10, 1969, approximately 15 persons arrived at MacArthur Park to participate in the DAC-sponsored Boston Tea Party. Two individuals rented a small boat and proceeded to the lagoon where they made speeches opposing the war in Vietnam. Other individuals dressed in various costumes of Revolutionary War era and semi-religious type stood on the shore of the lagoon and emptied tea from tea bags into the lagoon as a means of protest of the manufacture of napalm and the United States participation in the war in Vietnam.

"On July 11, 1968, the DAC announced plans to hold a fast and vigil to take place in front of the Dow Chemical Company, Western Sales Offices 2600 Wilshire Boulevard, Los Angeles from sunrise, July 12, 1968 to sunset July 19, 1968...."

Fasting as a form of demonstration became common practice for antiwar demonstrators. Kight fasted, refusing to eat quite a few times as a form of public demonstration against the war. (The longest fast Kight held was for ten days, during which time he had water only.) In July 1968, in *Open City Newspaper* (Los Angeles), Kight was quoted on the "last day of an eight-day fast to protest Vietnam defoliation," as saying: "Now they realize that 'Thou shalt not kill' means everybody, every time, every place, and that their mouthings [sic] to the contrary have been hypocrisy." The vigils were maintained around the clock with a total of 22 full-time fasters and an average of 16 people spending the night

1968. DAC-created informational sheet about the Dow boycott. 20th Century Organizational Files, Southern California Library (Los Angeles, California)

in sleeping bags in front of the Dow offices on Wilshire Boulevard. To avoid any trouble, Kight dealt directly with the LAPD's Rampart division in advance. He said, "It's better to inform them of our activities—although not our thoughts—to save ourselves lots of hassle."

The demonstration fast became a cause for spectator curiosity, with summer camp children coming to see a "real, live demonstration." Kight and others brought lawn chairs and set up a mini-gypsy camp. In time, Kight also brought his typewriter and office files to demonstrations.

The eight-day fast included, according to Kight, "some really horrible abuse. The usual stuff—'hippies, peace creeps, traitors, why don't you do something for your country for a change?' and so forth. It's absolutely horrifying, but it seems the older people get, the more they approve of the war and of killing. We got our harshest verbal assaults from old people." People shouted at them from passing cars and hurled verbal abuse from the sidewalk. They had cherry bombs and a few water bombs lobbed at them. At one point, a Hungarian refugee confronted Kight, saying that he wanted to punch Kight out; according to the *Open City* article, "Morris calmed him."

In an effort to use positive reinforcement, Kight complimented the LAPD on handling the situation "...marvelously. A member of the Rampart Division checks on us each morning at ten and asks if we slept well and if we had any trouble the previous night....We're building bridges of communication with the police wherever possible."

Always politicking, Kight used the fasting time to make friends and form new alliances. According to the article, by the end of the eight-day fast, they were receiving congratulations and good wishes from the passersby. "'In fact,' Kight said happily, 'some businessmen from the area have offered their assistance in any future enterprises we may undertake.'"

THE BIGGER PICTURE

KIGHT: "IN THE PROCESS, SINCE I WAS ALREADY DEALING WITH SO many gay and lesbian persons, they were invited to join me in the Dow Action Committee. Most turned me down, saying 'Well, you're a Communist and we want nothing to do with anybody who is as unpatriotic as you are.' Some said, 'It is none of our gay business. Let the straights fight it out.' And some said, 'Well, you're right and we'd like to join you.' And so quite a number of lesbian and gay persons came to the Dow Action Committee and quite a number of non-gay persons. (I've never used the word 'straight,' I don't care for it, straight sounds so square, so traditional, I use 'non-gay.') Quite a number of non-gay persons came in and most [of the non-gay people] just couldn't take it—the lesbian and gay people—and they fled. Some [were] wise enough to stay. And so we wound up with a group of quite sympathetic non-gay people.... So we then had a gay/non-gay collective combine."

Kight's old friend Gino Vezina remembered: "Morris Kight integrated the Vietnam war and gay liberation. He mixed those, and to a large extent that worked."

It stood to reason that Kight would include many young gay men and women who sought his solace and help. It gave them a focus for their anger and dissatisfaction with the establishment and it gave them a place to go and be with people. Kight instilled his brand of Gandhi pacifism in his young activist prodigies and it later served the gay liberation movement.

Kight: "Those who did [join DAC] learned how to leaflet, how to commit civil disobedience, how to confront the established order, how to confront the oppressor, how to deal with the media, how to practice nonviolence. It turned out to be a powerful training ground for the Gay Liberation Front because a number of those people joined me in the Gay Liberation Front.... So the gay and lesbian persons enjoyed being members of the Dow Action Committee."

Through working on the Dow boycott, Kight honed his media skills and proved to be a genius for effective publicity. He was known for his "inventiveness and rashness," and later in the gay movement, "campiness" in demonstrations. Jim Kepner echoed many when he swore that Kight "could smell the news media." His legendary handling of the media would become fodder for Kight enthusiasts as well as his detractors.

Kight always used phone trees to be certain that every day there would be picketers outside Dow corporate offices and the manufacturing site. Kight got a reputation as being able to rally a large number of people in a short amount of time; no one seemed to care or notice that the majority of Kight's group were gay men. Because he brought so many to the antiwar movement he was powerful. And he was becoming more powerful. Kight was cultivating a benevolent, if not entirely benignant, godfather mystique.

Kight: "Thousands of people, literally, thousands of people [were at] my house at 716½ South Bonnie Brae which was the headquarters of ... 'underground gay liberation.' Of course that was the only kind of social services [underground]."

Initially, DAC used a space at the Peace Action Council office at 746 South Alvarado Street, on the other side of MacArthur Park from where Kight lived on West Fourth Street. A few months later, Kight used his skills and knowledge in real estate and found a place for DAC headquarters at 619 South Bonnie Brae, a few steps away from his own residence. (This DAC location would become known as "Freedom House.")

Soon, Kight was full of force and passion and attempted to singlehandedly take over control of DAC. Perhaps through expediency, he elbowed the much meeker Marcia Silverstein to the side, delegating her to the more menial tasks. Initially, they shared responsibilities and were meant to co-chair DAC. Silverstein was politically astute, smart, and had been active in the Peace Action Council. She was a single, heterosexual woman and deeply committed to the antiwar movement, certainly passionate about her political beliefs, and she brought a lot to the successful organization, which included many coordinated national efforts. Still, Morris Kight pretty much barreled right over her. She did not have a large personality. She was demure where Kight was grand. She wasn't forceful; she was no match against Kight's self-importance.

Kight began coordinating demonstrations on his own. Where there were once two signatures on all memos, by 1968 there was only one signature on outgoing memos—Kight's. And shortly after that, there were simultaneous memos with just Marcia's signature. By late 1968, Morris Kight was signing his memos alone as "Chairman of Boycott."

Despite his inflated ego, Kight could still be quite charming. In late 1969, he easily convinced Marcia Silverstein (and many others) to follow him into the early gay liberation movement. Not for lack of commitment or belief in the cause, Silverstein didn't last very long in the Gay Liberation Front. According to Gino Vezina, "There were meetings [where Morris lived beginning in the early 1970s] and Marcia was on trial, like a Spanish Inquisition, accused of this and that [political incorrectness] and was ready to be discharged from pro activism because of 'her sins.'"

Vezina described the "kangaroo court" as it degenerated; it became "a radical fascist approach within a radical Marxist movement" for the purpose of raising awareness. These proceedings could get very personal and hurtful, sort of an unguided and unsafe radical truth-therapy, targeted at one individual. In a particular instance, Kight was acting as prosecutor, Marcia Silverstein was the guilty-without-defense defendant, and the jury and witnesses were all young gay men—Kight's lackeys. Vezina was the only person at the Silverstein trial who spoke out against the proceedings: "What the fuck is going here? What right do you have to pick on this woman?" he said to the room full of people. No one agreed with Vezina as most were Kight's sycophants. The verbal abuse continued until Silverstein left and never returned.

By the mid-'60s, Kight was appearing in newspaper articles and on television news reports as the spokesperson for the boycott. He appeared on numerous television shows, some local and a few national shows. He became a regular and favored guest, billed as a "liberal activist" for opinionated television host Joe Pyne, first on Pyne's local Los Angeles program on KTTV which was later syndicated nationally. Joe Pyne was pro-civil rights for African Americans and pro-Vietnam war. He hated hippies, homosexuals, and feminists. Kight appeared as a counterculture spokesperson for the antiwar movement (specifically the Dow Action Committee). He'd speak up for civil rights, feminism and labor. Kight's calm demeanor was the perfect counter to Pyne's acerbic personality.

In 1967, in a move unprecedented in television history, Harry Hay and John Burnside appeared on Joe Pyne's show as an openly homosexual couple. Kight was more publicly reticent about his own sexuality. Gino Vezina remembered Kight's appearance on a separate Pyne show: "Morris went on a talk show with people from *ONE* Magazine and the Mattachine and a few others, and there was a vicious commentator [who] went down the line and asked each person, 'Are you gay?' Most of them said, 'Yeah, and proud of it,' but Morris said, 'I'm too old to discuss my sex life.' He was cautious about being openly gay in the peace movement. [It's] hard to explain.

"Some of the older ones who were in Morris' group were always bickering over those kinds of things, which I always thought was ridiculous. I never took sides in any of that, but I had my own private feelings about it."

Kight's nonchalance regarding his sexuality was never remembered fondly by his peers. Kight pulled everyone he knew into the peace movement and everyone he knew were all people in gay circles. He was reticent about being openly gay with his peace friends. Harry Hay often told a story of John and himself being invited to Morris' house for a Sunday afternoon barbeque with his "peacenik crowd." Hay said that he and Burnside felt like the "token gay people" for Kight's peace friends and it could have been Kight's way of inculcating the consciousness of his peace friends. Hay didn't appreciate it, and in a typed letter to Don Slater and his partner Tony Reyes, October 1967, Harry quoted Morris thanking John and himself for "your attendance at our Peace Fair, and for your kind words ... for your general showing of love and loyalty."

Kight's alleged less-than-blatant sexuality during his involvement with the peace movement continued for the rest of his life. He wasn't deceptive about his sexuality. He later coined a term to describe himself during the 1960s: "I was a pre-gay liberationist." In Kight's mind, his sexuality was not the issue at hand; the issue at hand in the mid-1960s for Morris Kight was boycotting Dow Chemical Company until they ceased production of napalm and other war chemicals.

In 2003, former California State Assemblywoman Jackie Goldberg recalled meeting Morris in the 1960s: "I actually did not meet Morris with anything having to do with being gay or lesbian. I met him out in front of Dow Chemical, during the Vietnam War. [It was] Dow Chemical in Torrance, oh, what a terrible place it was, all these huge trucks going in and out, and police, it was really quite engaging to be there. I met him because, like he, I too had been drawn to complain about the fact that they were using the same process that they used to make Saran Wrap stick to bowls to create a weapon that came out of the sky and burned Vietnamese children, adults, women, and soldiers.... There were times we were picketing at Dow when there were eleven of us or six of us. And then sometimes there'd be 50 of us and we thought we had died and gone to heaven. It gave me a chance to get to know this guy, who I think may have actually been the first out gay man I had ever met, and certainly he was out then."

Miki Jackson first saw Kight in 1967 delivering an antiwar speech in the amphitheater at Westlake Park. Jackson remembered herself as a teenager "in the audience and I heard him as a gay person and said, 'if he can say that, if he can do that, then I can do that too.'" She made a point of introducing herself to the older activist and followed him into coalition politics. Kight described them as lifelong "solemn loyal friends."

Jackson and many others remember Kight as the first publicly open gay person in the peace movement.

In 1994, when asked point-blank if he had kept his "sexuality concealed" during the late 1960s, Kight answered: "No, I did not. That's more revisionism and revanchism. I was as up-front gay as anyone in the country. It's just that I didn't care to be in direct action with homophiles, because I felt, I felt that they were wasting their time."

Regarding his alleged closeted life, Kight said, "That's been a carefully manufactured image also, to have them seem as if [the homophiles] were all out. You understand that a number of them operated under pseudonyms. Some became better known under pseudonyms than they did with their regular names."

One example, a more contentious personality that Kight dealt with, was Mattachine alumnus and co-founder of ONE, Inc., William "Bill" Lambert, a.k.a. Dorr Legg.

From his many television appearances, Kight caught the attention of one young girl who was especially curious about the activist. Carol Kight couldn't have been much more than ten years old when she realized that it was her father who kept appearing on television. With no difficulty at all, she was given his telephone number and called him. Many years later, remembering the call, she said that she was very cautious and shy. A man, who she later learned was Robert Humphries, answered the phone and she asked to speak with Morris Kight. When asked who was calling, she said, "His daughter." The phone dropped; she heard the receiver land on the table or floor. Then she heard muffled voices and laughter in the background and eventually Morris came to the phone. He was happy to hear from her and they had a good talk. For many years following, their communication was intermittent and largely dependent upon her overtures.

By the mid-1960s and throughout the rest of his life, Morris Kight had a completely different closet door that remained mostly closed: that of his heterosexual past and two offspring. Except for a few close allies, he remained very tight-lipped about the details of his life in New Mexico. Though it's not out of the question that his reputation was a concern for him, it is also not complete to say that Kight made that decision simply because he worried that his heterosexual past might dampen his position as a gay leader. He was pragmatic and protective. Before his above-ground activities for gay liberation, he had made the decision to keep his family and knowledge of that family distant. He respected the fact that he was not wanted in that world and he did not want to cause further pain to those he had hurt. His primary concern, as he expressed it to a close friend, was that his present world was not suitable for children. He was involved with so many "colorful" and unpredictable characters, plus he was already receiving death threats, and he did not want his children exposed.

A PERSONAL TAIL

BY 1967, KIGHT'S 'RECENT PEACE ACTIVITIES' EARNED HIM A "Reserve Index-B" status with the FBI investigators. In 1996, Kight recalled how he dealt with the FBI.

"The FBI acted as if we were dangerously subversive. I had my own personal tail. A tail is somebody who follows you around. I was never alone. I really had no time to be lonely because I had a very attractive man, by the way—he was my personal tail. On Thanksgiving 1965 we fasted [for ten days] on this corner of La Cienega and Wilshire [Boulevards] by Lawry's [Steakhouse], protesting the fact that people were eating 4,500 calories of food at one sitting where there were people in the world that would consider that several weeks of sustenance. So we passed [Thanksgiving] there. He, being a loyal FBI agent, had to do what I did, and so he fasted with me, except he kept going home. We had a double sleeping bag, and I thought, 'Now I have him. He'll be forced to sleep with me. How ever will he handle this?' We had ten days to talk, and we talked an awful lot about what I believe in and who I am and where I came from. A few weeks later he was relieved as my tail."

"[Months later] I went to a civil rights trial. A marvelous black matriarch was arrested along with me for demonstrating at the 77th Street School. When we got to the 77th Street police station, they had Margaret Wright and me in the same cell together, saying we're old friends. Then when we got downtown, I as a white European, more privileged than she, a black American, was discharged and she was tried. So I went to her trial and testified for her. And here was my old agent friend and he came and said, 'I want you to meet some friends, FBI agent, CIA agent...' I said, 'I'm not supposed to associate with you people very much.' He let me say hello and go back.

"Then he followed me down the hall and said, 'Have you ever figured out why I was relieved as your tail?' He said, 'First off, when did you find out?' I said, 'Well, I found out very early on because I use investigative techniques to determine who you were. But since I knew there would be another one if it weren't you, I just put up with you.' He said, 'Well, I was relieved because we spent ten days together and you had me. You got me. You converted me. Immediately my reports changed and my supervisor in the FBI came to me and said, "He got you, didn't he? He changed your mind. Your reports are changed, so you're relieved."' He stayed on at his job [at the FBI]. He said, 'Don't get interested in education because that's my assignment.'"

Kight had more than one FBI tail and he realized the interest in him wouldn't soon abate. He was usually suspicious when someone around him who had had trouble with the law suddenly and inexplicably didn't have trouble with the law. He strongly suspected one of the transsexuals who hung around at his house of being an informant. Kight let his rascal nature loose and purposely fed false information to this particular informant. He would joke to close friends about telling the alleged informant of his plans for international travel. Kight never knew what happened to the false information that he purposely fed to the FBI, but it went on for two years and is recorded in his FBI file.

Entry in Kight's FBI file, dated November 27, 1968:

"...A source advised that Morris Kight has indicated that he will travel from Los Angeles to Montreal, Canada to attend the Hemisphere Conference to End the War in Vietnam..."

And some of the reports of intended travel were accurate and true. FBI entry dated January 10, 1969: "Reliable source advised ... that Morris Lee Kight ... intends traveling via air to Washington, D.C. to participate as a speaker in demonstrations at time of inauguration...."

Kight passed on a bit of information about traveling to Berlin, East Germany, in June 1969 to attend an International Peace Conference. Each report of Kight's intention to travel is followed by multiple copies of requests for an FBI Special Agent assignment to each destination.

FBI entry dated June 4, 1969: "Enclosed for the Bureau are five copies of an [internal request for travel] regarding foreign travel on the part of the subject to East Germany in June of 1969. Also enclosed for the Bureau are six additional copies of [requests] and two photographs of Kight for transmittal to Legat, Bern and Bonn [FBI's overseas offices]."

FBI permission was granted and Special Agents were dispatched to various locales.

FBI, dated July 25, 1969: "Enclosed for the Bureau are five copies of [a form] regarding subject's cancelled plans for foreign travel. Also enclosed for the Bureau are six additional copies of [another form] for transmittal to Legat, Bern and Bonn … Records, Passport Office, Department of State, Washington, D.C., were reviewed by a representative of the FBI on June 11, 1969 and June 24, 1969 and failed to contain any records for passport application or issuance in the name of Morris Lee Kight."

The FBI was irrepressible, and agents never showed any annoyance with Kight's antics.

It wasn't all business for Kight; there was some personal connection to the FBI. Well-known among the Los Angeles gay society was Clyde Tolson, professionally known as Associate Director of the FBI (1930–1972), but best known as a "close companion" of FBI Director J. Edgar Hoover. On his frequent trips to Los Angeles, Tolson was a regular at many gay hangouts and made no effort to conceal his sexuality when in homosexual company. Longtime Kight friend and confidante Miki Jackson recounted a story that Kight told several times over the years to different people: "Morris said he was acquainted with Tolson and with some gay men who knew him and Hoover but were really friends with Tolson. Morris would cast a sidelong eye and say archly, '*Friends* with Hoover?' with an emphasis on the word friends. Morris had been to social occasions with Tolson a few times when Tolson would come to L.A. Tolson, Morris would say, 'liked to come to Southern California in the winter to enjoy what could be enjoyed in Southern California in the winter.' [Kight] said Tolson and Hoover were a couple, but as is usual with many gay couples of long standing, had separate sex lives."

As it turned out, Hoover collected antiques and items of value in his own signature fashion. Jackson continued, "If [Hoover] saw something he wanted he would have the owner of the store 'looked' into. Hoover favored gay proprietors and dealers [whom Kight would know through his own antiques business]. Hoover would look at the coveted item and remark on his fondness for it and at a later date he would come back and ask to speak to the proprietor in private. He would chat a bit and then say he had a problem and perhaps the proprietor could help him with it. He had been provided with some troubling material. At that point Hoover would draw an envelope out and spread its contents on the desk—usually consisting largely of compromising photographs of the proprietor. He would chat on and say he wasn't quite sure how to handle the situation and so on. He would gather up the material and tuck it under his arm, saying he would have to consider the matter further, and leave, often stopping to [again] admire the item he coveted on his way out. Within days the item and perhaps one or two others would be delivered to Chez Hoover.

"Morris said he heard Tolson laughingly recount these machinations on a couple of occasions. Mutual acquaintances told him that Tolson sold many of these treasures before Hoover was 'cold.' Tolson was said to often complain of Hoover's gauche taste and how cluttered the place was with overly ornate items. Morris also said Hoover had a number of gays employed at the FBI and made great use of the gay underground network or 'grapevine.' Apparently Hoover liked using gays as he felt he could control them easily. Morris remarked that a person with a degree in psychology could have made much of that. Morris said that Hoover had a great deal on many people and seemed to favor targeting their sexual weaknesses. He wondered if—other than sexual scandals being great ammo—if that was because of Hoover's own complex sexual situation. [Kight] said what he heard Hoover had on Eleanor [Roosevelt] was material on her lesbian affairs. Whether that involved nude photographs or not was never mentioned."

In 1970, Kight received a letter from Georgia Congressman Julian Bond in response to a letter that Kight wrote to him regarding a small piece that appeared in *Hollywood Citizen News* where Bond is quoted as saying: "Among the most violent people in America [is] the little sissy who runs the Federal Bureau of Investigation."

"Dear Mr. Kight," Bond wrote, "I did in fact call J. Edgar Hoover a 'sissy,' but I meant no unflattering reference to his sex life.

"The word 'sissy' may mean one thing to you, but it means several to me.

"Let us simply say that in my opinion, Mr. Hoover is a 'sissy' by my meaning of the phrase; he may also be a homosexual as well.

"Sincerely, Julian Bond."

Regularly, Monday nights were the general meeting of the Dow Action Committee, followed by "good, cheap food" at a nearby Chinese restaurant called the Bamboo Inn. Over egg rolls, steaming noodles, and wonton soup—the "traditional soup of conspirators," as Kight called it—he and his friends discussed and analyzed the world's suffering and argued principles of the modern Western world with each other, other customers and the waiters. One night, when the meal was over and the dishes cleared, the fortune cookies were laid out on the table. One by one, Kight and his friends opened their cookies and each received the *same* fortune: "The FBI is watching you." They waited for the restaurant to close and once alone, Mr. Lu, the owner, locked the doors and came to sit with them at the table. He told them, in his strained immigrant English, that agents had been asking after DAC's business. Mr. Lu told them what Chinese people had learned after centuries of dealing with a rigid government: "good steady customers are a treasure worthy of emperors." Mr. Lu, according to Kight, said that dealing with the Dow Action Committee was "very painful." Every Tuesday, the FBI visited Mr. Lu and asked dozens of questions about who was with them and what was discussed and if they left any notes. In recalling the story in 2000, Kight said: "That's how the Syndicate [Mafia] got control of this country's politics [because] J. Edgar Hoover was so preoccupied with hating the labor movement, hating the feminist movement, hating the lesbian/gay liberation movement, hating the antiwar movement, that he totally ignored the Mafia, the Syndicate. They got control of our politics and they still control it because of his inattention. I carried that fortune cookie piece of paper in my wallet for 18 years until it finally turned to dust, it just wore out."

DOW SHALT NOT RECRUIT

DOW CHEMICAL COMPANY UNDERESTIMATED THE BOYCOTT AND pickets and never anticipated much repercussion. Dow's press relations department issued a statement saying the boycott was "a small group of activists, quite a fringe group, they are more against the war than napalm." Dow was wrong.

The Dow boycott provided an important focal point for the antiwar movement. Every household in America had something they could do (or rather, *not* do, as in "don't purchase Dow products") in support of ending the war in Vietnam. The boycott was quite successful. Corporate America, not just the Dow Chemical Company, sorely felt the adverse effects of the antiwar movement when protests against the war started happening on separate college campuses across the nation and headlined the evening news. In colleges and in the finest universities across the country, demonstrations against recruiters representing Dow and other companies were effective, and it became very unpopular for soon-to-be-graduates to be courted by the war industry—which Dow Chemical represented. For the most part, the demonstrations remained nonviolent and curtailment in recruitment was due to changes in consciousness. There was a new awareness among the youngest and brightest talent ready to enter the work force. It was, after all, a revolutionary time, and DAC propaganda was strong and relentless with signs such as "End University Complicity with Dow and the War Effort."

Even though Dow, other companies, and the military itself publicly denied that there was a drop in employment recruitment, by late 1967, the *L.A. Free Press* reported that "recruiters began to go 'underground' to conduct potentially conflagratory [sic] interviews. The CIA, notably, has taken its Harvard interviews off-campus to a Boston office. A spokesman for FMC Corp., which builds tanks, chuckled to a *Wall Street Journal* interviewer that 'these protesters probably don't even know we're in the defense business.'" The article ended, "They know now."

Kight's 1994 note to the archive: "[DAC] was totally nonviolent, indeed, classic pacifism. We worked very hard, were very creative, did many things."

The pickets and demonstrations kept the message in the news and encouraged more activism. The consumer boycott was effective, but nothing hit the corporation harder than curbing their recruitment efforts.

DRAFT RESISTANCE

ANOTHER FOCAL POINT FOR THE ANTI-VIETNAM WAR MOVEMENT was draft resistance. Peacetime draft begun in 1940 required all men between the ages of 18 and 25 to register. They were the first troops sent to Southeast Asia. Throughout the 1960s, America's young people were being drafted for compulsory military service and as U.S. troop strength in Vietnam increased, more young men were drafted for service. The unpopularity of the war in Vietnam created a viable anti-draft effort. Often called "draft dodgers," young men would seek counsel to avoid being drafted into the army or ways to get out after already enlisting. Many would find their way to Morris Kight or Don Slater.

Don Slater used his office at the Homosexual Information Center (HIC) on Cahuenga to counsel young gay men, the same office where he let Kight use a desk and a phone. It was never a secret that Kight believed Slater to be "very right-wing" and they had opposing views on most subjects. Still, there was a mutual respect, and they were able to work together on a few key undertakings, such as draft resistance.

Though Slater and Kight shared a common goal—to help people avoid being drafted—and were working against a common nemesis (the U.S. military), they did so for very different reasons. Slater was not ideologically opposed to the military as Kight was, yet they were happy to work together against a common enemy.

Kight always opposed war and aligned with pacifism. He would consistently oppose the draft on the grounds that it supported war.

Slater, on the other hand, was pro-government and he did not oppose the U.S. military involvement in Vietnam. His opposition was toward the military's treatment of homosexuals. Some homosexuals wanted homosexuals to serve in the military, to integrate into mainstream society; they felt it was a gateway to eventually being seen as honorable and accepted. He himself had served an "unexceptional" eight months in the military before rheumatic fever put him in the infirmary and then he was honorably discharged. Some of his friends, close friends, were terribly mistreated by the military and scarred for life by a "blue" or dishonorable discharge for no crime other than being homosexual.

There are different accounts of Slater's success rate with helping gay servicemen. Some documents say he rarely won a draft resistance case, and other resources say he had a hundred-percent success rate. In either case, it was unheard of for gay men to have a place to go to seek such counseling.

Most of the counseling activity took place at Slater's *Tangents* offices on Cahuenga Boulevard. Slater founded the Homosexual Information Center in the mid-1960s in response to a terrible breach with the then-board of ONE Archive. Soon after HIC began, Slater began publishing a monthly gay and lesbian magazine called *Tangents*. The editorial board of *Tangents* frequently crossed over with ONE. The pioneers of both organizations had a bitter falling-out and would draw lines in the sand that would go deep and hold for at least two generations. Kight put forth his best efforts to keep far away from the fight and remain cordial with both sides. Yet, every so often, and later more often than not, he could also alienate both sides of the same fracas.

Slater counseled men who wanted to resist the draft on the grounds of being a homosexual or who wanted a discharge because of the military's treatment of homosexuals. He knew which forms were required and helped the men to fill them out with the typewriter. He would go with them to the hearing, and he would seek outside [legal] counsel when necessary. Kight, working as a pacifist, counseled young men seeking refuge from the draft (not just gay men) citing various reasons. He would refer some to Slater or someone else who was doing the same kind of work. Kight also continued his other counseling for troubled men. In a typed note written to Slater (May 31, 1965), Kight says: "...since this morning before nine I had three calls from you-know-whoms asking for advice and assistance one of the requests to furnish free cab to someplace 35 miles away to one in imagined distress."

Jim Kepner: "Not all gays approached military counseling the same way: some used it to protect the right of privacy, some to oppose the war in Vietnam. Some began telling draft boards that they were gay, whether they were or not."

Kight's draft resistance activities were partially supported by the Peace Action Council, but funds were difficult to get from the Council. It wasn't unusual for the needs-agendas to overlap. For instance, Kight might get a call from someone needing to be bailed out of jail and, once out of jail, it was learned that the person also had not reported to the draft board. Kight and Slater would ask each other for help with certain cases. Some, but certainly not a majority, were losses. In August 1967, Kight typed a full-page note to Slater "Re: Gary Tayler bond jumping. Dear Don, Your kind note came this morning.

"Its [sic] just the kind of thing that you'd do, offering to absorb all of this, but no, I can't accept that. Gary was, and is, a friend of mine; though unless he's a far finer person than most he'll find somehow that he's been wronged and that we are the greater sinners. But surely he's too intelligent for that."

The letter goes on about other challenges that came up with Gary Tayler: "… hardly anyone writes traffic bonds and Gary is what might be called a 'floater.' Thus Mr. [Sheldon] Andelson, I, and you guaranteed it. I can't honestly ask Mr. Andelson to assist on the financial end since he's been just wonderful to me with the many cases he's handled so ably for me and our tribe."

Kight laid out his efforts to "ameliorate the damage."

"This failing, then we are down for the money. I realize that your little pittance there goes as quickly as it comes in, for rent, phones, printing, legal fees, etc. etc. and that you don't have it to spare, but then spare it must.

"So I will work out my end and will make some special effort to get the funds in. Perhaps we could have a hippy-type benefit called the 'Gary Tayler Redemption Day' and have the Mormon Tabernacle Choir to sing 'We Shall Overcome.'

"Worst of all is that this default, and another Bob Miller (you [were] not involved), has put me in a bad light and will affect the liberties of many more innocent victims of entrapment, who really deserve the help. I have bonded out 1500 people in ten years and to this date the losses have totaled only around $500, and all out of my pocket, heretofore."

Kight enjoyed a witty banter with Slater; they used their ideological differences to have fun with each other. He closed his note: "This brings up the question of Dropping Out. We must say to all and sundry, drop out all you want, but Baby, Do Your Own Thing and don't take the rest of us with you. PeaceThroughLove and Its Going To Take A Lot of Lovin' To See This Through, Morris Kight."

Perhaps antsy to try some street activism, in an atypical move for the more reticent Don Slater, he organized the "First National Homophile Protest" on Armed Forces Day in May of 1966 to protest the military's treatment of homosexuals. *Gay L.A.* referred to the organized motorcade as "the first gay parade on record." About a dozen cars honked horns and waved posters with statements such as "Ten Percent of all GIs are Homosexual" for 20 miles through the Wilshire district and into Hollywood, to loudly protest the U.S. military's anti-homosexual policy. Kight, always supportive of Slater, did not participate in this parade as he was opposed to the war, he was opposed to all young men being sent off to war, and he opposed the military industrial complex.

The demonstration did not receive much attention or press coverage. The local CBS television affiliate ran a quick clip and the *New York Times* ran a blurb, but the *Los Angeles Times* had a strict policy that they'd send a reporter only if "someone was hurt." Except for a few firsthand accounts, there is little record of the demonstration and Slater lamented the anti-climactic response to his brave act of radicalism. He expressed his disappointment, no doubt over a few cocktails, to Kight. Slater was becoming sour that Kight spent so much time and effort on "that other" civil rights movement and this was causing a ripple in their friendship. In November of 1966 Kight typed a very personal note to Slater:

> "Dear Loved One ... CORE [*Congress of Racial Equality*] in NY with some of the best minds in the country working on the problem. Not all of these people are raging angry, many are terribly hurt. And across here in Los Angeles are people whose families were living here before ours came even from Europe. Surely I can't have influenced all these people. But I am alert enough to observe what they are saying, to hear them in meetings, to feel their heartbeat as we move along together and thus I just must call it as it is.
>
> "FIRE.
>
> "I don't use that word in my personal or public or literary contacts for the reason that I do not wish to add to the conflagration." Kight was referring to the ubiquitous heat of potential violence in his activism. It was always present, even years later in the Gay Liberation Front.
>
> "But dear boy," Kight continued, "conflagration it is and it will take a lot of water to put this one out. So far we've been using cap pistols. Peace Through Love, Morris."

Kight read the temperament of the media and he knew they were not yet ready to report any positive news about homosexuals. That would come with a lot of time and effort. In the meantime, Kight continued to strengthen individuals; he tried to build a coalition of homosexuals, one person at a time, who could stand up for themselves and support one another and eventually create a more friendly world.

PEACE AND FREEDOM

THE REVOLUTIONARY TIDE OF THE 1960S HAD PEOPLE LOOKING IN new places for answers to old problems. Antiwar activists needed to *support* something and not just be opposed to everything. In response to Democratic Party support for the war in Vietnam and feigned support for the Civil Rights Act, the Peace and Freedom Party was founded on June 23, 1967. A new alliance was forged between the black civil rights movement, the labor movement, and the antiwar movement, and that pumped life into the Peace and Freedom Party. It began with a seven-month registration campaign to gather enough signatures to qualify to be on the ballot in California.

Ed Pearl, owner and booker at the famous Ash Grove nightclub (on Melrose Avenue in Los Angeles), got involved with the PFP through the antiwar movement.

Ed Pearl was new to political activism himself, though he had always allowed his club to be used for different group meetings and fundraising events. "Any group could use the Ash Grove anytime, anytime I wasn't putting on a show," he explained. "I always let people put on benefits, but I never got involved with anything until it was time with the Vietnam War—the escalation of the war—and it was time to do something." The Ash Grove attracted the top folk and blues talent of the day, from Muddy Waters, Doc Watson, Big Mama Thornton, to Bonnie Raitt and Joan Baez. Bob Dylan made his first West Coast appearance at the Ash Grove. Music began to blend with radical politics and the atmosphere at the Ash Grove evolved into a sort of cultural center where people exchanged ideas of politics and art. The rich sat with the working class, celebrities blended with hippies and truck drivers. It was a meeting place for Black Panthers and other radical groups of the time. The Ash Grove may be where Kight met and developed a relationship with the Black Panther Party. From the early Black Panthers he learned about community shaping, grassroots organizing, fundraising, and nonviolent lawful civil disobedience. The Ash Grove was also a social place for the Mattachine Society. Ed Pearl recalled, "a lot of gay men, and lesbians too, went to the Ash Grove because there was never any prejudice of any kind, that happened without my knowledge or caring about it."

The Ash Grove became more than a nightclub; it was an institution.

Pearl remembers first meeting Kight: "The Peace and Freedom Party opened an office on Western, and there was this man, an older man, he had some kind of human rights [organization] in the same building. Morris and I quickly became friends. I knew Morris for a solid eight months and became really good friends with him. He was much more knowledgeable politically than I was, so I learned a lot from him. I learned from him that it was human rights and it was also gay rights.

"I learned a lot about politics in general from Morris. I really didn't know a lot about the differences and the different groups and Morris seemed to know a lot more than I did. We talked about everything, it was a time of such serious politicization of the Sixties Generation, including me." Kight and Pearl had a semi-regular routine of going out for breakfast at one of the local cheap dives and discussing current events. "I had politics before, but that was only UCLA schoolboy politics and not living in the real world." Ed Pearl knew that Morris was gay; Kight told him. Ed also knew about Kight's underground help to gay people. "More than Dow," Ed remembers about Morris at that time, "it was Human Rights."

No question about it, Kight enjoyed his cocktails (rye and soda being his beverage of choice), but his true elixir was having intellectual conversations with radical people. He was attracted mostly to people on the left of the social and political spectrum, but he could talk to anyone about most anything. By the mid-'60s, activism had become his social life. And his social life had become quite active. The Ash Grove became another frequent watering hole for the activist.

Many of the same musicians and stand-up comedians from the Ash Grove came out to support the Peace and Freedom Party and the antiwar rallies. The Nitty Gritty Dirt Band and Pete Seeger were regulars at Sunday rallies at MacArthur Park, followed by a potluck at Kight's nearby house.

After a rigorous eight-month campaign, the Peace and Freedom Party qualified for ballot status with signatures of 105,000 registered voters. In early August of 1968, in an unprecedented move in American politics, the California Peace and Freedom Party held nominating conventions simultaneously in San Francisco and Los Angeles. Kight participated in Los Angeles as the potential candidates were discussed and eventually chosen. The California ballot listed Chicago activist Peggy Terry as the Peace and Freedom candidate for Vice President. The Presidential slot on the ballot was blank.

Ed and Morris kept in touch for many years and Ed got to know Morris as an art enthusiast.

Pearl explained: "Morris really adored the woman I was with all that period. She was a dancer and an artist, and an amazing person. Morris adored her, he got really close to her, she was really good at visual arts, she is a great painter, and she and Morris had a special relationship around art and culture. I sat there and viewed them both, admiringly, how much they knew about it and enjoyed being a spectator to that."

REVOLUTION FEVER

MOST OF KIGHT'S CONTEMPORARIES AND FORERUNNERS DID NOT understand him; they didn't appreciate his commitment outside of gay needs and most of them didn't see how it could connect to their cause. Many were single-issue politicos. And yet they knew him, his dark side, quite well; they saw his ego for what it was and they correctly sensed his competitive nature.

Gino Vezina: "Great people did what they did with a certain amount of humility. Because of Morris' egotistical drive, he did do things to promote gay lib, it may be because of ego. There were people who got involved with him, thought he was great at first, but when they got wind of his ego, they left. Several people, good people, antiwar movement [Civil Rights], after they saw the ego they left."

Kight developed an enviable mailing list and was disciplined about keeping people abreast of his activities. Included with a whole packet of antiwar materials that Kight sent to Harry Hay was an undated, typed, open letter for fundraising. Kight signed the letter with his name as 'Chairman of the Dow Boycott.' Harry Hay saved the letter and the many pages of 'peace happenings,' and scrawled in red ink in the upper right corner: "This is what Morris was doing in 1968—But NOT openly as a gay, as we were. —HH"

Hay responded to Kight with a typical four-typed-page letter with a lot of gossip and a little history, most of it gay.

Hay to Kight (undated letter): "So—when [Barbara] Gittings or [Frank] Kameny or [Foster] Gunnison trumpet forth with great knowledge about Mattachine or

Homophile beginnings—I always have to think 'jeez, ya pore opportunist bastard! Whattya tryin' ta prove? Ya don't know who first coined 'Homophile' or why? Ya don't know how long it took to sell the Minority on the fact that It was a minority … (yasee they [early homosexuals] wanted so desperately to be exactly the same as everybody else but maaayyybbbbbeeee they might be willing to be a kinda-sorta 'sub-culture, anyone?')"

Kight's and Hay's correspondence was rich and consistent and, as Hay pointed out in one letter he wrote responding to Kight, often consisted of "envelopes stuffed with warmed-over leaflets and other sundry printings from the big City."

The radicalized social climate of the time created a natural loosening within the gay culture. The injustices were obvious and many were getting fed up with the status quo for homosexuals, though most of the organizing was still underground.

On New Year's Eve going into 1967, Los Angeles had early kicks of the birth of the modern gay rights movement. LAPD raided two bars in Silver Lake, The Black Cat and New Faces. LAPD raids were fairly common occurrences in and around gay bars, easy busts for the police. It being New Year's Eve, New Faces hosted a costume party. At about 11:30 p.m., 15 or 20 men in full drag with wigs, makeup, and high heels walked across the street to check out the new gay bar, The Black Cat. Unwittingly, they walked into a sting operation by undercover vice officers at The Black Cat. At midnight, the bar was packed and the crowd went wild, cheering and belting out a version of "Auld Lang Syne." The bartender pulled a string that released a hundred colorful balloons from the ceiling into the crowd, and some of the patrons kissed.

Vice officers alerted uniformed police and suddenly the place swarmed with uniformed cops who, along with undercover officers, beat and randomly arrested people. Billy clubs swung, Christmas ornaments smashed. There were reports that one person was kicked so hard that "his bowels emptied," and another person was hit on the back of the head with a pool cue. Several people ran across the street to New Faces and police raided that bar as well, beating a bartender at New Faces so badly that his spleen ruptured.

Morris Kight: "Bars were the only places to go," in those days. "The only criminal behavior in The Black Cat bar that night was [by] the police."

Six of the men, who were seen kissing, were charged with lewd conduct. There were a total of 16 arrests with the added humiliation of having to lie face down on the sidewalk.

Before the bars closed that night, Kight received calls from people who were there or who knew what had happened, and by early morning calls came in from the jail. Everyone pooled their resources for bail and legal counsel; within a few weeks, San Francisco and New York activists sent monetary and emotional support. Protests outside The Black Cat began almost immediately. In an unprecedented move, homosexuals did not cower and quietly accept the police brutality. In what was probably the first massive gay public demonstration on the West Coast, the barebones gay community, as it were, publicly responded to the LAPD abuse with a picket outside the Black Cat bar on Sunset Boulevard that continued for several months and attracted support from all across town and all sexual identities, but it received no mainstream media attention.

Communication and publication became a key to gay organizing; silence and ignorance were old roadblocks. The local L.A. gay newspaper *Tangents* covered details of the raid and the angry aftermath. In addition, key members of PRIDE founded a newsletter called the *Advocate* with the stated purpose "to unite and inform the gay community of what was happening in their closed society." The *Advocate* would grow into the national newspaper-of-record for the homosexual community.

Morris Kight remembered, "Herbert Selwyn [from the ACLU], a non-gay man who had a long record on civil liberties, helped to present a legal challenge to the arrests during the 1967 raid at the Black Cat bar."

Tangents: "All over the city, homosexuals are determined that they will no longer 'cop out' to the lesser charge if they are arrested. And when someone else is arrested, they will come forward as a witness, even though police may bring pressure on their employers."

The protests signified the beginning of a new era for gays. Kight was also able to populate a picket line in a matter of hours with dozens of willing protesters. No one else had that capability.

Many years later, in a letter to Jim Kepner, Harry Hay wrote: "[Morris] brought some of the Queens of his entourage in the PEACE movement" to the demonstration line at The Black Cat. "My guess is that that night's effort was his first GAY Political Action Involvement. Later that Spring, the TANGENTS GROUP held an outdoor supper benefit in Morris's backyard and ... later that summer ... as part of the Peace Movement, Morris had us over for another benefit and I introduced Gay Civil Rights to this crowd, with Morris acting as a 'neutral' sympathizer. Of course, the 1965–68 DOW Protest Committee of which Morris was founder, key activist, and total puppet-master was made up primarily of screamingly obvious, but quite doggedly undeclared, Gays."

In the end, four of the six that went to court pled no contest, paid the fine, and went home. Charges of "common drunkenness" against the heterosexual married bartender were dropped. All the men who went to trial were found guilty by a jury. An unprecedented spark had been ignited across the country and gays were sneaking hope that there was indeed a better way of life for them. The LAPD, on the other hand, took the pickets and demonstrations as an affront to their authority, and with the proverbial line drawn, there began a virtual street war between the police and homosexuals.

A LOT WORSE

IN 2003, KIGHT RECALLED ANOTHER PIVOTAL EVENT FOR GAYS IN Los Angeles: "In [1969], gay men had liberated a hotel downtown called The Dover Hotel located at 555 South Main Street." Kight had a liberal use of the word 'liberated.'

"It belonged to a group of Asians and I never knew whether they had cured themselves of their homophobia and thought 'Why not?' or if they just didn't know what was going on. Whatever it was, we took advantage of it to make the five stories a cruising area. And so Howard Efland, a heterosexually married man—that also is part of our tragic past, as many of us carried on heterosexual marriages which really were façades, they really, they were travesties, they didn't really have mutual love. They didn't really have respect. We did it anyway.

"Howard Efland, leaving his wife and three children [Efland had no children] with an excuse he was going out of town, whatever it was, came to The Dover Hotel, laid down, got himself nude, which was the custom, by the way, and laid on top of the bed face down with his rear end showing, which was a hint that you were into mutual anal intercourse. If you lay on your back and exposed your private parts, the indication was that you were into mutual oral copulation. And so he was found."

As was common practice, Howard Efland registered under his common pseudonym: Jack McCann.

"Five police officers came into the room and hurled epithets at him, 'you faggot' and 'da da da faggot' and so on, and started beating on him with their truncheons and he said, 'Please, you're killing me, stop this. Why are you doing this?'

"So they drag him off the bed and dragged him by his hands or arms, dragged him down the hall. They dragged him all the way down the hallway to the fire escape [at the back of the building], and then out onto the fire escape. They dragged him down, feet first with his head hitting the steps as he went down. The fire escape was metal and his head hit the metal, him screaming 'you're torturing me.' So they dragged him feet first down the steps, with his head hitting the steps, bang bang bang. [He was] screaming, 'Stop this, you're torturing me,' losing his voice because he was losing his life. When they got to the bottom of the stairs, they started putting him in the back seat of the police car; happily [as the end of Efland's torture], his powerful heart gave out and he died.

"We [the bare threads of a gay community] were horrified and we did the first really organized protest about that in that we asked for a coroner's inquest, and a coroner's jury of civilians were put together and we appeared before them and they had two days of testimony about police brutality, us namely; police malpractice, us namely; and the police saying, 'He was a dirty faggot da de de da.' And so his homicide was called justifiable. We didn't believe that it was justifiable."

It being 1969, no media outlet would touch the story. Howard Efland's family could not withstand the public scrutiny, hence they chose to accept the coroner's report that said Efland died of "excusable homicide" caused by resisting arrest, with the exact cause of death listed as a "ruptured pancreas."

Troy Perry and Kight and others led the efforts to publicly demand an investigation. It was the first collective outrage that sparked an action beyond demonstration. Voices and paperwork went into the District Attorney's office demanding an investigation. The *L.A. Free Press,* the only above-ground newspaper to report the story, gave an account of the seven-man Coroner's Jury that conducted a perfunctory inquiry. "Non-police witnesses" testified about seeing police officers kick, slap, handcuff, and throw Efland against the walls and allow his head to hit the pavement. Witnesses told about the screaming in the alleyway of "God help me." Several of the witnesses were discredited when the D.A. introduced their criminal records. The officers all corroborated their stories and explained that Efland died after one of them "accidentally 'fell' on the victim's stomach." It took

15 minutes of deliberation for the jury to excuse the police of any wrongdoing and the department returned to "business as usual."

The inquest closed the Howard Efland murder investigation, but it opened up a very unstable and potentially volatile relationship with the LAPD.

Morris Kight continued: "And so one year later, the L.A. police killed a black male gay, somewhat cross-dresser … Larry Laverne Turner, at 42nd and Central Avenue. He was in female attire and was on the sidewalk, or the corner of the sidewalk, cruising, hooking, and prostituting himself. And the police came arrested him and claimed that he had a pistol on him, claimed that, and then shot and killed him. The pistol is probably bogus because he had recently been a member of the United States Naval Service and discharged from the Naval Service because he had an antipathy to weapons, he refused to bear arms. He had a psychic antipathy to that."

About a month after Larry Turner's death, a lesbian named Ginny Gallegos died under suspicious circumstances while in police custody.

Kight would recite the names Howard Efland, Larry Turner, Ginny Gallegos frequently during the late days of gay subjugation and in the early days of gay liberation. The deaths brought latent homosexuality to the surface. There were discussions and debates amongst gays, antipathy toward the police. Kight wouldn't let the names be forgotten and he gave them 'poster child' status in the incubating movement and would repeat their names like beating a drum. In March 1970, as a form of protest, there was a "Gay Memorial Service," officiated by Reverend Perry of MCC, in honor of all three decedents. Police harassments and entrapments were escalated and there was genuine fear for the lives of all gay men and women.

The constant threat of danger was not exclusively from the police. Certainly LAPD apathy toward crimes against homosexuals fueled more rage. Hatred directed toward homosexuals was rampant, from all races and all sides of the ideological scale. In the decade of free love and mind expansion, it was a very real hazard to be openly homosexual.

Kight experienced physical brutality in the 1960s. In 1994, he told another story to Paul Cain:

"And then, in 1965, I was on a picket line, opposing the war in Vietnam, and a stunningly attractive young man came and didn't join the picket line. But he stayed around, and we got acquainted. And I was very interested in him, personally and sexually. When we finished [at the picket line], I said, 'Why don't you come with me?' and so we went to a gay bar. We went to the Paper Doll, located at 1707 West Seventh Street. And when I got into the [bar] light, he just turned terribly attractive and that was pretty wonderful.

"And then we went to my house. And I fully expected, of course, to have sex with him. And then he wanted to talk because he found me interesting. And he wanted to find out why I opposed the war in Indochina. He wanted to find out why I said I was gay. Because, mind you, I was saying I was gay."

Sadly, in his later years, Kight did sometimes feel the need to defend himself in response to the accusations from Harry Hay and some others that he had operated "in the closet."

"He [the young man] wanted to find out why I was doing all these things. It turns out that he had been a recent returnee from Vietnam. He had been brainwashed into believing that that was an okay thing, and yet something had told him it wasn't. He was suffering terribly. And he leapt across the table, with a switchblade knife six inches long, and stabbed me in the stomach. It got awfully close to the peritoneum and I knew that I was in serious crisis. I rushed out of the house and got in my car. I didn't call an ambulance, I wasn't thinking, 'cause I thought he would finish killing me. So I sped away and went to the receiving hospital.

"The City of Los Angeles, in those halcyon days, had city health services and good ones, by the way. I was at the receiving hospital at 1606 West Sixth Street and went in and they said, 'Oh no, no, no, wrong place. Get on the gurney.' And they red-flagged me, put a red blanket over me, meaning that I was in crisis and took me to an ambulance ... I was in General Hospital three or four days."

Never one to miss an opportunity to boast, Kight added to the end of his story: "A team of marvelous doctors recognized me from television, and wanted to talk with me about my work, gay and antiwar and so on.

"And so, after three days, they said, 'Go home now, come back in two days and we'll take the stitches out. We believe that no further surgery is necessary. However, stay in touch.' A year later it herniated, so I had this terrible hernia. I went back there, went to see about the hernia, and all the doctors say that it looks like hell, but it's purely cosmetic, and there's nothing to be gained from further surgery. That was from the stabbing."

Not all of the threats against Kight were because he was gay. There are other factors, like his blatant antiwar activities, to consider.

"The following year, a car came in front of my house [on West Fourth Street], when the front door was closed, and they shot through the front door, and pierced the wood of the door, and pierced a Catholic woman's sodality [sic] banner, silk and embroidery, gorgeous folk art. I had no part of that, but it was interesting folk art. It had three bullet holes in it, and one bullet grazed my face. And then they went on. I never knew who it was. So I came awfully close to being shot and killed. I could go on, but I think that's enough of a litany of horrors."

CHICAGO 1968

KIGHT TRAVELED A LOT WITH THE DOW ACTION COMMITTEE. During 1967 and the Summer of Love, Kight spent a lot of time going back and forth between San Francisco and Los Angeles for demonstrations and meetings-of-the-minds and bodies.

FBI entry dated February 14, 1969: "No attempt has been made by the Communist Party (CP) or the Los Angeles Local-Socialist Workers Party to infiltrate or dominate the Dow Action Committee."

The FBI would know about such things because they had infiltrated the antiwar movement and by 1968 they targeted the DAC. Yet the FBI continually tried to link all radical and liberal causes and New Leftist movements and other revolutionaries as one and the same cause. To the FBI, they were one and the same problem.

Kight's FBI file: "In 1968 and 1969 [Kight] was extremely active in the Dow Action Committee (DAC). In April 1968, he indicated that he had decided to be arrested at some future DAC demonstration. In July 1968, Kight in describing attendance at a social function sponsored by the Los Angeles Committee for Defense of the Bill of Rights (LACDBR), reportedly stated 'true, there are a lot of old Communist Party member and activists, but if they are Communists, they are my kind of people.'

"In 1968 [Kight] attended functions sponsored by the Students for a Democratic Society, the 'Resistance' and the Los Angeles Branch – Young Socialist Alliance.

"In 1968 Kight was a speaker at an LACDBR sponsored rally....

"The above information was furnished by sources who have furnished reliable information in the past."

According to the evening news in 1967, the antiwar movement was having an impact on America's conscience and there was no pro-war machine for the news to report. J. Edgar Hoover, however, remained eager to ease the world of all ideological rebels who did not respect the status quo.

Beginning in late 1967, the National Mobilization Committee to End the War in Vietnam began planning an antiwar rally that called every antiwar organization and counterculture group across the country to be in Chicago during the Democratic National Convention in August 1968. President Johnson announced that he would not seek re-election. The 1968 nomination was particularly heated. The Democratic Convention promised to be an historical event inside and outside of the convention hall.

The plan was to be outside the International Amphitheatre and peacefully demonstrate and hopefully sway delegates and party leaders. They depended upon large numbers of people to peacefully demonstrate. Two large-scale marches were planned, ending with a rally at Soldier Field. For months ahead, the Yippies (The Youth International Party co-founded by Abbie Hoffman, Anita Hoffman, Jerry Rubin, Nancy Kurshan, Paul Krassner) had been creating "an experience" leading up to the Chicago Convention and the week-long event might have been compared to Woodstock's political action committee cousin. Chicago Police were well informed and summarily denied permits. In an eleventh-hour effort, the Committee to End the War filed an appeal in federal court, wanting to force Chicago to issue permits. The judge ruled in the city's favor, saying that the protest groups were being unreasonable. In preparing their city for peace protesters, Chicago PD prepared for everything but peace.

Kight: "Dow Action Committee went to the Chicago National Democratic Convention, suffered heavy arrests, most of us were arrested.

"We had a spy agent to go with us, a Commander Rock with the LAPD Red Squad. A real bastard, just knew everything. He subscribed to all the mailing lists. He knew the Communist Party USA, he knew who that was; Communist Party Marxist Label, he knew who that was; Socialist Workers Party, he knew who that was—he subscribed to their newsletters, he read everything. He was totally informed, and so he was sent to Chicago a week ahead of time to advance us. He was to be our liaison to the Chicago Police and he said [to the Chicago PD] 'they [DAC] are really a dangerous group because they are not Communists. They advocate a withdrawal of troops immediately, and they do that with great style. They advocate the Dow

Chemical Company stop the manufacture of what they call criminal elements, and they obey the law. They are just a dangerous group.' And so the Chicago Police gave us special attention. And wow, they attacked our bus. They came with tear gas and gassed Grant Park, drove us from the park. We had three buses in a row and they came and slashed the tires off the buses, used stilettos to slash the tires.

"Ever try to buy 12 tires in Chicago in 1968 on a limited budget? [It] took a lot of doing."

It was weeks before Kight physically, emotionally, and financially recovered from the Chicago assault. The organization was bruised but stronger as a result. Fallout from the police-incited riots in Chicago continued to reverberate in national discussion. For Kight, it put him on the national radar as an activist who appeared in the evening news and was often quoted in the press. He was not in the spotlight, but very close to the spotlight, and certainly he was on a first-name basis with celebrities of the peace movement (Jane Fonda, Tom Hayden, Dalton Trumbo, and others). Morris Kight was happy with that.

Into 1969, Kight continued to work hard for the peace movement. He sent out two- and three-page typed missives and organized a number of demonstrations with a single focus—to end the war in Vietnam. In early 1969, the Peace Action Council began making plans to lease a building and open a thrift shop to raise funds for their activities. It was a novel idea at the time and one that Kight would take with him into the gay liberation movement.

For the third year in a row, he organized an annual Memorial Day Rites demonstration at the Dow Chemical Company's Western sales office on Wilshire Boulevard. It had been popular in previous years and Kight wanted to do it again. In a flyer that he created and sent to a "small mailing—only to those who have supported us in the past," he promised to have:

"Speakers from the Peace Community, guitarists, singers, spiritual leaders, memorials to those killed in our senseless war in Vietnam, both American and Vietnamese. Special service of exorcism of evil from Dow's paper heart.

"OPEN MIKE POLICY WILL PREVAIL."

His flyer continued with a brief explanation about the Dow Action Committee's reputation as the "vanguard in demonstrating against chemical and biological warfare. Now the whole nation has found out, that of [all] things this is the worst monster of all.... Even the 'out-of-date' chemicals are a monster—current plans are to toss the old ones into the ocean—

"That's out of sight and out of mind!"

He closes with "Can we count on your support? Peace, Morris Kight."

The event that Kight organized was a "peaceful, loving, successful [day] that captured the imagination of the community."

In a December 1994 note to the archives, Kight wrote: "...We worked very hard, were very creative, did many things, and ultimately ... they abandoned the manufacture of napalm. I cried for a half a day."

Dow did cease manufacturing napalm in 1969. Unknown at the time to anyone who cared, Dow had a stockpile to last the U.S. military at least until 1972 or even 1973, by some accounts.

The battle was won, but the wars—the figurative antiwar effort and the actual war in Vietnam—continued. The boycott continued and slowly died out. Kight and Silverstein focused on the broader peace movement. It would take Dow Chemical Company years to fully recover favorable public relations. The U.S. government's response to the successful boycott was a private examination of corporate America's role in politics. Corporate attorney and tobacco industry lobbyist Lewis J. Powell shaped a new directive, crafting a long-term plan for American corporations to be more active in politics and legislation. The confidential memo that became known as the Powell Memorandum eventually made its way to President Nixon's desk with the title "Attack on the American Free Enterprise System." It directly addressed the toll the liberal revolution was having on the capitalist structure in a democratic society, and the U.S. Chamber of Commerce praised the document.

The Powell document was first leaked to the press and immediately ridiculed by syndicated columnist Jack Anderson. Subsequently, the Chamber of Commerce published the full document in the Chamber's newsletter, *Washington Report.* In the analog age, a copy of the Powell Memo was difficult to come by, but Kight and many other devoted activists shared a worn and faded mimeographed off-print copy of the document. The information was valuable to have; they were able to foresee major shifts in politics and social discourse in the coming years. The boycott clearly did more damage than kick the shins of the giant ("the establishment").

Kight was most proud that the Dow Action Committee remained nonviolent. Despite the police assault in Chicago, the FBI espionage and instigators, and ongoing challenges in being a revolutionary among revolutionaries out on the streets, Dow Action Committee never engaged in violence. Kight basked in that truth for the rest of his life.

Aside from all the press attention and rise in popularity, Kight was growing bored with the peace movement. There was no intellectual challenge and the spark was beginning to dim for him; it was becoming rudimentary. He triumphed in the Dow victory. Things were starting to shift for Kight personally and more broadly. A new revolution had been brewing for quite a while, going back to the Black Cat demonstrations in 1967 and the expressed outrage at the murders of three innocent homosexuals. Then, during the last weekend in June 1969, came the incident that would shift the consciousness of gay life forever.

Kight described it: "We started receiving several calls from Christopher Street Park, from pay telephones during the time, and frankly, it felt important. I wished I was there, but deep in my heart I could not sort it out. That sorting process came later."

History was being made on the other side of the country in New York City's Greenwich Village. It was another police raid on another gay bar. The police setup was exactly the same as it had been at the Black Cat bar in L.A. in 1967 and in thousands of other bars throughout America. Unlike all the other many raids and arrests that ruined so many other lives, this particular raid did not proceed as usual. The police met resistance—unprecedented in history. Gays would not take it anymore.

First reports were sketchy—the most reliable reports said that "a bunch of queens had barricaded a handful of police inside a bar called the Stonewall Inn."

L.A. activists were tethered to the phone and news reports even though there was no national press coverage. Other than some local New York coverage, only oral accounts on the phone were available at that point.

Morris Kight: "The New York Police Department, accompanied by the Alcoholic Beverage Control Board of New York, raided a gay bar, the Stonewall Inn at 59 Christopher Street in Greenwich Village, presumably to check on the unlicensed nature of the premises, but really to harass the customers.... [The bar patrons] refused, they refused to sneak away, refused to go away, they stayed and rioted and leafleted and organized.

"For days, they held the streets of Stonewall—from the Stonewall Inn in Greenwich Village, demonstrating. The police were inside, locked in the building. They called the police department on the pay phone from inside the Stonewall, saying, 'Send reinforcements. There's a riot going on.' 'Is it Chicano, Latino, Asian Pacific, African-American, peace, antiwar, labor? What was it?' 'No, it's fags.' 'You're kidding. You're kidding? Why would they be doing that?' 'Well they are. Send reinforcements.'

"Reinforcements came, flashing lights, sirens. That attracted more of a crowd."

The history of The Historic Stonewall Inn reads: "The police were then outnumbered by about 600 people. Ten police officers barricaded themselves inside the Stonewall Inn for their own safety. Garbage cans, bottles, rocks, and bricks were hurled at the building, breaking the windows. A parking meter was uprooted and used as a battering ram on the doors of the Stonewall. The Tactical Police Force of the New York City Police Department finally arrived to free the police trapped inside the Stonewall and with the larger police force they then detained anyone they could and put them in patrol wagons to go to jail."

The next night, rioting surrounded Christopher Street with thousands of people gathered in Greenwich Village. There were more fires in garbage cans and more than a hundred police tried to keep the crowd under control until four in the morning, and this continued for four days culminating with around 1,000 protesters and another explosive street battle with the police. There were injuries to demonstrators and police, looting in local shops, and five more people were arrested.

Kight: "I had a number of telephone calls from Christopher Park, which is a little piece of land across from the Stonewall Inn, while the event was going on, saying that it was happening.

"The second day, Allen Ginsberg, the famous poet, walked through the crowd [around the Stonewall] and said, 'Homosexuals do not have that hurt look anymore.'

"In making that very painful statement, and very true," Kight commented, "[Ginsberg] caught the spirit of liberation. It spread across the land and across the planet Earth."

Kight recognized that a new wave was taking shape, and reevaluated bigger goals for gay liberation. He saw himself as a different man. He was still restless—that came from a place very deep within him—but he saw himself as an accomplished man. He had been patient; he had planted seeds for a new kind of community by empowering one troubled gay man at a time; he had a strategy and the phone numbers of influential people. Kight had had a vision for some time and now he was ready to shape a new future.

On the heels of the very successful and yet quite violent demonstration at Stonewall, Kight was confident in and remained committed to nonviolent protest as a successful means of social reform. Nonviolence, Kight believed, was the most effective and produced long-term results.

Months later, Morris Kight would take his nonviolent activism on a new road toward gay liberation.

Chapter 9

Home to be Free

"In 1969 there was a monolith of oppression, repression, exploitation of lesbian and gay persons. It was assumed that we were sick, sinful, deviant, aberrant, and separable, that we could be separated and be ignored. There was no movement of any kind."
—Morris Kight

BY ALL ACCOUNTS, the Stonewall Inn uprising in June of 1969 was a turning point for gay liberation from which there was no going back. The Stonewall Rebellion heralded a new era, an epochal beginning to a new gay revolution, a post-Stonewall generation. It spilled past New York, had a rippling effect across the U.S., into Europe, and nothing would ever be the same politically, socially, and personally.

There had been decades of groundwork for change, yet it seemed like it happened overnight. In real time, it was three nights and four days to be exact. There would still be decades of work to adjust the consciousness of America.

It would later turn out that the *response* to the Stonewall Inn uprising became more important to gay history than the event itself. "It was," Kight wrote in 1989,

1970. Western Regional Homophile Conference at the First Unitarian Church, Los Angeles. Kight addressed the committee at his first public foray into gay activism. Kight had predicted that the group would be far more academic than active. Photographer unknown. Foster Gunnison, Jr. Papers. Archives & Special Collections at the Thomas J. Dodd Research Center, University of Connecticut Library.

"a bit of time before all realized the miracle of Christopher Street. And then began the legend about that night, and the following days of rage."

After Stonewall and through the summer of 1969, Kight continued to juggle his work with the National Mobilization Committee to End the War in Vietnam, his support of workers' rights, and his underground social services for gay men. The peace movement had built up nationwide momentum and by the spring of 1969, it had become a cultural staple and an unstoppable force. Kight's reputation was very much attached to the success of the peace movement and he was fully entrenched in the counterculture of the 1960s.

But Morris Kight was feeling the winds of change.

Kight: "October [15], 1969 I was an invited speaker at a major antiwar rally in San Francisco."

According to the *San Francisco Chronicle,* the rally was a "Massive national antiwar protest," launching the beginning of a new antiwar campaign called a "Fall Offensive," a nationwide "Moratorium Against the Vietnam War." Organized by the National Mobilization Committee to End the War in Vietnam (by this time informally known as 'The Mobe'), the day launched two months of daily demonstrations across the nation. *The New York Times* reported that there were "demonstrations ranging from noisy street rallies to silent-prayer vigils that involved a broad spectrum of the population ... and growing public opposition to the war in Vietnam."

It was reported that up to 100,000 people showed up in the San Francisco drenching rain on a Wednesday morning to participate in a peaceful march that started at the Embarcadero and convened at the end of the polo field in Golden Gate Park.

Among the speakers was David Hilliard, a militant member of the Black Panther Party, who made a speech condemning Nixon and the "capitalistic, fascistic American society" and was booed off the stage.

1970. Also at the Conference was (second from left): Reverend Troy Perry, Harry Hay, Jim Kepner. Photographer unknown. Foster Gunnison, Jr. Papers. Archives & Special Collections at the Thomas J. Dodd Research Center, University of Connecticut Library.

Moderates were taking over the antiwar movement.

Kight: "I was selected as the gay speaker and so I went to San Francisco with my associates from Dow Action Committee. I was up on the platform to speak. I looked out across the crowd. 350,000 people [Kight's vastly inflated figure] were out on the polo grounds at Golden Gate Park. [They were] scrubbed, bathed, [wore] clean clothes, saw the dentist twice a year—teeth much cleaner than ours—middle-class or upper-middle-class children of this country who had just had it with our lousy government making profit on people in Vietnam.

"And so I came across the platform and I started having what is called in evangelical circles, a Presentment."

This was quite an admission for a devout humanist nontheist as Kight. Still, he had an experience.

"I started dancing, leaping up and down. Dalton Trumbo was a speaker, Reverend Cecil Williams [pastor of Glide Memorial Methodist Church] and a number of other celebrities...."

Kight was often impressed by the company he kept.

"...they came to me: 'Morris, something has happened to you, you are so cheerful, you're smiling.' I said, 'Look, look, I'm having a dream, I'm having a vision, so get me on.' And so I came to the microphone and spoke.

"I said, 'I can tell that there are a great many Vietnam veterans in the audience. I can look you over and I can see that there are possibly a hundred thousand veterans of Vietnam. I believe that you are not proud of having gone there; I believe that you were ripped off; I believe that you believe that you were exploited. And I believe that you went to conquer a people who didn't deserve it. I think many of you have won medals and I think you're not proud of them and I think that you'd like to get rid of them. So we're going to ship them to the Pentagon. Throw them to the stage!' It was raining medals. The stage was covered with them. We had monitors scooping them up. We shipped them to the Pentagon, saying 'These people just don't want them anymore.' Well, I started singing a song."

In the middle of his nontheist epiphany, in front of more than a quarter-million people according to Kight, but factually at least 100,000 people—Morris Kight sang the song he'd heard his father sing when, as a child, Morris and his mother snuck up on him while working in the fields. The song was a spiritual from the Southern Baptist churches. Kight: "While I was up on the platform, I started singing to myself, 'I'm coming home to my Lord and be free.'

"Coming home, coming home
Never more to roam
Open wide thine arms of God
Lord, I'm coming home...."

As a humanist, Kight easily assimilated the word "lord" to mean what he considered to be a calling of a higher order.

"And so I felt that it was time I go home to Los Angeles and come back to—I don't like saying 'my people' because I don't own anybody—come back to 'the people,' the gay and lesbian people."

He spoke some, he sang a little and then Kight left the park and took a plane back to Los Angeles.

Rosa Parks once cited the same hymn as her inspiration.

In 1995, Ms. Parks said: "[The lyrics] gave me strength when things seemed bad.... So when I declined to give up my seat, it was not that day or that bus in particular. I just wanted to be free like everybody else. I did not want to be continually humiliated over something I had no control over: the color of my skin."

Kight could be faulted for "borrowing" from the black movement to service the gay movement. It is also very likely that the same hymn could inspire both civil rights pioneers.

Yet, if he "added" the hymn to his story for no other reason than to draw a comparison between the two civil rights movements, it could be forgiven. Kight saw injustice as injustice no matter the color, no matter the object of one's affections. Kight considered all forms of humiliation and degradation as wounds on the soul of humanity. He witnessed it daily on the faces of countless men who called on him needing help. He made no distinctions; it was human liberation and gays had a place in human nature, in society. Fighting one kind of inferiority was the same as fighting another kind of inferiority. He did not want gay people to struggle with inferiority any longer.

Kight returned to Los Angeles.

"I came back in the middle of the night. At daylight I started resigning from various commissions, boards, committees and so on—I was on the Executive Committee of the Peace Action Council, a distinguished group ...94 constituent groups—and each was entitled to two representatives, 190 people voted ... I resigned from that and it broke my heart because I didn't want to give that up."

He cleared his desk of everything and prepared for a new focus.

"So I told everybody, 'I'm going to found the Gay Liberation Front.'"

In actuality, he didn't have a name for it yet.

Most of his New Left friends thought he had gone mad.

Morris Kight had gone home—home to be free. Hallelujah.

Part IV

Gay Pride

GAY
LIBERATION
NOW

Chapter 10

Gay Liberation Front

IT ALL STARTED with a paid announcement in the back pages of the *L.A. Free Press*—which Kight often declared "the citadel of radicalism" and which the FBI called "an avant-garde newspaper."

"GSF [Gay Survival Front] is now seeking new members in LA area for weekly parties, discussion, nude gatherings, encounter groups, other activities for intelligent, aware, discreet gays who are interested in making new friends in a safe, free environment. Screened membership."

The October 1969 ad was more than a call for a meeting—it was an official proclamation of an above-ground gay liberation movement.

Kight to Paul Cain: "I'd been watching carefully to see when it would be ready. I knew that the homophiles couldn't be reformed. They had such a vested interest in their pretentiousness, that they couldn't be reformed. Decent, wonderful people, much to be cooperated with and honored, but they couldn't be reformed into any kind of radicalism, because they were too conservative."

1970. Joseph Hansen, Morris Kight picketing at Barney's Beanery.
Photo: Pat Rocco. Pat Rocco Papers, Coll2007-006, ONE National Gay & Lesbian Archives, USC Libraries, University of Southern California.

Three-line ads ran in the back pages for weeks: "GAYS-AC-DC Hear what GSF has to say about your social life" and for gatherings to rap about "a better life for lesbian and gay people." Every ad ended with either the phone number of the Homosexual Information Center or Kight's home phone number for "more information."

Los Angeles Times, December 9, 1988: "Those early years were 'magical,' says Kight, who set up what he says was the only hotline for out-of-the-closet gays west of the Mississippi. As many as 350 people a day called, mainly for help and reassurance they weren't alone."

Don Slater and Kight were political polar opposites; Kight believed Slater to be too conservative and Slater envisioned a more sedate, less chaotic, gay movement at a later time. Still, they were friends—they were good drinking buddies and Don let Morris use his offices whenever he needed. Slater would not stay involved, but the first meetings of the Gay Survival Front met at his Homosexual Information Center on Cahuenga Boulevard in North Hollywood, also known as the offices of the periodical *Tangents*. Slater was at early meetings and was overheard saying "It's easier to liberate yourself from a closet of shame than from a closet of fear."

The first meeting in December of 1969 had a total of 18 people and the group voted to re-name itself the Gay Liberation Front [GLF]. Some say that it was named after the Vietnamese National Liberation Front and some say it was the National Liberation Front of China. Either way, GLF had an immediate identification with the revolutionary "New Left" movement and China's Chairman Mao.

Kight soon went through his vast phone book and telephoned everyone he knew—fellow activists from left-wing leanings, politicos and socialites, those with "raised consciousness" is how he would describe them in order to stroke their egos. He told them all about his "new vision," a crusade to liberate gay people. He wouldn't do a hard push and was clear to his former colleagues that he wasn't recruiting anyone to be gay, he was asking for their support. He'd let the movement build steam before he'd push others to get on board or risk being left on the wrong side of history.

Even by 1969 radical standards, gay lib was considered extremely radical. Kight, appearing noble, rang bells and knocked on doors to signal the beginning of a new authentic movement, a gay rights movement, Kight introduced the counterculture to a whole new level of "radical."

Del Whan, one of the first women in the GLF, first heard of Morris Kight when he spoke at the USC campus auditorium.

Whan: "The auditorium was a quarter full of staff and students who sat individually far apart from each other. The topic was about coming out as a gay person. I had never heard anybody talk about this before. I was a USC staff employee (Director of the Foreign Language Lab) in the closet at the age of 30.

"Morris told the audience to come out, to tell their parents that gay was good; in other words, to come out of the closet and stop hiding. Other than going to bars at night, I was in the closet.... My self-esteem was shattered. I was afraid to come out because I thought I would lose my job. Nevertheless, about a month after hearing Morris speak I went to my first Gay Liberation Front meeting upstairs at Satan's Bar in Silver Lake."

A recent New York transplant, Karla Jay, "found this choice [meeting at a bar] odd because in New York so much of the thrust of the movement was to get gay men and lesbians out of bars," she wrote in her book, *Tales of the Lavender Menace*.

Jay commented that the seating arrangement in the bar was "problematic." New York gay meetings made a point of putting the chairs in a circle to suggest equality. Not so in L.A. GLF, where, as Jay put it, "there was no pretense of equality." At L.A. GLF, there was a large table for all the 'leaders,' while the assumed 'followers' were left to sit at the small tables.

Jay described Kight as "certainly no Dapper Dan." In the gay movement, Kight's wardrobe was much less subdued. Long gone was any trace of the acquiescent Albuquerque entrepreneur, and the image of the dignified peace activist was intermittent. When Kight came out of his political closet, he took the entire contents of the closet with him. Sometimes a shirt didn't quite fit or his khaki pants needed laundering. He could show up wearing a suit jacket, plaid shirt, sandals, and short-shorts or a knit top and sneakers. He always wore lots of rings, authentic turquoise and silver; often an oversized silver peace-pendant dangled around his neck. Karla Jay: "He always seemed to have a retinue of followers that included a young minion, over whose shoulder Morris would drape a friendly and paternal arm."

Whan's impression of Morris was that "he liked to hold court like a king or queen." She specifically noted his "tone, his accent, his physical demeanor all added to a persona of being somewhat above all other earthly mortals."

Kight described the first GLF meetings as "more about training classes," as most attendees just wanted to know, "What is radical, how do you get radical, what's that like?" Kight thought "it was great fun." Kepner's notes of an early GLF meeting quote Morris: "instead of over-politicizing our actions, we should emphasize the camp-bitch humor and not be too serious."

A letter to the editor of the *L.A. Free Press* referred to "Gay lib, a freaky little side show along the path to social change." Kight brought a lot of that "freaky" with him in his over-the-top appearance. After years of commitment to the antiwar effort and handling the daily affairs of the Dow Action Committee, which was mostly a lot of media contact, it seemed that Kight totally shifted his attention away from the peace movement and toward a gay rights movement in one split second.

The country was ripe with discontent and rebellion, people were already mobilized, and Kight seized the momentum, as he liked to put it, to "free my people." When Morris Kight shifted his thinking and refocused his energy, he made sure that it created a rippling effect. He tapped organizational muscle, skills, and funds from the Peace movement, Black Power, Feminism, and the L.A. Mission. Though gay lib, like any movement, couldn't be one man's mission, Kight might've fantasized otherwise. Kight brought years of experience engaging the media, organizing street-level and mainstream thinking and most importantly, fundraising. He brought together teams of eager activists. He inspired them and coached them. Ultimately, success would depend upon the efforts of many people.

Jon Platania opines that "without Morris there would not have been any gay lib. He was not divisive. People would have fought themselves into the ground."

Gino Vezina: "Morris Kight was very directly the original innovator of gay liberation, I was witness to this and I know that some of the things [he did] go back to the late fifties when some of those people who have taken credit were in diapers. I know these things. [And] some of the older ones who were in Morris' group were always bickering over those kinds of things, which I always thought was ridiculous."

Kight: "There were five [Gay Liberation Fronts] that first year, 1969: New York, Berkeley, Los Angeles, San Francisco, and San Jose—in that order." Post-Stonewall gay groups were popping up across the country. In addition to the original five Gay Liberation Fronts, The Gay Alliance and Gay Revos were active in New York City. In Chicago they called themselves The Freaking Fag Revolutionaries, while Weathersuckers-Berkeley and the Purple Panthers were in San Francisco.

In the early days, the gay rights movement was not popular in the mainstream. The issues that gay liberation raised were deeply personal. In the autumn of the sexual revolution, most people were still not comfortable discussing sexuality. Even for those who could support the civil rights of homosexuals, the words did not come easy. Folk musicians, ardent hippies, and antiwar activists did not immediately embrace the movement. The Black Panthers had their own unique relationship with the gay movement on both coasts. Before a healthy social discourse was possible, someone needed to demonstrate how to articulate and discuss the issues without shame. Morris Kight found his new calling.

With each meeting, GLF grew: more faces, mostly young—all curious. There were no membership cards, no dues or sign-in sheet. These were not the same meetings that Kight had previously participated in with the antiwar groups, farm workers, and the Black Panthers. The GLF meetings, like Dow Action meetings, employed Robert's Rules of Order, as best as possible, and rotated the group leader every month. The organizational part was purposely somewhat loose because the group was largely unstructured and unfettered youths looking for an outlet, a rebellion.

Howard Fox told Bob Dallmeyer: "GLF was about as unstructured as you could get. We had no formal membership. People were members because they said they were. People had a vote because they were there. We had no officers per se. We would elect a chairperson once a month to conduct the meetings for that month and most of the work was done in committees. Anybody could write a letter on Gay Liberation Front letterhead putting forth whatever thought they wished to convey, and that was okay. And if somebody didn't like it, they could write their own letter.... They were radicals. Morris, of course, was a radical.... He was a person who, for me, meant a great deal, because he put together the various strands of thinking and social concern that I felt were important."

During the same 1989 radio program with Dallmeyer, Rand Schrader remembered: "We met every Sunday, and that became the most important day of the week for me, because it is where I was growing in an area that I had held back, an area that I had repressed, and so it had a special significance and value to me.... Morris, I realize now, at that time was five years older than I am now. He was a person who, for me, meant a great deal because he put together the various strands of thinking and social concern that I felt were important."

Kepner's notes reveal the type of discussions at a fairly typical GLF meeting: "Action versus reaction ... Problem dealing [with] parents, 'I'm Gay & I'm proud.' Need for different programs, maybe for older & younger homosexuals. Question posed: how do you counsel people who have Bible homophobia? ... How to achieve gay dignity. How does one accept oneself? Dealing with guilt. Is exclusive homosexuality limiting? Put swishes & butches together? 'Closets are for clothes.'"

Some recognized Kight from his media exposure through the peace movement. John Effinger, who was in his mid-twenties at the time, remembers, "I first met Morris at the GLF meetings. [Earlier] I saw him often at a house in Central L.A. that was a sort of planning center for antiwar activities. I saw him there from time to time and saw him frequently in marches before they became so big one could not keep track. He was there before I formally met him, but he would have been 'not much on my radar.' I would have seen him as a fellow traveler from an earlier era and I was too stupid to realize how interesting *his* life must have been.

"Most great movements are built on sleight-of-hand and creating illusions of power.... I saw Kight at several antiwar demonstrations after the GLF meetings. He was invigorated by it all, especially by the youthfulness of those around him. I think he thought to some extent, 'I am really their age. I was just born early,' pure conjecture of course. He never sacrificed his earned wisdom to 'act young' however. I heard from some a bit about how open he could be. If he pressed himself on others he did not on me.... I don't remember Morris drinking.... I was not a free spirit in the sense that so many at the meetings were. They were willing to try anything. I was not. But I think I do remember Morris taking a little grass at a meeting. I am not sure of that. It would not have bothered me or caused concern."

August 1970 issue of *Gay* magazine has a photo of Kight with the headline: "Morris Kight: a beacon of light for today's youth."

Kight saw the big picture of gay rights as building up one person at a time, and he didn't let anyone leave those meetings without being affected in some positive way or learning something. Often described as a "warm and encouraging leader" and "father figure" in the Gay Liberation Front, Kight did a private appraisal of every able body that expressed interest in the movement and then found a specific function for each person to contribute to their liberation. He gave every young person at these meetings a direction or an assignment, to give them a new purpose.

Kight had just turned 50 years old and believed "the fact that I was older was no issue." According to Platania, "He wanted, in the worse way, to be the elder statesman and to be respected. People very often turned their oppressions in and upon themselves and Morris Kight was the brunt of that. He was an incredibly beautiful man. He was still an attractive man into his fifties. Morris did what he felt that he had to do and was kind of the heart and soul of calm and serenity in the middle of all this [calamity]. He'd say some outrageous things about what we should do and not do."

Effinger remembered, "Jim Kepner was also a member and added a scholarly air to the proceedings. Both men anchored our nascent radicalism, yet both still had a youthful passion for liberation politics. I got the feeling they felt very much in tune with the new thinking of the younger generation even though they could sometimes just manage to hide their amusement with our intemperance. I can still see Morris with that long grayish hair tied back in a ponytail, grinning though never condescending."

Borrowed from the women's movement were "rap sessions," which were about "consciousness raising" to bring awareness to overcoming suppression. It created a space to safely and openly talk about being gay and lesbian, coming to terms with a new era of gay. Some hated being gay; many expressed fear. It was all open—nothing was forbidden. The rap sessions were an integral part of early liberation, tapping into individual psyches in order to overcome generations of subjugation. It empowered a movement of unique individuals.

Kight to Cain: "I felt that a radical approach, at first, was necessary to deal with our concerns. The Gay Liberation Front was meant to be super-radical, and it was. And it was meant to go to the root cause—that's what radical means, radical means *radicale*... and we went to the root cause."

The root cause of gay oppression, as Kight saw it, was the homosexual's lack of self-acceptance.

John Effinger: "Morris struck me at the time as an old Will Geerish lefty from the '30s, someone who might have been in a Clifford Odets play. I could imagine him organizing longshoremen." For the record, Kight never organized longshoremen—though he probably would have if asked.

John Effinger continues: "In those days, we [GLF] were like AA members who tell their stories to a fascinated audience who have, in fact, heard nearly every possible variation on those confessions. We loved, loved, loved to hear and especially to talk about our 'coming out' stories. They were endlessly fascinating until they weren't. The GLF meetings tended to the business of the demonstrations pretty quickly, and back we went to the 'stories.' He was much younger then than I am now, but he seemed like a grandfather to me then. How he managed to listen to coming-out story after coming-out story I find hard to imagine."

Gino Vezina: "I don't recall any coming-out story from Morris."

Del Whan: "My overall impression of Morris was that he was a brilliant patriarch. I don't recall any coming-out story from him."

Lee Mentley reported that many were "shocked in encounter groups to learn how parents treated their [gay and lesbian] kids—throwing their own children out of the house, treating them in fashions to cause suicide."

Effinger: "Morris understood the radicalizing effect of all this and encouraged it. He did not spend a lot of time on theory. He was very oriented toward the needs of the individual—[he had] an empathy [that] radicalized leftists often could not manage."

There was probably never a brighter role model for self-approval than Morris Kight; liberal leanings, hippie style, and long association with radical causes worked to his benefit with younger people—who desperately needed a positive gay role-model. He made a point to always be a shining example of good manners, as well as a father figure, problem-solver, direction-giver, and Grand Poobah to all the young gay men and women. To any young people who were interested, Kight introduced specific Western philosophers, like Herbert Marcuse. But he never forced it on anyone.

Not all old hippies approved. In writing to a friend, Harry Hay wrote his concerns that Morris and Don were trying to take over the "'Stream's' theoretical direction." He wrote: "In all fairness to the ideas themselves I would like to see them begin to have National considerations through a Forum on Gay Consciousness or a couple of Summer Workshops—maybe we'll be able to come up with something." (1974)

Kight easily injected the gay rights movement with the ideology of antiwar, anti-establishment, and pro-civil rights. Kight's social reform was not about books and research, but about personality. A particular personality emerged from the early gay movement, a gay persona formed—it was a push to the spotlight, shameless self-love, flamboyant exhibitionism that became legendary and exemplary. It was Morris Kight. According to multiple accounts, he drove others to compete with him on this level.

If anything revealed the inner workings of the man, it was the one edict Kight had in the GLF: "We do not respond to criticism."

Howard Fox: "Uniquely, we did not respond to criticism. Boy, that sure freed us up to use our energies more creatively, more productively. There was a lot of criticism, in the *Advocate*—letters to the editor, and other places. We could've used up all our time and energies just answering all these criticisms, and [Morris] put forth that we did not respond to criticism, and I thought that just was great, and so we didn't."

Some of the harshest critiques of the gay movement came from homosexuals. Older homosexuals who were not politically motivated and were able to create comfortable lives for themselves feared gay liberation. Perhaps sensing a long hard losing battle, many did not want their own 'covers' blown. They didn't relate to "old hippie Kight."

Censure within the gay population from the more socially tame activists wasn't new nor did it deter Kight. He never expressed frustration. He did not focus his lessons of tolerance to those who had been so oppressed. Instead he served as a shining example of patience and self-acceptance to young social warriors to prevent further shame and self-hatred.

Leo Laurence, a San Francisco activist, was in his mid-thirties and considered himself much more radical than Kight. Laurence co-founded the Committee for Homosexual Freedom and impressed Kight early in 1969 with his articles in *Berkeley Barb* on a new phenomenon called "Gay Civil Rights." At the time, the concept was unheard of and Kight contacted Laurence to say that he was quite impressed and felt they were kindred revolutionary spirits. Laurence was perhaps the first journalist to publicly link gay rights to civil rights. Kight invited him to Los Angeles. Laurence remembers:

"The word 'homophile' was used by the closeted community, which, at the time, everybody [who was homosexual] was closeted. The idea of coming out of the closet was strongly and angrily opposed. And that's what those of us who were [starting Gay Lib] were facing [within the gay community]. We were vigorously condemned because community organizations worked very hard to protect the closet. That was extremely important. They used the word 'homophile' because it was a scientific term."

The word "homophile" was born because the U.S. Post Office would not deliver any materials (letters or publications) containing the word "homosexual." Laurence continues, "Late 1969, early 1970, I started using the word 'gay.' Homosexual has the word *sex* in it, suggesting that's the key focus of this whole community. Civil rights was not important, only sex."

FBI

THE FBI BECAME AWARE OF THE GLF THROUGH INDIVIDUALS (LIKE Kight) who were already under surveillance for other activities within the New Left movement. From day one, the FBI had operatives inside the GLF and continued to the final days.

GLF FBI file: "The Gay Liberation's purpose is to free homosexuals, transvestites, lesbians, and other sexual deviates from 'oppression' from the 'straight population.'"

Kight's FBI file: "The pyramiding of the Gay movement by its very nature confronts all authoritarian, conformist regimes including communism, as well as the juvenile American culture, and exposes the hypocrisy within these systems."

MEETING GAY

JON PLATANIA'S FRIEND, MICHAEL JOHNSON, INVITED HIM TO attend a meeting, as he put it, "to this thing called the GLF. I thought that compared to what was going on in the world it was kind of ridiculous to politicize yourself around your sexual choices and I was not interested. I was sexually active and out there. I split that off from public life, as was the style in the late '60s if you were going to get anywhere. I went [to the meeting] anyway. It was upstairs somewhere."

Platania describes it: "A ragtag group of people. Not too many women, mostly men. Bill Beasley was yelling at everyone in a somewhat manic state. Morris was kind of the heart and soul of calm and serenity in the middle of all this.... He lived in an old house and the old house was full of antiques and he would sell these antiques. He'd buy things from garage sales [and places like that] and he'd sell them."

Soon the GLF meetings were 30-strong. The nascent group organically took shape to mold an identity for the gay liberation movement. Harry Hay and John Burnside made a point to show up as a couple and participate in the early meetings. Harry chaired the first meeting. Hay tried to instill his wisdom and best understanding of the American Indian tribal traditions into gay liberation. Hay talked against "chauvinism, [which] in all its social and racial aspects, is the real enemy of all men and women who seek the one security that is viable—community—and the one freedom that is transcendent—individuation." Kight did not share Hay's desire to inject gay liberation with what he called a European-inspired version of Native American principles.

Difference between the two leaders were apparent from the first meeting. Kight eschewed spirituality while speaking about traditions set forth by Gandhi. Kight encouraged young gays to claim their rights by resisting oppressive legislation. The two men, who were just as much alike as they were unalike, were continually compared and judged against one another. Hay wanted a celebration of individual identities; Kight stressed individuals' civil liberties. Basically they had the same goal—drop cloaks of shame and live openly as gays and lesbians. Kight the devout socialist with a bureaucratic training was measured against Hay, a dyed-in-the-wool communist who was at a later point in his life leaning toward an examination of ancestral and spiritual natures.

Reverend Malcolm Boyd summed it up: "Morris and Harry Hay were so different. And were often advocates of each of them juxtaposed them against each other, made them compete. Even if they weren't competing. Morris and Harry were such different people personality-wise."

Kight would sometimes joke, "Harry will never forgive me for being right about communism." Though it's not likely that communism had anything to do with Harry not forgiving Kight, as pointed out in *The Trouble with Harry*: "Kight succeeded Harry as the town's grand old man of gay politics and attained almost the status of a gay godfather."

Kight's announcement that a "gay rights movement" had officially begun felt like a slap in the face to the early "homophiles," a word by which Kight still did not want to be referred. Kight respected them, but he never considered their activities "a movement." Just as quickly as he embraced gay rights, he was resented by his homosexual peers.

Hay and Burnside remained active in the Front until they moved to San Juan Pueblo, New Mexico, in the spring of 1970. Later, Hay did nothing to extinguish rumors that Morris had run him out of town by taking over the power of gay liberation. When asked directly about this, Kight said to Cain: "I think that's exceedingly unkind. I think that's a very cruel statement. I find that really, really terribly cruel and terribly insensitive. I did no such thing! I welcomed everybody to the table. But in coming to the table, I thought they all had to bring with them some credentials, some goodwill, some belief in the mystique of radical lesbian and gay liberation—not that he didn't. But he was perfectly welcome."

Kight expressed some misgivings about Hay's motive in going to San Juan Pueblo.

"[Hay] went to San Juan Pueblo of his own choice.... Somehow or other, the mysticism, the magic of the San Juan Pueblo—they're ancient people, by the way—that he would absorb some guidance and become a kind of white chief of honor. I'm not sure, that's what I thought he had in mind. And I think he also thought he was creating an ashram there, that people would come there and study, and so on."

GAY CONSCIOUSNESS-RAISING

KIGHT STRESSED THAT CONSCIOUSNESS-RAISING WOULD BE THE heartbeat of gay liberation. He had to literally convince homosexuals that it was acceptable to be homosexual, "to pronounce yourself gay." In addition to their "coming out" stories, everyone was encouraged to share information, political views and discuss a variety of topics, from racism to self-esteem. This was the first forum intentionally created for people to be seen and heard as homosexual without fear of reprisal. Creative expression was strongly supported; Kight encouraged the use of clever bon mots. There had never been a gay group consciousness and individual gays had been burdened by a veil of shame that would take time to eliminate. One anonymously written GLF position paper—written more as a therapeutic exercise that came out of a rap group—expresses the radical thinking of the time. "Look out straights, here comes the Gay Liberation Front… Understand this—that the worst part of being a homosexual is having to keep it secret. Not the occasional murders by police or teenage queer-baiters, not the loss of jobs or the expulsion from schools or dishonorable discharges—but the daily knowledge that what you are is so awful that it cannot be revealed. The violence against us is sporadic. Most of us are not affected. But the internal violence of being made to carry—or choosing to carry—the load of your straight society's unconscious guilt—this is what tears us apart, what makes us want to stand up in the offices, in the factories and the schools and shout out our true identities."

Following examples of the American civil rights movement, Kight began a master plan to shift social thinking. Borrowing from the women's movement, where knowledge had become power, he prepared young revolutionaries to reject all notions of inferiority and become powerful persons. He knew they'd face rejection and yet he never disavowed the belief that as a group they would rise above. He preached "accept yourself, reject the notion of inferiority, become a more powerful person." He knew of ways to enter the ranks of society despite being told to 'stay away.' He coached individuals and groups about not internalizing the brutality of the exterior world. A few years later, he soft-pedaled the reality in an interview with New York-based writer and historian Jonathan Ned Katz. Kight said "Society does tend to be a little homophobic. There is an institutional notion that it is sinful or sick to be gay." He completely rejected the idea that homosexuality was a sickness and he expressed that as often as possible. Kight recognized what he called an "unnatural fear of gays," and aggressively began to inculcate mainstream thinking with the idea that homosexuality was a "perfectly natural fact of life."

He had a plan. It is not known, or likely, that he pictured himself as the Johnny Appleseed of gay liberation, yet he knew that the gay movement needed to get a lot of attention. It's not certain if he made a conscious decision, although it seems likely, to become a model gay leader and spokesperson.

Kight encouraged young people's ideas and he pushed self-expression in public places. He knew about creating an infrastructure for community and voices in public protests. Whether speaking to young gay enlistees or to a reporter, he was always patient, spoke slowly and carefully enunciated. He was the perfect example of well-manners, a careful listener, and his ability to remember names made him easy to like. He reached a new peak in popularity. He hammered his ideas home with his many idiosyncratic on-the-spot sayings like "Accept yourself," "Don't conform," and "Gay is good." It is no surprise that so many young gay men and lesbians were in awe of the first "adult" to encourage their homosexuality, their "outness." In regard to his own homosexuality, Kight liked to say: "I'm a natural fact."

Morty Manford, president of the New York Gay Activists Alliance, wrote to Kight: "We can alleviate the pain they suffer as victims of that most debilitating of all diseases: homophobic hate … and so we address ourselves to both curing prejudice and the political realities of pressing for our civil rights."

In writing about the Los Angeles GLF, John Loughery quoted Kight in *The Other Side of Silence—Men's Lives and Gay Identities: A Twentieth-Century History*:

"We felt that we were an idea whose time had come, but the thrill it generated surpassed most people's expectations. That's because it wasn't *homophile education*. It was street theater and a call to change the world. It was an invigorating moment to be gay."

Another bigwig at the "adult" table was Jim Kepner, who took copious notes at every meeting and provided a historical context to conversations. Reverend Troy Perry attended early GLF meetings and sat at the bigwig table with Slater and others as they showed up. The leadership was complete when a young bearded graduate student who had just returned from working in Ethiopia joined the GLF. Don Kilhefner, whom Kight described as "a bright young man," had been a member of the Student Nonviolent Coordinating Committee and was an easy fit into the hierarchy of the GLF.

Don Kilhefner to Bob Dallmeyer: "In many ways, the GLF in L.A. was more or less the flagship of the gay liberation movement throughout the country, in that most of the seminal ideas involved in the liberation movement emerged from there. Now people might dispute that in New York, but that is my contention—that the GLF in L.A. played a seminal role. In Los Angeles, Morris worked tirelessly at giving gays what he called 'a place at the table,' creating public policy, and he hung to his belief in the importance and relevance of social services and legislative reform."

In and of itself, GLF's accomplishments were groundbreaking and sociologically impressive; considering the amount of dissension within the organization, its success was all the more amazing. From the very first meeting there was always the possibility of an unraveling.

One early disagreement would become an ongoing discussion—violent tactics or actions were always suggested and Kight calmly proclaimed gay liberation as a movement of nonviolent social reform. Not everyone agreed with him but certainly the bigwigs did. The *L.A. Free Press* printed predictions of gay riots, quoting a number of "gay militants as saying police repression had brought homosexuals all over the country to the verge of a bloody uprising." Some of the press reports were reactionary rhetoric from the rebellion at the Stonewall Inn the previous year. Across the country, arrests by entrapment and reports of young men dying while in police custody were increased. Kight held fast to his belief that gay liberation was a social reform of nonviolent means.

A *Free Press* article with the headline "L.A. Gay riots threatened" says: "A number of speakers, including Morris Kight said they thought this was going much too far. Kight described a rally the previous week at Oceanside, California, in support of the Movement for a Democratic Military, in which GLF'ers participated. 'It was one of the most disturbing rallies I've been to in years,' he said. 'Speaker after speaker spoke of shooting our way out. Not a word was said about love. Just remember, the man has the guns, the tanks, the tear gas. What do we have? You can't lift oppression by liquidating people. It's too deeply embedded in our society.'"

L.A. Free Press, January 7, 1970: "The GLF apparently does not advocate violence in the furtherance of its aims as the issue stated that 'First-time visitors to GLF attempted to promote violence as part of the demonstration and their views were entirely rejected by the GLF.'"

LAPD was aggressive in arrests and entrapments of homosexuals and notoriously lenient on perpetrators of violence against homosexuals. In the late '60s and early '70s, in response to the liberation movement, it became an all-out war between "the establishment" and gay liberation. With a ramped-up vice squad and an overzealous, homophobic police chief, by the spring of 1970 there had been three deaths of gay men while in the custody of L.A.'s vice squad, countless police beatings, and more bar raids. It was outright dangerous to be openly gay, much less part of gay liberation.

Kight addressed the possibility of an uprising in the streets in the previously cited *Free Press* article (May 1970): "We are fighting off a super-militant minority who want vengeance in these recurring incidents. The super-militants have threatened to turn Hollywood into a Gay Watts. Hollywood is the largest gay ghetto in the world. With a half-million homosexuals concentrated in one vast ghetto. L.A. is sitting on a bomb."

The article continues: "A super-militant, who calls Kight an 'Auntie Tom,' said 'I am sick of that old lady and her Martin Luther King methods....We've got the numbers and we've got the guns.'"

Leo Laurence in the *Los Angeles Free Press*: "There are violent people in the movement. If government doesn't change they will start moving and you won't be able to stop them.... If this oppression does not stop, these hostile people will start doing things and you can't stop them. There will be fighting in the streets, there will be sniping.... I'm opposed to violence, but if they don't change, that's probably what will happen."

Forty years later, Leo Laurence stressed: "Do not equate radicalism with violence."

The anti-violence advocates became known as "Auntie Toms," while the super-militants were called "fire queens." Some in the underground press fanned the flames of the possibility of violence with reminders and comparisons to the still-fresh memory of the Los Angeles Watts Riots and they gave ample press coverage to the feud that was brewing within the gay movement regarding the use of violence. A super-militant advocate told the press that he carried "an aerosol can of Easy-Off Oven Cleaner to spray in the eyes of pigs." Kight, Kepner, Hay, Perry and others would insist that true gay liberation had to be won nonviolently or it would be no victory. It would be years before violence against homosexuals was outlawed and multiple generations of activism for violence against homosexuals to noticeably decrease. It had to start somewhere.

Kight wanted to separate his gay movement from any form of violence, a hyper-critical point for many antiviolence activists coming from the peace movement. Many thought consciousness-raising was the linchpin to a profound psychic change. Morris Kight never believed that a revolution would happen while sitting around talking. As important as discussion was to get to the heart of the matter—which was the thinking—and for people to hear their voices proclaim to be proud to be gay, boots had to hit the pavement for there to be a true revolution. A theme of the early gay liberation movement was a demonstration-a-day, creative rapid response known as "zap." Street protests were clever and humorous, often theatrical. Kight's tactical goal was to catch as much attention as it took to get on the evening news—which was the best way to create dialogue at America's dinner table. Kight wanted, as the saying goes, to get the show on the road.

Effinger: "Morris used to tell us that the main battle was to get attention and we got that. It was harder to get the attention of the media."

REPARATIONS

ENTRY IN KIGHT'S FBI FILE IN EARLY 1970: "ONE ITEM OF INTEREST ... concerns a matter of reparations."

For Kight, gay liberation needed to be theatrical to attract media attention. By all accounts, Kight had an undeniable genius for publicity.

For months, Reverend Perry (of MCC) had been hitting the streets protesting LAPD's brutal treatment of homosexuals. On January 11, 1970, a cold rainy Sunday morning, Kight participated in one of Perry's protest marches. They were joined by Bishop Michael Itkin (Evangelical Catholic Communion of San Francisco), who was a fellow nonviolent revolutionist in "the liberation of all oppressed peoples." All three were dressed in ecclesiastical robes. It is anyone's guess what Perry and Itkin, both legitimate 'men of the cloth,' thought when Morris Kight joined them wearing his own ceremonial robes, robes he wore on occasion for the Church of the Androgen.

They led a candlelight march that stretched four city blocks; a few hundred "lesbians, transvestites, male homosexuals, bisexuals, and straight sympathizers" visited various churches, carrying signs that read "Gay Power" and "We're gay and we're proud." The churches visited on this particular Sunday were relatively friendly and there was no hostile reaction. Police cars drove alongside the marchers, who stayed on the sidewalks, and for two hours the cops did not interfere, there were no arrests, no violence.

Kight enjoyed marching the streets in his ceremonial robes. On the last Sunday in February, without Itken and Perry, he repeated the holy act. Don Jackson covered the event for the *Free Press*:

"His Holiness, Pope Morris I [The First] went to the First Congregational Church on Wilshire Boulevard to tack a bill for $90 billion on the door. His Holiness said, 'The Congregational or Puritan Church is one of the most guilty. In New England during the 18th Century, thousands of people were burned at the stake, charged with sodomy. I hope the straight Christians will pay their just bill and learn a little bit about love. Doing it in the missionary position all the time is a sin and a bore.'"

"The Gay Pope" presented other churches "who participated in the murder of 9 million homosexuals" with the same bill for reparations "for the genocidal acts instituted, perpetrated and perpetuated by the churches." Kight, in full ecclesiastical robes, was followed by 35 members of the GLF in the pouring rain.

Jackson continued: "His holiness has proclaimed March 1 to be 'Lavender Sunday,' and asks all Gays to come out of their closets and picket the Sunday services of the church of their choice before presenting the bill. Individual Gays are encouraged to prepare a bill for the damages they have suffered as a result of the hate against homosexuals perpetuated by the churches....

"Simultaneous press conferences are being arranged in New York, San Francisco and Los Angeles."

The March 1 demonstration was pure theatrics.

The original plan was to picket and tack the bill for $90 billion on the door of the First Congregational Church on Virgil Avenue. Church officials were forewarned and deluged the police with requests for preventive measures. The police put the area on tactical alert. The GLF quickly moved their demonstration a few blocks away to the enormous St. Basil Church on Wilshire Boulevard. Kight thumbtacked a post with a list of demands for reparations from all organized religion, including $90 billion.

The GLF was told that an anti-Castro group planned to "counter-demonstrate" the Sunday church rounds. If the anti-Castro group did show up, which they didn't, they would have seen gays carrying signs that read: "Castro Cuba murders homosexuals," and "Red Cuba keeps Gays in chains."

John Effinger remembers "a couple of Sunday demonstrations. The most hostility we encountered was from the Catholic cathedral on Wilshire. We would time our demonstration so that we would catch the crowd coming out of Mass or services, having just been cleansed of their sins. The signs were pretty tame: HOMOSEXUAL RIGHTS NOW! that sort of thing. But it was kerosene on the fire for some Christians. Little old ladies could be particularly ugly. That surprised me. The Jewish demonstrators were the least affected by this. I remember admiring them for not giving a damn what the Christians thought. I do remember one old codger yelling, 'I hope you burn in hell!' And this young man (let's face it, cute Jewish guy) retorted, 'There is no hell, old man!' I remember the old man's genuine puzzlement. What can you say if you can't agree on the basics? I remember this little scene pretty clearly because the Jewish guy was so good-looking. (I can think only of a few other movements that were so sexy—the women's movement qualified.) It was one of the fuels that fired our passions, [poured] kerosene on the fire."

Douglas Key, for the *L.A. Free Press* (March 6, 1970): "At the catholic church, hate and guilt exploded inside of a number of catholics. They screamed 'You will all burn in hell, perverts,' 'God hates you,' 'Commie faggots,' 'Who in the hell do you think you are?' 'You should all be killed,' and similar un-Christian statements."

It was a rainy winter in Los Angeles. Kight and his band of Sunday morning protesters were often marching in the cold rain—never deterred. It was suggested at a GLF meeting that they carry lavender umbrellas.

Key's article: "People leaving the church said, 'God bless you,' 'Christ is with you,' 'Wonderful,' and 'Thank you.' A man came up to some of the demonstrators and shook hands with them. Children in Sunday school buses waved peace signs and shouted 'gay power,' and asked for some of the gay power signs to 'put up in their rooms.'"

At St. James Episcopal Church, Key reported, "the reaction was almost as positive as it was at Christ Unity. Members of the choir waved peace signs. 'Freedom for gay clergy,' shouted the marchers. Many persons passing by in cars waved peace signs. More demonstrations against organized religion is [sic] planned."

Kight knew that "people need democracy, they have to have policy and clarity, and they have to have something to do." These Sunday zaps certainly gave them something to do, something to talk about, and something to organize around.

There was no plan or actual intention to collect a dime from the churches, much less $90 billion. The *L.A. Free Press* and the *Advocate* gave ample coverage to the activities and outlandish request. The Sunday demonstrations were fun and they continued for a few months. Demonstrations were for attracting media attention and Kight wanted a tangible victory for the GLF. It was important to the morale of the young social warriors. "A win" for Kight was about press coverage and how many people they reached. The Sunday protests never did garner mainstream press attention.

Effinger: "Of course, true to the times, the great conflict was between 'liberals' and 'the new left.' Morris tried to keep us all focused on the main prize. Ideas such as 'gay marriage' were never discussed and hardly imagined. It would have been considered too bourgeois. Our main goal, in a way, was to offend. And to get publicity. This [was] at a time when the *L.A. Times* could barely manage the word 'homosexual' in its pages. We often discussed the old demonstrations where high heels for the women and suit jackets for the men were required. We were more 'in your face' in our tactics. Sort of a 'we're queer and we're here,' though that was yet to be coined."

Despite the tepid press response, GLF continued to carry the message to wherever it needed to go. They created catchphrases and in-house support systems. They were trained in what to do in case of being harassed or arrested, and they knew that they never ever had to be ashamed to be gay. Everyone in the GLF knew Kight's home phone number and they could call at any time of the day or night. He quickly became known as a "fixer," or "the man who knew someone who could make things happen."

They needed allies. Early on, Kight introduced guests from the Peace and Freedom Party at a GLF meeting. The Peace and Freedom representatives proposed to strengthen their party position on gay liberation and invited the GLF to propose a party platform. Kight also brought in an old cohort from the Dow Action Committee, Marsha Silverstein, to talk about organizing and boycotts. Kight also brought in Dr. Martin Fields, UCLA social psychiatrist, who was a specialist on protest to address the GLF.

Everyone agreed on a common enemy—the suppressive straight society. Their movement needed a focused target so they could direct their energies on one goal.

FAGOTS STAY OUT

WITH INSTRUCTIONS TO DO "A ZAP A DAY," GLF'ERS USED THEIR creativity to do individual and group demonstrations, nonviolent street protests, and small actions to begin society's inculcation of homosexuality. It was an exciting time. They demonstrated against an employment agency because they segregated in hiring with a code "33." Kight explained to Cain: "If you applied at an employment agency, and you were obviously gay, they coded you at the top of the page, '33.' I never knew where that came from. Were you a third of a person, or what? I don't know. In any case, we demonstrated at an employment agency, we demonstrated at colleges because they were teaching that we were abnormal, we demonstrated at the neuropsychiatric [associations], because they were 'curing' us, and so on."

Jon Platania: "Morris would say some really outrageous things about what we should do or what we shouldn't do. Morris was part of this thing we called the 'agitprop committee' [agitation and propaganda] and I wanted to stay as far away as I could because I had this wonderful job to think about, and so I did. But Morris was really really out there."

Platania, a young ambitious man with an impressive upwardly position in Los Angeles had aspirations, as he put it, to "move up the political bureaucratic ladder." Because of his ambitions he chose to stay out the public light with GLF. Platania liked Morris. "He was not a druggie like everyone else was. Morris would have a drink (a beer) and he was still an attractive man into his fifties." Platania saw the elderly statesman with "no real means of support" and as a father figure who was really "out there," trying to help others. Platania had money, Kight had none. Platania would slip the old man a few dollars, nothing was ever mentioned and Kight never asked. Kight recognized Platania's enormous potential contribution to the cause, but he wouldn't push the young man beyond his comfort level.

Platania: "I agreed that the contribution that I could make [to the group] would be part of a Consciousness Raising program where they asked people who had group facilitation skills to head these groups, men's groups, it was quiet and we could do that in our apartment. I enjoyed doing that and thought that's the right contribution for me."

In late January of 1970, the GLF voted to launch its first organizational demonstration, picket and boycott at a local restaurant-bar to demand the removal of a handwritten sign that hung above the bar that read: "Fagots Stay Out."

Barney's Beanery, a working-class neighborhood bar with a kitchen that featured chili hot dogs and chili fries, was a great catalyst for the gay movement.

Kight to Dallmeyer: "Sometime in the 1950s Barney Anthony, a *bonne à moi*, a host, a gracious person had a visit from the Sheriff's Department and the Alcoholic Beverage Control Board saying his place was a known homosexual hangout, and it really was. [That area] had cheap rents near Hollywood, near downtown, it had ambiance, it had quietude and it attracted writers, actors, artists, it attracted a number of gay people of course, and they did go to Barney's Beanery. It was a fun place to go, a little rundown, a little tacky, nonetheless fun. And Barney Anthony, being a tower of strength, totally agreed with the ABC of the Sheriff's Department and then he whipped out a pencil and made a sign, 'Fagots Stay Out,' and it hung there all those many years, an insult, much like the infamous 'colored only' signs in the South."

In 1993, Kight reminisced for a special issue of the periodical *Planet Homo*: "In those faraway days any place of public accommodation which had more than three identifiable gay customers could be closed down—and almost invariably was—under the Red Light Abatement Act. And yes, Barney's had picked up a big gay clientele."

In January 1970 the GLF began holding "shop-ins" (where they'd sit in a booth for hours, sipping a cup of coffee) and let their displeasure with the sign be known. Over the next few weeks, they added "change-ins" (forming a long line at the cash register to ask for change), and finally when they had become an obvious nuisance they did a "sit-in" (only ordering a glass of water), and finally an outside picket.

Anthony's spelling of *fagots* never bothered Kight. The sign itself never bothered Kight—he encountered it so rarely that it hardly mattered to him. What mattered to Kight was finding something for the liberation movement to rally around.

Once again labeled a "security matter," an FBI file entry dated March 9, 1970: "KIGHT led a GLF demonstration held in Los Angeles on February 7, 1970, to protest a sign apparently reading 'fagots stay out' which was placed by the management of Barney's Bar and Café, 8448 Santa Monica Boulevard, Los Angeles."

In actuality, Kight showed up at Barney's from time to time, as he was mostly at home manning the phones, alerting the media, and issuing press releases that had to be hand-delivered by one of his many lackeys. He kept the home fires burning for the GLF.

During the time, the police raided his house three times looking for subversive mailing lists. Many in the gay community were terrified. People were saying, "He is embarrassing us all with those radical ideas," "He is going to get us killed. We'll all be killed. This fool is killing us."

The national gay movement had unofficially adopted the color lavender, so for the Barney's protest Kight, the publicity strategist, had lapel buttons made—a white background with a solitary outline of a purple handprint (fashioned after the Black Panthers' symbol). Kight explained in the press that it represented the purple handprints protesters made on the walls of the *San Francisco Examiner* because the newspaper used terms like "Queers," and "Semi-males," in reference to homosexuals. There were other lapel buttons that the GLF wore and handed out to bystanders. Some buttons used the outline of the purple fist and read, "Come Together, LA GLF," while others said, "Better blatant than latent."

Kight kept busy on the phone all day, delegating. He'd take and make calls in between one-on-one counseling, showing genuine interest and concern with each individual.

In early 1970, everything was happening at Barney's Beanery and everyone was showing up—Harry Hay, John Burnside, all the gang from ONE and Tangents, plus the county sheriff and the local media. Early on there were a few arrests for unlawful public assembly; the offenders were detained and quickly released. The best record of the event is a 20-minute film by independent film maker Pat Rocco called *Sign of Protest*. In documentary style, Rocco reports directly from the demonstration on one particular evening. Most of the employees and patrons at Barney's were getting "a kick" out of the protest. There was no overt hostility, just simple people who simply could not understand "what's the big deal?" The first person Rocco interviewed was the new owner of Barney's, Irwin Held (coincidentally the escrow and license transfer wasn't complete when the protests began), who was described by the *Advocate* as "a large, genial, nervous man, with a mercurial temper." In the beginning, he didn't mind the pickets as there was no evidence that the few dozen marchers hurt his business. He offered free beer to any of the picketers who came inside.

Held said to Rocco, "We hope to continue everything as it has been in the past. We didn't anticipate anything like this. Anybody who comes in here is welcomed to be served food or drink—as long as they behave themselves and don't interfere with anybody else, it's their privilege and the sign will continue as it is. Anybody who doesn't like it or enjoy it or feels ill at ease—it's a two-way swinging door—they can walk out as easily as they can walk in. No hard feelings on anyone's part."

On film, as he continued to talk, Held became ill at ease. Rocco next turned the camera to interview Barney Anthony's daughter, Joan, sitting in a booth with a few friends who were all enjoying the excitement. Joan was light-hearted—not confrontational—and flatly explained to Rocco:

"The sign went up in 1950 to discourage the faggots from coming in. Vice squad had a raid and it took two years to clear the [business'] name. There were eight or ten signs in the bar, now there is one. If they don't like it, they don't have to like it. The only reason would be a legal reason [to take the sign down]."

In the film, the offending sign is seen prominently displayed behind the bar and Rocco maintained his journalistic neutrality throughout. He and his cameraman walked through the restaurant and talked to a few more patrons, some too inebriated to make much sense. One patron, Fred, shrugged and told Rocco, "Hey, they're out there in the street. I'm in here. That's my wife. I just like my wife, that's the premise," and he put his arm around his wife, "this is my only protest." His wife, just as intoxicated, added, "It's Barney's Beanery's law."

Rocco walked outside, following his cameraman. About 50 protesters circled in front of Barney's carrying signs that read: "Faggot Nigger Kike Gook, It's all the Same," "Gay Liberation Now," "Gays are Here to Stay," "Give Me Sex or Give Me Death," and "Give Queens Beans!"

Protesters made more comparisons to Jim Crow signs that once dominated the South. One demonstrator, writer and radio show host Joseph Hansen (a.k.a. James Colton), said, "This is discrimination on a very basic level." Rocco waited for his old friend Morris Kight to come around in the circle of protesters. Kight, wearing a beret-style worker's cap, was more than happy to saunter up and speak on camera. In his patrician intonation, he introduced himself to Rocco:

"I founded the Gay Liberation Front because it was time for one. My position here is just to be along, to march with my associates here who complain about this particular injustice. And that's why I'm here. We have about 50 people here. We march until 10 p.m., and it'll grow up to a hundred, a hundred and fifty, who knows. It's a determined group and that's what's important, the spirit, the determination. [Rocco doesn't ask the next question quite fast enough, so Kight pushes ahead.] Yes, we're just delighted with how it is going. The issue here is that this restaurant has been here a long time, 50 years, and they have a sign saying "fagots stay out." The sign doesn't offend me awfully, but it offends everybody else. I think it's sort of funny in a way. I don't need to come here, but a great many people would like to. And they think this sign comes out of an antique American idea that should have gone out of style along with [emphasizing the malice] 'Niggers stay out,' along with 'No Mexicans or dogs allowed.' And these kinds of things have to go. And what we really want, Mister Rocco, is to have the sign retained—but changed. To have the 'Stay Out' X'ed out and change it to 'Fagots Welcomed,' *that* we would consider a victory. Thank you."

The interview abruptly ended, Kight turned and sauntered back into the picket line.

"Two, four, six, eight—gay is just as good as straight. Gay is good and gay is great. Gay is good and so is straight. Bring that sign down," chanted the protesters going around and around in the same circle, alternating their chant with: "Hey, hey, hey, we are proud and we are gay."

Rocco interviewed sheriff officers who were assigned to keep a watchful eye on the protest. A male officer explained to Rocco: "Mister Kight and his Gay Liberation Front is protesting that sign, discrimination against homosexuals. We don't expect any incidents. We spoke with both people concerned and they are going to cooperate with us fully and we're going to cooperate with them."

Rocco found Reverend Perry among the marchers carrying a *Life* Magazine from June 26, 1964, and pointed to an article about the original owner of Barney's Beanery, Barney Anthony, who had said, "Homosexuals should be shot."

Perry to Rocco: "We are told today that the sign is a joke. We don't consider the sign a joke any more than 'Whites only' signs are ... or 'Mexicans and dogs keep out.' Homosexuals are people too. I haven't talked to the owner personally. Mister Morris Kight, I believe, has talked to the owner and the manager of the place, who said the sign isn't coming down. We think it's going to. We think it's a good focal point for the community."

Boycotts, pickets and sit-ins continued for weeks, then months. The sign stayed and Held made six similar signs and added them throughout the bar and café. Kight appointed himself spokesperson and began a communication with the L.A. County Sheriff's Department, who from the beginning of the protest wanted to negotiate a peaceful resolution, ironic since the sign came into existence by order of either the Sheriff's Department or the Alcohol Beverage Control Board, depending upon which version of the story is being told.

Though he wouldn't allow schemes of violence or destruction, Kight encouraged plans of mischief and comic relief. Jaime Green remembers an elaborate scheme, in the middle of the Barney's protests. "Irwin Held had two passions in life: his stupid bar and his pristine, beautifully manicured front lawn at his home in Hancock Park."

Jaime Green: "A few of us organized vans to bring some people who owned dogs [to Held's Hancock Park home]. We bused them around the corner of his fancy house and they took their dogs for a walk on the lush green lawn. The van came back a half-hour later, sometimes with a second crew of dog owners."

Held's prized lawn was covered in dog feces, "Looked as if it had actually fallen out of the sky." This continued for a few weeks. No one witnessed Held's reaction to the defecation on his front lawn.

For three months, protesters were at Barney's Beanery, day and night, sometimes just one protester and sometimes there were dozens. The press showed up regularly—often alerted by Kight. A few times, the number of demonstrators grew and as a preventive measure, sheriffs lined up and stood between the picket line and the restaurant. Tourists gawked and snapped photos of the homosexuals—who didn't look any different from the average person. Religious fanatics were the most antagonistic toward the protesters, screaming insults to which some gays responded with blowing kisses, "We are in a state of grace, judge not lest ye be judged" and almost sparked a violent reaction from the religious groups. It was an odd, unexpected sighting—to see homosexuals picketing. Sometimes there was confusion. In the beginning it was truly groundbreaking; after three months, the situation was less of an attraction and more of a nuisance. The tension was mounting inside and outside the café.

During the sit-in, demonstrators threw dimes in the jukebox to continually play the French song "La Vie en Rose," sung by Edith Piaf, about every 20 times in succession. Held, losing his casual stance, refused to serve a number of people and kicked out a woman he believed to be a transvestite.

According to the *Advocate* (April 29, 1970), the woman Held accused of being a transvestite left the café, furious, and later returned to "explain most seriously that she was not in drag and [she] was a regular customer."

Held was unraveling. He raised his prices, tried setting minimum purchases, and instead of offering free beer as he did at the beginning of the demonstration, he cleaned away half-full mugs of beer and threw people out. He knocked a beer from Cliff Lettieri's hand, snatched brochures from him and grabbed Lettieri, picked him up from the table and began to swing with closed fist.

Los Angeles Free Press, March 20, 1970: "…Mr. Held went berserk and physically assaulted a gay just as a deputy sheriff entered the café, who observed the attack. Held actually shoved the gay into the officer. The deputy restrained Held from further violent acts and then attempted to calm him down. Held, claiming the Gays had defaced his property, was demanding payment for a hand-lettered cardboard sign which had become wet with beer. He demanded five dollars for the sign. The sheriff said the sign was worth about ten cents, but Morris Kight of the GLF paid $2.50 for it and after a short conference between the GLF and the sheriffs, the GLF decided to leave the café, went outside and resumed picketing.

"Held is being charged with criminal assault by Cliff Lettieri, the Gay who was attacked inside the café…. Held is also being taken to small claims court for the damages incurred when he deliberately spilled beer on a number of Gays."

Barney's regular patrons stayed away. More demonstrators showed up, taking up more seats in the café and more room on the narrow sidewalk out front. The smooth coordination of the effort was remarkable and unprecedented. Demonstrators were orderly and non-hostile. Many homosexuals were able, for the first time, to explain their case directly to customers and onlookers. They calmly and sensibly articulated their opposition to the hateful sign.

L.A. Free Press (March 1970): "While most of the Gays were inside the café, one of the few pickets who remained outside was physically attacked by a black man who objected to the use of the word 'nigger.' He had asked the picketer what the protest was for and the picketer said, 'Faggots stay out is as bad as niggers stay out.' The Gay told the black that he didn't like the word 'faggot.' The black suddenly understood, apologized, and then sat down on the steps of the café and wept."

Held was nervous and less controllable.

Kight got the attention of a booker for a local TV talk show, *Tempo* (hosted by an up-and-coming talk show host named Regis Philbin). For the on-air confrontation with Irwin Held, Kight recruited Rand Schrader, a young articulate law student, to present Gay Liberation's objection to the sign. On camera, Irwin Held shifted nervously in his chair as he first said that everybody was welcome at Barney's. Then he said that anybody who didn't like the sign could leave. Next, he announced that Barney's planned to hang more and bigger signs, and then he said, "Some of my best friends are queers." In perhaps an attempt at humor, Held said that he himself was a member of the Canyon Club, a gay social club in Topanga Canyon that "excludes Negroes," but that he only went there to swim and didn't associate with other members. Then he returned to his main message: that he didn't want a lot of queers in Barney's because "they would make passes at the customers."

Schrader, while not making any personal statement, served as the perfect lieutenant, stayed focused on the offending sign, and made a great impression on-camera. The whole *Tempo* interview was a marketing success and Kight was thrilled. Held was the embodiment of the anti-gay mindset. For Kight this fight was never just about a sign behind a bar; it was much bigger than that. It was an opportunity to grab attention for the movement, a pitchman's dream. The TV show presented people a clear choice—to align with the brash old man or see their way to join the side of the young, handsome, suave guy.

During the peaceful civil protest at Barney's Beanery, the Los Angeles Sheriff's Department was uncharacteristically "good-natured" toward the demonstrators. One sheriff's officer asked Kight for a "Purple Hand" button as a souvenir. For as long as the demonstrators remained nonviolent, they held a powerful position with the Sheriff's Department. Kight was aware that the only way for perceived sexual deviants to make a huge social shift was by the high road. The sheriff's office tried many times to mediate a solution with Held and with Kight representing the interests of homosexuals. Held wouldn't budge—until he blew his cool. That moment finally came as a result of the resourceful leaders of the gay movement working on Held from various angles—not just abusing his front lawn.

Kight drafted the help of heterosexual ally attorney Al Gordon to closely check Held's permits for a planned addition to Barneys. Cliff Lettieri had Irwin Held arrested and taken into custody on assault charges. While in custody, Held was notified that there would be a special hearing with the State Alcoholic Beverage Commission to consider his application for a license as new owner of Barney's Beanery. Troy Perry and his contingent filed separate petitions with the state against granting a liquor license to Held.

Once released from custody, Held came back to his café to find it more than half-filled with protesters sipping glasses of water. He called the Sheriff, and asked to have some of the nonviolent protesters arrested.

Advocate: "The dozen Sheriff's deputies were getting tired of the whole affair. It obviously was an explosive situation which could lead to real trouble. And it didn't seem worth it!

"The deputies went back into the kitchen with Held—for a long time. They first had asked spokesmen for the demonstrators just what they would accept.

"Kight, Perry, Lettieri, and others said [they] had no desire to turn the Beanery into a gay establishment, that they would leave peacefully if the signs came down [and] the charges against Held would be dropped. They also said they would like to have the signs.

"After about an hour of conferring, an employee came out and took down the original sign over the bar, but left it face out on the back bar. There were cheers, and a few grumbles from diehard regulars, and some doubted that the sign would remain down. A few minutes later, the new signs, all on cardboard, came down, and these were handed to the demonstrators. The old wood sign was taken out of sight. The group had a last rousing cheer out front, then disbanded."

L.A. Free Press: "Morris Kight, GLF secretary, said: 'To pursue this matter further in the courts would have taken us into the area of vengeance. It was a most significant victory over oppression, and now we can turn our attention to other items on our long agenda.'"

Kight did take the original sign home with him that night and it became what he'd sometimes refer to as the "numero uno piece of the Morris Kight Collection."

In retelling the story in 1993 for *Planet Homo*, Kight added: "It would be wonderful to say that was the end of it, but oh no! Irwin Held broke his word."

As traumatic as the whole ordeal was for Held, it had also provided phenomenal media exposure and publicity for the restaurant. Barney Anthony had learned in 1964, when a photograph of the sign had appeared in *Life* magazine, that any publicity was good for business. Held made a new "fagots stay out" sign that was put up and taken down many times over the next 14 years. In the mid-'70s, Held brazenly made matchbooks bearing the same statement. Barney's was a curiosity for out-of-town tourists, gay and straight. It's hard to say if Held was homophobic, insensitive and backward, or if he was just a savvy businessman exploiting an opportunity.

For the new gay movement, the Barney's protest was an important springboard that proved working together against a shared enemy was far more productive than arguing internal differences. The *L.A. Free Press* described the demonstrations as "Southern California's first encounter with the new homosexual." Victory over the sign itself may have been short-lived, but the whole campaign served a very important purpose—it put the Los Angeles gay revolution on television in an assertive, non-victimized position.

RADICAL VS. VIOLENT

MORE THAN IRWIN HELD AND HIS SILLY SIGN, IN MORRIS KIGHT'S view the biggest deterrent to the success of gay rights was the continued threat of violence within the movement itself. There were no rules in the GLF but Kight did maintain a firm decree of nonviolent social reform. He knew nothing would be more antithetical to promote gay rights than bloodshed, as that would foster what he called an "unnatural fear of homosexuals," not respect. Kight exampled himself a calm demeanor and remained above the fray. Yet the possibility of violence was ever-present—either as retaliation for anti-gay violence that had been perpetrated, or as a response from newly radicalized-liberalized amped-up young men and women. Kight was painfully aware that the threat also came from moles within the organization who called for militant violence, rationalizing that violence was needed to provoke radicalization of both gays and their oppressors.

A special 'note' at the bottom of an August 1970 GLF flyer announcing a "People's Army Jamboree":

"Please remember that the Jamboree does not wish to initiate violence. Those who do so in a potentially dangerous situation may bring down some heavy shit on their brothers and sisters, and may be viewed as Pig provocateurs trying to cause an excuse for the Pigs to come down on us. So please use your head."

It is not clear how many, but there were definitely FBI informants in the Los Angeles GLF. FBI recruitment was easy enough during any of the nearly 4,000 arrests of homosexuals in Los Angeles (mostly on trumped-up charges of lewd conduct and many cases of entrapment by undercover police officers).

Bill Beasley: "Informants were around the whole movement—the antiwar movement, the Black Panther Party.... Anybody who was protesting against the activities in the world.... The government tried to put an end to it."

Kight was familiar with the FBI's counterintelligence program in the peace and civil rights movements. Planted moles from inside the groups inject inflammatory rhetoric and stir up internal conflicts. They promote disturbances and violence to create confusion and instability. In some cases, the disruption was successful. True activists always went on to find another forum and regroup. Kight knew this same sort of counterintelligence was in the gay liberation movement and he expected that it would have some success.

There were few good reporters covering the gay rights scene. Kight's FBI file relied most heavily on information from "Informants from within the GLF" and the "alternative press." The FBI often quoted details from Douglas Key's *L.A. Free Press* articles.

Being a reporter, Key caught Kight's attention early and even if Kight had been able to predict the drama that Key would bring into his life, he could never resist a member of the press. Douglas Key was one of the more colorful and emblematic figures in Kight's life at that point.

John Effinger: "I remember one member named Doug who was an attractive, masculine, muscular young man who always wore a dress to the meetings. Sexual attraction was always a feature of these get-togethers."

Key, a pre-op transsexual, was still writing under the name "Douglas Key" in 1970 and may have had a hormonal reaction to gay lib. Key reported thoroughly on GLF meetings, gatherings, schedules of upcoming events, and wrote eyewitness accounts as well as editorials. Key, who was not homosexual, pushed for the inclusion of 'trannies' in the gay movement; it was not an automatic love-fest. Transsexuals and transvestites were not guaranteed the understanding and acceptance in a room full of out-of-the-closet gays and lesbians. Douglas Key, perhaps not an ideal ambassador for any cause, was described by a prominent Professor of Gender Studies as "A really important figure in the gay lib history of Los Angeles."

Key is also described by Del Whan: "A pre-op trans white guy who was very male and loud. A royal pain in the ass—had male privilege written all over him. The women did not want him in their group. He was upset that Morris made some funny comment about 'transsexuals need to learn how to keep their seams straight,' referring to Key's inability to keep facts straight."

Key was one of the more vocal members within the movement, eventually becoming disruptive at meetings and proving "too difficult" for many to deal with. By early 1970, Key reported on the "unity" within the GLF, whenever possible, including reports of violence against transvestites and violent reactions from gay libbers. Key made a point to include transvestites in all of his articles on gay liberation and frequently mentioned a trannie organization called The Society of Anubis. Key reported that Anubis had "eight hundred members in southern California. About half ... is composed of male Gays and female Gays, making the SOA rather unique among Gay organizations." When Virginia Price, a pioneer in the transvestite movement, was introduced at a GLF meeting and received "an ovation," Key made it news.

Kight would have liked to have his "standing ovations" recorded in the press. He respected the way Key used his byline to advance his personal agenda. Key compared gender re-identification issues with homosexuality. Most homosexuals did not agree that the two were the same, acknowledging that transsexual is not homosexual. The gay movement had never before embraced gender issues—role-playing, yes. But not gender.

This may have been the "seam straightening" that Kight referenced.

In 1994, Kight said: "Transgender is very real. Whatever that may be, that's transvestites, cross-dresser, male/female trans—female to male. And there's transvestite heterosexuals, male to male, female to female. I created 'transgender.' I've been recreating the language, and that's one of the terms. First, I tried 'transpeople,' and that didn't fly. Then I created 'transgender,' and that flew, and it's now in the language. I think that's appropriate."

Kight frequently took credit for the creation of nomenclature.

Key instigated what was perhaps the largest "ripples of discontent" in the early movement when he reported that "transvestites and transsexuals have come to the conclusion that the Gay movement is not valuable to their manifestations." Key pushed it at GLF meetings for quite a few months and the tension mounted on both sides of the "discussions."

Active GLF member Craig Hanson wrote to Kight: "What should we do with Angela Douglas (née Mr. Douglas Czinki)? I discussed her/his case with Connie Vaghn, MCC transsexual member, on Sunday. Connie doesn't believe Doug is a real transsexual but he/she does have a very severe gender identity problem, complicated by paranoid fantasies."

Karla Jay (*Tales of the Lavender Menace*): "When Angela [Douglas Key] told me that she wanted to become a lesbian and that it was my political duty to help her with her sexual transformation, our friendship came to an abrupt end."

Douglas Key (*Los Angeles Free Press*): "The necessity for an immediate cessation of the present internecine struggle within the Gay community was stressed, and 'the energies of the gay community should be directed against the enemies of Gay

Liberation,' according to one of the speakers. A macadamian [sic] Gay Movement, composed of at least fifty organizations in the United States working to alleviate the oppressed condition of the homosexual, appears to be headed for a loosely coordinated grouping with the primary attribute of flexibility...."

Flexibility, according to Key, meant the full inclusion of transsexual heterosexuals in the gay movement.

Advocate headline: "Gay Lib survives bitch fight only slightly shrunken—so far."

The consequent article reports on Douglas Key as an outspoken dissenter, creating chaos at GLF meetings. Kight was frequently breaking apart ruckuses.

Key often forecasted the end of the GLF. He'd publish that he was quitting the GLF, and then be back at the next Sunday meeting. After a particularly violent outburst, Key didn't show up at the next Sunday meeting and the *Advocate* reported, "Sunday was orderly and amiable. Key was not present."

Douglas Key left the GLF and soon left Los Angeles for Miami, Florida, via Chicago, New York City, and Atlanta. Key felt that completing her transition was easier with new associates and a new social circle. According to the *Advocate,* Key "quit the group to found the Transvestite-Transsexual Action Organization" [TAO]. Key unsuccessfully tried to add TAO's agenda and interests to GLF.

In July 1970 Kight received the first of many rambling letters from Angela Douglas in New York after visiting Chicago, which "was hell." She described GLF Chicago as "quite right-on and [they] have begun to form self-defense groups.... Help them if you can.... The entire trip was very enlightening. We all bitched at each other etc and it was ... so much fear. But here I am in N.Y. and diving into the scene here; I hope it is worthwhile for all concerned. Take care, love to all. Love & Peace, Angela."

Angela reported many adventures and encounters to Morris; she did not have a simple or easy life.

In September 1970, Angela wrote a typewritten letter to "Morris and everyone" from Miami where she sought and befriended the pastor of MCC for "desperately needed assistance ... I am a physical wreck—horrid leprous sores on my feet and legs. The sun, air and cleanliness of the city is curing me quickly."

Douglas' letters were four to five pages, many handwritten on single-spaced lined paper, some typed single-spaced. She became increasingly distraught and paranoid.

Angela referred to "a few days of intense depression (my monthly)." In another letter, she elaborated, "I am really quite the lesbian now, very well accepted as such by most gay sisters and I am most happy about this. I do not hate men, just male chauvinists. It is so hard to be a woman, so hard and I am proud to be even a partial one, inside me, I am a woman, my exterior is beginning to match this inside. It seems you understand me better now—I miss all of you, of course, very much. You are all such a big part of my life. Yes, freedom, Morris. Freedom to be a man or a woman, to be gay, to be straight, whatever ... the gay girls are great! We're all witches, y'know. Good creative vibes."

Invariably, Angela found herself in serious legal troubles and was a victim of beatings. Her letters became more desperate and she needed "lawyers, psychologist etc." She asked Kight for help. A few weeks later Angela wrote again: "No money and I'm living on the street. Where are the so-called brothers and sisters? Bullshit....

Thank you so much; what I need now is a hell of a lot of publicity. You could have done it, but for some reason, did not."

These letters to Kight continued for years, maniacal and removed from reality and yet astute in current events and politics.

GAY-INS

TWO TEXAS TRANSPLANTS, DAUGHTERS OF A SOUTHERN BAPTIST preacher, caught Kight's eye early on in the movement. He could immediately envision many uses for Brenda Weathers and her younger sister Carolyn. They were smart, articulate, good-looking, "fem" enough, not too butch. And they were from Texas. Brenda was already a rebel, having been kicked out of Texas Woman's University in 1957 for being a lesbian—the sort of thing that brought pedigree to a revolutionary movement such as the GLF. Carolyn moved to Los Angeles later, in 1968, focused her energies in the antiwar movement, "marching up and down Hollywood Boulevard and smoking grass with strangers," as she described it. She later added, "It was probably General Hershey Bar who I used to hang out with on the Boulevard."

Carolyn Weathers remembers an early GLF meeting: "One afternoon in 1969 or early 1970 when [everyone] was hard at work, building things in the meeting, a longhaired lesbian hippie chick popped in just long enough to tire of the serious, shoulder-to-the-wheel politics, to run to the front door, turn around and make a 'charming' hippie-dippy impromptu speech about how everybody, men and women, gay and straight, black and white, should all stand on a hill together, holding hands. Oh dear, that was *me*! As I recall, some of the listeners grew starry-eyed but many rolled their annoyed eyes to heaven, as in, 'Jesus, get the airy fairy out of here!' which I now don't blame them. I can imagine [Morris] being among the irritated, not among the starry-eyed. Yet I don't see him rolling his eyes or blowing out his breath or doing anything of common rudeness. I picture him loftily amused as he assessed the situation, expressing how nice to have a visitor, but now we must return to the important work we had at hand, and allow ourselves no more distractions. I can almost hear him adding, 'And then, when the first work is done, we will take up the next and the next, until we perhaps go up the mountain and hold hands briefly for those who like that sort of thing.' Then I fled out the door, leaving the hard workers to do the hard work."

Gay people knew how to have a good time. As it turned out, Morris Kight could exploit that too for their liberation.

Borrowing from the famed "love-ins" of the 1960s hippie movement, where it was encouraged to love in the open, Kight came up with "Gay-Ins." The idea was to create an environment, out in the open, in public, where it was safe to be gay. It was a novel, revolutionary, and dangerous idea.

In March 1970, one-inch ads appeared in the *Los Angeles Advocate*: "Out of the Closets and into the Park!"

The *Advocate* item gave further clarification: "L.A.'s Gay Liberation Front is sponsoring a Gay-In at Griffith Park's merry-go-round area on Sunday April 5, from noon to 6PM. The event, GLF says, 'will be an attempt on the part of the GLF to offer a radical alternative to the closeted existence which homosexuals have been forced to live.' The accent of the Gay-In will be on 'spontaneity and creativity.' The sponsor urges everyone to bring food, games, streamers, banners, musical instruments, incense, and other contributions to the 'festive, colorful, peaceful afternoon.' Besides wandering musicians, guerrilla theatre, and dancing, at least one gay marriage ceremony will take place."

Kight (to Dallmeyer): "I felt that if we went into public parks and enjoyed ourselves, played kickball and badminton, had food and music and danced and so on, that we would be indicating that we had every right in the world to use the parks and that we liked to gather together and that it was great fun. Maybe 1,500 people came to the first Gay-In and we were at the merry-go-round all day. We had a wonderful time. There were flags and banners, music, dance, rapping. Some played cards, others played tennis."

Pat Rocco: "They were just fun. They were just meant to be blatant fun, where people came out and dressed the way they wanted to. They were just fun affairs."

The *L.A. Free Press* reported that "close to 2,000 persons—most of them homosexuals" turned out for the first Gay-In. Key reported: "Almost half of the homosexuals were females." People came from San Francisco and San Diego to participate.

To Kight, the point in having an event like this in a public area was to create an opportunity to demonstrate something very basic—gays are not to be feared. Right in the middle of an ordinary family day at the park, there was a kissing booth, body-painting, gay guerrilla theatre, and (decades ahead of its time) gay marriage ceremonies.

Kight dressed for the event in a short T-shirt and white shorts—too short and too tight by anyone's standards. Kight's round stuffed-pillow shape with his belly hanging out brought additional attention. His personal liberation involved shameless exhibitionism often expressed through his piebald wardrobe.

Helen Niehaus of the Society of Anubis and Kight performed five gay marriages. He called them "mateship" ceremonies, to de-heterosexualize the event. "In a heterosexual ceremony," the *Advocate* quoted Kight, "the minister will say, 'By the power invested in me, I pronounce you, etc.' I don't have any power invested in me. The power is in you. Not the love of power, but the power of love. And by the power of love, you can join these two." It was theatrics for Kight; there was no political force behind the mock ceremonies because he personally didn't much care for the heterosexual institution of marriage. He never saw it as a valuable or immediate goal in radicalizing homosexuals.

Someone counted seven uniformed policemen and a dozen plainclothesmen scattered through the crowd. A few straight families at the park got involved with the Gay-In; everyone got along with lots of milling around with other "hip" straight groups in the park.

Gay-In One was a success.

That night, about a hundred homosexuals demonstrated outside the Hollywood police department to protest the one arrest made at the park earlier in the day.

A young man charged with "desecrating the flag" was released and the charges were dropped.

A second Gay-In was quickly set for Memorial Day weekend. The *Advocate* announced that it would be held in the Greek Theatre area of Griffith Park with the theme "Come Together." Plans were "fluid," with an open invite to everyone to play instruments, dance, perform or just "do your thing."

Resemblances of 1950s Albuquerque echoed in the *Advocate* report that Kight wore "a tapestry robe and wide-brimmed [velvet] hat rimmed with pearls."

Novelist Christopher Isherwood made an appearance at Gay-In II, a rare showing of celebrity support. The apolitical Isherwood disappointed some in the gay movement who wanted him to be more openly supportive of gay rights. In his diaries, Isherwood wrote about the day: "May 31 … In the afternoon we [Isherwood and his partner Don Bachardy] went with David [Hockney] to Griffith Park, where there was a Gay-In. Only it wasn't very gay or very well attended. The police had been by, earlier, harassing them because they were distributing leaflets without a permit. Nobody got arrested but it scared a lot people off. Lee Heflin was there, and a friend of his stamped our hands with the sign of a hand in purple ink, denoting some gay-liberation front group; they took a lot scrubbing to get off. Lee introduced me to an elderly man named Morris Kight who was wearing a silk dressing gown and a funny hat and who appeared to be directing the proceedings. He married two pairs of girls, explaining that this wasn't a marriage but a 'mateship.' We had to join hands and chant something about love. Kight also introduced me publicly and called on me to speak, so I said, in my aw-shucks voice, 'I just came here because I'm with you and wanted to show it.' There were several journalists with cameras and quite possibly Don and I will appear in the *Free Press* or the *Advocate* or elsewhere. Well, at least it was a political gesture of sorts."

The *Advocate* quoted Isherwood exactly as he said it, "I just came here because I'm with you and wanted to show it." The author's absence in the movement was noted. In Isherwood's September 18 diary entry, of the same year, he writes about attending a Society of David meeting. "As far as I was concerned, this was a kind of trap; my being there was turned into a confrontation between an old liberal square celebrity and the young activists of the Gay Liberation Front. A big swarthy baldish guy named Don Kilhafter [sic] (I think) put me down, without absolutely directly attacking me personally. Old Kight aided him without seeming to. Most of the others were genuinely friendly and pleased that I'd come."

At Gay-In II, body painting was popular again, and guerrilla theatre put on a well-received re-enactment of police beatings at the Dover Hotel. Tables with literature, posters and buttons accepted donations, and the Peace and Freedom Party was registering voters. The kissing booth was less popular this time, however—probably because of the presence of plainclothes policemen.

Being openly gay in a public park, in broad daylight, was probably too much "liberation" for the authorities to handle. The *Advocate* reported: "The Los Angeles Police Department was well represented and there were several instances of harassment. But no arrests were reported."

Kight to Dallmeyer: "The Los Angeles police department came. Forty-five officers in riot gear lined up on one of the hills overlooking us, holding their batons

at the erect. I thought, good grief, the police are here to interfere in a lawful, legitimate picnic of people having fun, doing nothing unlawful in any way. And so I went up to see them. We had alerted the TV and radio stations that this might happen, by the way, so the [media] were there in some numbers. And so I went along the long line of police officers and said [softly], 'I urge you to leave. Your presence is making a lot of people very nervous. You're interrupting a lawful picnic. People are having fun. Surely, the Los Angeles Police Department doesn't object to people having fun. I feel a great tension in the crowd. I feel that violence is just below the surface. Your presence is really, really dangerous, really offensive. You're not here to control any behavior that is within your jurisdiction. I urge you to start to quietly withdraw.' And they did. They went. The audience gave them an ovation."

The *Advocate* reported that early in the afternoon, "Kight was handed a cease-and-desist order against accepting donations—on the complaint, according to police, of a park ranger." The donations ceased. A little while later, citing rarely invoked park regulations, the police verbally warned Kight that the posters, literature, and a huge orange and lavender "Gay Liberation Front" banner had to be taken down and removed. Trying to prevent a riot, Kight argued with his constituents that defying the police order "wasn't worth it."

The *Advocate* quoted Kight: "'The Gay-In had been intended as a peaceful affirmation of the rights of homosexuals. This view prevailed and the signs came down.'"

Kight's decision to abide by the LAPD order was judged and argued for weeks within the ranks of the GLF. It would launch a new accusation—that Kight was an "assimilationist" for going along with the police.

Howard Fox (to Dallmeyer): "We announced Gay-In Three, which was Labor Day weekend, 1970 and that one I really did do all the planning. We had rock bands and it was widely publicized and we had a tremendous turnout and frankly there were lots of illegal things going on at that event."

1970. Morris Kight in fancy drag at Gay-In II. Photo: Pat Rocco. Pat Rocco Papers, Coll2007-006, ONE National Gay & Lesbian Archives, USC Libraries, University of Southern California.

Gay-In III was at the carousel area in Griffith Park. A requested $1.50 donation was implemented to raise funds for "free social services for our brothers and sisters in the gay community." For an additional 25 cents, a plate of spaghetti and cold cuts were offered ("while they last") and beer and soft drinks were sold. There were the usual Gay-In trappings—body painting, dancing, a deejay and as the *Frontlines* newsletter later reported, a few announcements by Kight "and other leaders of the movement, urging greater open support for and involvement in GLF." A common moniker on GLF literature was: "None of us are free until all of us are free." Gay-In III attracted the most people, from different walks of life, who showed solidarity with the Gay Liberation Front and their determination to establish their rights.

The goal was simple—get "gay brothers and sisters out of their closets and show society again that we intend to claim full participatory rights."

FUNKY DANCES

ONCE UNLEASHED, THE NOISE OF GAY LIBERATION WOULD NOT BE silenced. In the early days there was equal attention given to both "inculcating the idea of community," and opening up the thinking of the outside world. In a 1988 interview for the *Los Angeles Times*, Kight said that his most important contributions to the early movement were attitudes and ideas.

No longer a theoretical movement, in 1970 any shift in thinking had to be experiential as there was no empirical data.

Carolyn Weathers: "Occidental College put flyers all over town that they were having a student dance and everybody was welcome. They're having this dance out on the tennis courts. Somebody at the Gay Liberation Front got hold of the flyer, and so we all went. Great, everybody welcome. We went out to the tennis courts and we kind of lurked about waiting for the dance to begin. And then we all went out there and started dancing—men with men and women with women. At first some of the students were just really pissed off and appalled, particularly I noticed the young guys who were trying so hard to be masculine and the young women who were trying to be ultra-feminine, they were the ones who seemed more upset than any of the regular kids who in time would join us in these big whooping circle dances that we would do. It all turned out to be kind of a happy experience except for those at the extremes of, you know, trying to be masculine and feminine."

Within a month, flyers appeared on college campuses and in bars announcing the "People's Funky Dance." Always looking for ways to be "gay" without having to go to the bars and needing to raise funds, the GLF found Funky Dances were multi-purpose. Probably no other grassroots movement put more "fun" into fund-raising than the gay community and much of it had begun at the Funky Dances. The Dances were so successful that the concept was easily adapted to help the Women's Caucus of the GLF and later the Gay Community Services Center.

Kight always provided a brainstorming venue for eager GLFers to create an image to present to the world; usually it was his home. Whoever showed up to brainstorm would become the current GLF marketing committee. They put together invitations for people to join or get to know gays. Kight would be the adult and, because of the Doctrine of Shame that they were letting go of, if anyone needed permission to do anything, Kight was there to oblige. It was pretty much an "anything goes" regulation. One flyer said: "All we want is freedom—an end to all laws against us—and, every now and then, a FUNKY DANCE." Some of the flyers used original cartoons, while others used characters from popular strips like *Peanuts*. Charlie Brown says: "Good grief! What am I doing in a bar again? The same old people, the same old games..."

The handbills were elaborate, eye-catching, informative, and always invited non-homosexuals to join in the fun: "All people welcomed—gay and straight—black, white, brown, yellow, red, and blue—in drag, in costume or just plain naked—but come!"

Del Whan: "Ralph [Schaffer] put in an appearance nude at a Funky Dance in the early 1970s. No one seemed to object."

The earliest Funky Dances were held at Larchmont Hall, 118 North Larchmont Boulevard in Hollywood. They quickly outgrew that space and moved to the "Funky Ukranian [sic] Cultural Center," further east at 4315 Melrose Avenue. Finally, the Funky Dances found a permanent home for semi-regular events at Troupers Hall, 1625 North La Brea in the heart of Hollywood.

Platania: "The Gay Funky Dances, even I who lived it and was there to see it, don't believe that it really could have been quite how I remember it...

"Dances bridged gay lib, they gave people an alternative to the bars. Morris would stand outside of the bars and tell people, 'you can't go in there, they won't let you touch in there and the only thing they want is your money and you'll become alcoholic, come to this dance.' We got the reputation that we were more fun than the bars."

Lee Mentley: "I went to a Funky Dance and spent the night at Morris Kight's on McCadden Place. We stayed up all night talking—talking gay stuff, drinking and silliness. I passed out on the couch, got up in the morning and drove home."

STUDENTS FOR GAY POWER

AN IMPORTANT TOOL IN KIGHT'S ARTILLERY, DISCOVERED FROM Dow Action Committee, was the power on college campuses. He wanted to establish chapters of gay liberation on college campuses and he didn't need, nor want, to do it himself. He needed one good warrior. As it turned out, he had many.

One typical campus flyer read: "Cal Poly is nice and straight, but if you're not, it can be a problem! Help us get started, now! Write: GLF..."

At the bottom of the flyer was the standard asterisk notation: "All mail held in strictest confidence."

Kight and Kepner did not always see eye to eye, yet they were able to appear simpatico to create a synergy that encouraged younger members to create gay studies departments on college campuses. It was a long-range plan that could not have been conceived in the university system.

Passionate sentimentalities emerged when gay liberation expanded to college campuses. At a National Student Gay Liberation Conference in San Francisco, a 20-year-old militant leader, Charles Thorpe, was quoted in the *Advocate*:

"I never saw any choice but to fight for our people … violence is a means of oppression used on us, and we are told we must accept that.… As violence shall oppress us, so shall it liberate us."

The *Advocate* article continues: "However, said Los Angeles Gay Liberation Front founder Morris Kight, it seemed to him that Thorpe was not so much calling for violence as predicting its inevitability if 'oppression' of Gays does not end in the near future. 'Even so,' [Kight] said, 'there is, so far as I can see, no popular support for his statement.'"

Kight was forever stomping out embers of violent rage.

In handwritten notes to himself are Kight's talking points for speaking to student groups: Twenty-minute talk about "civil rights," "civil liberties," "human rights," clearly state that the antiwar movement cannot be separate.

Kight used the Watts riots as an example of productive nonviolent action. He introduced a "vast spectrum of nonviolent techniques" to campus groups saying, "Homosexuals do not use violence or it might easily be self-defeating."

Throughout the '70s, colleges around the world were participating in gay liberation. Students were vocal about the rights of homosexuals and college newspapers were filled with news of gay liberation events and activities, task forces, and gay awareness. Once successful on campuses, Kight knew there was a future for gay liberation in society.

At USC, Del Whan wrote an anonymous letter to the student paper, the *Daily Trojan,* saying that "she could not come out.

"Nevertheless, I went to the GLF meetings Morris spoke about [while speaking at USC campus]. Soon after, I took the first small steps to come out at work. I quickly became an activist and started the USC Gay Lib Forum as an Experimental College class in 1970. It later turned into the Gay Students Union."

For years, Whan was the only woman and the only USC staff person openly involved with the campus group. She explained to Glenne McElhinney: "My direct boss, Professor Larue in the Department of Religion, was extremely supportive and knew all the facts about the Biblical origins of anti-homosexual prejudice going back to the early Hebrews. His boss, Dean David Malone, of Humanities, was secretly supportive too (as I heard later). As a group, we had to meet off campus in the Religious Center due to USC's anti-gay policy. We sued USC for recognition as a student group around 1971, 1972. Justin Dart and the Board of Trustees finally permitted recognition without going to trial after some gay alumni threatened to cut off funding."

Around the same time in the early '70s, Richard Gollance, an undergraduate film student at UCLA, wrote an op-ed piece for the UCLA *Daily Bruin* campus newspaper titled "The Problems Facing Gays," which was later found in the GLF FBI files. Gollance articulates many of the shortcomings in the educational system at the time: "Intellectually, spiritually—most of my growth, my increased awareness of myself and the world, has been outside of school. And the most important—to me—and the most difficult, was to buck the odds and learn to like and to appreciate myself. Not despite being gay. Maybe because of being gay. But certainly to be able to include my gayness as part of my positive self. Not only did the educational system ignore that need—in myself and my many gay brothers and sisters—it actively worked against that need."

Forty years after writing that Gollance said: "A lot of young people used the liberation movement as a coming out process. Morris Kight put it into a context. He gave it a political and social influence. He most definitely indirectly influenced who I became."

LAWFULLY GAY

GLF-LA ATTRACTED PEOPLE FROM ALL WALKS OF LIFE AND FROM around the country. Barry Copilow and his best friend Steve Berman were new arrivals in Los Angeles when they attended their first GLF-LA meeting. Copilow, who had just graduated from Northwestern where he'd been active with Tom Hayden in Students for a Democratic Society, recalled his first GLF-LA meeting: "I remember sitting around, not on chairs, not on benches, like sitting on a kitchen sink and counter tops, there was clutter. I remember yelling at everyone, I thought I was the cat's meow, I thought I knew everything. I remember yelling, 'You're too passive.' What a jerk I was. Morris was amused."

Copilow and Berman arrived to the movement with their own battle scars, having been beaten up and arrested in Chicago demonstrations and later arrested in Texas. The eager young men impressed Kight. Kight and Berman had an immediate close natural alliance, a symbiotic bond. Copilow described it as "a strong father/son connection. Steve would do anything for Morris."

Many years later, Copilow recalls Kight's advice to the young activists: "Don't just do something, stand there." Kight was suggesting be openly gay, present to the world as gay, and resist being anything other than gay. Stand there and be present as homosexuals.

Kight saw great potential in the two friends and he said, "We're going to do something with you, Copilow." Looking back, he realizes that Kight saw that as a young man he could be manipulated—and hence would be very useful to their mutual cause. Kight and Berman encouraged Barry Copilow to go to law school which was another part of Kight's grander vision for gay liberation.

POLICE HARASSMENT

KIGHT TO JONATHAN KATZ (1976): "AS A GAY, SIMPLY BEING A CITIZEN in society has a certain amount of hazards."

Historians may debate exactly what set off the Stonewall Inn riot in New York. There is, however, no argument that organized mobsters monopolized control of gay bars throughout New York City. The mob paid off the police so that the police would not raid inside the bars, but instead would wait and arrest patrons outside the bars. Every so often a bar raid was staged, for appearances' sake—but it never included a fine to the bar owner. Only the patrons were selected for arrest, often beaten, and always heavily fined. To the NYPD, it was sport. A win-win for New York's finest, also known as "the establishment," as well as for the mafia bar owners.

The exact same situation existed in Los Angeles. There was no gay "community"; homosexuals depended upon bars to socialize. For those who didn't have access to elite private parties, generally held behind high-hedged walls, there was nowhere else to go to congregate, be entertained, comfortably have a drink with a friend, or meet a new intimate. It was guaranteed that the still-closeted population would not attend GLF functions, much less spend Sunday afternoons frolicking in the park, but they'd go to a dark bar.

According to *Gay L.A.* (2006), in 1969 there were 162 bars "in and around Los Angeles" that "catered to gay men and lesbians." Kight had come to despise the bar scene and yet quite by design it never disturbed his social life or his drinking. Though he'd later revise his stance, in the mid-'60s through '70s, gay bars represented a no-win situation for the struggling gay population. The bars promoted alcoholism, contributed to personal and societal problems, and exploited their customers by enforcing antiquated "no touching" rules. Kight could see the long-term effects this would have on the gay populace. In the abstract—it further disempowered an already deprived collective, and in the flesh—one arrest could ruin an individual's life. One police beating could permanently dissuade a young activist. The LAPD aggressively pushed against the momentum of liberation. In one 12-month period, there were three deaths of homosexuals while in police custody.

A demonstration flyer that Kight wrote: "Stop police murder, brutality and entrapment of homosexuals!"

GLF planned a "tin-can demonstration" around the Rampart police station (encouraging participants to "bring a small, empty tin can and a pencil to beat it with. It will make an ominous and interesting sound").

"During the demonstration we will attempt to raise (by Magick [sic]) the Rampart Police Station several feet above the ground and hopefully cause it to disappear for two hours. If the GLF is successful in this effort we will alleviate a major source of homosexual oppression for at least those two hours. A large turnout might do the same thing for a longer period of time. Support this action with your presence."

Centered and prominent at the top of many flyers was a familiar memorial:

"Larry Turner: Black Street Transvestite killed by Los Angeles Police March 8, 1970.

"Howard Efland: Gay Brother killed by Los Angeles Police March 7, 1969.

"Ginny Gallegos: Gay Sister killed by Los Angeles Police Spring, 1970."

At the bottom of the flyer was the customary GLF proviso: "A peaceful, non-violent demonstration."

Los Angeles Police Department exhibited a top-down patent intolerance of homosexuals and blatant antagonism. The vice squad used some questionable methods of entrapment. The District Attorney's office processed a mountain of arrests on charges of lewd and lascivious behavior. Del Whan remembers men in the GLF "seemed to me to be much more organized and angry in 1970 because of their frequent contact with police harassment and the LAPD practice of entrapment."

Kight (1998): "I didn't keep records because the Los Angeles Police Department raided my house and went through the files and read everything. So I learned not to maintain files. I learned to burn documents. We had a little fire pit outdoors that we used to burn documents, letters, and addresses. We burned it all because I didn't want the LAPD to spy on my friends."

Los Angeles Advocate (1969): "'Stay out of Barnsdall Park at night!' That's the message the LAPD has been trying to get across for two months."

By mid-1970, *Los Angeles Advocate* reported so many raids and arrests that it resembled a police blotter. One week's report including a raid on the Little Cave, a bar that netted seven arrests on "647-A" lewd conduct charges and one arrest for possession of marijuana (a felony). Vice raided a gay bathhouse shouting: "I smell faggots," "Is this the fruit playroom?" and "There's a whole nest of them over here..." Another night, there were six arrests on 288-A, a felony charge of oral copulation and two arrests on misdemeanor charges. Police harassments and arrests were commonplace and city officials gave tacit consent to the mistreatment of homosexuals.

Police in wait outside gay bars to pick off homosexuals was one problem. Another problem was the mafia-owned and operated gay bars. Bar owners were happy to take their patrons' money and enforce "no touching" rules. The GLF, Morris Kight, told bar owners that the rules were discriminatory and violated customers' civil liberties. Bar owners didn't care. They were aware that gay men had no alternatives.

Kight coordinated volunteer law students like Barry Copilow. GLF printed a one-sheet reduced to a wallet-sized informational handout, "What to do in Case of Arrest." Seven bullet points about what to do, what to expect, and what *not* to do under headings: "If you are stopped by the police," and "If you are arrested," and the final topic: "If you are beaten."

The information was straightforward, practical advice on how to handle any of the mentioned situations without making the situation worse, including "Whatever happens, you must not resist arrest even if you are innocent."

Kilhefner to Dallmeyer: "I can still remember in early 1970 when I first began handing out little printed cards that said if you are arrested by the police this is what you should you do. One person came up to me and actually grabbed me by the shirt and said, 'You're going to get us into trouble, you're going to bring the police coming down on us,' and almost beat me up. He certainly did threaten me. The closet mentality at the time was 'be quiet, be clandestine, stay in the shadows, don't rock the boat.' [LAPD] never expected—that gay people would have the self-respect [to] come out and organize. They simply did not know what to do. They knew how to intimidate us. They knew how to scare us, threaten us, cause us to lose our jobs, arrest us and beat us. But they never expected us to come out and organize."

From the early days, GLF-LA organized to educate, troubleshoot, and end blatant civil rights violations. Kight considered options and realized that a complete boycott of gay bars could be marginally successful, if that.

In a letter to Kight from Craig Hanson (October 26, 1970): "Dear Morris: Last night after GLF I visited the Klondyke [sic] bar on La Brea and three bars on Santa Monica's 'gay strip,' Hub, Stampede, and Jaguar. I asked thirty-five customers in

A. WHEN THE POLICE CONFRONT YOU:
1. STAY CALM. Think before you speak.
2. NEVER RESIST PHYSICALLY. Say it in words.
3. DON'T TALK. Except to give your name, address and age, and if you happen to be in an unusual place at an unusual hour, you should explain your presence. Say you will answer no more questions until your attorney arrives, or if you can't afford one, until you are provided a free attorney. You are not required to provide your occupation or place of employment.
YOU HAVE THE RIGHT TO REMAIN SILENT AT ALL TIMES.
4. NOTE THE NAMES AND BADGE NUMBERS OF THE OFFICERS. Remember them and write them down as soon as possible.
5. If the officer is not in uniform, you are entitled to see his identification.

B. IF THEY WANT TO SEARCH you, your car or your house, whether or not you have anything to hide, say loud enough for any people in the area to hear you: "Where is your search warrant?" "You don't have my permission to search!" "What are you looking for?"

C. IF THEY ARREST YOU:
1. Tell them you want to know the charge, as required by Penal Code section 841.
2. Yell your name and age to bystanders and tell them to contact the Gay Liberation Front immediately.
3. You have the right to make two completed telephone calls at your own expense at the station within 3 hours of your arrest; one to your attorney, employer or relative, and the other to a bail bondsman as required by Penal Code section 851.5. Always carry two dimes with you.
4. If you are booked on misdemeanor charges, bail is automatically set and may be posted at the station. If it is a felony charge, bail will not be set until your arraignment in court(unless your bondsman or attorney runs a writ to set bail).
5. If you are not released on bail, the police must take you to court for arraignment within 48 hours of your arrest(not including holidays or weekends) as required by Penal Code section 825. Don't get busted on Friday night.
6. While in jail, do not discuss your case with anyone other than your attorney, including other prisoners, or take "friendly" advice from officers. Pay no attention to promises and threats if you are questioned; the police will say anything to get your confession.
7. Contact the Gay Liberation Front as soon as possible.

D. IF YOU WITNESS THE BUST OF A GAY SISTER OR BROTHER:
1. Tell the arrested person to give you his name and age, note the badge number and names of the arresting officers, time of arrest, and remember exactly what you saw.
2. Get names, addresses, and phone numbers of other witnesses, and report immediately to the Gay Liberation Front.
3. Be careful that you do not physically interfere with the arrest; keep at least 25 feet away. If the police threaten to arrest you for obstructing an officer, tell them only physical interference is unlawful. But don't argue; the police might arrest you anyway.

the above bars what they thought of GLF. Five hadn't heard of it at all. Thirty were very hostile towards GLF (including long-haired types), and only five had any favorable comments.... My feeling was that LA GLF's anti-bar activities are doing far more bad than good."

Platania: "It was Morris who said practically we cannot make every decision by consensus. Those of you who want to participate in the closing of the bars,

1970. Letter-size information about what to do "when the police confront you," distributed by the Gay Liberation Front.
Foster Gunnison, Jr. Papers. Archives & Special Collections at the Thomas J. Dodd Research Center, University of Connecticut Library.

IF YOU ARE A JUVENILE(under 18):

1. Section C inside does not apply to you, except for the right to remain silent. You should say you will not answer any questions about your case until you have an attorney.
2. After you are arrested and taken to the station, the police may release you, usually to your parents, or send you to a juvenile hall(not an adult jail), depending on your record and the seriousness of the charge.
3. If you are not released, the police must notify your parents or guardians, as required by Welfare and Institutions Code section 627.
4. You do not have the right to phone calls or bail.
5. A petition must be filed against you in juvenile court within 48 hours of your arrest(not including holidays or weekends) or you must be released, as required by W & I Code section 631.
6. You must be taken before a juvenile court for a detention hearing the next day after the petition is filed(not including holidays or weekends) or you must be released, as required by W & I Code section 632.

The Gay Liberation Front CANNOT provide you with an attorney. We can offer our brothers and sisters legal information, help to co-ordinate your legal defense, and stand by you when necessary.

1970. Wallet-size legal information, for juveniles, distributed by the Gay Liberation Front. Foster Gunnison, Jr. Papers. Archives & Special Collections at the Thomas J. Dodd Research Center, University of Connecticut Library.

come on and let's do it. And those of you who don't, don't. We will never come to agreement on some of these things. So Morris was, to that extent, very practical."

Kight prepared to reach out to the opposition and negotiate a livable arrangement.

First he reached out to the incredibly homophobic chief of police, Ed Davis, but, as expected, it was to no avail. No one from the city council would take his calls. An incredibly frustrating situation; it could have been a standstill and the arrests and police harassment would have continued.

Kight had an uncanny ability to distinguish the "true believers" of bigotry from those who just required enlightenment. He could convert an ambivalent adversary just by exercising bottom-line pragmatism and some good manners.

Kight wouldn't linger long with those who allowed a personal salvation or religion to define their political beliefs or justify their opposition to civil rights. With those types, Kight saw an unwinnable argument and he consciously chose not to engage the morally motivated. He quickly assessed LAPD Chief Ed Davis as one such futile case. In 1970, Kight needed an ally for gay liberation. He didn't need a politically perfect, lily-white champion. He didn't need someone with faultless nomenclature or the same objective.

Eddie Nash was such a person. Kight understood Nash's personal house of worship—the Holy Dollar.

Ten years younger than Kight, Eddie Nash was born in Palestine as Adel Gharib Nasrallah. He came to America in the early 1950s, according to Wikipedia, after he was almost gunned down by Israeli soldiers. In Los Angeles, he had a few bit parts in television shows, once playing a character named "Nash," which provided his Americanized moniker. He focused on owning multiple bars and nightclubs in Los Angeles exclusively catering to every crowd with a thirst—blacks, whites, straights, gays. Nash owned strip clubs, dance clubs, jazz clubs, blues clubs, discos, restaurants, back alley bars, and high-end establishments that featured curbside service. At one time, he had the reputation as the wealthiest and most dangerous gangster on the West Coast.

Kight took it upon himself to reach out to Nash, the person who owned the most bars frequented by the most gays. Kepner's meeting notes clearly state, "Morris negotiates for GLF groups."

Kight didn't expect to sell Nash on a better quality of life for gays and lesbians. He needed to speak in terms that Nash understood: revenue. They had a shared interest, the gay community. Before Kight did anything, he had to show Nash some muscle.

In September 1970, GLF men and women began a long series of peaceful but noisy demonstrations inside and outside the Farm, Eddie Nash's most popular gay bar. Demonstrators were thrown out of the bar and they focused their picketing outside. The bar remained mostly empty.

Del Whan: "I went with GLF men to picket a gay bar called the Farm, to protest its "no touching" policy. During the protest Ed Nash came out and began to hose off the sidewalk as we marched up and down yelling and carrying signs. It was a crazy scene, even a bit humorous. The poor man finally gave up as we were not deterred by the water treatment."

Kight telephoned an introduction and educated Nash about the success of the Dow Action boycott. He kept himself available to negotiate a resolution whenever Nash was ready.

The Farm's business declined dramatically with a reported two hundred protesters outside. GLF threatened a civil rights suit against the establishment, an important and unprecedented force by gay customers.

After about a month of demonstrations and boycott, Nash was ready. Kepner's handwritten note: "Ed Nash called GLF yesterday." Kepner noted that Kight, Howard Fox, and Tony DeRosa met with Nash for two hours. Nash said, "Let's make an agreement."

Nash agreed to rescind the "no touching" policy if they called off the boycott. GLF wanted announcements in the bar every hour that "holding hands, light kissing, and on shoulder touching" was permitted.

To permit touching, which was never illegal, was not enough to define the new, albeit unconventional, terms. Kight agreed to call off the boycott in exchange for "further cooperation" with the management. GLF would encourage patronage of the Farm and continue to boycott other gay bars. In exchange, Nash agreed to discreetly pay the bail for any persons arrested in and around his bars. No one would interfere with the other surreptitious arrangement that Nash had with the LAPD. In exchange for a sum of dollars, LAPD minimized busts inside his clubs. The GLF and Nash had a separate agreement. That night there was expected to be up to two hundred demonstrators at the Farm. Instead, Eddie Nash had more than two hundred patrons in his bar.

Every morning, Kight would phone Nash's office with a number—it was the number of arrests that were made the night before in and around his bars. Kight often fudged the number to include one or two arrests made at other bars not owned by Nash, but no one would check or argue. The money would be ready for pickup later in the morning.

Jaime Green: "Morris used to send me to [Nash's] office at Seven Seas [nightclub] and I would come back with, you know, thousands of dollars in an envelope or a brown paper bag. Cash, it was always cash. I was the bag man. He would send me to these bars or these places to meet these strange guys in parking lots and bring home cash."

It was a beautiful arrangement and much of the reason it worked so well was because Kight and Nash were able to sit across the desk from each other and hammer out a mutually beneficial agreement. It might not necessarily be a compliment, but no other prominent person in the gay movement at the time could have done the same thing.

Of course, some thought Kight was nuts to undertake the negotiations. A common sentiment was expressed by Craig Hanson in a letter to Kight (October 1970): "You dared to take on the Mafia ... the Black Hand ... at the Farm? My God, man, you might find bullets ripping through your house some night! My fear of the Mafia is much greater than that of the police."

It was a strategic advancement. The arrangement stayed in place for a few years. The relationship between the two men continued and Nash frequently responded to Kight's numerous fundraising requests.

Flyers were quickly printed to announce: "Victory! The Farm is liberated! You can now show affection in The Farm by touching ... holding hands, kiss a friend, put your arm around a stranger. Another groovy freedom brought to you by the Gay Liberation Front. More to come! Gay power to Gay people! All power to all the people!"

A separate flyer: "homosexuals have all the rights our straight sisters and brothers enjoy ... if a bar denies you your basic human rights, contact the Gay Liberation Front."

Del Whan: "We were rowdy and took to the streets. Most closeted GLBT people did not want to be seen in our company. We did not care to fit in any longer with society's rules. Those with good jobs and businesses were loath to be associated with us."

GAY SURVIVAL

LOS ANGELES GAY LIBERATION FRONT DIFFERED FROM ALL THE other GLF groups around the country in one very important way: it took up social services.

Kight to Dallmeyer: "That made the L.A. GLF different from all the others, in that [while] all the others promised justice and freedom and liberation down the road, we promised justice, freedom, liberation and instant services right now. It was also fortuitous in the early '70s we developed the notion that *we* could serve one another best. That we could do that with love, tenderness and caring and

thoroughness, and so we trained a decade of lesbian and gay persons to serve one another."

He addressed raw needs of people who had been ignored and hidden for far too long. Much of it was not pretty work. Most people didn't want to know about anal warts or a recurrence of gonorrhea. Nor did they want to receive an after-midnight call about an arrest for an ill-advised tryst. Morris Kight took those calls.

He himself provided counseling over the phone and in person. He always had a meal to offer or a sofa on which to sleep. He knew which places a young, obviously gay man could safely apply for employment and oftentimes he knew someone who was hiring or just needed help for a few days.

Kight to Dallmeyer: "I have a social service component built into me. I am deeply concerned about the welfare of people and I don't think that anyone runs their life so well that they can govern their affairs all the time. [Everybody] has to have assistance. Lesbians and gay people were a sick, sad, sorry lot because we had been so thoroughly messed over. So I brought the notion of social services to Los Angeles and started out doing that, providing direct for-free, non-judgmental,

1970. "Gay People's Victory": after negotiating with the owner, the Farm agreed to work on behalf of their gay clients' best interests. Left: Morris, unidentified, Don Kilhefner, unidentified.
Photo by Lee Mason, *Advocate*. Lee Mason Photographs, Coll2012-078, ONE National Gay & Lesbian Archives, Los Angeles, California.

non-threatening, non-exclusionary services to lesbian and gay people and then brought that to the Gay Liberation Front."

Platania: "Morris filled this really important role of finding [professional people] who could help other people. He really did that more or less single-handedly."

Through years of good deeds, Kight had amassed favors and people—some important people and some who went on to become important—who may have felt that they owed him a great debt. Kight's style would not allow him to imply that anyone ever owed him anything; he would simply, at some point, request a favor, a good turn, from them (although it was more than likely he was actually asking a favor for someone else, who would then also feel indebted to Kight). He did this before anyone had coined the phrase "pay it forward." It was just how Kight's world spun.

He kept track of everything, without written records. Much how Bessie worked her domain in Hell's Half Acre, Morris became the "go-to" person in the GLF. He knew how to keep secrets—and not just his own. Since he never wanted to leave a trail of incriminating evidence of doctors who provided underground services for free or the clients who received them, Kight regularly purged his files. The most sensitive information was stored in between his ears.

Kilhefner realized that the first thing they needed to do in order to help people on a substantial scale was to write things down.

Kight: "I had destroyed all documents, because my house was raided regularly by the police and I was spied upon by the FBI. I couldn't afford to have documents. So I destroyed [them]. [Kilhefner] sat down and said, 'Let's get it out of your head and onto paper.' So we sat for three days and de-computerized me onto paper. And that became the Gay Survival Committee. People admired that."

Unlike any of the other cities with a Gay Liberation Front, Los Angeles provided social services. They had employment and housing services, treatment for syphilis, gonorrhea, body lice, scabies; provided succor, personal counseling, a shower and a cot, and other personal needs. "And that," Kight frequently reminded people, "as you well know, became the model for the Gay Community Services Center."

To the best of his ability, Kight remained true to all his self-imposed edicts. For the next 30 years, each time he talked about the model he used, the underground social services he had provided, he'd specify each individual component

GAY LIBERATION FRONT

SURVIVAL COMMITTEE
577 1/2 North Vermont
Los Angeles, Calif. 90004

665-1881

Legal Advice

Draft Counseling

V.D. and Drug Problems

Personal Counseling

Job Co-op

"None of us are free until all of us are free."

1970. Wallet-size "business card" for Gay Liberation Front Survival Committee. Foster Gunnison, Jr. Papers. Archives & Special Collections at the Thomas J. Dodd Research Center, University of Connecticut Library.

(physical health, mental health, legal help) that he envisioned—always free, non-judgmental/non-threatening/non-exclusionary. It was unprecedented at the time. And he bragged about it.

Kight passed along all that he knew from his experience helping thousands who had come to him for help. Now it was a full-scale division of the GLF headed by Kilhefner known as the Gay Survival Committee.

PERSON-TO-PERSON

THE GLF OFFICE WAS ACTIVE SEVEN DAYS A WEEK WITH A FULL weekly calendar of group meetings. Mondays, "Issues and Actions Committee," Thursdays, "Gay Group Encounter," Fridays, "Survival Committee," Saturdays were for "gays under 21, girls and guys, no adults allowed," and Sundays were general business meetings.

1970. Wallet-size invitation to "information talk group" distributed by the Gay Liberation Front. Foster Gunnison, Jr. Papers. Archives & Special Collections at the Thomas J. Dodd Research Center, University of Connecticut Library.

From the GLF Weekly Calendar of Meetings: "Saturdays: Gays Under 21. You're not the only one in the world! Give each other the answers that older generations can't or won't give to you. Girls and guys. No adults."

Kight always stressed, "we have to do the counseling ourselves." In 1970, Harry Kaplan was a 16-year-old high school student who read about the GLF in the *L.A. Free Press* and expanded on a peer-to-peer counseling group in his liberal San Fernando Valley high school. Kaplan became the GLF's "Youth Coordinator" and headed the youth rap sessions in the second-floor Vermont offices on weekends.

Kaplan: "Most guys discussed issues [they were having] with their parents and many used the group as support and leverage for coming out to parents and friends. It became popular for a while, very personalized. One [member of the rap session] had his mother call my mother to try to sort things out when her son was coming out."

Jon Platania and his friend Paul Olson rented a "broken-down house on Edgemont Street," and called it "Liberation House." The men had begun communal living arrangements in Liberation House, Freedom House, and Van Ness House. All these efforts served the men and strengthened their grassroots efforts. In a September 1971 letter to Foster Gunnison, Kight wrote:

"The Liberation Houses: our miracle. People change, become someone new, take responsibility for themselves, and for others, and all in all I feel great about both of them [Van Ness House and Liberation House]. Other groups here now propose to do the same thing, and I am pleased. We are usually pointing the way, and this we did."

Most of the young men who sought assistance were displaced youth, transients, runaways, street hustlers, boys who had been discarded by their families. For them, GSC was a literal lifesaver with unprecedented employment and housing opportunities. Temporary housing—"collectives," as they were called: residential flophouses that provided meals, showers, and temporary lodging—was set up following the model set by the U.S. Mission (whereby each house became self-supporting).

Kilhefner lived in a collective; Kight did not. Kight was sometimes criticized for not living in a collective, preferring instead to be the master of his own humble hippie domain. A collective was not the kind of living arrangement that appealed to Morris Kight. He worked from his home, worked the phones, counseled in his home and had some of those infamous "back room meetings" in his home. He was far more productive than collective living would allow.

Most of the GLF's medical services continued to be provided anonymously, in the back room of Kight's home on Fourth Street. By 1970, a number of medical doctors and practitioners were writing prescriptions and providing free "samples" of medications in Kight's back room. Medical Board protocol still required that treatment for any sexually transmitted condition had to be reported to the County Health Board. A teacher could lose credentials, a lawyer could be disbarred, and none of that helped the growing hepatitis concern. Doctors who agreed to Kight's crazy scheme to circuitously see patients risked their medical licenses, their careers, their livelihoods.

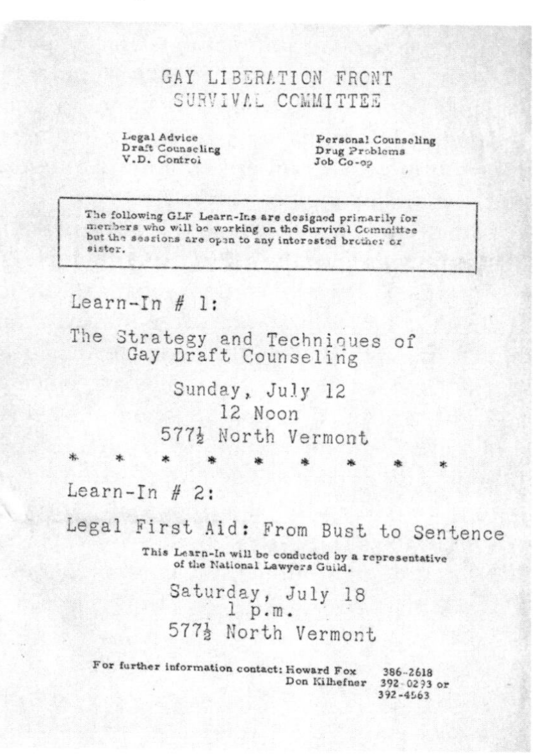

GAY LIBERATION FRONT
SURVIVAL COMMITTEE

Legal Advice
Draft Counseling
V.D. Control

Personal Counseling
Drug Problems
Job Co-op

The following GLF Learn-Ins are designed primarily for members who will be working on the Survival Committee but the sessions are open to any interested brother or sister.

Learn-In # 1:

The Strategy and Techniques of
Gay Draft Counseling

Sunday, July 12
12 Noon
577½ North Vermont

* * * * * * * * *

Learn-In # 2:

Legal First Aid: From Bust to Sentence

This Learn-In will be conducted by a representative of the National Lawyers Guild.

Saturday, July 18
1 p.m.
577½ North Vermont

For further information contact: Howard Fox 386-2618
Don Kilhefner 392-0293 or 392-4563

1970. Flyer for first "Learn-In" of the Gay Liberation Front, Gay Survival Committee.

Foster Gunnison, Jr. Papers. Archives & Special Collections at the Thomas J. Dodd Research Center, University of Connecticut Library.

GLF and specifically Gay Survival Committee regularly ran classified ads in the gay press regarding upcoming meetings and "free social services to the gay community … Also the 24-hour telephone for the gay community."

Listed in the white pages as "Survival Phone," 665-1881 was a well-known number. By the time the Gay Survival Committee had the line set up in the Vermont Avenue office, the phone calls had reached a hundred a day. Volunteers did their best to man the 24-hour hotline.

December 1970 *Frontlines*: "Due to the large number of calls coming into the GLF office, we are adding another line. Since this is a business phone, we are listed in the L.A. Yellow Pages under MARRIAGE AND FAMILY COUNSELING! ?????"

Kight burst with pride that his humble one-man operation had a 24-hour hotline.

He didn't like that most of the calls still came from jail.

With the advent of gay lib the need for bail funds and legal assistance increased. Kight's underground bail fund was expanded to its humble limits. The opposing forces to gay liberation were organizing and Kight did not want individuals' legal troubles to weigh down the forward movement. If gay liberation was to succeed, homosexuals needed to be functioning participants of society and not outlaws. GLFer Larry Townsend and a few others founded an underground organization called HELP (Homophile Effort for Legal Protection) described as "basically a gay ACLU," to cover bail and recruit (so to speak) a group of 20 to 30 local attorneys (gays and straight libertarians) who would represent homosexuals. Some cases were pro bono. Those who could afford to, paid for services. Attorneys Sheldon Andelson, Al Gordon, Alan Gross and a few law clerks handled every kind of case, from entrapment, disorderly conduct, wrongful eviction, to discriminatory hiring practices and wrongful termination.

Jaime Green: "Before there was any intervention at all, people used to stay in jail two or three months without any charges."

Another GLFer, Cliff Lettieri, organized an action committee of gay leaders to deal with police harassment. After months of talks with owners of bars that were predominantly supported by homosexual customers, the Tavern Guild created specific funds for legal defenses against police brutality and entrapments.

Kight continued to provide counseling services from his home, which was always open, and refer people with other legal difficulties.

Handwritten note to Kight from Stan B (February 14, 1971): "Just a line to say 'thanks' for past, present and, I hope, future courtesies. You have been invaluable in a project—and maybe several—which perhaps will bring ¼ of one ounce of understanding into the atmosphere of Planet Earth. P.S. Please call if I can do anything at all for you."

FAMOUS GAY

JON PLATANIA'S LIFE TOOK AN UNEXPECTED TURN ON OCTOBER 29, 1970. In a typed two-page statement for his GLF sisters and brothers, Platania provided a verbatim account of his arrest—a typical entrapment and how he utilized GLF techniques to survive.

In summary, while relaxing in Griffith Park, Platania was approached by a man "in a Texaco jacket" who was "doing all he could to look sexy, up to and including placing his hands in an obviously provocative position on the lower half of his anatomy.

"...Less than 'turned on' by all of this," Platania explained that after some direct flirtation, "feeling sorry for the guy," Platania "wanted to invite him into my van to smoke a doobie."

Less than 20 feet away and five minutes into the conversation, Platania was grabbed from behind and they "pulled my wrists up between my shoulder blades, slapped on the handcuffs, pushed me across the street." Platania shouted: "Do you see what's happening here? I'm being unjustly arrested! Call the Gay Liberation Front! My name is Platania! Call the Gay Liberation Front! My name is Platania!"

Handcuffed and shoved into an unmarked car, arrested, booked, and held in jail, Platania was charged with violating penal code 647-A—lewd conduct.

Platania was fired up, screaming in Rampart police station, and "in comes Tony DeRosa, Lee Heflin, and Don Kilhefner, led by Morris Kight, to spring me out of jail, the same day." They posted a $625 bond with an arraignment scheduled for November 4th.

When Jon Platania was released from jail, his promising political career was over, but a new political activist was born.

"I told my boss and gave my resignation, because this was going to be a public thing." Platania didn't want to compromise his executive supervisor—he personally knew his boss and his family. As a friend, his boss tried to talk Platania out of fighting the charge: make a deal, take a reduction in charges, a leave of absence, and it could all go away.

"No," Platania said, "this is what I want to do."

Kight personally took Platania to meet attorney Sheldon Andelson, emphasizing to Andelson that this was an important case. Platania wanted to take an affirmative defense: "I wanted to charge the police department with lewd and dissolute conduct, unbefitting to the people and the dignity of the State of California.

"Sheldon said, 'That sounds like a good idea politically, but do you realize that if you lose this case you will have to register as a sex offender for the rest of your life?' I said, 'How many people in Los Angeles are arrested in just this way and have their lives ruined?' Sheldon said, 'More than you care to know.' [I said,] 'Exactly, and until some of us stand up and bring this to the public's attention, it's going to go on forever. I will survive one way or the other.'

"Sheldon said, 'I can't in good conscience defend you.'"

Several other attorneys refused to represent him. A sharp guy with a master's degree, Platania decided to defend himself in court. Kight offered every resource the GLF could muster, a few law interns, and even Sheldon Andelson agreed to advise Platania, "against [his] better judgment."

Platania remembered that "Morris was more personally understanding: that here I was, a man with aspirations, a family, plans, a nice house in Berkeley and not at all prepared to have my life turned inside out, upside down and everything else. It wasn't easy to do what I did. It was very costly in terms of my profession, my money, everything."

Kight alerted the media. The *Advocate* and the *Los Angeles Times* picked up the story. There was standing room only in the courtroom with lots of people outside;

as Platania put it, "Overnight, I was a famous faggot." Platania remembers Kight's consistent, daily support.

The jury trial began in January 1971 with 25 prosecuting attorneys and one person at the defense table, Jon Platania. Unfamiliar with court procedures, Platania scored points in the jury selection by getting a pledge from each juror that they had no bias against homosexuals or any belief that homosexuals were especially prone to commit criminal offenses, and that they didn't consider homosexuals to be sick or depraved.

After five days of testimony, the jury, previously unfamiliar with the details of gay life, had a lot of information to consider. The jury went out midday Friday and returned four hours later with a verdict: "not guilty."

This not guilty verdict was monumental and seen as the beginning of a gradual shift in relations between the LAPD and gay people. "Not guilty" put the police department on notice that gay lib was not going away and a new era had begun.

Though Platania's arrest was a typical case of entrapment, his trial and outcome were atypical. Kight seized the momentum of Platania's victory as belonging to the movement. Through Kight's view, Platania was a valuable warrior in the nonviolent crusade to free all gay people.

GAY, BLACK, RADICAL

THE FBI HAD ONE BIG STEW OF ALL LEFTIST ORGANIZATIONS. Anything that slightly resembled anti-establishment was thrown into the same pot labeled "Security Matter." With Richard Nixon in the White House and J. Edgar Hoover dressed up as the country's chief detective with a personal commitment to eradicate all odds and ends of the New Left, it is easy to see how the GLF was clumped together with the Venceremos Brigade (Americans in solidarity with the Cuban Revolution), Brown Berets (young Mexican American community organizers), National Chicano Moratorium Committee (Chicano antiwar activists), Socialist Workers Party (born out of the American Communist Party), and Young Lords Party (Puerto Rican nationalists based in New York and Chicago). These groups had little or nothing in common except maybe a random member having used the same pay phone at Union Station.

Gay liberation was a blend of activists from the antiwar, civil rights, and women's movements, and yet many within those movements, at that time, didn't have a warm reception for the gay movement.

GLF FBI file entry: "The Gay Liberation's purpose is to free homosexuals, transvestites, lesbians, and other sexual deviates from 'oppression' from the 'straight population.'"

Leo Laurence: "The New Left was essentially hippies, the black movement, women's movement, then eventually, of course, the homosexual movement. The Old Left were the communists, socialists, Trotskyites, Stalinists and so on."

Kight described GLF (to Dallmeyer, 1989), speaking in rapid-fire cadence: "The GLF [was] not Marxist/Leninist-oriented nor is it capitalist-oriented, nor reform capitalist. We don't even have capitalism in this country anymore, we have corporate socialism. And the socialist countries certainly don't have anything that Marx ever wrote about. No, the system that the GLF, in my opinion, my observation based upon what I hear them say, the system they're searching for hasn't yet been invented or written. We're hoping it will evolve. If homosexuals are not, within a measurable length of time, able to achieve their rights within this system, they will demand that this system be remade in their image. That's how militant this struggle is going to be."

Kight's friend from the peace movement, Bill Beasley, who was often the only or one of two black people at GLF meetings, spent a lot of time at Kight's house having potluck meals and working on different campaigns. Bill considered Kight "a good friend." Beasley was definitely one of the more vocal members of the group and didn't suffer foolishness. Kight and Beasley agreed that revolution was serious business. To that end, there was a constant lookout for infiltrators in the GLF. Kight didn't want to allow them to derail gay lib with a call for violence.

Yet, he was always ready, if needed, to recreate gay liberation.

Beasley: "People came around pretending they were personal friends. I was always suspicious. Morris was suspicious too. He knew the kind of agents to expect. We talked about it, a lot of times after meetings we'd go to his house and talk about the infiltrators."

Kight was always supportive of the black civil rights movement and the Black Panthers in particular. Many homes of homosexuals were used for early Panther community meetings. The Black Panthers, as an organization, had never addressed homosexuality as an issue of their concern.

GLF FBI file: "The BPP is a violence-prone black militant organization headquartered in Oakland, California, with chapters located throughout the United States."

It took a man like Morris Kight to confidently and imperfectly navigate the perilous political hierarchy of the New Left movement. Kight hadn't been trained by the Panthers—as Leo Laurence put it, "he was much too old for them." Kight had his own training—he knew and respected the Panther organization, but he had his own methodology very similar to that engaged by the Panthers. The Panthers built communities one neighborhood at a time by showing true concern for people's welfare, providing social programs, bail, and addressing police brutality.

Laurence: "The Government tried to make [the Panthers] out to be very violent, dope addicts who went around murdering people, and I knew otherwise. Morris wasn't on the inside, but he knew Panthers and Panthers knew him."

A particularly important and sensitive alliance for gay liberation, it was natural for Kight to reach out to his brothers in the L.A. Panthers to support his new mission to liberate gay people. Kight saw it as a natural alliance. Gay rights belonged in the radical world of antiwar, women's libbers, and black power. Kight very much wanted the GLF to be included in the broader revolutionary hierarchy. It would prove far more complicated.

The mainstream media, for the most part, contributed to the vilification of the Black Panther Party by reporting whatever information the government provided. In 1970, UPI ran the headlines: "Panthers 'Most Dangerous,' Hoover Says."

Kight continued to support the message of civil rights and espoused pacifism. He protested alongside Black Panthers often times in close range to violence that erupted between police, FBI plants, and the militant radicals.

Stanley Williams: "When Morris urged us to join antiwar and civil rights demonstrations, I always stayed near him. He instinctively knew when to leave, just before the police would start cracking heads."

Kight supported Panther Minister of Information Eldridge Cleaver in his brief run for the U.S. Presidency on the Peace and Freedom ticket after Cleaver had publicly said that homosexuality was a sickness and compared it to "baby-rape." Kight kept his eyes on the mission of civil rights. In the hierarchy of the radical left, the black civil rights movement as a whole—Black Panthers specifically at the time—was at the top. They were the most radical, well-organized operation of the New Left, the most respected organization, most feared, and the most successful. The Black Panthers was the organization to replicate. To be "trained by the Panthers" had clout in radical circles—though it was sometimes "too radical" for nascent activists. Kight trusted the innate nonviolent nature of the Panther movement.

Leo Laurence, trained in radical organizing from the Black Panther Party, said: "[The Panthers] liked what we were doing. They thought that gay activists were more radical than they were, because we can hide it if we want to—they couldn't [hide their blackness]. They thought that made us more 'revolutionary,' a word that at the time, with the New Left, was very popular."

Stanley Williams: "One of the things Morris organized was a dance in cooperation with the Black Panther Party. A small group of us went to Compton and met with Angela Davis, a prominent leader of the Black Panthers. The meeting was in an ordinary-looking house, but inside it was heavily fortified and guarded with armed men. We were thoroughly frisked upon entering. We did arrange for a dance at the Polish Hall, but it was a colossal dud and accomplished nothing."

Del Whan recalls a GLF meeting at a BPP house in central Los Angeles: "We were a handful of people from GLF; besides Morris and me I think there was another woman. We went down a long, very dim hall in a regular house in South L.A. We passed some of the Black Panther men and women who were lined up in the hall very close to us as we marched past. One young woman gave me a very angry look that spooked me. If looks could kill, hers sure did. At least it killed my brain and my vocal cords. It was clear to me that she had a special dislike or hatred for white women.

"We all sat in chairs, in a circle, in a small brightly lit room. I just remember chairs, no other furniture. It was clear to me that I was just along for the ride so I did not say a peep. It was the Morris show. He and the guys talked about something for about an hour, I think. Then we left; it is all a blur to me.

"Afterwards I mulled over the flash of fury I had seen in the woman's eyes and came to a few conclusions. I was surprised that she appeared to hate me without knowing me. I decided that she must have seen me as a threat. It did not matter to her that I was gay and not a sexual rival. She did not like or trust me. What she probably saw was a young white female tourist who might be bopping into South Central to have an experience with a black man.... I knew I would never go back. The gulf was too big for words to bridge."

Like many women, Whan read Eldridge Cleaver's book *Soul on Ice* and was familiar with his past conviction for rape. "He confessed to thinking that by raping a white woman he could steal the property of the 'Man,' like a trophy prize."

Panthers co-founder Huey Newton was much more philosophical and well-read than Cleaver, and saw the homosexual issue differently. As "Supreme Commander" of the Party, he expressed as much in an August 1970 speech given to the Black Panther Party.

"During the past few years," Newton began, "strong movements have developed among women and among homosexuals seeking their liberation. There has been some uncertainty about how to relate to these movements....

"...we should try to unite with them in a revolutionary fashion.... We want to hit the homosexual in the mouth because we're afraid we might be homosexual, and we want to hit the woman or shut her up because we're afraid that she might castrate us, or take the nuts that we might not have to start with."

It was the most genuine effort on behalf of Panthers to reach out to the gay movement. "We haven't said much about the homosexual at all, and we must relate to the homosexual movement because it's a real thing. And I know through reading and through my life experience, my observations, that homosexuals are not given freedom and liberty by anyone in the society. Maybe they might be the most oppressed people in the society...

"...maybe I'm now injecting some of my prejudice by saying that 'even a homosexual can be a revolutionary.' Quite on the contrary, maybe a homosexual could be the *most* revolutionary..."

Newton's closing salute: "All power to the people!"

Kight had an advance copy of the speech, a two-page letter addressed to all members of the revolutionary movement. He ran to the closest Xerox machine, but first he had to add his commentary. Typed in italics at the top of Newton's letter, Kight added:

"The Gay Liberation Front is indebted to Huey P. Newton, Supreme Commander of the Black Panther Party, for the following letter which he sent to the Panthers about the Women's Liberation and Gay Liberation Movement."

After Newton's closing, Kight typed, in italics: "None of us are free until all of us are free." He then included GLF contact information and the 24-hour Survival-Phone number.

To Kight, this was an important validation of the gay movement.

In the fall of 1970, Regis Philbin again invited two representatives from the Gay Liberation Front to appear on his local Los Angeles TV show *Tempo*. This time, Kight chose himself to appear, representing gay men, and he left it up to the women to choose their representative. They decided that Carolyn Weathers was the best spokesperson.

Weathers: "I was scared to death, not because of coming out as a lesbian, but because I had stage fright. But Regis and [the female co-host] were extremely kind with me. They were more argumentative with Morris because Morris was more assured and was able to bring up points more than I was. I was just talking about how we were tired of people thinking that we were just these women hanging around on street corners with Girl Scout cookies in our pockets, stuff like that—trying to get rid of the stereotypes of homosexuals as depraved child molesters or something."

For television appearances Kight "straightened up," dressed in khakis, closed-collar shirt with a peace pendulum hanging around his neck, and a sports jacket. His hands comfortably folded on his knees, he leaned forward in his chair to listen when other guests spoke and then he'd lean back in his chair and fold either his arms or legs as he spoke aloud and clearly enunciated every valuable word.

Weathers: "That's when Morris mentioned that Gay Liberation Front was going to join the Black Panthers. He said the GLF was going to 'hook up with the Black Panthers.' I didn't know, he hadn't told me that. He threw it out on the program at Regis and that woman.

"I had no idea. He didn't prepare me. I was stunned, but I couldn't act stunned. We're supposed to show unity. In a spirit of gay-lesbian unity, I tried to act unfazed while making no comment. I quietly nodded while Morris was going on about how gay liberation was by God gonna join the Black Panthers. I guess it stunned everybody except Morris, who knew all along that he was going to be saying this. I think he was such an ultimate politician. He had a good political sense."

The announcement on the *Tempo* show spurred more controversy in the GLF. The same Thanksgiving 1970 weekend that GLF pioneers hit Alpine County, Kight also sent a carload of gay libbers to Washington, D.C. for the Black Panthers Revolutionary Constitutional Convention. "Sure enough," Weathers recalls, "I got sent as the woman delegate from the Gay Liberation Front."

Carolyn Weathers: "I think of Morris as the father of it all. He was someone who reached out everywhere."

In late summer of 1970, Kight got itchy for the GLF to join an important rally in Washington, D.C. in November. Organized by the Black Panther Party, the "Revolutionary People's Constitutional Convention" was expected to be *the* radical-activist gathering of the year. Kight talked it up at GLF meetings and prepared a working list titled "Statement of the Male Homosexual Workshop" for the D.C. convention. Typed in all capitals, it listed 18 "demands," with number 17 being: "The full participation of gays in the people's revolutionary army."

Weathers, Platania, Bill Beasley, Ralph Schaffer, and a fourth gay man drove cross-country to represent the GLF at what would basically turn out to be a New Left's Woodstock.

Weathers remembered Bill Beasley, the only black man on the journey, as "very energetic" and that he "frequently mentioned Morris and all the important stuff Morris was fomenting and organizing and orchestrating, which important pies Morris had his fingers in, and what he was working on with Morris. He always extolled Morris with his special brand of energy."

Bill Beasley asked to get out of the car at some point in Texas and took a bus the rest of the way to D.C., explaining that he wanted "to avoid problems that could come up" with one black man riding in a car with three white men and one white woman.

In D.C., Weathers was initially blown away by the gathering: "What a story. The Black Panthers and the hippies, it was just amazing. Commies and Panthers marching through the streets, and this gymnasium full of feminists. It was quite an experience. But I knew we weren't really gonna change the [U.S.] Constitution. There were some people who went there truly believing that's what we were going to do. I knew that that really wasn't gonna happen."

Kight prepared a "Statement of the Male Homosexual Workshop," typed in all capital letters, that was to be read at the D.C. convention. He framed the "homosexual" issue as "sexism" using some Panther jargon: "All Power to the People. The Revolution will not be complete until all men are free to express their love for one another sexually." Five short paragraphs proclaimed that "sexism is irrational, unjust and counter-revolutionary. Sexism prevents the revolutionary solidarity of the people. We demand the struggle against sexism be acknowledged as an essential part of the revolutionary struggle. We demand that all revolutionaries deal individually and collectively, with their own sexism.

"...No revolution without us."

The statement was not read at the convention.

Gay representatives received a lukewarm reception. It was more like "lukecool." GLF's proposal received no consideration for inclusion in the planned revolutionary constitution.

Weathers: "I know it must have been for a really good political purpose or, to [Kight's] credit, some good political purpose to move us along, to shock. I'm sure he realized that it wouldn't go anywhere, but just to show that we tried. We were not getting enough response, so we're gonna get really radical and hook up with this really radical group."

Leaders of the gay movement, on both coasts and everywhere in between, came away from the D.C. convention with a new and profound awareness that attending other people's caucuses with other people's agendas simply did not address the needs of gay people. In the hierarchy of the revolutionary movements of the time, homosexuality was on the bottom rung of the ladder, with transsexuals and transgenders just below that. Even the radical boisterous New Left homosexuals knew that being heard was not the same as screaming and yelling. Kight himself had to admit, sometimes showing up and just being there wasn't as effective as he'd like.

Despite the outreach, the Black Panther Party never did embrace the Gay Liberation Front; even the spark of Huey Newton's speech couldn't ignite much warmth between the two revolutionary factions. Gays remained supportive of (if not a bit confused by) the black civil rights movement.

At the same time, something else was happening on both coasts in gay lib—a loud, more aggressive voice from youth pushing their way to the surface and grabbing control—if not a bit haphazardly, certainly brash and rude. They blamed the Old Left for all the problems of the ubiquitous closet. And the Old Left, if it truly existed in the homophile movement, resented the new movement of street theatrics and public demonstrations.

ALPINE COUNTY

"BROTHER DON HAS A DREAM," SO WENT THE HEADLINE OF THE two-page press release, which appeared in its entirety in the *Los Angeles Free Press* on August 14, 1970. Don Jackson wrote: "I have a recurring daydream. I imagine a place where gay people can be free."

A sparsely settled, rural area in the Sierra mountains in Northern California on the Nevada border, Alpine County had a population of slightly more than four hundred with 384 eligible voters in the June 1970 election. Jackson first proposed his novel idea in December 1969 at the Gay Symposium at Sherwood Forest in Berkeley. He reasoned that lesbian and gay folk could move there, quickly become a majority, govern themselves, and "be free at last." Jackson envisioned a Gay Colony as a "quicker way to freedom."

Kight immediately opposed the idea saying that it smacked of "cultural nationalism," separatism, and would reinforce stereotypes posed by the oppressor culture: "I thought they were all crazy. We can't do that, we can't go into the country. We'd starve to death. I pooh-poohed it. I didn't say that publicly. It was just my private thing."

Fed up with oppression, many still wanted to go away and just be gay. They thought it was a good idea and Jackson discreetly proceeded with his plan for a Gay Mecca with a gay government.

Frustrated by the lack of mainstream media coverage given to the gay movement, about a year later Kight rethought his reaction to the Alpine scheme; he recognized the potential publicity value.

Kight: "I thought, wait a minute, Don Jackson has a capital idea. So I brought together Jon Vincent Platania, Stanley Williams, and Don Kilhefner. The four of us met over at 1501 North Hoover, next door to KCET-TV, and I said, 'Let's do it. Let's take over Alpine County, but don't. Let's agree among ourselves that we'll fake it. That we're going to be serious, we'll stare into the camera and we'll say that we're taking over Alpine County, we're creating dah dee dah dah dah.' And so we held a press conference." (1989, *IMRU*)

A carefully crafted two-page, single-spaced press release said, "A county in California where 200 gays would constitute a majority of registered voters. 479 homosexuals had already signed up to move to Alpine County. Their plan is to demand a special election, vote out all the elected officials and occupy every office, including judge, sheriff, and supervisors—with homosexuals. After the elections, they would make use of the $2 million the county receives annually from state and federal sources."

Jon Platania: "People were just homophobic enough to believe and fear it. We made flyers saying, 'Come to Alpine County, the new Gay Mecca.'"

Harry Kaplan: "There was a great debate going on at the time about whether we should try to separate ourselves as homosexuals from the oppressive rule of straight society and form our own social unit both politically and geographically."

Years later, Kight still laughed when recalling his press conference to say that "the Gay Liberation Front of Los Angeles has met and has voted among ourselves (unanimously, we might add), to take over Alpine County. Very quickly we have

1970. The first gay pride parade (Christopher Street West) on Hollywood Boulevard. Photo by Pat Rocco. Pat Rocco Papers Coll2007-006, ONE National Gay & Lesbian Archives, Los Angeles, California.

1979. CSW Parade, West Hollywood. Photographer unknown. Christopher Street West Association Records, Coll2012-134, ONE National Gay & Lesbian Archives, USC Libraries, University of Southern California.

1990s. CSW Parade, West Hollywood. Photographer unknown. Christopher Street West Association Records, Coll2012-134, ONE National Gay & Lesbian Archives, USC Libraries, University of Southern California.

1979. Steve Berman, Tony Sullivan, Morris at the Oregon/California Border during Briggs Initiative. Photographer unknown. Morris Kight Papers and Photographs Coll2010-008, ONE National Gay & Lesbian Archives, USC Libraries, University of Southern California.

1979. Roy Zucheran and Kight at CSW Festival. Photographer unknown. Christopher Street West Association Records, Coll2012-134, ONE National Gay & Lesbian Archives, USC Libraries, University of Southern California.

1977. At a fundraiser for The Center, Morris appears in Pat Rocco's production of *Brigadoon* at Troupers Hall. Photo by Pat Rocco. Pat Rocco Papers Coll2007-006, ONE National Gay & Lesbian Archives, Los Angeles, California.

1985. Kight and Jim Kepner. Photographer unknown. Christopher Street West Association Records, Coll2012-134, ONE National Gay & Lesbian Archives, USC Libraries, University of Southern California.

1983. Morris and Troy Perry at CSW Festival in West Hollywood. Photo by William S. Tom. William S. Tom Photographs Coll2008-017, ONE National Gay & Lesbian Archives, Los Angeles, California.

1990. TV news cameras look on at Troy Perry, Kight, Bob Humphries at CSW festival opening ceremony. Photographer unknown. Christopher Street West Association Records, Coll2012-134, ONE National Gay & Lesbian Archives, USC Libraries, University of Southern California.

1995. Morris in CSW Parade, West Hollywood. Photographer Jason Whittman. Los Angeles Event Photographs Coll2012-102 ONE National Gay & Lesbian Archives, USC Libraries, University of Southern California.

1982. Back row: Wallace Albertson, Kight, Jim Kepner. Front row: Rand Schrader, Gene La Pietra, Councilwoman Peggy Stevenson, at Circus Disco fundraiser. Photo by George Lear. George Lear Circus Disco Photographs Coll2012-045, ONE National Gay & Lesbian Archives, USC Libraries, University of Southern California.

1979. Morris Kight Tribute at the Ambassador Hotel with (l-r): Sheldon Andelson, Rand Schrader, Wallace Albertson, Troy Perry, Jim Kepner, unidentified male, unidentified male, unidentified female, Ivy Bottini, Gloria Allred, Al Gordon, Pearl Gordon. Photo by Pat Rocco. Pat Rocco Papers Coll2007-006, ONE National Gay & Lesbian Archives, Los Angeles, California.

1977. "No on 6" fundraiser. Unidentified woman, Mervin M. Dymally, Morris, Frank Vel, Gene LaPietra, unidentified man. Photo by Pat Rocco. Pat Rocco Papers Coll2007-006, ONE National Gay & Lesbian Archives, Los Angeles, California.

1991. Outgoing Chief of Police Daryl Gates puts his arms around Councilman Joel Wachs and Morris after Police Commission meeting on August 9; Gates was told to allow police to wear uniforms at Street Fair recruiting booth. Photo by Karen Ocamb. Harold Fairbanks Papers and Photographs Coll2016-009, ONE National Gay & Lesbian Archives, USC Libraries, University of Southern California.

1977. Kight and Mayor Tom Bradley at Mayor's Annual Meeting at Carriage Trade Restaurant. Photo by Pat Rocco. Pat Rocco Papers Coll2007-006, ONE National Gay & Lesbian Archives, Los Angeles, California.

1976. Supervisor Ed Edelman and Morris facing each other at GCSC fundraising drive. Photo by Lee Young for NewsWest. Harold Fairbanks Papers and Photographs Coll2016-009, ONE National Gay & Lesbian Archives, USC Libraries, University of Southern California.

1982. Morris Kight accepts Eason Monroe award from ACLU President Samuel Paz. Photo by Sydney Lee. Sydney Lee Photographs Coll2012046_001, ONE National Gay & Lesbian Archives, Los Angeles, California.

1974. Kight addresses the L.A. City Council at City Hall regarding an employment bill. Photo by Pat Rocco. Pat Rocco Papers Coll2007-006, ONE National Gay & Lesbian Archives, Los Angeles, California.

1974. "The Felon Six," Barbara Gehrke, Jeanne Cordova, Troy Perry, Kight, Al Gordon, Jeanne Barney, Frank Brighamand. Photo by Pat Rocco. Pat Rocco Papers Coll2007-006, ONE National Gay & Lesbian Archives, Los Angeles, California.

1980. Regis Philbin interviews Kight during the pickets at the opening of the movie *Cruisin'*. Photo by Pat Rocco. Pat Rocco Papers Coll2007-006, ONE National Gay & Lesbian Archives, Los Angeles, California.

1974. Morris, Al Gordon, Jeanne Barney (of the Felon Six) at the Police Commission hearing on the Mark IV raid. Photo by Lee Young for NewsWest. Harold Fairbanks Papers and Photographs Coll2016-009, ONE National Gay & Lesbian Archives, USC Libraries, University of Southern California.

1976. Pat Rocco, Sharon Cornelison, Morris at L.A. City Clerk getting parade permit. Photo by David Ghee. Pat Rocco Papers Coll2007-006, ONE National Gay & Lesbian Archives, Los Angeles, California.

1992. At his 73rd birthday celebration, Morris flanked by Sandra and Stephanie Farrington-Domingue. Photo by Karen Ocamb. Harold Fairbanks Papers and Photographs Coll2016-009, ONE National Gay & Lesbian Archives, USC Libraries, University of Southern California.

1997. Michael Weinstein and Morris at AIDS Healthcare Fundraiser. Photographer unknown. AIDS Healthcare Foundation Archive.

1992. Morris bookended by Cate Uccel and Miki Jackson at "The Stoney Awards" for Stonewall Democratic Club. From the personal collection of Miki Jackson.

1979. Morris with Zev Yaroslavsky at Morris Kight Tribute at the Ambassador Hotel. Photo by Pat Rocco. Pat Rocco Papers Coll2007-006, ONE National Gay & Lesbian Archives, Los Angeles, California.

1981. Morris with Ken Schnorr, the first close AIDS casualty. Photo by Pat Rocco. Pat Rocco Papers Coll2007-006, ONE National Gay & Lesbian Archives, Los Angeles, California.

1978. Morris, Harvey Milk, Christopher S. Dogg at McCadden Place. Photo by Elmer Wilhelm. Morris Kight Papers and Photographs Coll2010-008, ONE National Gay & Lesbian Archives, USC Libraries, University of Southern California.

1994. Quentin Crisp, Steven J. McCarthy (a.k.a. Madame Dish), Morris, Charles Chan Massey at Stonewall 25, Waldorf Astoria New York. Photographer unknown. From the personal collection of Charles Chan Massey.

1985. Morris with Julie Harris at AIDS fundraiser. Photo by Pat Rocco. Pat Rocco Papers Coll2007-006, ONE National Gay & Lesbian Archives, Los Angeles, California.

1976. Jane Fonda (center) with Frank Zerilli (Troy Perry's assistant) and Morris Kight. Photo by Pat Rocco. Pat Rocco Papers Coll2007-006, ONE National Gay & Lesbian Archives, Los Angeles, California.

Circa 1980. Gore Vidal with Morris in the yard at McCadden Place. Photo by Pat Rocco. Pat Rocco Papers Coll2007-006, ONE National Gay & Lesbian Archives, Los Angeles, California.

GAY LIBERATION FRONT
SURVIVAL COMMITTEE

Legal Advice
Draft Counseling
V.D. Control

Personal Counseling
Drug Problems
Job Co-op

The following GLF Learn-Ins are designed primarily for members who will be working on the Survival Committee but the sessions are open to any interested brother or sister.

Learn-In # 1:

The Strategy and Techniques of
Gay Draft Counseling

Sunday, July 12
12 Noon
577½ North Vermont

* * * * * * * * *

Learn-In # 2:

Legal First Aid: From Bust to Sentence

This Learn-In will be conducted by a representative of the National Lawyers Guild.

Saturday, July 18
1 p.m.
577½ North Vermont

For further information contact: Howard Fox 386-2618
Don Kilhefner 392-0293 or 392-4563

1970. Flyer for first "Learn-In" of the Gay Liberation Front, Gay Survival Committee. Foster Gunnison, Jr. Papers. Archives & Special Collections at the Thomas J. Dodd Research Center, University of Connecticut Library.

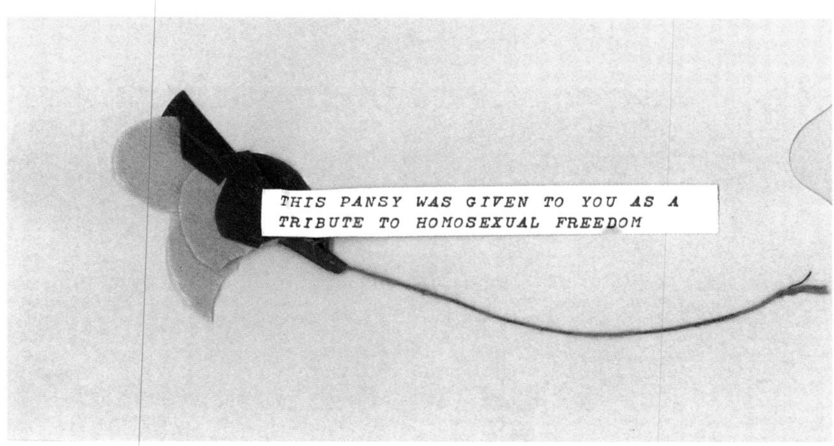

Purple papier-mâché and felt pansies that were made by volunteers and distributed for donations at the first Christopher Street West Parade, June 28, 1970. Foster Gunnison, Jr. Papers. Archives & Special Collections at the Thomas J. Dodd Research Center, University of Connecticut Library.

Post-1970. After the picket and boycott at Barney's Beanery, the owner created matchbooks with the infamous sentiment. From the private collection of Richard A. Meade.

1992. Portrait of Morris Kight by Don Bachardy. ONE National Gay & Lesbian Archives, USC Libraries, University of Southern California.

1995. Morris Kight and Mary Ann Cherry. As the photo was being taken, Morris whispered in my ear, "You're going to want this photo someday." Photographer Unknown. From the private collection of Mary Ann Cherry.

recruited pioneers ready to move and very quickly we expect to move there and establish homes, a university, the first American Lesbian and Gay university where we will teach gay studies. We expect to have farms and ranches and craft shops and we expect to be a citadel of intellectual and activist activity of the part of the lesbian gay community." Kight continued, "The following morning, NBC with one of their famous reporters standing on a piece of land in Alpine County saying, 'I'm standing on the land which has been bought by the Gay Liberation Front. It is here where they are going to build their homes.'

"And I thought, 'Good grief, if he can tell that big a lie, I feel less of a liar than him.' So then, we just held a daily press conference."

It was a media coup. By mid-October, United Press International (UPI) and Associated Press (AP) picked up the story, drawing national attention. Over a hundred local and city newspapers and radio stations covered the Alpine County story, including the one outlet whose refusal to report about gay liberation irritated Kight the most—the *Los Angeles Times.*

"Gay Front move worries Alpine County," was one headline. The Alpine powers-that-were-in-office expressed concerns. "Naturally," the chairman of the board of supervisors was quoted, "We'll do anything and everything we can to prevent anyone taking over our county." According to the *Bedford Gazette* in Pennsylvania, Alpine County's "top elected officials" said that "residents will resist a possible political takeover by the Gay Liberation Front." A week later, the same officials were quoted in a different Pennsylvania newspaper (*Lebanon Daily News*), "There is no way to prevent hundreds of homosexuals from becoming residents and laying the groundwork for a political takeover. If these people come up and abide by the laws there's nothing we can do to prevent them from becoming residents."

Gays and straights were taking the scam seriously. Many lesbians and gays began to organize around it, making plans to uproot their lives and relocate to the region where the sun is seen for only 90 days and the snow falls 25 feet deep.

Howard Fox: "Alpine County, which is really a godforsaken place, not too far from Lake Tahoe, it's a ski resort at times, it's just freezing and no place anybody gay would want to live. But we carried forth with this whole sham. And Morris was giving press reports about how 'the penetration of Alpine County had commenced.'"

The momentum of the scheme was buoyed by Kight's natural humor.

Carolyn Weathers: "We, the gays and lesbians, were going take over Alpine County. We were going to be like the pioneers in the covered wagons. And of course, there was all this brouhaha … we, the Gay Liberation Front were running around [handing out] these buttons saying 'Alpine County or Bust.' People took it up as a great idea. There'd be a guy at GLF sewing blankets and quilts and people were sending food supplies and all this for when we took over Alpine County. [My sister] Brenda thought that actually it was never meant to be, in other words, it was just agitation propaganda to get attention and to further the cause. They never intended for us to really do it, but it got its own momentum. That doesn't mean it wasn't a great idea. Many people took it seriously."

Gay people were quitting their jobs, putting their homes on the market and getting ready to put down deposits on property in Alpine County.

Del Whan: "Morris cooked up the takeover scheme of Alpine County as a publicity stunt, agitprop to get the media attention and bring GLF to public attention. Many gay people took the plan to set up a Gay County seriously and were very upset when they eventually realized that Morris was just making waves to stir up public attention for gay civil rights."

Meanwhile, the Berkeley and San Francisco gay libbers, where Don Jackson was based, were fully engaged in promoting the takeover of Alpine.

Jackson was genuinely excited and inspired by the possibility of a Gay Colony. He wrote or spoke to Kight almost daily with updates and ideas. "Events have changed my concept of what Alpine will be. It has grown into a bigger issue than just Gay Lib or even just Gays. Now, I visualize it as a liberated territory, a bastion of liberty in the status sea, based on the basic libertarian doctrine that a person has a right to do anything he wishes so long as he doesn't harm anyone else…I think the name of our organization should be 'the Alpine Liberation Front.' It is better than Alpine Mobilization Committee. I visualize it growing into a national organization." And "I know it will be a big strain on you, but the Alpine Mobilization may be the biggest accomplishment of your life."

Jackson added a P.S.: "I heard the Alpine County Sheriff on TV last night. He said 'folks are already startin' to move out.' It may be deserted by the time we get there."

Mother Boats, longtime activist and Vice President of Sexual Freedom League, promoted the Alpine Liberation Front in the Bay Area. No one from Los Angeles told their Northern California counterparts that it was an agitprop joke. The scheme was out of control.

Kight was having fun, enjoying the press coverage and being quoted in the news constantly.

"Morris Kight told newsmen Wednesday about a dozen of the GLF members would be on the steps of the [Alpine County] courthouse … Kight said the GLF owns a small tract of land in the area and has options on other property. 'The Washoe Indians have a private alliance with us,' he said, 'and we have a 5-to-20-year plan to preserve the environment of Alpine County.'"

Mother Boats in *Berkeley Barb*: "Gay Liberation is somewhat embarrassed at their omission of the Washoes from their plans to liberate Alpine. A 'faulty intelligence report,' based on typically racist establishment records, caused the mistake."

Jeff Poland of the Berkeley groups wrote to Kight: "Dear Morris—We haven't actually contacted any Indian groups yet (Boats too busy with nude Halloween dance), but this clipping should show them [the Native Americans] how we feel."

A note to 'the file' in Kight's handwriting, dated November 12, 1970: "With tongue-in-cheek [heavily underlined]: Do you think the splendid (future) success of the Alpine County project will cause the U.S. government to send all gay people to Alpine County as a 'reservation'?"

Years later, Kight to Bob Dallmeyer: "Thanksgiving Day 1970, June Herrle, Steve Morrison Beckwith [and Rob Gibson] wanted to have a holiday in the country, so they thought they'd go to Alpine County. They packed picnic lunches and we sent gifts for the natives. There is an Indian family in Alpine County and we sent gifts from gay people, 'giving to our spiritual brothers and sisters' gifts."

The same weekend that car full of GLFers went to D.C., a small caravan of GLF-LA members made its way to Alpine County. Two men and a woman from GLF-LA who posed for photographs in front of the Alpine courthouse were introduced as an advance party to "scout conditions for a planned takeover." (*Times Reporter*, Dover, Ohio).

Kight timed the trip to Alpine for Thanksgiving weekend because holidays are traditionally 'slow news days,' and there was a better chance for coverage. In addition to exercising his media savvy, Kight's natural radar for infiltrators went off.

Kight to Dallmeyer: "In the meantime, we had been infiltrated by an FBI agent, who thought we might really be about to take over the government and he wanted to go along. I said, 'You're welcome to, we welcome everybody. I tell you what you do, there is a pay phone on the main drag in Markleeville [the largest town in Alpine]. You go there and commandeer the phone, and we'll use that as our method of communicating with our troops.'"

In retelling the story, Kight overdramatized the setup. He was not physically in Alpine County.

Kight: "So here was this FBI agent with the phone, 'Hi, NBC, just a moment, here is Mister Morris Kight,' and for three days he was there staffing the phone. And we were using his good offices, FBI has more and better equipment than we have, they have more trucks and everything than we have. Then Steve, June, and Rob had their picnic lunch on the steps of the Alpine County courthouse, munching away."

Howard Fox: "Because it was Thanksgiving Day there was no news, so the networks sent crews to photograph them live from Alpine County. This story made news for weeks and weeks throughout the world. *Time* Magazine wanted to interview us....We told them that we are doing what Ronald Reagan and Richard Nixon and Spiro Agnew have told us to do—that if you are unhappy with the system, use your votes to bring about change. And we were doing this by peaceful means. This was the American way. It was wonderful."

Kepner's copious notes of the GLF meeting include detailed short-term and long-term plans. They had plans for sponsors, legal defense, election coalition strategy, and they even asked themselves: "What are our legal & moral responsibilities to people already there?"

Letter to Kight from Craig Hansen (October 22, 1970): "Alpine County takeover has really caused a ruckus. Why? GLF has done a lot of crazy things which deserved news before and received the silent treatment from the Establishment media. I believe the reason is that we have threatened straight America. We are taking over!"

This was by far Kight's biggest publicity success. Kight already had a reputation as a master manipulator, a practical joker, a little bit of a con man.

Eventually, Kight contacted the Alpine County sheriff, once again introducing himself as a representative of the Gay Liberation Front. Kight suggested they have a town meeting, "a truce session with the county's residents." The sheriff outright rejected the offer.

By mid-December, weather in the high Sierras was quite harsh; temperatures slid down to 15 degrees. No one from Southern California, GLF or otherwise, would be found in Alpine County. "The windy weather," the sheriff was quoted in a newspaper, "was not conducive to visitors." The sheriff felt "the gays have been defeated and repelled.... There's deep white snow on the ground and the icicles are two feet long—Alpine County is a virtual fairyland, but not the kind they want."

In December 1970, Kight's friend Reverend Itkin asked him, in a three-page letter, "out of the spirit of warmest friendship for you," for ideological clarity on why he chose to support the Alpine County project: "Cultural nationalism, by its very nature, is counter-revolutionary." Itkin reminded Kight that he vocally had been opposed to the entire idea. "We were," Itkin wrote, "at that [previous] time, in perfect agreement."

Kight received a lot of mail, anonymous and otherwise, regarding Alpine County—pro and con.

Kight: "Then it was time to blow the bubble. We announced that our forces had grown too large and Alpine County simply wouldn't hold us and we were moving on to somewhere else. And we gradually killed the story off."

Kight made up a story that "real estate agents returned deposits on property when they discovered that the prospective buyers were homosexuals."

UPI and AP reported Alpine County's "Victory over homosexuals." Mid-December mainstream news headlines began to read: "Gay Front Delaying Invasion," quoting Kight, "'We'll have to take the real estate agents to court on a civil liberties issue just like the blacks did in the South—because we're an ethnic minority, too.' Kight, 51, a former hotel operator who says he 'dropped out' 10 years ago to organize against sexism, poverty and racism, said the planned migration to Alpine will attract about 1,070 'pioneers.'

"'The earliest possible date for the migration will be sometime next spring if the courts clear the way for homosexuals to purchase Alpine County property,' Kight said."

In the spring of 1971, UPI reported, in usual Kight humor: "New site eyed by Gay Front," naming Bankhead Springs, a 224-acre town just east of San Diego, as the new target for the Gay Liberation Front. The article said that real estate inquiries were made by "the homosexual group" and that if the purchases happened, "the town would be exclusively for homosexuals. It would be called Mt. Love and would be divided into 1,000 quarter-acre lots."

As late as August and September 1971, newspaper stories continued across the country.

A huge publicity success for the gay movement did not boost Kight's reputation among his gay lib peers. Kight didn't want to risk ruining the scheme if he let Jackson in on his real intention to use Alpine County solely as an agitprop tool. Jackson sent Kight typed letters to keep the Bay Area press alerted as Kight instructed, often stroking the older man's ego: "I gave the *Chronicle* your phone number. The people giving interviews should be rotated. The young longhairs are best for relating to the younger Gay Lib types, but you do some of the interviews to give dignity to the project. Your name won't have to appear in the press very many more times before you are listed in 'Who's Who.'"

Don Jackson, more philosophical and idealistic about the Alpine plan, wrote to Kight: "It's getting so your name is in the paper every day. Both of our names have become household words in the Bay Area. Radio and TV talk shows discuss our ideas. People on buses talk about Alpine. That's what barbers and hair burners discuss with their customers. If the Alpine project succeeds, it will be an event of profound historical importance. Historians will write books about it. School textbooks will contain its story. Biographers will come to write the life story of Morris Kight. Alpine County, Gay Liberation Front, Morris Kight and Don Jackson will all be listed as subjects in the encyclopedias. Enough of this ego tripping and down to immediate issues.... If the Alpine project fails, it will have a very demoralizing effect on the Gay Community, causing immense disillusionment, disappointment and return to the closets. If it succeeds, Gay liberation will become the most powerful movement in America. The whole future history of this nation depends on what happens at Alpine."

Kight and Jackson's relationship never recovered from the betrayal. It achieved what Kight set out to achieve—worldwide coverage of gay liberation. In mid-1971, Kight wrote: "A vast number of stations have all but ignored our existence, except the recent 'Alpine County' news story which was covered well."

Gay liberation was no longer ignored by the establishment media and it was becoming a topic of conversation in American homes. Another of Kight's goals achieved.

Del Whan: "Morris preferred to manipulate the nascent gay liberation movement and affairs of state from his home base."

Rob Cole: "I found Morris to be a charmer, a bit of a con man who actually delivered most of the time.... He had a genius for getting media attention."

Platania: "That is what makes Morris the ultimate trickster. He was a man of spirit, politically sophisticated, outraged, outrageous, and maligned."

Kight ran two demonstrations, Alpine and D.C., from his home phone in Los Angeles.

People not familiar with Kight's abstract thinking could easily confuse his antics as mean-spirited or self-serving. Certainly, many of his detractors were quick to note, and often, that Kight received as much press attention as gay liberation. The confusion continued for years: was it a joke or was it a genuine effort that backfired; was it a joke *on* gay people or a joke *by* gay people? All the critics pointed out that Morris Kight's name appeared in every press release. There were no press releases until Kight became involved. He crafted a strategy and parked gay liberation into the consciousness of America. It wasn't always delicate. Other leaders of the movement partook in the sham, yet all responsibility for the collapse of Don Jackson's dream was placed heavily and solely on Kight. The media coverage wasn't always appreciated as the great triumph.

Kight's reputation as being stubborn and self-aggrandizing was sealed at the expense of what Kight saw as a huge success. New York activists were appropriately impressed with the amount of attention the zap garnered; Alpine County received far wider press coverage than the rebellion at the Stonewall Inn. The crazy idea stirred discussions about civil liberties and the constitutional rights of homosexuals. Whatever his intentions, the Alpine County demonstration would follow Kight for the rest of his life—for better and for worse.

In 1975, in a follow-up to the Alpine County scheme for the *Los Angeles Times*: "Both Kight and Kilhefner admit the announced move was 'pretty much guerrilla theater from the beginning.'"

In the same article, an Alpine County resident said, "I don't think they're as dangerous as we thought at the time," and that he had come to realize that probably homosexuals already lived in Alpine. "But none are 'out of the closet' that I know of," he added.

One raised consciousness at a time was the best they could do.

LESBIANS AND FEMINISM

MEETING SPACE WAS ALWAYS AN ISSUE. ANY MODEST VENUE WOULD do; by late summer 1970 the GLF had outgrown every meeting location, including Harry and John's Kaleidoscope Factory. A sublet from the Peace Action Council opened up (555 Vermont Avenue), and Kight grabbed it for the GLF. At the same time, the GLF rented a storefront, 4400 Melrose Avenue, for its main headquarters and intended for it to be used as a coffeehouse.

Kight (to Cain): "We decided to also open a coffeehouse and were trying to provide hospitality at a low cost. And since we had lots of space, there were so many homeless people, an apartment house next door had declared their mattresses and mattress pads surplus. And we went over and salvaged them and at night put them on the floor. And as a result, it became a 'death trap.' The Los Angeles police came to see me at my home, and said, 'Mr. Kight, we know of your low opinion of us. And we're trying to deal with that, and we know you're trying to deal with it. We also can be right. Pay attention to us. You have created a monster. There are going to be killings. There are going to be deaths.'"

Male domination in the GLF created the most complicated and divisive internal discussions. The women's liberation movement preceded gay liberation by almost a decade and ushered in a time of profound personal examination and social change. All women were forced to examine their personal decisions under a new light of choice, and not all women were drawn to "liberation" or to join the rank and file of feminists. Deeply committed individuals corrected outrageous inequities toward women.

Kight intellectually understood the need for a feminist movement. Even though he described himself as "always feminist," he did not innately embrace the women's cause, not in the same way he embraced the antiwar, civil rights and gay rights movements. Always the gentleman, Kight could support a woman's abilities—though not all women's. It is not likely that he ever had a female superior except for Bessie; his relationship with the one female co-worker that is known about—Marcia Silverstein in the Dow Action group—would not be considered equitable.

Little is documented on the subject of women in the GLF. Kight's "tentative suggestions" dated April 1970, with his handwritten note in the margin: "proposal MLK adopted" (before he abandoned his middle name Lee). The second item on his suggestions is "Women: More and more are coming to us. Would they like an all-female caucus, and if so, what do they want? This would represent the female viewpoint within the total framework of GLF/LA."

His abilities to shepherd the women the same way he helped young men through this revolutionary period were limited. Ironically, because it was similar to the approach the early "homophile" movement used toward gay rights, his approach was weighted with intellectualism. He was onerously academic, so he could at least give lip service to the feminist movement.

Kight often spoke of the women's suffrage movement and their "major major revolution in getting women the vote.... The right to vote is only just a tiny part of feminism. And so, then we had to have a new movement, a brand new one. Which is not nearly, nearly done."

The feminist movement was incredibly well-organized and by many measures successful, but fractured under the conflicts between lesbians and heterosexual women. Not all feminists had the same concerns. When gay feminist women in New York expressed their unique concerns within the broader women's movement, the lesbian activists were quickly labeled the "Lavender Menace" by their feminist counterparts.

Conditions were not better for women within the gay lib movement where they were outnumbered by a ratio of sometimes 20 men to one. Sexism was rampant in the GLF. The women were called "girls" and the men didn't like being labeled "male chauvinists." Gay men, with a few exceptions, didn't immediately identify with the feminist movement. Gay men were oppressed and could not see themselves as oppressors. Many rationalized that they needed to undo their own oppression first, then they'd help women.

Men wanted to have GLF meetings at Liberation House, which was not an appropriate venue for public meetings—meetings that included women-slash-feminists-slash-lesbians.

In the midst of a unique revolution against patriarchal principles, women's voices were not soft; their voices were scarce and easily discounted. They remained patient, constantly waiting for their turn to set an agenda or create a goal that addressed their needs. It was not to be. Lesbians who came to the GLF soon realized that they were inferiors to the men. The social services in GLF, while unique and much needed, were geared almost exclusively to men. Lesbians realized their unique needs would not be addressed in the general population of the movement.

Women tried to communicate with men. Minutes from one July GLF meeting note Del Whan's comments: "We are tending more and more to treat each other and all outsiders as enemies. Need to do more welcoming." She proposed a rap session between men and women before the meeting. The minutes read: "Ralph opposes, but suggests going to a restaurant afterwards."

Examples set by The Daughters of Bilitis (the first lesbian rights group formed in San Francisco, 1955) gave lesbians an organizational backbone. It was never likely that they'd stop organizing. They walked out of the GLF in August of 1970 to form the Gay Women's Caucus.

Del Whan: "The women met about three or four times at the GLF office on Vermont, but then the group moved to the Women's Center on Crenshaw. Some of the women were not comfortable meeting at GLF because of the men."

From the GLF Weekly Schedule, August, 1970: "Tuesday nights, 7:30: 'Lavender Menace' rap sessions dealing with personal and social liberation of the minority within a minority. Male chauvinists beware!"

Whan: "I wanted to start a center just for gay women. I felt that lesbians were somewhat hidden in the closet (even at the Women's Center on Crenshaw). Eventually we moved our meetings to an upstairs apartment above a store at 1910 South Vermont.

"As there were so few women in GLF, I ran an ad in the *L.A. Free Press* for 'the Women's Caucus of the Gay Liberation Front' to have its initial meeting. Art Kunkin, the publisher of the *Los Angeles Free Press*, actually called me to see if I was a real person and not a crank nut. Satisfied that I was really a movement activist, Kunkin ran the ad."

Amid the split between men and women, gay liberation versus feminism, the Gay Women's Caucus found their footing through their own leadership. Some women still attended the general GLF meetings, but all the women were militant with men, and with each other, about root causes of oppression, which seemed endless. Under the self-imposed burden of good manners and democracy, they just "talked themselves to death."

Women's liberation was partly about nomenclature and the Gay Women's Caucus would argue among themselves about being called a gay women's group or a feminist group.

Whan: "After much debate about names the women decided to change their name to Lesbian Feminists. I did not care much what we called ourselves so long as we got our members out of the closet and were able to help other women still suffering from homophobia, low self-esteem, alcoholism, drugs, [suicidal thoughts], and discrimination."

Kight had been impressed by the few women leaders who were around at the time. He watched very closely as the women organized, waiting for the natural leaders to rise to the surface. He wanted to work with them. He continued to invite women to the GLF meetings and zaps, and some women continued to participate, and some preferred to organize on their own.

Sandy Blixton, a young man active in the GLF, wrote (in *Out of the Closets: Voices of Gay Liberation*): "Many of the men resented the departure of the women and held fast to their sexist behavior. Other brothers began to deal with their own sexism and found a new revolutionary method of updating Marxist class analysis."

The men missed the organizing muscle that women brought to the movement. Attempts to reconcile were unsuccessful. GLF member Craig Hansen wrote an open letter to the "Women's Gay Liberation," in an attempt to better resolve the issues. It illuminates the men's attitudes.

Hansen's four-page analysis, typed single-spaced, details similarities and differences in their shared oppression followed by a telling four-point summarization of a solution "for the women."

Sandy Blixton: "It seems that as long as gay liberation is a male-dominated movement, we will not be able to win the battle against sexism."

Kight and all gay men made women's liberation and lesbian needs a new frontier. Over time, gay men changed their rhetoric, using "women" and "sisters" when addressing their fellow revolutionaries. After many hours of consciousness-raising, gay men came to realize that they shared a common oppressor with women—the sexist, male-dominated culture—and that, in fact, freedom for one without freedom for everyone was no freedom at all.

Mina Meyer: "As time went on and feminism left its mark, they [gay men] knew not to fuck with [feminism] too much."

The division was not resolved and would become more antagonistic and counterproductive before unity.

Whan: "Despite his non-democratic tendencies, his insensitivity to women's issues, his behind-the-scenes manipulation of events (he was always on the phone with public officials or the *Los Angeles Times* or other movers and shakers), I always had deep respect and gratitude for Morris because he lit the spark in my consciousness about my own oppression as a gay person. He was the first publicly 'out' gay person with such an affirming and militant pro-gay-rights approach to life. Morris was a phenomenon!"

Meyer: "It's easy to disagree with Morris and still be friends with him."

DIAGNOSIS: GAY

PROBABLY NO MAINSTREAM PROFESSION, INCLUDING LAW ENFORCEment and organized religion, administered crueler treatment or did more harm to homosexuals than those representing the mental health profession. The psychologists and psychiatrists of the twentieth century adhered to draconian beliefs, without any medical basis, declaring homosexuality abnormal and something to be "cured." Modern barbaric treatments included electroshock therapy, isolation, and sometimes lobotomies.

In 1965 Dr. Evelyn Hooker, psychologist and an early non-homosexual advocate, began significant research to support the removal of homosexuality as a diagnosed mental illness.

With few exceptions, the psychiatric profession posed serious hazards to the survival of homosexuals. Kight and other leaders recognized that the diagnostic code needed to change before gays could be safe with headshrinkers and the like.

In 1970, protests began against the American Psychiatric Association in San Francisco and Chicago, and at the Federal Building in downtown Los Angeles. Nothing garnered the desired response nor was given any media coverage.

Stanley Williams: "Morris arranged for a 'Scream-In' at the office of a psychiatrist who claimed he could cure homosexuality with a 'Primal Scream.' That demonstration drew about ten people."

The American Psychiatric Association slightly upgraded homosexuality as a "perversion" in its list of disorders. GLF-LA responded with a one-page "Position Statement," clearly penned in Kight's voice:

"Let it be known that the Gay Liberation Front of Los Angeles categorically opposes the NAMH's 'Position Statement on Homosexuality and Mental Illness' on all counts. At best, it is only token liberalism and does not deal with the real problems of the homosexual community in the United States; at worst, it is constructed on a basis of out-and-out lies.

"If the NAMH has a sincere desire to understand and aid the homosexual in the United States, it should spend its time less on such meaningless paper and closed conferences and more in open honest communication with the homosexual community at large. It is long past time when the homosexuals should cease being considered in such terms as 'mental illness,' 'deviational behavior,' and 'abnormal.' The truth of the homosexual lifestyle as an acceptable sexual alternative must be made clear once and for all.

"WHO HAS GIVEN YOU THE RIGHT TO ESTABLISH THE DEFINITION OF OUR BEING?

"WHAT HOMOSEXUALS WERE CONSULTED CONCERNING THE VALIDITY OF YOUR POSITIONS?

"WHY WAS NO MENTION OF THE FEMALE HOMOSEXUAL MADE?

"Homosexuals in America are at last standing up and demanding the right to define their own humanity. No longer will we stand by passively and allow you to tell us who we are. YOU WILL DEAL WITH US OPENLY AND HONESTLY OR BY DIRECT CONFRONTATION—BUT YOU WILL DEAL WITH US.

"LET MY PEOPLE GO!"

Kight to Dallmeyer: "The American Psychiatric Association ordered its annual convention to be held at the Biltmore Hotel in downtown Los Angeles. We learned that a British psychologist was coming to do a slide show on curing homosexuality. How this monster was doing that was through aversive conditioning, behavioral modification-aversion therapy. He would have you describe a gay experience [and] in the meantime, negative things would be going on, very glum music would play and you'd be seeing ugliness on the slides.... This monster was interrupting a natural evolutionary process. And so we of the GLF planned to attend his lecture. The men wore jackets and ties—well, some of the women wore jackets and ties too, by the way—and off we went to the Biltmore Hotel."

In contrast, Carolyn Weathers remembers gay libbers dressed in hippie clothes with roach clips. When the lights were down, Kight and the band of GLFers surreptitiously snuck in through a series of doors and quietly sat down, dispersed throughout the lecture room.

Weathers: "Dr. Philip Feldman from England was presenting this program. And he had a video of this young man who [he] was trying to cure of his homosexuality. And he would show the young man a tape of a beautiful woman and there would be no electric shock. He'd show him a tape of a handsome young man, he'd [receive an] electric shock. I remember Sharon turned to me and said she was curiously offended because lesbians weren't even in it."

Howard Fox: "I have this friend Steve Morrison who has a loud booming voice, and as the film was being shown he shouted out, 'How much of this shit are we going to sit here and watch?'"

Weathers: "And that was our cue. The rest of us stood up. It was mixed men and women, [maybe] 30 of us. And we all stood up and said, 'Hell no,' and we got out of our seats and walked up to the stage and would not let Dr. Feldman proceed with his presentation. He wasn't pleased about that."

Lights came up and "GLFers started agitating for an end to this nonsense."

Weathers: "We would stamp our feet on the stage too, for the hell of it, I guess, it was revolutionary-like. And then, one by one, whoever felt like it would go up to the podium and tell the people, 'You've been, excuse me, you've been fucking with us for so long and telling us that we're not worth a shit, you have screwed up so many young gay and lesbian people, you're gonna listen to us for a change.' It was that kind of [demonstration]. Brenda went up and said something, and of course a lot of the guys did. And when we saw people in the audience weren't listening, we stamped our feet again. And finally we were able to end this presentation. And those who came to see Dr. Feldman had to accept that. We just were adamant that that would not take place that day."

Fox: "Don Kilhefner went up to the microphone and made an announcement that we were the Gay Liberation Front of Los Angeles and we were taking over the meeting. That we were going to divide the participants into small groups and that there were going to be workshops and that we would reconvene in an hour or two to discuss what had taken place. In the interim, we were going to teach them about something that they knew nothing about, which was, what it is to be gay. Some of the doctors were incensed and outraged. One man in particular was just livid [and] furious that we were doing this to them, and finally his colleagues calmed him down. He threatened to call the police, and we said 'Fine, go ahead. The media needs to see how professionals treat people whom they claim are sick.'"

Brenda Weathers addressed the room of mental health professionals with a few words on behalf of lesbians. The lecture portion of the GLF demonstration was over.

Carolyn Weathers: "We did ask the people who attended the psychiatrists' convention to join us in small groups, talk to us. And eventually they did decide to do that. The men and women of the Gay Liberation Front would talk to groups of three, five, six of the psychiatrists. And many of them said it was the first time they realized they were talking to well, and happy, gays and lesbians. They'd always only encountered people who'd been made so miserable by it [because of homophobia]. But they did come seeking cures, [their] so-called cures. Contact was made and it was the beginning of contact with the American Psychiatric Association."

Del Whan: "We gathered in groups around the room to discuss our concerns and answer their questions. After an hour of this peaceful encounter, Morris [from the podium] thanked everybody ever so graciously for listening to us and we left. What a great success."

Kight had prepared a typed two-page leaflet detailing the GLF's position to distribute to the mental health professionals: "Homosexuality is not a sickness," ending with: "Recommendation to Psychiatrists and Behaviorists: when a client suffers from stress resulting from oppression of homosexuals in our society, she or he should be referred to: Gay Liberation Front [with complete contact information]."

In November 1974, psychologist Albert R. Marston, who was chairman of the same meeting, wrote: "That workshop, led by M.P. Feldman, of the University of Birmingham in England, dealt with his research on using aversion therapy for the treatment of homosexuals. About 45 minutes after the meeting began, during a film showing aversion therapy, about 50 to 60 members of the Los Angeles chapter of the Gay Liberation Front stood and protested Feldman's presentation, and particularly the film. Taking over the microphone, they demanded to speak to the mental health professionals. After some heated moments, during which there was a threat of police intervention, a plan to complete the meeting was agreed on. The plan involved an hour of small-group interaction between the mental health professionals and representatives of the Gay Liberation Front (GLF). During that hour of small discussion sessions, a number of ideas were presented by the members of the GLF. In addition to these ideas, other thoughts were stimulated by the discussion."

Marston and most of the other professionals at the meeting came to learn that "many homosexuals feel that psychology has been used by the state and society as a means of punishing the homosexual, often through imprisonment or institutionalization."

There were many nonviolent protests. Eventually mental health professionals developed new positions regarding homosexuality. In 1973, the American Psychiatric Association removed homosexuality from the list of mental disorders and in 1975, the American Psychological Association followed suit.

In January 1971 Kight spoke at a symposium hosted by the California State Psychological Association in San Diego under the name "Morris Kight, PhD." It was not an uncommon mistake and one that Kight never corrected.

MILITARY AFFAIRS

MORRIS KIGHT ENVISIONED A GAY LIBERATION MOVEMENT THAT purposely didn't allot for gays in the military—because his utopian gay world was one without war. For better or for worse, the early gay movement was very directly infused with Kight's ideology of pacifism.

Kight to Cain: "I believe the military should be eliminated in this country and all other countries. I think it's an anachronism, and a vulgar excess, and it costs a lot of money, and it drains away person-power."

Despite his personal feelings about the military and war (the Vietnam War in particular), his experience taught him that many people found valuable opportunities in the service. He recognized the value of an honorable discharge and that it was important to avoid a "dishonorable" discharge on the grounds of being homosexual. Kight dealt with the mountains of paperwork that any discussion with the Defense Department would entail. Kight did not take this effort on by himself—the U.S. Military was a Goliath of an opponent and the fight against it would require a small army of Davids.

In the Vietnam War era, as an extension of the work that Kight began in the 1950s, the Gay Survival Committee offered draft counseling and help to gays who were already in the military. Men, gay and straight, paused in a 'moment of truth' when faced with the final box on the military intake form asking about "homosexual tendencies." At the time, it was not uncommon for some heterosexuals to exploit the Armed Forces' disdain and rejection of "sexual deviants." Some "straights" attempted to "queer out" (pretend to be a homosexual) to avoid the draft. This tactic was not always successful.

Rob Cole for the *Advocate* (July 8, 1970): "The rule of thumb is, you're straight unless you can prove otherwise—at least, until you're actually in the service. 'We've had some weird ones in here,' said the [Army station] spokesman. 'Some come in claiming to be card-carrying members of a "homo" society; several arrived dressed in women's clothing, and some carry on as effeminately as possible to impress us.' Many of these were inducted anyway."

Kight received letters from all over the world and he responded to every single request for information on "your organization." There were pleas for help with parents, friends or colleagues, from confused men in small towns living heterosexual lives curbing, or perhaps denying, their homosexual instincts, and weighing their options in life. One letter-writer said that he was "still feeling (if not groping) my way." Perhaps the most heart-twisting of the letters came from servicemen—confused, frightened, and without guidance.

The GLF draft counseling differed from Don Slater's efforts through the Homosexual Information Center (HIC). Slater focused on respectability for gay servicemen, GLF focused on a dual-pronged problem: there were homosexuals who didn't want to be drafted and there were homosexuals already in the military who wanted out.

Peter Sorgin and Dick Nash, a Unitarian minister, ran the draft counseling arm of the GLF. The Military Affairs division of the GSC benefited from Slater's and Kight's counseling experience. Kight also lent his public relations expertise, consulted with them when asked, and did whatever was requested. He used his few valuable connections in Washington, D.C. to make introductions and then he stepped out of the way and let it happen. He very much wanted this program to be successful, but he felt his skills were best used developing other social service programs; Kight felt his strengths were program creation and development and some administration in the beginning but he liked to keep moving. It was his personal style to not stay on one thing very long past the launching.

The GLF-LA professionally printed an impressive three-fold hand-out titled "Revolutionary Homosexual Draft Resistance." It outlines: "The Gay Liberation Front of Los Angeles follows the general guidelines for the method of homosexual draft resistance initiated in 1967 by the Homosexual Information Center. Of the thousands of men who have followed these procedures, NOT ONE HAS BEEN INDUCTED!"

The GLF-LA also mimeographed and sent to other gay organizations around the country a five-page document with very specific instructions on "How to Organize a Draft Resistance Program."

All appeals to the Justice Department were "handled free of charge by GLF."

The GLF of Los Angeles ended the important document with a final statement:

"If he gets 'cold feet' and decides not to follow our advice, we will not hold it against him. He can come to us for help at any time, even after he is inducted, and we will do everything possible to assist him. But as a civilian agency, it is harder for us to protect a man's right once he is in the service."

In October 1970, the Gay Liberation Front sent the first of many letters addressed to the Secretary of Defense, Secretary of the Navy, Surgeon of the Commanding Headquarters of the Army, Naval Commanding Officer, U.S.S. *DeHaven* Commanding Officer, Congressman Beall Jr., ACLU c/o Frank Kameny, and the Committee to Fight Exclusion of Homosexuals from the Military Service c/o Don Slater. A well-written, concise two-page letter from the "Chairman of Military Counseling of The Gay Liberation Front of Los Angeles" was the first of its kind, and explained that they provide assistance in arranging the immediate separation from the United States Naval service for a person whose name has since been redacted from the file.

"Our goal," the GLF letter explained, "is to protect the civil liberties, civil rights and human rights of homosexual men and women. This we have been able to do in many creative, legal and non-violent ways. [This] request is based upon his proclaimed homosexuality, and strong Department of Defense and Naval Regulations regulating such conduct. His statement to us is: 'Since coming into the Navy, I have discovered that I am a homosexual.'"

The GLF tipped the argument in their favor by using the military's own rules against them.

"'I didn't realize this at the time I enlisted,' the 'Subject's' statement continued. 'It was something I now realize I wouldn't admit to myself because of the social stigma attached to homosexuality. With constant contact with other sailors in the Navy, I began to feel more and more pressure on myself, especially during extended periods at seas, and I finally came to realize and accept the fact that I am a homosexual.

"'I am aware that homosexuals are not wanted in the service and that homosexual acts constitute a court martial offense, and because of the increasing emotional and mental pressures I am facing, I request assistance from Morris Kight and the Gay Liberation Front in securing a discharge.'

"...Therefore," the letter continues, "we ask that [Subject] be honorably discharged, and at the earliest possible time from the United State Naval Service."

The Commanding Officer of the U.S.S. *DeHaven* issued a three-page, 12-point report on the case, including a request for an immediate FBI investigation.

Probably nothing could get the ire of the FBI more than GLF's involvement with military affairs. In November 1970, the GLF warranted its very own FBI file, which began with this entry:

"Requesting desired investigation based upon receipt of a letter written on the letterhead of the GAY LIBERATION FRONT OF LOS ANGELES (GLFLA), requesting subject be given a honorable discharge from the Navy, in view of being a homosexual."

Please note: the GLF brought many cases to the attention of the military, representing young men on both sides of the draft notice.

Jerry Denning was one of many that came to the GLF for help with military problems and stayed with the organization to help others. "I had heard about, through the *Advocate*, a certain organization called the GLF—I felt it was necessary to have some kind of organization behind us. In October 1970 I made my initial foray into the battle with the Air Force by contacting the GLF and asking them if they could be of assistance. I became in rather steady contact with Peter Sorgin, who was then in charge of the Military Affairs Committee of the GLF, and through the course of things, I met the energetic and the irrepressible Morris Kight."

Denning told Bob Dallmeyer: "In the early days, everybody [in GLF] had a job to do. I was living in Santa Monica on the beach in rather grand style and I met a man at a local bar ... heard him discussing at the other end of the bar with some friends about how difficult life was for him. He was an attractive young blond fellow wearing eyeglasses.... I decided in the conversation with Jeff, his name was Jeff, to counsel him and guide his course through a petition to the Air Force for an honorable discharge on the basis of his incompatibility because they would not have homosexuals in the service. We decided to really go for it. One of the little hooks in all of this was that Jeff's father was a Lieutenant Colonel, still active in the service, also in the Air Force. Jeff decided to go for it and be brave."

Jerry Denning proved to be a valuable asset to the GLF. He had served in the military on staff for a U.S. four-star general and studied law in college. He was quickly drafted by the GLF to write all the legal briefs for the Military Affairs division of the GLF, not just for his friend's case.

Denning: "[Jeff Orth] became a rather celebrated case. At Christmastime of 1970, the Air Force had already been informed for one month that Jeff had intended petition for discharge from the Air Force. He was on the security police [force] at Edwards AFB. They immediately suspended his action and put him into a holding facility, where he had a room to himself. Actually it was kind of convenient."

Denning: "[The GLF] thought that [a Christmas Day picket of the Commanding General's residence] was a spectacular idea. We bought a bunch of Christmas trees—naked, empty Christmas trees—and signs that we had made up ourselves saying 'Free Jeff Orth," and 'Happy Christmas General So-and-So.' We really had a fun time of it. The GLF ... got about eight or ten persons—they were drag queens and longhairs and the strangest group of people that I have ever anticipated seeing. And every one of them was deeply and profoundly committed to the support of this effort, on behalf of a stranger who they had never met, they had never seen, or never heard of.

"The Commanding General ruled in favor of the petition and shortly thereafter Jeff received an honorable discharge on the basis of his incompatibility with the service."

The Military Affairs department of the GLF helped many homosexuals extricate themselves from the military's grip.

The FBI made many notes of this service provided by the GLF.

MORRIS AND THE PRESS

IN A 1988 *LOS ANGELES TIMES* PROFILE ON KIGHT, JIM KEPNER talked about Kight's highly effective "inventiveness and rashness and campiness," and added, "I swear he could smell [the news media]."

As already discussed, Kight had earned considerable clout with the press during his efforts with the Dow Action Committee and he used those connections for gay liberation. He appeared a number of times on national television and radio programs. In January 1969, he appeared on the Joe Pyne show sitting opposite Alan Stang who was speaking on behalf of the conservative advocacy group, the John Birch Society. Kight and Stang debated who was at fault in the riots at the 1968 Chicago Democratic National Convention.

Joe Pyne liked Kight. As the innovator of debate-style talk-shows, he only wanted the most articulate and controversial as guests. Kight could take the mandatory acerbic insult at the top of the show and cleverly debate whoever sat across from him. Sitting across from Alan Stang no doubt contributed to Kight's false reputation as being communist, as anyone who opposed the views of the John Birch Society was automatically labeled "communist."

The media connections paid off immeasurably in the Alpine County scheme. It increased Kight's profile and his ego grew exponentially, as did resentments from the homophiles. Harry Hay was overheard saying (he probably said it many times), "Don't ever get in between Morris and a camera."

Platania: "Everybody in those days was kind of a media freak. We laid it all on the line so if we were going to get anywhere, we needed media attention."

Kight to Cain: "I was looked upon as a father figure, because I was old enough to be the father of most of the people who joined. I was admired for my long association with radical causes. I was admired because I'd been much in the press and on the Joe Pyne Show many times. NBC, CBS, and so on. I was admired for that. I was admired because people thought I had ideas."

Kight kept contacts for every media outlet handy. A neatly handwritten list of names and numbers on one of his many yellow legal-sized notepads, with cross-outs and scribbles as people left one outlet for another.

Jeanne Barney: "For a time I was editor of *Newswest*. He used to call me every day and he'd say, 'This is Morris Kight…', and he'd [list the pertinent happenings or events that he was involved with] and he'd hang up. No pleasantries, pretty much the first call of the day. And then [after] I left *Newswest*, we didn't talk anymore."

The first time that Barney met Kight in person was at an open house at the Center. "In the old Victorian building," is how she remembers the meeting. At the time, Barney wrote a popular advice column for the *Advocate*.

"I don't think there were any chairs in the room," Barney recalls. "The only chair I remember was a peacock chair in the corner and that was where Morris was sitting, wearing as much turquoise as he possibly could. I went over and introduced myself to him and he said, 'Oh yes, my dear, we tried to get you fired.' He and Craig Schoonmaker [of Homosexuals Intransigent] tried their darnedest to get me fired because I was a heterosexual woman. Dick Michaels wouldn't do it. My column was the most popular thing right after the personal ads."

Because of Kight's "pushiness," he got a lot of GLF members on television, on radio, and many were quoted in the press.

Leo Laurence: "Morris arranged for me to appear on a TV show—don't remember the name of the show, the moderator liked to have opposing groups. I clearly remember the moderator got an outspoken homophobic on the same show; when I talked about gay rights he would interrupt and talked crazy. Whenever he would start getting crazy I would just look at him and say, 'all right, so you're a bigot.' The show got out of hand."

Del Whan: "I spoke on a Sunday night radio show (to represent lesbians) with Morris, who represented the gay male, Virginia Prince (represented as a transvestite male), and Christine Jorgenson (male-to-female transsexual). Morris set it all up, I believe. I was amazed at how little we had in common [within the GLBT community]."

In fact, sometimes it became obvious across the airwaves how little the various factions within the gay movement had in common with each other.

On another occasion, at Kight's behest, Del Whan appeared on a local Los Angeles television variety show to debate the prim and properly coiffed Helen Andelin, author of *Fascinating Womanhood* and founder of the Fascinating Womanhood Movement. Andlein, in her white kid gloves, was a prominent spokesperson for traditional women's roles, advised women to fulfill their obligations within traditional marriages and advocated living "as God intended." In other words, she was the antithesis of a lesbian feminist.

Whan: "Maybe it was because I was feeling a bit intimidated by Helen in her pink dress and high heels. In that situation I forgot to hit any political rhetoric high notes. Morris had not prepped me for what I should say. I was just a gay woman and about the only one available for such a mission.

"Morris didn't think I did a very good job. Our segment followed an act where a guy swallowed a live goldfish."

Through the 1970s Kight kept a busy and open schedule of public appearances. If invited, he'd be there. He was a featured speaker at the People's Army Jamboree to talk about Gay Liberation. He and Troy Perry spoke at Valley College for a program titled "20th-Century Dialogues." In December 1970, Kight appeared on a local KRLA public service series, *The Communication Gap*, speaking on behalf of all gay persons.

Daily, he received requests for information on gay liberation and "your organization" from all over the world, including the Playboy organization.

Flirting with the media was a double-pronged challenge. The effort to get media attention for gay lib needed to be balanced with an effort toward getting the right kind of attention. The goal was a positive representation of the gay community with stereotypes in perspective. As much as Kight courted the attentions of the press, he was not shy about writing a letter or calling in to a radio program to complain about the mainstream's mistreatment of homosexuals. The GLF on both coasts were sensitive to how they were portrayed in pop culture and the mass media. In comedy, they were easy targets and often the brunt of cheap jokes. In drama, homosexuals were still commonly portrayed as child molesters, suicidal maniacs, or simply lunatics. In the 1970s, Hollywood publicists were not yet pursuing gay causes as it was not yet fashionable to have gay friends, much less support gay liberation.

How homosexuals were portrayed became an ongoing cause within the movement. Spunky activists were dogged in responding to disparaging attacks and jokes. Often it required a little "consciousness-raising" for mainstream society: letter-writing campaigns to editors, producers, TV studios, and ad agencies on both coasts.

New York activists created the National Gay Task Force and invited other activists to join the effort. West Coast activists organized the Gay Media Task Force.

Morris Kight was at the ready with an eight-point statement that was sent to all networks, studios, production companies, and media outlets. It diagnosed the problem as ignorance rather than calculated bigotry and stressed that "Gay people do not want to return to media invisibility." By 1973, well-meaning portrayals of homosexuals came across as condescending and limited. When asked by the *Los Angeles Times* if there had been any acceptable portraits of homosexuals on television, Kight emphatically replied: "No, I can't think of one. Though we thank them for the ones that are least bad." (December 10, 1973)

The coalition of gays from both coasts met with representatives of the Association of Motion Picture and Television Producers, the three major television networks, and the Writers Guild, the Directors Guild, and the Motion Picture Production Code. Kight explained the communication as "an attempt to develop confidence and to sensitize them to the issue. We wouldn't want censorship. We don't want to say, you can't do this, you can't do that. That's a bad way of doing it."

The meetings were described by both sides as "cordial and beneficial" and more meetings were promised. The professional guilds alerted their members to the "informational resources in the gay community," to answer any questions and concerns from writers, directors, and on-air personalities. Along with a few other innovative producers of the time, Norman Lear participated in the "gay awareness" workshop with his staff. The most useful information to the entertainment industry was learning which words were offensive. They were surprised to learn that "fag; faggot; dyke; queer" were terms of abuse. "If you don't want to insult," the task force statement said, "the words are 'gay, lesbian, and homosexual.'"

"There's been a conspiracy of silence," Kight was quoted in the *Los Angeles Times*. "It's been easy for gay people to hide. We're trying to create an atmosphere for them to come out. Instead of ripping open the closet door in their faces, we are quietly oiling the hinges....

"While gays and the entertainment industry may have achieved a certain rapprochement, it is unlikely that they will become bosom buddies in the immediate future."

Another of Kight's stunts, created just to get in the news, was in May, 1974. Not far away from the flash bulbs and glitz of the annual Emmy Awards (the TV Academy honors) at the Pantages Theatre, Kight and a coalition called "counter-Emmy" presented a sardonic non-award to the LAPD as "Best Actors of the Year" for their portrayal of "Return of the Gestapo," referring to its standard "ungenerous tactics."

Across the street from them was another peaceful demonstration of Chicanos and feminists who, according to the *Los Angeles Times,* were "embittered by the television industry's treatment of minorities."

Discussions about the portrayal of gays in the media would continue for decades.

Morris Kight continued to court the *Los Angeles Times*. The paper of record would not return his many advances; they did not respond to his daily phone calls and written press releases. In typical Kight fashion, he waited for the right reason to demand a meeting.

Tangents Magazine decided to advertise more broadly asking the venerable liberal weekly, *The Nation,* to accept a small ad for the ambitious homosexual magazine. The second largest newspaper in the country, the *Los Angeles Times,* refused to print the ad because it contained the word "homosexual," offering the explanation "we are a family newspaper." Don Slater, Joe Hansen, and Kight went to the *Times* offices, in what Hansen described as "an enormous office high up in the *Times* building with men from the advertising and public relations departments, and even an editor or two." Five company officers were in the room, describing themselves as "the committee which guides the affairs of the advertising department." They were asked if they were a censorship committee.

The officers were stone-faced; HIC representatives talked about freedom of the press. The *Times* officers would only repeat their committee title and explain that the ad would offend their readers. They were reminded that many of the *Times* readers were homosexual and were being denied needed services by the newspaper's refusal to run ads for legitimate affairs. Hansen: "We were not asking for sex ads. They wouldn't dare say such a thing to any other minority, black, for instance."

In the meeting Hansen's language was "not refined," by his own admission. He recalled the scene, "Poor Morris Kight nearly fainted from embarrassment, not at the self-righteous hypocrisy of the power in the room, but at taking part in a protest with such a foul-mouthed lout as me."

Hansen once described Kight as the "self-declared gay community ombudsman"; he didn't completely understand the older gentleman. Kight would not "faint from embarrassment" at the use of foul language—he was, after all, Bessie Kight's son. He cursed in his private life. But cursing and losing his temper was not Kight's negotiating style; he wanted to appeal to the officers on their intellectual level. Kight commanded respect in the way he spoke and handled himself, that was how he wanted to represent the gay community and the strategy he used to engage in conversation around homosexuals; the powers-that-be did not want to acknowledge gays, much less discuss them and their rights. Only on rare occasions did Kight lose his cool and never in the first meeting. He wanted to be invited back. He was, after all, creating a place for homosexuals at the table of social reform.

The three men left the office unsuccessful and feeling defeated. On their way out, Don Slater told the suits that he had no choice but to picket the *Times.*

Slater had never picketed anything; he was always opposed to street protests as an avenue to social change and often ribbed Kight about his demonstrating. Slater organized the entire protest, picked the date, got the police permit, made the posters and showed up at the big bronze doors of the *Times* in downtown. It was a sunny weekday afternoon and about a dozen protesters showed up to join the cause and handed out flyers explaining their grievance to mostly good-natured passersby. Morris Kight was not there. Slater was disappointed in the response to his new cause and he felt slighted by Kight. It's easy to reason that the protest was not well covered by the media, least of all the *Los Angeles Times.*

Slater couldn't understand why Kight had supported the Barney's Beanery protest whose, according to Joe Hansen, "…picket line had twice, no, three times the number of protesters we'd mustered in favor of the freedom of the press." Slater didn't picket Barney's Beanery because his ideology led him to believe "the owner has a right to choose his customers." The discussion between Kight and Slater, as described by Hansen, sets a great divide in the political theory of America's civil rights movement.

"The *Times*," Slater said, "had no right to deny me freedom of the press. It's a First Amendment guarantee. I have no right to deny Barney freedom to use his own property as he chooses. That is a Fourth Amendment guarantee."

Hansen said, "Morris Kight blanched under his freckles ... and said, 'You're saying that blacks cannot eat in a white man's diner?'

"'A black cannot conceal his blackness,' Don said. 'A homosexual can conceal his difference. The black's problem is real. Homosexuals are creating a problem here, where none exists.'"

The rift was never fully repaired and the two men grew apart.

By mid-1970, Kight was getting notes like: "Dear Morris, thank you very much for your kindness and coming out to San Bernardino last week for our '20th-Century Dialogues' program. I certainly thought that you and Troy did an excellent job in presenting your point of view."

The letters of appreciation poured in for all sorts of reasons. Robert Richards, a priest with Community of St. John the Beloved (one of the first Catholic churches to serve "the homophile community of San Francisco"), wrote: "Dear Mr. Kight, you are beautiful. Thank you for your past support and for your friendship. Your letter proved very helpful. You seem to have a sincere and a real ability to understand the total 'scene' in the various Gay groups and Gay movements... O you man, you're terrific."

Bob Ennis sent Kight some heady remarks (September 24, 1970): "Your work is un-ending and beautiful, many rewards lie ahead for you. I appreciate your honesty and your consideration for others, it is basically through these means that you have achieved your successes of today and those to come."

Kight saved them all for the archives.

NACHO AND ECHO

KIGHT BRIEFLY TOUCHED TWO PROMINENT HOMOPHILE ORGANIzations: the National Association Conference of Homophile Organizations (NACHO), and the Eastern Conference of Homophile Organizations (ECHO, a.k.a. Eastern Regional Conference of Homophile Organizations). Both had grown from the Mattachine Society.

Like a lot of the old homophiles, Kight loved control and loved building organizations with acronymic names. Kight didn't share the old-timers' labor-intensive mechanics in organizing. The homophiles were heavy with formalities: resolutions, lists of commonalities, goals followed by discussions and disagreements about the goals (which apparently were not that much in commonality), committees within committees, guidelines, rules, affiliations, discussions of exceptions to the rules, qualifications for membership and conferences and symposiums to discuss all of the above. At one point, "hotel secrecy" became a concern. There were serious discussions about rules of behavior, sincere attempts to construct a "respectable" public image for individual homosexuals. There had been genuine and decent effort to cohere East and West Coast groups and maybe some in between.

Packets of material sent from East Coaster Foster Gunnison required a timely and time-consuming reply. Jim Kepner obliged, saying, "Few of us have time to read all that! True, the issues are complex, details tortuous, opinions endless and your persistence admirable—but it needs condensation and a sense of proportion…."

Kepner's letter is six single-spaced typed pages.

Kight's one brush with ECHO was in February 1970. While the Barney's Beanery pickets were still going on, Los Angeles homophiles hosted the Western Regional Homophile Conference at the First Unitarian Church. This would be Kight's first true public foray into the academics of the gay movement, or the "homophile" world.

Writing for *L.A. Free Press,* Douglas Key wrote: "Attempts to obtain the use of the Masonic temple were crushed when temple officials discovered 'homophile' was not 'hemophilia' and rejected the WHC request."

Eighty-four delegates from 22 separate homosexual organizations gathered together. Kight played it cool with Harry Hay, Jim Kepner, and certainly Troy Perry, but it was important to him that he speak—and that he be heard. None of the men tried to silence Kight (up to that point) and the conference welcomed him—as a new member.

Hay spoke first as the highly regarded founder of the American homophile movement. He expressed his "tribal" inclinations and coined the term "Gay Window" to shake off homosexual tendencies to identify themselves as through hetero-sensibilities.

Kight spoke next and immediately called for a revolution. In his best rhetoric, he addressed the crowd: "We insist that there is no homosexual problem, and that's how we expect to solve it…. We have to quit reading history and start living it. We are not going to cry anymore. We intend to be treated as human beings," followed by an eruption of applause.

Speaker after speaker called for compromise with each other and unity within all gay groups and by the end of the weekend, the conference was "deep in angry terminology" over categorizations and priorities and eventually more than two dozen resolutions, including Kight's resolution to collect $90 billion from all the churches (clearly a theatrical stunt to attract the media).

As it turned out, this was the last Western Homophile Conference. One radical summed it up: "They'd been around a long time and were designed to protect the closet."

Kight never used the scientific word "homophile." In his notes to the archive, he consistently referred to the title of the conference as "Western *Homosexual.*"

Later in 1970 was an infamous North American Conference of Homophile Organizations [NACHO] meeting in San Francisco. There were lengthy discussions at GLF business meetings regarding a request from NACHO for $45 for dues. Ralph [Schaffer], who was a Kight acolyte, said "a deceptive homophile organization," and moved to take the show by storm without application or payment of dues.

Kight, familiar with but fairly new to the fundamental organizational wrangling of the national homophile groups, decided to wrangle it in his own way and wrote to Foster Gunnison (July 27, 1970): "Dear Foster, one of the characteristics of GayLib is that everything is done out in the open, no secrets, and thus I send this letter for the archives knowing it's part of the scene.... On the GayLib national thing: I had said that [Jim Kepner] should take seriously your, and other, notices that NACHO was aware of its stodginess, pokiness, hangups with form, credentials, etc., that people in leadership were willing to talk and to perhaps change it. Again I urge [you] to wait until after August before going on. It's far better in my opinion for NACHO to join the 20th century than to form a new organization. NACHO has an excellent start, has good press, and become vital if enough reasonable people reason together. Peace."

In 1994 Kight recalled what happened at the 1970 NACHO conference: "I was invited to come up as the keynote speaker. I went, but could not stay ... so I spoke, and I said, 'Listen, everybody, you've had it. You need to pay attention to the fact that it's a new ballgame. If you wish to join us, you're all welcome. You're all bright and alert, and we could use your bodies. But you have to change your ways!' And they applauded me, simply because I'm a forthright figure.

"I simply wanted to persuade them to join the 20th century and they couldn't hear it."

Kepner's notes at the time: "'It's time for the old groups to leave the field,' Morris Kight said. NACHO was already torn by conflict between the east, which had marching orders for the rest of us, and pluralist west, over litigation strategy and over whether NACHO should admit organizations which 'damage our image,' or which engage in 'extraneous or deleterious issues.' Anarchy faced off with arrogant conservatism, and anarchy won."

In 1997, Kepner recalled the NACHO meeting: "In 1970, Gay Liberation crazies recruited by Morris Kight and others from the streets trashed and destroyed NACHO. The debates between NACHO's East and West blocs paled in comparison with the post-Stonewall, hippie-counterculture-New Left radicalism. Here was real diversity!"

Kight: "It was, that day, the homophile effort died, never to be reborn again."

In 1994, Paul Cain asked Kight about Kepner's claim that Kight wanted "to bury NACHO."

Kight said: "No, that's not true. That's more revanchism [sic], and more revisionism. I went up to do just what I said I'd do. I went up to, not to destroy it—it was dead anyway. The corpse was laying there, and they hadn't put the makeup on. It's just nobody had buried it yet. They died of their own inertia."

In late October 1970, Kight sent a missive to all "Gay Liberationist" groups, titled "Preliminary Call for National Gay Liberation Conference." Kight planned to have a new kind of gay "conference" so that different groups "know one another, to develop trust, love, respect, and to share our successes and failures." Kight invited over one hundred groups to have 25 major demonstrations during the week of June 28, 1971, "and that each group in the country conduct some kind of action—be it a teach-in, fund raiser, rally, raps, or organizing meetings."

GLF-LA voted unanimously to host a National Gay Liberation Conference. "…At such a conference we would hear reports, discuss mutual problems, form liaison, and project the massive national effort for June 28, 1971."

This stirred up the homophiles around the country. They saw Kight trying to push his radical agenda on young people and called out his recent claim that "most of the younger generation was not interested in a 'conference.'" They always accused Kight of ruining their conferences, their caucuses, their way of doing things. Kight wasn't intentionally ruining anything; he had an overt, radical, steadfast agenda to keep the movement affirmatively progressing.

Eventually, after New York activists called for a larger effort, GLF-LA 'postponed' the conference indefinitely.

Kight continued to irritate the original homophiles—it wasn't intentional, it was simply his nature. He genuinely did not believe in their methodology. He was genuinely a pushy guy who worked hard. Often, he pushed himself to the front and center of attention; no one in gay circles had ever done that before and certainly not with Kight's panache. They suffered with fear and shame. Kight was shameless and fearless. Kight saw them as conservative conformists, or more accurately "assimilationists." They all bandied that word (non-word) back and forth as the ultimate slap across a gay activist's face. Kight, like many others, did not experience gay liberation as a way to assimilate with heterosexuals.

His particular personality with his casual-hippie appearance, or maybe it was lucky timing, made Morris Kight the match that struck gay liberation on the West Coast afire.

Kepner and Hay wrote long letters to each other, newsy and gossipy. By the time GLF was closing its doors, Kight was a separate and constant topic, sometimes comical, always acerbic.

Kepner to Hay: "Morris is terribly distressed now because some of the younger radicals want to organize something without him doing the friendly puppetmaster job … Morris does a great job himself, but he can't abide the idea that somebody else might get credit for doing something. I was a bit embarrassed at one conference … Morris did the honors introducing me, taking the occasion to talk at length about how we had worked together for 20 years. I didn't contradict him, but I don't recall even hearing of him before he came around the CRH in 1966, and it wasn't until GLF started that I knew of him associating himself openly with the homophile/ Gay movement, other than at things like the anti-draft committee autocade. I know he did show up at ONE sometime earlier, but I don't recall meeting him there." (July 22, 1974)

Hay responded to Kepner:

"Now for Morris: Although we'd heard about him from Don Slater and from Guy Strait in S.F.… [Morris] had brought some of the Queens of his entourage in the PEACE Movement … Later that spring the TANGENTS GROUP held an outdoor supper Benefit in Morris's backyard, and he Circle participated ["Circle" is Harry's version of consciousness-raising or sharing from one's inner self]. We all became life-long friends that night. Later that summer … Morris had us over for another benefit, and I introduced Gay Civil Rights to this crowd with Morris acting as a 'neutral sympathizer.'"

Almost five years later, Hay recollected events in a letter to Kepner:

"In 1968 we started, Johnny and I, to go to his Dow Action Group, attempting to persuade Morris and his crowd to join us at some political action. To no avail—we didn't get anywhere. In 1969—when the Flower Children were zapping the Cops with Love, the Panthers were becoming big stuff, and Dow Action decided its time was past, Morris was at loose ends. Johnny and I tried like crazy to get Morris to—with us—set up an avowedly GAY Chapter of the Peace Movement." (August 2, 1974)

A Gay Chapter of the Peace Movement is exactly the "separatism" that Kight "pooh-poohed."

Hay's letter continued: "Again we got nowhere. Morris had made up his mind he was going to uproot, go up to San Francisco, and get involved in the 'Ecology' Movement. We said, 'Morris, the Ecology Movement ain't going anywhere unless it politicizes.' 'Okay,' sez Morris, 'I'll take a week off and brush up on my Marxism.' That knocked me cold—in his condition I would have estimated he needed about two years to brush up. However, instead he suddenly had to rush off the [sic] NYC on business and ... whaddyaknow, while he was there STONEWALL happened."

It is not clear what Harry Hay refers to here—Kight was not at the Stonewall Rebellion and being at Stonewall is probably one of the few things that Kight never tried to claim.

From time to time, up to mid-1973, Kight would toy with the idea of reorganizing himself in San Francisco. After his old friend from the peace movement, Tom Dunphy (street performance artist a.k.a. General Waste-more-land), relocated to Berkeley, Kight wrote to him:

"You are right its [sic] time to move out of this city. The deterioration is more noticeable each day, little things. Stored [sic] being boarded up, garbage in the street, obscenities on walls, arson, lack of trust, the air worsens each day. I do want to move to SF, but the time is not yet right. Have not forgotten that I want to move; of course its got its problems but all of America is in trouble. The Sins of our past have caught up with us."

Hay's letter to Kepner continued: "Morris didn't really begin to dig the significance of 'Stonewall' until after Leo Laurence began to come down exhorting [the] Movement in September of 1969, at that radical Coffee-house on north of Hoover which got burned."

In addition to Harry Hay and Morris Kight, Leo Laurence also claims to be the first person to introduce the concept of gay rights as civil rights. Laurence is the first to articulate the principle in print (the *Berkeley Barb*). Leo remembered that Kight had initially contacted him when reading his civil rights slant and invited him as a houseguest whenever Laurence visited Los Angeles.

Hay continued: "As I understand it, Morris had always been a one-man Midnight Mission for street hustlers who needed to be sprung outta pokey or who needed bail or a place to crash after they were sprung. I think he'd been doing this in L.A. since about 1960 ... Don Slater would know. And in the '40s he'd been doing the same here in Albuquerque [sic]: he worked for the Bureau of Indian Affairs, in the offices both in Albuquerque and in Taos.

"However Mattachine never knew of him, or had correspondence with him. He was primarily one of the many 'Anty Bountifuls' who dotted Urban Areas from

'Ellis Island to the Golden Gate' (but who wouldn't be caught dead being political ... back in the movement's formative years). When you come right down to it, his wheeling-dealing method of operation isn't really political NOW."

In the early '70s, New York-based historian Jonathan Ned Katz contacted all the homophile leaders to gather information in the interest of research for what became his book *Gay American History: Lesbians & Gay Men in the U.S.A.* (Penguin Books, 1976).

Kight, like Hay and many others, was in correspondence with Jonathan Katz regarding his historical perspective on American gay life.

Naturally, Kight felt that he belonged in the history and courted Katz through letters starting in July 1973. Jonathan Katz was 20 years Kight's junior and Katz was an established American historian of human sexuality with a focus on same-sex attraction.

"Dear Jonathan," Kight's first letter begins, "What do your friends call you for a first name? I would like to be among those."

Kight wrote to Katz (December 13, 1973): "Mine has been largely a spoken revolution ... I am stunned at how much of my rhetoric has gone into the thinking of the community and how many phrases I hear coming back." Kight told Katz that as of 1956, "I became an almost full-time gay libber, having that interrupted from time to time for other issues that I believed in." Kight did believe himself to be "one of the old folks in the movement," and generationally he certainly was—but there was a legitimate argument to be made that he wasn't one of the older folks of the movement (and Hay articulated that argument in letters to Katz). Kight sent Katz his full activist résumé going back to his arrest for serving a black family in Fort Worth.

Later that same month, Katz was included in Kight's personal year-end review sent to everyone on his mailing list.

"I think my life has been in almost five yearly cycles, I am starting a new one now. Leaving the Center in January 1974, will remain a member of the board and will do [some] daily work without pay."

Two weeks later, Kight wrote to Katz regarding Harry Hay and the Mattachine Society.

"[He is] Probably the man who could be called its 'founder,' though I shy away from the term. Heaven only knows I have founded a lot of things, largely because in the far-off days of the past, my ideas were so unpopular that I had to create something and then attract others to the cause to make it happen at all.

"[Harry] has largely been expunged from the history of the movement since arch-conservative forces took over what he was doing and warped it into conformity. That we didn't conform is obvious."

In that same letter, he wrote: "I do not like to analyze my own thoughts, my own doings. I am a far more private person that anyone knows. I am not the driven persona that some think I am. I find it easy to say where there were failures and why they were." Kight also included a typewritten résumé/bio for Katz's perusal.

At some point, before the publication of his book, Katz wrote to Kight regarding the challenge he faced to keep "lesbian and gay history from becoming exclusive property of academics." Later in the same letter, he prepares Kight: "I've recently reexamined, cut back, and refocused my plan for [the book] after having unrealistically laid-out as too complicated a plan for the contents."

Katz's *Gay American History: Lesbians and Gay Men in the USA* (1976) is a seminal collection of documents and first-person accounts of the foundation of American queer history covering the period from 1566 to 1976.

Kight is not mentioned in Katz's final book. Still, Morris arranged a "high literary tea" for Katz in Los Angeles in 1977 on his book tour.

In October of 1976, Katz recorded a radio interview with Kight via telephone.

Katz asked about the "troubled people" who go to the Center needing help.

Kight: "Society does tend to be a little homophobic. There is an institutional notion that it is sinful or sick to be gay.

"There are problems in an urban society, how to survive. Gay people did that for themselves. There are enormous changes, we're coming to help, there is a social consciousness that entails what I can see as other gay persons addressing more needs. I tend to address myself as to the needs of my own people."

Katz asked who was more oppressed: blacks or gays, and speculated that black gays are probably oppressed "in their own community."

Kight: "There are higher rates of suicide and higher rates of alcoholism among gay people than non-gay people. The only place that gay people have had is gay bars."

Katz: "Bars?"

Kight explained that bars have traditionally been the only place for gay people to meet, to socialize with one another, and this contributes to a higher than average rate of alcoholism. Later in the interview he outlined for Katz the "alcoholism abatement" program that the Center had "following AA's 12 Steps, calling it Gay AA." When responding to Katz's next question regarding the way the media treats gays, Kight blatantly exaggerated.

Kight: "One of the major networks asked me to do a treatment of four scripts: a supposition of who we used to be, what we've done in the last five years, where we're going. I'm doing my best to come up with something."

Katz asked Kight to explain "common attitudes toward" gays.

Kight: "It stems from the decline of the matriarchy, rise of patriarchy, and the rise of nationalist regime. Soldiers were told to defend then breed. We didn't have children and we're hardly the subjects of producing an army, that's why it was written into the religious philosophies that it was an abomination [to be homosexual]. It was a guarantee survival of heterosexuality. We must reject the idea that it's a sickness, [to be gay] is a perfectly natural fact of life.

"Gay people must reject the notion of inferiority and lead with 'I'm a natural fact'—you become a more powerful person."

Kight clarified: "The point is not to breed more armies, not to breed more people but to accommodate what we have now. Apparently, by the year 2010 the population will have doubled. If you believe that we're doing a lousy job now, think what it'll be like with the decline of fossil fuel, deterioration of air and water, worldwide wars. A lot of troubles are coming. We can attempt to bring population under control, it's a worldwide problem. Society can be conned into believing a lot of lies—that we are sick, sinful, it's a lie. There are a lot of other lies. Do not depend upon other people. Gay people are self-reliant."

Kight continued his communication and typewritten letters to Katz for years.

In 1975, Harry Hay wrote (from San Juan Pueblo, New Mexico) to Don Kilhefner (in Los Angeles), in a postscript:

"Hey—have you been getting any more flack from Morris's insistence on being one of the Grandpa's of the 'Homophile Muvmint'? Of course, he was one of the last of the TRADITIONAL OLE TIMEY QUEENS taking responsibility for the hustlers and the belles in the downtown area. If I'm not mistaken he was Guy Strait's 'eyes-n-ears' for the South Coast for CRUISE NEWS & WORLD REPORT. But the first time Morris himself ever participated in a 'Movement' happening was when he brought his little quorum of querulous queens to join our picket line for the Black Cat New Faces Bars on the night when there were five demonstrations (by the Flower Children on Sunset Boulevard and in Venice, the Blacks in Watts, and the Chicanos in East L.A.) simultaneously against police brutality. This would have been circa February 1967...."

Hay continued: "... All during 1968 John and I were trying to get Morris to come out openly in the Peace Movement as a Gay Activist—but he never would. He didn't start being an active gay until Leo Laurence started coming down to L.A. in the fall of 1969. Oh well—enough of this gossip."

Many of the men of the early homophile movement would perpetrate rumors about Kight's gay political activism, how far his closet door opened and when, until over time it became gay folklore.

LET'S HAVE A PARADE!

A LOT HAD HAPPENED SINCE THE STONEWALL INN UPRISING.

A bicoastal gay revolution, with a few pockets in between, was on a vigorous simmer. Stories came in from all over the U.S., Alaska, Europe and Eastern Europe about gay activism in the cities. Kight's living room was a round-the-clock think tank with letters to the editors, personal notes, press releases, and telephone calls. Young people learned that every walk to the store was an opportunity to re-educate the public, to show the world they need not fear gay people. Every public kiss was a social protest.

In July 1970, Kight wrote to a friend:

"Many encouraging signs here of change ... GLF/LA much good news in its continuing, and never relenting efforts to get people out of the closets."

The first anniversary of the uprising was approaching. Los Angeles and San Francisco activists did not want to celebrate the Stonewall rebellion as the launch of gay liberation, seeing that it was a 'New York thing.' The good folk in New York saw it first and foremost as a 'gay thing.' There was consensus for a cohesive national celebration of gay liberation, but exactly what was never cohered.

NYU's Student Homophile League crafted a resolution that was presented at the November 1969 Eastern Regional Conference of Homophile Organizations [ERCHO] that read, in part:

"We propose that a demonstration be held annually on the last Saturday in June in New York City to commemorate the 1969 spontaneous demonstrations on Christopher Street and this demonstration be called CHRISTOPHER STREET LIBERATION DAY. No dress or age regulations shall be made for this demonstration."

New York activists passed the resolution to form a Liberation Day Committee and seek nationwide support.

Kight received a letter from New York and liked to describe it in his best Edwardian style:

"On watermark-embossed paper from a law firm on Madison Avenue," [paraphrasing] 'Dear Morris, we in New York are going to have some kind of celebration of the anniversary of Christopher Street. What are you going to do in Los Angeles?'"

Kight didn't mince words with his immediate response: "I thought, 'What an arrogant New York letter.'" By the following day, he had rethought the idea and said to himself: "Gee whiz, that person didn't mean to be arrogant. That was just my failing." Probably with the help of a phone call or two from New York, Kight came to realize that a national commemoration would exponentially propel gay liberation. Stonewall was a victory over police brutality; the very same kind of victory Los Angeles had two years earlier, in 1967, at the riot in the Black Cat bar. It was a smart strategy. As it would turn out, the long-term value of the Stonewall rebellion would be in the commemoration of the event.

Kight: "And so on May 10, 1970, I knew that I had to do something. I took the phone off the hook, because it rang constantly, and put the draperies over the front of the house and a big note on the front door, 'Please do not disturb me. I'm in consultation.' And all morning long, I thought of what to do. The script that almost won was to have 25 separate demonstrations. Before the day was out, I thought, Fuck it, that's kind of old-fashioned [demonstrations]. We've done that. And so we won't do that again. Instead, we'll have a parade! Down Hollywood Boulevard."

It was a crazy, radical idea. It would require a great deal of planning, resources, and courage. If it worked, it would be brilliant. Kight never imagined it any other way. He cleared off the big table in the main room and settled in for a long brainstorming session.

"So I whipped out the butcher paper, put it on the table, and started fantasizing names. And in came Bob Humphries. I said, 'Bob, you won't believe what it is I've dreamed up. And please don't reject it until you've thought it through. We're gonna celebrate the Stonewall uprising with a parade on Hollywood Boulevard. Yes, that's what we're gonna do. And right now, I am engaged in trying to find a name for it. Join me.' And he said, 'Oh, that's a wonderful idea.'"

Kight continued: "[Bob] came to the butcher paper and looked at the 65 names I already had down. Bob added a name, 'A Festival in Lavender and White.' I said, 'What namby-pamby, mincing, prancing, Nelly conversation is that? What are you talking about, Festival in Lavender? What is that?'"

According to Kight, he and Bob marched around the house, going around and around in circles, figuratively and creatively, when suddenly Bob came rushing in and said, "I've got it. Christopher Street West!"

Kight said, "Roll up the paper and put it away. That's it. Now we've got to sell the idea."

Kight's dramatic punctuations to the story are valuable details as they differ so greatly from other people's recollections about where and how the idea for Christopher Street West parade originated.

Kight: "Bob Humphries, Donald Dill, and I called Troy, I said, 'Troy, I'm coming over.' So Troy and Bob Ennis, an African-American man who was Troy's secretary, Donald Dill, Bob Humphries, myself, and that's it."

"I didn't have an African-American assistant at the time," Reverend Troy Perry clearly remembers.

A minor detail, but one worth noting, is that Kight was confused. In fact, Donald Dill was a Reverend of the United States Mission and served as Secretary on the U.S. Mission board.

Perry continued, "MCC was pregnant with Stonewall. We started nine months before the Stonewall Riots. [The gay revolution] was going to start on the East Coast or the West Coast, but [in 1969] it was ready to start."

Perry remembered the discussion "generated towards holding demonstrations. We were already holding demonstrations. But then we came up with the idea 'Let's hold a parade.'"

Kight: "I said, 'Troy, we're here to sell you an idea which you probably won't like. It's probably much too radical for your tastes. But we're gonna have a lesbian and gay parade. And we're gonna call it Christopher Street West. And we're gonna march on Hollywood Boulevard. And we'll get a lawful permit to do that. And it will be the first ever. It will be very dangerous.' He said, 'Shut up, hon! Good God! Let's do it! Oh, mercy. Let's do it!'"

Fact is, Troy Perry had been demonstrating in the streets of Hollywood for gay rights for more than a year.

Kight, in his aristocratic best: "The Gay Liberation Front of Los Angeles met that night at Satan's, a nightclub over on Sunset Boulevard, itself a radical place. The people who ran Satan's were non-gay Satanists, and they mistook us for Satanists. Which, I guess, some of us were, and some of us, many, were not. But what the hell? ... The Gay Liberation Front met that night and quickly voted to have a parade down Hollywood Boulevard to commemorate the anniversary of the uprising at the Stonewall Inn. I had to be saved from the mob! They wanted to tear me apart, they were so thrilled."

Los Angeles city required 40 days to apply for a parade permit. Kight filed for a permit the following day, 43 days before the parade.

Kight: "I went to City Hall, to the City Clerk, which I had done for years because I was involved in so many radical causes, and bought a $50 parade permit. They said, 'Mr. Kight, you know how it works. This is usually police [business].' I said, 'Well, I'm just reversing it. It was easy to park here.' It was right across the street. So I bought a $50 permit and went over to the police station and I saw Sergeant Sherman, who was Events Coordinator for LAPD, a closeted right-winger, he said 'Well, you know all about how to do it. So here are the forms. Fill 'em in.' I said, 'No, that's not what I want. I want to take them with me.' 'You've done this so many times, what's this about?'

"So I got the four forms and went back to my house, I typed them out, 'Christopher Street West, a Lesbian and Gay celebration.'... on Sunday June 28, 1970. The permit had the question, 'Will you have animals in the parade?' What the hell, we would barely be able to do it in the time we had. Animals, elephants and tigers and lions—where the hell would they come from? I said, 'Yes, we'll have a trained flea circus of 5,000 fleas.' Just to be very gay, I put it in."

Kight envisioned "everything from fleas to elephants."

"I took it back and handed Sergeant Sherman the parade permit. He looked down and he said, 'Let me see you in the office.' He said, 'You've demonstrated against the war, and [supporting] black power, and brown power,' and so on.... This is something else, isn't it? I know you've been associated with gay and lesbian causes, but this is something else.' I said, 'Well, yes, this is something else. We are determined to have a parade. And we're here to get your cooperation to have one.' He stalled for an hour and a half, trying to figure out how to stop it. Well, he couldn't stop it. He said, 'Well, I'll take it under advisement.'"

On the Parade Permit Application, dated May 14, 1970, there was no mention of 5,000 fleas. There was listed, however: two bands, three sound vehicles, one hundred musical units, three dogs, and three horses, several small pets in cages, and ten auto-sized floats, plus eight marching units, with five hundred people in each unit. Reverend Troy D. Perry signed as "applicant" and Metropolitan Community Church was listed as Sponsor. Robert Humphries was Parade Chairman.

Question [from permit application]: "purpose of parade." Answer [by Kight]: "A joyous celebration of the total freedom of homosexuals in Los Angeles, with their families and friends, indicating that they are full citizens of this community and their rights to use the streets in the city of Los Angeles."

Kight: "So we all gathered at the [MCC] Virgil Street Parsonage and talked it out. Every organization around was represented, representing the many tendencies in our community. To this day, I wonder why not one of us said: 'It can't be done.' And so we did it. We raised sufficient money to get it going, someone loaned $500, which was repaid one year later, for leaflets, groups mobilized, and the show was on the road."

Morris Kight Ringmaster-Provocateur was alive, like never before.

Kight: "We suspected the police might not like to issue such a revolutionary permit."

LAPD was notoriously resistant to the gay movement, more than the NYPD. Two weeks after turning in the parade application, on June 10, all the principals in the parade effort were called to a police commission hearing.

Reverend Perry: "Morris and Bob Humphries said, 'We want you to do the talking in front of the police commissioner.' Now, you know Morris. Morris was not afraid to speak. This was the first big-time demonstration like this, and he wanted me to talk. That's because I think he wanted to make sure that they saw somebody in a [priest's] collar."

Troy Perry stood before the commission representing the gay community's request for a parade permit with all the other key figures seated in the observation galley behind him.

Another shared goal of early gay activists on both coasts was to get public officials to say the word "gay" or "homosexual," thereby entering the words in public record, nomenclature, and discussion.

Reverend Perry: "Morris and Bob Humphries told me, 'Don't mention the word *homosexual* when you go to the police.' It was bizarre. That lasted about an hour but after being browbeaten, I finally used the word 'homosexual' to describe us. 'You know who we are,' I said, 'we're representing the homosexual community of Los Angeles.'"

Perry was surprised to see Chief of Police Edward M. Davis in attendance at the hearing, and was even more stunned when the Chief said:

"Did you know that homosexuality is illegal in the state of California?"

Reverend Perry responded, "No, sir, it is not."

The commission and the parade applicants debated the legality of homosexuality in the state of California for the next few minutes until the homophobic Chief of Police pulled in the reins of the meeting by saying:

"We have a request from the gay community for a parade permit."

Chief Davis, no doubt familiar with Kight's criminal record, glared at Morris Kight seated in the front row and said: "I'd sooner grant a parade permit to robbers, burglars, thieves, liars, cheats, murderers than discommode the decent citizens of the city to grant a permit to fund this."

The Chief publicly chastised the entire gay population, and ironically his remarks ultimately served a constructive purpose: when his comments were made public, many of the more politically moderate homosexuals, the law-abiders and folks who preferred to follow the rules and blend in, who were at first cool to the idea of a parade, quickly became supporters. The biggest promoters of the parade were, in fact, the LAPD.

Suddenly, according to Kight, Commissioner Cohn waved a typed resolution in the air and said, "I move that Christopher Street West be granted a parade permit."

Cohn then quickly introduced a resolution, which was added to the parade application as a condition of the issuance of the permit: "Public liability and property damage insurance in the amounts of $500,000 and $1,000,000 respectively, shall be posted by applicant, naming the City of Los Angeles as an additional insured."

The resolution also required a $1,500 deposit to cover the cost of additional police officers with the understanding that any amount in excess of the $1,500 would be paid by applicant within three days after the parade. And the third and final zinger:

"In the event the number of participants in the parade is fewer than 3,000, applicant shall use the sidewalk, rather than one half of Hollywood Boulevard, and shall obey all signals."

The group sitting behind Perry shouted that these extreme and unusual requirements were impossible to fulfill. The Commission went on to explain that the insurance was necessary to indemnify the property owners whose property would be damaged in the rioting which would, no doubt, ensue.

Perry: "Because they assumed there was going to be so much damage done to storefronts from people throwing rocks at us, we would duck, and it would break out the glass. We said, 'Just like Nazi Germany.' The Germans did the same thing to the Jews. The Jews had to pay for the broken glass when people threw rocks at them and they hit the glass instead."

Kight left the meeting, saying, "This is unacceptable"; quoted in the *Los Angeles Times,* he described the city's position as "Another blow for human rights."

Kight went into the lobby of the so-called 'glass house,' Parker Center Police Station, and telephoned Eason Monroe, the Executive Director of the American Civil Liberties Union. "A slight homophobe, but I called him up and I said, 'Eason, it matters not what your opinion of us is, we have rights too and you know that. I'm a vigorous advocate of the First Amendment. I'm a member of the ACLU, as you know. And we're in serious trouble. We have to have this parade permit in a hurry.'"

Monroe called Herbert Selwyn, a non-gay man who had a long record on civil liberties and had helped to challenge the arrests during the 1967 raid at the Black Cat bar.

When Kight learned that Herb Selwyn had agreed to take the case, he called Selwyn and said, "Stay at your office. I'll be right there."

Selwyn had an incredible reputation. Kight rushed to the Wilshire Boulevard office to say, "We just have to have you in a hurry, because you're the best in town."

Selwyn said, "I'll be happy to take your case," except that he had a heavy workload and needed clerks and typists to come in and do the research and do typing.

Kight promised, "We'll furnish them."

They worked all day and night to file a restraining order against the LAPD. Selwyn called the city and requested to be put back on the agenda.

At a second Commission hearing, with less than two weeks before the anniversary date of Stonewall, flyers printed and distributed announcing a parade, Selwyn argued that it was unprecedented to charge one group of citizens for the costs of protecting them from another group of would-be attackers, whether real or hypothetical.

Reverend Perry remembers Selwyn said to the Commission, "These ridiculous conditions make it impossible to hold a parade. They violate these law-abiding citizens' right to peacefully assemble."

Selwyn got the bond requirement reversed, but not the charge for police protection. They wanted $1,500 cash for the policemen's protection.

Selwyn was prepared to file an order to the California Supreme Court (writ of mandamus) to compel the local authorities to follow the constitution. Two days later Judge Richard Schauer granted a temporary injunction ruling that the parade permit must be granted without conditions unless the police could "show cause." The judge reviewed both sides of the argument and said that he would render his final verdict within a week.

"Show cause" only slightly bogged down the preparations for the parade that might or might not happen. Without the permit, the contingent plan, which did not get discussed very much, was to use the sidewalks. They needed a permit; a permit would validate gay liberation.

Flyers, posters, and press notices continued. "Christopher Street – West, a Freedom Revival in Lavender." "Celebrate your freedom! Affirmation and joy! Make Hollywood Boulevard gay, at least for a day."

With Grand Funk Railroad and John Sebastian preaching from every transistor radio, in keeping with the times the parade announcements said: "Bring: Incense,

Music, Wear Colorful Attire, Costumes, Flowers and perfumes are encouraged! Let us drive sexual repression from our lives!"

Kight always stressed "peaceful and nonviolent"; in particular the Christopher Street West parade needed to be nonviolent. The full bulletin that announced the parade read: "A Love-In, entirely peaceful and non-violent, which is the essence of love."

There was just as much support as there was distortion about the upcoming gay parade. From the beginning, some gays accused Kight of "getting them all killed," there were rumors of riots and conflicts between gay people, and different fringe groups came together for the first time to participate as a collective. The celebration did commemorate an angry outburst, a rebellion—what happened at Stonewall was violent. No matter how much Kight preached nonviolent social change, people talked about fighting, mostly fighting back. Kight buffered the truth by saying the Stonewall rebellion was a "nonviolent riot," rationalizing that not a gunshot was fired and no one was killed. The idea didn't stick.

Kight was busy with graphics. He traced a circle using the bottom of a pop bottle to sketch out a button that read "Gay Power Christopher Street West '70." Ever the optimist, he brought his prototype to Achievement Badge and Trophy Company on West 7th Street in Los Angeles and placed an order for three thousand buttons. The printer made a mistake in the first short run, misspelling Christopher as 'Chritopher.' Kight was just as pleased to have the misspelled extra buttons.

Kight faced the never-ending task of raising funds. He dusted off an old idea from the Veterans of Foreign War that had been somewhat co-opted by the peace movement: volunteers made purple papier-mâché pansies that were distributed for donations. Each pansy had a small paper sash attached to it that read, "This pansy was given to you as a tribute to homosexual freedom." Kight later said the idea "came off fairly well.

"A good many of the ideas I originally projected and which were adopted never came off because of the time, a shortage of volunteers, and mostly few [participants] were able to grasp what we were doing."

The lead-up to the parade was the first solid, mainstream media coverage for the Los Angeles gay movement.

Kight articulated the position to the *Los Angeles Times*: "This is a colossal piece of ignorance that goes to the root of misunderstanding in the community. Nearly all homosexuals are house-owning, law-abiding people who disobey the law only in their choice of sexual outlets. Heterosexuals violate these same archaic, puritanical laws, which have nothing to do with 1970. It would be a joyous affirmation of self-respect. We want to peacefully honor the impressive show of strength made by rioting homosexuals on Christopher Street in Greenwich Village last year. And we want to simply affirm the fact that Hollywood is a homosexual ghetto with many of the businesses supported by us."

Kight pranced around, on a natural high from his two favorite inebriants—gay people and the media. In July, he wrote to a friend: "The overground press is giving gay news big play. Each day a new media thing or person calls in for another story, another thing, and this duplicated all over."

Never one to think small, Kight told the *Los Angeles Times* that he had originally envisioned: "A massive street march—Mardi Gras, New Year's, Hallowe'en—community-wide block-party celebration all rolled into one.... They could not be done because much of our creative effort was expended in fighting for the right to parade in the first place."

On June 24, in the back pages of *The Paper* was an announcement for a Saturday gathering on Hollywood Boulevard, an event in advance of Sunday's parade.

"CHRISTOPHER STREET WEST: Celebration of Homosexual freedom. Mill-in, Picketing, leafleting, rapping. McCadden Place and Hollywood Blvd. 7pm-10pm. Info: 484-1094 [Kight's phone number]."

Finally, Friday, June 26, two days before the parade was scheduled, the California Superior Court heard the case. Superior Judge Richard Schauer ordered the Los Angeles Board of Police Commissioners to issue a permit for a "Hollywood Blvd. homosexual-oriented parade without requiring a $1,500 cash bond."

Los Angeles Times, June 27, 1970 headline: "Bond Dropped for Homosexual Event."

The accompanying article read: "A judge, citing the constitutional guarantee of freedom of expression, ordered the permit issued without conditions."

Troy Perry: "It was amazing to me, the Judge found in our favor. He said, 'these are citizens, they don't have to put up extra money, they pay taxes. I don't care if you have to call out the National Guard, you are to protect these people and they can have their march.' And my God, we started planning for our march, Morris and everybody."

A huge victory, the parade promised to be as prominent as the event it commemorated.

Kight: "We got the permit. I went out, the press was in the hall and we held a press conference."

Kight's love affair with all recordable devices was just coming into full blossom and had become 'an obvious little secret' among insiders.

Kight received death threats right up to the morning of the parade. He was very casual about death threats and bore them like an ordinary risk for an effective social rabble-rouser.

"Someone telephoned in the morning and said, 'How would you like it if I came over and killed you today?' And I told him, 'No, I cannot do that today. I have a very big day ahead of me and I must attend a parade.' And I hung up."

All things political, social, and existential came together for Morris Kight on that Sunday afternoon, June 28, 1970. He described it as the "happiest moment of my life." Kight was reborn or became a believer. He was a changed man. Everyone who marched in that first parade was changed as a result of it. They were, for the time, empowered. They held a gay rights banner for less than a mile and carried it into the next generation and beyond.

People came in droves from as far away as San Francisco, San Diego, and Las Vegas. There were slogans like "Out of the Closets and Into the Streets," "We Are Not Afraid Anymore," "In Memory of Gays Killed by Pigs," "Homosexual Equality Now," and "I'm Gay and I'm Proud." There was a lax organization to the parade formation, most people marched with whatever group they most identified. MCC,

GLF, SPREE [Society of Pat Rocco Enlightened Enthusiasts], U.S. Mission, and ONE were represented. Some people had never heard of the fringe groups, subcultures sprouted from within the subculture. People were coming out of the vaults from behind the closets.

They convened on the corner of McCadden Place and Hollywood Boulevard. As far as parades go, it was very quiet.

Participants had no idea what to expect. They slowly moved up McCadden Place with Kight and Bob Humphries in the lead. His soft white hair swept off his forehead and touching the back of his neck and ears, a bit portly-shaped with perfect posture, Kight walked with his arms at his side, index fingers and thumbs gently touching with palms open and facing forward in the universal stance of passive resistance. He was 50 years old and one of the few senior members.

More than a few participants had to consider their professional careers, families, and personal safety. Some men and women who were not yet 'out' to their families, employers and co-workers marched. It was an unprecedented expression of gay pride—a truly radical idea for a radical movement. Specters of their fallen friends hung low: Larry Turner, Howard Efland, Ginny Gallegos—three of the hundreds of homosexuals and transgendered who had been battered to death while in police custody just for being queer.

No one could know what was around the corner, as they carefully marched east onto Hollywood Boulevard.

Kight: "I had no idea what we were facing. There might very easily be people with guns or bricks, there might easily be nobody, or there might be a handful of gay people. So march we did, with butterflies in our stomachs, with legitimate doubts and fears, but with enormous courage and devotion. I rounded the corner [at McCadden and Hollywood Boulevard] and there were 35,000 people lining the sidewalks. They were all applauding, they were chanting, they were singing. The people left the sidewalk and came into the middle of the street to touch us. They wanted to be a part of what they knew was history. And it was history. I must have had—there were 350 camera people, of one kind of another, a block of cameras, straight ahead of me."

As the formal introduction of homosexuals to the general public, the official coming-out party, Kight said "It will be dangerous," he did not exaggerate.

The parade marched east on Hollywood Boulevard and then turned south on Vine Street and continued one block to Selma Avenue.

Los Angeles Times: "Spectators greeted the marchers with nothing more than boos, catcalls, and wolf whistles mixed with cheers and applause."

Jim Kepner, writing under one of his many pseudonyms, Lyn Pedersen, reported: "Spectators were not exceptionally warm. There were a few catcalls, but most watched quietly and responded in a friendly manner when approached. There were few shows of outright hostility. Comments ranged from 'it's all right, let them do their thing,' and 'it's disgusting!'"

Marching in any of the first gay pride parades took unprecedented displays of courage. No one was surprised to see African Americans marching in Black Power parades. People expected to see women march in favor of women's liberation.

Women and blacks were born that way. The common perception was, however, that gays had a choice to keep it private. It took extraordinary bravery, deep commitments to voluntarily come out as gay when there was still so much hostility, misunderstanding, toward homosexuality. To "come out" in 1970 could be seen as openly admitting to being a deviant, evil, or perverse; but to march down the street declaring oneself a homosexual would surely mean the mark of insanity. When the history of twentieth-century heroes is complete, let these people be remembered as raw courage for a greater cause at its very best.

The public's reaction to open homosexuality was unpredictable. Kight had to conquer the fears within the collective of the GLF and prepare them, as best as possible, for whatever was around that corner and the subsequent consequences the parade might bring.

Pat Rocco: "The Boulevard was packed solid from one side of the street to the other."

Kight: "Well, what awaited us were 30 to 50,000 delighted residents, spurred on by the radio and television campaigns brought on by the Police Department's attitude. So there it was! The thing that we could not do for ourselves, the police did for us. Who would make a public issue of a gay parade? A lawsuit to demand one, ah, that is news!"

Howard Fox: "It was just a sea of people into the street, we could hardly get the parade down the street and people were cheering and there were helicopters overhead and the streets for miles around were jammed up because the police hadn't taken it seriously and they had done nothing and now they were left with this headache. And it was just the most thrilling day of my life. It was just really wonderful."

'Lyn Pedersen' reported to hear someone say: "I'm not gay, but I think this is great."

Most would agree with the other statement overheard: "The best thing that ever hit Hollywood Boulevard."

Carolyn Weathers: "It was very exciting—kind of scary too. There was a lot of tension walking down the street. I remember specifically walking down Hollywood Boulevard with a bunch of lesbians and the gay men behind us and this silence from the bystanders. Silence. One guy threw a full can of beer at us. It was not a celebration. It was a pretty gutsy thing to do, to walk in that parade, but I felt good."

That would not be the last beer to be thrown that day.

Kight said, "Eighteen hundred people walked. We know that's true, because Magnus Marcus Overseth, a man from Minnesota, had an athletic counter, the kind used at major sports events. And he counted the crowd as they went down the street. And he counted 1,800. Thirty-five thousand people watched. And the rest of the story is history."

Magnus Marcus Overseth was quite active in GLF, was at the parade and did use an athletic counter. Shortly after the excitement of the Hollywood parade, Overseth moved back to his native Minnesota because, according to Kight, he had "the idea, not a wild one at all, that the Apocalypse is soon to strike us, and that [Minnesota] will be a sane area that will be spared." Overseth founded a small farming community back in Minnesota and kept a regular correspondence with Harry Hay for many years.

The reported numbers of participants varied like reported numbers of spectators. the *Advocate* and the *Los Angeles Free Press* both reported 1,200 in the parade, and they both claimed to use the same counting method—Magnus Marcus Overseth's athletic counter, though totals vary.

The *Los Angeles Times* reported:

"Police estimated there were 500 demonstrators and 4,000 bystanders, but other observers felt there were many times more. The parade sponsors, an umbrella group known as Christopher Street West, used a mechanical counter and said there were 1,169 participants. It estimated that the crowds of onlookers lining the sidewalks five and 10 deep numbered 25,000 to 30,000."

Kight stuck with the figures of 1,800 participants and 35,000 spectators. There is no estimation if this was the largest group of openly homosexuals to publicly assemble in Los Angeles legally.

There was nothing subdued or gray about Gay Pride. From the very beginning, it was a societal array of everything from fleas to elephants and everything in between. The closet door had fallen off the hinges and hit the cultural pendulum. Floats and posters were wild, dramatic, and humorous to extremely conservative. There was no trained flea circus that first year, but there was a woman on a horse, a Tarzan carried a five-foot boa constrictor, a raccoon, and a monkey. There were a few duchesses, butch types, leather-clad motorcyclists, and quite a few transvestites. Guerrilla Theatre presented "vice cops chasing screaming fairies wearing paper wings." Two handsome men walked sheepdogs and carried signs that read, "Not all of us walk poodles." One float read "Homosexuals for Ronald Reagan," and another, "Heterosexuals for Homosexual Freedom." A local Hollywood street character known as General Hershey Bar, whom Kight had privately counseled, carried a sign that read: "If you can't be free to be gay, you aren't free at all." An offshoot group calling itself The Militant Gay Movement showed up with a super-sized Vaseline jar. The typical force that emerged from the early gay liberation movement was irreverent, unapologetic, lots of energy and fun. Right behind Kight, the Gay Liberation Front marched and shouted: "Two, four, six, eight—gay is just as good as straight."

Descriptions of the parade were as unique as its participants and spectators. Joseph Hansen, one of the worriers about the parade who stayed on the sidelines, described it to C. Todd White:

"Super silly and very ragtag. Nobody had any money for floats or anything but somehow or other, they threw out a few sequins and a bit of tulle, and some paint, and got out there and did it the best we could.

"Nobody knew what to expect."

Joseph Hansen, not a big fan of Kight's revolution and the gay parade, did concede that the event was: "Electrifying. It startled people, but I think the most amazing thing about it was its effect on homosexuals.... I think it just showed homosexuals that being bold, being brave, and coming out was not going to have the awful results that everybody always feared. Those days were past; they were behind us. And that was a thrilling day."

Terry Le Grand remembers there were "a lot of hecklers" at the parade. Terry was holding the GLF banner marching behind Morris Kight when a spectator threw dog feces on him. Aggravated and appalled, Terry stopped walking, dropped the banner and was ready to have a few words with the assailant.

"Morris Kight grabbed me and said, 'Terry, for crying out loud it's just shit. Wipe it off and keep walking.'" Terry snapped to his better judgment, right action in the name of a greater cause. He returned to the line-up and continued walking. He took off his shirt and didn't say another word about the assault.

Los Angeles Times said: "One thing the hour-long, mile-long procession lacked was a violent reaction from spectators, which the Police Commission had predicted in requiring a $1,500 cash bond for the parade permit."

The *Advocate*: "The turnout appeared to catch the Los Angeles Police Department largely unprepared. [The police] had blocked off only one side of the boulevard, as specified in the permit, and permitted traffic to proceed on the other side. As a result, cars were trapped in the crush of spectators who surged into the street along the parade route, despite the efforts of a few squad car units and motorcycle-mounted patrolmen to force them back to the sidewalks. Shortly after the parade started, the police gave up and began diverting all traffic, except the paraders, off the boulevard. There was no violence of any kind, and police would acknowledge only three arrests."

The parade's second greatest success was that it had begun a shift in social awareness. Hansen wrote, "The fact that nobody threw eggs or rotten tomatoes, nobody jeered—people stood and smiled as it went by—was a huge shock and a very pleasant one."

1970. "Gay Liberation Front" banner that led the parade. Photo: Pat Rocco. Pat Rocco Papers, Coll2007-006, ONE National Gay & Lesbian Archives, USC Libraries, University of Southern California.

New York GLF did not prevail as well. They were unable to get a permit that first year. On that same day, June 28, 1970, thousands of homosexuals, a historical turnout, marched for three miles on the sidewalks from Greenwich Village to Central Park. There was no violence and it was reported to have had "lots of good vibes."

Historical scholars agree, for the long-term success of gay liberation, it was strategically necessary for the Stonewall commemoration to be successful outside of New York. A 2006 article in *American Sociological Review*: "Los Angeles activists, by participating in a Stonewall commemoration the first year, played a crucial role in the survival of the Stonewall story.... The first commemoration of Stonewall was gay liberation's biggest and most successful protest event."

Ultimately, Los Angeles defined the Gay Pride Parade.

At Selma Avenue, the parade turned west and dispersed before Las Palmas. Many people streamed south to Sunset Boulevard where there were more crowds of spectators. Bystanders were curious. They couldn't imagine who would march down the street professing to be homosexual. On Sunset Boulevard, cars and floats, spectators and participants stuck together. It was a festive chaos that continued west a few blocks to Highland Avenue. There was disorder, pandemonium, no hostility. It was a sweet frenzy, a mill-in, blending different kinds of people with total peace. It couldn't be awkward because there was no social protocol. For the first time, there was a celebratory atmosphere between gays and straights. Homosexuals stood face-to-face with heterosexuals, right there in the middle of Sunset Boulevard in Hollywood. Not a single person was hurt. The LAPD was prepared for a riot. Instead they got a traffic jam.

It was a profound, euphoric experience and a growth spurt for gay liberation.

Los Angeles Times: "After the parade several hundred of the participants gathered at Las Palmas Ave. and Hollywood Blvd. to stage a sit-in on the sidewalk."

Reverend Troy Perry, with a handful of supporters, began what became a 16-day hunger fast to protest the abuses by the L.A. Police Vice Squad.

Reverend Perry: "I made up my mind that somebody was going to talk to me after all this, it wasn't going to just be a parade.

"Morris immediately came along. I said, 'Morris, help keep the people away from me.' I sent my lover and my mother away, because the police were moving in now, and I said, 'Morris, whatever you do—I don't care about these heterosexuals ... but tell our community to get away from here. Because the police, all the motorcycles came up Hollywood Boulevard and we thought they were trying to have a riot—that they were trying to do something to us. So immediately I said, 'Morris, you gotta help me.'"

Kight knew what to expect. Reverend Perry didn't think they would get arrested. "This Sergeant came up and said, 'You do know that you can be arrested for doing this.' I said, 'if fasting and praying is a crime then I'll be arrested, I guess, but I'm not budging at all because I have a constitutional right to be here.' Morris asked, 'If they take you to jail, what do you want to do?' Keep everybody away from the jail; I don't want a problem where the police hurt people."

Perry and two women were arrested and taken to jail. The women posted bond and were released that night. Perry refused to be released and spent the night in jail.

Reverend Perry: "I said, 'No, I can fast in jail. I'm not putting up any money. You can let me go. I haven't done anything wrong so I'm leaving anyway.'

As this was happening, post-parade activities and parties continued into the night, throughout the city.

Reverend Perry heard this story from a few friends: "Morris walked into Satan's Bar and says, 'They have arrested Brother Troy and the two women.' People started saying, 'We're going down to the jail' and Morris immediately said, 'We're not going down to the jail. Brother Troy has said he does not want us to go down to the jail. We're not to go down to the jail.' This young gay man walked over and threw a beer in Morris' face and said, 'You're just a coward.' This is the truth. With beer running down his face, Morris looked at the young man and said, 'That may be but Brother Troy has said we are not to go down to the jail and we're not.'

"The crowd was upset that this young man had thrown a beer at Morris. They started clawing, and whoever the young man was, he got pushed by somebody who was very upset that he'd thrown a beer on Morris, saying, 'That's not how we're going to start doing things in the Gay Liberation Front.' I don't know who the person was, Morris never told me, but everybody told me about this, that a young man did that. Morris handled it."

Kight had dealt with rowdy drunks since he was a child.

1970. Bob Humphries, left; Morris Kight, center. First Gay Pride Parade, Hollywood Blvd., Los Angeles. Photo: Mother Boats C.P. (Brian Traynor), © Brian Traynor and Australian Lesbian and Gay Archives.

Perry continues: "The next day they took me from the jail and they sent me down to the court where Morris had stayed up all night, finding out what they were up to."

Morris had contacted Troy's lover and mother, who lived with him. They called other church members and people from GLF showed up at the courthouse. Perry: "While I'm in the jailhouse, Morris is taking care of the crowd out front. We really did work a lot together. I didn't see this, but when the judge had come in, Morris had told everybody to stay seated so nobody stood. In other words, they refused to stand and the judge had to see it when he came in. I had no idea.

"So when I came in, they all stood up. [Because I was behind glass] I didn't know why they stood up. I saw my mother and she was crying. She was a Southerner, and once you get over the fear of being arrested, you got to remember for most people it is the most frightful thing, because they don't how you're going to be treated and it's on their record and things like that."

Kight directed special attention to Troy's mother. He knew how to soothe her fears. Perry continues: "The judge was upset, I'm in my collar—I know he thought I was a Roman Catholic priest—he was eating up the City Attorney alive for having me appear, 'Why did you just—even if you wouldn't sign him out last night—why didn't you just let him out on his own recognizance? I don't understand. This is stupid.'

"When we got home, Morris, my mother, my partner, and others said, 'Brother Troy, are you going to continue fasting?'

"'Yes, I am.'

"Because of [his previous experience with] the Dow Company, Morris said, 'there are two places that you can go where they probably wouldn't bother you. One is First Unitarian Universal Church, but nobody would know you were there. The other is the Federal Building because the LAPD cannot arrest you on federal land. There are Federal Marshals there.' So we agreed that would be the place to go. And then Morris said, 'What do you think, Mrs. Perry?' and Mother just broke down crying, 'Oh, I wish he wouldn't do it.' She was so afraid that I was going to get hurt. I said, 'Mother, it's okay. We're all going to be all right.'"

Reverend Perry and five men and the same two women fasted on the steps of the Federal Building in downtown Los Angeles for 16 days. Morris visited them every day. "There were a lot of things that were going on. Finally, on my twelfth day of fasting, a city council member had come by and left me a note while I had gone to the restroom. A woman said I want to talk to you, she said, 'Martyrs are soon forgotten. Don't kill yourself, I want to talk to you.'

"So Morris and I met with Robert Stevenson, a real hero and a city council member from Hollywood, to talk to him about what it was we wanted and how can we start opening up the city. That started the negotiations. LAPD still was not ready to talk to us."

The first gay parade opened up the argument in the gay community regarding 'more radical' versus 'too radical.' In a 1970 "Gay Liberation Supplement" of the *Los Angeles Free Press* Morris Kight wrote:

"As for the radical content, the sky's the limit, but that gays proudly announced their Gayness and proudly paraded it in the streets, was considered by many as the most radical goddamned idea they'd ever had."

In 1994, Kight recalled the argument of "right-wing assimilationism and accommodationism [sic]. In 1970, we wanted to overthrow repressive laws, which have now happened in nearly half the states. We wanted the police to stop harassing us so badly, and while they still do, it has greatly diminished. We wanted a sense of community, and we said that GAY P-O-W-E-R meant something! We were self-affirming."

The day after the parade in Los Angeles, the *Advocate* attempted to contact L.A. Mayor Sam Yorty and Police Chief Davis. "Neither could be reached for comment."

The Gay Liberation Front Los Angeles was in the national news. The liberation of homosexuals was in the streets and living rooms of America.

Reaction to the parade within the gay community was mostly positive except from some of the more conservative contingent. One letter to the editor of the *Advocate* said: "That parade did more harm than good. By showing us off as a group of silly freaks those queens sure lowered our public image to the level public opinion has had it set for years. How can we make demands for equality, based on our rights as normal citizens, when our public image is constantly destroyed by flamboyancy and poor taste?"

Kight would not respond to criticism, especially from within the gay community.

Within two hours after the parade, plans were being set for an annual event. It didn't take long before Christopher Street West was declared "an institution."

In August of 1970, Kight announced the Christopher Street West coalition:

"[It] worked so well, that it has now become thirty-six organizations, naturally called 'Christopher Street West.'" Kight may have formulated this idea directly from his Career Services Training handbook.

Kight added: "Just about everybody in the United States who reads a newspaper, listens to the radio, or sees television knows about it. An example has been set, and a great one it was!"

Historians Armstrong and Crage in *The Making of the Stonewall Myth* (2006) acknowledge the power of gay pride as an institution: "Had the parade occurred only once, the Stonewall story would likely not be repeated today."

Los Angeles Free Press (July 3, 1970): "The chrysalis nature of the gay movement has begun to manifest itself. An incredibly intense display of creative freedom was observed and shared by many thousands of people in Los Angeles on June 28 as 1200 gays freed themselves of almost all inhibitions and fears and paraded down Hollywood Boulevard."

Using the U.S. Mission's tax-exempt status, the first Los Angeles Gay Pride Parade was underwritten by The Mission and Metropolitan Community Church. There was almost $200 in direct business donations and about $300 was raised by the sale of buttons and paper pansies. Bob Humphries' detailed financial report, sent from the United States Mission to the General Committee for Christopher Street West, was a perfect balance of assets and liabilities, each totaling $973.51. The bulk of the expenses, which was $520.22, went to "Expenses per Morris."

Kight wrote a personal thank-you letter to Herb Selwyn of the ACLU: "Without your assistance we would have been denied the right to parade, the considerable numbers of people who came would have been denied that pleasure, and the untold millions who thus heard our message, would never have done so."

Kight crafted a public letter of appreciation to "To the Homosexual Community," thanking: "All those persons, businesses, and organizations which contributed to the success of the parade this year."

At the bottom of his letter, he included a thanks: "to Edward Davis, Chief of Police, the real Publicity Chairman."

In the early days of liberation, Kight's goal was to create visibility and the first Christopher Street West parade went beyond that goal. The public persona of the gay movement was humorous, good-natured—making "good copy" for the media.

Regarding permanent markers in gay liberation, history will show, as Armstrong and Crage have surmised: "As the Stonewall riots recede into the past while gay pride celebrations flourish, there may come a time when the parades lose their connection… The vehicle may outlast the memory itself."

Kight in the *Los Angeles Free Press*, August 1970: "We are on the march, on the offensive, and one of these days some bright guy will say: 'what was all the fuss about?' What has it been about, indeed? The idea that the law, the courts, the police, an employer, the church, your neighbor, your family should ever have dictated your choice of love, has been of the most maddening irrelevance of the last six thousand years."

In a July 1970 letter to a friend Kight wrote: "As for Christopher Street 1969 I realize that all kinds of misconceptions exist, nobody will ever agree how many were there, what was or was not done, surely no one would defend the management of the bar itself. But is all that important in a changing world? Is folklore a bad thing? I think not. It's folklore that made some of the more enjoyable legends of our time. Somebody could probably make a living for a year or so in doing research and writing a book about it, but then time moves so fast that it would be out of date shortly, by more important events to come."

Kight was plucky about creating history as much as he was about creating a myth around the history.

THE END OF THE BEGINNING

IN MID-SEPTEMBER 1970, THE *ADVOCATE* RAN THE PRESCIENT heading "GLF programmed to destroy self."

In October 1970 Kepner wrote to Hay and Burnside (who were, by this time, comfortably settled in New Mexico):

"Things still bubbling here—I'm halfway out of it with Gay Lib, since some of the shouters took over and got things tightly under their control. But they're doing a fair job in some areas. If Morris doesn't keep you posted, I'll send along a batch of miscellaneous announcements and flyers."

Alfred Craig letter to the *Advocate*, in part:

"As a result of personality and political differences, GLF's membership has plunged from about 100 to 15 since Memorial Day. It could hardly afford to lose any more and remain viable. Nevertheless, the Marxists who now operate the organization … have programmed the Los Angeles group for self-destruction. The residue remaining after most of the rational people fled consists of a 'Chosen Few' who act as if they were some superior form of being with knowledge denied us ordinary mortals. Having attained this state of enlightenment, they assume the right, nay, the *duty* to force others to adopt their superior way of life."

Consciousness-raising groups had transgressed into "kangaroo courts" or also known as "star chamber trials." This practice continued for years after the GLF dispersed and were more like group-scrutinizing an individual's beliefs with the intention, as Craig inferred from his own experience, to "make certain that other dissidents toed the official line or left the organization."

GLF had become intolerant of criticism.

A lot had been accomplished because of the GLF cohesiveness, sporadic as it was. Gay Liberation as a social movement was set in motion and would not end without the GLF.

The national Gay Liberation movement was extremely successful. What had begun on both coasts of the U.S. was now awash through the consciousness of America.

Del Whan (2010): "I remember thinking that we were all working so hard at building the movement that we had not time to be sexual people, just movement people. Fun was not my focus. It was all about coming out, getting others to come out, organizing, paying the rent, going to the printers with the leaflets, getting announcements in the *Free Press,* getting the license to sell beer at the Funky Dances."

Christopher Street West. Tony Derosa; Christopher Street West. Peace Press. Offset, 1971. Los Angeles, CA. Courtesy of the Center for the Study of Political Graphics. ID 9505

To relieve stress, some people go shopping, some go bowling, others may go dancing—Morris Kight went protesting. He loved to be out on the streets, marching with fellow activists, signing and passing petitions, sharing war stories from the frontlines of the peace movement, a little gossip and perhaps a joke or two. It was sincere and it was also incredibly social. The gay movement couldn't always provide that kind of ideological camaraderie for Kight; there wasn't consistent solidarity within the movement. So Kight went to peace rallies and he invited gay comrades.

New York Times, April 22, 1972, headline: "Old Timers Join Newcomers in War Protest in Los Angeles."

"'Well, we're back marching again,' sighed Morris Kight. 'I don't know why we do it.' A few seconds later the veteran activist answered his own question. 'We must continue to try,' he said, fingering the peace symbol that hung around his neck. 'The truth is, if it weren't for us the war would have spread throughout Asia. We have been the conscience of the nation.'"

Particular entries in the GLF FBI file details homosexuals in the antiwar movement. Special agents were coordinated in multiple cities' antiwar rallies that took place on inauguration day, January 20, 1973.

"At Los Angeles (Pershing Square Park): Between 12:30AM and 1:32PM another contingent of antiwar demonstrators was forming at Pershing Square Park, Sixth and Hill Streets, in Downtown Los Angeles. At about 11:55AM a stake body truck loaded with approximately 25 uniformed members of the National Socialist White People's Party (NSWPP), wearing white crash helmets and Nazi swastika arm bands, was observed circling Pershing Square. As they rounded the southwest corner of the park, a group of individuals identifying themselves as being members of the Jewish Defense League (JDL) congregated on the corner and yelled epithets at the truck load of 'Nazis' calling the latter 'fags' and 'Queer Nazis.' At this point female members of the demonstrators representing the Gay Liberation Front (the self-styled 'Dike Brigade') appeared on the scene taking exception to the epithets being hauled by the JDL at the Nazis, saying, 'you can call them filth, animals, pigs, or whatever else you like, but don't refer to them as "gay," as we are representatives of the truly "gay" people here.' Then they demanded verbal apologies from the JDL'ers which were quickly received.

"The Gay Liberation Front is a loosely knit group of homosexuals and other individuals seeking to legalize homosexuality and further the cause of both male and female homosexuals. Secondarily they seek an end to American involvement in South East Asia."

GAY VERSUS GAY

"THE SAME TENSIONS HAVE TORN AT GLF FROM THE BEGINNING—basic disagreements among right- and left-wing radicals, hippie types and the more conservative members, compounded by GLF's lack of structure and concern for order." (Jim Kepner for the *Advocate*).

John Effinger: "As one in the *liberal* camp I was never in the middle of this storm, but was more observing from the edges. This eventually led to disillusion. Though our first meetings consisted of from 10 to 20 (mostly) men the GLF grew very quickly and we eventually moved our meetings (of a hundred or more) to a building on Vermont near the Hollywood Blvd., where the meetings became free-for-alls as the various leftwing factions went to war with each other. At the last meeting I attended, a discussion of a demonstration was hijacked by a group of guys in women's clothing (some wearing tutus) who INSISTED that nothing was to go forward until ALL agreed that the men would be required to wear skirts at the next demonstration. After that I would see Morris at various events, mostly at Vietnam War demonstrations. Over the years I would see him from time to time and have never felt less than affection for this good man who tried to keep his eye on the prize (to steal a phrase)."

In February 1971 Craig Hansen wrote in a letter to Kight: "I believe the Los Angeles Gay Liberation Front has become an exclusive and excludive [sic] organization. It has failed to serve the civil rights needs of the greater Los Angeles homosexual community because the leading members are so insistent on preserving the proper 'long-haired image.' Persons who do not fit that image are told by characters such as [Chuck] Avery that they are unwelcome. It is very unfortunate that you have not been able to use your influence to stop this practice, but perhaps it is impossible, considering the composition of the organization.... I feel disgusted with the hippie-snobs in Gay Lib who tried to push [Hansen's friend] back in [the closet]."

In early 1971, Gay Liberation Front L.A. was still organizing peaceful, nonviolent demonstrations. Speaking to Mitch Grobson in 1998, Kight recalled: "One day in 1971, mind you Gay Liberation Front was November/December, 1969, the 12 months of 1970, and three months in 1971, I brought together a meeting of the Gay Liberation Front, we met on Vermont Avenue ... and said 'Look, we've done our work, and I recommend we dissolve ourselves.' Well, I almost had to be protected from the mob, 'Why you rat fink, how dare you give up.' I said, 'If you think we have work to do, let's do it, but I think we've done our work, we disabused lesbian and gay people of any notion that they are less than inferior.' And so I said, let's dissolve ourselves. And so then the GLF ran itself back out of existence.

"Maybe he's right, [others reasoned] we have disbanded, disavowed our relationship with inferiority. We went around believing that we were sick because the psychiatrists said we were, sinful because the Church said we were, we represented a birth defect because our family said we were, unemployable because employers didn't hire us, we couldn't rent property because we were obvious and the worst thing you could be was to be obvious, and we've just done something about that. We have found a way to bring order out of the homophobic camp. We're beginning to cure our own internalized homophobia. When it was agreed that we would dissolve, we paid our bills and gave our office furniture away to other groups, and announced to everybody that we were going out of business."

Kight fully believed in the longevity of gay liberation and saw the GLF as a group was descending into a manic rube. Every day he received numerous letters from Missouri, Arkansas, and beyond, mostly handwritten, from people of all ages, races, creeds asking for "more information concerning your movement."

Some people blamed Kight for ending the GLF; many of the same people who accused Kight of ruining homophile conferences. Kight wrote off the conjecture as more of Jim Kepner's "revisionism, reconstruction, and revanchism."

Kight to Cain: "All the GLFs died in 1971. All of them! I didn't kill the GLF. I didn't close down the GLF. Toward the end, it became a death rattle." Kight described "a lumpen proletariat, who had ever so many more needs than we could fulfill. They had a desire for food, and clothing, and housing, and so on."

GLF closed the storefront at 4400 Melrose and the 555 Vermont office space.

Kight had bigger organizations to build and fires to control. When asked in 1994 if he envisioned, when he began, that the movement would grow into what it is today, Kight's unequivocal answer was: "Oh, absolutely. My answer is terribly ego-stricken, but it's true. Yes. I believed that we would be big, big, big, and we are big, big, big." (Cain)

The Los Angeles GLF Help Hotline stayed open and manned by volunteers from Kight's home and, whenever possible, Kight took calls. The FBI continued to keep the GLF file open and identify GLF as a "subversive" organization. Only the FBI documented GLF activities past 1971 until mid-1975, by which time it had become clear that Gay Liberation was no longer an organization, but a substantial social movement.

1973

FOR THE FIRST TIME IN HISTORY, OPENLY GAY POLITICAL ORGANIzations were formed. Divisiveness threatened every single one. The organization known as Christopher Street West which took charge of the Gay Pride Parade and celebration was terminal.

Appealing to the wider community, Kight wrote an open letter and had it signed by the 16 members of the Christopher Street West Planning Committee.

"What exactly is Gay Pride? It is no secret that our community is quite diversified when it comes to politics, religion, lifestyle, etc. Thus, Gay Pride will mean many things to many people. But out of our great diversity and creativity, we are putting together an event, which belongs to ALL gay people. In doing so we are learning more about each other and generating an awareness of what pride and unity means to all of us as gay brothers and sisters."

Kight was pulling away from the parade in late 1971. He wrote to Foster Gunnison: "As for 1972 I do not know. I will not run it again. I am tired of it now, and feel that fresh blood is necessary to keep it going. Enough, I created it, and coordinated it two years. Many worked, much good came of it."

For the 1972 parade, a giant papier-mâché dragon with a penis head accompanied the giant Vaseline jar. The Cockapillar ejaculated a white fluid as it weaved down Hollywood Boulevard.

In 1973, sponsors pulled financial support because of parade content. Gay bathhouse owners were outraged about the vulgarity in the parade; the consensus was that it left the gay community open to harsh criticism from the neighborhood. Censorship was discussed and Kight, to some people's dismay, did not oppose it. He claimed that he was "annoyed with critics of the parade within the gay community."

Despite his best efforts, there was no progress toward resolutions to have a parade. The planning committee couldn't agree, much less the community. Kight blamed the "blunting of the parade's political focus." He threw his arms up in the air, feigning boredom with petty differences and dismissed any possibility of a cohesive effort.

Pat Rocco: "One thing I remember was, well actually two things I remember were disagreements, and we should have them too. There were outstanding disagreements between the two of us. One had to do with Christopher Street West. There were parades, of course, in 1970, '71 and '72. There was no parade in 1973, somehow it just got by us. It just went by. Nobody organized it. There was no official organization."

Jim Kepner's notes blame Morris for sabotaging the parade the third year.

The cancellation of the Los Angeles parade freed Kight to go to New York City to celebrate Gay Pride East Coast-style and be wined and dined like gay royalty. The last weekend in June of 1973, he and Barbara Gittings co-Grand Marshaled New York's Gay Pride Parade and rally in Washington Square. All weekend, Kight was the guest of honor of Dick Leitsch, Morty Manford, Vito Russo, Bruce Voeller and others. One night, two o'clock in the morning, they surprised Morris with a walk to the Stonewall Inn, where he "burst into tears."

Two days later, June 23, 1973, Vito Russo introduced Kight as the second keynote speaker at the rally in Washington Square Park: "The man who founded the GLF of Los Angeles, the president of the board of directors of the Gay Community Services in Los Angeles, and was in the peace movement before most of us were born. He is the silver thread, as he calls it, from southern Los Angeles to New York City, and he comes bringing us love, the dean—as John Francis Hunter calls him—of the gay liberation movement, Morris Kight."

1971. "The Cockapillar" appeared in the 1970, '71, '72 Gay Pride parades. Photo: Pat Rocco. Pat Rocco Papers, Coll2007-006, ONE National Gay & Lesbian Archives, USC Libraries, University of Southern California.

Addressing the largest crowd of homosexuals he had ever faced—maybe 50,000—Kight's tempo was more hurried than usual. His enunciation was less patrician, more proletarian.

"Brothers and sisters, I bring you greetings of love ... There was in this demonstration a picket sign which I think is classic. One of the best I have ever seen in my life. 'Don't pretend to be somebody else. Be yourself.'

He offered greetings from the West Coast.

"Now, let's talk. In New York, I have been the recipient of the most hospitality that I have ever received in my entire life. Don Goodwin of the Mattachine Society has had me to the society's offices and to a lovely dinner. I was at the westside discussion group FAIR yesterday. I couldn't have enjoyed myself more. Last night I was at the Gay Activists Alliance of New Jersey for a thrilling and beautiful march, and afterward a delightful party. Billy Russo, one of my coworkers in Los Angeles, is in the city and he has provided transportation for me, and I thank you, Billy. Beyond that, two beautiful people, and many joining them, Jonathan Katz, and David Roisensack, had me to Coming Out, and I never had such an emotional experience in my lifetime.

"Beyond that, the Gay Activists Alliance has had me to the Firehouse time and again, and I've enjoyed it. My host in New York has been Morty Manford. Thank him. OK."

After all the back-slapping, he continued.

"At this time every year throughout America, there is held graduation exercises. And they always talk about promises. They are going to promise you a lot of things—the universe, dominion, progress, domination over women, over blacks, over Chicanos, over us, over children. Domination, domination. I call it the great bullshit revelation of June each year.

"So that's not what we are talking about. We are talking about not dominating. We are talking about sharing and loving and caring."

Getting down to basics, his speech sharpens—consonants are hard and the vowels drag.

"So we have a promise that we should make one another. Other minorities have had those that promise them things. Sojourner Truth said to black women, 'that white man over there says that woman, that lady must be lifted into a carriage.'"

Kight shifted gears and turned on his Southern drawl to create an energetic rhetoric.

"Nobody ever lifted me into a carriage and ain't I a woman? Marcus Garvey said, 'liberty and justice for all.' Well, they must be talking about white folks because us black folks never had no liberty and justice."

His speech resumed the original inflection.

"Unfortunately nobody promised us anything except misery and destruction and genocide. We have been promised a life of death and destruction and despair. Until this generation in which we have joined together to promise one another, that should never happen again.

"In that context, we must remember Dachau, Bełżec, Pilsen, Auschwitz, Buchenwald, in which a million of our brothers and sisters were scooped up off the streets of Europe and taken to that place and there submitted to the ultimate solution to gayness, incinerated, and turned into soap."

He paused to place an emphasis on his next line.

"Never again [a-gan]. Never again [a-gan] will we allow this to happen.

"Never again will you be allowed to take our children from us. You will not be allowed to take our dignity. You will not be allowed to take our lives. You will not be allowed to deny us a home, a job. And we demand that you give us the room that we want. Not to be part of your society.

"I do not wish to work at the White House because I don't want to be a thief. I don't want to work at the Pentagon because I don't want to be a murderer."

For a New York crowd, they loved it and they loved him. He shouted over their cheers:

"I don't want to work at the National Institute for Mental Health because I don't want to treat dissidents and gays as if they were sick.

"I want to make a world in which we say, 'No more can you do that.' The mental health industry must get off our backs. The Church must reform itself. The nuclear family must give way. All of this society must give us room, room, room. And you have taken it for yourselves.

"And thus, as long as there is a breath of life in Barbara Gittings and me, any one of you, we will not allow it."

The speech wound down with "an exercise in love. Touch. Feel. Talk to somebody. Kiss somebody. Caress somebody. Enfold somebody into your love…"

With a double scoop of irresistible hippie love magic on top of gay pride, Kight closed, "Brothers and sisters, I bring you nothing in the world but total mad love."

Vito Russo articulated the crowd's reaction: "Thank you Morris. We love you."

Kight had the time of his life. He held court, soaked up every watt of the spotlight and enjoyed being royalty. He was around people he could converse with, not argue. The New York activists seemed so much more mature, in Kight's eyes, than their West Coast counterparts. There was no fighting, no backbiting—at least not around visiting royalty.

Kight to Cain: "It had been such a high-energy day—of course, it had been the largest demonstration ever. Everything had been absolutely correct. It was thrilling. It was the perfect day. And so we ate and drank. And we drank a lot. And along about two o'clock Igal Roodenko, a gay man, pacifist, now dead of old age from a heart attack, Igal said to me, 'We need to get out of here.'"

They left the party and together headed up to 72nd Street.

"To the most strange apartment I've ever been in my lifetime. It was three stories tall. And elegant, the most elegant I'd ever been in. It had a two-story bed. A bed that was built up with a rack of books and a rack for fish tanks, and then a sleeping pad here and a sleeping pad there, and so on, and so forth. I went up all through this bed."

Later they went to the Boat Basin on the Hudson River, and enjoyed a Greek-Roman style building with a fountain inside. About five o'clock in the morning, Kight said, "I've just got to get some rest. I've just got to get home to Morty [Manford]."

Kight went back to the Village and as soon he entered the apartment, Morty Manford greeted him, "Oh, thank heavens you're here! The phone has rung all night! They're searching for you. People at the Center and your friends have been calling to say there's been a fire in New Orleans. We don't know if it's a gay bar or not, but it sounds gay to us."

It was a gay bar. The Upstairs Lounge was a popular second-story gay hangout in the French Quarter of New Orleans. Later it would be determined that the fire was caused by a firebomb thrown into the stairwell, the only exit and entrance. During peak business, the fire hugged the heavy drapes and flew through the crammed bar with no emergency exits and barred windows. The few who survived did so by squeezing through the bars of the second-story windows and jumping onto the sidewalk.

Manford suggested that Kight re-route himself to go through New Orleans on his way back to Los Angeles. Before afternoon, both men were at the airport boarding a flight to New Orleans.

Kight: "I notified the press that I was coming. When I got to Atlanta, the press was at the airport and they interviewed me, and so on, I said it was a national day of mourning. And then I went on to New Orleans and Troy was there, along with some other people from Los Angeles."

There is no record of media waiting at the airport to greet them.

Reverend Troy Perry's pastor assistant and two church members died in the fire.

Reverend Perry remembers, "The Police Department called a press conference, said they found out it was a gay bar. They said it was only thieves and queers and they don't carry ID. Once they found out it was a gay bar, we didn't exist."

Up to that point, it was the largest bar fire in American history. It was national news for exactly 24 hours when suddenly the news media stopped reporting the catastrophe. News of the disaster continued to spread through gay communities by phone calls and underground press.

Kight and Perry held a press conference at the local Marriott Hotel. Identified as "president of the Gay Community Services Center and reputed founder of the Gay Liberation Movement," Kight was frequently quoted in the *Times-Picayune*: "Kight called the fire 'the worst single tragedy to befall the gay community since Nazi Germany.'"

Twenty-nine people had burned to death at The Upstairs Lounge. Kight and Perry counseled families who were finding out for the first time that their loved ones were gay. They helped fire victims in the hospital and immediately began raising funds.

Kight: "The police were making the most terrible statements. The Fire Marshal was making homophobic statements, such as, 'We will never know who they were because gay people don't carry identification.' And we were holding a quick press conference to correct them."

Reverend Perry: "Here again, Morris was right. He said, 'Troy, you have more power than you know. If you tell people to send us money, they will pay for these hotel rooms.' I got on the phone.

"I called Clay Shaw to hold a memorial service if I could not find a church. But I found a church. Morris and Morty Manford came in—and then I brought in two other clergy, one who worked for Social Security so we'd know how to deal with the bodies. Morris again was working his way with the media. We were all interviewed. We all knew how to talk. They got more than they knew what to do with. We verbally attacked the Police Department right off the bat."

The local press coverage was horrific, from dismissive to a cursory mention. The print media was downright hateful in its coverage. At one point, Perry and Kight had to blast the local press for repeating distasteful gags and pejorative statements from homophobic locals.

Eventually, Kight and Perry met with the Fire Marshal of New Orleans Parish. They were able to direct him away from more mean-spirited statements.

Reverend Perry: "Well, the police tried to backpedal but it was too late—it was amazing how we turned them around. We all held a press conference and said 'Those were human beings.' The bodies were so burned the FBI has had to use skulls, the bodies were completely cremated and everything was burned up including their ID. These were people with real names, with families."

By the next day, the final count was 32 dead and numerous serious injuries. Charred bodies were stacked in the city morgue as the drama played out. Three fire victims remain unidentified to this day.

Kight: "We stayed for a week, burying the dead. I fantasized about creating a National New Orleans Memorial Fund to raise money and contribute it to a Trust.

"One of [the New Orleans belles] came and said [in a Southern accent], 'Mistah Kight, we must meet with you. You must meet with the people from this city. You're out there, holding press conferences to say all these radical things. We're unused to radicalism. You have to bear in mind that many of the people who burned to death in the fire are sons and daughters of distinguished old Southern families.'"

Kight recognized those Southern ways. He and Troy were seen as carpetbaggers. Kight perceived the locals as financially unhelpful and internally impoverished; he resented their meddling in his good deeds.

"And so, of all the money raised for the National New Orleans Memorial Fund, none came from New Orleans. None. They didn't want to hear it. They didn't want to deal with it. We were an embarrassment to them. I am convinced that we were absolutely correct and right. And moreover, we used mountains of tact in dealing with those who were not supportive of us."

Funds were raised. Kight asked Dick Michaels, publisher of the *Advocate,* to "conduit the money." Kight explained: "Michaels was a very conservative, very decent, wonderful man." After an hour-long phone conversation it was agreed that the donations would be sent to the *Advocate*, using their Post Office box, accounting, and banking. "We trustees, seven of us, would dispense the funds." They contributed to such costs as burial, medical, utilities, and rent.

"And the final, last act of the National New Orleans Memorial Fund, a year and a half later, was a brother who had been badly burned, lost two fingers on his left hand, and one or two fingers on his right hand, and his shoulder was badly damaged, and his leg was badly damaged, he hobbled." The man would never be able to work again and knew people in El Dorado, Arkansas, where he wanted to move. "So the last money was to help buy a house for him. And the last time I talked with him, he was living in peace and love in El Dorado.

"It was a shattering experience. We were unbelievably inspired. We were unbelievably brave. We were pushed beyond ourselves." (Paul Cain, '94)

In a private condolence letter to Reverend J.E. Paul Breton (MCC Washington, D.C.) Kight wrote: "New Orleans was a unique experience for me. I shared some of it with Morty, when we talked a long time on the phone and became very emotional. It has affected my life. Idea to dust off and present to you. I am only awaiting that to dust off … for the highly evolved there is no death, but only spirit everlasting. And [Reverend] was all that."

The New Orleans fire was a turning point.

Before he went to New York, Kight was indifferent about an annual gay pride celebration. He was prepared to abandon the idea altogether. If no one else wanted to quarterback the event, he was just as pleased to see it fade away. He was a peripatetic activist; he'd flit from crisis to crisis, identify a need, cite a solution, organize something new, create some jargon, write a few press releases, wave a magic wand, make a difference, and then move on. He'd leave it for others to carry through or not. He'd say, "Let's move on," to the next challenge or instigation. He was still impetuous, a bit immature in his efforts to keep things moving, just to keep "gay" in the public consciousness.

On the flight back to Los Angeles from New Orleans, for the first time, Kight longed for tradition, a bit of a routine. He wanted stability. He appreciated what ritual brought to a community and he wanted that for his community. He finally saw a gay community where none had existed in 1957 and he looked deeper into the purpose of that community. He craved the feeling that he had on June 28, 1970. He vowed never to miss another hometown Gay Pride parade. He never again talked about uprooting and moving to San Francisco or any other place. He was home. Los Angeles was as much of a home as a tumbleweed like Morris Kight had ever known. It mattered not what the content of the parade was—just as long as it was big and gay and colorful, and it needed to be a regular event—to inculcate the celebration of being gay and allow gay to permeate mainstream consciousness, not once and for all, but habitually—a reliable stream of gay pride celebrations everywhere.

He returned to the West Coast with new insight and inspiration. He was ready to pass the leadership baton and let Gay Pride become its own entity and have a life.

The following year, Christopher Street West formed a new Steering Committee with Pat Rocco the first official president. They went through the parade permit process and again met objections—Police Chief Ed Davis criticized the "unsavory" content of the 1972 parade.

The 1974 Gay Pride celebration was a week-long festival, closer to the Mardi Gras atmosphere that Kight had originally envisioned, and culminated with a parade. In 1976, Pat Rocco brought in circus animals, including elephants (and fleas no doubt), a circus tent, and gave his old friend Kight a Ringmaster baton to exercise or exorcize his full P.T. Barnum.

In 1977, Kight served as the first official Grand Marshal of the parade, followed by Harvey Milk in 1978.

Over time, the parade gained respectability. Kight reached beyond the homosexual parameter to include hetero supporters. In 1974, Jack Albertson (prominent character actor) and his wife Wallace Albertson joined the parade and celebration.

"I will never forget that first CSW parade," Wallace Albertson explained, "where my late husband, Jack Albertson, and I and some of the other political figures in L.A. marched and it wasn't easy to do it then. But Morris galvanized us all."

Kight served on the Board of Christopher Street West for the rest of his life. Commemoration of the Stonewall rebellion survived and proliferated and sprung forth an institution of gay culture. Annual Gay Pride celebrations became international events and remain famous for the "adventuresome" spirit. Kight predicted in 1970: "The vehicle may outlast the memory itself."

Through the 1970s, the young gay community became more flamboyant, more celebratory. It grew stronger in numbers and organized as best as any of the other civil rights movements of anytime. Like the women's lib and the black civil rights movements, Gay Liberation did not move directly or easily toward equal rights.

After GLF closed its doors and had opened a generation of young minds, it was a particularly exciting time for Los Angeles, and for Morris Kight personally. There was still so much that needed to be done, so many needs to be addressed, and their community was growing every day. It would all get done. It was all very positive and colorful. There would be many stepping stones on the road to liberation and with each success, the opposition's resolve strengthened.

Unnoticeably the hippie movement receded to the sale racks and thrift stores. The 1970s were waking up with a bit of a hangover.

No one, not Morris Kight nor any of the great thinkers and intellectuals of gay liberation, could have foreseen the many challenges that still lay ahead.

Chapter 11

Gay Community, Gay Services, Gay-Centered

THE END OF the Gay Liberation Front did not signify the end of the liberation movement. The "social services component," as Kight liked to call what they did, quickly made Los Angeles a leader among other cities with active gay lib movements. To Kight's thinking, the next phase of the gay revolution must be to expand social services. For as much as Kight and the others had accomplished in GLF, they discovered a black hole of need among their people.

The early days of liberation uncovered a desperate, marginalized slice of society, an underserved population of gays, lesbians, and transgenders. Kight knew the gaps and pitfalls for gays, most especially personal shame. For about every two people who "came out" to their family, as encouraged by the GLF and specifically Kight, there was another youth who was left unsupported and often dispossessed and disenfranchised. An unfortunate effect in this revolution was mainstream thinkers' rejection of their own children—even if temporarily, most often permanently.

The streets of Los Angeles flood with more than the local youths; Hollywood notoriously entices young kids from all over the world, kids with big dreams, broken hearts, and chips on their shoulders. As Stuart Timmons described them: "If the Dream Factory of Hollywood made industrial waste, they were it."

Hotline phone calls with requests for bail, counseling, or treatment for a venereal disease never stopped. There were endless calls for help to get back home or to find

a way to stay. They saw a marginal pauper population with basic needs—places to sleep, work, and eat.

In October 1973, the *Los Angeles Times* published a letter from Kight responding to criticism in a multi-part investigational series on runaways. "We know the words harsh though they may be," Kight wrote, "are true." He elaborated:

"The [Gay Community Services Center] hears about some of them when they first come to Los Angeles and is able to come to their aid ... some we hear about for the first time when we find them in Juvenile Hall, sleeping in abandoned cars, or near death from accidental overdoses or from attempted suicide from their 'failures.'

"In some cases, the center has stood as guardian to enroll them in school. In every case we have been responsive and responsible and have given the young brother or sister an opportunity to make decisions for themselves without pressure from older people."

1971. The founding board of the Gay Community Services Center. Left: Executive Director Don Kilhefner, Vice President Morris Kight, Jim Kepner, June Herrle, Dr. Martin Field, Jon Vincent Platania. Photo Lee Mason. Lee Mason Photographs, Coll2012-078, ONE National Gay & Lesbian Archives, Los Angeles, California.

He closed the letter with the standard appeal for funds and he asked for "community's support in such humane, innovative work."

Liberation had taken its toll on everyone. After his arrest and subsequent acquittal, Jon Platania, once a rising professional with sights on a political career, managed a group of parking lots in downtown L.A. Platania became a highly motivated activist. He and his friend Paul Olson continued to rent broken-down houses to serve as crash pads and temporary housing for the indigent youth. They had slack rules about no drugs or alcohol in the houses and a fairly strict regulation that each resident had to pay a nominal fee per day while living in the house. It was suggested that residents be living as an "out" homosexual, but it was never mandatory. The crash pads gave a much-needed hand-up to an entire generation of brave young people who bucked the status quo and dared to live as homosexuals.

The owner of the Van Ness house died. Kight learned that the Johnson brothers, Mormon laypersons, took over ownership and he immediately phoned them to continue the lease on the house, "and I told them who we were. They didn't bat an eye to hear we were gay. They said, 'Well, fine,' and we leased the house for $300 a month.

"At one point, we had five Liberation Houses around the city. In those foregone days we were deeply concerned about crisis housing. I made a lot of mistakes in my time and I dreamed up that we would make the Van Ness house into an organic collective. Rather than to have a crisis house, people were going and coming, residents would work and pay a rent sufficient to pay the bills. Thus a dance of death started all over again. We got a group of exploiters who claimed they were gay liberationists when they had no spirit of gay liberation. They exploited us horribly. Didn't pay their rent. We had to pay the bills with our money. So we served them notice that they had to move, 'cause we were to make it the Van Ness Recovery House.

"To get even with us, they dumped a one-hundred-pound bag of cement down the sewer, stopped up the sewer out into the street. We had to dig up the sewer and replace it. We finally got them out of the house. Then we made it the Van Ness Recovery House. These recovering alcoholics were so excited about it; they were energized. They sanded and painted, brought in furniture, and so on. We opened with three residents."

Van Ness Recovery House became a viable independent nonprofit 20-bed facility to help recovering alcoholics and addicts. It continues to thrive and serve the GLBT community in Los Angeles 50 years later.

Every idea preceded the availability of funds. Lack of assets never deterred their ambitions or dictated their direction. Platania and Olson continued to take turns signing leases on the early Liberation Houses. Soon they rented a storefront at 1519–1521 Griffith Park Boulevard and hung a shingle naming it "Gay Will Funky Thrift Shoppe."

Platania remembered: "Morris, Stanley [Williams], Ralph Schaffer and I were busy setting up the Gay Will Funky Thrift Shoppe. Lee [Heflin] made Indian-styled beaded leather pants and shirts. People donated clothes. Morris found all the furniture. It was a used upscale Hollywood hand-me-down shop. Morris was in heaven. And we did marvelously well." This became the first steady source of income for gay services. Ralph Schaffer and Stanley Williams volunteered to manage the secondhand store.

Ralph Schaffer was Morris' roommate/custodian/assistant. In addition to managing the thrift store, Ralph ran Kight's Fourth Street home. Out-of-town guests knew to contact Schaffer, not Kight. He handled all household duties, shopping, meal prep, as well as Kight's phone calls and correspondence. Schaffer sometimes represented Kight at meetings and events. Del Whan and Carolyn Weathers remembered Schaffer "as a kind man and feminist."

Del Whan remembered Kight's house as "always full of men. One was Ralph Schaffer and I recall an angry abrupt guy named Don Johnson. They were both close to Morris, and they had almost totally different ways in how they related to [women]. Ralph was very kind to me and all women. An effeminate male in his forties, he seemed to understand female sensitivities and discrimination by gender.

"Ralph used to come to all the Funky Dances put on by GLF and all the dances that I put on for the Gay Women's Service Center as fundraisers at Troupers Hall in Hollywood. Ralph once put in a nude appearance at a dance in the early 1970s. No one seemed to object."

Schaffer was every bit as politically and socially active as Kight, publishing several articles for *Gay Sunshine Press* and writing a few articles for *Free Press* that were unpublished. He wanted to replace Douglas Key (Angela Keyes Douglas) on their masthead.

By default, Schaffer became an extension of Kight, or at least Kight's household. He was indispensable. Kight could be abrupt and dismissive of Schaffer. Kight could be oblivious, appearing ungrateful for Schaffer's efforts. Schaffer was even-tempered and knew how to navigate Kight's temperament.

At the same time, Platania shared a house in Silver Lake with June Herrle, near Kilhefner's and Steve Morrison's Hoover Street Collective, frequented by many GLFers including Lee Heflin, Tony DeRosa, and Stanley Williams. Platania described their house as a "more middle-class version of the Hoover Collective." It was a tight-knit, fun, passionate group of innovators, "a cheap way to live for people who are activists."

HUMBLE BEGINNINGS

THERE ARE AS MANY DIFFERENT VERSIONS TO THE BEGINNINGS of the Gay Community Services Center as there are people to tell the tale. What is consistent in each telling: at the time it was an outlandish idea. Genuinely humble in every way, the spirit was to be support of community over personality. However, the individual personalities involved did not make for a completely altruistic venture. There was the requisite infighting, eventual competition for recognition, power plays, and games for ego tender. It is likely that Kight's nature brought out a competitive cockiness in others. No matter the individual and group strategy, while all of this was taking place, it was audacious just to imagine a not-for-fee social services agency geared specifically for the needs of homosexuals. It might have been a collective delusion. In any case, success would depend upon a Brobdingnagian ego. Morris Kight may have been grooming himself years for this challenge. Gay and lesbian liberation had nothing to lose from Kight's ego. Any collateral damage would be internal.

Despite the strong personalities, they usually worked well together, sharing a goal and mutual respect that allowed constructive critique. When the chemistry worked, it worked brilliantly.

Platania: "The Center grew out of our collective response to our collective sorrow, anger and determination."

Kight: "In April and May of 1971, a number of us met to fantasize what was then called Gay Community Services Center [GCSC]—lesbian was added later. Attending those meetings were Jon Vincent Platania, who was a psychologist [Platania became a psychologist a few years later], a terribly bright man, great at manipulating governments to give money, and so on. Dr. Donald Kilhefner, one of the brilliant geniuses our community has created. June Herrle was a master of social work, who had a child during that time. Stanley Williams, who had been from Gay Liberation Front. Tony DeRosa, an artist and a superb liberationist, attended some of the founding meetings."

Stuart Timmons described Tony DeRosa as a "swarthy and intense artist who also created some of the movement's most powerful images."

Another prominent activist in the early days of the Center was a law student named Rand Schrader. Schrader went on to become the second openly gay judge appointed in California and many years later, a street in Hollywood was named after him.

Also at the meetings was Martin Field, a medical doctor who had been "consulting" with MCC and, more discreetly, with Kight and his "clap shack."

Kight: "Ultimately, a think tank of about 15 emerged. We met at my house, 1822 Fourth Street and at Kilhefner's, 1501 North Hoover, and other people's houses.

1974. l to r: Morris Kight, Don Kilhefner (standing), Ken Bartley, on the porch of the original Gay Community Services Center, Los Angeles. Photo: Walt Blumoff for the *Advocate*. Walt Blumoff Photographs, Coll2012-056, ONE National Gay & Lesbian Archives, Los Angeles, California.

We agreed that we were writing history. We agreed to that, because we knew that's what we were doing. We also agreed that we could go crazy and [should] not judge one another. And we would dream up programs. And then we'd get it so in our head that we could peddle it to the others.

"And so then we—knowing full well that it was a radical idea which needed to be packaged and so on—sought a meeting with the board of directors of all the homophile and gay outfits in town. There were only eight, so it was easy enough to meet with them. We met with MCC, we met with ONE, Inc., Dorr [Legg] attended the meeting—and we said, this is what we were going to do. If you hear criticism [from anyone inside or outside the community], don't answer it unless you wish to. Have them call us and we'll answer it."

Dr. Betty Berzon recalled: "In the summer of 1971 a rather ragtag band of people came to my house to talk about what I thought was a wild scheme. They wanted to open a center, like a Jewish Community Center, only for gay people. Their leader was a round little fellow with longish blond hair and twinkling eyes. Morris began, 'My dear Miss Berzon,' and he delivered an eloquent oration on the fact that the planet was in dire peril and we had to do something about it. He outlined the many ways in which the situation could be rescued. Eventually he got to the importance of establishing this gay and lesbian center in Los Angeles and how I might possibly help since I had been involved with Human Growth Centers around the U.S. I listened, he hooked me, and I became a part of this crazy scheme."

Terry DeCrescenzo recalled, "Betty wished that people wouldn't give her credit for founding the Center, [because] she didn't. The group came to her."

Berzon, who had studied at the Western Behavioral Sciences Institute (WBSI), was probably the most pedigreed of the bunch. She joined their effort in the second year to "help define programs and counseling techniques," as Kight described it.

DeCrescenzo continued, "Betty became the informal psychologist for the Center. She created peer counselor groups, counselor training, and they mapped the outline for the Center's programs. She developed a series of programs, created leaderless groups, to encourage natural leaders to emerge. In addition, they continued the rap groups."

Soon, the executive committee had their meetings in her comfortable home located in the hills.

Berzon described the founding team as having "unbelievable ingenuity and chutzpah." In a 1997 interview she recalled that "watching Kight, Kilhefner, Platania, and June Herrle as they sat in my living room and planned this organization was an inspiring, exciting adventure. They created something that had every reason why it should not be successful, and they made it happen and made it grow."

"So we met," Kight recalled, "and we wrote a charter and mission and incorporation and bylaws and a 65-page document projecting what the Center would be—programs, numbers and names, the philosophy, and the mission. I was already performing the services. Some of those services were already performed by Don Kilhefner, by Jon Platania, and others."

Based on the consciousness-raising groups and the work done by the Gay Survival Committee in the GLF, Platania and Kilhefner created a first draft of the Center's bylaws to give to Kight. Del Whan, who had founded the Gay Women's

Services Center in February 1971, remembered that Kight and Kilhefner borrowed the GWSC draft constitution and bylaws. Platania "dictated it. [Kilhefner] typed it. Morris gave his suggestions, of course."

Each draft of the new vision for a social services agency tailored by and for gays was passed around. It took months of revisions. Kight, Platania, Kilhefner, Stanley Williams, June Herrle, Troy Perry and others from MCC wrote notes in the margins and made suggestions for programs. MCC had been providing many similar services since their inception in 1968, so they were very familiar with the particular needs.

Kight: "Those services that the Center now renders were in some primitive form already being rendered… However, Don felt it would be more helpful if more people shared in the execution of those responsibilities."

Kight insisted that the structural formation of the Center, including the development and evaluation of programs, be easily replicated. He immediately envisioned others duplicating the idea in other cities, and as early as July 1972, Kight was receiving letters from activists wanting to open Gay Centers in other cities. He was generous with information and taking time to consult and give encouragement. To whomever asked, Kight would send instructions and the exact Articles of Incorporation.

Over time, the Center has been replicated around the world.

Platania: "Morris needed to be 'founder' of the Center, it gave him a forum. Really looking at the long range of his life, there is nothing wrong with Morris laying claim [to being founder]." Though the truth was, as Platania said, "We all did it."

Platania described himself "an administrator of some note and was ideally suited" to serve as Executive Director of the Center. "Morris, June Herrle, and a number of other people asked if I would serve as [first] Executive Director. Donald [Kilhefner] came to me and said that he 'had always seen himself in that role.' So I tossed it off.

"June was disappointed, but agreed that Don would be the first Executive Director. She rationalized that 'for Don and Morris, this was their whole life.'"

The founding board members were: Morris, Jon Platania, June Herrle, Jim Kepner, Lee Sansen Sisson, and the founding Executive Director was Don Kilhefner.

For Platania, it was an early chapter in his life. Platania resolved that he had other plans for his own life. "I want to walk down the street and hold the hands of my boyfriend, but I didn't want to define myself in that single-dimensional way" of gay liberation.

Kight contributed many ideas to the Center, including the prisoner, probation, and parole program. At that time, at least one-third of all people in prison were lesbian and gay, and were looked down upon by prisoners and guards.

Under Kight's guidance, Jaime Green and John Kerr developed relationships with probation and parole officers. In one memo to Kerr, Kight wrote: "Need to share with you what is being done and the kind of high level political intervention we are plugging for."

Kight: "The military and draft affairs was a big issue then. That was a major issue."

Unitarian minister Dick Nash was quickly on board to operate the Conscientious Objectors and Military Affairs division that had begun in GLF. In actuality, Nash had continued to oversee draft counseling and never ceased providing services.

All the programs were created to address real needs, and the most pervasive need was to address the psychic damage done by the corrosive social environment of pre-liberation, "the closet." Hostility toward liberationists was rampant and that needed to be addressed as well.

The need to create innovative programs was essential. The American Psychiatric and Psychological Associations were still two years away from leaving the dark ages in their analysis and treatment of homosexuals. As a result, conventional treatment was rejected by some doctors.

Platania: "Back in those days Donald [Kilhefner, who is and was then a licensed PhD] just hated, and for very good reason, anything that had to do with psychologists, psychiatry, or any of the rest of the mental health programs that would make of us some sort of psychopathology."

The program creators carefully found language that addressed the issues without perpetuating the condition as "personality defects." The organizing committee quickly agreed to avoid more "pathologizing." A common catchphrase became "growth without pathology."

To give liberation a chance to take hold, they wisely avoided terms that might backslide into old ideas about being homosexual. Along with June Herrle and Steven Berman, who was a young psychology intern at the time, they created the term *Self Development Program* to invite people to address their personal issues with peers, to find new approaches and support. It outlined the basic fundamentals of how to reform a previously repressed society.

Kight: "Peer counseling was and is a major part of the Center."

June Herrle, Don Kelhefner, and Betty Berzon trained peer counselors in techniques and terminology—a tactic taken right out of the feminist women's movement playbook. The programs utilized a few gay professional volunteers to facilitate small group therapy sessions to provide an experience of change and personal growth. Basically, it created the first self-aware generation of openly gay men.

Platania recalled that "people came in droves" for the Self Development groups. "A hundred per night [came] and the whole point was the emphasis had nothing to do with pop psychology. It was to recognize what internalized oppression was doing to us. [Kilhefner] founded the whole thing. He didn't want to have anything to do with the psychological efforts of the day that were being co-opted by the worst of the professional oppressors."

It was easy for Morris Kight to say that he did not internalize his trauma, but that was not the norm; even he recognized that he was not a reliable barometer for how others reacted to perverse rejection. He labeled "oppression sickness" as what he saw as a destructive force within the community—the self-hate and judgement furthered oppression of homosexuals.

In 1972, Betty Berzon and Steve Berman wrote and distributed a training model for facilitators of "Peer-Directed Gay Growth Group[s]." It contained seminal research based on their programs at the Center in response to the fact that gay people had begun to reject the traditional and formulaic response to their search for greater self-awareness: "become heterosexual." If this new and unique gay center would do anything, it would have to avoid "heterosexualizing" its client base. The Center would be created and run by and for gay people.

As a student at Cal State Long Beach, Lee Mentley became a peer counselor. He first met Morris Kight in late 1969 at a GLF meeting that he saw advertised in the back pages of the *Advocate.* Mentley ran into Steve Berman on campus and Berman invited him to the Gay Center on Wilshire Boulevard. "I met everyone," he remembered, "I led encounter groups.... The only qualification for this job was to be happy, gay, articulate. [Berman] said 'Get everyone in there, get them in a circle and give everyone a chance to talk.'" Mentley was "shocked in the encounter groups to learn how parents treated their [gay] kids—throwing their own children out of the house, treating them in fashions to cause suicide."

Mentley: "I saw that not everyone had it as easy at home as I did. I took it all much more seriously because I didn't have that kind of drama at home. Family was always wonderful to me. We sat on the floor in a circle and talked. I didn't have those problems, so I tried to show them everyone was unique, that we are all supposed to be different, 'Gay people are special.' They were real 'encounter groups.' They told each other, 'Straighten up your back and love yourself.'"

Platania remembers: "I looked on the exterior a lot crazier than I was."

Like all new paths, at times there were breaks in the road.

"By and for gay people" did not exclude the professionally credentialed. Dr. Evelyn Hooker—a heterosexual woman who was "gay-friendly" before there was such a term—became prominent in the late 1950s for an unprecedented study that concluded that homosexual males and heterosexual males were quite alike. It was well funded and highly respected research. Hooker was invited to be a part of the pro tem board of directors of the Gay Center. It was quickly apparent that her counsel was for appearance's sake; they really wanted the use of her name.

In the development materials, under the heading "Outside Professional Staff and Development," Platania recalls that Hooker took issue with the idea that heterosexual professionals would need to 'deal with their own sexuality.'

Platania: "She looked around the room and said, 'Now, if you mean that until and unless somehow I and other heterosexuals are able to—as you say—'act upon and even celebrate' some sort of bisexuality, that there is something pathological about *us*?'"

Platania, tacitly encouraged by Kight and Kilhefner, affirmed and responded, "If gay liberation means anything at all, it applies to everyone's sexuality, not just to those of us who have gone to jail for expressing an

1971. Front entrance of the original Gay Community Services Center at 1614 Wilshire Blvd. in Los Angeles. Photo: Pat Rocco Papers, Coll2007-006, ONE National Gay & Lesbian Archives, USC Libraries, University of Southern California.

impulse common to all people everywhere. Freedom, Dr. Hooker, is something that we took."

Hooker stood up and announced, "If this is what the Gay Community Services Center is about, I am afraid that I cannot lend my name to this enterprise."

Kight barely peered over his reading glasses as the good doctor exited.

Even though Hooker was no longer involved in the founding of the Center, she remained supportive of the continually evolving organization. Kight eventually got her permission to use her name on the inaugural letterhead.

The founders needed a physical structure to create a permanent headquarters, or home. With 20 dollars in their bank account, Kight and Platania set out to find an affordable location. Kight found an ad in the back pages of a little weekly newspaper called *The Independent*: "'Victorian house, suitable for bookstore, boutique, dress shop, tea-room ...' I said, 'My God! It's a stereotype! They're talking about us!'

"So Jon and I called up the man, and it turned out to be a doctor. He officed nearby, at Alvarado and Wilshire. I went to see him. Being out of the closet about everything, we didn't want to obfuscate, so we told him who we were. And he said, 'That house has belonged to my family since 1875. I was born on the second floor of that house. And I do not know if I wish to have my ancestral home used by you for such a purpose. You'll have to give me a day to think about it.' So [Platania] and I went back the following day at 4 o'clock to meet him and he, wishing to insinuate himself into sexual liberation, introduced his companion, 'This is my woman-companion. We're not married, you know. We're companions.' Wishing to insinuate himself in, he said, 'I've thought about it all night. And I've decided it's a perfect thing to do with my family's home.'"

Platania remembered, quite differently, that he and his friend Paul Olson found the house. "The moment of glory arrived when Paul and I rented an old Victorian building on Wilshire Boulevard."

Kight: "The building was called in the press a Victorian mansion. I never knew where they got that language from. It was a Philadelphia architect/designer [Charles] Eastlake who did the first pre-packaged houses ever in history. He published a book of hardware you could buy, a furnace here, a design there, and so on, and designs of how to do it. And whoever built the house brought it to Wilshire Boulevard in Westlake Park. As a result, it had marvelous furbelows and incrustation and serpentine, and had a gorgeous lamp fixture that hung on the front porch. The building was used up. But we wanted it desperately, and so we went in there."

The first evening they had the keys to the house was a warm Friday evening in October 1971. Dry Santa Ana winds swept through the city, rearranging the preconceived order of all things not nailed down. With Platania and Kight's companion, Larry Edward Allen, Kight recalled, "Believing that we were forebears, that we were making history, the three of us huddled together in the big room, and chanted, 'Amen, om, liberación; Amen, om ...' The three of us danced around, hugging one another and chanting."

Platania remembered about a dozen people standing in a circle: "All of us standing in a circle did om, om, om. Then we sang an old Black spiritual altar call: 'Just As I Am, Without One Plea.' Yup. We did that."

They also sang the second verse of the spiritual:

"Just as I am, all tossed about, with many a conflict [they changed it to 'affliction'] and many a doubt; fightings and fears within, without … we come … we come."

Platania: "That sort of thing can inspire or alienate. It all depends on who is do'n the singing and who is do'n the lis'nin." Accent was added for effect.

It can be said on that evening in 1971 the toddler gay liberation movement for the first time had a home. There was no turning back. Being gay in America would be forever changed. At some point soon after opening the doors of the old house on Wilshire, Kight sat back in his big squeaky wooden desk chair, put his feet up on his desk, leaned back and finally, as a gay man, he belonged someplace.

The phones were turned on the evening they took over and immediately the hotline rang for referrals and counseling.

Kight: "The lights had been turned on, and the water was already on. We had no gas yet. We opened the door that first evening and without a trace of public notice but word of mouth, 19 people came to the Center that night. They wished to come and serve. They wanted to be part of that magic."

Sometime the next day they hung a sign over the door at 1614 Wilshire Boulevard that read "Gay Community Services Center." An oft-repeated tale is that soon after the founders hung up the sign, a man visiting the Center said to Kight, "That sign is going to get us killed," to which Kight dryly replied, "Not a chance of that happening if you don't stand directly under it."

As the *Advocate* reported in a later 1974 piece, "when the sign went up … traffic slowed to a crawl as motorists heading downtown did a double-take. One man reportedly pulled over to the curb, got out of his car, walked up to it and stared."

In a 1995 interview with Karen Ocamb, Thom Mosley recalled: "I had just gotten out of the military and trekked down to the [Center] and sat outside, terrified, watching who was going in and out. There were so many people of color, I didn't expect it. But I was horrified that so many were effeminate. There was a preponderance of transgender—it was a haven for them. It was scary-looking, but I couldn't escape it. There was an energy there. I originally went for the men's rap groups to meet other gay men. We talked about coming out to the family and interracial dating. They also talked about police harassing bar patrons. I thought: what's this place about? It's not so much about social services as being a leader in what was about to be this glorious movement."

Also with Ocamb, Deborah Johnson recalled being an 18-year-old political science major at the University of Southern California: "The Center saved my life. I don't know what I would have done if it hadn't been for the Center, if there had not been someplace that I could go, where I could walk in the door and just explore what it meant to be a lesbian. It didn't really matter what you did for a living—whether you had a doctorate or whether you never graduated from high school. We were just glad that you walked in through the door."

In November 1971, The Center received approval from the *Advocate* with a one-page editorial titled "Love Project."

"Various projects in the gay community are begun for various reasons. Some because certain individuals like the limelight; some because they are angry over unjust laws; some because they want to reform the world; some because those involved just don't have anything else to do; some are built only on hate and will end quickly.

"L.A.'s Gay Community Services Center is a brave and bold venture, and it is built on love. We know some of the people most deeply involved in this project, and we know that they are motivated only by a deep love and concern for all fellow human beings. They see their new Center as a means to help Gays at many levels and in many ways—to help them to solve problems, large and small, and to fill needs that are not problems at all but only aids to a satisfying life.

"GCSC has not chosen an easy role, and its plans are ambitious. So far, its budget far outpaces its visible means. But the needs are great, and we wish the hard little band on Wilshire Boulevard every success. But wishes aren't really fulfilled by the type of Fairy in *Cinderella*. The support of the entire gay community will be necessary. We urge all gay organizations and individuals to help in whatever way they can—furnishings, equipment, time, and even money." (Nov. 10, 1971)

The *Advocate*'s was a powerful endorsement. The Center was validated. Kight ran to the printer, had hundreds of copies made and used it in his fundraising.

There was paperwork, and legalities to be addressed. Alan Gross, a heterosexual attorney, had volunteered his services to incorporate the Center. Articles of Incorporation were signed by Kight, June Herrle, James Kepner, and Jon Platania, filed in the office of the California Secretary of State within the first month, and days later endorsed by Secretary of State Edmund "Jerry" Brown Jr.

Alan Gross then volunteered to guide the Center through the process of obtaining a federal nonprofit tax-exempt status. It became a two-and-a-half-year process and without it they were limited in fundraising options. They were building more than an organization; the Center would become an institution. The thrift shop and occasional donation were not enough.

Working pretty much around the clock, they were relentless in legalizing and funding their collective dream. Kight amassed long handwritten lists of people to solicit for funds. He was bold and shameless, working the phones and his old Smith-Corona typewriter. A typical Kight group solicitation letter would begin with "Dear Gentle People." A personal letter would begin with a private referral such as "[He] has told me that you might be persuaded to be of assistance to us during a time of rapid growth, and commitment."

Kight: "People were quite generous with such a brand new idea—lesbian/gay people serving one another."

They passed the hat at all meetings, and sometimes young people would solicit door-to-door with coffee cans, following the model of the U.S. Mission. Fundraising dances held at Troupers Hall on Highland Avenue were also an alternative to the bar scene.

No one was immune to being hit up for cash or an in-kind donation or volunteer services. It was not unusual for Kight to call Sheldon Andelson or Steve Lachs. Usually the first call of the day, he was direct: "We cannot seem to find a way to pay our telephone bill this month." Kight solicited Eddie Nash, the mobster owner of multiple gay and non-gay bars and nightclubs, to donate to the "Wilshire Volunteer Fund," a bank account created by Steve Lachs and Rand Schrader to enable discreet donations without a connection to the word "gay." Nash knew what the Wilshire

Volunteer Fund was (Kight never deceived the mobster), and he continued to be an anonymous donor for many years.

Of course, not everyone was willing to donate.

Christopher Isherwood diary entry dated December 24, 1972: "I was just about to send some money to the Gay Community Services Center—the outfit run by Kight and Kilhefner—when something made me call Bill Legg at One Incorporated. (Actually, I had a reason for calling him, I wanted to know how to make the check out to One so that it is tax-deductible.) In the course of our conversation, he told me that he and Troy Perry have lately been seeing Yorty [Samuel Yorty, then mayor of Los Angeles] and also the District Attorney, and have arranged to consult with them on gay problems. 'Some people tell me, "They'll use you politically," and I answer, "Why not, we're going to use *them*,"' Legg said. So then I asked him about the Gay Services Center, and he said that whenever anybody applies to them for help, they try to make him into a revolutionary activist; they are radical about this and declare that anyone who isn't with them is against them. Of course, Legg is prejudiced. He sees all other gay groups as Johnnys-come-lately, trying to grab the credit away from Veteran Warrior One [referring to Legg]. But what he said was just what I suspect about Kilhefner—Kight I'm not so sure about, but he's certainly slippery. So the rest of talking to Legg was that, rightly or wrongly, I didn't send the Gay Services any money, after all. I must go down there, though, and see for myself."

Kight was on the phone at his home all day and into the night at home raising funds and researching both private and government grant sources.

Lillene Fifield, Morris, and Don wrote grant proposals. "On clunky old typewriters," Lillene recalls. "We couldn't actually get the grant until we got the 501(c)(3). We just sat there and wrote them. The three of us [became] really close."

Lillene Fifield remembered, "Morris was not a worker bee. Don and I were the worker bees. I worshipped Morris. I liked his ideas. I was one of the people that surrounded him to make sure that it happened. Morris did the footwork, he'd come up with the ideas, make phone calls, bang on doors. Morris was a launcher. I know clearly because I saw that develop in myself. I never wanted to run one of those organizations, never wanted to be a president or even a director. I wanted to do footwork, be a grant writer. Morris needed people to do the detail stuff, grounded in reality, so that his pie in the sky actually got implemented. He could shake people up. Whatever was needed, he was at the front of the line."

The Center was turned down for almost every grant it applied to during that time.

Miki Jackson remembers, "Of course there was never enough money in the whole outfit. Morris had insisted for as long as I recall that if we were to make progress with the government we would have to get their attention in a new way. Money was the way. He said, 'They don't recognize you until either you give them money or they give you money.' It was obvious which way that would have to go. He was sure that once the government had invested some money in gays that that would be the way in. Practical old fox."

Fifield: "One strategy that Morris used was to identify gay and lesbians in institutions and government places who could give us information."

In mid-1973 Kight received a surreptitious call from a person who worked for the County of Los Angeles who said that federal grant dollars intended for human services were being diverted to police and roads.

Armed with this information, Kight and Fifield dreamed up the "Community Coalition for Equitable Revenue Sharing," and invited all the social services agencies in L.A. to a joint meeting. Fifield recalled: "This was bigger than us."

Over 120 people from different agencies showed up to the meeting at the Center and it was very successful. The Coalition solicited the County for an accounting of the funds. Fifield remembered that "Not one single penny of that money was diverted to other projects, just went to many different social human services." Ultimately 375 not-for-profit community-based organizations benefited from the effort, which eventually afforded the Center's first executive director, Don Kilhefner, a $100-per-month stipend.

Soon the Center was offering 30 separate programs including emergency housing, a confidential medical clinic, peer counseling, and nonstop requests for legal help.

Many legal interns and law students jumped on board to form a legal services division. Each volunteer was another brick on the path to complete liberation.

Steve Lachs worked in the Los Angeles Public Defender's office at the time and called himself "socially out," but in 1971 he was definitely not out at work. He lived a careful life. At one private gay party he met a law student named Terry O'Brien who told Lachs about the Center. O'Brien asked Lachs if he would speak to the group as a full-time lawyer. Without thinking about it, Lachs agreed.

"I drove to the Gay Community Services Center on Wilshire Boulevard at night. I parked across the street from the old Victorian with this huge flight of stairs going up. I sat in my car for a good 15 minutes and I looked at that staircase. I sat in my car thinking if I go up that staircase everything's going to change. Do I have the courage to do it? I was in such a dilemma about it. Finally I got out of my car and walked up the stairs and went in and went to the meeting."

In addition to Terry O'Brien, Lachs met an old friend from law school, Barry Copilow, at the Center. He also met Rand Schrader, Tom Coleman, Rick Angel and "some guy from San Diego who wouldn't give his name, and a handful of others."

And he also met "two other guys, Don Kilhefner and Morris Kight. It was one of the most wonderful and really magical times in my life. I had heard of them and I knew that they were on the cutting edge of gay life and liberation and all of that. I was a middle-class, yuppie-ish kind of guy and I wanted nothing to do with protesting and getting arrested. I had some trepidation about meeting them.

"Morris and Don took me, they hugged me, they told me that they wanted me to be included in their lives, in what was going on. I could do things at whatever pace I wanted. If I wanted to be out, I could be out; if I didn't want to be out I would not be out. If I wanted to march I could march, and if I wanted to sit at home, I could do that. A huge weight dropped off of me. It was just remarkable. Both of them were great, they just welcomed me so warmly."

Years later, Lachs could still articulate the profoundness of the meeting: "If you're black, your parents are too. If you're Jewish, your parents are Jewish. If you're gay, you don't have that. You don't have your parents to sit down and tell you what it was like, or your grandfather to teach you, you don't have that feeling when you're gay. You lose that sense of continuity, of feeling who are my people, you are not going to sit around the dinner table and learn about the suffering of your ancestors. Many don't realize the consequences of coming out of the closet [in the early 1970s]."

The law students at the Center started a program to provide legal counseling one night a week. "People would come in with their legal problems. This was the early days and they couldn't afford furniture so there were pillows thrown around."

Lachs advised Kight and Kilhefner that it could create a litigious problem for the Center to offer legal advice from non-lawyers. Immediately Kight suggested that Lachs come on board as legal advisor. Lachs agreed. He helped clients solve all kinds of problems, not necessarily problems stemming from being gay—but everything from landlord and tenant problems to fights between partners and lovers, employment problems, problems that dealt with "more disputes than breaking the law." But he also dealt with problems with the police and entrapments and 'lives being ruined' kinds of cases.

For years, Lachs spent every Monday night at the Center, providing free legal advice. "It was important to me, personally, that I do this. You didn't know Morris Kight for long and not be out."

In 1979, Steve Lachs became the first openly gay judge appointed to the Superior Court of California.

Kight told Paul Cain in 1994: "Never, ever did I want anything in my life so badly as I wanted lesbian and gay liberation, and I wanted to found and see the Center through to fruition. And the next great passion was to create a sexually communicable disease control project and clinic. I had to create that language."

The concept of a free health clinic was not a new phenomenon as part of a growing movement in America called "the free clinic movement." Non-supporters of the movement called it "do-it-yourself medicine." Kight immediately registered the GCSC clinic with the National Free Clinic Council, which operated under the principle that "Health care is a right and must be free at the point of delivery." A year after GCSC opened their doors, the NFCC gave the Center their first grant of $20,000 for the clinic.

Kight served on the board of directors for the NFCC "representing gay male concerns," describing it as a "mystical and magical time." Kight told Cain, "I rose very quickly in the ranks of the National Free Clinic Council to become not only the lesbian and gay spokesperson, but spokesperson for health issues in general. So I would show up on the faculty of what is now Health and Human Services … teaching lesbian and gay concerns all around the country."

Kight: "I had great passion for all of that, but the greatest passion I had was for the venereal disease control project, the health services of the Center."

Linked to his one-man mission in Fort Worth in the 1930s to cure prostitutes and his work in the 1950s in New Mexico to reduce tuberculosis, the Venereal Disease Control Project was the feather in Kight's social services cap.

Jaime Green: "Those of us working in the Center during 1971, 1972, 1973 remember the single-mindedness Kight manifested in wanting the clinic. He worked at it very hard, brought together volunteers to rehabilitate the space for the clinic and persuaded the first Medical Director, Dr. Ben Teller, to be the head of the clinic."

Dr. Benjamin Teller, a former public health physician, was the founder's dream come true. Teller volunteered his services, created relationships with pharmaceutical companies for donated drugs, and recruited an entire staff of volunteer doctors, nurses, technicians, and administrators.

Richard Little had not seen Morris Kight since 1966. In 1972 he went to the Gay Center on Wilshire Boulevard. With a few dozen other men who were there to be treated for gonorrhea, he remembered that "the place was packed." He signed in and sat on the floor. Morris Kight came down the stairs of the big old house "carrying armloads of blankets and sleeping bags. He threw them [from the landing of the stairs] out to the homeless boys." Richard did see a doctor that night in a makeshift room that had probably been a den; it was "tiny and cramped." The best description a farm boy from Ohio could offer of the exam was: "The doctor sat on a milking stool" to do the exam and confirmed the case of gonorrhea. He gave Little an injection and a prescription and sent him on his way.

The Venereal Disease Control Program specifically earned support of local politicians. The Center, as it turned out, was able to identify and treat sexually transmitted diseases earlier than the Los Angeles County Health Department could. County Supervisor Ed Edelman noticed the success of the program and reached out to Kight and was immediately added to the mailing list. City Councilwoman Peggy Stevenson also took note of the burgeoning community service agency and the middle-aged, white-haired hippie at its helm.

Kight: "It grew so fast that we then took the house next door, at 1620 Wilshire Boulevard. Then we took two houses behind us on Lexington Avenue, and then we took a house at 1624 Wilshire Boulevard, exclusively for women—a women's housing project, called Sappho House."

Sappho House was to be the counterpart of the numerous programs that had been designed specifically for men, including the gay men's collectives. Sappho House was short-lived, as it immediately became a threat to the only other gay women's service agency at the time, the Gay Women's Service Center.

GWSC was the first social services organization for lesbians to be incorporated in America. The organization successfully sued the phone company to be listed in the phone director using the word "gay." GWSC already addressed many of the same needs as GCSC (coming out, suicides, arrests, and harassment) and some issues unique to lesbians, such as child custody. GWSC bailed women out of jail, signed releases from mental institutions, and were called by parole officers when a lesbian was getting out of jail.

Del Whan: "We [at GWSC] had a policy that it was better to have someone sleep on our floor than be left in the parks and streets."

GWSC, like the Center, held fundraising dances at Troupers Hall.

Del Whan: "We had lesbian policewomen who came to our dances undercover. They were nice to us, of course."

Whan and others remembered, "I don't recall that Morris was supportive of the Gay Women's Service Center. When the men decided they needed women to attend the newly-forming GCSC, they scheduled their women's rap events on the same nights as the Gay Women's Service Center potlucks."

Kight and Kilhefner were often cited for not having many women in the planning of GCSC.

Del Whan remembered: "Morris and Don Kilhefner came to the GWSC one evening around the time they borrowed the bylaws and rules of incorporation. I asked Morris why they had the women's raps on Tuesday nights in competition with the GWSC. He replied, 'Well, we don't discriminate,' implying that the GWSC was discriminating against men. So that meant the men intended to compete with the GWSC for women and they continued to have their women's rap on Tuesday evenings."

Ultimately, GWSC closed its doors within a year and nothing could match the long-term success of the Center.

Whan: "Also, [by the end of 1972] lesbians in L.A. had more and more places to go. Lots of groups were starting on college campuses. The GCSC on Wilshire had become very popular with women as well as men. The Center had many more donors and soon was attracting professional women to volunteer with their programs."

Whan remembered that just as quickly as Mina Meyer and Sharon Raphael closed the doors of the Gay Women's Service Center, "Morris and Don came over and talked the GWSC partners into coming over to the GCSC. There was little women's involvement in upper level at that [early] point." Meyer served on the board of directors of the Center and was Kight's "co-operator" on the National Free Clinic Council. Meyer and Raphael served as co-VP of the board of directors to Kight's term as president. Kight also put Meyer in charge of the women's programs at the Center, which gave her a double function

1974. Morris Kight shakes hands with Mayor Tom Bradley at first public meeting between gay community and city leaders.
Photo: Pat Rocco. Pat Rocco Papers, Coll2007-006, ONE National Gay & Lesbian Archives, USC Libraries, University of Southern California.

as a full-time employee and a member of the board, "which," Whan recalls, "was in direct conflict with the bylaws. But we didn't pay much attention [to that]."

Though they were still many years away from adding the word "lesbian" to the name, the Gay Community Services Center began to attract a new group of gay women to their center.

When Lillene Fifield first met Morris Kight in 1970 she was at a GLF meeting that "was full of men," and she "wasn't so excited about the reception I got, so I went away." Traveling around the country in a VW van during the summer of 1971, she had what she calls a "cosmic experience." She came back to Los Angeles and "the first thing I did, I went looking for Morris Kight.

"Once he found out who I was, what my skills were and what I was studying, in typical Morris fashion he said, 'Well, here's what we need.'

"From that time on I was intimately involved in so many activities, just about any demonstration that was happening..."

Kight: "Lillene is a brilliant social service advocate. Brilliant analyst, brilliant community organizer. Lillene was the principal author of the Fifield Report, done under the auspices of the Center in which she studied the incidences of the cause and cure of alcoholism among lesbian and gay persons."

Fifeld recalled that Kight was "extremely important to me. He was an incredible mentor, helped me to grow up and make good choices to become who I wanted to be in the world. He was involved with my coming out as a human being." Kight became the 30-year-old woman's role model and mentor. "Morris Kight was always the one to call to say, 'Lillene, this is what is happening. Come.' [It was] his one-word summons."

1972. Cover of the first annual newsletter sent by the new Gay Community Services Center. Foster Gunnison, Jr. Papers. Archives & Special Collections at the Thomas J. Dodd Research Center, University of Connecticut Library.

In addition to Kight, Fifield spent a lot of time with Kilhefner, Troy Perry, Pat Rocco, and Jon Platania.

Fifield: "I decided [during the summer of 1972] that I'd get myself placed in the Regional Research Institute in Social Welfare [at USC] where I was a student," and she learned to write grants.

Fifield, Kilhefner, and Kight formed a team that was dedicated to getting the Center funded. Fifield: "The three of us would visit funding agencies of all kinds. And of course, Morris would be the 'pie in the sky' kind of guy in all his grandiosity and [say] 'Absolutely, we need to have this.' Don would be the second character in the whole thing, he would come through angry: 'We've been oppressed for years, we deserve this, we got to make up for all those lost years of all that addiction,' and on and on. And I would be the voice of reason. [Because] we had already established a plan for how much money we wanted, I'd be the person who would propose a compromise. We ran our little pony show a lot in those early years. Ended up getting the Women's Clinic funded [from the Regional Research Institute], convincing them that we could handle sexually transmitted diseases and the etiology of all that."

Kight: "A great many things happened. For one, we grew terribly, terribly fast. And that was okay."

In the first 12 months, the Center served approximately nine hundred people and more came to hang out and volunteer. The first year, the Center still had to depend entirely on community donations. It was difficult, but the struggle solidified the organization's roots in self-sufficiency. When they opened the Center, they had (depending upon whose report is referred to) $20 or $35 and they signed a lease for $300 per month. Through 1972–73 the Center served approximately 50,000 to 75,000 persons with a full-time staff of 85 volunteers and a bare-bones annual budget of $30,000. In 1972–73, its income was $41,678. In 1974 the *Advocate* reported the Center as an "institution to be reckoned with.... The center claims to have given direct services to the minds, hearts, bodies, and souls of over 75,000 Gays in each of the past two years," yet, "To put it mildly, the center is no goldmine."

Kight was frustrated by all the government funding that was passing them by because they still needed the 501(c)(3) certification from the Internal Revenue Service. Denied their first petition for nonprofit status, Alan Gross made several trips to Washington to plead the case on behalf of the Center. Gross warned his pro bono clients at the Center that the IRS would try to find reasons to deny them a tax exemption to avoid the appearance of impropriety in what was a very anti-gay time. After a few more denials, in 1973 Kight and Kilhefner scheduled a face-to-face meeting at the IRS offices in Hollywood. (Coincidentally, a few years later, the same building would become the home of GCSC.) Always certain to stress that the Center was a non-exclusionary human service agency, the two founders rolled up their sleeves and were willing to do anything to get the IRS certification. The IRS requested an assurance that the Center did not "promote homosexuality." In a written letter to the federal agency, they wrote: "The Center does not advocate any sexual orientation or lifestyle." The IRS responded with many pages of "conditions" for the Center. They wanted the Center to agree they "would not advocate the practice of homosexuality or contend that homosexuality is normal ... your officers and directors are not avowed homosexuals." They agreed.

In 1975 the GCSC became the first organization with "gay" in its name to be granted nonprofit status by the Internal Revenue Service. This was a huge victory. The 501(c)(3) legitimized the Center and gave credence to the gay community. Kight knew that this was becoming a great legacy, solidifying his long-term vision for the Center and for the gay community.

Fifield remembered, "Morris was always on the long-range and what needed to happen for the long-range to happen."

Uncharacteristically, Kight never commented on the tactic used with the IRS, but Kilhefner often bragged that it was another "guerrilla theatre trick."

With the 501(c)(3) in hand there were no roadblocks to fundraising; possibilities for expansion were endless. Kight and Fifield had been researching grants long before they received the tax-exempt status. The fundraiser in Kight was a dog with a new bone.

The Center steadily grew. The annual income for 1975 was $527,050; by 1976 it was $645,306 and the number of professional and nonprofessional volunteers had grown to 250, with a salaried staff of 44.

Kepner wrote in a letter to Harry Hay: "The Center's growth is simply fantastic, though I hope they aren't making a mistake tying themselves to Federal/State/County grants. But that's their decision, and the corner of Wilshire and Union is certainly a dynamic place."

Hay to Kepner: "When you come right down to it, [Kight's] wheeling-dealing method of operation isn't really political NOW. Like you, we also hold our breath with the way GCSC is entangled in Government Grants.... I shudder to think just what lists their personnel records have leaked and leached out onto: here I'm inclined to agree with ole Slippery-fingers Slater."

Don Slater's ideology was simply opposed to government funding; he preferred all independent social service organizations, including the Center, to remain autonomous and to some degree anonymous. A conventional kind of gay guy, Slater never fully embraced the vision that gays would be accepted and safe to openly operate in mainstream society.

The Center had become a huge vessel that needed to be maintained and kept afloat. Kight: "We never spent time to integrate the new programs. Somebody would come and say, 'I'd like to do this.' 'Fine, do it.' And so a new program was born. We didn't check them out. We didn't really put them to the test. And so by April of 1973, we had 32 separate services with one or two or three people heading each, and one program, the medical services, with three hundred [people working or volunteering].

"And then we started competing for public funding which we'd always planned to do. And we had a road map for that."

As a brick-and-mortar entity, the Center had become a major institution and central to a much larger cultural movement. Kight was at a peak in productivity and at the eye of every storm that passed over the community. This may be the happiest period in his life.

Writing to Harry and John, Morris always began his letters with cursory flattery and expressions of love. He began a 1973 letter with the salutation "Dear Loved Ones," then immediately launched into news from the Center, always with a little bragging. "It goes on day and night, literally. I am never not a gay liberationist, never not involved in the struggle, never not on call at the Center. I go in and out of there all day long, and am on the telephone much of the rest of the time doing community organizing." In a rare moment of sentimentality, Kight also added (regarding New Mexico): "I miss the piñon, the ristras, the brown hills, the Ceremonials, but I am where I can do the most work."

John Rechy recalled a visit to the old house on Wilshire Boulevard, in the early days, when it was the Center: "I called to arrange a meeting about something or other, [Kight] must've heard my footsteps because when I entered the room where we were to meet, he was reclining on a couch with a hand planted on his forehead [with open palm facing north], his eyes fixed, not on the ceiling but on heaven, and he sighed, 'So much to do, so much to do.' And there was [so much to do]."

SLAVE AUCTION

"THIS HAS TO BE THE MOST BIZARRE THING I HAVE EVER SEEN IN my life," is how one vice officer described the scene.

"It started out innocently enough," is how organizer John Embry described it, "if a slave auction can be called innocent."

Embry, founder of the gay leather magazine *Drummer*, created an event that would bring together the leather community. "To keep it out of the realm of crass commercialism," Embry decided the proceeds would go to charity, including GCSC, MCC, and HELP. A mock slave auction was held, with each winning bidder designating the charity he wanted his funds to support.

"My biggest fear was that it would bomb," Embry said of the private party that was held in the spring of 1976 on the patio of the popular Mark IV bathhouse.

Embry described that around midnight, "All of a sudden, a plaster-cracking voice from the heavens thundered down for everyone within a ten-mile radius to hear: 'This is the Los Angeles police department conducting a felony arrest. Stay where you are. Do not move.'"

Pat Rocco: "It was a fundraiser at a bathhouse, and it was meant to be fun. Somehow the police got wind of it, raided it and arrested 40 people."

An army of a hundred police officers broke down doors and bellowed orders through bullhorns while police helicopters hovered overhead. Many speculated that Police Chief Davis wanted this raid to help his political career (he had an unsuccessful campaign for Governor in 1978).

In addition to the 40 arrests, an additional 80 patrons were detained and questioned.

The raid proved to be a public relations disaster for the police department, and a rallying point for the gay community and local media.

Sensing a galvanizing opportunity, enter Morris Kight.

In less than 24 hours, the 39 men and one woman arrested were bailed out, and Morris Kight, who was not at the auction, greeted them with a press conference.

Embry said, "Morris could fill a room."

Embry recalled leaving prison: "Morris Kight was before the television cameras, eloquently decrying the illegality of the caper and the police tactics. He was a very effective speaker, a powerhouse, and the place was packed with newspaper and TV reporters, gays and gay-friendlies."

In the press, Morris "Knight" [sic] was quoted: "'No one was sold' and maintained that all involved were voluntary participants in an affair similar to 'slave-for-a-day' auctions often held at schools."

Jeanne Barney: "Morris knew everybody because he wasn't afraid to be pushy, and that's how a lot of things got done. He was fearless, would not take no for an answer. People finally said yes to him just to get him off their backs."

From Los Angeles' early, minuscule, ad hoc gay-straight alliance, attorney Al Gordon stepped in to arrange lower bail (awakening one judge in the middle of the night), and handled the subsequent legal charges. The LAPD, not amused by the slave auction gimmick, convinced the D.A. to prosecute and treat the event as actual human slave trafficking—a felony arrest for 40 people. It was definitely one of Gordon's most memorable cases.

In addition to all the positive national press, the *Los Angeles Herald Examiner* published the home addresses, provided by LAPD, of every person arrested in the bust. Local news stations showed clips of the arrestees over and over.

Newly-elected City Council member Zev Yaroslavsky described the bust at the slave auction as using "heavy artillery to kill a mosquito."

Yaroslavsky: "It was an absolute outrage." As a protest to that incident, Morris and a number of others organized a mock slave auction to take place at Troupers Hall, nine days hence.

Kight's point in doing the second mock slave auction was to call attention to the absurdity of the bust on the first slave auction—and to raise money as a fundraiser for the Mark IV legal defense.

Pat Rocco remembered, "We did it publicly and openly. I got a bunch of entertainers and we got the word out. It didn't take long. We were interviewed on television about the upcoming event. It was called a slave auction."

Yaroslavsky: "I was a new City Council member at the time, I didn't know any better. I said to my staff, 'I'm going to go to this thing as a sign of solidarity.' I was being advised, 'Don't go, this is not proper.' I thought about it and decided to go, but the typical early Zev way, I went with my wife. I told Barbara, 'You're coming with me.'"

Yaroslavsky telephoned Morris ahead of time to let him know that he'd be there. He knew who Morris was. "Anybody who was paying attention in town knew who Morris Kight was. He was one of the pillars of the gay and lesbian community."

Yaroslavsky explained to Kight: "Just coming as an act of solidarity with what's happened. I think it's outrageous. He said, 'That's wonderful. Would you like to say a few words?' I said, 'No no no. I'll be in the back, no recognition. I wanted you to know that I'll be there.' We showed up, Barbara and I, and about ten television cameras, every camera in town is there, and we're standing in the back, just minding my own business. I'm standing close enough to my wife so that any picture had me and her in it. Everything was going fine. Morris started the evening out by saying, 'Before we begin I'd like to introduce a man who has had the courage to come out here today. Zev.' Every camera in the place pointed at me. At that very moment, I said 'Screw it, I'm here. I know why I'm here and I'm going tell everyone why I'm here.'"

Still, Yaroslavsky felt blindsided. His first thought was, "Why did he bother to ask me if I wanted to be called?"

In the time that it took for Yarovslavsky to walk from the back of the room to the stage his political persona was shaped. "[Morris] outed me as someone who was willing to push the envelope, take risks, stand up against repressive behavior.

Within 24 hours, I realized he had done me a favor. As the years went on, I realized more that he did me a favor."

Jeanne Barney: "The Troupers auction was the first time that we had the West Hollywood sweater and the gay leather in one room, and everyone got along. When you think about all the different bastions within the gay community, they said it wouldn't work. And it hasn't happened since."

Attorney Al Gordon supported the event by going on the auction block himself. He was sold for $369 to his wife, Lorraine. Privately, Lorraine referred to Morris as "First Fag" because, she noted, "everything gay that happened, he did it first."

The Troupers Hall event was a huge success by all measures. Privately, however, Al Gordon told his client John Embry, "You may end up with all kinds of things out of this case, but justice will not likely be one of them."

Eventually, the defendants were offered a deal—the charges were dropped to a misdemeanor and they would serve a hundred hours of community service each.

Newly appointed City Councilmember Peggy Stevenson, who had replaced her recently and unexpectedly deceased husband on the Council, questioned LAPD on how much was spent on the Mark IV bust. The police department refused to answer. She held up the passage of a $4 million budget until the total for the bust was revealed. Later it came out that 107 uniformed officers were used, two helicopters, two of the largest police buses, and untold personnel overtime.

There were other times when gay activists couldn't get arrested, even when they tried.

Since 1970, Assemblyman Willie Brown introduced legislation called the Consenting Adult Law to repeal the sodomy law and effectively decriminalize gay sex. Every time he introduced the bill, it was voted down.

In 1974 Al Gordon and Kight had come up with a way to challenge the 1915 California law that also made fellatio a felony.

Jeanne Barney remembered a phone call from Gordon who told her that "Troy Perry and his lover Steve Jordan, [as well as] Jeanne Cordova and her lover Barbara were going to the police station with signed affidavits, admitting to terrible perverted acts of sodomy."

1975. l to r: Morris Kight, Gerry Parker, State Assembly member Willie Brown at California Democratic Convention.
Photo: Pat Rocco. Pat Rocco Papers, Coll2007-006, ONE National Gay & Lesbian Archives, USC Libraries, University of Southern California.

Jeanne Barney said, "You really need a non-gay couple."

When Al asked if Jeanne's heterosexual partner would do it, she responded, "Frank'll do anything that I tell him to do." Al added, "We're going to include Morris because if we don't, he'll bad-mouth us."

Jeanne Barney: "The six of us, and Al and Morris and Pat Underwood, went to the police station. First we had a press conference. Morris, bless his heart, went to every newsperson and he said, 'How do you do, my name is Morris Kight,' because he wanted to make sure he got covered in the news. One channel identified him as Morris *Knight* and another channel identified him as 'an unidentified man.'"

The six 'felons,' however, became known as the Felon Six.

Al Gordon liked antics as much as Kight.

Gordon informed LAPD that "six felons" would be turning themselves in at the Los Angeles Press Club. No police showed up, but the media didn't disappoint and immediately got the point—it was about the hypocrisy of the law as it applied to gay men differently than how it applied to heterosexual or even lesbian couples.

Once the media was assembled, Gordon presented the affidavits and Kight made a citizen's arrest. The three couples were driven to the Rampart police station. The station commander wouldn't arrest the couples.

With the media still in tow, the band of activists went to the City Attorney's office. No charges would be filed. They were told that prosecuting private sexual acts between consenting adults was against the District Attorney's policy.

Jeanne Barney recalled that at the D.A.'s office, "Somebody came out and said that the D.A. would not prosecute such cases.

"Then we went to Evelle J. Younger, California Attorney General. We weren't going to leave until we were arrested. We were there for a long time. Younger said that they wouldn't prosecute any cases statewide even if the law didn't pass."

Gordon and Kight argued with Attorney General that the penal code should be changed. The state did revoke the laws against consensual homosexual acts in May 1975, removing a big weapon in the police harassment tool kit.

It went into effect January 1976.

Dramatics aside, they did accomplish a lot. There were a lot of serious discussions, and also they fought. A common source of disagreement were the basic differences in meeting the needs for females and males in the gay community. There was no equivalence in women's programs to the men's programs.

Mina Meyer spent considerable time and effort to found the first women's health clinic at the Center. Kight had recruited Meyer specifically to start a women's clinic and, Meyer recalled, "They went ahead and provided it for the men. Morris said, 'We don't have the money, go out and find doctors and nurses, get your own volunteers, we'll provide the space.'"

Despite initial resistance from the male-dominated board, who believed that "women don't get diseases like men," Meyer prevailed. She found lesbian doctors, nurses, and technicians willing to volunteer their time and create a women's clinic based on their Feminist Women's Health Clinic. This was a time when "women's health" was not accepted terminology.

The women's health clinic at the Center was a great success from the beginning. One night a week, Thursdays, they provided free services. Meyer: "Fifty- and sixty-year-old women who had never had a pelvic exam were finally comfortable with a lesbian doctor and nurse."

Kight found they could get funds from the county for medical supplies if they put up posters around the neighborhood, in the downtown area, announcing their free clinic providing birth control.

Meyer remembered, "Big posters with a man and a woman—put them all over the neighborhood. That neighborhood is filled with mostly Central American people with large families who need birth control. And sure enough within weeks, Thursday nights, when the women's clinic was open, the place was filled with families—a mom, dad, and six kids. About a month or so, the doctors and nurses who volunteered said, 'No more.' They weren't up for this, they were doing it on their day off and it was an extra shift for them. They were doing this for their lesbian sisters. There was no way they would come in to give birth control to the local folk. That wasn't what they signed up for and within a short amount of time there were no volunteers and the women's clinic closed."

The heterosexual posters came down, but Kight continued to successfully solicit funds for family planning programs at the Center, saying, "The program had been conceptualized to deal with lesbian women, bisexual women, and for men not aware of their responsibilities in sexual matters."

The Center continued to develop, as did resentments.

Mina Meyer remembered that she and Sharon were irritated by Morris in the 1970s. "He'd make things up," she said, and explained that everyone would compare his stories. "His ability to exaggerate was unbelievable. He changed history. He'd fudge things for his own aggrandizement. Having been a witness and knowing the truth, I know he lied. He was a narcissist."

In late 1973, Mina Meyer resigned from the Center to go back to school. She felt that initially the internal problems at the Center stemmed more from classism rather than sexism. "Shelly [Andelson] never came to the meetings, never saw him. He just sent money. Morris Kight would drive up to Betty's [Berzon] condo in the hills and he'd report to her what we were doing. She didn't come off the hill to the scuzzy house on Wilshire."

Still, claims of sexism slowly percolated among staff and volunteers. Sexism was easier than classism for people to understand and recognize.

The internal conflict simmered just below the surface as upper management strategized the first major growth spurt for the Center. They were being forced to make the first big change. It was like navigating a large boat and had to be planned and steered way in advance.

Kight: "We rented five houses. *Then* we learned what nobody had told us: that all five houses had been condemned." The Center had to vacate the Wilshire Boulevard house and consolidate all the programs under one roof. It would take over a year to navigate the move and raise the unprecedented funding.

Kight: "[Building and Safety] said, 'Please! We worry about you, we worry about the fact people might be burned to death, [because] it's so dangerous, you couldn't get out of there.'"

Reminiscent of the GLF Melrose crash pad condemned by the city in 1970, Kight negotiated time to exit the buildings. "And so, I went before the city Building and

Safety Department and used my political power, of which I had accumulated a lot, and urged them to give us time. So they gave us time, and they kept extending our time."

There were many postponements while Kight and city officials worked together for the good of the clientele being served at the Center.

McCADDEN PLACE

THERE WAS A LOT OF MOVING GOING ON AROUND THE SAME TIME. Morris himself needed to find a new home.

The redevelopment of the Bunker Hill section of downtown Los Angeles destroyed much affordable housing and displaced many families and individuals, including Kight. He joined the opposition with pickets and petitions, and did everything possible to stop the inevitable development of downtown and Dodger Stadium.

In July 1974, Kight wrote to Morty Manford about being unhappy in his Fourth Street apartment and the landlord was "unhappy with me. Having a renowned gay liberationist on his property has finished freaking that poor man's mind." In referring to the landlord, "The poor man there suffers from such debilitating homophobia that it makes it difficult for me. I discovered also that he does not know how to use alcohol and that makes it difficult for him too."

Kight described a house in Hollywood as "ideal." He was "working towards it. It has enough room, windows, opening onto a lanai and greenery. A bit rough, but I am prepared to do interior redecorating for a few days to make a home of it." Before Kight moved in, 1428 McCadden Place was known as Unique Love Playhouse.

Located in the heart of Hollywood, a few steps south of Hollywood Boulevard where the first Gay Parade was launched, the three-thousand-square-foot rental house was the most spacious and important place Morris ever lived. For the first time in a long time, he settled in and put down roots. Within weeks, it became a most important address for gay liberation.

Kight decided the upstairs loft, overhanging one-third of the main room on the ground floor, was what he needed for living, sleeping, reading, and privacy. The rest of the house and the backyard, including a small shack, were delegated to be open-use space.

A quick assemblage of befriendees donated labor and creative ideas to create a lush and functional environment. Fred Bradford remembered crawling under the house to install an additional telephone connection for the "Gay Helpline." Volunteers kept the place going for as long as Kight lived there. They served as caretakers of both the property and Morris himself. The rent remained affordable, parking was easy for many visitors, and it was close to public transportation for Kight. The property also provided ample room for Kight's four-legged friends—domestic and feral.

Kight wanted for nothing while living on McCadden Place.

It was described in the press as "a big old barn of a house full of small noisy dogs, assorted cats and a fourteen-foot dining room table," used for brainstorming, production, dining and entertaining. A few couches and overstuffed chairs aligned with side tables and a coffee table created an ideal meeting space.

Gino Vezina remembers that Kight "always kept the front door open on McCadden Place." Safety was precarious in that location. "He didn't care. He'd say, 'I'm not going to worry about it.' He was indifferent to danger."

Kight explained it this way: "I want to indicate through example that I'm not afraid. I don't have any draperies or shades on the windows. I never have in any house I've ever lived in. Gays like openness. It's a metaphor."

Over the years, Kight played host to literary, political, and entertainment elite, including, to name a few, Mayors Sam Yorty and Tom Bradley, Representative Bella Abzug, L.A. politician Zev Yaroslavsky, Governor Gray Davis, President Jimmy Carter's son Chip, writer Gore Vidal, and pivotal Chicago gay activist Dr. Howard Brown. Simultaneously, the house provided a safe harbor for displaced youth or a newly sober and unemployable middle-aged gay man.

Kight moved into McCadden Place with few personal possessions. Within a few years, the walls were covered with art, memorabilia, and political posters, while the rooms were full of sculptures and unique objects and furniture pieces. Prominently displayed was the original "Fagots Stay Out" sign which Kight had negotiated off the wall at Barney's Beanery a few years earlier.

There had never been a place like McCadden Place. Eccentric, open and free, it provided stability and an opportunity for a disenfranchised community to establish traditions. Kight enjoyed the limelight, the attention, and he especially liked being at the center of a very powerful wheel.

Barry Copilow remembered the parties at McCadden Place as legendary. "Morris Kight could party and loved to watch everybody else party. He brought a lot of people together."

Steve Lachs remembered a "kangaroo court, when there was a dispute between a nasty man who wrote for one of the bar papers and one of the clubs, who threw him out of the club. They were about to go to a lawsuit, and Morris spoke to the lawyers involved and said, 'This is a terrible, terrible thing to have in the press.' It was a *New York Post*-type of story. Morris came up with the idea of convening a three-person court, and both parties agreed.

"At McCadden Place, we had a trial, listened to testimony and we came to a decision. Not a bad way of handling disputes, binding, and everybody got to vent and tell their story. And three people were neutral. A very practical way of doing things."

The first December that Kight lived on McCadden Place began an annual solstice celebration. December 21st was an open invite to local gays and businesses and community leaders, elected officials, and those hoping to be elected. There was an open fire pit in the backyard, more food than necessary prepared by a small army of helpers, and an open bar prominently stocked with gallon jugs of bourbon, cheap beers and whatever else anyone brought with them. Kight entertained and connected people from all walks of life and all shades of beliefs.

Steve Lachs fondly recalled, "Parties at McCadden Place—they all blend into one another. I was really, really fortunate in that I was able to meet people there, from the highest hills, directors and writers, and at the same time we'd meet street people there. The parties at McCadden were all fun. Anything that Morris touched was fun. He was bigger than life. Grander without any money than a lot of people who had tons of money; he was grand in his nature."

Pat Rocco remembered, "McCadden Place had this interesting setup that made it really conducive for meetings. It wasn't like a house at all. The ground floor had a little balcony overlooking the situation, and the ground floor was wide enough to have pretty darn good-sized meetings. Morris' house was just better, so many things that happened in that house though. I remember Mayor Tom Bradley coming there, Gore Vidal coming there, I remember a whole array of Congresspersons and Senators coming there at one time or another. It became a very famous place. Just everything happened there."

The small shack in the large backyard was transformed into a guesthouse that became familiar accommodations for many out-of-town guests.

Ann Bradley started and ran the "Lesbian Writers Series" at A Different Light bookstore and had the occasion to ask Morris Kight for a favor. Bradley, who had been at an event that she described as "extraordinary" in 1984 at McCadden Place, approached Kight in the fall of 1988 about hosting a similar event for Joan Nestle, a New York writer and founder of the Lesbian Herstory Archives whom Bradley was hosting in Los Angeles in early 1989.

"I asked him if he would host a reception for her," Bradley recalls, "and MECLA would pay. Morris said, 'That sounds like a lovely idea.' And he hosted the whole night and it was just spectacular. We had a large number of people invited. He had a banner made for her and then gave it to her for the Lesbian Herstory Archives, inscribed, 'L.A. and The McCadden Place Collection Welcomes Joan Nestle, our spiritual sister.'

"It was also amazing to have Joan Nestle and Morris Kight standing together. It meant so much, not just politically but also for equality and justice for the Gay and Lesbian community."

Bradley explained that a day or two after the party, Joan Nestle, who had been on an exhausting schedule, had an inflammation of Epstein-Barr. "On Saturday, I called him and explained that she had a restricted airline ticket and needed a medical authorization. 'Oh darling, you call Ben Teller,' Morris said.

Ben Teller saw Nestle and gave her the necessary letter to change Nestle's restricted ticket to get on an earlier flight.

Bradley continued, "You wouldn't want to abuse that kind of power [that Kight had]. He was a person of action. Very extraordinary person."

A typical thank-you note from one of the thousands of houseguests through the years went: "Dear Morris, your home is the warmest, most peaceful and spiritual. My favorite place in L.A."

FIRST TUESDAYS

ONE OF THE FIRST THINGS KIGHT DID IN HIS NEW HOME WAS TO create "First Tuesday." The first Tuesday of every month was a meeting in his home, open to all gay, lesbian, and trans persons with needs or with services to promote.

Bob Dahlmeyer remembered being taken to a First Tuesday meeting when he first came to Los Angeles and how he met Morris Kight. "It was the ultimate in networking within our community. Unbelievable needs were addressed, and everyone got their needs met. People also came to promote themselves. It was a public address system specifically for gay people."

It was Kight doing what Kight did best—connecting people who can help one another and who will then help others.

Dahlmeyer continued, "Morris had control of everything going on."

First Tuesday carried on for years on McCadden Place. Over time, Kight relinquished his control and allowed others to host at McCadden Place. Eventually, it moved to another location and the idea of community helping each other evolved into other variations. It became an institution, an insiders-club institution.

First Tuesday also birthed many activists. Writer and actor Michael Kearns received a phone call from Morris Kight, whom he had known of since before he moved to Los Angeles. Kight called to compliment Kearns on his new book and on being on the cover of the *Advocate*. He invited Kearns to join the First Tuesday crew, and thus began Kearns' commitment to activism and advocacy and a lifelong friendship with Kight.

Without the benefit of a crystal ball seeing into the future, one might have assumed that this period was the pinnacle of Kight's popularity. It was a heady time for sure. In addition to a growing list of benefactors, Kight had a steady stream of befriendees. There were a lot of people coming and going. Gino Vezina called them 'pixies,' while many others saw them as Morris' 'followers.' Whatever they were called, they waited for Morris to delegate to them some task, some menial and simple assignment that would allow them to participate in their own liberation. Gino, who was never one of them, remembered that "Morris' ego was a bottomless pit" and described them as "people who surrounded him and kowtowed. He was a great friend but I never catered to his ego like that. Morris always wanted a great deal of attention. Sometimes he got it, sometimes he didn't."

Jon Platania remembered Kight "as a very complex man." He understood and loved Kight like few others. "He was both Father and Mother to a whole community of lost souls making our way toward freedom." Kight served as a sounding board for the young Platania; he was a confidant and a mentor. "He was an incredibly beautiful man, as a young man. His lack of self-care, [his] smoking and eating didn't help, but he was still an attractive man into his fifties. I think at a certain point Morris did what he felt that he had to do."

Steve Berman and Kight also grew very close during the 1970s. Barry Copilow described them being like father and son, they had "a natural alliance." Kight would imply that his and Berman's relationship was much more intimate. Copilow insisted that "Morris Kight was the non-sexual love of Steve Berman's life. He was a mentor, a guiding light, and Steve would do anything for Morris." Lee Mentley echoed the same sentiment, that Berman would've done anything for Kight. Berman gave Morris an older orange Toyota for his use.

While working at the Center, Berman went back to school and studied to be a psychiatrist. His degree would help the Center to expand its services.

Morris Kight told Barry Copilow, "You're needed in the community." Copilow finished law school and remembers that Morris saw that "I could be manipulated." Copilow continued to be a legal counselor at the Center and worked as Legal Director under Steve Lachs and then later Roger Colgan, who served merely as more of a 'face' for the position since he was, according to Copilow, "ineffectual."

Platania recognized something else happening around this emerging community. The established professionals, lawyers and doctors, found an upsurge of needs to be met. "They saw an opportunity for a lot of client referrals in this great untapped gay community resource and wanted to be a part of that. It wasn't altruistically motivated. [It was] inwardly motivated by their careers."

It was standard and advisable to steer a number of entrapment cases to Sheldon "Shelly" Andelson. Preceding the founding of the Center, Shelly and Kight had an agreement. Two of every ten cases Andelson was to charge full rate (often Kight would let Shelly know which ones were able to pay, or were "good for it").

How Sheldon Andelson and Morris Kight ever crossed paths is worthy speculative fodder. The exact circumstances of their introduction has never been clear. They moved in different social circles, but it is safe to say it occurred in the mid- to late 1960s. "Shelly" was the founder and chairman of the Bank of Los Angeles, and owner of the notorious gay bathhouse 8709. Later Andelson became the first openly gay Regent of the University of California. He and Kight were as close as two people could be, though their closeness was rarely seen in public. There was a definite class distinction. Kight respected Sheldon. Andelson appreciated Morris' impunity. They genuinely loved one another.

For a 1979 dinner honoring Kight, Andelson took a full page in the program with:

> Thank you Morris
> For enriching my life
> By being the one
> Who opened my closet door
> And began my involvement
> With our wonderful community.
> Shelly Andelson

When he came to meetings at the Center, Andelson showed up in a Jaguar, sporting tasseled loafers and two dogs. Clearly, he was a big shot.

Kight and Andelson were fond of each other. They were a brilliant political strategist team. Andelson called most of the shots.

Steve Lachs served on the board of the Center while Sheldon was chair. "It was an informal organization and Shelly was big on micromanaging, like what flavor frozen yogurt should we have.

"I always had the feeling that Sheldon had a great deal of admiration of Morris. He saw Morris as capable of doing a lot of the things that he couldn't do. Sheldon couldn't be Morris, he didn't have the freedom of Morris, he was bound by being an attorney, a businessman, a person of affluence and connections, and he didn't have that bohemian freedom that Morris had, and I think he always loved that with Morris—the yin to his yang. Morris was always the person with the freedom

to say what he wanted to say, when he wanted. Sheldon loved that Morris had that kind of freedom. Shelly didn't have that."

Sheldon's influence and contacts made him a prolific fundraiser.

Lachs: "Sheldon was a threat—he could easily compete with Morris in terms of influence in the community. Morris was a really smart, practical person. For all the grandeur and theatre, he so thoroughly understood what Sheldon brought. Morris treasured him. He saw clearly. They had their differences, particularly at the Center. Sheldon was chair and he was doing things his way. It led to an occasional conflict."

As Copilow said about Kight, "[he was] a control freak. He knew what he was doing, always had a twinkle in his eye and he did what he had to do. He used his gifts and if he was the face of the gay community, wonderful. The gay community needed a face. Back then, any publicity was useful, there was no such thing as bad publicity. Anything that got 'gay' out there was worth it."

Copilow said that Morris "did not have a tremendous presence at the Center, Don [Kilhefner] was more visible. Morris was the face of the Center, he'd do interviews and be quoted a lot. Don was the organizer." Copilow remembered a favorite saying of Kight's: "Don't just do something, stand there." Young people interpreted it as "hold your place, be out, be present, stand there."

One of those young people was Jeanne Cordova. She met Kight in the early 1970s. Morris immediately recognized her as a leader and set about to cultivate that quality in her. "All of a sudden," Cordova recalled, "Morris Kight was in my life. He saw me as a lesbian activist. I was 22 years old and he saw a lot of potential." Thirty years her senior, Kight tapped into Cordova's strong personality and helped to shape a powerful community organizer and activist. He also used her positions as publisher and editor of *Lesbian Tide* (known as "the newspaper of record for the lesbian feminist decade"). She was also editor of the progressive weekly, the *Los Angeles Free Press.* "He'd call me and say 'I need X amount of lesbians to be at X place'" and she'd have them there. "I would give him feedback on what he was missing [in dealing with lesbians] and would often end up at his house, strategizing." Initially, they strictly had a

1974. Spree Awards and fundraiser (for the Center). l to r: Jim Kepner, Troy Perry, Kight, Gerald Strickland, Dick Summers. Photo: Pat Rocco. Pat Rocco Papers, Coll2007-006, ONE National Gay & Lesbian Archives, USC Libraries, University of Southern California.

political relationship. After "being at his house for many late-night sessions, talking and strategizing and getting phone calls at all hours of the day and night about different things … we had a real personal relationship." Cordova came to think of Morris as her "political Godfather." She also regarded Kight as the "father of Los Angeles/SoCal gay liberation movement. He built the infrastructure."

Cordova noted Kight's Southern gentlemanly way of speaking. He always pronounced her name using the Spanish pronunciation: Cor-doe-Bah.

In her 2011 memoir, *When We Were Outlaws*, Cordova described Kight at the time: "He knew how to plan large-scale demonstrations and keep them peaceful. In a fledgling movement filled with 20- and 30-year-olds, he was unquestionably our leader, although he did not necessarily look the part. Of medium height with an ordinary, middle-aged potbelly, he had a shoulder-length white mane so wispy that the wind blew it in all directions at once. Usually, he wore the simplest of thrift-store khaki pants and shirt, one grade up from vagrant."

Kight quickly became her mentor. She learned a lot of her politics from him, particularly tactical. Over the years, if Jeanne had any difficulties, she'd call Morris. Kight had a list of who to call—councilpeople, straight people for particular reasons. He taught her the importance of allies. "He was the first one to teach 'coalition politics.' The gay movement was part of the large liberal civil rights agenda." She called Kight for help: "'Morris, we need about 30 guys down there' and he could do it and he did do it, and he'd come himself."

With the exception of a single two-year falling-out, Cordova and Kight worked together for the next 40 years and remained close.

Kight's connection and influence were not limited to the West Coast. He had an ongoing correspondence with Foster Gunnison, an incipient East Coast archivist who had been active in the Mattachine Society, NACHO and ECHO (as discussed in a previous chapter). Gunnison later founded the Institute for Social Ethics (ISE). Kight enjoyed a polite letter exchange where they mostly discussed the tedious organizational aspects of the gay movement—"rules" and "guidelines." Their exchanges were polite and purposeful, not so much personal or too informal. Ordinarily, Kight avoided this kind of talk but he liked Gunnison. In the mid-1970s, during one of his many fallings-out or fed-ups with ONE Archive, Kight sent boxes of original documents and memorabilia to Gunnison's nascent archive (among the documents was everything he had concerning the founding of GCSC). Gunnison's archive never did materialize and Kight expressed disappointment that he never heard anything more from Gunnison. Years after Foster Gunnison's death in 1994, his collection of historical data from the early gay rights movement appeared at the Thomas J. Dodd Research Center, University of Connecticut Libraries. Gunnison did preserve Kight's material, though no one else donated to Gunnison's presumed archive.

Kight met Morty Manford in Chicago at the 1972 National Coalition of Gay Organizations Convention. A New Yorker, Manford was a college student who helped to found the first gay group at Columbia University. He was present at the 1969 rebellion at the Stonewall Inn and later was founding president of Gay Activists Alliance (GLF's East Coast counterpart).

Manford and Kight became very close. They were intimates as well as political comrades. For years, they shared an ongoing letter-writing exchange, along with the occasional long-distance phone call. Their communication was relaxed, personal, philosophical, pontificating and theorizing. Manford was Kight's East Coast organizing and strategizing counterpart, often staging 'zaps,' and they linked a broader movement across the country. Manford served as a sounding board for the older activist's bigger dreams for the movement.

They shared an intellectual respect and a mutual admiration. Kight encouraged Manford to go to law school when Manford pursued an indictment against Michael Maye, president of New York City's Uniformed Firefighters Association, who had beaten Manford at a gay rights protest. Even though Maye was eventually acquitted, it remained a landmark case for the advancement of gay rights in New York.

Kight could not have had the kind of rapport with Harry Hay, Don Slater, or even Jim Kepner that he enjoyed with Morty Manford. Perhaps it was the advantage of Manford's youth, but more likely it was his willingness to buck the status quo. Kight let his full vision and socialist shirttails hang out with Manford. In comparison, his letters to Hay seem guarded and ideologically restrained. With Manford the long typewritten letters delved deeper into high-minded issues from a place deep within him. Manford always responded in kind.

Kight wrote to Manford (July 1974): "There is much more to go into, of a substantive nature [regarding the Center]. I hope the agenda now being fed into me from several sources will be tight enough to get at these issues in an orderly manner, but with quite enough room that anyone wishing to add on can do so easily."

They shared their frustrations with their respective organized gay activist groups and with "the way things are done." Kight was a strategic liberationist. He saw the long game.

In keeping with his GLF dictum "we do not respond to criticism," Kight advised Manford how to deal with recent criticism from the *Advocate*: "I would try to keep my shirt on about that. It's just not that big. If you allow it more room than it needs in your fine brain, then there's just not room for other things. Put it behind you. Be done with it. I recall their launcheds [sic] into me, but just barely. Too much to be done to give it time and space."

Kight wrote regarding the Center's IRS tax-exempt status, "So the good work for us has a rippling effect in that many can be benefited ... our information from IRS is that 15 gay groups are waiting in line, many more in preparation, many groups stalled because they do not have IRS 501(c)(3) and will surely come marching into DC with requests."

Not often, but the two men did have misunderstandings.

Kight experienced the early pangs of ageism in the gay community. After a particularly hectic visit Manford made to Los Angeles in July 1974, Kight wrote to him: "We didn't have a chance to talk things out. Sorry I spoke harshly regarding youthist [sic] commentaries I was hearing and realize I could have been more prudent in reacting to them; it is not necessary to speak harshly to co-workers, but only lovingly. I did ask your forgiveness and presume I got it. I am sure you begin to notice the degree of youthism [sic] that prevails in our community."

Manford responded to Kight: "I am reminded how dedicated movement activists have a duty to ourselves to enjoy once in a while and not allow ourselves to become 'movement objectified.'

"[We] didn't spend as much time together this past visit. I truly feel your love, commitment, kindness, and hospitality are something special for which we are all the beneficiaries. I hope you do not mind that I actively sought to broaden my contact amongst LA gay community and around the city. Because our longtime affection, respect and friendship stands rather firmly on its own deep merits."

Their friendship was solid, and communications continued for many years.

Not all the long-term correspondents were amicable. Angela Keyes Douglas was described as having "a difficult personality who saw conspiracies everywhere." The general consensus about Angela was that she was "nuts." One prominent historical researcher also described her as "a really important figure in the gay lib history of Los Angeles." Certainly, Douglas was on the frontier for transgender recognition. The GLF rejected the transsexual movement, yet Douglas raised awareness to transphobia [sic] both inside and outside the gay movement. Angela Douglas claimed that she had to leave Los Angeles after she and a trans singer were attacked at a gay lib dance. She referred to the "antitransvestic" attitudes of some gay men: "I'd had my fill from gays, all demanding I be a man, stop dressing as a woman."

Kight recognized that Angela was a pioneer in her cause for transgender civil liberties and that it was a difficult battle fraught with peril. He knew the fight would take a very long time, and that Angela probably did not possess the right temperament to achieve the goal. When Douglas left Los Angeles, she insisted they stay in touch and Kight was very patient with her. Douglas admonished Kight for using the incorrect pronoun while addressing her. Douglas remained connected to Los Angeles through Kight.

Angela: "It is so hard to be a woman, so hard, & I am proud to be even a partial one. Inside me, I am a woman; my exterior is beginning to match the inside. It seems you understand me better now—I miss all of you, of course, very much. You are all such a big part of my life. Yes, freedom, Morris, freedom to be a man or a woman, to be gay, to be straight whatever."

Douglas was intelligent and politically astute, often asking Kight to "help promote us, will you?" and did not have a smooth gender transition. Her abrasive personality made her an unsympathetic character. Kight may have taken sympathy on her as he tolerated an enormous amount of verbal and written abuse from Angela in a steady stream of phone calls and handwritten letters from her travels.

She settled in Miami and set up a chapter of the GLF and wrote for the Transvestite-Transsexual Action Organization newsletter *Moonshadow* and a "mini-magazine" called *Mirage*. She set up a "security force to stop police abuse of transsexuals and gays." After the American Psychiatric Association removed homosexuality from its list of mental illnesses in 1973, Douglas opened discussions to also remove "trans" from the list of mental disorders.

In 1976, Angela Douglas completed her transition with 'vaginoplasty' surgery by Berkeley doctor John Brown, who was later dubbed "Butcher John Brown" and "The Worst Doctor in America." In the 1970s, gender reassignment surgery was still quite risky and could be crude under the best of circumstances. Dr. Brown did gender reassignment surgery in a small clinic for a desperate and disparate minority group on an outpatient basis. He also performed surgeries in his garage and in motel rooms. He operated on anyone who paid his $600 fee—far below the going rate at Stanford University and Johns Hopkins Hospital that offered the same surgery while meeting much stricter criteria. An "incompetent and inept surgeon," Brown later lost his license to practice medicine. Though some of his patients were pleased, many, including Angela Douglas, were not happy with the results.

The botched surgery did not help Angela's disposition. She became more desperate and involved herself with multiple lawsuits, claiming people had "ripped her off." Kight was patient, though he didn't always respond to her letters as promptly as Angela would've liked. She was emotionally needy. Kight also saw her as mentally wounded.

According to more than a few sources, generally speaking once transsexuals received genital surgery, often their interest in political organizing dissipated as they wanted to live quietly and blend in unnoticed, hoping to no longer feel like misfits. Not so with Angela Keyes Douglas.

After her surgery, Angela returned to Miami and remained a presence in Kight's life through mail and phone calls. She had become more mentally unhinged; her letters demonstrate a constant emotional pendulum swinging from lonely and distraught to sociable and manic.

Gino Vezina remembered: "For years, Morris would get a phone call almost every day of the week, [saying] 'Morris Kight, you cocksucker, I'm going to come over and kill you today. You son of a bitch, you better watch your step, asshole. Today is your last day on earth.' He had the calls traced. Finally, he found out that it was post-op transsexual Angela Douglas calling from Florida. That went on for a couple of years."

Douglas often asked Kight (and others) for funds for various legal fees or living expenses and always made big promises of returns: "We can sue the City of Miami for millions. If we win, will give most to gay lib, etc. Can you dig it?"

Things heated up in 1984 when Kight became aware that Angela, now going under the birth name of Douglas Czinki, began communication with intelligence agencies, FBI, CIA, Secret Service, regarding Kight. In a memorandum to Jim Kepner (dated 3 October 1984) Kight cautioned Kepner regarding careful maintenance of all correspondence from and regarding Czinki. Angela/Douglas told the Secret Service (which seemed to be the agency that listened to the nonsense) that Kight was a "well-known Libyan connect, particularly with Moammar Khadaffi [sic] … I have no contact with the government of Libya and know not Khadaffi."

Kight tolerated the mood swings, the love fests and tirades, and the anonymous phone calls for years, until Angela Douglas won the lottery in 1991 and ceased all contact with Kight.

Douglas won $232,567 in the Florida state lottery which netted her $186,000. After squandering the money and most of her relationships, Angela returned to

Jackson County, Florida to live in near-poverty. Though she continued to write and market herself, except for an occasional fax promoting herself, Kight didn't hear from Angela again. From time to time, Angela would appear on national radio programs more as a novelty act than a serious spokesperson.

It is worth noting that Angela Douglas lived the last few years of her life seeming more male. Newer acquaintances weren't sure about Angela's gender as she continued to use her name "Angela" but dressed as a man. Her gender wasn't obvious. After her death in 2007, Angela was remembered for her "many contributions to a little-appreciated and generally misunderstood social issue."

DREAMS AND DEMONS

KIGHT PREENED AND PLUMED HIS ESCALATING VISIBILITY. THE public profile was as much to serve Kight's ego as it was to force the establishment to respectfully deal with "a gay"—if just one gay person, let the consideration begin with Morris Kight.

Gino Vezina: "Had Morris Kight lived his life in a different way, [had he] stayed in Texas, he could've ended up as governor. Instead, he came here [to Los Angeles] and got involved with the gay thing. The basic problem with Morris Kight [was] he was greedy for attention. Activists had to have a certain amount of humility. Morris Kight did not have any humility."

Outside, Kight remained gracious and present. Some have said that his ego grew in accordance to his prominence, but the truth is that Kight always had a healthy ego. In the early days, his ego fed the gay rights movement. His ego envisioned a better world for the disenfranchised and he envisioned raising them up from lower-class citizens. And, he assumed, they would be grateful. He had an ego large enough to support every displaced teenager who didn't have an ounce of self-worth, much less pride. His ego would pull drunks out of gutters and bail unfortunate souls from jail and not get sucked under with them. His ego allowed him to lend endless emotional support to his generational peers of lonely, bitter old men who had long ago lost their true selves to mind-numbing jobs and cheap booze. If ego were physical strength, Kight could have bench-pressed the bench, the press, and all the weight it could hold.

Yet Kight grew impatient with bureaucratic problems, which is what GCSC had become. So for fun he went to peace rallies and he'd invite gay comrades along. Some people unwind by going shopping; some go bowling, or sit at a bar; others go dancing. Morris Kight went protesting. A die-hard activist, he never tired of street demonstrations. He enjoyed the rush of being on the streets with fellow activists and, for the most part, like-minded individuals. He loved passing petitions and engaging strangers on the street. He'd introduce himself and quickly open their eyes to new ways of looking at the world, or not. As an institution, the antiwar movement was serious and it was also incredibly social. In the early days the gay movement couldn't always provide that kind of street connection and amity; there wasn't as much consistent solidarity within the gay movement. Still, Morris always shared camaraderie with other demonstrators, a little gossip, and a joke or two.

Kight expected to speak at every peace rally in Los Angeles. In the early 1970s, when he spoke from the dais, he always included gay rights in his litany of grievances against the status quo. Not everyone in the antiwar movement liked that Kight tried to integrate the antiwar movement with gay rights. Some antiwar activists didn't want to mix gay rights with their cause for peace, while others didn't want to deal with what had become Kight's well-known idiosyncratic ego. Kight was growing out of favor with some peace activists.

In January 1973, the kingpins of the antiwar movement gathered outside of City Hall in downtown Los Angeles for a demonstration. Dalton Trumbo, Raoul Teilhet (president of the California Teachers Union) and Milton Zaslow (from Peace Action Coalition), Anthony Russo (of the Pentagon Papers fame) all spoke and many others, all Kight colleagues. Morris was not asked to speak.

Gino Vezina arrived late to the rally and found Kight behind the staging area, "so enraged about not being asked to speak, he was purple."

The Peace and Freedom Party, however, embraced Kight and his high visibility in gay rights. In the summer of 1973, after he addressed a meeting of the California Peace and Freedom Party, a group from the Party approached Kight privately, to urge him to run for Governor of California. It was appealing. He wanted it. He wouldn't have to be obvious about wanting it, but he also didn't play it too coy. No one could have known that it resuscitated an unrealized dream to run for an elected office, one of the many dreams thwarted when his marriage ended. So he thought about it, he talked it over with a few of his trusted inside circle, and he let it be known beyond his circle.

After a few months, Bishop Mikhail Itkin of the People's Church in Hollywood publicly announced his own candidacy for a U.S. Congressional seat, running on the Peace and Freedom Party ticket as an openly gay candidate. In December, Kight announced that he would run for Governor of California on the Peace and Freedom Party ticket.

The press wouldn't give attention to one openly gay candidate running for office. But two openly gay candidates were newsworthy to the *Free Press.*

In February 1974, Harry Hay wrote a letter to Morris, discouraging him from running.

"Dear P & P 'prospective' GUV: Read about your plans and considerations in the FREEP."

In a two-and-a-half-page typewritten, single-spaced letter, Hay pleaded and reasoned with Kight not to run for Governor. It was written hastily with a lot of typos and crossing out and liberal usage of underlining and all capitals and, at times, embellished with his humorous slang (e.g., "Bi-Shit Opkin in L.A. and Rev-ray in S.F." when referring to Bishop Itkin and Reverend Ray Broshears, respectively).

"No, Morris, please ... NOT YET!

"You're moving too soon. There are a couple of steps which must be taken first."

Harry Hay saw things happening very fast and worried that too much too quickly could take the gay movement in too many different directions. Hay was generous with his wisdom and reasoned a more effective strategy for a long-term liberation movement that did not include homosexuals assimilating to heterosexual norms. Hay did not want homosexuals to blend in with the status quo heterosexuals. Hay, like Kight, wanted his community to have a place in society, to be counted. Hay eschewed assimilation as much as the closet. Harry wrote that he did not consider Morris one of the "Bullshit Liberals," or the "Queers, Homos, and similar Freaks (all of whom are the same as everybody else except in bed)."

"The GAYS," Harry reasoned, "must first demonstrate as a closely-knit cohesive group, as a political club … [and demonstrate] their political acumen."

Harry was confident when a Gay Consciousness was manifested with respect "for what they are, for what they see politically and socially, AND FOR WHAT THEY CAN DO … THEN YOU CAN RUN FOR GUV if you're still so minded."

It's not likely that Kight had received Hay's letter in time to influence his change of mind. Yet around the same time, in February 1974, Kight crafted a letter to "Members of the Peace and Freedom Party, Co-Workers and Friends in various Community causes." He sent a copy of the four-page, double-spaced, typewritten letter to Hay and Burnside in San Juan Pueblo, New Mexico. Their letters crossed in the mail.

"Certainly, I have thought over the years, of running for office. This was not a new idea and, frankly, was, and is, an appealing one…. In December, I had finally made the decision to run for governor of the state of California.

"Now I see that this decision was a mistake, and the very best way to rectify it is to say so—ask for understanding and to bow out."

He reasoned that the Gay Community Services Center, where he "worked for two and half years as a volunteer," forbade the Center from endorsing political candidates. Kight said that he had been "gradually easing myself out of the Center. Yet, in fact, I find that I cannot—in the public's eye—be totally separated from the Center.

"While I have pride in that association, I feel it far too hazardous to the Center's work to risk having an insinuation of partisan politics placed at its door."

He mentioned the exhaustion that he experienced from his current schedule.

"I think also that I might have to work harder than the established party candidates, since I would not want to sling mud nor engage in personal brawls…. To talk about this with reason, and candor, and love, and concern, would take a lot longer, however, I think would have longer-lasting possibilities."

He asked for kindness to "let me drop out."

He privately mentioned to a close friend that he worried that in the course of a rough-and-tumble campaign, his past and his former family would be ensnarled in his political ambitions.

Kight ended his letter with a reaffirmation of his commitments to the Annual Conference of the National Free Clinic Council, the Annual Christopher Street Liberation Day Celebration, and "now-in-the-planning National Conference of Gaypeoples and Organizations."

Kight took a little time off, as he said, to "finish certain projects, take some time to look after some very personal matters, have a bit of time to rest at the ranch of old friends in Northern California."

Pat Rocco's Mount Baldy cabin, about an hour and a half north of Los Angeles city, served as a retreat for Kight and other gay men. The cabin was used for meetings and fun and restoration. As Rocco described it, "Morris went up there for play, and nobody cared about whether we were running around nude or not up there, or who we were playing with, or what combinations of people we were playing with because we were. That was the place to be open and free and as gay as we wanted to be, and not worry about ... This was pre-AIDS."

Rocco had the Mount Baldy cabin for 30 years, 1959–1989. They sometimes had meetings there, meetings that didn't include all the key people. Rocco said, "we had Gay Community Services Center meetings up at this cabin and Christopher Street West meetings, of course. It was totally hidden away. You had to hike in to get to it, that kind of thing.

"But we also had times when we just went, we just went up there for friends, for play.

"I saw Morris in some interesting and fun, frivolous situations where he was able to have fun and let his hair completely down. So after it was over and done with, [the fun] was never talked about except between us. After it was over and done with ... you know, fun times. Fun times."

FICTIONALIZATION

IN HIS 1975 DAVE BRANDSETTER NOVEL *TROUBLEMAKER*, AUTHOR and local L.A. activist Joseph Hansen described a setting with "three distinguished members of the Southern California Gay Community." Thinly disguised in Brandsetter's description: "First was a minister, complete with dog collar, though he'd got his training in the backwoods Baptist seminaries in the deep South [Reverend Troy Perry]. Next was a moon-faced man with a belly who had begun as a gay activist at fifty after a lifetime of bailing out likely youths from jail, and now spent his nights on television talk shows explaining the gay mystique, whatever that was [Morris Kight]. Last was an acne-scarred publisher who served the homosexuals of fifty states with a sleek magazine that glamorized sadism and Texas mass murderers [Jim Kepner and *ONE* Magazine]."

EXIT THE CENTER

IN 1974, KIGHT WROTE TO MANFORD: "OBVIOUSLY IN A HOMOPHOBIC world, highly disciplined organizations are needed, those who can carry the flag. While I felt GLF/LA had passed its usefulness in that form, and I am convinced that was a good judgment, we still need such an organization here for specific purpose of being action-oriented."

Kight was fatigued, and he was having health issues. Skin cancer on his face and upper torso required almost five years of treatment. About two years after the same diagnosis he required extensive surgery at UCLA whereby his forehead and nose were reconstructed using a fold of skin from his front scalp. This created an obvious six-inch vertical scar on his forehead and added a task to his daily personal grooming; he had to shave the top of his nose as the hair follicles from his scalp were active.

This also began his penchant for wide-brim straw hats.

It was time to make changes, personally and professionally.

To Manford, Kight wrote: "Stress and strain, this does seem to have some validity but even that goes away when one does not allow it into the mind.

"Body and soul: I have faced up to the fact that loss of energy, constant headache and temperature are not going to go away. Thursday a bunch of medical tests as a guest of one of the local hospitals, and a bug has been found, and a spectrum of antibiotics found, and soon I shall be bouncy, bouncy and no more cancelled dates for out of town."

In January 1974, Kight resigned his day-to-day administrative position at the Gay Community Services Center. He continued to fundraise and serve on the board and consult.

Others were leaving the Center under much more tragic circumstances.

A 1975 *Gay Sunshine* newsletter described it as a "typical day at the Gaywill [sic] Funky Shoppe. Ralph Schaffer … stayed in the Shoppe [long after the 9 p.m. closing] to prepare his merchandise for the next morning."

It being a hot summer night, Schaffer left the back door open. Later that night, Ralph was found inside the Shoppe "slumped to the floor," shot twice from behind with no struggle.

Platania said, "Ralph Schaffer was shot and killed. It was hate, plain and simple. And nobody gave a shit. LAPD investigators speculated that 'He must've tried to molest a customer.' The murder was never solved, and nobody cared. Morris was devastated."

Kight added another name to his running list of casualties in the struggle for gay liberation: Larry Turner, Howard Efland, Ginny Gallegos, and now Ralph Schaffer.

Soon after, the Silver Lake collective disbanded. June Herrle chose to have a child as a single woman and she moved back to her hometown in Ohio and no longer participated in gay activities.

WILL SUCCESS SPOIL THE GAY CENTER?

IN MAY OF 1975, THE CENTER MOVED WEST OF DOWNTOWN TO 1213 North Highland Avenue in Hollywood. As they unpacked and settled into their new surroundings, there was an uneasiness among personnel. A revolt was percolating just below the surface, though it hadn't yet been articulated.

By this time, the Center had more than 32 separate programs and it continued to grow. They were applying for larger funding grants. The Center was lax in organization. Staffed by mostly part-time volunteers with everyone doing whatever they wanted to do, there was no coordination. Once they moved to the Highland location, no attention was paid to the day-to-day operations. It was a productive and innovative time, yet along with the many new programs and many newly liberated gay people, resentments were building.

What was *not* happening was just as significant as what was happening at the Center. Inter-personnel dynamics were being revealed. There was a definite hierarchy in the staff; even volunteers were hierarchical. Oddly enough it reflected the same hierarchy as found in the 'establishment' mainstream society. White men stood at the top and front, always. Non-white males were next in order for receiving preference and recognitions, and last—always last—were women.

At this time in history, both nationally and at the Center, Kight and many of his peers were viewed as sexists. They didn't see themselves that way because they were, after all, left-wing activists fighting in the name of civil rights.

Meyer: "Don and Morris were two very different people. They were the bosses and [they had] condescension toward everyone."

Though he no longer kept an office at the Center, Kight was still very much involved. He was known to be a bit imperialistic with underlings—it was his way of keeping the workflow moving forward. That never changed with him. Gripes brewed among the staff, and management had nary a response. Kight claimed he knew nothing of the growing problems until everything blew up. The Center acquired a reputation of having a duplicitous nature. The management at the Center was high-minded and appreciated a self-deprecating staff despite their mission to build personal pride. Management planned for some disgruntled staff, thought of as 'collateral damage.' Staff, probably more so volunteers, did not expect inconsistency with the organization's stated mission and the behaviors of individuals.

Their noble mission was at risk, due to a collection of overblown egos and an unenlightened managerial style.

Around this same time, Kight wrote to Manford, venting about personnel at the Center:

"We've been peacefully serious all these years and [staff] are beginning to move against us. So we must stick together as we never have before. Each of us must be efficient, loving, brave, and we must be totally honest with one another. In the aftermath of that honesty, it would be so helpful if everyone learned to speak well of one another, to find our differences, our beefs, and to settle them quietly in private and move on."

Later Kight recalled: "One day, Rita Saenz, who headed Governor Jerry Brown's Alcoholism and Drug Addiction Services, said, 'Morris and Don, if, within two weeks, you can produce a program, a proposed document, to create an alcoholism demonstration project for women, Lesbian women, we can fund you at a million bucks. You have to work fast. I'm telling you that there's a million bucks waiting.'

"So we said, 'Thank you. We'll do it.'"

They immediately assembled about 15 people who worked full-time—many without salary—to fulfill the task put before them. Lillene Fifield, Don Kilhefner and Kight agreed to write the program itself, which was to be called the Women's Alcoholism Program of the Center. They recruited the best among them to undertake the various tasks of research and analysis. One of these was Brenda Weathers, who had been working with Romaine Edwards, a director of alcoholism programs in Los Angeles, trying to set up a treatment program for women. They had no funding.

Carolyn Weathers remembered, "In her own recovery process [Brenda] noticed that there just weren't any alcoholism treatment programs for women. Lillene knew this and she asked Brenda if she would like to help with the grant writing."

Lillene Fifield led the group effort. Ken Bartley, Brenda and Kilhefner gathered data and together they assembled a grant proposal. They used a number of social workers from USC School of Social Work to help write the technical aspects. Lillene would write the testing component; they expected to be subjected to a lot of analysis and testing.

Kight was most involved with the program design; he also accumulated supportive letters from the community.

They worked day and late into the night, many at typewriters, many scoring books and charts. People brought in food.

Kight: "We didn't have lots of chairs, so we sat on the floor."

Lillene, Morris, and Don spent a lot of time in her small office at the Regional Research Institute in Social Welfare, where she was a student. They became quite close.

"On about the seventh day," Kight recalled for Paul Cain, "we produced a 385-page document for a world-pioneering program, the women's alcoholism program of the Center, to deal with oppression/repression/exploitation of women, which would lead to alcoholism and drug abuses."

They used the Xerox machine at the Health Services offices on Wilshire Boulevard. Kight: "It took all day long and night, looking at the ceiling, printing 80 separate copies" of the 385-page document.

Sitting in the back of Jon Platania's truck on the way to the airport, they read the document and still debated it. Once at the airport, they mailed ten copies to the National Institute of Health and Human Services in Washington, D.C.

In retelling the story to Paul Cain in 1994, true to form, Kight embellished the details. "[They] read our proposal. It was ultimately reviewed by a 15-person peer review panel, peers from alcoholism services, and they read it. And when they finished, they leapt to their feet and gave our proposal a standing ovation."

Carolyn Weathers recalled, "In early 1974, the NIAAA wrote back that the proposal had been accepted for the creation of a women's recovery house and outpatient center with specific outreach to the lesbian community, with GCSC as the parent agency.

"The program was named the Alcoholism Program for Women, and GCSC appointed Brenda Weathers as its director."

Kight remembered, "The director of NI Triple A [*National Institute on Alcohol Abuse and Alcoholism*] said, 'All your enthusiasm is really great and I share it, but let me tell you, I have a question to ask you. Will success spoil the Gay Center?'"

STRIKE AT THE CENTER

THE NET AMOUNT OF THE GRANT WAS $350,000, AN ENORMOUS amount for the time, the largest grant ever given to any gay organization anywhere up until the 1980s. Still, Kight had to exaggerate, claiming it was a million dollars.

Kight: "Yes, a million bucks was a lot of money. For women exclusively, and sexual orientation was a big issue, because it was exclusively lesbian."

Lillene remembered that "Morris and Don were always supportive of women's activities, even though their consciousness could've been raised a little more."

None of the women denied the existence of sexism at the Center, but the mistreatment was not exclusively directed toward women. "An awful lot of men who Don was with were very resentful," Mina Meyer recalled.

In 1972, a 19-year-old Michael Weinstein fell upon GCSC on Wilshire Boulevard. A recent New York transplant, Weinstein was drawn to the "lefty orientation" at the Center. "The fact that there was Gay Center felt miraculous, that they created this space, it was very moving and a very big deal. I was initially scared, in a good way. It was an interesting environment. Southern belle drag queens, diesel dykes, there were hippie elements, lesbian-feminists. It was a great hangout. For all its leftist leanings, it was very male-dominated.

"I became involved romantically with Don Kilhefner and was introduced to the inner circle of friends." These included Mina Meyer and Sharon Raphael, both of whom became lifelong friends with Weinstein.

"Ken Bartley had a ranch in the San Gabriel Valley, where there was a lot of taking advantage of boys. It was quite a sleazy atmosphere, a lot of inappropriate touching. It was out of control."

"Morris Kight," Weinstein remembered, "had flair, charisma, and he mentored a lot. I never saw him take advantage of boys. He also didn't discourage it."

Barry Copilow had similar memories: "Morris Kight was not a lech. A lot of the [men] who worked at the Center would take young boys home. I never heard a story like that about Morris Kight."

Kight didn't go to the San Gabriel Valley ranch. He preferred the atmosphere and company at Pat Rocco's Mount Baldy cabin.

Weinstein was not the only young male at the Center who felt "taken advantage of" at the time.

Miki Jackson: "I was out of town for a while in 1974. I got my regular Morris calls, but I was a little out of touch. I know Don was being a problem. The women were getting tired of his chasing boys—along with other things."

Meyer felt "a closeness with Morris that I didn't share with Don." There were those who shared a real commitment to the cause of gay liberation—"we respected each other."

Jeanne Cordova worked with Kilhefner. "We disagreed about a lot of different things, occasionally about sexism and gay liberation." They were never personally close, not like the closeness she and many of the other women describe having with Kight.

The gay men had a *tribalness.* Cordova agreed "with the tribalness," but she didn't always agree with the gay men. She found herself to be what she coined a "lesbian primarist."

"Sometimes Morris was a little sexist, but most men were at that time. Gay men came to that thinking much later." Most of the women forgave a lot from Morris. Cordova explained that they blamed "his era, he was 30 years older," and the "sexism of that generation. He was born into an era that dismissed women."

Consensus among the women was that Kight slowly came to a feminist awareness sooner than a lot of the other men of his era.

Mina Meyer: "Morris was an old-line movement person who wasn't a bureaucrat, but he knew how to get things done and he knew how to make the world move. Don was more of an intellectual and he also knew how to get things done. No one would get in their way."

Michael Weinstein said, "Don was the organizer. Morris didn't sweat a lot of the organizational details. He had political connections. He was the spokesperson."

Steve Lachs recalled, "Don and Morris worked well together. Don was more methodical and concerned with operations. They were both filled with the dream of a community. They respected each other's abilities."

Whatever dynamics Don and Morris had, gay men and lesbian feminists were about to cross into unprecedented territory; core issues met fundamental differences. The leaders were about to find themselves at cross-purposes within their own liberation movement.

"Before the Center," Weinstein says, "there wasn't that much overlap between lesbians and gay men. Then lesbian-feminists were on the rise. I don't think Morris understood it. There were prerogatives that men assumed that were objectionable to women. Also, it was almost exclusively white—so it wasn't really representative of the community at large."

In the summer of 1974, the women searched for a building for the alcoholism program and decided on 1147 South Alvarado Street.

Carolyn Weathers: "I remember how incredibly filthy the kitchen was, the scum and grease from what looked like decades covering the floor, the counters and sink. But, God, the house was grand!"

Around the same time, in a rather unceremonious and offhanded way, Brenda Weathers was told that the grant money earmarked for APW would be shared with other programs at the Center, all of which benefited only the men.

Carolyn Weathers: "Brenda was informed of plans to 'spread the paper,' that is, apply some APW funds to other GCSC programs."

There was no formula for this "sharing." It was not unprecedented for an agency to use a small percentage of funds earmarked for one program to support the organizational structure that was used to seek the funding. But that wasn't how it was presented to Brenda Weathers. No one involved at the time, who survives to chronicle the event, is willing to go on record as to exactly who delivered the 'spread the paper' message to Weathers. All agreed that it could have been handled better. So much trouble could have been avoided if the message had been patiently and respectfully explained. Instead, the women, once again, felt beneath and betrayed by their male comrades and a few of the female managers. Gratitude was in short supply.

Caroline Weathers: "Brenda Weathers said, in effect, 'Over my dead body.' She insisted that these funds be spent for nothing less than an alcoholism treatment program for women, as per terms of the federal grant.

"There followed some rocky times."

Miki Jackson: "As I heard it at the time, whatever project got a grant—if one, or more did—the whole Center would benefit and share, since they had written the grants together and used Center resources [to write them]. At the time it seemed very unlikely that a grant would be given at all. It was easy to see it as a cooperative project with the real goal of priming the pump and using it to widen the population the government would give to, to include gays and lesbians, to take that and use it to get more and so on, when no one thought any real money would ever materialize.

"Money showed up, history got rewritten, memories blurred, and serious fighting started in earnest. It never stopped."

There had already been rumblings of discontent, but as Weinstein put it, "The final straw was the grant money. As money came in, the culture changed."

Jeanne Cordova talked one-on-one with Morris Kight about the grant money and came away with two thoughts: "Morris wants that grant money. Women should be independent."

Meanwhile, GCSC was in the middle of a big move and expansion.

Lillene Fifield: "The problems began on the day of moving from Wilshire to Highland. There was a 'refusal to move.'"

Some of the employees began a work slowdown.

"As we were moving into a new building [on Highland], we started getting phone calls from funding agencies that they wanted to come and inspect, do an audit. The programs [were] not [active]. Men's clinic, women's clinic, alcohol program for women wasn't going yet."

The executives soon learned that a group of employees and volunteers, dissidents as they'd become known, wrote a massive report, a newsletter called *It's About Time,* complete with handbills, flyers and backup materials detailing various misdeeds by Center leaders, including growing deficits, "misappropriation of funds," and a multitude of other transgressions assumedly committed by the executive committee.

The report quickly became known as the Blue Paper (for its blue cover), supported Brenda Weathers' position, and was mailed to leaders of the gay community, gay media, and all funding agencies. Copies of the Blue Paper were sold at the Highland Avenue Center for ten dollars a copy. Inevitably a member of the executive committee found a copy of the Blue Paper. The Center executives were outraged.

In addition to the scathing content, the dissidents used Center offices and equipment to print the newsletter.

Pandemonium was inevitable. As a result of the distribution of the Blue Paper, the Center was thrust into many audits by multiple agencies simultaneously.

In a 1975 interview for the radio show *IMRU,* Kight explained, "After being funded for [just] a few months, having survived for four years through great denial, giving up many things, being very prudent, we survived, and now suddenly we get a pittance of public funding. The county spent enormous amounts of money auditing that mere pittance. Then we're accused of misappropriation of funds.

"I think that really is shortsighted. I think that those who made those accusations would have been well put to hold off a while, until they could really get some substance and information."

Once the Blue Paper was public, the board met privately for six days in marathon sessions to decide what to do.

Carolyn Weathers: "Each side saw the other as obstructive to good purposes. One saw insubordination and impediment to general funding for its bouncing, 'revolutionary toddler' agency [GCSC]. The other saw misdirection of earmarked funds that would endanger an extraordinary program [APW] before it got off the ground. There was profound need for both of these entities. Months of struggle ensued."

The Center's administration called a special meeting with the staff of the Alcoholism Program for Women. According to Carolyn Weathers, they "strongly suggested that job termination was possible if the staff continued their support of Brenda and her 'interference' in the parent agency's handling of APW's business.

"[In response] the staff immediately wrote a letter of support for Brenda and 99 percent of the APW staff signed the letter."

Morris: "They started meeting and subverting us."

The board addressed every question from every funding agency and made adjustments where required. In every instance but one, each individual accounting agency from various funders found there was enough money in the general account to cover each deficit for individual programs, but not collectively.

The audits didn't prove anything. They concluded that while there wasn't mismanagement, the Center was under-managed. In addition to being understaffed, the accounting system wasn't sufficient to handle its operations.

The County Auditor was quoted as saying, "We can't decide whose dollars are whose."

The one exception was the Alcoholism Program for Women.

Next, the board made the questionable decision to terminate seven paid staff workers (out of a paid staff of 40) and seven volunteer staff (of almost two hundred volunteer staff). The specific reason given for the firings was "failure to accept the limitations in power and control of the job description."

Kight: "All I had in mind was to save the Center ... Decent people were hurt, and I'm really sorry about that. Nonetheless, my passion was to save the Center."

Jeanne Cordova was fired from the board of directors. The reason given for her dismissal was that she was unable to work with other board members; they found her hostile and adverse to the interest of the Center. Later Jeanne made public her unwillingness to "work with the present board members."

Cordova and the other dissidents became known as the "Feminist 15."

David Glasscock, a well-meaning aide in County Supervisor's Ed Edelman's office, saw the newsletter and, overreacting, made a statement suggesting that future funding be held in suspension until certain conditions were agreed to, which included the requirement that staff members had to sign a loyalty oath.

Privately, Kight and the board members were horrified at the mention of loyalty oaths, yet didn't hesitate to pass the idea on to the staff that loyalty oaths might be required. They were secretly relieved when the staff refused to sign.

Dissension increased.

Lines in the sand became deeper, each side more resolute in their position.

Personnel policies and procedures were rewritten specifically regarding terminating employees. Whatever policies were in place were nullified and removed, thereby not in effect at the time the workers were fired.

Morris Kight was caught between the proverbial rock and an obscure hard place. He suddenly found himself, a lifelong anti-establishment rebel, on the side of bureaucrats. A longtime proponent of workers' rights, he was being accused of being opposed to workers organizing. Not tacit or the slightest bit self-conscious, he was mostly shocked at the complaints lodged against him. He thought of himself as a feminist, a radical, the anti-authoritarian authority, an anarchist's anarchist, the resident expert on social discourse. He was a coalition-builder—a lover, not a hater. He missed the irony.

Jim Kepner: "Morris seems to be a person who can change his mind in the twinkling of an eye, yet never know the meaning of self-doubt."

The workers organized and did exactly what Morris Kight would have done or advised them to do, if Morris Kight had been on the other side of the argument. About a dozen of the remaining workers declared a strike and organized daily pickets outside the Highland Avenue offices. Joined by some disgruntled gay men, over a short time the picket line grew. It was relentless, lasting every day for close to a year.

Steve Lachs lamented, "We were paying people nothing compared to the work they were doing. We attracted some really good people. And there were lots of personality clashes, lots of political disagreements. We were always able to hold the Center together."

It was a coming of age, of sorts, for lesbian feminists and gay men. It could have led to a hallelujah moment if it hadn't become so terribly hurtful, mean, and personal.

No longer about grant money, this was a faceoff between the new feminists who became known as 'womyn' versus the old patriarchy. The picket line became vicious and personal. Some of the original allegations began to recede.

One picketer's large sign bore the bold letters "K-K-K," and in softer print included the full words "Kight, Kilhefner, Ken [Bartley]."

Kight recalled: "The worst picket sign I've ever seen in my life. I went out in the street and burst into tears, and even now, 15, 18, 20 years later, I cry. A picket sign ... 'K-K-K.' I have been a vigorous enemy of the Ku Klux Klan all these years, and seeing a sign insinuating against me in that kind of way—it was very painful."

1975. Picketers outside the Gay Community Services Center on Highland Avenue in Hollywood. Photo: Pat Rocco. Pat Rocco Papers, Coll2007-006, ONE National Gay & Lesbian Archives, USC Libraries, University of Southern California.

Picketers spoke with delight about the extensive damage they were doing at the Center. They targeted clients who were trying to access the Center's services.

Center employee Bob Sirico to *IMRU*: "In the evening, a black, blind lesbian walked into the Center with a seeing eye dog. One of the women on the picket line grabbed the harness of the dog and walked her down the street. One of the sisters from the Center had to go out, find her wandering in a circle on the corner, and bring her into the Center."

June Suwara, who had once vied for a top management position at the Center, stood before a rally in De Longpre Park in Hollywood: "We're succeeding. We're cutting down the services. We're cutting down people going into the Center to receive services by scab people, people who are not trained."

The Center's existence was threatened and the building vandalized by the picketers' antics. There were numerous examples of bitter mischievousness.

The picketers filed a fake Change of Address with the post office so that Kight's mail was forwarded to a nonexistent address. It took weeks to discover and reverse.

There were prank phone calls, harassing calls, and bomb threats.

A window at the Center was broken and two Selectric typewriters were stolen.

Individuals' homes were picketed with signs bearing false accusations.

The controversy was everywhere in the community, though it especially burned among lesbian feminist women. There was outright exclusion and verbal attacks against women who stood in solidarity with the Center administration; they were accused of anti-feminism.

Steve Lachs: "The Center walkout was about women, as w-o-m-y-n. It was a huge fight with the gay *womyn* versus lesbians. There was a fundraiser at Sheldon's [Andelson] house. The invitation said, 'gay men and women.' Sheldon got shit on by half the women there because he said gay women instead of 'lesbian.' It had to play its course, which it eventually did. It was very, very difficult, tough times."

Jan Ora for the 1975 *IMRU* interview: "Viciousness is a cancer in our women's community right now. Some women who have decided that if they don't support the picketers who were fired, then they aren't politically correct or feminist."

Ora continued: "I do not want the women's community to become isolated and desperate, and I see this happening as women react to the judgmental, restrictive energy of some women in the community. Sisterhood is more than a word. As a radical feminist, I call for an end to the destructive energy which is tearing apart the women's community and attempting to tear apart individual sisters."

Center staff employee Johnnie Sue Hyde told *IMRU*: "When I decided to stay inside the Center when picketers first began forming, my decision was shaky. I was unsure, untrusting of the side with which I found myself allied, several times angry enough to consider joining the Feminist 15, et al.

"What has kept me inside that building, and what I feel is the real issue, for me has to do with the attitude. The picketers would have won me if they had approached me with concern, with love, or at least respect, to make changes, to admit errors, to grow. I need to feel that I can be vulnerable.

"The feminist's blanket condemnation of GCSC workers as male-identified, bourgeois, capitalist, sexist, lackey pigs made it impossible for me to be vulnerable with them. If the Women's Movement had begun with the policy that all housewives are just hopelessly fucked up and politically incorrect, and if the first feminists were so disgusted that they screamed 'Pig' every time that they saw a housewife, instead of perceiving her as a sister, our struggle would never have begun."

Betty Berzon recalled, "It got very crazy. We on the Board received death threats. When we entered and left the building, we were shouted at, spit upon, and shoved [by picketers]."

Soon after that, the Board met in Sheldon Andelson's office.

Terry DeCrescenzo was another casualty in the crossfire. Fairly new in town, Betty Berzon invited her to help at the Center which meant that sometimes she took minutes at the board meetings, typed them up and distributed them to board members.

Perhaps wanting to deflect attention, Morris Kight told Jeanne Cordova that Terry "created the list of names of people to be fired." This led to DeCrescenzo being alienated by Cordova and many in the lesbian community.

DeCrescenzo was clear that she "did not dictate the names. My role at the Center was peripheral at that time. I was a nobody."

During the first month of the strike, the Alcoholism Program for Women launched. Because of letters written to funding agencies trying to get the Center defunded, they jeopardized funding for APW as well.

Agencies were at the offices every day to go over everything with "a fine-toothed comb," Fifield remembers.

Brenda Weathers left the picket line after 30 days. She needed to be in the office to tend the program she so desperately wanted. Fifield said that "Brenda was really committed to the recovery of alcoholic women."

The strike lasted more than a year, "the most miserable year of my life," Lillene recalled. She was banned from many lesbian organizations and exiled from closed-door meetings with the Alcoholism Program for Women, which continued with Brenda Weathers as Executive Director.

"It totally ruined us [key executives and board members]," Lillene described it. "A lot of the allegations were manufactured. Morris was furious, as was Don, as was I."

Kight: "It led to the near-collapse of the Center."

Lillene and Brenda eventually patched things up, but it took longer than the length of the strike.

The Center side said that APW was originally conceptualized to interface with all the other programs at the Center. The men, or the Center, construed the APW's need for a separate facility as a desire to secede and become its own entity.

Brenda Weathers insisted that separating from the Center was not the APW's original plan. The women had little choice but to form their own incorporated Board of Directors with legal nonprofit status.

Brenda Weathers to *IMRU* said, "Then president of the Board of Directors for GCSC, Terrance O'Brien, threatened to have the funding source rescind the grant, [to] not give us [APW] the grant money unless certain conditions were met. That was kind of scary, because there we stood upon the threshold of having our grant turned back."

Speculation was that all funding might be withdrawn if the Center was not asked to remove their fiscal sponsorship of APW (using GCSC tax-exempt status).

Kight to *IMRU*: "Funding could only be held up for some stated and specific cause, and no cause has been found to suspend funding. Indeed, that funding, and other funding, has passed its audit. It should be borne in mind that each of these audit reports contains recommendations for improvement of procedures—some of them quite sane and saleable, some of them quite reasonable. Some of them, however, I think have to be read in the terms of 'bureaucratize,' that is, auditors have a habit of making all kinds of recommendations for all kinds of things."

Kight said to Cain in 1994: "We learned that [ACW] were subverting us. They formed a separate Board of Directors and they got a separate 501(c)(3) and they hired separately. They were subverting the whole thing because the program was vast."

ACW did separate from the Center. It broke off and became an independent entity with its own nonprofit status.

With ACW separate from the Center, the pickets died down, and everyone went their own ways. Life and liberation continued.

According to DeCrescenzo, Betty Berzon came to realize, with the benefit of reflection and not being caught up in the moment, that it was "so wrong to fire the people because they disagreed. She had been persuaded by Morris. He could be very manipulative and Machiavellian.

"He manipulated Betty, who was no slouch. She did not believe in subterfuge—she believed in transparency. She may not have ever articulated that she felt conned by Morris Kight."

Years later Kight reflected on the strike: "Nonetheless, we withstood it. It was horrible. Even now, these years later, I stammer and stutter to think about it.

"We were convinced we were right. Then and now."

AFTER THE STRIKE

AFTER THE STRIKE, TERRY DECRESCENZO WAS INVITED TO JOIN the board of directors. She developed a series of programs for the Center, "leaderless programs," she described them, where "natural leaders emerged from the groups."

When the strike was over, Kight didn't hold a grudge. He turned away from the conflict and never really spoke of it much. He wouldn't forsake the coalition opportunities.

In 1977, Morris babysat Daisy, Brenda Weathers' four-legged family member, while Brenda was away arranging her relocation to the East Coast. He was happy to add Daisy, a purebred, to his mutt and the couple of semi-feral cats he fed regularly.

Carolyn Weathers made a note in her diary dated December 3, 1977 regarding a visit Brenda made to see her dog while briefly back in L.A., but still moving to the East Coast: "B[renda] and me to see Daisy at Morris and Larry's. Warm. Just us four. Morris wants to see B[renda] as a spokeswoman going around [the] country, pulling folks together, getting others to run for office."

Years later, Betty Berzon recalled visiting Morris during this time and asking about the purebred. Kight explained that he was helping Brenda Weathers while she got resituated. Berzon was shocked, "Why would you do such a favor for one of our enemies?"

Morris explained, "We're all on the same side. We have disagreements, then we come back together. And then we fight again."

1979. A no-charge Thanksgiving dinner organized by Kight and the U.S. Mission became a city tradition. In De Longpre Park, l-r Frank Vel, Tony Sullivan, Morris, unidentified, unidentified. Photo by Pat Rocco. Pat Rocco Papers Coll2007-006, ONE National Gay & Lesbian Archives, Los Angeles, California.

Chapter 12

Gay-gencies

THE FOLLOWING YEARS were the most prolific and monumental for Kight both personally and politically. In advancing the gay rights movement in America, he conceptualized a community by and for gay people, and developed a long-range strategy to build coalitions inside media, politics, and pop culture. It is easy to affirm that all roads led to liberation and equality but in the mid-1970s, that eventuality was still a long way off. Kight accepted that it would require patience and expected setbacks along the way.

MEDIA

CLEARLY, PORTRAYAL OF GAYS IN POP CULTURE NEEDED TO CHANGE. Ordinarily depicted as homicidal, suicidal, unhappy, troubled, and often the fool, homosexuals were the brunt of jokes and ridicule, and the few news stories about them were negative and adversarial.

Morris set out to target TV networks regarding specific portrayals while also putting local channels on notice that gays would no longer be silent.

1981. Morris Kight holding court at his annual Solstice party. Photo: Pat Rocco. Pat Rocco Papers, Coll2007-006, ONE National Gay & Lesbian Archives, USC Libraries, University of Southern California.

Once again, through a series of "zaps," homosexuals across the country raised their collective voice and would be heard.

In 1972, through Troy Perry, Kight met East Coast activist Mark Segal who already had a reputation for disrupting TV shows, having interrupted a live broadcast of the *CBS Evening News with Walter Cronkite* and the *Today Show,* both filmed in New York. While visiting Los Angeles, Segal acquired passes to most every ABC show (his prime target). The general plan was to sit in the audience and disrupt the live studio tapings in order to end the invisibility of gay people.

Segal visited Los Angeles a few times. Each trip was a unique adventure and not just for the many zaps or the panel discussion on gay rights that they participated in at UCLA.

On Segal's first visit he was with Morty Manford, and they both slept on the floor or a few worn sofas at the Center. Kight showed them around town driving a gold Lincoln Continental. Kight explained that the car had belonged to Bing Crosby and had been donated (likely donated to the Center) by Crosby's manager. No one could ever check if the story was true.

Segal and Manford wanted to visit Disneyland. Segal recalled that "Morris said, 'you can't go there, that's a capitalist's heaven.' All the way to Disneyland Morris goes on and on about how awful it is that we're all going to Disneyland. We get there and as soon as we get in, Morris said, 'all right, the first thing we do is go to Pirates of the Caribbean....'" Apparently, Kight knew his way around the "awful Disneyland."

In his 2015 memoir, *And Then I Danced: Traveling the Road to LGBT Equality,* Segal recalls a subsequent visit to Los Angeles.

Segal said that Morris took him to "a campaign cocktail party for a homophobic candidate for city council [who was running against Joel Wachs]. [Kight] telling me en route that the woman had no idea that she was about to enter a party of gay men ... the next issue of the *Advocate* headlined the event as, 'Candidate Flees Gay Party.'"

Segal describes another time when Kight took him to a fundraiser in the Hollywood Hills at the home of the GCSC Chairman of the Board, Terry O'Brien. On the way to the party, Kight told Segal that Terry had gotten his parents' permission to hold the fundraiser at their home.

"I walked around the tastefully decorated home, several items caught my eye. The first was sitting on the fireplace mantel. Slowly approaching the statuette and looking at it closely to see if it was indeed what it seemed, I picked it up. Within an instant Terry appeared out of nowhere to take hold of the statuette and said, 'My father doesn't let anyone touch the Oscar, it belonged to a very close friend of his.' As I glanced over to the corner of the room I could see Morris smiling. I walked over to him and asked who Terry's father was. Morris looked coyly at me. 'Pat, of course.' He was talking about the actor Pat O'Brien."

The following week, Segal recalls, the zaps were to begin and he had audience passes to studio tapings of most every ABC TV show, their prime target.

First on the list was *Merv Griffin,* a syndicated talk show taped in Hollywood. The producer of the *Griffin* show, Dick Carson (Johnny's brother), got wind of the plan and told them, according to Segal, that if they agreed not to disrupt the show,

Griffin would have a gay spokesperson on the show. Within a week, Troy Perry appeared on the show to talk about gay rights.

Next, according to Segal, "We called Av Westin, the vice president of Network Standards and Practices, and requested a meeting. That was the first meeting between a national network and the LGBT community. While Westin agreed to change entertainment policy, he was honest in explaining that the news divisions of the networks operated separately and he could not assist with our negotiations with them."

Segal says that NBC and CBS quickly agreed to change programming in their entertainment divisions. It seemed the campaign was a near-success. Next, they had to deal with the news division.

In 1975, Kight and 25 gay men and women snuck into KCOP television station and took over the studio to oppose demeaning remarks made by Mort Sahl on his program *Both Sides Now* with co-host George Putnam.

Pat Rocco: "Mort Sahl, the comedian, had made some terribly homophobic remarks on his talk show and we just got incensed. Morris and I got people together. I happened to know the layout of this particular station and knew a way that we can get in." Some protesters posed as audience members and others snuck in through a working gate. "We went to the offices and said, 'We're here because we want to protest the Mort Sahl situation.'"

From the *Los Angeles Times*: "The protesters demanded that Sahl be fired, that they be given another taping session with a 'fair moderator' and that KCOP apologize to the gay community. A spokesman for KCOP said station executives were discussing the matter with the protesters."

Rocco: "[The producers] said, 'Well, we're not going to be bullied by this.' We didn't leave. We stayed on the grounds, slept there overnight. We got the word out through the fence to tell the community that we're here. Other television stations showed up and photographed us through the fence, and as people were throwing food to us we said, 'we're not leaving, and they're not going to put us out.' We made the biggest splash. I'll never forget sleeping overnight on pillows [that were dropped over the fence] in a television station. [Finally] Mort Sahl apologized on the air. It was a marvelous thing. That was a wonderful experience."

1975. Appearing on *Both Sides Now* with Mort Sahl and George Putnam, Kight is second from right. Photo: Pat Rocco. Pat Rocco Papers, Coll2007-006, ONE National Gay & Lesbian Archives, USC Libraries, University of Southern California.

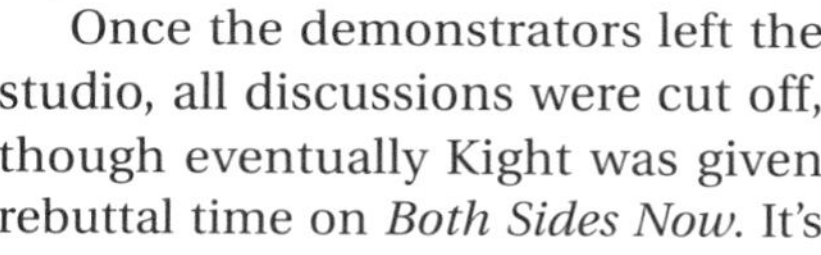

Once the demonstrators left the studio, all discussions were cut off, though eventually Kight was given rebuttal time on *Both Sides Now*. It's estimated, by an industry source, that in the mid-1970s disruptions at tapings around the country caused nearly $750,000 in delayed productions.

Obviously, breaking the media dysfunction would not happen with one demonstration or one argument. It would take decades of consciousness-raising and re-educating the media, print, radio, television, and feature films. It would be years of phone calls, letter-writing and petitions from activists on both coasts citing offensive behaviors and crude remarks. Kight became adept at the tightrope walk of diplomacy with a big stick, namely his reputation for being able to call an effective picket and boycott *overnight*.

Always polite, concentrated, and to the point about the umbrage, Kight never shied away from offering possible solutions to the plot or suggest alternative portrayals (not wanting to erase gays altogether from the cultural fabric). Often, the studio or producer would respond to Kight either with a phone call or letter to thank him for bringing this to their attention. No matter the response, the show always made concessions to story lines or, sometimes, they eliminated a fictional character.

In a *Los Angeles Times* article featuring the headline "Gays Lobby for New Media Image," Kight was asked if there have been any acceptable portraits of homosexuals on TV. He replied: 'No, I can't think of one. Though we thank them for the ones that are least bad.'"

In a note "to the file" dated September 1976, Kight documented a phone call with an ABC television executive: "Called with reaction to the 'Family' show on gayness, expressed our appreciation for parts of it, in depth discussion [and] my resistance to the homophobia in it."

POLITICS

WHEN LOS ANGELES ELECTED AMERICA'S FIRST BLACK MAYOR, TOM Bradley (who unseated notoriously conservative Sam Yorty), Kight promptly reached out. Bradley was open to better relations with the gay community and agreed to meet with Kight publicly. At the meeting when Kight extended his hand to Bradley, the mayor responded, reaching back across a table to shake Kight's hand. This was the first kind gesture made toward the gay community from a high-ranking public official, a huge advancement. Kight would frequently call upon the mayor to discuss issues affecting homosexuals. In turn Mayor Bradley appointed a liaison to the gay community and his office remained friendly with Kight; it was hard not to be.

Another advocate was State Assemblyman Willie Brown who worked very hard on the Consenting Adults bill that repealed "all laws against homosexual acts" between consenting adults. For five years the bill failed to pass the legislature, with Brown reintroducing it every year until it passed in May 1975. For the first time in California history, gay sex acts were decriminalized. Additionally, in 1977 Brown voted against AB 607, which specifically banned same-sex marriage.

Willie Brown continued to talk about issues that affected gay communities, specifically issues with police departments in the state. His reputation as a supporter of the civil rights of gays and lesbians was strong and consistent. Willie Brown was partially responsible for Kight joining the Democratic Party.

In 1976, Kight told an interviewer, "there is a growing populist movement inside the Democratic Party ... and I think [it] has the makings inside it somewhere for the germination of a new idea."

Kight immediately became active in state party politics. As a member of the California State Democratic Central Committee, over the years Kight served on several subcommittees for human rights and affirmative action. He remained active in the party selection of candidates and endorsements.

1979. Kight demonstrating at the Federal Building, Los Angeles for "Sullivan-Adams immigration case." Photo: Pat Rocco. Pat Rocco Papers, Coll2007-006, ONE National Gay & Lesbian Archives, USC Libraries, University of Southern California.

STONEWALL DEMOCRATIC CLUB

THE ONLY REASON FOR KIGHT JOINING THE DEMOCRATIC PARTY was to shape a Gay platform within a major political party.

Wallace Albertson, an old friend and straight ally who had just become the first woman president of the California Democratic Council, recalled, "Morris was very anxious to have a gay caucus, to have a political voice which he could carry to... the Democratic Party and also the national committee in Washington."

As president of the Council, Wallace was proud to help establish the first gay caucus to the Democratic party: "There weren't enough openly gay people in the organization to come forward. We were short a couple of votes, because there was a minimum, a quorum.

"So my husband Jack and I joined the gay caucus in order to have them qualify."

Once the Gay caucus was established, a Gay-centric political club was the next step.

Harry Hay wrote in a letter to Morris, "The Gays must first demonstrate as a closely-knit cohesive group, as a political club ... the HENRY COWELL Democratic Club, let's say," referring to one of America's leading composers who in the 1930s served four years in San Quentin on a 'morals' charge.

"You have to...try to undo the harm to the political integrity of Gay Consciousness."

Harry described the foundation for what became the Stonewall Democratic Club.

Kight reached out to Anne Marie Staas and husband Dr. Saul Niedorf whom he knew for years through organizations like Americans for Democratic Action, of which Kight had been a member since its founding in 1947. Passionate supporters of social justice issues, Staas' and Niedorf's Hancock Park home was frequently used as a place for quiet political introductions as well as large fundraisers. Anne Marie considered the current Democratic party leadership "homo-clueless" and gay rights the last frontier of civil rights. She was immediately on board with helping to have a gay platform for the Democratic party.

Along with Howard Fox, who not coincidentally had also become a powerful operative in state Democratic politics, Morris and a few others set off to found the Stonewall Democratic Club—the first gay club in a major political party. They openly stated their purpose was to elect Democrats in federal, state, and local elections who will best serve the interests of gays ('lesbians' was later added). Wallace Alberston said, "Stonewall Democratic Club played a very significant role in California politics producing I think a lot of well-schooled activists."

Kight and Fox served as founding President and VP respectively, and both men continued to serve on the Board for the rest of their active days.

As a member of the California State Democratic Central Committee, Kight served on just about every one of its subcommittees for human rights and affirmative action.

Kight: "I don't think gay people have so very much to gain now from being involved with continuing socialist movements," because socialists had not treated gays very well. "At this time in our history, we're going to move more people inside the Democratic Party than we are elsewhere and surely that's reformist and that used to be an ugly word. I don't think it is anymore … and hopefully the Party will respond to gay people and there's some evidence that it is."

Through Stonewall, Staas and Niedorf got to know Morris much better and they embraced him and his many quirks. Saul in particular "admired Morris very much." In the early Stonewall meetings, they found Kight's tone "imperious," to "befit his knowledge, experience, accomplishments." They both noticed that he seemed to reinvent his accent according to the situation.

Kight: "Legitimizing the word 'gay' and politicizing the word 'lesbian' was an important part of [liberation] because before that time we had been homophiles, or just homosexuals, or queers or a number of things. We legitimized those terms and raised the gay and lesbian consciousness. We established a notion that gay is, lesbian is, we established the notion that we are a community, common unity, that we are bound together in common destiny.…We started to establish a community that has grown and grown until now there are millions of out persons, not to go back into the closet. To serve one another, to serve society, and part of that is to move up in the world, get better jobs and perfecting their skills and hiring other people."

For those professional and conservative homosexuals who weren't comfortable being associated with a blatantly gay organization but who wanted to participate politically, the newly formed committee, MECLA, created a way for affluent gay men to donate to gay-friendly candidates without having to identify as 'gay.'

Founded in 1977, MECLA (Municipal Elections Committee of Los Angeles) initially came together to support a candidate running against a homophobic incumbent. Steve Lachs, who has a fundraising background, described the group as "gay yuppies" who wanted to do good, and "the nicest people you could meet but they were talking bake sales. Next morning, I called Bill, the organizer, and said 'forget it, it's not worth it,' opting instead for an intimate fundraiser in the Hollywood Hills for wealthy gays."

At the private dinner Lachs gave an impassioned speech and eventually raised $20,000. Lacks remembered that it was "unheard of in our community. Next day we opened a bank account, we couldn't have the word 'gay' in it so we came up with MECLA." Later meetings were held at the Carriage Trade restaurant where people were told to go in the back door. "There were no windows. People couldn't deal with being seen."

Of course, Sheldon Andelson was active in MECLA (though not a founder), and that was as good a reason as any for Kight to play nice with the organization.

"This was not Morris Kight's thing. He understood it. He appreciated what was happening, but he wasn't into fundraising in the Hollywood Hills.... There was some distance there. Part class distinction. There would have been discomfort on both sides." Truth is, it wasn't Kight's crowd. He wouldn't have fit in. He'd have stood out like an old veteran uncle at a high school dance. Nonetheless he stayed supportive. Kight to Manford: "One of the most rapidly growing groups in California—Gay Republicans. I swear to god if you went to one of their meetings you'd fantasize that you're in a GAA meeting in 1970. It's exciting. Any activism should be encouraged."

As the mid-1970s ushered in a new era for the gay rights movement and metaphorical closet doors were flung open and off the hinges, a new wave of opposition to homosexual freedoms manifested, and no one was more galvanizing than orange juice pitchwoman and former beauty queen Anita Bryant.

Bryant created the "Save our Children" campaign in Florida in order to overturn legislation that banned discrimination in housing, employment, and public access based on sexual orientation. Bryant claimed the ordinance discriminated against her and her children's right to a "biblical morality."

Ivy Bottini recalls: "It was 1976 and I read an article, it wasn't even an article, it was a couple of little paragraphs in the *L.A. Times* talking about Anita Bryant, that she was trying to do some initiative against gay men in Florida. I remember reading that and it sent a chill through my body. I thought, we'll be next. Whatever happens there, we'll be next."

Bottini first met Kight while visiting Los Angeles from New York in the early 1970s, shortly after the Center opened. Ivy borrowed her friend's car to go see the "big old house on Wilshire."

Ivy remembers that Morris was sitting on the porch and they introduced themselves, and Morris invited Ivy to join a rap group that was just beginning. Bottini: "So I went inside and joined the group. It was small, maybe five or six of us. And then I went about my business, flew back to the East Coast and I didn't see Morris again until maybe 1975.

"There was a fundraising benefit at one of the theaters downtown. I think it was [a production of] *La Cage Aux Folles*. I somehow ended up in the front row on the side. I heard people talk, I turned around and here's Morris coming down on my side of the aisle, where I was sitting. He was in a tux, a black bow tie, and his hair was quite white. He looked so distinguished. And I thought, I know him. I didn't know anybody as I seriously moved to California in '75."

Kight: "I felt Ivy was somebody I ought to get to know. We got acquainted and found every reason in the world to cooperate [with each other]. We worked together on Proposition 6, the Briggs Initiative, and tried to collaborate as much as we could."

Bottini knew that she needed to get politically involved with gay men, "because," she said, "that's where the organizing would start.

"It was funny because in all my arrogance coming from New York as a lesbian feminist and having headed up the march for 50,000 women down Fifth Avenue, I thought, I gotta get over there and help them because those guys are gonna fuck it up."

At a meeting held at Morris' house on McCadden Place they formed an ad hoc committee called the Coalition for Human Rights whose purpose was to organize a nationwide gay and lesbian community and effectively *prepare.* "Something's coming at us," Bottini recalls. "We don't know what it is, but we need to be able to contact our community...we literally organized the state."

And then it hit: the Briggs Initiative.

In 1978, conservative Orange County legislator John Briggs sponsored Proposition 6, which would ban gays and lesbians from working in California public schools, when it qualified for the November state ballot.

The Coalition for Human Rights was ready and the "No on 6" campaign became the most open and aggressive resistance up to that time. "John Briggs," Bottini recalls, "*just* had *no* idea what he was walking into!"

Kight quickly solicited the support of East Coast activists. Florida's Dade County had received $20,000 in donations from California to oppose the "Save Our Children" anti-gay initiative. In return the "No on 6" campaign received an unprecedented amount of out-of-state donations.

As the coalition grew, Bottini recalls, "Morris went off on his own." Troy Perry remembers that Kight "was used to sometimes being the Lone Ranger." Kight followed his own strategies and preferred to handle his own funds. Not everyone was comfortable with that. Tony Sullivan recalled: "When I was the Treasurer of the 'No on Briggs' Initiative Committee, Susan McGreivy called me 'the conscience of the movement.' One day, she walked in, and I'm with Morris and I'm saying, 'Morris, you *cannot* have a check; you *cannot* have money.'"

In a recorded phone call with Morty Manford in 1978, Kight expressed his concerns about the general direction of gay liberation, advocating "for basic education of the non-gay public" rather than trying to legislate. "Having people meet 'out-gays,' 'up-front-gays' and meeting them with gay awareness, we'd be light years ahead...We're being licked here and there by 'being reactive.' We move, they move with larger forces than we do, then we move back again. It makes us eternally reactive. I wish we'd done it differently—[wish] we had never even tried all this legislation. It hasn't changed the quality of life for gays one damn bit. But education has changed the quality of life enormously."

The "No on 6" campaign became very one-on-one, it was about 'being out' and 'being proud,' it involved a lot of handshaking, door-to-door speaking directly to

people about the harm the initiative would cause. There were efforts to encourage people to 'come out' to their families, co-workers, friends—to create an opportunity for straight society to personally know gay people.

Frank Wels walked from the Mexican border to the Oregon border to personally speak to people about the bill, he'd shake hands and let them meet an openly gay man in a non-threatening way. Morris drove alongside and acted as Wel's guide and guard as he walked 1,200 miles in 83 days, stopped in two hundred communities and met about five thousand persons, to a mostly positive response. Kight: "My vision and my dream told me that if we worked hard, California would vote against this." Because the bill concerned schoolteachers, the Teacher's Union was opposed. Still in late September, polls showed the bill passing

Zev Yaroslavsky debated John Briggs on the Sam Yorty TV show. "They could've had Harvey Milk, but they wanted a straight politician." Yaroslavsky recalls that in late summer and early fall of '78, Proposition 6 was still winning.

Christopher Isherwood diary entry, October 27, 1978: "Feeling depressed. Morris Kight just admitted to me that it looks like we'll lose on Proposition 6. I certainly realized this to begin with, but had then begun to hope—and indeed things have been looking much better. Of course, it's also true, and not just a phrase, that we have won a victory of sorts just by getting ourselves into so much prominence."

A turning point was when it was revealed that the poorly written Briggs Initiative would include heterosexuals for possible termination, just for knowing or associating with a homosexual.

1977. "No on 6" gathering at McCadden Place.
Photo: Pat Rocco. Pat Rocco Papers, Coll2007-006, ONE National Gay & Lesbian Archives, USC Libraries, University of Southern California.

After much debating, petitioning, and letter-writing pleas, when the inclusion of heterosexuals in the bill became known, Democratic Governor Jerry Brown and President Jimmy Carter came out against Proposition 6, soon followed by Republican former Governor and soon-to-be presidential candidate Ronald Reagan. The threat to heterosexuals made it easy for them to stand up for civil liberties.

Perry: "It was very interesting, we got all three of those people to [oppose the measure]."

Bottini recalls, "When we got Reagan, we knew we had it."

By November, public opinion in general support of Proposition 6 swung fairly quickly to what became overwhelming opposition.

Bottini: "And, you know, we beat them. We beat them really good."

In a note to his files titled "Praising Morris and righting the record," Jim Kepner wrote:

"...five months after Stonewall, until 1977, Morris Kight was an inventive leader of the newly radical gay liberation movement in Los Angeles, an embarrassment to gay conservatives who disliked his funky style and whom he denounced with rare invective, but he knew how to get headlines our movement had rarely had before, and to keep his own name in those headlines. Since Anita Bryant shifted our movement's center of power, he has increasingly railed at the new people who came along and took charge of what he'd considered his private front puddle."

Kight was not in the headlines as much as he was in the body of the text. By this time in history, the gay liberation movement was self-propelled and required some steering.

Kight talked about his personal circumstance and overall assessment of the gay movement with Morty Manford in 1978: "[I am] Physically excellent. Working blastly [sic] hours. Got rid of the cancer totally, the last six tests not a trace of it. Other than being fifty-eight and a half and having worked like furious for years and years, which takes its toll by the way, I'm all right. Almost everything that I take on turns into a major victory. The Stonewall Democratic Club is the most important political power base in the nation—just unbelievable.

"The annual Gay Pride Parade, CSW, seems healthy enough with plenty of money.

"We haven't had any significant change in movement [leadership] except driving people into greater organizations which has its value."

Six days after defeating the amendment, with six days of unprecedented jubilation, the national gay community suffered a punch to its collective gut when Harvey Milk was assassinated on November 27, 1978.

An openly gay San Francisco politician, Milk had been instrumental in defeating Proposition 6. He and Kight had brainstormed during the Briggs challenge, spoke on the phone and visited each other's homes. They were both mavericks, both socialists, both ambitious, they were each good at organizing large groups and preferred to act solo. The biggest difference between them: Milk was a charismatic political leader with potential for a national platform. A potential that had been cut short.

A sampling of the headlines: "Officials Across Nation Deplore S.F. Slayings" and "President, Political Leaders Throughout Nation Mourn Slain San Francisco Officials," gives pause to demonstrate the great advancements in the homosexual presence in society and the great respect for the beloved Harvey Milk.

Los Angeles had a candlelight vigil. Kight, like the rest of his community, grieved him as family.

Even John Briggs was quoted: "I liked Harvey Milk. I disagreed completely with his lifestyle, but you can't debate a man as often as I did Milk (seven times) without finding redeeming features."

DAVID GOODSTEIN

AFTER YEARS OF LOBBYING, GAY RIGHTS HAD BECOME A LEGITIMATE civil rights issue and was prominent in the media. And so had Morris Kight. His public profile grew exponentially with the causes he espoused. He was often quoted in the press and his name became synonymous with gay pride. His already large ego became just as well-known. Prompted by resistance from within the gay community, his adversaries mostly came from personal jealousies and resentments and worked against the bigger picture of gay rights in America.

In 1975, the founding owner of the *Advocate*, Dick Michaels, sold the magazine to David Goodstein, a Wall Street investment banker. Michaels had been a realist about Kight—he understood the man's ego and also appreciated his efforts toward forwarding their mutual cause. Michaels had no problem giving Kight ink.

Steve Lachs remembered: "I used to run down to Crescent Heights on Sunset Boulevard and buy a copy of a cheap little magazine called the *Advocate* before it became a national magazine. Morris was at the pinnacle of that and more and more as he became a spokesperson of the gay and lesbian community. If you wanted to write an article about gay in L.A., you'd have to quote Morris, Don [Kilhefner], or Sheldon [Andelson].

1997. Kight talking to State Senator Tom Hayden.
Photo by Anne Marie Staas.

Goodstein, on the other hand, came to activism much later in life and had an automatic competitive dislike of Kight. Goodstein wanted to advance gay rights and at the same time, he wanted to cultivate a much more subdued gay identity, *dignified*. He envisioned a prefab gay community.

In a 1976 interview with the *Los Angeles Times,* Goodstein explained that he purchased the *Advocate* for the specific purpose to influence social change.

Goodstein had zero publishing experience and even less journalistic backbone. Mark Thompson, a cub journalist for the *Advocate,* explained that "David thought it would be fun to run a newspaper."

His first edict was to ban any mention of Morris Kight.

Thompson: "[Goodstein] put a moratorium on all gay activists, the meddlesome types. He said they were trying to run everything according to their dictums. Top of the list was Morris Kight and it was a short list." Tony Sullivan added: "Goodstein said, 'The only time this publication will ever mention Morris Kight again is when we write his obituary.' It was really vicious and uncalled for."

Richard Adams: "Well, Morris outlived him by many years."

Thompson, who did not personally know Kight at the time, explained it like this: "David Goodstein wanted to go national, he thought the paper was provincial. He wanted to bring the middle class into the movement; he believed without the middle class the movement wouldn't succeed. He said that hardscrabble street activists, the type who scream and are angry, will alienate the middle class. David's mission was to attract large numbers of people from all walks of life. He thought people like Morris would alienate new people."

In addition to doing a disservice to the community that he claimed to help, Goodstein broke all journalistic standards. Thompson said, "The News Editor at the time, Scott Anderson, fought it and took umbrage. It was journalistically unfair. It was a contentious go-around with Scott referring to David as 'Citizen Hearst'" [a wry reference to Orson Welles' movie *Citizen Kane* which is based on the real-life newspaper giant William Randolph Hearst].

Goodstein honestly did not understand or appreciate what Kight did to help the gay community. Bail money and doctor's care were never issues for a man of Goodstein's means. He didn't understand the value of coalition-building and legislation-shaping. In short, he took for granted "the community" that he so easily came to know, as if a gay community was always accessible.

Goodstein wasn't completely alone in his lack of appreciation for history. Prominent openly gay *Village Voice* journalist Arthur Bell proclaimed that "most of the gay political activists 'make me want to puke.'" Politically ignited post-Stonewall, Bell was a harbinger of a new generation of young homos who would never be closeted. Bell criticized the gay community: "How many times can you write about a parade?" He refused to write what he called "gay propaganda." Not naming names, Bell declared, "Gay activists are some of the most boring people around."

From the beginning, Kight knew that it was personal for Goodstein. In a 1974 letter to Morty Manford, he tells about an earlier encounter with Goodstein: "Oddly enough, in a meeting after a major antiwar rally in San Francisco, years ago, where I was a speaker and where a lot of love was manifest, he was present and I had heard of his resentment and felt it might be time to talk. And so I gathered together a handful of very old, close, loving supportive and non-judgmental friends and asked him to come with me, to their house. A huge room facing the bay, filled with greenery and tapestries, contemporary art. Love, love, love and in that atmosphere we talked quietly and lowly, hoping that a bit of 'illumnure' [sic] would happen.

And for a moment it almost did. And then at the very end, David stood to his feet and said, 'What I want more than anything in the world is to be a Morris Kight.'

"From that," Kight continued, "I took so much pain that only you could guess what it meant."

Goodstein didn't stop at the print ban. Goodstein engaged a tabloid mentality; he wanted to destroy Kight's credibility. He hired his top freelance investigative reporter, Randy Shilts, to investigate Kight. Shilts and other staff at the *Advocate* were very uncomfortable with Goodstein's mission.

In late April 1976, Shilts billed the *Advocate* for "Research on Morris Kight."

Kight recalled, "Goodstein hated me because he never could understand who I was and what I was doing. He couldn't understand that I had little money. Oh, I had some money and discretion as an operator. But not without free will. Or in seeking those saturates of power, [I] emerged such a powerful figure. And so it really bothered him horribly. Again, this is the scoop. David Goodstein hired Randy Shilts in 1976. Randy Shilts was hardly heard of at that time, was virtually unknown. He hired him and gave him a great deal of money to investigate Jean O'Leary and me. I never knew why he would make it any of his business. I never knew why he would be concerned about [us]. I would think he would be concerned about overpopulation, deterioration of the environment, the war in Vietnam. I thought he would be concerned about the disparity in politics and population and income and so on.

"Randy published, for David Goodstein's eyes only—ONLY, marked that way—a nine-page, single-space typewritten document in which he had investigated me, and he had gone far, far afield. People would come, they would call [me] and say, 'Randy Shilts is investigating you. Good grief! Why would he do that? You're the most public person of them all. How in the hell do we deal with that?' I said, 'Tell them the truth.' And so, he got paid, and got paid well, but I always had a fantasy that that was what made Randy Shilts what he became. He became a prominent author and spokesperson."

Kight continues: "Members of the *Advocate* staff were so horrified at David Goodstein's subversion that they pirated a copy of the report out of the *Advocate* and gave it to me. I read it and I do not believe that of all the attacks upon me, in my lifetime—oh, there have been so very many—I do not believe that any of them ever hurt me so badly as that one. I was pained. I am a positive, outgoing person. Dale Carnegie's *How to Influence People* is one of my bibles. And yet, that one pained me horribly. And I simply screamed, literally screamed, at the perfidy of that.

"Two months later, *Blueboy*, a major gay magazine in Florida, asked Randy Shilts his opinion of me and he said, 'Oh, he's a marvelous person.'"

After laughing, Kight continued: "I thought it was the lack of honesty and sophistication, and sense of brotherhood/sisterhood on the part of Randy Shilts. I thought he should have said to David Goodstein, 'Oh, please! Come on! Use your money for something else! Cure poverty, or cure hunger, or do something about the hunger in Somalia. Morris is an okay person, he's the most public person in the world. No one in the world is more public than he, his records and everything are available to everybody. And who cares about what Jean O'Leary does or doesn't do.'

"It indicated a great weakness on the part of David Goodstein that he would fantasize that getting some evidence about me would destroy me."

In 1978 Goodstein (along with Dr. Ron Eichberg) pioneered a series of personal growth seminars called The Advocate Experience (later known simply as The Experience). Fashioned after Werner Erhard's popular movement of the time called est, which was an outgrowth of the 1960s Human Potential Movement, both programs offered seminars to bring personal transformation through self-acceptance. Goodstein tailored the est prescripts to specifically address what he perceived as the needs and shortcomings of gay men who had experienced shame in the straight world.

In *Out for Good* (Simon & Schuster, 1999), Dudley and Nagourney explained: "Goodstein's Advocate Experience may have had some influence on the gay movement, many gay leaders went through the rigorous weekend experience, yet it seemed to do little to soften the bitterness within the movement."

When invited, of course Morris went to a meeting with David. "Goodstein called me in 1979, 1980 I guess, and he said, 'Morris, I really desperately need to meet with you.' I said, 'Well, that's fine. That's neat. Your place or mine? Doesn't matter.' So I met at his office over on Wilshire Boulevard. I went over and found him and a group of stereotypical young men, all between 21 and 23, all Western European, all dressed exactly alike, all cloned. Khaki pants and desert boots, and modish shirts. All busily typing away, all busily fabricating busy-ness, with him in a vast office, reigning supreme over them. It was somewhat like a George Orwell-type production. And it was. They were all hushed: 'David is coming in his car now. He regrets that he's a little late.' I said, 'Fine. Never mind.'

"'David is on his way now. He'll be here in a minute now. He'll see you. He apologizes.'

"Please! So I was there. I would treat the subject of conversation as totally privileged. Then and now, I've never quoted from the conversation, ever. I just would risk—because, mind you, it was a counseling session. I've always respected confidentiality. I would risk just one quotation from it. At the very end, he said, 'Morris, I would like for you to be my guest to take the Advocate Experience.' I said [laughs] 'Thank you, David, no. I don't care if you run a cult.' And with that, we said goodbye."

A few years later, Rob Eichberg invited him to be a guest of the Experience. "Since I should delve in all experiences," Kight said, "I don't want to be arrogant or hostile to any idea, however good it may be. I hardly needed the three-day Intensive." He laughed and continued.

"Some people did. I went to see what it was like. Yes, it's a stunningly important experience. Really worth your time and trouble. And yes, you're made a better person by it. I have nothing but praise for the Experience."

Without a pause, Kight adds, "By the way, they created the Morris Kight Humanitarian Award. Did you know that?"

Kight told Cain that he "didn't care for [The Experience] very much, because I felt that David Goodstein was trying to make it into a cult. And the last thing in the world I ever wanted to do was be a member of a cult."

Community scuttlebutt posed the rhetorical question if Kight would and should forgive David Goodstein for barring his name from the *Advocate* and for hiring Randy Shilts to investigate his personal life?

In a recorded phone conversation with Morty Manford in 1978, Morris summarized another private meeting with Goodstein:

"David has apologized to me for something he said about me. I said, 'David, thank you very much. Enough. Let's not discuss it anymore. Let's get on with something else.' But the getting on with something else doesn't seem to be working. We just don't have anything in common except that we are both on Planet Earth."

Goodstein did take the *Advocate* national. He also diluted the journalistic quality. Kight would never go on record or publicly state what he told Manford and others in private: "the *Advocate* is a massive embarrassment to us all."

After years, Scott Anderson's relentless efforts to restore some journalistic integrity to the magazine had an impact. He was able to include Kight in an affirmative profile on Movement Elders.

Then, in 1984, the *Advocate* moved its offices from the Bay Area to Los Angeles.

Mark Thompson, by this time an editor of the publication, describes a big catered open house to welcome the magazine to its new home base. "Vito Russo flew in from New York, the mayor's office was represented, several hundred people dressed to the nines. I was standing in the doorway to my office with Vito and Malcolm [Reverend Boyd, Thompson's longtime partner] when we heard a big commotion at the front door. We looked at each other and asked each other who is this character galloping down the hallway like he was a prince creating a big fuss. 'Hello, hello,' he said holding out his hands, like some grand duke and dressed like one.

"Vito and Malcolm at the same time said, 'Oh my God, I think that's Morris Kight.' He made it to my office and introduced himself. 'Yes, yes, you're the wonderful news editor that everyone is talking about.'

"Without another word, he strode into my office, like it was his own, and with a flurry went around the desk and 'kah-plunk,' he sat in the chair and put his feet up on the desk, threw his arms back like he owned the place."

Kight was, as Thompson remembered, "So pompous. Lovable. Spoke very courtly. A refined gentleman. Very grandiose.

"And then he got up and said, 'Well, it's very nice to meet you, I must be going.'"

Not long after that, Thompson and Boyd started to get invites to McCadden Place. They admired Kight and were "also was a little scared of him," Boyd remembered. "We didn't know exactly what he did [for a living], he was a mystery man. We went over [to McCadden Place], looked at the art and thought it was wonderful, a really grand place."

Reverend Boyd recalled Kight's soirées: "It was kind of a salon, you'd meet very interesting people there. He was the great gay host."

Thompson continued, "He was one of the most complicated creatures I have ever met. Admired him but also wondered sometimes. There was a lot of smoke and mirrors and I didn't always understand him. When he could be sincere with me, I thought this was, at heart, a good man. He was also a wily cat. Cat in many senses of the world."

Mark Thompson described Morris Kight as "a fantabulist."

The way he presented himself was a bit of sleight of hand, as he was much sharper and shrewder than most would have assumed. He forced a response from people, and pity the person who landed on the wrong side. He was never belligerent or argued his point. He persuaded people, or blindsided them, with an assumption that they were on a higher ground, that they were principled enough to see the wisdom in his argument. As an outspoken champion for nonviolent social change, he was exemplary.

APPOINTMENTS

KIGHT NEVER RAN FOR PUBLIC OFFICE. IT WAS THE SORT OF THING his ego would have craved, but the scrutiny into his past and the intrusion of his former wife and family would have made it not worth the trouble. He did however enjoy two political appointments: one, to the newly created California Governor's Task Force on Civil Rights, came from then-Governor Edmund Brown Jr. Short-lived ('81–83) but impactful, the Task Force was given the assignment of addressing an increase in threats and violence against racial, cultural, and religious minority individuals and groups. The Ku Klux Klan had an unexplained revival and similar groups were of great concern to civil rights advocates.

The Task Force interfaced with the California Fair Employment and Housing Commission and the California Commission on Crime Control and Violence Prevention, and established liaisons with numerous government and private entities that were concerned with civil rights, including various county Human Relations Commissions.

In an undated "Memorandum for Archives" Kight wrote about the Task Force:

"Held a three-day symposium at Chaffey College, Alta Loma, California. Six members of the Task Force were present, among them me. We got much hard work done."

At the workshops at Chaffey College, Kight explained, "People got going on some synergistic kinds of ways and everyone's space was respected. In the ones I did, I used my one-on-one technique [of] going into each person's agenda. It worked, and we came out with 31 resolutions each with suitable debate. We did go on record to support inclusion of Gay and Lesbian concerns in the report. By staying on top of that it can happen."

Though Kight did not enjoy a high profile on the Task Force, his very presence at the table kept gay rights included on every list as targets of hatred and at-risk.

"But the real question is," Kight continued, "what of the report? What can it do for the improvement of the quality of life in California? I have proposed that we really take a hard look at the content of the report and hope that a paperback book can come from it."

He compared the proposed book to be as significant as the Kerner Commission (1967) and McCone Commission (1965). "And certainly hopefully more honest than the Kennedy Assassination Commission report."

In 1982 the Task Force submitted its two-volume *Report on Racial, Ethnic, and Religious Violence* to Governor Brown.

Kight ended his memo to the archives: "I am troubled about the emergence of three classes of people in society: super-rich, the haves and the have-nots. Right now I think that society has written the have-nots off, and those who are escaping into walled communities can hire people to come down into the ghetto to do their dirty work."

▲

The other appointment was more fruitful and long-lasting: In 1979, long-term and respected Los Angeles County Supervisor Ed Edelman selected Kight to serve on the Los Angeles County Human Relations Commission, a position he held for two decades.

Founded in 1943 in response to the infamous Zoot Suit riots, and still going strong, the Commission consistently works to improve intergroup relations in the increasingly complex multicultural environment of Los Angeles County. It is the oldest of its kind in the United States.

During his tenure, Kight implemented the promise of protection based on sexual orientation, brought gay concerns directly to straight people, and developed many important heterosexual allies. He also involved gay people in other civil rights issues not exclusive to homosexuals thereby infusing all corners of society with open homosexuals.

The commission, under his influence and guidance (he was elected the first gay President in 1988), accomplished numerous 'firsts.'

Kight kept a full and active agenda while serving on the Commission. In 1984 the Commission held a public hearing on Prejudice and Discrimination Based on Sexual Orientation, the first of its kind in the nation; added gay students to a hearing on "Minority Youth Unemployment"; formed the Media Image Coalition with Gay and Lesbian participation; added "gay bashing" to its annual report on hate crimes; conducted the first in the nation school hate-crime survey, which included gay and lesbians and which resulted in the founding of Project 10 by Dr. Virginia Uribe, a lifesaving program for generations of Gay and Lesbian youth; published a brochure, "What Can I Do About Bigotry Toward Gays and Lesbians"; held a Corporate Advisory Committee panel discussion regarding discrimination against gays and lesbians in the private sector, and a hearing titled "Effects on Prejudice on the Lives of Gay and Lesbian Youth"; endorsed a boycott of the State of Colorado for their passage of anti-gay Amendment 2; collaborated with Los Angeles Unified School District to develop policies and procedures for data collection and reporting hate crimes and bias-motivated incidents (including race, gender, disability, ethnicity, religion, and sexual orientation); corresponded with Peter Hoskstra, Chair on the House Committee on Oversight and Investigation in Washington, D.C., and requested that a proposed hearing on homosexuality include expert witnesses on discrimination based on sexual orientation with a copy of the Commission's report on Gay and Lesbian Youth.

And so it went for the 22 years that Kight served on the Commission, during which time he became known as "the longest-seated openly gay appointee in the history of the United States."

Ann Bradley remembers that Kight "changed the hearts and minds of the Commission…. He used his power in a very generous way, not just to mentor younger people and create opportunities, he did sweet things. I had a couple letters in the *L.A. Times* and I always got a call from him, so sweet. He'd say, 'Oh darling, it's the second most important thing, people read the front page and then letters to the editor'… Many people are always waiting for the right time. There is no right time for people who do not want you to have full civil liberties and civil rights. I think Morris Kight got that at a very concrete level. He was not waiting for the right time."

Through his work with the Commission, Kight grew close to City Councilman Zev Yaroslavsky (later Supervisor of the Los Angeles County Board of Supervisors).

Yaroslavsky recalled, "Morris was a legend in his own time. An icon in the community … You knew when he was expressing his views that he wasn't just another guy. He was a proud Gay man. Even people who weren't inclined toward Gay people, who didn't agree with him, respected Morris. He was a symbol … The personification of the cause."

Whenever Yaroslavsky ran for re-election on the City Council he always counted on Kight's endorsement. Instead, in 1989, Yaroslavsky recalls, "he endorsed my opponent. I called Morris and asked him about it and he said, 'well, she called me and asked. I said yes.' 'Well,' Zev reasoned with his old ally, 'she's running against me. Does anything we've done together matter?' 'I hope you win,' he said and then added, 'it's good to get change.' He had an independent mind and it didn't tarnish our relationship. He was embarrassed, he did it impetuously."

In 1999, then-County Supervisor Yaroslavsky (who won the election when Ed Edelman did not seek re-election) reappointed Kight to the County Human Relations Commission, citing, "He has served our community well for many, many years as an appointee." Yaroslavsky reappointed Kight for every subsequent term that Kight was willing to serve.

In the last days of April and the first few days in May of 1992, the city of Los Angeles was besieged by race riots. In response to the acquittal of four white police officers in the brutal beating of a black motorist, the city erupted in anger, hate, and a rage so vile it was humbling.

Miki Jackson recalls the afternoon that the verdicts were read when initial reports of disturbances on the streets came in, including the uneasy absence of a police presence.

"I called Morris and we went back and forth a couple of times. There were no cell phones, so we had to phone-tree and listen to the news. Morris called his contacts in the African American community, friends from the peace movement, specifically James Lawson, and head of the First AME Church, Reverend Cecil L. 'Chip' Murray. They all agreed that we should meet at First AME Church in South L.A. and call for the rioting to stop, call for peace."

As a Commissioner of the Human Relations Commission, it made sense that Kight would engage with other city leaders at First AME.

In her van, Jackson picked up Morris and their friend Julie Schollenberger and they drove to South Central L.A. to the First AME Church which, as it turned out, was "the axis of the riot." There was an "eerie feeling" in the streets.

Once in the church, a bunch of them decided to march down the street. Kight stayed at the church as part of the core group of speakers and planners.

Jackson describes what happened next: "Most businesses had already closed. Walking down the street, a lot of small pick-up trucks and other vehicles, came toward us. They were full of youngish men, not all but a lot were wearing white, they had clubs and bats and what have you. They stopped in front of the liquor store. They jumped out of the trucks, maybe 25 of them, they beat in the windows of the liquor store.

"The people who were leading our march, who were from that neighborhood and who were leaders in the church, told us all to turn back. We went back to the church. As this happened, the streets started to fill up. It just ballooned."

Karen Ocamb remembers pulling into the AME church parking lot as a couple of people pulled signs from a car trunk to nonviolently protest the verdict. They saw a crowd coming toward them.

Ocamb: "I pulled out my little *Frontiers* press pass, thinking it would 'protect' us so we could get into the church. A few neighbors saw what we were about to do and urgently told us to get the hell out of there. We all got back into our cars and left." As they left, they passed "a caravan of cars with angry young men."

Jackson: "We were at the church, inside, for a while. It was still very active. Networks were set up [to check on each other] and then it came time to go home, it was already dark.

"People from the church insisted that any non-African Americans were to be accompanied by African Americans until they got out of the neighborhood. We took side streets back to Hollywood and got Morris home, it was very late. The whole city was strange, little groups of people walking around, prowling storefronts. It was still bubbling up. Hollywood was mostly deserted. Very eerie, like a science fiction movie."

"Morris was on the phone at 5 a.m. for the next two or three days of the riots," Jackson remembers.

Because of his position on the Human Relations Commission, he had a vast and valuable list of contacts. Phone trees and organizing were set in place. They checked on people and helped people and Kight could monitor the police activity.

Jackson: "Morris was a nerve center. Because of his long deep relationships in the African American community, he was on the ground, it was grassroots all the way with close intimate contacts in the police, with the County Commissioners, City Council. He patched a lot of people together, he was communications central."

By the middle of the second day, the rioting in Hollywood grew more intense. Kight lived one half-block away from Hollywood Boulevard which was burning down. Storefront by storefront, the fires ruined what was once a neighborhood inside a city.

The next day more fires started. Kight often talked about the fires and the destruction that fires caused to gay liberation. These fires were a lot closer to home.

Jackson and her partner Cate Uccel went to Kight's house later in the day when "things were burning all around him," is how Jackson recalls.

"His house was a woodpile so we were all very concerned about the fires. Inside Morris' house was a couple of people, all there to help. There were cinders in the air from the fires, it was very smoky and police had cordoned off the boulevard.

"We went outside and hosed down the roof of the house.

"Next door to his house was a tall apartment building, maybe eight stories. Some of the people from the building had gone up to the boulevard and looted the shops wholesale. It was a mad rush of people grabbing stuff from the stores. His neighbors, who were not people of means, young working-class mostly, started to flood into the apartment building, from the storefronts, carrying new TVs, stereos, what have you.

"And then we hear crashing noises. TVs and other large electronics were being tossed out the windows. They were getting rid of the old equipment.

"People were scared, mad, and partying."

Best description of the circumstances is surreal. Where Morris Kight was situated was close to ground zero in Hollywood and required a survivor's skill.

Kight asked the same neighbors who were tossing their old TVs if they'd use their advantage of height to watch out for tinder on his roof or on his property. They were all happy to oblige the nice old man next door.

Everyone stayed the night at Kight's. They took shifts to keep a lookout. Jackson remembers Jaime Green was there, Al Atwood, David Frater. Morris "was adamant" that Roy remain at his apartment and stay inside.

The team started to stack up Kight's art collection by the door. They all agreed that they would load as much as they could into Jackson's van and other vehicles, and leave the rest by the door for a quick escape.

Not soon enough, Rodney King, the victim of the brutal police beating, was able to make a televised statement (viewed on many new televisions) for the public: "Can we all get along?"

The rioting died down, the National Guard left town, and people swept up the remains of their livelihoods. Eventually, a few things went back to the way they were before the riots, but nothing was ever really the same in Los Angeles.

As Commissioner, Kight was immediately engaged in finding the right guidance to recover and repair the city. Few have experience in post-riot recovery. The Commission invited Sherry Harris, a councilwoman from Seattle, Washington who had, as a child, witnessed the Newark riots, and subsequently became a community activist and the first black out-lesbian elected to public office in the United States and the first African American woman elected to office in Washington State.

Harris stayed at a nearby hotel in Hollywood and Kight was in charge of showing her around the city. He organized meetings with various groups who then listened to her suggestions for repairing their city.

Jackson: "People were asked to volunteer and come into the hardest-hit neighborhoods to clean up. Morris came with us and others. He couldn't do much physical work but he counseled people who'd been traumatized. He spoke with shop owners and others, he counseled people and he got a very warm response for being this old white guy."

The city remained traumatized for a very long time. City efforts coupled with nonprofits and churches joined together in the endeavor to clean up and help the city recover. Kight participated with community leaders and leaders in the African American community, he broadened his contacts and, as Jackson remembers it, "he maintained those contacts very scrupulously. A lot happened because of his community outreach. To his great frustration, the white gay and lesbian community had always been so divorced from other racial communities and other activists. He tried to get people together more, to include people from gay and lesbian communities. It was not very successful. Some successes, but not too much. Everyone was so divided, insular. It was a very difficult time and coming out of it was quite a process."

Kight didn't indulge in much worry or fortune-telling. He remained pragmatic. He understood that the city was in chaos, there were crises of all kinds of faith, and that if allowed to continue, it couldn't lead to a good place.

He continued to network with grassroots leaders such as Helen Hernandez, who had worked with Cesar Chavez and Dolores Huerta. They put a number of community outreach events and symposiums together and they re-examined hate-crime laws and worked to strengthen legislation.

Over time, subtly and slowly, the city exhaled and people became less afraid of each other.

Later in 1992, the Commission published a brochure, "What Can I Do About Bigotry Toward Gays and Lesbians," to address prevention of gay-bashing.

In 1993 the Commission held a Corporate Advisory Committee panel discussion regarding discrimination against gay and lesbians in the private sector. The same year, the Commission also held a hearing, "Effects on Prejudice on the Lives of Gay and Lesbian Youth" followed by a released report in April 1994. In every instance, Kight was involved in setting the criteria for and the selection of who would serve on panels.

The Commission collaborated with Los Angeles Unified School District in 1994 to develop policies and procedures for data collection and reporting hate crimes and bias-motivated incidents (including race, gender, disability, ethnicity, religion, and sexual orientation).

In 1995, the *Los Angeles Times* reported that hate crimes against gays and Latinos were up in Los Angeles County. That could be accounted for by the organization of compiling the information from various police departments and private watchdog groups as well as an increase of reporting the crimes.

COORS (DOW WITH A BIBLE)

KIGHT NEVER MINCED WORDS ABOUT THE INTENTIONS OF THE Gay Liberation Front of Los Angeles: "Businesses making money in the Gay community should share a reasonable amount of their profits with groups doing social services in that community."

In an October 1970 letter addressed to the owners of the Ballenger-Dawson Agency, Kight wrote, "Dear Brothers Tom and Ray:

"We are aware of the long and expensive campaign you launched to get agency contracts to service advertising in the publications that serve us.

"The Hamm's Brewing Company is to be roundly thanked for this showing of faith in you, and through you, all of us. We note that more and more Gay bars are carrying the product, the Society of Anubis has installed Hamm's in their handsome clubhouse. We have adopted it as the official beer for our legal and licensed bar concessions at our dances."

This was, as Kight noted in the letter, "the first time that we [GLF] have endorsed a product. Some will think this odd; we think it not since it fits our notion that some sums taken from our community, be ploughed back into it. Peace, Love, Joy, MLK."

No peace, love or joy were to be found, however, when it came to his disdain of the Coors Brewing Company, the Coors family, and the Adolph Coors Foundation of Golden, Colorado. Sometimes one could forget that he was a pacifist.

In 1974, AFL-CIO declared a strike against the ferociously anti-union Coors on behalf of brewery workers, a move that galvanized gay and lesbian union workers to assert their role in the labor movement. The AFL-CIO boycott ended in 1987 after Coors allowed a union organizing effort, which eventually failed.

Company bias was directed toward homosexuals as well as Latino labor (paid significantly less), and female workers were also maligned. Prospective employees were required to submit to a lie-detector test and answer a 178-item questionnaire which included the question: 'Are you a homosexual?' If the answer was 'yes,' the application was promptly refused.

Kight and Howard Wallace (an openly gay Teamster in San Francisco) joined together in 1977 to found the Gay and Lesbian Response to the "depredations of the Coors Family on Gay/Lesbian issues," and to organize gay distributors to boycott Coors in gay bars. Gay bartenders stopped serving the beverage; some reports had bartenders dumping bottles of Coors into the sewers. Soon, with the support of high-profile leaders such as Harvey Milk and endorsements from influential organizations such as Stonewall Democratic Club, there was a full-on, across-the-nation boycott, clearly demonstrating the gay community's consumer power and cohering an alignment between labor and the Gay community.

The first 20 years, the boycott was mostly self-run. It didn't require much effort except to keep the word out that Coors beer was bad for the gay community. From the beginning, Kight knew this boycott would not be the same as the successful one against Dow. This was a post-'Powell Memorandum' era and there were new, more sophisticated methods to right-wing organizing. Joe Coors, grandson of the brewery founder, had bankrolled the founding of the ultraconservative radical right think tank the Heritage Foundation, and would soon fund many other conservative organizations and help to join the staunchly conservative right with the Christian conservative movement.

Baum explained in *Citizen Coors: An American Dynasty*: "Until the Heritage Foundation came along, funded by Coors money, there was no address for the conservative movement, no place from which to launch moral crusades against homosexuality."

Throughout the '70s and '80s, Coors continued to fund the most ultraconservative movements in order to agitate public opinion, filing multiple lawsuits against the rights of homosexuals. These homophobic positions, which were freely shared with elected representatives, eventually influenced policy and laws. At least 75 members of Congress and/or the Senate voted to oppose much-needed social services and health programs for gays and lesbians based on information from the Heritage Foundation.

Then, in the early 1990s, Coors Brewing Company separated itself from the family, making overtures to minorities and specifically gay customers. Press releases argued that the company should not be held responsible for what individual stockholders chose to do with their own money. And while Coors made some changes regarding discrimination and sexual orientation policies, instituted a corporate ethics program and a code of conduct (no more lie-detector tests), and offered benefits to same-sex couples, the family continued to donate millions of dollars and occupy dozens of board seats promoting the ultraconservative Christian right agenda.

Kight and others immediately recognized the underhanded strategy: Appeal to gay customers while still funding initiatives to curtail gay rights. Stuart Timmons summed it up in a 1997 *Frontiers* article: "they still fund phobes."

In a letter sent to the City of West Hollywood, Kight wrote: "$1 coming from COORS to a Lesbian/Gay effort had $5 going out the back door to fund anti-gay causes," and told a reporter for the *San Francisco Bay Times,* "The Coors family and the Coors Foundation have every right in the world to contribute their money to whatever cause they want to. Lesbian and gay people have the equal right, if not the duty, to deny them access to consumer money in the first place."

Regarding the brewing company's domestic partner benefits, Kight quipped, "How many gays and lesbians do you think there are in Golden, Colorado? Why should the lesbian and gay nation pay tribute when it only affects eight couples?"

The deep-pocketed brewing company eventually hired Mary Cheney, daughter

The Strike Is Not Over. Carlos Callejo. Silkscreen, circa 1970. Los Angeles, CA. Courtesy of the Center for the Study of Political Graphics. ID 28055

of Vice President Dick Cheney and an open lesbian, as their liaison to the gay and lesbian community. With her pedigree she was able to tout the company's employment record, court gay dollars, and convince some younger gay leaders that the boycott could end.

Cheney didn't impress Kight or anyone else on the Boycott Committee. She was new to gay politicking and certainly not a gay activist.

Meanwhile the Coors company donated big money to gay causes, aggressively marketed to gay consumers with ads in the *Advocate*, at Outfest, and the Christopher Street West Gay Pride Parade, and launched an advertising campaign which featured openly gay Olympic swimmer Bruce Hayes and a series of print ads of restyled classic paintings featuring white gay male couples.

Even so, the Boycott Committee stuck to their guns.

Kight: "Lesbian/Gay peoples, in their political wisdom, and innate sense of self-protection, simply knew that the COORS family were bad news." Asked when the boycott would end, he said, "When the COORS Family halts all anti-gay political activities and halts its funding of homophobic causes."

But being courted by Coors money posed big-time influence on the gay community and battle scars began to form. The pro-Coors faction described it as a debate between the old homosexuals and new blood. West Hollywood Mayor Steve Martin said, "Old gays and lesbians are totally anti-Coors. The rhetoric you hear against the company is like something from another era. It's this recycled leftist, anti-corporate, conspiratorial view. The people who are opposing Coors are old leftists."

When Outfest, the highly successful gay-focused film festival, accepted Coors funding, Kight organized a large demonstration in front of the premiere event, using it as an opportunity to educate the community about how the Coors company was using them to fix their public image. The demonstration was successful and Outfest agreed to no longer accept funding from Coors.

Then, in 1997, after West Hollywood (America's first "Gay City") passed a resolution from the city's Gay and Lesbian Advisory Board to send Coors an acknowledgment of the company's efforts and a commendation for their progress, the Coors Boycott Committee asked them to reconsider the resolution and a public debate ensued: Should the gay community and its organizations continue to accept funding from Coors when the Coors family continued to fund anti-gay organizations? Or would rescinding the commendation send the wrong message to Coors and other companies that were making strides toward equal treatment of gay and lesbian employees? The matter was sent back to the Gay & Lesbian Advisory Board who voted 5–4 to rescind their original resolution outright. When asked to recommit to the Coors boycott, however, the City Council of West Hollywood refused to take a position and left in doubt whether or not they would follow the Advisory Board's vote to rescind the commendation.

On June 1, 1998, Kight and many other Coors Boycott Committee fellows attended a standing-room-only West Hollywood City Council meeting. Kight showed up in a suit and tie, meaning all business. He always wore his numerous rings, tortoiseshell aviator glasses and his brilliant white hair.

Councilmember Steve Martin was surly when he introduced "Morris Night" purposely mispronouncing the elder's name. With a big yawn, he cautioned, "Morris, stay within two minutes."

Kight: "Good evening councilmembers, I hope this is the beginning of the end." He then went on to condemn the City Council's waffling over whether or not to follow the Advisory Board's recommendation: "The Gay and Lesbian Advisory Council is an important component of your government … and they are accumulating at last a bit of moral authority. Do not deny that moral authority, by a clear majority they have voted to have this resolution withdrawn by you."

Next, he attacked a component of the City Council's motion in which they proposed to ask Coors: "Nice-nice 'Oh gee whiz dear Coors, please don't give any more money to right-wing organizations.' Good grief, you're blowing in the wind. We have carried on a 21-year nonviolent intensive boycott of Coors and they haven't given one inch."

As Kight was airing his final grievance (about the council's decision to 'compliment the Coors family for their creative personnel policies'), Steve Martin brusquely interrupted, "Thank you … your two minutes are up.…"

Kight: "Oh, thank you."

Martin: "You need to wrap up, Morris.…"

Kight: "I feel really cheated because I worked for years to get to this moment and you are allowing me two minutes. Wow. Says something about discourse, doesn't it." He ended by reiterating: "I hope that you validate the Gay and Lesbian Advisory Council and that you vote to rescind the frightful mistake that you made on 5 of May 1997." With that, Kight grabbed his cane and left the podium.

More speakers followed with comprehensive and impassioned pleas for the City Council to rescind the resolution and reinforce the boycott. After 15 speakers, Mayor Pro-Tempore John Heilman admitted that upon being "educated by Morris, Don [Kilhefner] and others, the resolution was a mistake. The company and the family that profits from the company are still our enemies."

Councilmember Paul Koretz put forth a substitute motion, a reworded, compromising letter to Coors asking the Coors family to cease funding and providing leadership to "organizations whose missions include the denial of fair and equitable treatment of gays and lesbians and other minorities."

Kight stood up and shouted: "I think that the motion by Paul Koretz is probably meant in the spirit of peacefulness. However, I would totally reject it as apologetic as saying something that is not true, that the Coors family have a progressive personnel policy. It's a smokescreen. You're being covered over by smoke. I would simply urge you to rescind the pro-Coors resolution and boycott Coors. Anything else is not acceptable to the Coors Boycott Committee, make that clear.

"We'll keep coming back and coming back. We-will-wind-you-down.

"We simply will not allow you to abuse gay people."

Kight sat down.

After Councilmember Jeffrey Prang commented on the "unpleasant process," Steve Martin doubled down on his desire to commend Coors for the changes in corporate policy, and for "doing the right things."

Kight yelled from the galley: "Can't you hear what's going on?"

Martin: "You're out of order, Morris."

Voice in the galley: "He's been out of order his whole life."

Martin: "Yeah, he has been."

Voice: "That's why he won."

Martin: "The hardest part of this process has been the *absolute* lack of love and absolute lack of consideration for other people's opinions, the intellectual violence, the intellectual fascism, the character assassination ... from day one—"

Kight: "Steve, you said once we are eating our young."

Martin: "You are, Morris."

Kight: "How dare you...."

Martin: "It cut because it's true, Morris."

Crowd boos, shouts: "Shame on you."

Kight stood up—everyone stood. Kight shouted, "How dare you, shame on you, you should be boycotting Coors. You should rescind!" His raised voice cracked.

Martin: "Morris, you're out of order and I don't want to have you removed."

Kight: "Have me removed...."

Crowd: "Have all of us removed."

Chaos erupted, then Morris sat down and eventually the crowd settled down. Councilmember Paul Koretz withdrew his substitute motion that he thought was "undivisive and painless," saying "The hell with it," and the Council quickly voted unanimously to rescind the motion and to withdraw the commendation of Coors company. One battle victorious.

A few years later, the Coors family produced its first known gay offspring, Scott Coors, great-grandson of Adolph Coors Sr. He wasn't the first of the prominent conservative family to try to counter the boycott, but he was the first gay family member to do so by stepping in when Mary Cheney left the company. By 2001, the company had recast itself by changing its policy to be gay-friendly. The tall, handsome, Stanford-educated Scott Coors was the perfect stand-in for the uncomfortable "stuck in the middle" position he presented for himself and the Coors Brewing Company. Scott carried the company's message while trying not to mention the family's mission.

Kight told the *Advocate*: "Scott Coors is a very good-looking, well-spoken, charming fellow. But he has delivered nothing to help gay people in this situation. He keeps saying to me, 'Let me talk to Papa about the foundations,' and then nothing happens. He seems to side entirely with his family."

In the early 2000s, Stonewall, the famous gay bar on Christopher Street in New York City, had been designated an historical monument as the site of the Stonewall riots. It also began serving Coors beer.

To this date, the Coors Beer Boycott is still active.

GAY ASIAN PACIFIC

PRIOR TO 1980 THERE WERE FEW PLACES FOR GAY ASIANS TO MEET, and by and large they were geographically spread out. There was an informal network in place, but for the most part Asians felt isolated from the larger organized gay community. Morris Kight was instrumental in changing that dynamic.

During the late '70s, as Jaime Green described it: "We made these, what we used to call dog and pony shows when we were at the Center. We would go out to a university, it would be sponsored by the Gay Students Union or some faculty, et cetera." At one of the engineering schools, Roy Zucheran walked up to Kight. Green continued, "This very young, very attractive Asian boy. And from the minute he met Morris, there was an instant bonding.

"Morris brought him home, to where we were staying, and the hostess made him go to a hotel or a motel because Roy was just a college kid. Morris was genuinely upset about it."

Gino Vezina remembers Kight always as a "one-at-a-time [lover]. He was not prone to promiscuous activities; he was more of a passive partner. Roy came along, extremely closeted, and knew about Morris Kight. He initially came to Morris for counseling and he never left." Kight described Roy to Nicholas Snow in 1997: "I have a companion now, a marvelous man, the kindest, the most decent wonderful man."

They were polar opposites in temperament and needs. Roy worked and functioned in the nine-to-five corporate world. He paid the rent at McCadden Place whenever he lived there. He was quiet and preferred to stay in the background.

David Frater: "Morris and Roy had a deep and spiritual relationship that probably had a very strong physical component at one time. There was love and deep admiration for each other. [Roy] made good money, he was very thrifty, and was able to help Morris."

Both Vezina and Green recount a superior/inferior dynamic in the Kight/Zucheran relationship. Vezina said, "Morris was only interested in people he could use."

Pat Rocco described Roy as "a godsend ... he was the person who saw to it that Morris' things were kept in order, kept a good house for Morris. He saw that he was fed, because Morris didn't care about these things. And of course, at the end he saw to his health care, all those things. Roy was really there."

1983. Morris Kight in fancy drag at a holiday formal. Stephen Stewart Photographs, Coll2010-006, ONE National Gay & Lesbian Archives, Los Angeles, California.

Though Roy moved out a few times over the years, they spoke by phone every day at 8 a.m.

Sometimes Kight would tell the story that it was his idea and at other times he'd say that it was Roy's idea to organize the gay and lesbian Asian community. *The Making of a Gay Asian Community* (by Eric C. Wat) expresses that Morris was involved in setting up the first meeting and he had his own personal reasons for doing so. Roy Kawasaki explained, "Morris' main concern was Roy Z. He was anxious about Roy's welfare because he didn't have any Asian friends. He would always say, 'When I pass on, make sure you don't forget Roy.'"

Together they organized and hosted the first meeting of Asian Pacific lesbians and gays at McCadden Place in 1980. June Lagmay: "To me this was like going to the house of God because Morris Kight has such a wonderful reputation and deservedly still does for being such a patriotic father of the [gay and lesbian] movement. The way he would say, 'You got to have a way of expressing yourselves and don't depend on the European community to do that.' He was so charming."

There were close to 20 people at the first meeting; within a month, the group had grown to nearly 80. Eventually they formed a board, had potlucks, weekend retreats in Big Bear, and printed a newsletter. Roy was the editor.

Paul Chen: "Morris wanted to turn [Roy] into a political animal ... He sort of pushed Roy into it and Roy went in reluctantly ... He thought the organization would be a good place for Roy to blossom." Ting described Kight as "extroverted, daring, very bold. He liked the limelight a lot, loved being in front of a camera. He was a ham. We all know that.

"Roy was the complete opposite."

An apt quote, attributed to various sources: "Morris could spot a camera a mile away."

An offshoot group called Gay Asian Pacific Support Network started in Los Angeles and quickly spread to other cities on the West Coast. In 1999, GAPSN presented Morris Kight with the Pacific Bridge Award.

CROSSROADS

KIGHT ENJOYED SERVING AS PRESIDENT OF THE U.S. MISSION Board of Directors; overseeing the tax-deductible social service agency gave him the autonomy he desired.

In 1978 the U.S. Mission established Hudson House (named for the address of the first house on Hudson Boulevard in Hollywood) to provide emergency housing for the homeless. Through public grants the organization quickly grew to six homes and up to 43 residents. Over the next four years, with Pat Rocco as Executive Director (a title given to him by Kight), the organization was responsible for helping nearly four thousand individuals find shelter, food, clothing and emotional support.

In 1980, four of the six rental houses were sold for real estate development, leaving just two Hudson Houses, both in Hollywood, and a lot of city funding on the table—funding which Kight put to use. His plan was to expand the U.S.

Mission umbrella by adding a job counseling and placement service for gays and lesbians, which Kight later described as "an urgent and irresponsibly unmet need." He used the corporate name "Hudson House, Inc. dba Crossroads Employment Services" and the U.S. Mission IRS tax identification number (operating as Hudson House) for their nonprofit status, eventually creating enormous confusion and an appearance of impropriety.

Named for its location in the historically significant "Crossroads of the World" building at 6667 Sunset Boulevard in Hollywood, Crossroads Employment and Job Counseling Services opened its doors for service on July 20, 1981, with Kight, Bob Humphries, Karen Kircher, Pat Lenhof and Sallie Fiske sitting on the board, and Pat Rocco, Valerie Terrigno, Rene Joubert, Frank Vel, and Tomalina Herrera as staff.

Rob Cole: "[Kight] was on a first-name basis with city, county and state political leaders and was able to get city funding for [Crossroads], the first such agency with a specific outreach to gays and lesbians." Jobs were also found for members of the straight community. According to Rocco: "Because it was a gay employment agency, it was the first of its kind," and word of mouth spread quickly.

In November 1981 when $140,000 in anticipated funding wasn't received, Crossroads was unable to meet their payroll, an unacceptable situation for Kight. Rocco, whom Kight had appointed as Director of the organization, made a $1,000 personal loan to Crossroads and was repaid from HUD funding that came in for Hudson House. This would later cause confusion, as the two organizations were separate and provided different services. The funding agencies would not look kindly on the commingling of funds. And more confusion was to follow.

Pat Rocco had opened an account with First Interstate Bank for Hudson House in 1978. Crossroads opened its own account at Security Pacific Bank in '81 under the name Hudson House Inc. dba Crossroads. In 1982, an urgent mailgram was sent to Kight, from First Interstate. "We find that your account has been unlawfully opened, there is only 1 Hudson House Incorporated under the State of California and since we have a lawful account at Security Pacific Bank, kindly close the account."

Kight immediately sent off a mailgram to Reverend Donald Dill, Secretary of the U.S. Mission: "Urgent that the role of the Mission and the Hudson House be totally clarified to the satisfaction of several parties, demand to know why the houses maintain a bank account under a title which does not belong to them. Seek total separation of housing facilities and job counseling. Wish it made clear that I am not an authority of, nor a spokesperson for the houses, since however my name was used in connection with the houses, I demand an accounting of all revenues from residents or the giving public...."

An immediate handwritten note from Bob Humphries was sent to all involved to declare that according to "the bylaws of the United States Mission, it is forbidden for any officer or member of the Mission to maintain, affirm, or support by word or deed, the insufferable notion that Hudson House, Inc. is an incorporation of the Hudson Houses."

About this same time, the city funding agency decided to take a closer look at the little organization that was making such a big impact. The CDD [Community Development Department] Human Services Division asked for clarification on the name conflict. Giving Kight every benefit of every doubt, they later concluded that "some procedural abnormalities may have taken place during the formative stages of reaching contractual agreements."

But first, CDD needed to know what organizations were providing what services using what funds. Rocco responded with a detailed eight-page typed letter while Bob Humphries promptly separated the U.S. Mission from the job counseling service, not allowing the board to use the same 501(c)(3) tax exemption. Humphries also insisted that the housing services program known as Hudson Houses was in no way legally bound to Hudson House, Inc. dba Crossroads. The two entities were entirely disassociated.

Upon a closer look at the staff, the CDD learned that Pat Rocco did not possess a college degree, which was required for the position of Company Director, and found a previous guilty plea of a federal charge on his record. Within two weeks Kight handed Rocco a written termination notice and the name "Hudson House" and "Hudson House, Inc." were removed from all utilities and accounts.

While a new board of directors was installed, Valerie Terrigno was appointed Project Director. Crossroads received its own corporate tax-exempt status, separated from the U.S. Mission and Hudson House, Inc., and continued on with funding from CDD. Kight remained on the board but pulled back from the day-to-day operations of Crossroads. He handed the reins to Terrigno.

It would later come out that Terrigno also lied on her résumé and that she too did not have a college degree. Kight later said, "We took her on face value. You have to have some faith in this world."

Using her position at Crossroads to elevate her profile in the gay community, Terrigno was elected president of Stonewall Democratic Club in January of 1984 and by that November she was running to become the first mayor of the newly created city, West Hollywood.

From the beginning, she dominated the race. Dynamic, charismatic and media-savvy, she retitled herself executive director of Crossroads and touted her experience running a small social service organization that did outreach to homeless and street youth. Clearly, she learned from Kight, employing "coalition politics" by getting endorsements from every major political club.

After seeking and being turned down for campaign support from Sheldon Andelson, Terrigno (on an annual salary of $11,500), somehow financed her own campaign by making a $20,000 loan to herself. Much later, federal prosecutors would insist that the money came from funds embezzled from Crossroads.

After winning the election, Valerie Terrigno became a national figure with an international gay and lesbian following.

Her first act as mayor was to have the "fagots stay out" sign taken down forever. (After the initial confrontation in 1970 when the original sign was removed, the owner of Barney's Beanery had enjoyed the media exposure so much, no matter how negative, he put another sign up and added collector's matchbooks printed with the degrading statement.)

While Terrigno toured the country touting West Hollywood as a "gay Camelot," and planting seeds for her own political ambitions, the FBI raided the Crossroads offices looking for evidence and explanations.

Since 1983, city officials and CDD had multiple red flags going up about Terrigno's handling of the company. She began doing all the bookkeeping and, in short, took advantage of confusion within the agency and began embezzling funds.

In February 1985, West Hollywood officials became aware of the federal and Los Angeles city investigations and began to take notice of her poor administrative abilities, and by October Terrigno was indicted.

At first, she blamed her lack of bookkeeping skills; at her sentencing, she insisted that the agency was a financial mess when she took over and that she was forced to juggle funds to keep Crossroads alive. Yet, Crossroads was still run aground.

Her blatant disregard for rules and responsibilities was clearly the cause of her undoing. One investigator noted her lack of discipline both as an administrator and as a thief.

Terrigno was convicted for embezzlement of $7,000 from Crossroads, though the actual figure was much higher. Her sentence was nominal: 60 days in a halfway house, five years of probation, and she was prohibited from profiting during the probation from books, movies, speaking engagements or other coverage of the case. Terrigno was also banned from holding any employment where she would be responsible for public funds. She was ordered to pay restitution of the federal and city funds and one thousand hours of community service

There was a lot of blame to go around. Gay leaders never asked the tough questions or went beyond the exterior to peek under the hood of a candidate. Despite numerous mentions of her experience at Crossroads, no one asked anyone at Crossroads about her performance. Gay leaders admitted that they went on trust alone.

Then there was the question of who might have tipped off the FBI, with speculation falling on Kight as the possible informant. Realistically, if Kight had called the FBI, they easily could have found a number of contract violations prior to Terrigno's tenure at the agency. Kight preferred to stay silent on the issue but he was quoted in the press as calling her "Salary Terrigno," expressing some disappointment at what she had done in her position.

Rocco said, "We were blindsided. We didn't know that she would steal. That was awful. A terrible thing."

Ann Bradley recalled that Kight "was devastated … that she was not handling the position with complete veracity."

Tony Sullivan speculated that Kight was in contact with the FBI. "I'm sure the FBI were quite capable of manipulating Morris … I've always felt that Morris was involved with that. And that is sad. Morris fucked people over. And Morris also deserted people that he shouldn't have."

Ivy Bottini: "I felt really bad about what happened to Valerie. I watched the community turn their back on her. Nobody—almost nobody that I can think of fell from grace faster than she did. And when she did, there was no net for her. I can't say that I would be a hundred percent sure that he was not capable of [turning Valerie in to the FBI], I would like very much not to think it was true. But knowing how he claimed everything for himself … there is a little piece of me that goes. . . it could be one of those quirks that somebody has. You really don't know them. Yeah, I think maybe. I hope not."

After 1985 Kight would refuse to talk about Valerie Terrigno. He wouldn't speculate, he wouldn't elaborate, he wouldn't say anything. He did, however, leave a paper trail.

A "Memorandum for Archives" from Morris Kight dated 22 February 1984 begins: "I have held this document for several months, holding in rage, and near horror at what this represented. These photocopies of bank records are from Security Pacific Bank, Highland at Willoughby, Los Angeles."

Attached to the memo are copies of a World Money Order drawn from the Royal Bank of Canada for 20 dollars. A copy of the backside shows an endorsement made out to "Hudson House Crossroads for deposit only," and an illegible signature.

Kight recalls: "I had a call from Valerie Terrigno who had been recently hired as the replacement for Pat Rocco ... She wanted to know if I had run the check through our account. I had not. The only checks we received during the year and a half that I was responsible for the program were from the U.S. Government via City Treasury. That is all I had ever wanted us to receive. So I said no. And she said, 'But the bank says that is your signature and I just want to know what is going on. If your account is being used for forgeries, I want to know it.' I was just horrified. I never trusted her again and felt that she either had an agenda which was to shut everyone out or she was lacking in taste, tact, and downright common sense."

To the naked eye, it does not look like Kight's signature. A copy of the Security Pacific deposit slip for 20 dollars is also attached.

Perhaps it was Kight's proximity to Terrigno that made him unfair game for the speculators. He had acquired a reputation as being fast with cash that came in from various sources, and his well-known ego made him easy fodder for gossips. But none of that ever made him a co-conspirator with the FBI against a community leader. Perhaps the fuel of the rumors was not so much as Kight's jealousy of Terrigno as it was jealousy of Kight.

The fact that there are rumors does not make rumors fact.

UNPOPULAR CHOICES

THE THORN IN THE SIDE OF THE HOMOSEXUAL REPUTATION, THE common thread of bigots and homophobes, was the ignorant idea that homosexuals were pedophiles. Homosexual pedophilia is no more prevalent than heterosexual pedophilia.

In the wake of gay liberation, a group formed in 1978 that aimed to exploit the liberation movement for their own nefarious purposes. They called themselves NAMBLA [the North American Man/Boy Love Association] and described themselves as a civil rights group who sought to decriminalize age of consent to support and promote consensual man/boy relationships.

Personal judgments aside, this was a public relations cold sore for every gay activist and gay ally.

Kight saw NAMBLA as a red herring. He knew that Anita Bryant and company would try to use the organization's mission to represent the entire gay movement and divert gay liberation. Kight's strategy was not to outright dismiss NAMBLA—he wanted the broader gay community to have a discussion about the matter, he wanted to help shape a way to deal with the matter of intergenerational consensual sex. The broader gay community did not want to be affiliated with this fringe element.

Elders Kight and Harry Hay saw a larger problem in the gay community: the community was too quick to dismiss, to discriminate against, to not make any effort to understand—exactly what had been done to homosexuals in the not-too-distant past. The tactic to reject and hide from NAMBLA was, in the civil rights warhorse's view, small-mindedness, an erasure of things that we do not understand and an unwillingness to address the situation. There was no conversation, no townhall, no discussion.

John Embry said, "Harry was quite a powerhouse. Harry was dedicated to things. He had a proclivity to join things that were at the rock bottom of the pile, NAMBLA for instance."

Hay did not join NAMBLA, neither did his partner Burnside nor did Kight.

Their approach to the controversy was far too sophisticated and nuanced for most prosaic activists to understand. Kight and Hay didn't suggest that the group be embraced or even accepted. They wanted to have an open conversation about sex, marginalized sex that is uncomfortable to talk about, and it can be said the younger generation of activists weren't having any conversation.

NAMBLA did apply for a place to march in the CSW parade, hence there were discussions about the parade and how to discourage them.

Troy Perry recalled (2006): "NAMBLA wanted to march and we said 'no.' We have this group of child molesters who only go to bed with prepubescent kids and who want to use us and attach themselves to us—these men who look at little boys and little girls, it doesn't matter, the kid is the thing. So I said, 'they are not going to march with us.' Morris, again, had voted to permit them to do it. They didn't want to see anybody arrested who showed up. Well, they showed up."

NAMBLA showed up at the CSW Parade, an annual Gay Pride celebration in the late '70s, holding their "NAMBLA" banner and dressed for a good time.

Troy Perry: "Pat Underwood was the President of the Board that year and had them arrested when they stepped off the curb. I didn't find out until later that it was Harry Hay and John and whoever else, it was like two or three people. What I mean by arrest, they were removed. They didn't take them to jail; the police just held them until the parade started and made sure they were out of the parade until the parade was over. They talked to them in the car is what they did."

Kight participated in the parade on his own float and he didn't stand with Hay in support of NAMBLA, though he was supportive of NAMBLA marching in the parade.

Kight: "We have to be on the side of those who say that having sex with our unwilling, or ill-informed, younger brothers or sisters is exploitation. I think we have to agree with that. It is an important point, is there informed consent? At what point are you old enough to say 'yes, I would like to engage in dah-duh-dah-duh-dah.' At what point? I don't know, I'm not wise enough to know that. What I advocate that we do is to lower our voices, stop the segregation, stop the shibboleth of discussing it. We seem unwilling to do that. Indeed, a call that we discuss it, just bring it up and, 'oh Morris, don't talk about that. We're not going to talk about that.' It's a terrible, terrible thing."

The following year when NAMBLA made their way to San Francisco's annual pride event, Kight marched in the parade next to the small group representing NAMBLA.

Stanley Williams recalled, "There were still those who equated homosexuality with child molestation, so what Morris did was unforgivable. He was roundly booed. I personally walked out into the street and expressed my disgust at his attempt to include pedophilia in the parade."

When he was invited, Kight spoke at a private NAMBLA meeting in 1982.

He was asked about that in 1994:

"Yes, I spoke before them as their invited guest. I was keynote speaker. I went there to say a lot of things that I believed then and now, is that all beings, of any age, are sexual. And that the richest sexual experience in anyone's life is before he/she is 18. Never again, from that day forth, from the time you're 18, 19, 20, 21, 22, you deteriorate slightly, a little bit each day, in your sexual appetite and your sexual energy. And then since our young brothers and sisters are richly and fiercely sexual, something should be done about that. What to do about that is the subject of discussion.

"I'm simply saying that somebody, somewhere must bring sexual freedom to our young brothers and sisters, and then from that point on. I think I remained intellectually pure. I was saying how to do that is yet to be decided. There are people who think that intergenerational sex is a bad thing. I'm not saying it is or isn't.

"People are saying that sex should be with one's peers, within two years of either age. Sixteen to eighteen, within two years. I'm not sure if that's the solution. But we all ought to engage in intellectual discussion. I received a standing ovation [at NAMBLA], because they thought I was making sense. Even though I was not specifically advocating nor opposing intergenerational sex. I was simply saying that we ought to do better. Now, that speech comes back to haunt me, because there are people who say 'Morris is soft on sex among adults and children,' and that's not so.

"The North American Man-Boy Love Association has become the number one shibboleth of the organized lesbian/gay community. It's the most unpopular issue. It is absolutely the subject of total condemnation. Rather than war, and abortion, and overpopulation, and the deterioration of the environment and a whole variety of life-and-death issues: the fact that the atom bombs are leaking, and the air every day is becoming electrified, until we all finally turn green from leaking atomic energy. We don't spend much time on that. We spend a lot of time on NAMBLA."

In 1996, Kight accepted an award from and addressed the Humanists Society, followed by a question-and-answer period. He was asked, "How can gays and lesbians counter the propaganda that gays and lesbians are out to proselytize and make more gays and lesbians?"

Kight answered, "Thank you. It's a very serious question. The child molestation, unwanted sexual approaches by adults to children are offensive, destructive. However, 96 percent of those [crimes] belong to the non-gay community, not to us.

"So it's okay for us to say that we're sorry that it's happening. If it's happening in your community, go and clean it up. The business that they worry so much about, we lesbian and gay folk training children, being with children, being teachers and so on. They say that we're attracting them, that somehow or another that they come in our orbit and catch it. Like it's smallpox or some communicable disease."

Beyond unfounded assertions, there is no evidence that Kight sexually favored young boys. There is not one first-person claim, either as witness or participant, that Kight had young boys around for sex. The young men who were in his company were more often boys who had been either abused at home or turned away by their families for being gay. They were more attracted to Kight as a patriarchal figure. There is a report from a younger man who made an advance toward Kight; he did not return the interest. He was kind, he was direct, and he declined.

He gave young men a safe place to stay and made them feel useful. Many of the young men genuinely loved Kight and believed they could never do enough for him in return for his kindnesses. Some adored him. Unfortunately, and sometimes comically, that adoration drew a good deal of ire from his homosexual contemporaries. Most unfortunate were those who did not understand his way of thinking, who added rumors and disrepute simply because they didn't want to discuss the issue.

In 1994, the ILGA [International Gay and Lesbian Association] expelled NAMBLA, GLAAD [the Gay & Lesbian Alliance Against Defamation] adopted a position statement that deplored NAMBLA and its goals, NGLTF [National Gay and Lesbian Task Force] adopted a resolution that condemned "all abuse of minors, both sexual and any other kind, perpetrated by adults," and NAMBLA was banned from participating in the Stonewall-25 march in New York. Kight did not come to their defense.

As of 2006, according to various media reports, NAMBLA only exists as a well-maintained website with a few enthusiasts.

AIDS

AFTER THE FIRST FEW YEARS OF LIBERATION, SOME OF THE YOUNGER activists realized that with all the hard work, the brainstorming, the demonstrations and the devotion to advancing gay rights, they forgot about sex. By the late 1970s, the gay social scene had become very cosmopolitan, urban, and trend-setting. Enthusiastic with promiscuity and experimentation, gays were making a splash in most every corner of society. It was a pinnacle time for the gay movement.

Then gay men began to get sick and die in major cities and large towns across America without explanation.

"From very early on," Ivy Bottini said, "I had a feeling about this. Morris wouldn't accept that it was sexually transmitted. He just wouldn't say that it was possibly sexually transmitted."

Kight did not want to be the person to tell people to stop having sex. Sexual freedom was a goal, not a life sentence. He couldn't fathom that a virus would attack the very thing they'd worked toward. There had to be better answers. Kight: "I urged us to cool it. Not to guess at what it was. But instead offer all the assistance to those who had it that we could."

Bottini said, "I used to wonder how much more quickly we could've gotten it under control if more people took it seriously as being sexually transmitted."

Miki Jackson recalled going to visit Ken Schnorr, president of the Stonewall Democratic Club, in the hospital. "Around that time the medical people came up with this name for the disease, GRID, Gay Related Immuno-Deficiency. Morris was appalled. He said 'Imagine—naming a disease after a class of people.' He rallied people to get the 'gay' out of the name of the disease.

"He also used to say 'They named it over Ken Schnorr's body.'"

Schnorr died in January 1982 at age 35.

By that time Kight couldn't ignore the obvious. He, and everyone else in the community and medical establishment, had to accept the bitter truth that the virus was spread, not caused, by sexual contact. Ivy Bottini, who hadn't spoken to Kight for over three years over the disagreement, said: "Morris had to reverse his statement."

When one of Kight's helpers, David Spencer, became ill, Kight and Roy took care of him at McCadden Place for over a year. When David died in 1987, his cremated remains were buried in the McCadden Place yard. Soon to be joined by many others.

According to Jackson, Kight used his position on the Human Relations Commission and Stonewall Democratic Club. "He worked on elected officials and staffers to help with funding and policies." This would prove to be a long and difficult path.

1983. Morris in the garden of his McCadden Place home. Photo by Stephen Stewart. Stephen Stewart Photographs, Coll2010-006, ONE National Gay & Lesbian Archives, Los Angeles, California.

Sheldon Andelson died in December 1987 at 56 years old.

Howard Fox, Kight's co-founder of Stonewall Democratic Club, died in 1989 at age 52.

It was a call to action for all hands on deck to address the crisis. Civil rights attorney Al Gordon stepped up to help many people who were dying of AIDS get their affairs in order. Family abandonment and outright rejection for being homosexual continued to happen. Some young men, deathly ill, were turned away by their righteous relatives. It was heartache on top of heartache with a desperate need for pragmatism. Most of the pragmatic help came from a coalition of lesbians who did not organize as much as they mobilized themselves. They rolled up their sleeves and did what needed to be done for men wasting away alone in their apartments or just as alone in hospital wards. They brought food and comfort, they did laundry, light housekeeping, and they contacted family members and whoever else needed to be contacted. There is no name for this group of people, perhaps angels.

They also healed a divide that had always been between gay men and lesbians, with no known cause. A rift with no argument. The surviving gay men acknowledged with respect and gratitude the fortitude their sisters brought to the crisis.

Kight and others were met with brick walls when they tried to mobilize nationally, seeking government funds for treatment, medical research, prevention, and education. President Ronald Reagan was briefed on the crisis but would not address the issue much less say the word "AIDS." The White House responded with an unfortunate lightheartedness, humorously referring to a "gay plague."

Meanwhile fear and misinformation led to a noted increase in homophobia and gay-bashing. And the death toll continued to rise. Steve Lachs remembers a period of time when "a friend was dying every ten minutes."

Los Angeles had the third largest concentration of AIDS cases in the U.S., only behind New York and San Francisco. Hospitals were overcrowded. Dying men were 'stored' in hallways with no one willing to treat them. Large cities set up "AIDS wards" that were difficult to staff, and patients were never touched by a human hand, unless it was a visiting loved one. People were losing their housing from being unable to work or were refused housing based on their health status. People were literally dying in the streets.

In 1982 the Gay and Lesbian Services Center held an emergency meeting to address the many needs that were coming in their doors and to vote on whether or not the Center should become exclusively about AIDS services. Kight was concerned that limiting their focus would sacrifice other concerns of the gay community.

The board voted that in order to effectively battle the disease on all fronts there needed to be a new organization with its own funding and its own corporate status. In January 1983 they founded AIDS Project Los Angeles [APLA]. It was a defining moment for the GCSC and for the ultimate success in handling the AIDS crisis.

Early on, word came around that Paul Olson, who was responsible for the early Liberation Houses, had succumbed to the illness, a few years shy of his 30th birthday.

In 1983, Steve Berman decided he would run through Northern California to raise money and awareness about AIDS. Kight often described Berman as a "companion, one of the two loves of my life, the light of my life. I loved Steve more than I've ever loved anybody in my lifetime."

Kight told Nicholas Snow: "He engaged in a 5K run to raise money for AIDS research. He did very well. And when he got to the finish line, he marched 75 more yards and fell dead of an aneurysm in the brain. It nearly drove me crazy, I loved him so much." Steve Berman was 36 years old.

Barry Copilow explained, "In 1973, Steve had a cerebral hemorrhage, an aortal malfunction, at 26 years old. No one knew about his health condition. His brain couldn't function on the level that was required to go to school. Steve wouldn't let anyone know about his impairment. He couldn't function fully. Had to put everything down in meticulous notes. He made copious notes how to walk to different clients' houses.

"Steve loved Morris very much, but they were not lovers. He loved Morris like a father. They did not have a sexual relationship. Steve was on an anti-seizure medication which was a libido suppressor."

For two years Kight was in "deep personal grief." Subsequently, Kight created the "Steve Berman Award" at Christopher Street West Gay Pride Parade. He made the nominations. The first Steve Berman Award was presented to Mina Meyer and Sharon Raphael.

Steve Berman is in-urned in Hilltop Memorial Cemetery in Richmond, California. Kight planted a bottle brush tree in the McCadden Place yard in his memory.

Miki Jackson: "It was intentionally planted right outside the window behind the huge old table he used as a desk—so he could look out on it when he worked. He sat for quite a while under it and looked at it for a long time that day. He mourned Steve's death the rest of his life. That was a loss he really didn't get over."

By 1985, there had been more than 5,600 U.S. deaths from AIDS and still no action from the White House.

Then in 1986 things went from bad to worse when extreme right-wing ideologue and three-time failed presidential candidate Lyndon LaRouche and his supporters were able to get Proposition 64 on the November 1986 California ballot. Proposition 64 was written with the tagline: "Spread Panic, not AIDS." And that is what they did.

LaRouche had a following of lobbyists who named themselves PANIC [Prevent AIDS Now Initiative Committee] and they covered the state spreading his hate-filled and shameful rhetoric, most of it misinformation and outright lies. The "Yes on 64" initiative called for a multi-billion-dollar budget to eradicate the disease by classifying AIDS as easily spread; to require mandatory HIV testing of various 'high-risk' groups; and to publicly name and quarantine all those who tested positive.

Ronald Reagan's lack of leadership on the federal level made LaRouche's campaign frighteningly effective. One poll, three months prior to the election, had half of California voters in favor of quarantining.

The "No on 64" and "Stop LaRouche" campaign set up offices and modeled their efforts after the successful statewide anti-Briggs effort. Call centers were set up around the state to systematically call every phone number in the phone book to discuss the initiative with whoever answered the phone. They made flyers, posters, mailers, and T-shirts with a simple message: "No on 64." They wrote position papers and editorials.

Fortunately, the California Medical Association, the California Nursing Association, and the Centers for Disease Control all refused to support Proposition 64, and the measure failed by 71% to 29%. And the country was no closer to a cure or an effective treatment.

Los Angeles was far behind New York and San Francisco in providing hospice and home health care services. With Kight's guidance, the "No on 64" campaign rolled into an organized coalition called "Los Angeles AIDS Hospice Committee" that included, among others, Michael Weinstein, psychologist, author Laud Humphries, and Jackie Goldberg of the Los Angeles School Board.

On February 16, 1987, the AIDS Hospice Committee held a public hearing in West Hollywood to convince the Los Angeles County Board of Supervisors to provide funding for a rational, non-moralistic, and compassionate approach to dealing with the AIDS crisis. Kight opened the meeting with a true story of a young man found dead in his apartment. "He had spent the last four days of his life alone and unable to move. When his body was discovered, it was mired in human waste. A civilized society does not allow this to happen."

Kight was followed by 30 first-person eyewitness testimonials that went on for seven hours detailing the bureaucratic governmental red tape that held up grant requests for needed AIDS support services, research, and education, and the atrocious conditions and care for people with AIDS—"the worst care in the country, it's a scandal" is how Weinstein summed it up. They requested a two-pronged approach: establish an in-home hospice program and shelters for homeless AIDS patients.

Before the meeting ended, the AIDS Hospice Committee announced the creation of the AIDS Hall of Shame. The first inductee was Ronald Reagan, followed by California Governor George Deukmejian, and the Los Angeles County Board of Supervisors, with the exception of Supervisor Ed Edelman, who had testified during the day. Michael Weinstein directly called out supervisors Pete Schabarum, Deane Dana, Mike Antonovich, and Kenneth Hahn for allowing the county to provide a "a very low level of care." (Antonovich had suggested in a 1985 interview that "all the gay people turn straight" as a solution to the crisis.)

After the testimonials, Antonovich held a news conference wherein he stated, "The responsibility for the AIDS epidemic does not belong to the Board of Supervisors. It belongs to the heterosexuals and the homosexuals who are drug users and engaging in promiscuous sexual behavior." He went on to say that they must adopt "abstinence or monogamous relationships to stop the transmission of the disease."

Hours later the AIDS Hospice Committee and over one hundred protesters were outside Antonovich's Glendale home, staging a peaceful demonstration "to call attention to the board's insensitivity to the care of AIDS patients," Weinstein was quoted as saying.

Secretary for the hospice committee, Paul Coleman, met with Antonovich and County Health Director Robert C. Gates to reach an agreement on hospice funding. "It was like talking to a brick wall," Coleman was quoted, and described the meeting as "a total failure."

Less than two months later, in May 1987, AIDS Hospice Committee with two hundred supporters marched to Governor George Deukmejian's home in Long Beach. Chris Brownlie presented him, in absentia, with a symbolic "Heart of Stone" award and officially inducted him into the "AIDS Hall of Shame." Another candlelight vigil this time accompanied by chants of "shame, shame, shame."

Supervisor Edmund Edelman, who had appointed and reappointed Kight to the Human Relations Commission, stepped up and demanded the board address the issue in helpful and meaningful ways. It was, after all, their responsibility to respond to the community's needs.

The Director of County Health Services also recommended the supervisors provide funding and coordination of services for AIDS.

In December 1987, the Board of Supervisors voted on a plan presented by Ed Edelman to set aside $1.5 million dollars for hospice care. The plan was passed unanimously.

In January 1988 the county supervisors awarded, without debate, two contracts totaling $500,000 to two nursing agencies in Los Angeles and Long Beach.

The hospice at Barlow Hospital in Elysian Park, near Dodger Stadium, opened in September 1988 with $200,000 from the county and a $200,000 donation from gay businessman Gene LaPietra. It was named for one of its founders, Chris Brownlie. The Chris Brownlie Hospice could care for 25 AIDS patients and was the second exclusively AIDS hospice in the county.

In March 1988, the Los Angeles County Board of Supervisors surprised everyone with a unanimous vote to commit $2 million from the following year's budget to pay for AIDS programs. This quadrupled the county's level of support for hospice programs, including an additional $400,000 toward the Chris Brownlie Hospice.

Over the next 30 years, the AIDS Hospice Committee (with its name changed to the AIDS Healthcare Foundation) became the largest global advocate and provider of HIV/AIDS medical services with the very clear mission "to rid the world of AIDS."

In June of 1988, AHF threw a special luncheon to honor Supervisor Ed Edelman with a "Heart of Gold" Award. "His heart has always been on the side of the people," Kight said as he introduced the Supervisor.

The Gay and Lesbian Community Services Center named a new medical facility after the supervisor, the Edmund D. Edelman Health Center, to acknowledge his leadership.

In October 1989 Governor Deukmejian signed legislation authorizing uninsured Californians suffering from serious illnesses, such as AIDS, to purchase state health insurance paid for through tobacco tax revenues. That created more funds for medical care and hospice.

In addition to Kight's long list of daily phone calls and meetings, every weekday was filled with hospital visits, and weekends were reserved for memorials. Bob Dallmeyer recalled coming back from a memorial in Pacific Palisades with Morris: "He said, 'You know, if horseshit could stop AIDS I'd be putting it in capsules.' We used to go to an average of three to four memorials services a month. We became professional eulogists. Morris' brain was so fecund, his humor—he came up with a totally patented ending. He always wanted to speak last in the remembrance, and he'd say, 'I am sure [Bob] never got that true meaningful standing ovation in his life. Let's give him that standing ovation now, everyone up on your feet.' And he'd leave them to a standing ovation."

For his part, Kight would support any fledgling organization by providing a meeting space, referrals, and funding ideas. He was involved in the founding of "Aid for AIDS" in 1983 which provided funding for emergency rent, mortgage and utility payments. It was another way to allow people to die with dignity, ideally in their own homes. Since its founding, AFA has helped more than 16,000 men, women, and children.

In 1986, Kight helped found "Being Alive," a militant activist group that came together over the civil and moral rights of PWAs, "not a burial society looking for tea and sympathy as the callous might assume," as Bob Dallmeyer described it. At a gathering in West Hollywood Park with 2,500 PWAs he exhorted the crowd: "on behalf of death with dignity, more hospices and better health care. Take to the streets, demonstrate, sit in, chain yourselves to the front door of any clinic that treats you like vermin." The crowd thanked him with a standing ovation.

In March 1987, a national organization began in New York called ACT UP. They were more militant and radical than anything before or since. They did not bar civil disobedience, even property damage. Their immediate goal was "greater access to experimental AIDS drugs and for a coordinated national policy to fight the disease."

Miki Jackson remembers attending one of the first Los Angeles meetings for ACT UP with Morris. "We quickly realized that this was going in a different direction" than they would choose. A focused national effort to access drugs was to be commended, but Kight made the decision not to participate though he was supportive of the hugely successful ACT UP.

The national death toll was on the kinder side of 16,000 in June of 1987 when President Reagan appointed a President's Commission on the HIV Epidemic. It was a small move in the right direction and began the myriad political battles for funding, appointments, and priorities.

Reverend Nancy Wilson (MCC Los Angeles) said, "It is not the Lyndon LaRouches that we have to worry about in our state, it is our elected officials, and even those persons who will call themselves our friends." Wilson was among many others who called for massive protests.

Chris Brownlie, an AIDS Hospice Committee member and person with AIDS, said, "There is an enemy we fight that is more deadly than AIDS, it's homophobia. We don't count, our lives don't matter to them. We have to tell them our lives do matter. I don't want to see another person, gay or straight, die of this disease on the streets. That's inhumane. That's a crime against humanity. It's our responsibility to stop it."

Los Angeles County Board of Supervisors ignored the many pleas for help and dragged their funding feet to take a vote for emergency funding.

In November 1989, about a year after opening the hospice in his name, Chris Brownlie died at his home at the age of 39.

Kight did not like that his community was being consumed by all things AIDS. He still counseled people on a variety of topics. Michael Kearns was one of many who turned to Kight for help, to clear the fog on an important personal life-altering decision: adoption. As a single, HIV-positive man, Kearns was determined to become a parent. It was always a personal goal of his. "When I began thinking about adoption," Kearns wrote for Gaytoday.com, "I sought Morris' opinion. He was one of a very few gay men who didn't attempt to dissuade me. Since I was considering parenting prior to the 'miracle' of protease inhibitors, many labeled my actions as 'selfish.' Morris chose to rivet on the bigger picture: was I going to adopt a child who otherwise might be one of society's routinely discarded? Yes, of course. When hateful judgments of my ultimate decision to adopt appeared in print, it was Morris who consoled me."

A quick update: as of 25 years after the adoption, both father and daughter thrive and enjoy individual successes in life, profession, health, and love.

In 1990, while on a day trip to San Diego for Morris to do another eulogy at another memorial, Kight told Miki Jackson about a laundry service for people with AIDS in San Diego and, Jackson remembers, "he wanted to visit it, he said that he wanted to see the program. It was called Auntie Helen's and it was supported by a thrift store with washing machines in the back." It was self-supporting and provided a much-needed in-home supportive service. "On the way home, I told Morris that 'I want to do this. I want to give this a try in L.A.'"

Kight helped to raise funds for the laundry service from grants for small programs. Ed Edelman helped with a $5,000 grant from the county. They rented a small space on Santa Monica Boulevard and hung a sign. Soon Aunt Bee's Laundry Services and Thrift Store was open and providing the same valuable laundry services in Los Angeles. They picked up soiled bedding and linens from homebound patients, washed, dried, and folded, then delivered back to the home. It involved sometimes two pick-ups a week and, of course, expanded into checking on clients. By the end of the first year, Aunt Bee's moved to a much larger storefront and functioned seven days a week.

Morty Manford had become New York state Assistant Attorney General. He died in May 1992 at age 41.

The first National March on Washington for Lesbian and Gay Rights took place in October of 1979 to protest Anita Bryant's attacks on homosexuals. Subsequent marches were focused on raising awareness about the national health crisis and combating irrational fears. In 1987, Kight was featured speaker to 650,000 participants. Again in 1993, when attendance at the march was closer to one million people, Kight addressed the crowd who shouted for "justice."

By the end of the twentieth century, gay life had an identity in the world. Gay politicians were not rare and gay causes not unusual. Political and public gay allies were more common than not. Gay life had been organized and mainstreamed.

In 1992, Kight said: "A generation ago it was not very gay to be gay. Since then, a worldwide, nonviolent revolution has brought millions out of the closet and created wholesale change in societal attitudes."

Randy Shilts died in February 1994 at age 42.

Over the long years of the AIDS crisis, many bodies of young gay men were left unclaimed at the city morgue. If Kight knew them or knew of them, he'd claim the remains and bury them in his yard at McCadden Place. Along with his numerous four-legged housemates, the garden at McCadden Place was the final resting place for many who had succumbed to AIDS.

A necrology of AIDS up to 2015 would bring the estimated total of deaths in the United States on the darker side of 659,000.

1999. Kight, Pat Rocco, Michael Kearns with daughter Katherine. Photo: David Ghee. Pat Rocco Papers, Coll2007-006, ONE National Gay & Lesbian Archives, USC Libraries, University of Southern California.

Part V

The Proud Generation

Chapter 13

A Doddering Old Man

AS THE GAY COMMUNITY matured, Kight often stood back, assessed and admired it much the same way that he had admired the cottonwood back in Proctor. Proud and paternal, he appraised the yields of his labors in the name of equality and justice for all gay persons. He saw what had become "a community" where there once was none. And he never hesitated to remind everyone he encountered of his participation (at times exaggerated) in the liberation and cohesion of a magnificent and powerful people, of his place in a history yet to be told.

In his own odd way, he was being pragmatic. He rationalized (having unified arguably one of the strongest financial power bases in history) that he should "return to the well," so to speak.

"The Community" as a cohesive whole was in the age of adolescence. Some decision-makers at various organizations responded to its founding father like petulant teenagers—gossipy and refusing to communicate. At the Gay and Lesbian Community Center (the elder and more successful of his progeny) Kight no longer knew everyone on the Board of Directors; he didn't understand the mindset that was taking over. There were huge philosophical differences between the old guard and the new: for instance, in 1992

1994. Morris Kight's 75th birthday. Harold Fairbanks Papers and Photographs, Coll2016-009, ONE National Gay & Lesbian Archives, USC Libraries, University of Southern California.

the Center (which then operated with an estimated annual budget of $14 million and employed close to a thousand people throughout the city) gave honors to a publicly closeted lesbian and supported another well-known (yet closeted) lesbian running for City Council. These kinds of actions outraged true political activists. Grassroots people knew the collateral damage instigated by any one person living in the closet. Ann Bradley remembers, "Morris Kight did not support the closet. He didn't out anybody, but I don't think he ever supported anyone staying in the closet. He was very clear about not being a supplicant."

"Outing" in the 1990s became a political act in the war against AIDS. Kight believed "outing" to be "crypto-fascism. It's an arrogant act. One needs to out oneself."

But there was a new sentiment sitting at the board table; new values were making decisions. And the matter was more about economic priorities than social principles. It was perfectly acceptable among board members (who were described as "men [and women] of money who were very aware of their money") to not "come out" if it would adversely affect one's ability to earn or inherit. The people who had put their livelihoods on the line to create true opportunities for gays and lesbians found such attitudes offensive. It was a long way from the radical left, grassroots, activist mentality that had started it all.

And as the community 'matured,' Kight, inevitably, aged. He was well into his seventies when he began to plan for his golden years.

No one person was ever privy to all his finances. Although everyone knew he received a modest Social Security check, they didn't know where the rest of his money came from or how much there was. David Frater remembers bringing the mail to Kight at McCadden Place and some days, "he'd open envelope after envelope with cash and checks and notes saying 'thank you for your good works' or 'thank you for your help.' I have no idea how much there was."

In actuality, there wasn't a lot of money. There was a little from a lot of different people and that added up to be enough for him to "do his good works" and live modestly. It wasn't consistent and sometimes he still got into a jam with a utility bill.

Kight hadn't held a legit job in years so a formal retirement was not in the cards. The idea of slowing down never crossed his mind. He was getting around on the bus or via arranged rides and never missed a board meeting or Human Relations Commission event. During his regular check-ups, the doctor said that he was doing remarkably well. Still, Kight would not escape the realities of old age.

In late 1991, he had a health scare, a mild stroke. The prognosis was positive as long as he kept his stress level down and made some dietary changes; he did neither. He never viewed his life as stressful, partially because he ate whatever he wanted. Nonetheless, he acknowledged that he was approaching a time in which he would need more help and personal assistance. He made a point of this to his inner circle. Then he made a plan and reached out to the Gay and Lesbian Community Center.

In typical Kight style he grandly summoned the entire board to "a private tea and tour of the McCadden Place Collection," his vast assemblage of objects, art, and artifacts, mostly from the gay and lesbian struggle for equality. Many board members had already been to the grand old man's manor, some had not; in any event, it was always a treat.

Rose Greene, co-chair of the Center from 1990–93, described it. "Of course, it was an honor to meet this icon of the community and get to know him and see what he had acquired of our cultural artifacts over the decades. From what I saw, what was on the walls, I thought the Collection were absolute treasures. He explained how much more he had."

During tea, in his most noble way, Kight proposed a novel idea: the Center could purchase the property at McCadden Place or pay his rent and allow him to live there; in exchange he'd continue to curate it and bequeath the Collection to the Center. Together they would share fundraising responsibilities to support the Collection.

Rose Greene: "He was, in his own way, shopping the community. I thought it was a perfect match."

Torie Osborn, Executive Director of the Center since 1988, and a close progressive ally of Kight's, was also very much in favor: "It's sort of funny, when you have an eccentric, brilliant, unusual character in your midst—it is too often too easy to take for granted that character, the richness of the treasure ... it would be nice to let him live out the rest of his time in a secure situation."

Ann Bradley thought, "To be honest, he really was offering them something quite magnificent ... If you asked me point-blank, 'Do you think the Center should take care of Morris Kight?' Heck yeah. The Center wouldn't be here without him."

Some of the newer guests, however, wrongly perceived that what Kight really needed was different living quarters. They viewed the house as an "old barn" that had become unsuited even for its aging bohemian resident.

What they didn't know or consider was that the 'old barn' was perfect for him as a home, workspace and meeting place. At 1428 McCadden Place Kight had more than 3,000 square feet of house on more than 7,000 square feet of land in the middle of bustling Hollywood. It was built in the 1920s and rumored to have been part of the Buster Keaton film studios. A petition was made with the Los Angeles Historical Society to have it declared an historical landmark. The rent was affordable. Kight himself paid to get a new roof and with his ragtag band of helpers and dedicated caretakers, he could keep the place up.

He was still mentally sharp and there was no imminent need for change, but the idea had been on a few people's minds; some felt an obligation to him. And no doubt, Kight expected things of his progeny.

"At about that same moment in historical time," Rose Greene remembers, "the Center became the beneficiary of two cottages," in the tony section of West Hollywood, from the bequest of Doctor Lawrence Linn. A single gay man from an era when it was common for families to disown homosexuals, Dr. Linn left everything he owned, which was quite a bit of Los Angeles County real estate, to various agencies within the gay community. He also left pages of stipulations and restrictions. 1443 and 1447 North Martel Avenue had to be used for "educational and cultural purposes" and could not be sold in order to enrich an endowment. Additionally, these two houses were protected by the Historical Society, which further restricted their uses.

Rose Greene: "When I saw the two [Linn] homes themselves I thought, Morris could live there for the rest of his life and it would be a win-win situation for him, for the Center, for the community. It just felt like, what a great way to pay respect and honor to him and his Collection, his life's work. And of course, as one of the founders of the Center, it made perfect sense."

According to Miki Jackson (who tape-recorded a meeting at McCadden Place with Kight, Rose Greene and her new co-chair, Ed Gould), "They told him outright that they couldn't inherit the houses without his Collection. They came to Morris and asked him to move into one house, live there and curate his Collection, [and] do some educational programs in the other house."

Next, Kight gathered his small circle of confidants (the self-titled "McCadden Place Group") and asked them to help him "make a number of important decisions." This was their first glimpse of Kight's concern with his legacy. Bob Dallmeyer spotted Kight's "fear of dying and being lost in memory and in the annals of history. I forgave it because he had accomplished so much for the community." Dallmeyer called it a "Machiavellian enlightened self-interest."

Kight asked his people what they each thought was the best long-term plan for the Collection. He was patient and listened to everyone's opinion but he had already made up his mind. He knew that his legacy depended upon other people's support. So he autonomously negotiated a deal with the Gay and Lesbian Community Center, using his historical value and memorabilia as bargaining collateral.

A series of private meetings between Kight and co-chairs Rose Greene and Ed Gould took place. Gould was a recent addition to the board, recruited by Rand Schrader in 1990; he became active in some Los Angeles gay groups but he never organized and had no personal link with social justice or activism. Gould had corporate executive experience, a privileged

1984. Kight (center) at CSW parade with his recurrent banner/greeting. Stephen Stewart Photographs, Coll2010-006, ONE National Gay & Lesbian Archives, Los Angeles, California.

background, and a handsome trust fund from a Chicago banking family. He had never met Morris Kight prior to the initial tea at McCadden Place. However, he seemed to go along with the idea of the Center helping the 'elder.'

Miki Jackson laments, "It didn't feel good. It made me uncomfortable. Morris really wanted this to happen. Of course he wanted to do things with the Center because he had such an attachment to it, which is ultimately what caused him to be so abused because he didn't do the things you need to do to protect yourself." In his zeal to create a working relationship with the Center, he seemed to acquiesce to every request.

In the autumn of 1992, Rose Greene made a formal proposal to the board.

"I pitched it and passionately sold the concept: In exchange for the Center getting the archives, Morris Kight would be the curator, and he could do that in a physical place where he could also *live*. What could be better than that?"

The Center board wasn't as enthusiastic as Greene, but nevertheless they voted to allow Morris Kight and his 10,000-piece collection of art, artifacts and memorabilia to occupy the two Martel properties. Greene: "If there were any negative votes, I don't remember."

In his third-person persona, Kight announced his gift to the Center in a press release: "Morris Kight felt it time for the Center to return to one of its roots—namely vigorous support of the arts."

He signed a written agreement in January 1993 that he would take over both houses on Martel Avenue, live in one home and conduct educational and counseling programs in the other, and house the McCadden Place Collection in both cottages.

According to the agreement, over the next years and concluding upon his death, the Collection would gradually become the property of the Gay and Lesbian Community Services Center. Without citing specifics, both parties agreed in principle that they would do all they could to raise funds for the Collection.

The deal came about after the election of the first Democratic president in over a decade, which had an immediate impact on the Center's board. Torie Osborn accepted a position in Washington, D.C. as Executive Director of the new National Gay and Lesbian Task Force. Rose Greene and Ed Gould agreed to co-chair for a few months while the Center did a long nationwide search for a new Executive Director. Ann Bradley politely resigned from the board to refocus her attentions on community activism.

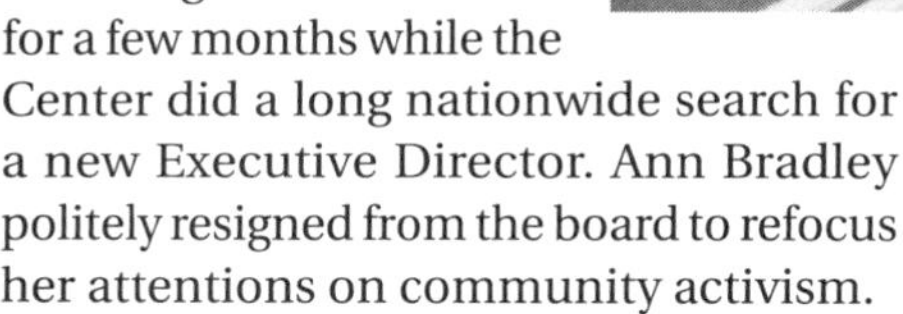

1987. March on Washington, Kight Center in beige shirt holding banner. Photographer unknown. Morris Kight Papers and Photographs Coll2010-008, ONE National Gay & Lesbian Archives, USC Libraries, University of Southern California.

Concurrently the building on Highland Avenue was sold, and the purchase (and total renovation) of a much larger modern building, in the heart of Hollywood on Rand Schrader Boulevard, was being completed.

After a protracted national search, Executive Director Lorri Jean was handed the reins. Except for serving on the board of Lambda Legal, she was from outside the gay community. As a Deputy Regional Director for FEMA, Jean had a reputation for being fiscally astute, which was pretty much everything the Center was looking for. She walked through the doors ready to take control.

Meanwhile Kight proceeded to organize himself and his Collection to move from McCadden Place to Martel Drive. David Frater and his lover worked for weeks to sort, sift, dust, give away, throw away, or pack valuables and perceived valuables: ten thousand pieces of every form of art and memorabilia from over 20 years of political and social activism and vigorous collecting. Volunteers came from every area with their sleeves rolled up, ready to work.

Up to that point, the Collection had been almost exclusively on display in the McCadden Place house and back barn. One day an anonymous office employee called Kight from the Center and requested a catalogue of the Collection. There was no catalogue; no such thing existed. Kight himself was the living, breathing catalogue. In his most archaic way, he communicated to the caller that a catalogue was *essential*. He tried to enlist the caller's participation—he could come off as obsequious. He cited the historical value and importance of both the Collection and his own story. He looked forward to working with the caller; the anonymous office employee did not reciprocate the enthusiasm. Back at the Center, the absence of a catalogue led to questions about the validity and "actual value" of the Collection.

On moving day his usual mixed crew of volunteers and borrowed employees from Aunt Bee's Thrift Store showed up with a rented truck and a few dollies. Many of the old gang were sad to say goodbye to the beautiful, ramshackle house, and paid their final respects to the many cremated remains buried there: numerous early AIDS victims along with Kight's four-legged friends. Kight was not sad. He was rarely sentimental, and certainly not over what he saw as simply a structure. It was a unique house but he knew that he was what made it special, plus he owned the memories. He looked forward to the next stop on his journey and probably the last chapter of his yet unwritten memoirs.

By all accounts it was a horrific move. He had so much stuff, between his living area in the loft and the galleries in the back. "It was crazy," Jackson remembers. "It was like moving the Augean Stables without Hercules." Plus, the Center was suddenly unaccommodating. "We had a plan for two houses and they refused to send someone with the keys. It became obvious that something was going on."

In the plan (sketched on a yellow pad) Kight was to reside and set up a counseling center in the north house. The majority of the art collection and history center was to be in the south house.

Instead, once the movers and everyone got there, they only had access to the north house, the smaller of the two.

On the spot, the movers re-sorted and pared down. Kight's personal belongings and some pieces of the art collection were moved into the 1,640-square-foot house. The rest was put into the two small garages. The south house remained locked.

Despite numerous calls from Kight, Jackson and others, the only information that came back from the Center about the south house was that it was "being worked on." Kight himself thought it was simply a temporary miscommunication. He always assumed the best of people, especially gay people. He believed the misunderstanding would soon be rectified.

It was like living in a warehouse. "Martel really didn't work. It was impossible for [Kight] to continue his majordomo role," Dallmeyer remembers. There was no large work table for brainstorming. McCadden Place had ample parking; Martel was permit parking for residents only and was strictly enforced by the parking-ticket-rich City of West Hollywood. Less than half a block south of the infamous Sunset Strip, visitors soon discovered they were in a hotbed of homelessness, prostitution, and drug dealing. Safety became an issue.

Before Kight, the houses had been vacant for quite some time and attracted a group of homeless men who found refuge in the bushes. Jackson remembers that Kight called them "weed bums."

"He gave them food and they were okay. They slept in the greenery and hedges. He couldn't do anything about it so he just made friends with them and asked them to watch out for who was breaking the windows in the other [locked] house."

Nonetheless, they cleaned up the outside area, hauled away debris, planted the garden. Frater worked tirelessly to restore the natural wood in the home. He ripped out closets, stripped the floors, and discovered architectural aspects like a built-in drying cabinet and window screens that rolled up into the framework. "It was an upscale, beautiful Craftsman-style home—woodwork, big beam ceilings, fireplaces," Frater recalls. After weeks of hard work, the north house was a showcase and "activity center" to ultimately fulfill the Center's obligation to the Linn bequest.

Ivy Bottini: "He created a lovely atmosphere of art and sculpture and the beautiful garden; [Morris] had at least one garden party there. He believed that he would be living out his life on that property."

Inside the house were Don Bachardy's two portraits of Kight, one in pencil and one acrylic. Every few feet in the tiny space was another artist's depiction of him either on canvas or on paper; there was even a sculptured bronze face mask by Philip Hitchcock on a pedestal.

The "Fagots Stay Out" sign from Barney's Beanery was on the wall: an old piece of cardboard with the words written in crayon, mounted and encased in Plexiglas and prominently displayed, it was the centerpiece of the Collection.

Soon after the move, Kight received another anonymous call from the Center. This time they wanted to "borrow" a few pieces from the Collection to feature in the reception area of their new offices on Rand Schrader Boulevard. Kight quickly complied and a messenger from the Center was at Martel that same afternoon to transport more than 40 pieces of furniture, wrought iron and tile garden pieces, original sculptures, paintings, fine art photographs, and posters that Kight carefully chose.

Jackson remembers, "He was acting in total good faith, wanting [the arrangement] to be a success." The messenger drove off and the only inventory of the pieces that were taken existed in his 73-year-old mind. He didn't think a receipt was necessary or warranted. In Kight's view, he and the Center were in a partnership.

Finally, after months, the Center gave Kight a key to the south house but told him, according to Jackson: "…not to move anything in there. They let him in there because he was paying David Frater to do repairs."

According to Jackson, "Morris nicknamed the second house Los Puertos y Las Ventanas [the doors and the windows]. It was a dizzying maze of doors opening into facing windows. We had to laugh; he pointed out every two feet another glass door or window—there was nothing but glass. And there was a lot of broken glass. The house would get broken into by the local vagrants and David [Frater] would fix it. Morris told the Center that it'd be better if he could at least give the place an appearance of habitation to keep people from breaking in, but [the board] didn't care." His requests for assistance with the restoration and upkeep went unanswered. It didn't take long before he got a reputation at the Center as "demanding."

Frater and Jackson remember that early on in the arrangement, the Center would send representatives to small events at Martel—usually perfunctory interns and assistants. But they soon stopped coming at all, perhaps uninterested in the eccentric old man with his history.

"We had corporations giving us [the LGBT community] money, lots of money," Dallmeyer remembers. "They had begun to bring in the suits. People who never went near the Center before were now contributing to the Center." Big bucks were coming in and "big bucks provide better opportunities and also philosophical differences."

For his part, Kight tried to operate as usual. He continued to do what he had been doing at McCadden Place. Dallmeyer remembers, "When he first moved in [to Martel], we immediately started having meetings there [at the north house] and it became Meeting Central. Any group that wanted a place to meet had a place, just a million different kindnesses that he could perform there. And then he was cited for having too many parties, too many gatherings. They were little meetings. It wasn't noisy, and the Center got on him. It was a sad chapter."

Jackson concurs, "He was trying to make it a public space, honoring the mission of the Linn bequest, while it was still his home."

After a few months, Kight received a written notification from the board that he was in violation of their agreement because he wasn't in the south house [doing educational activities], yet the Center wouldn't let him function in the south house.

Members of the McCadden Place Group came to believe that the Center didn't care about Kight: he had served his purpose for them to inherit the two Linn houses and now they wanted to get him out and keep the Collection and the properties. Kight wouldn't listen to pessimistic speculation. But the McCadden Place Group would not be ignored.

Rose Greene describes the Center's perspective: "He created his own kind of board and his group assumed an autonomous attitude. If the Center said we can't do this or we can't do that and it didn't suit what they wanted, they dug their heels in. There's Morris living there, and he continued to violate the specifics of the contract." No one can explain how Kight was in violation of the agreement. "I am not knowledgeable of the specifics of how that agreement got unwound, but I can tell you it was bitter and unpleasant."

After Green resigned from the board, "Lorri Jean and Ed Gould were left with the problem. It was my pet project and I have to accept the consequences," admits Green. "But Morris Kight marched to his own drummer and he just stopped abiding by the agreement. And then it started. The misery began."

Ann Bradley: "It could've worked out great except that Lorri Jean had no relationship with Morris. She wasn't educated on who Morris Kight was. No one made a case for his value."

So despite all the doors that Kight had walked through, all the hands that he shook, and all the negotiating tables that he was invited to join, Lorri Jean, for reasons of her own, would not open her door to him. This prevented Kight from using his most potent tool: his one-on-one dynamic powers of persuasion.

Jean remembered first hearing about Morris Kight during her job interview when she originally toured the old Center on Highland Avenue. By the time she arrived at her first Board of Directors meeting, "they were already fighting with him" because Kight was not living in the "right house," as agreed upon. Jean wanted to stay out of it and recalls, "I was as green as I could be."

There was also the matter of the "Royal Morris," as he was sometimes referred to. Despite, or perhaps because of, his lessening majordomo role, he was all the more pushy with his Edwardian-inflected gay history lessons. Not waiting to be asked, he'd cite the broader context of gay history and always include his place in it. To those who cared, the behavior revealed a deep, personal streak of insecurity in the elderly gentleman. And to those who did not care for him, it supported their argument that Kight was a self-obsessed bore.

By the end of 1993, there was still no inventory of the contents of the Collection. And Morris still hadn't received a return call from anyone at the Center.

"There were all kinds of problems on Martel," Dallmeyer says, "problems with neighbors, with parking, the church next door, and the street people. It was a dark house on a dark street, whereas McCadden Place was light."

1994. Dubbed the "Supreme Court Photo," l to r: Robert Arthur, Ivy Bottini, Quentin Crisp, Morris Kight, Pat Warren. Photographer unknown. ONE National Gay & Lesbian Archives, USC Libraries, University of Southern California.

The Center never sent anyone to Martel to inspect the Collection. If they had, they would have viewed a horrid display with an undetermined historical value being stored in two leaky garages and throughout the small home, impossible to completely access, much less assess. Over four hundred posters and canvases were rolled up, innumerable framed fine art photographs and paintings were stacked and pieces of sculpture were all protected under tarps and sheets—not circumstances conducive to a proper display, storage, or cataloguing.

By late 1993, Kight admitted that he was reexamining the wisdom of his decision to leave McCadden Place and move into Martel. It was a rare look back and acknowledgement of a mistake. Yet, he was not ready to concede.

Torie Osborn: "It makes me sad. No one called me. Not that I had power to do anything."

It was Kight's habit to refrain from nasty verbal barbs. He kept his tone and manner gentlemanly, which could frustrate some people and confound his adversaries. He maintained a Gandhi-like pacifist stance with a quill pen dialect while he pushed his way to the center of attention. He tried to appear as if he was always one step above the fray and he was impervious to criticism.

The Center continued to ignore him, ignored his proposals and summarily accused him of being in breach of contract.

"It was crazy-making," Jackson remembers.

Ann Bradley: "Lorri Jean was treating this in a very business-like manner—that is her strength. She had a fiduciary responsibility and no history with him. She was appropriately looking at it, as well she should. The problem was lack of clarity."

The other problem was Ed Gould.

Initially supportive, Gould shifted his support as sentiments modified. Repeatedly described as a "troubled person," Gould used his seat on the board for status. AIDS fundraising created many A-list events and a position on the Center Board came with social status. Gould had wealth, but not the kind that could have bought his way into that sexy, flashy crowd. Loyalty to an old radical hippie like Morris Kight was unlikely.

Meanwhile the stress of living on Martel took a heavy toll on Kight's health. In September 1994, there were rumors that the Center was planning to relinquish its claim to the north house. They made sure the unverified news got to Morris.

For a few weeks, Kight tortured himself with worry about what the Center was about to do. Kight learned that a court hearing was set to transfer the Center's interest in the north house (the house he was living in) to the next beneficiary in line under the Linn Trust, the West Hollywood Presbyterian Church (owner of the adjacent property).

Once he recovered from the initial shock, Kight quickly snapped into action and organized his group of confidants. No one knew of his previous experience in real estate. They didn't expect an immediate sound and supportable argument of the Center's fiscal imprudence by relinquishing the property. Kight reasoned, based purely on fiscal responsibility, that the Center had an obligation to hold on to the property. It was a sound argument.

Kight then reached out to *his* community with a two-page missive that detailed the horrible situation. Pragmatic and unemotional, Kight outlined the history and multiple problems with the Center relinquishing the Martel properties. Intended for people who had known Kight for many years, written in standard third person, he boasted about his good works and the historical value of the McCadden Place Collection.

He mentioned his 1992 stroke as impacting his decision to gift the Collection to the Center. He made mention of the Center's $14 million annual budget and real estate holdings. "Morris was sentimental about the Center," he wrote about himself, "since he was a major founder and it was based on his hands-on, not-for-fee services in Los Angeles from 1957 to 1971."

All of it true.

It was a long, wordy missive with the bottom line that Kight was asking the community for help in having use of both houses. Without personal rancor, he presented his best argument why the original agreement with the Center should still be upheld. Kight asked everyone to take action. "Please be conciliatory" and "be polite."

From one of his allies, Kight found out that board member Ed Gould consistently referred to the Collection as "a bunch of dusty old posters." Out of everything that was happening, this hurt Kight's heart more than anything else. He wrote to a colleague that he was baffled and drained by "dealing with people who simply have not kept their word, and worse, those who seem to have no understanding or appreciation of the magic of the Collection."

As pre-internet social scandals go, Kight's community missive spread faster than a cyber-virus. Fax machines around the country were burning with Kight's letter. He had a healthy mailing list of over five hundred names and he sent it to everyone, including all Center board members. He left copies on bus benches, in office waiting rooms, and in retail stores. Responses were quick and filled with love and best wishes; the rally of support was impressive. There was outrage at the callous treatment of a community elder and questions about the handling of a nonprofit's assets. A steady stream of calls, letters, and faxes from across the country poured back to Kight and into Lorri Jean's office at the Center.

Kight recruited his old ally Alan Gross to help prepare for the Linn Trust hearing. He persisted with his positive attitude fully expecting to say a few words in court. As it turned out, Kight was not given an opportunity to speak or present any documents since he had no direct standing with the Trust. The court referred the matter to the state Attorney General, postponing a decision.

Gross convinced Kight that it was time to go public. Days after the hearing, all concerns were publicly aired in a *Los Angeles Independent* article: "Gay center, founder wrangle over property." Kight described the situation as being "reduced to trench warfare," comparing it to his battles in days of yore with "hawks and homophobes. I would rather not engage in trench warfare with my peers," he said.

For the first time publicly, Lorri Jean spoke about Morris Kight. "We have never once entertained the idea of putting Kight on the street." The front-page article was the first and only communication from Jean and the explanation that the Center offered Kight rent-free housing in the south property but that the plan to "create a museum and education center out of both houses have been scrapped.

"Originally, he had a grand vision," Jean was quoted, "to enhance the image of Morris Kight. Frankly, I'm not sure any of it could have ever come to fruition. But the truth is he couldn't raise any money and we couldn't raise much. There are a lot more critical life-and-death needs that take precedence."

Kight insisted, "It would be so easy for them to raise the money needed to sustain this place if they wanted to. I have accumulated a collection of vast historical and artistic interest. I wish I could convince them of that.... Somehow or another, I failed to infect them with the vision of what this place could be."

Jean claimed that the Center spent $36,000 on maintenance and mortgage. "We're just getting it off our books," she reasoned. "He is a pioneer of the movement. If we had a way to go along with him that wouldn't cost us so much money, we'd be happy to."

Jean used the media to present a customized, handmade picture of the situation. Kight was being beaten at his own game, in his own playing field, with his own toys.

The *Independent* article ended with Kight: "'Why do they want to make me miserable?' he says. 'Twenty years ago I had enormous drive and vigor, but now I've become old... There are more than 10,000 pieces on the property here. I don't know where I'd move all this. I'm terrified, just terrified.'"

The floor beneath him was falling away, a frightening prospect for any senior citizen. And the article touched a fresh nerve, forcing discussions about aging in the gay community, a largely disenfranchised population. For the first time, people talked about what if anything is owed to elders.

Eventually, the Gay and Lesbian Community Services Center and many other gay organizations would create strong support services, networks and communities aimed to address the needs of the elderly. It would not, however, happen soon enough to help Morris Kight.

In 1993, superficial values and a heightened emphasis on youth and beauty dominated. Troy Perry: "It could be said in many pockets of society that age is simply a state of mind; but not in the gay community. Stereotypically gay men view age as an atrocity. Morris was 50 years old when he marched down Hollywood Boulevard, and he was already experiencing the stings of ageism within the gay community."

If ageism was the elderly Kight's Achilles heel, the cultural fixation on perfect physicality was the poisoned arrow. Except for his brilliant white hair, Kight had long ago lost any vestiges of his good looks. His body did not age well, though it certainly withstood much demand for many years. In old age, Kight's peaches-and-cream complexion was bloated and blotched with skin moles and growths. His belly flapped over his belt, he was hunched and kept steady with a cane.

"People liked to laugh at him behind his back. They had no idea," Ivy Bottini adds. In the early 1990s there was a new generation of homosexuals who were never in the closet, they did not relate to the closet, and had no sense of history about what made closet doors open and stay open. He was often outright rejected by the same youth he worked tirelessly to liberate from the closet. It never deterred him one step.

By late 1994, the McCadden Place Group referred to themselves as a Task Force. The Task Force wanted to protect the Collection from the Center and from Kight himself. In his best interest, with his consent, they rented a truck, gathered some strong volunteers, and removed his most valued and valuable possession, the McCadden Place Collection, from the Martel properties to an undisclosed, secured, off-site storage facility so that even Kight himself didn't know where it was, "or he'd have done something foolish, like give more pieces to the Center," Jackson recalled.

Having helped so many who were on the fringe, Kight was sometimes mistaken as being part of the fringe himself. On first impressions, he was consistently perceived as an eccentric and extremely smart character. This eccentricity may have become a handicap in his old age. People close to him feared that Kight was in serious danger of becoming "one of them"—one of the street characters who roamed Hollywood and hung out in the public library to read the newspaper, the same kind of individuals that he had counseled away from suicide and depression.

An anonymous witness tells of sitting in his air-conditioned automobile on a hot, dry day and watched Kight exit a city bus, saying he looked as if "it was all over. It was a terrible look of despair. He looked like he was extremely depressed."

In early October, California Attorney General Bill Lockyer approved the transfer of property to the West Hollywood Presbyterian Church.

A lot of things happened very fast and the exact order of events is recalibrated with each telling. At some point Kight received notice from the Center that they relinquished the property and voided their January 1993 agreement. Soon after, Kight received a notice from the Church that he needed to move "in the next couple of months." They also informed him that as of January 1, 1995, his rent was "$1400 per month, payable on the first of each month."

As usual, first order of business was fundraising. Pat Lenhof allowed Kight to use the Mission's tax-exempt status. The Martel Task Force formed a new ad hoc group and by sundown they called themselves 'Friends of Morris Kight.' Now a legitimate nonprofit entity with all donations tax-deductible, the group had two co-chairs, Miki Jackson and Bob Dallmeyer, 26 advisors, including two PhDs and two JDs. Kight made his way to Charlie Chan printers and ordered a couple dozen boxes of new letterhead for Friends of Morris Kight, with the same post office box number that was used for at least a half-dozen of his other 'causes.' At 75 years old, Kight's newest call to activism was, in effect, himself.

By late October 1994, Friends of Morris Kight introduced itself to the world with a page-and-a-half "Call to the Community."

"As you have no doubt read in the press or heard by the grapevine, Morris Kight—one of the founders of the gay and lesbian civil rights movement and the Los Angeles Gay and Lesbian Community Services Center, a fellow warrior in almost every social justice battle in the last fifty years, and a valued friend and counselor—is facing difficult times."

Mostly dictated by Kight, in the third-person voice and signed by co-chairpersons Jackson and Dallmeyer, he pled to his community for help, for care. "He will soon be vacating his residence. He is searching for a small place to live." He suggested monetary birthday gifts for Kight's upcoming 75th birthday and requested a commitment of a 12-month pledge of financial support: "You will have the opportunity to renew your pledge at each future birthday celebration."

Some read the letter and saw a new desperation from an old coot, yet most heard an old warrior's roar for help. The immediate situation, however, would not be solved by sitting back and waiting for the checks to roll in. There was, in Kight's own words, "much to be done."

In December, Kight wrote a letter to Reverend Dan Smith.

In his best Edwardian-speak, he began "Dear Gentle People," and continued with detailed responses and requests: Kight asked to negotiate the rental sum. He mentioned the garden maintenance and the enormous amount of work already done on the house.

"We maintain the property in all matter[s] that are within our competence to take care of.

"One last thing: I am working very hard on various issues from this address and find this place very compatible with my work. I love this house and find it very efficient for my commitments."

He closed: "In concern, Morris Kight."

During the December seasonal holidays, Kight and a few friends were able to sit down and have a more casual chat with several of the amicable board members of the Center. Jean did not socialize in this way and was not present. This was officially an "unofficial" discussion. The board members explained that they were surrendering the property to get rid of mortgage payments and insurance and the responsibility of caring for Kight, should he become incapacitated. The Center didn't want to take that on and insisted they could not risk that others would soon expect the same treatment. Kight, in his most patrician tone, responded "Madam, have you ever heard of actuarial tables? Here, let me show you," and handed over the most recent data for his life expectancy, taking into account his many health ailments and family history. The board members did not understand what he was talking about.

"Basically, he was saying, 'how long do you really think I'm going to be a problem?' It was so Morris," Ann Bradley recalls.

A week later, the Center softened their position and agreed to give Kight $5,000 in relocation funds, return whatever art pieces they had in their possession, and relinquish all rights to the Collection (now officially titled "The Morris Kight Collection"). In the eyes and hearts of the board members, Morris Kight was now the West Hollywood Presbyterian Church's problem. As Jean said, the Center "never once entertained the thought of putting Kight out on the street."

In March 1995, Mary Newcombe, the attorney representing the Center in this matter and another old Kight ally, wrote to Alan Gross that Kight's continued tenancy in the north house cost the Center "$3,658 to the Church for utilities and upkeep of the property since September." The Center wanted to deduct that money from the original $5,000 relocation funds promised to Kight.

"I assure you that we are anxious to forward Morris whatever money is left from the $5,000."

Weeks of quiet, justifiable outrage followed.

And then a $25 check came from a 72-year-old lesbian who lived in Arizona.

"It is painful to feel that our lesbian and gay community is willing to 'honor' us as role models from time to time, but not yet willing to confront ageism in its own ranks. For it is ageism in our nation which is responsible for the fact that a 'national treasure' like Morris comes to the end of his life with so few financial resources. Best wishes for this birthday and many, many more to come. Morris, you are a true warrior. We all salute you!"

A note like that, from a stranger, could buoy Kight for days.

Still, with all that was going on, Kight needed more legal help than one pro bono attorney could provide. Bottini recruited her partner Marge Rushford to deal with the return of the art pieces and the full payment of the relocation fee; meanwhile Alan Gross would deal with the eviction by the church.

At one particular casual meeting with board members, which Kight purposely did not attend, Jackson remembers asking point-blank why the Center was doing all this to Kight. "Ed Gould articulated his strategy. He said, 'Morris Kight is a doddering old man with no money and a contract is only as good as your ability to enforce it. He can sue us for anything he wants, any stipulations. We are a 40-million-dollar corporation with Century City attorneys [in addition to their downtown law firm], and he's going to die before he can enforce it.'"

When asked in 2012 about what Ed Gould had said, Lorri Jean responded, "That's really weird because we were not a 40-million-dollar organization, we were an eight-million-dollar organization at that time. There is something odd there. It doesn't sound like Ed, to me. I never heard, in the board discussions, disrespect to Morris Kight in any way. I heard exasperation about what we could do because it was illegal."

In 1995 things came to a head when Kight's doctors wouldn't allow him to have minor cataract surgery because he was too anemic. Jackson recalls: "They gave him some blood transfusions and sent him home with strict doctor's orders to do whatever he had to do to get out of his present situation.

"That did it," Jackson continued. "Ed Gould was right. Morris would be dead before we could get him out of there and the Center would end up owning the Collection."

The Friends of Morris Kight banded together. There was no time to patronize the old man so they gave him an ultimatum: give up the battles with the Center and the Church, or they would not help him. He didn't argue or question their loyalty. In a moment of humility, he agreed to accept their guidance.

Jackson immediately coordinated a series of yard sales and donations to Out of the Closet thrift stores. John Ferry took on the task of finding Kight a new apartment within his price range that could accommodate his declining physical condition.

Almost overnight, Kight began to stumble and falter. His razor-sharp mind, the only real tool left in his bag of tricks, was dulling. In mid-sentence, he would stop talking and freeze for a moment, mentally drift away, and maybe 30 seconds later he'd snap back to attention and pick up where he left off in mid-sentence. Sometimes he'd excuse himself by saying, "Now, where were we?"

"He was having mini-strokes," Jackson remembers. The neurologists at Cedars Sinai Hospital explained that Kight had a "general neurological disorder," as well as peripheral neuropathy and edema. This could go on for years, but stress exacerbated the condition and the strokes could eventually have a permanent effect on his mental capacity. The doctor's strongest recommendations included a drastic reduction in stress.

Despite it all, Kight never had an emotional crack. He had a rare cry on the phone to a few close friends and verbally expressed his sadness that the situation could not work, but there were no overindulged moments of self-pity. He kept whatever disappointment he may have had private. Friends of Morris Kight knew that before he left McCadden Place, Kight's health was fine, he was strong and capable and independent. After living on Martel, he truly did need assistance.

In mid-April, Kight 'crafted' another two-page letter from Miki Jackson and Bob Dallmeyer to Lorri Jean at the Center.

"A Crisis Exists," the letter begins, "indeed, a panic: We took the offer of $5000 seriously and have factored it into every plan we have made. Therefore, this is a firm request that the Center issue a check, forthright, for $5000 that we might follow some kind of orderly schedule for removal."

A copy of the letter addressed to the Center was sent to the West Hollywood Presbyterian Church. The copy that was sent to the Church was accompanied by a letter, on Kight's behalf, to Reverend Dan Smith and David Buller at the Church. It was much shorter, quick and to the point: "The Crisis Situation" detailed the $1400 per month rent that was paid for January, February, and March…. "We are eager to move from 1447, but our funds flow is only sufficient to maintain day-to-day output for expenditures, and thus we have appealed to the Center for what we believed to be a commitment."

The Church responded by serving Kight a stream of eviction notices. Attorneys for the West Hollywood Presbyterian Church filed so many orders against Kight in such a short period of time that a clerk at Los Angeles City Hall flagged a ploy and refused to accept any more motions from the same plaintiff naming the same defendant. It was litigious harassment.

Kight fired back with his own five-and-a-half typed pages to the court. "Physically challenged" became his new buzz phrase, and rightly so (though he often used his cane more as a talking stick than a walking aid). Kight also made sure his answer contained a one-page declaration from Dallmeyer and Jackson (of course, penned by Kight himself) regarding his fragile health: "It is our opinion that the strokes are as a result of the tension caused by his struggle to get out of Martel Avenue and the actions taken by his landlord in these matters."

And the Center, through its attorney, Mary Newcombe, steadfastly refused to release the relocation funds or return the borrowed art. A June 16th letter from Mary Newcombe said: "It appears that Morris may be mistaken as to the quantity of materials held by the Center … Morris will not need a truck to gather the few pieces still held by the Center…. In addition, please remind Morris that he has been using one of the Center's conference tables in [the north house], and that the Center will arrange for its pickup with the Church."

Like adult children caring for an aging parent, Friends of Morris Kight made some decisions, put down some new ground rules and faced the inevitable. Morris had to move quickly. Levelheaded, good-hearted people reached into their wallets, gave of their time and resources, to buoy a leader of their own liberation.

Kight had to forget about whatever pieces of the Collection the Center was holding. Eventually, he was able to retrieve his items from the south house and it would be weeks after he moved that the Center sent him any portion of the five thousand dollars.

John Ferry found a one-bedroom apartment that had been upgraded for handicapped access in the foothills of Beachwood Canyon, looking at the world-famous Hollywood sign. Kight took one look at the 550-square-foot apartment on the ground floor of a 1960s multi-unit apartment building and quickly said, "Let's take it." It had everything he needed, most importantly close access to public transportation. Kight would make the most of the minimal space.

In the end, he reasoned aloud, this was just one more sacrifice for the struggle for equal rights for all gay persons, as exiting the Martel living situation would "extend his life by a few years."

The move into the new apartment was fast and easy with one vanload—mostly boxes filled with his yellow notepads of scribbling and a few personal belongings. With a desk and a chair from Aunt Bee's Thrift Store, the help of a few handy volunteers, Kight squeezed himself into his final location: 1956 Beachwood Drive.

There was no large workspace or room to roam around or entertain in, and not much room for art. He tried in vain to find space for the Philip Hitchcock bronze mask of himself. Spatially and stylistically it didn't fit. With a wave of his hand, he quickly and unsentimentally dismissed it to the storage facility with the rest of the Collection.

Around this same time, at least two professional copies of the "Fagots Stay Out" sign were made. The original stayed in storage, one copy was for public viewing, and one hung over a small sofa that closely faced a large television in the new apartment. Once his desk and chair were moved in, Kight plopped himself down and immediately got to work, making phone calls and notes on the yellow pads.

What was left of three thousand pieces of the Morris Kight Collection was sorted and properly stored in two units at a public storage facility. Kight knew where everything was with easy access to key pieces for public showings. Over time, from the comfort of his Beachwood residence, he did complete a catalogue and a narrative of the Collection.

He showed confusion and hurt to a few friends about the betrayal and the pressure of having to move again. But after the move, Kight never expressed a grudge or any regrets and he rarely discussed it.

Ann Bradley comments, "Is it 'taking advantage' for him to think, 'I gave a lot to this community and I'd like to be comfortable in my twilight years?' When that happened [to Morris] is when they started talking about the need for elder care within the community."

In June 1996 the Center invited Kight to participate in a grand gala media event to commemorate the 25th anniversary of the Los Angeles Gay and Lesbian Community Services Center. They planned a year-long celebration with a time capsule that would be opened 25 years later at the 50th anniversary.

In the same invitation letter, they announced they would unveil a new name and logo for the organization. This immediately concerned Kight: "What are they doing to the name?"

The new name would be the Los Angeles Gay and Lesbian Center.

His first call was to Don Kilhefner; they shared an outrage.

The two principal founders joined forces and strategized to protest the loss of the words "Community" and "Services."

An open memo from Kight and Kilhefner to the gay and lesbian community, addressed "Dear Brothers and Sisters," arrived on everyone's fax machines and in mailboxes.

1984. Morris sitting inside his home on McCadden Place, Hollywood.
Photo by Don Saban.

With deliberately selected words they carefully expounded on the importance of the two words in relationship to what the center provides for homosexuals and the creation of a community.

In 1971, they wrote, "there was no gay and lesbian community. Today there is a real and growing community where 25 years ago there was none....

"Likewise, 'Services' implied that as the projected new community would emerge, there would be a critical need for attending to the myriad needs of that emerging community."

The founders expressed disapproval over the Center's process in deciding on the name change. Two national, heterosexually identified PR firms conducted a marketing research study "as if it were getting ready to sell a new brand of breakfast cereal."

"We owe it to those who have gone before us to honor their labor of love and their fierce determination to build for future generations of gay and lesbian people."

It closed, "In gay struggle and spirit."

Kight sent this to his entire list of media outlets. Not one picked it up.

On the day of the grand event, June 19, 1996, Kight and Kilhefner coordinated a small band of supporters outside the Schrader Avenue offices at eleven o'clock in the morning, before the scheduled noon event. They set up a card table on the sidewalk directly outside the entrance with hundreds of copies of Kight's and Kilhefner's Open Letter to the Community.

The invitations instructed event guests to check in at the lobby desk where Executive Director Lorri Jean would greet them. Perhaps the handful of protesters upset the planned check-in procedures because no one from the Center was available to greet the invitees. Celebrities and politicians wandered around the lobby, lost. Peaceful protesters seized the opportunity, stepped in and took control at the front door. They greeted guests and directed them inside to the staging area, while everyone got a copy of the Open Letter.

After all the guests had arrived, Kight and Kilhefner went into the event, as invited guests. Their assigned seats had been moved far in the back of the room—where they were ignored and never called to the dais to speak.

Jean thought it "very unfortunate" that they decided to picket the event.

There was never any formal communication between the two sides, only an unofficial letter from board member Ed Gould.

Gould wrote on his personal stationery that he was "personally affronted by your letter and its implications. The entire tone suggests that you have lost touch with the community which you allegedly represent. And you certainly have lost touch with the Center."

Gould's venom and disapproval were unquestionable. It was personal.

"You do not have any idea of the process involved and to state that we approach this work 'as if it were getting ready to sell some brand of cereal' is wrong and suggests you have no idea of process but simply want to inflame a community. And, you have no idea what community input was done. Because you were not asked, does not mean the community was not represented.

"Lastly, I personally take great umbrage at the suggestion that we have 'disrespect for our roots.' Nothing could be further from the truth. The only disrespect shown is yours. Your comment that we are 'destroying a part of gay history' is irrational and wrong."

Kight and Kilhefner responded to Gould individually. Kight's written response was historical, analytical, uncompromising, and deliberately ignored Gould's personal attacks.

For the Center, this was nothing but a public relations snag.

After a few weeks there was a single official response from the Center posted on the Center's brand new website: "Though we have engaged in lengthy conversations with [the founders] regarding the reasons for the change, they have chosen to invest considerable time and effort to attack us."

The new name became permanent and people adjusted.

One year later, Kight still called the Center regularly, with carefully chosen words to request a meeting with the Executive Director to "discuss a number of matters."

Jean's only message back to Kight was always the same: "There is no time available for a meeting."

Finally, in June 1997, Kight and Kilhefner met with the board of the Center. They mostly listened; Jean said nothing at all.

Personality and ideological differences continued and Kight remained estranged from the board of the Center.

Lorri Jean maintains that she and Kight were on good terms. Kight was popping into the new Center offices, without appointment. When Lorri Jean's schedule allowed, she said that she'd spend a few minutes with him. She ran into him at various events because he was, as Jean says, "out and about a lot." She never felt that he was mad at her personally.

According to Jean, eventually Kight told her that he forgave her for the name change because he saw that the Center was still dedicated to community and services.

EPILOGUE

IN NOVEMBER 1996, ALMOST EXACTLY A YEAR AFTER ED GOULD was appointed to President Clinton's Presidential Advisory Council on HIV/AIDS, he was identified as the anonymous man found face down, naked, on a cot in a rented cubicle at a gay bathhouse called Club Palm Springs.

Weeks later, toxicology reports came back and the Coachella Valley's *Desert Sun* reported on page one that the County Coroner had determined that 53-year-old Ed Gould died of "cardiac arrhythmia due to acute chloromethane intoxication." The paper reported that Gould had inhaled 'Hard Drive,' an aerosol spray labeled as a cleaner of electronic devices that had an off-label use as a sexual stimulant, mostly found in gay bathhouses.

Kight never publicly commented on Gould's death; there was no point. They were far out of each other's social orbits. He did once elbow a close friend and mention the *Desert Sun* article and shook his head, clicked his tongue and made a remark about the tragedy of another drug casualty in the gay community.

In 1999, the Los Angeles Gay and Lesbian Center hosted Kight's 80th birthday celebration at their new seven-million-dollar facility, "The Village at Ed Gould Plaza," posthumously named for its generous benefactor. The facility, located at 1125 North McCadden Place in Hollywood, was a few yards down the road from where Morris Kight convened the first gay pride parade and only a few blocks from where he once played host to the movers and shakers, political luminaries and celebrities who helped to shape, facilitate, and fund the early days of gay liberation. Kight didn't look back.

This event and three more birthday celebrations Morris would have were all fundraisers for the Morris Kight Collection.

The problems at the Center had knocked the stuffing out of him, and the two moves knocked out all the superfluous material. He no longer needed a large kitchen for entertaining or space for a house guest. He began a new campaign to bring awareness to the very real needs of aging gays. There were no services for or even much regard paid to elders in gay communities. It has changed some over the past decade.

During the next few years, Kight slowly went from being the spokesperson for elder care to being the poster child.

Chapter 14

The Venerable

AS ONE GENERATION of activists and leaders prematurely died, new unprepared leaders quickly rose to prominence. The rooms became bigger, full of unfamiliar faces, and *egos*. Kight's unfamiliarity with the new group may be one reason why his ego overcompensated for their lack of knowledge of his accomplishments.

Steve Lachs: "For him, it must've been a mixed feeling. It's a blessing to see all these organizations and people flowering and blooming—that's what you worked for—at the same time you're not necessarily the person they're coming to anymore ... I don't know if he felt in the end that he was honored as he should've been."

Kight was an easy target for opponents. He was bored by personalities that wanted to compete with him, much preferring to be complimented or, best yet, emulated. He didn't argue, he didn't respond to insults. Which sometimes raised the ire.

Steve Lachs: "Morris' ego wasn't the elephant in the room, it *was* the room ... Look at the cast of the time ... It would be hard to be humble around Troy and Sheldon, Harry Hay, and all the others—the movers and shakers. They all had ego that it was probably necessary for them to put themselves in the spotlight at a time when people were getting killed for being gay."

Though some considered Kight's ways 'old-timey,' they still served him well. He was known to remember everyone's name, and was a stickler for formalities and manners. Writer Perry Brass: "What impressed me were his simple, decent manners—he thanked everyone who had been nice to him by name."

In 1983, Kight was pointedly asked by an interviewer for the *Advocate* about criticism that his leadership approach was old-fashioned. He bristled: "I totally disagree. What has this 'new' brand of politics gotten us? Just tokenism. The current political methods simply aren't bringing results."

Kight exampled the Los Angeles Board of Supervisors restricting CETA funds (discretionary government grants) to 'intact families.' All alone, he went to protest, worried the new restrictions would negatively impact lesbians, especially those of color.

Kight: "Now I realize that that was a kind of quixotic romantic thing to do. But goddamn it, it was just me there! The supervisors can be conned by the assimilationists in our community—the enemies of gay liberation." He was aware of how some people reacted to his physical appearance—overweight and disheveled. "They'll say to the supervisors, 'Wasn't it embarrassing seeing him shuffle in here doing his same old shtick? Ten years ago he was doing it, but we don't do that now. We're *sophisticated*.' And meanwhile, the lesbians without CETA money are left to wander around without any support. If people say that's old-fashioned, let them. I think the *new* fashion should be for us to defend all sectors of our community."

Troy Perry: "Times change. As new professional groups started up here in the city ... Morris didn't fit in."

However, the people who wanted to scratch him off the list for being 'too old' to make a difference were making an unwise bet: he never stopped being committed to activism, never ceased to believe in the inevitable equal rights under the law for all genders, for all sexual identities. And in his final years, he found himself focusing on a new unaddressed need within his community and beyond: ageism.

OLD/OLDER/AGED/AGING/SENIORS

KIGHT'S LAST CAUSE WAS, AS IT TURNED OUT, FAR MORE FORE-shadowing than anyone would want to admit. As older and wizened voices in the world are silenced, the worst parts of history are at risk of being repeated. Communities may find themselves reinventing the wheel as they shut down their less attractive and more experienced forces.

This was not a new rallying cry from Kight. In a 1977 article for *NewsWest*, Kight, a spry 57-year-old, sounded the alarm at this impending threat to civil liberties, personal dignity, and individual freedoms: "Do you know where gay people begin to be objects of prejudice among their own people? A subculture within a culture that emphasizes physical youth and beauty, 30 is over the hill." In gay communities, loss of physical prowess is often considered one's expiration date, a pitiful statement on a society that does not treasure and respect their old. Kight: "With all the goodness of gay liberation, the situation for older lesbian women and gay men has only worsened."

The genuine needs among elder gays and lesbians led Kight and Kilhefner to put forth a service proposal in 1977 to fund a pioneer outreach program for older gays to the Gay Community Services Center. They presented the situation as critical.

Then AIDS happened and funding priorities quickly shifted. Needs of aging gays were still apparent, they just went unaddressed on a community level.

Kight later spoke to a group at the Penguin Place Committee for Older Gays and Lesbians in Philadelphia: "In the thousands of years that people have been on the earth, there have been old people. And they were honored people. We, however, didn't have old people in our community because we were killed off early. We drank ourselves to death, or we died of drugs, or somebody murdered us. Or we were unidentified. We lived lives of quiet desperation. Until this generation ... Still, an older lesbian or gay person may face challenges somewhat different from that of a non-gay older person, who may have a traditional family to help ease the way into elderly status. Some things are important, no matter what a person's sexual preference.... It's too easy to focus on the *problems* of getting old, instead of the *possibilities*."

In 1991, Kight rolled up his sleeves and had new letterhead printed (as was his pattern when he was starting something new): "OLD/OLDER/SENIOR LESBIAN/ GAY ADVOCATES." He gathered a group of like minds (Al Best, Ivy Bottini, Chuck Bowdlear, Dorr Legg, Sandra Teignor) and set about championing for older gays. In October of that year, The Senior Advocates came together to outline their purpose, agenda, and a call for dialogue with "our young/younger Sisters/Brothers to bring about urgent changes in our interrelationship."

The next year Kight presented a position paper to the CREATING CHANGES/ WEST second annual conference in Los Angeles. "After twenty-three years of a world-wide, massive non-violent movement for Lesbian/Gay rights, we are changed people. Millions and Millions of us are 'out,' and the number increases. Among all these committed people are millions of Old/Older/Senior Lesbian/Gay people. We are an asset, a resource, role models, and are capable of mentoring our young/ younger sisters/brothers."

Kight proposed creating an ongoing workshop for elders to air concerns and needs, find support and camaraderie, and "to commence a change in our dealings with one another." He suggested that "an old woman, an old man, and a woman and man of youth be invited to be keynote speakers," in order to create a new lesbian/ gay family. The proposal was unanimously passed, but the group was short-lived. Perhaps due to inconsistent and dwindling membership, the idea faded away.

In 1993, Kight was invited to contribute to the publication of *LAMBDA Gray, A Practical, Emotional and Spiritual Guide for Gays and Lesbians Who Are Growing Older*.

Kight's essay hit on all the predicative marks: the history, hostility, criminality, intimidation, social ostracization, family alienation, etc. Once again, Kight explained 'oppression sickness' and how it has failed liberated gays stuck with low self-esteem from years of living in the closet "where we learned to deceive all those we dealt with by pretending to be something we simply were not: heterosexual."

And then the rebellion: "...demonstrations, lawsuits, civil disobedience, conferences, teach-ins, and service-delivering organization, the creation of a movement and of a community. We have lobbied the federal, state, and city governments to include us in civil liberties, civil rights, and administrative services. There have been massive reforms in the law to decriminalize our behavior, and to include us in protective procedures....

"Capitalism and socialism have done a near total turnaround in their attitudes toward us. Capitalism has found that dollar bills have no sexual orientation and is increasingly fighting for those bills."

The reviews of Kight's essay were very positive. "Morris Kight is a living legend in the gay world," a *Chiron Rising* review begins. "We all owe him a debt. Few gays under 30 realize that the right to gay normalcy they take for granted today, they owe largely to this man. Mr. Kight's essay is a staggering overwhelming recitation of gay/lesbian accomplishments." Accomplishments that didn't seem to benefit older homosexuals.

In a 1997 interview for *Gay Today* with Jack Nichols, shortly after his 79th birthday, Kight said, "I enjoy being an elder of our tribe. That is something for us. A new class of wise out women/men who are a witness for our past of horror and veterans of our new life. There are a mere handful left of the pre-liberation gays/lesbians prior to 1969.

"We are a changed people. No longer hating ourselves. We are light years ahead [since Stonewall]. But we have miles to go before we sleep."

Kight continued to enlist help from legal professionals for issues facing older gays. He recruited help from housing communities, rehabilitation centers, the medical community. He continued to raise awareness to the marginalization of older gays and lesbians.

It wasn't until 2005, two years after Kight died, that ground broke in Hollywood for a gay senior housing complex. Spearheaded by the nonprofit group Gay and Lesbian Elder Housing Corporation, it was one of the nation's first affordable housing complexes for gay seniors and it began construction two days after Los Angeles City Council unanimously voted to support a new California state measure that would grant marriage rights to same-sex couples.

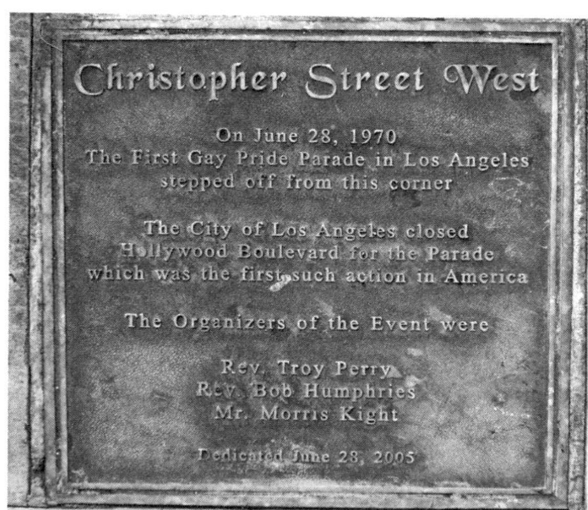

A plaque embedded into the sidewalk on McCadden Place at Hollywood Blvd. to commemorate the first gay pride parade, 1970, which began on that corner.

An executive with the development corporation said that the housing complex was inspired by "a need to protect the lives of those who have fought for the rights of gays and lesbians since the 1960s and 1970s."

VENERABLE

IVY BOTTINI: "EVERYBODY SEES MORRIS AS THIS EGOMANIAC. I don't. Maybe in the beginning, but that's not how I see Morris. Morris, to me, had low self-esteem. His ego was so fragile that he had—he was compelled to do, to get more and more and more to satisfy what could never be satisfied. I honestly believe, internally, he was a little boy at his mother's dress going, 'Mommy, Mommy!' But, having said that, he did amazing things.

"Morris, to me, was the ultimate loner."

Jeanne Cordova: "Morris was a very charming guy. I needed a dad, that was probably the reason that I took to him. Told him as much that he was my political godfather. He half-bowed and smiled, it pleased him. He wanted to be seen in that light. He had a number of acolytes. Sometimes I thought that Morris Kight went around picking talented people to groom.

"A lot of lesbians didn't like my close relationship with Morris. Some people [in the lesbian movement] were opposed to it. They were more separatists."

Miki Jackson remembers that for years, "Morris received Father's Day cards saying, in essence, 'You're the father I can talk to about sex.'"

Kight became "a father figure in not only the gay community but in the human relations community," said Los Angeles County Supervisor Zev Yaroslavsky in a featured profile on Kight for the *Los Angeles Times* in 1999. "Morris comes from an era where to be openly gay, you were putting your physical safety on the line," Yaroslavsky reminded the readers. "People today forget that. When the history of civil liberties is written, he'll be on the list."

In his last years, Morris Kight spent a lot of time doing what he always had done. He made 6 a.m. phone calls and typed long missives, went to meetings and events, and he sat on the sofa in his small apartment playing the television too loud. Late at night, his upstairs neighbor reported, he played the televangelists preaching and belching in the background as he made notes on his yellow pads or he pecked at the keys of his old Smith-Corona typewriter. He often fell asleep on the sofa to the televangelists howling. He continued to enjoy his evening rye and soda. "He was quite Spartan," is how Bob Dallmeyer recalled, "he didn't need a lot, he wasn't high-maintenance."

Kight never aged out of ego-neediness, attention-seeking, awards-whoring, and nonstop self-promotion. Passionately focused on his legacy to the point of obsession, he remained vigilant with the media and his press releases, trying to preserve his place in history.

It could be argued that Kight's personal "oppression sickness" manifested through his vast ego needs. His appetite for attention and appreciation on a grand scale was ravenous. Kight wasn't over-sexed or over-boozed, he was prone to overexposure.

He had the idea that he should be nominated for the Nobel Peace Prize and commenced to ask everyone he knew who carried any little bit of clout to write a letter to the nominating committee on his behalf. He was happy to provide a sample letter and the address in Oslo, Norway.

Gino Vezina recalled, "Morris was delusioned [sic] that he could do some groundwork to get that Nobel Peace Prize. When Mother Teresa got it, he called me and referred to her as 'that rat,' for winning the Nobel instead of him."

After numerous unsuccessful campaigns, his old friends at MCC church honored Kight with the title "Venerable." It was a quick ceremony after Sunday service, a genuine and sweet overture from Reverend Troy Perry. The salutation was deserved as much as it was needed. Kight took the salutation and ran with it. He tucked it under his arm and wobbled away leaning on his walker.

Troy continued: "He was like a favorite uncle. I would invite him to come in and speak at MCC. He got me one time, I always laugh. He was helping to support the baby doctor, Doctor Benjamin Spock (from the antiwar movement)." Kight asked Troy Perry if Doctor Spock would address the congregation, to "bring greetings" to everybody. "Greetings to me meant two to three minutes. Spock gets to the church, and Morris told him to take your time. The man spoke, he had the first real crowd he had evidently in quite some time, we had a thousand people. He had a captive audience. Finally, after 35 minutes, I got up and said 'I am so sorry, but we have a service. We are in the middle of our worship. You're going to have to wind this down.' So he took another five minutes to wind it down. I went on with the service with a quickie little three-minute sermon. So I told Morris that I didn't appreciate that—I was going to introduce him and let him speak for three minutes. That's as much as I let any politician speak. 'Oh well, Brother Troy, he doesn't get a lot of speaking.' He was so cute. But having said that, he genuinely loved MCC."

And the awards and recognitions did not stop. He wouldn't allow that to happen.

In 1982, Kight was the recipient of the ACLU Eason Monroe Courageous Advocate Award; in 1992 Southern California Americans for Democratic Action honored him with the Eleanor Roosevelt Humanitarian Award; in 1995 the Valley Business Alliance named him Man of the Year; in 1997, for his 79th birthday, the City of West Hollywood presented him with a Lifetime Achievement Award on the unanimous recommendation of the Gay and Lesbian Advisory Council; in 1999, the City of West Hollywood named a pocket park on the corner of Santa Monica Boulevard and Crescent Heights Boulevard the Matthew Shepard Human Rights Triangle. The dedication ceremony in April 1999 included the dedication of a Chinese magnolia tree to Morris Kight with a bronze plaque that read:

> "The Venerable Morris Kight
> In Recognition of your tireless, peaceful
> efforts to liberate gay, lesbian, bisexual
> and transgender people and others from
> economic and societal oppression.
> Thank you Morris for your courage, your
> leadership, your insights, and most of all
> your kindness even as you forcefully stand
> up against discrimination on behalf of those
> still to [sic] frightened to speak for themselves.
> You are our hero."

Kight liked to visit the magnolia tree. He'd go to the florist across the street and get water and perhaps a new plant to leave near the magnolia. Sometimes he planted new seeds. He arranged to meet people there before going to lunch or he'd talk to strangers while sitting on one of the three benches. He encouraged everyone to continue to take care of the small triangle of a park.

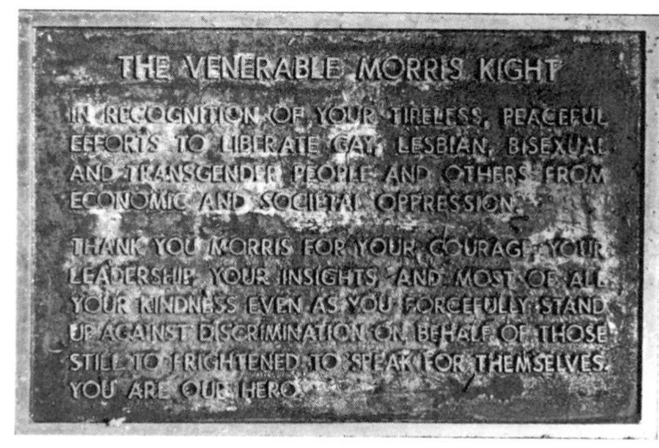

STONEWALL 25

"STONEWALL 25, I'M REALLY PROUD OF THAT," KIGHT EXPLAINED to Nicholas Snow. "I went to Fort Lauderdale in 1985 with a six-page proposal to suggest that in the 25th anniversary of the Stonewall uprising. And that was adopted and we worked on that for nine years."

In 1991, Kight and a group of delegates from around the world met in New York to plan and coordinate the 25th anniversary of the Stonewall Rebellion in 1994.

New York was also the chosen site for Unity '94, the 1994 Gay Games and cultural festival which would overlap with the Stonewall 25. It promised to be a no-stops celebration with a parade, book fair, exhibits of art and archival materials, community theater productions, history project, and much more. And, of course, Kight used the occasion to bring awareness to the plight of old/older gays and lesbians.

Kight: "Let us treat this event as the first day of our newly found international association, the first day of our forever," Kight said in his speech at the Stonewall 25 Rally in New York City on June 26, 1994. "This worldwide and joyous event, again a 'first,' calls upon us to recall the 25 years since the Stonewall Rebellion. We have created a massive nonviolent revolution and good for us. Never again will concerned lesbian/gays hide.

"Never again will we allow ourselves to be treated as inferior.

"Never again will we be the subject of malpractice and abuse.

"Never again will we allow the church to make judgements against us.

"Never again will we allow genocide.

"Never again will we allow ignorance to sap our strength.

"Now go into the world and take the message. We are a force to be dealt with. We are on the move. We have something outstanding to contribute to society and WE ARE EVERYWHERE!"

"Isn't it a joyful feeling to be a member of a 'First' Generation!"

The Venerable Morris Kight marker from the City of West Hollywood, located on the Matthew Shepard Triangle Memorial on Santa Monica Blvd. and Crescent Heights.

Speaking on *The Nicholas Snow Show* in 1997, Kight said: "And so on the 25th anniversary of the uprising, we marched the streets of New York and I floated above the street. My feet never touched the street. I felt that I was walking on sacred ground. That people had been there and had said something and had done something that had significantly changed the course of our lives. I'm really proud of that credential. It's a good credential."

In 2000, at the Millennium March on Washington for Equality, Kight addressed a crowd of over 300,000 gay people and supporters of gay people, from the podium. With his arms waving in the air like a victorious prizefighter: "I'm the happiest old man in the world." He meant every word.

Being "a first" became very important to Kight. He never tired of repeating his credentials and accomplishments. If people weren't irritated by Kight's constant reminders of his great part in a grand history, they were alienated by his exaggerated claims of involvement. He sometimes devalued legitimate points of pride on his activist résumé. For instance, there was never a mention of the celebration of Stonewall 25 without also knowing that Morris Kight 'founded' that celebration.

Tony Sullivan remembers, "I kept saying, 'Morris, you don't have to take credit for everything.' This tells you how close our relationship was because I said, 'Morris, you don't have to take credit for that other stuff. What you have done in itself is great!'"

Troy Perry recalled: "It was only when Morris got older that he would claim to do things that I and others didn't remember him doing. I always thought it had to do with age. He did so much, he never had to take credit for those [other] things ... But it came across as if he needed it, he was very hungry in his later life."

Gino Vezina: "He did care what other people thought, because of ego gains. He had enemies and he catered to that. Morris didn't have any other way to be fabulous. He would call and say, 'Is anybody saying bad things about me? Who said it and when did they say it?' And he kept repeating it.

"He said to me, 'So-and-so calls me up every day to see if I passed away. I want you to call that person every day to see if they have passed away.'

"I wouldn't do it. I'm not calling anyone to see if they've passed away."

Tony Sullivan: "I think he was a lonely old man before the end."

In the last few years, Kight's health took precedence over his activism. The invitations slowed down a little, but he didn't stop extending himself and his many kindnesses on a personal level. For all his foibles and flaws, and there were many, a consistent motivator for Kight was kindness. Even at its worst, he believed in the best of humanity. He understood the scared runaways with veneers of toughness as much as he cared for the young men wasting away from an inexplicable illness. An outsider's view might say that Kight was a bit broken in his final years. Kight was always a bit broken, skewed, off-center, odd.

When he was no longer able to host his annual solstice celebration in December, Kight began hosting a Christmas Day dinner at the Yukon Mining Company Restaurant in West Hollywood. Amid the frequent clientele of trans and gay men, Kight would reserve a large table in the center of the main dining room and be surrounded by his invited guests. He liked to hold court, be the center of attention, and treat his guests to a good meal. It was his way. No one had an excuse to be alone on a holiday.

The left side mini-strokes continued with the most prominent effect being aphasia. Kight's ability to speak clearly suffered, and he'd sometimes pause an unusually long time before responding in conversation. His mind still sharp, his overall health began to suffer. In November 2002, doctors ordered Morris to Cedars Sinai for observation and further tests.

Troy Perry was one of his first visitors at Cedars: "He was not a religious person. As he lay dying, in fact, I went over and had prayer. I prayed for him like I do everyone else, I said, 'This is for me more than it's for you.' And he said, 'But Brother Troy, there is something I want,' and he started telling me everything that he wanted at his funeral … He wanted his funeral at MCC, he could've had it anywhere. And of course, we had the mob scene, the governor and everybody showed up. I said, 'No, he didn't have a death bed awakening.' It was the same old Morris, but he loved this church. He wanted his funeral held here. He was my mentor when it came to organizing. Morris taught me about demonstrations."

Michael Kearns visited Kight the week before he died. "He was, of course, dictating instructions about his memorial. He was luminously Morris: grandiose, funny, dramatic, tender, dictatorial, curious, sentimental. We held hands, he looked way into my eyes. I kissed his head of snow-colored hair. Words were no longer necessary."

Of course, his dear friend Wallace Albertson visited: "Morris had no fear of death. As a matter of fact, we did discuss religious matters—frequently over the years. But he did have a concern that social evolvement may diminish over the years to come through apathy or worse, a misguided appetite for aggression. Morris wished to be remembered, yes, we all know that. He relished his recognition as a role model—and rightly so. But his best legacy will be when an enlightened youth steps forward to pick up the torch and advance our progress in human affairs."

The last time that Barry Copilow saw Morris Kight was at Cedars, five or six days before he passed away. "I heard that he was holding court, I got there just as he found himself alone. 'How could that be?' he joked. We talked and laughed, he was jovial. He knew exactly what was going to happen. He had planned stuff and laughed about it. He wanted to have 14,000 dancing cowboys [at his funeral].

"When I went to leave and was walking toward the door, I reminded him of the first time we met, when he said, 'We're going to do something with you, Copilow.'

"Last thing he said to me: 'We did it, Copilow.'"

Malcolm Boyd and Mark Thompson had a lengthy visit. Boyd recalled, "At that moment, at that time, I got the impression that he was hurting a great deal. His pride, his prestige and the way the community had treated him. He was lonely … He was bitterly disappointed in certain people and how he had been treated by the community, to which he felt he had given his life. He was letting off some steam. It was an odd moment. It's awfully hard to be a spokesperson, a leader, identifiable … The role of leader is supposed to be savior, the person who gives. And the person who gives, in a mythological sense is not supposed to have any needs. And that day, I got the impression that he felt that he had given more than he had received. That is the experience of many people in leadership capacities. I was sorry."

Bob Dallmeyer saw Kight a few times in the last weeks. "We were the outlaws, we had a sense of camaraderie and hanging tough. Morris Kight is in bright, bright colors—not a man in grays, blacks, not even pastels. A man in Day-Glo."

In a 1997 interview with Nicholas Snow, Kight said: "Yes, I have had wonderful love and as much I love, I think the love that I have received from the collective lesbian and gay community is the light of my life."

In the last couple of months of his life, Kight confided to Miki Jackson: "I can't say this in public because it just wouldn't do, but after all these years I have come to the conclusion that being gay isn't such a big deal."

From his hospital bed, the Morris Kight Collection (fine art, craft art, artifacts and memorabilia of his activism, posters, buttons, banners, and his papers) was signed over to the ONE Institute National Gay & Lesbian Archive, housed at the University of Southern California. Kight entrusted the institution founded by his old friends and sometimes adversaries with his most prized possession: his legacy. He shared no inner thoughts as he made the bequeathment. It was the end of the road for Morris, and he'd go out the way he lived it—in control and bringing people together.

In January 2003 arrangements were made to move Kight to Carl Bean Hospice in mid-city—an AIDS hospice, founded and run by AIDS Healthcare Foundation. Kight was treated as a regal guest with Roy by his side at all times. He passed away quietly in the early morning hours of January 19, 2003. Cause of death was respiratory failure due to pneumonia and carcinoid tumors.

His legacy, however, shall never die. For every gay boy who walks down the street holding his boyfriend's hand, Morris Kight survives.

At Kight's request, Ivy Bottini served as Mistress of Ceremonies at the memorial to end all memorials. Ivy recalled, "I actually loved him. He was like a brother. When it was my turn to get up and say something at the memorial, I said, 'You know, I can't honestly say what I would like to say because I won't get through it. So let me just ask this. Did he *ever* say 'Goodbye' on the telephone?'"

Zev Yaroslavsky remembered: "My first impression of Morris is the same as my last impression. From the time that I met him in 1975, he's been a character, a personality, free radical. He was his own person, spoke his mind, was not intimidated by power or powerful people. He was a force of nature ... The community became more emboldened and empowered. He rose to this exalted level of gay leaders. People treated him with respect. He sometimes mocked the powers that be; in a positive way he ridiculed some of the inane things that government apparatus did. He was still respected. He was a symbol. A statesman while he was alive. He knew it. He used that exalted position for good purposes."

County Supervisor Sheila Kuehl: "In honor of Morris I have to tell you that if you ever get a standing ovation don't say 'oh, sit down, sit down.' Because he never would."

It is only fitting to give Morris Kight the last word on Morris Kight. In 1994, wrapping up a portion of their long interview, Paul Cain asked Kight how he would like to be remembered.

"Oh, I'd like to be remembered for, 'He tried. He tried. And sometimes he won. He was liked. And often he prevailed. He was strange, it's okay to be strange. He was different and it's okay to be different.' If there is any historic justice, I'll be considered a dynamic figure. A unique figure. If there were real justice, I would be cast in the role of Gandhi, or Thoreau, or Martin Luther King, or so on.

"I am, indeed, a renaissance person. I advocate wholeness. I advocate libraries, and archives, and study, and reading, and traveling, and going to the theater. How did the pyramids survive, for example? The seven cities of Troy, one on top of the other. Now it's a mud mountain. . . What caused the pyramids to hold together. . . They survived, even though nature should have dictated that they would be long since gone. That's what I'm talking about. I'm talking about survival of our culture, survival of our artifacts. There's a great joy in being, a great joy in sharing."

Every story beckons a happy ending. Life stories sometimes beg consolation and perspective. Morris Kight wasn't perfect, but he was perfectly Morris Kight.

Gay or straight, shy or shining, European or Asian or African, smart or dim, funny or dull, loyal or traitor—there will never be another person quite like Morris Kight. No matter what else he was, he will be remembered as a person who made a difference. He left the world improved for him having been here. There is the consolation.

If having made a difference in the world, if having had a positive impact on many lives, and yes, if being first a few times in life, if knowing that one is loved and appreciated is the conclusion of a man's life, Morris Kight's is a happy ending. A very happy ending, indeed.

In June of 2003, a few months after Kight's celebrity-studded memorial at MCC, Troy Perry and the Los Angeles City Council dedicated the corner of Hollywood Boulevard and McCadden Place, the launch for the first gay pride parade, as Morris Kight Square. It is marked by a plaque with a city seal attached to a light-pole, above any average human's eye level:

"Morris Kight Square: Co-founder of the world's first street-closing gay pride parade on Sunday, June 28, 1970."

1984. Morris Kight photo by Don Saban.

1984. Morris Kight photo by Don Saban.

Highlights of Morris Kight's accomplishments:

1965 Co-founder of DOW Action Committee

1969 Founder of Gay Liberation Front/Los Angeles

1970 A Principal Founder of Christopher Street West

1971 A Principal Founder of Gay Community Services Center/Los Angeles

1973 A Principal Founder of Van Ness Recovery House

1978 Member of the California State Democratic Central Committee

1979 Appointed Commission on Human Relations/County of Los Angeles

1980 Co-founder of Asian/Pacific Lesbian/Gays

1980 Ongoing Advocate for the needs of Old/Older/Senior/Elder Lesbian/Gay peoples

1981 Appointed to California Governor's Task Force on Civil Rights

1980 Co-Chair/Delegate, Affirmative Action Committee of the California Democratic Party

1984 A Principal Founder of McCadden Place Collection, known as the Morris Kight Collection

1985 Founder of Stonewall 25

Endnotes, Resources, Bibliography

CHAPTER 1: THE END

Martinez, Al. "No Sad Songs for Him." *Los Angeles Times*, Jan 24, 2003.

DeCrescenzo, Terry. Notes on a conversation with Morris Kight. Los Angeles, Jan 3, 2003.

DeCrescenzo, Terry. Added a personal note. Los Angeles, Aug 7, 2010.

Grobson, Mitch. Videotape of MK Memorial. Personal footage. VHS. West Hollywood, Feb 2003.

Cherry, Mary Ann. Personal Notes from Metropolitan Community Church. West Hollywood, Feb 1, 2003.

CHAPTER 2: PROUD SOUTHERNERS

Kight, John Lewis. *Kight Family History*. 1952. Nome, TX: Personal handwritten notes. Feb 1, 2010.

Kight, Morris. Interview by Paul D. Cain. Transcription. Los Angeles, Jun 6, 1994.

Sullivan, Tony and Richard Adams. Interview by Paul D. Cain. Transcription. Los Angeles, Nov 11, 2005.

Kight, Morris. Interview by Mitch Grobson. VHS. Los Angeles, Feb 22, 1998.

Kight, Morris. Interview by Miki Jackson. Audio recording on cassette. Los Angeles, Aug 10, 2002.

Kight, Malcolm. Interview by Author. Phone conversation with handwritten notes. San Antonio, TX, Jan 30, 2006.

Lane, Kight (family historian). Interview by Author. Phone conversation with handwritten notes. Lubbock, TX, Jun 21, 2005.

Los Angeles Regional Family History Center, the Church of Jesus Christ of Latter-Day Saints: Kight family, Howell family, and Smith family immigration, census data 1700 onward. 2005.

Ancestry.com

Kight family, Howell family, and Smith family immigration, census data 1700 onward. 2005.

Rootsweb.com

Kight family, Howell family, and Smith family immigration, migration 1700 onward. 2005.

Comanche County Clerk, Public Records, Comanche, TX, Kight family census, 1891 onward. 2005.

CHAPTER 3: BESSIE

Carnegie, Dale. *How to Win Friends and Influence People*. London: Vermilion, 1936.

Limmer Jr., E.A. *The Story of Bell County, Texas*. ed., s.v. Burnet: Eakin Press, 1988. p. 575.

Byrd, Greg. "Profile of Morris Kight," *Frontiers*, 1984.

Kight, John Lewis. *Kight Family History*. 1952. Nome, TX: Personal handwritten notes. Feb 1, 2010.

Kight, Morris. Interview by Paul D. Cain. Transcription. Los Angeles, Jun 6, 1994.

Kight, Morris. Interview by Andre Ting. *ONE, Gay Asian Pacific Support Network Monthly Newsletters*. Los Angeles, Dec 13, 1999.

Kight, Morris. Interview by Miki Jackson. Audio recording on cassette. Los Angeles, Aug 10, 2002.

Kight, Morris. Interview by Mitch Grobson. VHS. Los Angeles, Feb 22, 1998.

Kight, Malcolm. Interview by Author. Phone conversation with handwritten notes. San Antonio, TX, Jan 30, 2006.

Kight-Fyfe, Carol. Interview by Author. In-person interview recorded on cassette. Houston, TX, May 26, 2004.

Lane, Kight. Interview by Author. Phone conversation with handwritten notes. Lubbock, TX, Jul 2, 2005.

Peters, Stanlibeth. Interview by Author. In-person interview recorded on cassette. Houston, TX, May 25, 2004. Apr 7, 2010.

"Bell County Probate Records," s.v. "Grimes Family" available at East Bell County Genealogical Society. Jun 2005.

Bell County Clerk's Office, Grimes family, Bland family census data, 1870 onward. 2005.

Comanche County Clerk, Public Records, Comanche, TX, Grimes family, Bland family 1891 onward. 2005.

Los Angeles Regional Family History Center, the Church of Jesus Christ of Latter-Day Saints: Grimes family, Bland family census data 1700 onward. 2005.

Ancestry.com. Grimes Family, Bland Family. 2005.

Rootsweb.com. Grimes Family, Bland Family. 2005.

"Hells Half Acre – Fort Worth." The Online Handbook of Texas History: TSHA.org www.tshaonline.org/handbook/online/articles/HH/hph1.html, Sep 19, 2009.

"Texas Centennial in 1936." www.texascentennial.com/index.php, Sep 19, 2009.

"North American heat wave, 1936." wikipedia.org, Jun 2004.

Repeated efforts to contact children of John Lewis and Lucy Mildred for this biography were not acknowledged. One niece, who chose not to be named, had a few sweet memories of their Uncle Morris, but opted not to be interviewed further, saying, "We didn't much care for a lot of what he got himself involved with."

CHAPTER 4: THE BEST THING TO EVER HAPPEN

Carnegie, Dale. *How to Win Friends and Influence People*. London: Vermilion, 1936/2019.

Ward, Emily. "Ending Isolation, Kight Encourages Gays, Lesbians to be Proud of themselves, stop Oppression." *TCU Daily*, Nov 17, 2000. (reprinted eQ Alliance newsletter, 2005).

Kight, Morris. Interview by Paul D. Cain. Transcription. Los Angeles, Jun 6, 1994.

Kight, Morris. Interview by Mitch Grobson. VHS. Los Angeles, Feb 22, 1998.

Kight, Morris. Interview by Ryan Robert Gierach. *Gay & Lesbian Times*, Jul 18, 2002.

Kight, Malcolm. Interview by Author. Phone conversation with handwritten notes. San Antonio, TX, Jan 30, 2006.

Kight-Fyfe, Carol. Interview by Author. In-person interview recorded on cassette. Houston, TX, May 26, 2004.

Lane, Kight. Interview by Author. Phone conversation with handwritten notes. Lubbock, TX, Jun 21 2005; Jul 2, 2005.

Peters, Stanlibeth. Interview by Author. In-person interview recorded on cassette. Houston, TX, May 25, 2004, Apr 7, 2010.

Texas Christian University Transcripts (1937–1942), Fort Worth, Texas. 2004.

University of Texas, Austin. Transcripts. s.v. "Morris Kight 1940–1942." Registrar's Office, 2004. Austin, TX.

Bureau of Indian Affairs, St Louis, MO. Morris Kight military records and personnel files. FOIA, May 2005.

CHAPTER 5: LAND OF ENCHANTMENT

Nardi, Peter M., David Sanders, and Judd Marmor. *Growing up Before Stonewall: Life Stories of Some Gay Men*. London: Routledge, 1994.

Weisel, Al. "LBJ's Gay Sex Scandal," pp. 77–131. *Out*, Dec 1999.

"The Administration: The Jenkins Report." *Time*, Oct 30, 1964.

"People, Parties in the News…" Kight-Peters engagement announcement. *Albuquerque Journal*, Dec 15, 1950.

"Miss Peters, Morris Kight Wed at St. John's Cathedral." *Albuquerque Journal*, Dec 19, 1950.

Duke, Alan. "New tapes show LBJ struggled with aide's sex scandal," © 1998 cnn.com, Sep 21, 2005.

Kight, Morris. Interview by Paul D. Cain. Transcription. Los Angeles, Jun 6, 1994.

Kight, Morris. Interview with Ryan Robert Gierach. *Gay & Lesbian Times*, Jul 18, 2002.

Peters, Stanlibeth. Interview by Author. In-person interview recorded on cassette. Houston, TX, May 25, 2004, Apr 7, 2010.

Jackson, Miki. "What Morris said about Clyde Tolson and J. Edgar." Email. Nov 9, 2011.

Fergusson, Erna. "Erna Fergusson's notes on [unpublished] biography of Clyde Tingley." Jun 22, 1961. Albuquerque Library. 2004.

Albuquerque Public Library, Special Collections. 2004.

Albuquerque Police Records Department, Albuquerque, New Mexico. 2004.

Calvin Horn Collection. University of New Mexico, Special Collections Library (Coll # UNMA 108). 2004.

City of Albuquerque, Cultural Services Department, Special Collections Genealogy Library. 2004.

Museum of Albuquerque Historical Society, Albuquerque, NM. 2004.

New Mexico State Records Center and Archives, Museum of New Mexico, Palace of the Governors, Santa Fe, NM. Census data for Kight, Peters, 1941 onward (2004).

State of New Mexico Public Records, Santa Fe, NM. 2004.

Special Collection Center for Southwest Research, New Mexico State Library, Santa Fe, NM. 2004.

Zimmerman Library at University of NM, Albuquerque NM. 2004.

John Donald Robb field records, DVD [sound recording] 2001. Recorded in 1952 and 1953 in Taos and Albuquerque, New Mexico. 2004.

CHAPTER 6: THE KIGHT FAMILY MUSEUM

"Fire Destroys Old San Felipe Hotel and Kight Family's Historic Museum." *Albuquerque Journal,* Sep 10, 1956.

Edwin Steinbrecher. Obituary. *Los Angeles Times,* Jan 30, 2002.

Ciotti, Paul. *Los Angeles Times,* "Morris Kight: Activist Statesman of L.A.'s Gay Community." Dec. 9, 1988.

Kight, Morris. Interview by Paul D. Cain. Transcription. Los Angeles, Jun 6, 1994.

Kight-Fyfe, Carol. Interview by Author. In-person interview recorded on cassette. Houston, TX, May 26, 2004.

Peters, Stanlibeth. Interview by Author. In-person interview recorded on cassette. Houston, TX, May 25, 2004, Apr 7, 2010.

Albuquerque Public Library, Special Collections. 2004.

Albuquerque Police Records Department, Albuquerque New Mexico. 2004.

CHAPTER 7: ANGELS OF THE CITY

Ciotti, Paul. "Morris Kight: Activist Statesman of L.A.'s Gay Community." *Los Angeles Times,* Dec 9, 1988.

Potvin, Ernie. "Gay Friends to Serve 600 Free Turkey Dinners in Park." *Frontiers,* Nov 9, 2016.

Mitch Grobson, *MK addressing the Valley Business Alliance.* (Feb 10, 1998; Los Angeles. Live Footage) Videotape/VHS.

KCET "Out in Front" profile of Morris Kight, Los Angeles, CA. 1992. VHS. 2012.

Kight, Morris. Interview by Paul D. Cain. Transcription. Los Angeles, Jun 6, 1994.

Kight-Fyfe, Carol. Interview by Author. In-person interview recorded on cassette. Houston, TX, May 26, 2004.

Peters, Stanlibeth. Interview with Author. In-person interview recorded on cassette. Houston, TX, May 25, 2004, Apr 7, 2010.

en.wikipedia.org/wiki/Tavern_Guild. 2010.

www.foundsf.org/index.php?title=Society_for_Individual_Rights_(SIR). 2010.

www.planetout.com/news/history/archive/08021999.html. 2010.

For more information: D.O.M.E. The Inner Guide Meditation Center. general correspondence from Ed Steinbrecher Jan 3, 2002

CHAPTER 8: DOW SHALL NOT KILL

Faderman, Lillian, and Stuart Timmons. *Gay L.A.: A History of Sexual Outlaws, Power Politics, and Lipstick Lesbians.* Berkeley: University of California Press, 2009.

Hansen, J. *A Few Doors West of Hope: The Life and Times of Dauntless Don Slater.* Universal City: Homosexual Information Center, 1998.

White, C. Todd. *Pre-Gay L.A. A Social History of the Movement for Homosexual Rights.* Chicago: University of Illinois Press, 2009.

"Conference 'near-perfect' meeting of minds in L.A." *Advocate,* Apr 1970.

"They Said It." *Hollywood Citizen News,* Jul 13, 1970. (Julian Bond quote)

Kight, Morris. "Dow Action Committee Fasts." *Los Angeles Free Press,* Jul 26, 1968.

Ciotti, Paul. "Morris Kight: Activist Statesman of L.A.'s Gay Community" *Los Angeles Times,* Dec 9, 1988.

Editorial. "Protesting Napalm." *Time* Magazine, Jan 5, 1968.

Becker, Jack. "Fast Against Napalm." *Open City Newspaper* (Los Angeles), Jul 26, 1968.

Nichols, Jack. "An Elder of Our Tribe." *Gay Today,* 1997/98.

Kight, Morris. "Special to Planet Homo." *Planet Homo* #042. Sep 1, 1993.

Suderberg, Erika. *Somatography.* Independent film project. Los Angeles, 1999.

Colville, Andrew. *Live on Tape: The Life & Times of Morris Kight, Liberator.* A short film project. Los Angeles, 1999. Courtesy AIDS Healthcare Foundation Archive.

"Ford laughs as Dow burns." *Los Angeles Free Press.* Nov 19, 1967.

"'Obnoxious' Parade Request." *Los Angeles Free Press.* Dec 1, 1967.

"Flammable Ingredients expected at weekend Dow protest." *Los Angeles Free Press.* Dec 15, 1967.

"Peace and Freedom Party registration expected to 'barely squeak through.'" *Los Angeles Free Press.* Dec 29, 1967.

Kunkin, Art. "Peace and Freedom chooses candidates." *Los Angeles Free Press.* Aug 2, 1968.

Kight, Morris. Interview by Paul D. Cain. Transcription. Los Angeles, Jun 6, 1994.

Kight, Morris. Interview by Mitch Grobson. VHS. Los Angeles, Feb 22, 1998.

Kight, Morris. Interview by Miki Jackson. Audio recording on cassette. Los Angeles, Aug 10, 2002.

Beasly, Bill. Interview by Author. Phone. Los Angeles, Jan 11, 2010.

Green, Jaime. Interview by Author. Phone. Los Angeles, Oct 4, 2004.

Jackson, Miki. Interview by Author. Phone. Los Angeles, Nov 1, 2011.

Perry, Troy D. Interview by Author. In person on tape. Los Angeles, Astro Diner. Mar 16, 2007.

Platania, Jon. Interview by Author. Phone. Los Angeles, Jan 26, 2010.

Vezina, Gino. Interview by Author. Phone. Los Angeles, Jan 12, 2009; Jan 13, 2009; Jan 22, 2009; Jun 10, 2010.

VonHamhorse, Kaplan, Harry. Interview by Author. Phone Interview. Los Angeles, Jun 6, 2008.

Jackson, Miki, 'RE: What Morris said about Clyde Tolson and J. Edgar.' Email, Nov 9, 2011.

Efland, Steve, 'RE: Seeking info on 1969 L.A. Murder/Howard Efland.' Email, Nov 9, 2011; Mar 26; Mar 27, 2014.

U.S. Federal Bureau of Investigation. Morris Kight File. FOIA, 2005.

U.S. Federal Bureau of Investigation. Dow Action Committee File. FOIA, 2005.

Bond, Julian. 'Letter to Morris Kight.' Letter. Jul 30, 1970, Foster Gunnison Collection at University of Connecticut. Ink on Paper.

Kepner, Jim. "Gay Movement History & Goals Why Can't We All Get Together?" Speech given at the ONE Institute in Los Angeles, Apr 28, 1997. Printed in *Badpuppy Gay Today.* 1997. 2005.

Kepner, Jim. "My First 65 Years in Gay Liberation." Unpublished personal essay. 1980. ONE.

Thank you:

Center for the Study of Political Graphics, Los Angeles, CA

Thomas J. Dodd Research Center, University of Connecticut, the Foster Gunnison Papers at the Natural History and Rare Book Collections Archives & Special Collections, Hartford, CT.

Harry Hay Papers. San Francisco Public Library. James C. Hormel LGBTQIA Center.

Morris Kight Papers (Collection 354). Department of Special Collections, Charles E. Young Research Library, University of California, Los Angeles.

Morris Kight Papers and Photographs (Coll2010-008), ONE National Gay & Lesbian Archives, Los Angeles, California.

20th Century Organizational Files, Southern California Library for Social Studies and Research, Los Angeles, California.

For more information regarding the Stonewall Inn Rebellion: www.thestonewallinnnyc.com/StonewallInnNYC/HISTORY.html

For more information and a copy of Powell Memorandum:

Archives at Washington and Lee University, the Lewis F. Powell, Jr. Papers: law.wlu.edu/powellarchives/page.asp?pageid=1251

CHAPTER 9: HOME TO BE FREE

Hansen, J. *A Few Doors West of Hope: The Life and Times of Dauntless Don Slater.* Universal City: Homosexual Information Center, 1998.

Findley, Tim. "The Big Anti-War Offensive Opens." *San Francisco Chronicle.* Oct 13, 1969.

Raudebaugh, Charles. "Massive U.S. Anti-War Protests—Rallies, Marches in Bay Area." *San Francisco Chronicle.* Oct 16, 1969.

Findley, Tim. "Bay Area Leaders Elated at Response." *San Francisco Chronicle.* Oct 16, 1969.

Flynn, William. "Tens of Thousands Echo the Cry for Peace." *San Francisco Chronicle.* Nov 16, 1969.

Findley, Tim. "A Festival for Peace Makes Political Point." *San Francisco Chronicle.* Nov 17, 1969.

Kight, Morris. "How It All Began." *Planet Homo.* Sep 1, 1993.

Kight, Morris. Interview by Paul D. Cain. Transcription. Los Angeles, Jun 6, 1994.

Kight, Morris. Interview by Mitch Grobson. VHS. Los Angeles, Feb 22, 1998.

Laurence, Leo E. J.D. Interview by Author. Phone Interview. Los Angeles, Sep 10, 2010.

Little, Richard. Interview by Author. In Person. Los Angeles, Jun 6, 2012.

Brass, Perry. "Morris Kight." Email. Aug 15, 2012.

Colville, Andrew. *Live on Tape: The Life & Times of Morris Kight, Liberator.* A short film project. Los Angeles, 1999. Courtesy AIDS Healthcare Foundation Archive.

U.S. Federal Bureau of Investigation. Morris Kight File. FOIA, 2005.

U.S. Federal Bureau of Investigation. Dow Action Committee file. FOIA, 2005.

Thank you:

Morris Kight Papers and Photographs (Coll2010-008), ONE National Gay & Lesbian Archives, Los Angeles, California.

Morris Kight Papers (Collection 354). Department of Special Collections, Charles E.

Young Research Library, University of California, Los Angeles.

San Francisco History Center, San Francisco Public Library.

20th Century Organizational Files, Southern California Library for Social Studies and Research, Los Angeles, California.

CHAPTER 10: GAY LIBERATION FRONT

Armstrong, Elizabeth A. and Suzanna M. Crage. *Movements and Memory: The Making of the Stonewall Myth.* American Sociological Review 71, no. 5 (2006): 724–51. doi.org/10.1177/000312240607100502.

Clendinen, Dudley, and Adam Nagourney. *Out for Good: The Struggle to Build a Gay Rights Movement in America.* New York: Simon & Schuster, 2016.

Duberman, Martin B. *Stonewall.* New York: Plume, 1994.

Faderman, Lillian, and Stuart Timmons. *Gay L.A.: A History of Sexual Outlaws, Power Politics, and Lipstick Lesbians.* Berkeley: University of California Press, 2009.

Hansen, J. *A Few Doors West of Hope: The Life and Times of Dauntless Don Slater.* Universal City: Homosexual Information Center, 1998.

Jay, Karla. *Tales of the Lavender Menace: A Memoir of Liberation.* New York: BasicBooks, 2000.

Parks, Rosa and Gregory J. Reed. *Quiet Strength: The Faith, the Hope and the Heart of a Woman Who Changed a Nation.* Zondervan Press, Aug 1994.

Kenney, Moira. *Mapping Gay L.A.: The Intersection of Place and Politics.* Philadelphia: Temple University Press, 2001.

Loughery, John. *The Other Side of Silence: Men's Lives and Gay Identities: A 20th Century History.* New York: Owl, 1999.

Perez, F., and J. Palmquist. *In Exile: The History and Lore Surrounding New Orleans Gay Culture and Its Oldest Gay Bar.* Hurlford: Logical-Lust, 2012.

Timmons, Stuart. *The Trouble with Harry Hay: Founder of the Modern Gay Movement.* Massachusetts: White Crane Books, 2012.

White, C. Todd. *Pre-Gay L.A. A Social History of the Movement for Homosexual Rights.* Chicago: University of Illinois Press, 2009.

Young, Allen, and Karla Jay. *Out of the Closets Voices of Gay Liberation.* New York: New York University Press, 1992.

WVUE-TV Channel 8 News transcript from New Orleans news footage, 1973 from WVUE archives (courtesy Robert Camino).

"Gay groups win; signs come down at Barney's Beanery." *The Advocate.* Apr 29, 1970.

"Conference 'near-perfect' meeting of minds in L.A." *The Advocate.* Apr 29, 1970.

"L.A. Gay-In set for April 5." *The Advocate.* Apr 29, 1970.

"Gays 'liberate' psychologist's homosexual talk." *The Advocate.* May 27, 1970.

"Court okays Christopher West parade." *The Advocate.* Jul 8, 1970.

Cole, Rob. "Military policies on Gays make no sense" *The Advocate.* Jul 8, 1970.

"L.A. Gay groups weigh information clearing house." *The Advocate.* Jun 10, 1970.

"Second L.A. Gay-In Set For Memorial Day." *The Advocate.* Jun 10, 1970.

Tucker, Nancy. "GAY PRIDE Thousands march in New York, L.A." *The Advocate.* Jul 22, 1970.

Stienecker, David. "Several hundred Gays march in Chicago pride celebration." *The Advocate.* Jul 22, 1970.

"Cops raid Regency, harass Corral Club." *The Advocate.* Jun 24, 1970.

"Big L.A. Christopher St. W. parade planned." *The Advocate.* Jun 24, 1970.

"Gay-In brings 'em out (cops, too)." *The Advocate.* Jun 24, 1970.

"Perry busted as he, 7 others start fast." *The Advocate.* Jul 22, 1970.

"Historic Day!" *The Advocate.* Jul 22, 1970.

Name Withheld. "MailBag. Letter to the Editor." *The Advocate.* Aug 5, 1970.

"L.A. Gay Lib pickets theatre, bar charging community exploited." *The Advocate.* Aug 19, 1970.

"Gay Lib in L.A. Starts own 'hotline' service." *The Advocate.* Aug 19, 1970.

"Rocco agrees to give GLF film premiere." *The Advocate.* Aug 19, 1970.

Martello, Dr. Leo Louis. "MailBag. Letter to the Editor." *The Advocate.* Sep 2, 1970.

"Bar police harassment of Gay-In, court asked." *The Advocate.* Sep 2, 1970.

"Court rejects GLF plea to bar Gay-In harassment." *The Advocate.* Sep 30, 1970.

"Cops fade out at gayest Gay-In." *The Advocate.* Sep 30, 1970.

"Tiny Town in Sierra Nevada Relaxes When Cold, Mosquitoes Stall Invasion." *Amarillo Globe Times.* Aug 25, 1971.

"Alpine County invasion. Victory over homosexuals?" *The Argus.* Dec 19, 1970.

"Alpine County Weather Helps Defeat Perverts." *The Bakersfield Californian.* Dec 21, 1970.

"Remote County to Battle 'Gays.'" *Bedford Gazette.* Oct 19, 1970.

Jackson, Don. "Gays Blast Barney." *Berkeley Barb.* Feb 13, 1970.

Editorial. "Alpine Co. Here We Come!" *Front Lines,* GLF newsletter. Dec 1970.

Gierach, Ryan Robert. "Interview with Morris Kight." *Gay & Lesbian Times.* Jul 18, 2002.

Chinn, Henry C., Jr. "Bayard Rustin: Six Decades of fighting for What We *All* Need." *Gay Community News, The Weekly for Lesbians and Gay Males.* Jun 29, 1986.

"Mountain Folks Fear Influx of Homosexuals." *Lebanon Daily News.* Oct 22, 1970.

Ribbel, Arthur. "Mosquitoes Nip Gay Liberation Invasion." *The Lima News.* Lima OH. Aug 19, 1971.

Hammond, John. "A Quarter Century of Liberation – Plus. *Talking with Morris Kight.*" *New York Native.* Feb 18, 1991.

"Homosexuals Plan to Flood Country, Direct Government." *Ogden Standard-Examiner.* Oct 22, 1970 (7A).

Applebaum, Jerry. "Peace movement to take to the streets again. Monster demonstrations planned for this fall." *Los Angeles Free Press.* Oct 10, 1969.

Back page advertisement. "Gays-AC-DC." *Los Angeles Free Press.* Oct 31, 1969.

Back page advertisement. "Gays-AC-DC." *Los Angeles Free Press.* Nov 7, 1969.

Key, Douglas. "Gay power groups pull it together." *Los Angeles Free Press.* Dec 19, 1969.

Key, Douglas. "Homophiles hassled in San Dimas." *Los Angeles Free Press.* Jan 2, 1970.

Douglas, Angela Key. "Gays Plan to seize Gov't." *Los Angeles Free Press.* Jan 9, 1970.

Dittus, A. Lee. "Letter to the Editor." *Los Angeles Free Press.* Jan 9, 1970.

Jackson, Don. "Homosexual violence predicted." *Los Angeles Free Press.* Jan 16, 1970.

Key, Douglas. "Gay solidarity march." *Los Angeles Free Press.* Jan 23, 1970.

Douglas, Angela Key. "Gay Lib Front meets; plans to picket Barney's Beanery." *Los Angeles Free Press.* Feb 6, 1970.

Jackson, Don. "Gays Demand Ninety Billion." *Los Angeles Free Press.* Feb 20, 1970.

Film review. "Pat Rocco's new film view of 'Homo Love." *Los Angeles Free Press.* Feb 27, 1970.

Key, Douglas. "Gay liberation." *Los Angeles Free Press.* Feb 27, 1970.

Key, Douglas. "Lavender Sunday—Gay spirit inspires Catholic Rage." *Los Angeles Free Press.* Mar 6, 1970.

Key, Douglas. "Gays plan marches, Leather Sunday." *Los Angeles Free Press.* Mar 13, 1970.

"GLF meets, plans more protests." *Los Angeles Free Press.* Mar 13, 1970.

Jackson, Don. "Don Jackson investigates entrapment of Gays by vice officers." *Los Angeles Free Press.* Mar 13, 1970.

Key, Douglas. "Gay News." *Los Angeles Free Press.* Mar 20, 1970.

"Jean Genet for Black Panthers." *Los Angeles Free Press.* Mar 27, 1970.

Key, Douglas. "2,000 Homosexuals hold Los Angeles Gay-In." *Los Angeles Free Press.* Apr 10, 1970.

"20 gays picketed Ft. MacArthur on Apr 22." *Los Angeles Free Press.* May 1, 1970.

Jackson, Don. "L.A. Gay riots threatened." *Los Angeles Free Press.* May 15, 1970.

Craig, Alfred. "Letter to the Editor." *Los Angeles Free Press.* Jun 5, 1970.

Overseth, Marcus Magnus. "Letter to the Editor." *Los Angeles Free Press.* Jun 12, 1970.

Douglas, Angela. "Gay-in a Success!" *Los Angeles Free Press.* Jun 19, 1970.

"Gay Liberation newspaper proposal." *Los Angeles Free Press.* Jun 19, 1970.

"Gays picket theatre supporting the local projectionist's union." *Los Angeles Free Press.* Jun 24, 1970.

Douglas, Angela. "Gays to march on Hollywood Blvd." *Los Angeles Free Press.* Jun 26, 1970.

Douglas, Angela. "Gays march on Hollywood Blvd." *Los Angeles Free Press.* Jul 3, 1970.

Kunkin, Art. "Gays crash Hilton 'Some of our people are sick.'" *Los Angeles Free Press.* Dec 4, 1970.

"Gay Task Force Due to Visit Alpine County." *Long Beach Independent Press-Telegram.* Nov 26, 1970.

"Gay Front Delaying Invasion." *Long Beach Independent Press-Telegram.* Dec 17, 1970.

Houston, Paul. "Homosexuals Receive ACLU Aid in Fight for Parade Permit." *Los Angeles Times.* Jun 13, 1970.

Houston, Paul. "Court Kills Bond for Hollywood Parade Permit." *Los Angeles Times.* Jun 27, 1970.

"Sunday Parade: Bond Dropped for Homosexual Event." *Los Angeles Times.* Jun 27, 1970.

Houston, Paul. "Homosexuals Stage Hollywood Parade." *Los Angeles Times.* Jun 29, 1970.

Kilday, Gregg. "Gays Lobby for a New Media Image: New Gay Image." *Los Angeles Times.* Dec 10, 1973.

Brown, James. "Super Emmy—It Had Its Moments." *Los Angeles Times.* May 30, 1974.

"Say 200 Could Control Government. Homosexuals Weigh Move to Alpine County." *Los Angeles Times.* Oct 19, 1970.

"A group of homosexuals, anticipating a legal battle…" *Los Angeles Times.* Dec 17, 1970.

Ciotti, Paul. "Morris Kight: Activist Statesman of L.A.'s Gay Community" *Los Angeles Times,* Dec 9, 1988.

"New Site eyed by Gay Front." *Nevada State Journal.* Apr 4, 1971.

Roberts, Steven V. "Old Timers Join Newcomers in War Protest in Los Angeles." *New York Times,* Apr 23, 1972.

Back page "Forum" classifieds. *The Paper.* Jun 24, 1970.

Kight, Morris. "How It All Began" essay for *Planet Homo*, 1989.

Kight, Morris. "A Special" essay for *Planet Homo*, Sep 1, 1993.

Bess, Donovan. "Gay Advance Guard Will Visit Alpine." *San Francisco Chronicle*. Nov 10, 1970.

Lind, Angus. "Fire Bares the Grisly Face of Death." *States-Item*. Jun 25, 1973.

Bouden, Mrs. Barbara. "Views of Readers. Fire Reveals Bias." *States-Item*. Jun 29, 1973.

"200 Attend Service for Lounge Victims." *States-Item*. Jul 2, 1973.

Segura, Chris. "Black, Empty Windows Stare. Worst Fire in History of New Orleans." *The Times-Picayune*, Jun 26, 1973.

Lee, Vincent. "Gay Leaders Plan Aid for Victims of Bar Fire." *The Times-Picayune*, Jun 27, 1973 I,14.

Segura, Chris. "Cleric Says Oppression Problem for Homosexuals." *The Times-Picayune*. Jul 2, 1973.

Editorial. "Gay Pride." *Time* Magazine. Jul 13, 1970.

Gollance, Richard. "The problems facing gays." *UCLA Daily Bruin*. May 16, 1972.

Dallmeyer, Bob, "Salute to the Pioneers of Gay Liberation Front 20th Anniversary," Audio File, aired on *IMRU*, KPFK, 1989. Cassette, Los Angeles, 2009.

ERCHO. "Meeting Minutes," Nov 1–2, 1969. Retrieved from Mattachine Society New York files.

Cole, Rob. "Remembering Morris," essay, *www.lapride.org*, Feb 2003.

Kight, Morris. Interview by Paul D. Cain. Transcription. Los Angeles, Jun 6, 1994.

Kight, Morris. Interview by Mitch Grobson. VHS. Los Angeles, Feb 22, 1998.

Barney, Jeanne. Author's interview. Phone. Apr 15, 2009.

Beasley, Bill. Interviewed by Author. Phone. Jan 11, 2010.

Copilow, Barry. Interviewed by Author. Phone. Oct 14, 2010.

Embry, John. Interviewed by Author. Phone. Apr 15, 2009.

Gollance, Richard. Interviewed by Author. Phone. Jul 3, 2010.

Green, Jaime. Interviewed by Author. Phone. Oct 4, 2004.

Laurence, Leo E., J.D. Interviewed by Author. Phone. Sep 10, 2010.

LeGrand, Terry. Interviewed by Author. Phone. Apr 20, 2009.

Mentley, Lee. Interviewed by Author. Phone. Nov 26, 2005.

Meyer, Mina. Interviewed by Author. Phone. Jan 27, 2009.

Perry, Troy D. Interview by Author. In person on tape. Los Angeles, Astro Diner. Mar 16, 2007.

Pearl, Ed. Interviewed by Author. Phone. Sep 15, 2009.

Platania, Jon. Interviewed by Author. Phone. Jan 26, 2010.

Rocco, Pat. Interviewed by Author. In person on tape. Los Angeles, Victor's Square. Aug 31, 2003.

Vezina, Gino. Interviewed by Author. Phone. Jan 12, Jan 13, Jan 22, 2009; Jun 10, 2010.

VonHamhorse Kaplan, Harry. Author. Phone. Jun 6, 2008.

Weathers, Carolyn. Interviewed by Author. Phone. Mar 13, 2005; Feb 12, 2006.

Weather, Carolyn. Interviewed by Author. In person on tape. Long Beach. Apr 9, 2005.

Bradford, Fred. "Morris Kight." Email. Jul 14, 2005.

Effinger, John. "Morris Kight." Email. Oct 13, 14, 2009.

Jackson, Miki. "What Morris said about Clyde Tolson and J. Edgar." Email. Nov 9, 2011.

Platania, Jon. "Remembering Morris." Emails. Jan 30, 2010; Aug 22, 201; Jun 26, 2015.

Stryker, Susan, PhD. "Angela Keyes Douglas." Email. Nov 15, 2007.

VonHamhorse Kaplan, Harry. "Morris." Email. Jun 4, 2008.

Weathers, Carolyn. "Morris_Brenda" Emails. Jan 28,2009; Jan 29, 2009.

Whan, Del. "GLF." Emails. Jan 4, 2009; Jan 25, 2009; Jan 27, 2009; Jan 31, 2009; Jan 23, 2009; Jun 13, 2010.

Williams, Stanley. "Remembering Morris." Emails. Jan 28, 2010; Jan 30, 2010.

Whan, Del. "GLF." Whan email to Glenne McElhinney (Impact Stories), May 08, 2008 cc: author.

"Morris Kight Collection," raw footage. VHS. 1999. Courtesy AIDS Healthcare Foundation Archive.

Colville, Andrew. *Live on Tape: The Life & Times of Morris Kight, Liberator*. A short film project. Los Angeles, 1999. Courtesy AIDS Healthcare Foundation Archive.

Jonathan Katz radio interview with MK, Oct 1976. Jonathan Ned Katz Papers, Manuscripts and Archives Division, The New York Public Library.

MK New York City speech, 1973. Israel David Fishman Papers, Manuscripts and Archives Division, The New York Public Library.

U.S. Federal Bureau of Investigation Morris Kight File. FOIA, 2005. Gay Liberation Front File, Part I, II, III. FOIA, 2005.

Letter from Director of FBI to Special Agents (RE: Counterintelligence Program Black Panther Party), dated 2/27/69. Center for Study of Political Graphics.

Los Angeles City Hall, Public Records, parade application, FOIA, 2005.

Anonymous letter to Kight, Nov 13, 1970. FG

Hanson, Craig. Letters to Kight, Jun 17, Sep 29, Oct 15, Oct 22, Dec 16, 1970. FG

Itkin, The Right Reverend Michael Francis. Letter to MK. Dec 31, 1970. FG

Kight letter to Craig Hanson, Jul 15, 1970, Morris Kight Papers, ONE.

All correspondence between MM & MK. 1973 onward. Morty Manford papers, Manuscripts and Archives Division, The New York Public Library.

Dowling, Arthur. Letter to Kight. Jul 2, 1970. FG

Hay, Harry. Letter to John O'Brien, Sep 21, 1998. Hay Papers, SFPL

Hay, Harry. Letter to Jeanne Cordova, Jan 29, 1974. Hay Papers, SFPL

Thank you:

Carolyn Weathers Personal Archives.

Historic New Orleans Collection, Williams Research Center. (2009).

Foster Gunnison, Jr. Papers, Archives & Special Collections at the Thomas J. Dodd Research Center, University of Connecticut Library.

Morty Manford Papers, Manuscripts and Archives Division, The New York Public Library.

Jonathan Ned Katz Papers, Manuscripts and Archives Division, The New York Public Library.

Israel David Fishman Papers, Manuscripts and Archives Division, The New York Public Library.

Harry Hay Papers. San Francisco Public Library. James C. Hormel LGBTQIA Center.

Harvey Milk Archives - Scott Smith Collection (GLC 35), Gay and Lesbian Center, San Francisco Public Library.

Morris Kight Papers and Photographs Coll2010-008, ONE National Gay & Lesbian Archives, Los Angeles, California.

Christopher Street West Association Records, Coll2012-134, ONE National Gay & Lesbian Archives, USC Libraries, University of Southern California.

Jim Kepner Papers, Coll2011-002, ONE National Gay & Lesbian Archives, Los Angeles, California.

Pedersen, Lyn. "A New Day for Gays," unpublished essay, 1970. ONE.

"Who is CSW." *www.lapride.org*, undated. ONE.

wikipedia.org/wiki/Eddie_Nash (Nov 30, 2010)

For more information on Eddie Nash:

Van Hoorelbeke, Jerry. *Underworld Secrets.* (ISBN 0932438474). 2006.

Gilmore, John. *L.A. Despair: A Landscape of Crimes & Bad Times. Bad Eddie & Other No Good People.* (ISBN 1878923161). 2005.

20th Century Organizational Files, Southern California Library for Social Studies and Research, Los Angeles, California.

Stryker, Susan, PhD. Women's Studies, Simon Fraser University, Burnaby, BC.

Note regarding Clay Shaw, whom Reverend Perry contacted for help to find a church in New Orleans: Clay Shaw was a prominent local businessman who was charged, and later found not guilty, of conspiracy to kill President Kennedy. At the time of the investigation of JFK's assassination, New Orleans District Attorney, Jim Garrison, believed that Clay Shaw was the man named as "Clay Bertrand" in the Warren Commission Report. Garrison claimed that Shaw used the alias "Clay Bertrand" among New Orleans' gay society.

For more information:

A Huey P. Newton Story, by Roger Guenveur Smith for an original video production of Black Starz with PBS and the African Heritage Network.

Newton, Huey P. *Huey Newton Speaks.* Oral history by Huey P. Newton. Paredon Records, 1970.

Newton, Huey. *To Die for the People* (City Lights Publishers, 2009).

Seale, Bobby. *Seize the Time: The Story of the Black Panther Party and Huey P. Newton* (Random House, 1970).

wikipedia.org/wiki/Daughters of_Bilitis

lapride.org/pages/cswhistory

en.wikipedia.org/wiki/

en.wikipedia.org/wiki/UpStairs_Lounge_arson_attack

Albert, Marston. "Reflections After a Confrontation with the Gay Liberation Front." *Professional Psychology.* Vol 5(4), Nov 1974, 380–384. Abstract (PsycINFO Database Record (c) 2009 APA, all rights reserved).

Glenne McElhinney (Impact Stories).

In remembrance of three people who died while in police custody in 1969 and 1970 (and so many more whose memories have been lost in history):
Howard Efland, died Mar 7, 1969
Larry Turner, died Mar 8, 1970
Ginny Gallegos, died spring 1970

CHAPTER 11: GAY COMMUNITY, GAY SERVICES, GAY-CENTERED

Bucknell, Katherine (editor). *Christopher Isherwood: Liberation Diaries - Volume Three 1970–1983*, Chatto & Windus, London, 2012.

Clendinen, Dudley, and Adam Nagourney. *Out for Good: The Struggle to Build a Gay Rights Movement in America.* New York: Simon & Schuster, 2016.

Hansen, Joseph. *Troublemaker, A Dave Brandsetter novel.* Harper, 1975. p. 142.

Stein, Marc. *Encyclopedia of Lesbian, Gay, Bisexual, and Transgender History in America.* USA: Charles Scribner's Sons, 2004. pp. 259–260. ISBN 9780684312613

Cordova, Jeanne. *When We Were Outlaws: A Memoir of Love & Revolution.* Spinsters InkBooks. 2011. ISBN 9781935226512

Editorial. "Love Project." *Advocate.* Nov 10, 1971.

Sarff, Doug. "A Pattern for Progress." *Advocate.* Feb 13, 1974.

Thurman, Nita. "Gay leader discusses lifestyle." *Denton Record-Chronicle.* Oct 26, 1980.

Kepner, Jim. "Morris Kight Strikes Again." *Drummer.* Mar 1973.

Editorial. "The Center." *Edge.* Mar 5, 1997.

Editorial. "The Way We Were: Morris Kight." *Genre.* Jul 1994.

Stumbo, Bella. Letters section. *Los Angeles Times.* Oct 7, 1973. Regarding Kight's response to a *Times* series: Sep 16–20, 1973.

Ciotti, Paul. "Morris Kight: Activist Statesman of L.A.'s Gay Community." *Los Angeles Times,* Dec 9, 1988.

Wride, Nancy. "The Liberator." Profile of MK. *Los Angeles Times.* Jun 8, 1999.

Maxwell, Evan. "Police, Gay Leaders to Cooperate in Investigation." *Los Angeles Times.* Feb 1, 1975.

Shuit, Doug. "Bitter Fight Expected on Gay Teacher Issue." *Los Angeles Times.* Mar 25, 1975.

Editorial. "Sex: A Commonsense Standard." *Los Angeles Times.* Apr 30, 1975.

IMRU radio program (air date Aug 2, 1975) hosted by Gary Taylor regarding strike at Gay Center.

"Wild Out West: A Rough History of the Early Center," undated essay by Stuart Timmons, unpublished. (JP Personal Archives)

Whan, Del. "Gay Women's Service Center in L.A., 1971–1972." Notes from panel discussion at June Mazer Lesbian Archives, West Hollywood. 2008.

Freeman, Chris. "Christopher Isherwood Diaries." (Unpublished.) 2017.

Ocamb, Karen. Essay, "From Dream to Bedrock Beacon: A Short History of the L.A. Gay and Lesbian Center." Includes 1972 Center annual figures. Unpublished. (2016).

Kight, Morris. Interview by Paul D. Cain. Transcription. Los Angeles, Jun 6, 1994.

John D'Emilion: Oral Histories, Sep 22; Oct 2, 1976.

Dallmeyer, Bob. "Salute to the Pioneers of Gay Liberation Front 20th Anniversary." Audio File. Aired on KPFK *IMRU.* 1989. Cassette, Los Angeles, 2009.

Barney, Jeanne. Interviewed by Author. Phone. Apr 15, 2009. In person. On tape. West Hollywood, CA. Oct 9, 2009.

Bottini, Ivy. Interview by Author. In Person. Los Angeles. Jan 23, 2009.

Copilow, Barry. Interviewed by Author. Phone. Oct 14, 2010.

Cordova, Jeanne. Interviewed by Author. Phone. Feb 18, 2014.

DeCrescenzo, Terry. Interviewed by Author. Phone. Jul 30, 2010.

Dilkes, Ed. Interview by Author. Phone. Feb 9, 2012.

Embry, John. Interviewed by Author. Phone. Apr 15, 2009.

Epstein, David. Interview by Author. Phone. Oct 10, 2012.

Fifield, Lillene. Interview by Author. Phone. Oct 12, 2011.

Gollance, Richard. Interviewed by Author. Phone. Jul 3, 2010.

Green, Jaime. Interviewed by Author. Phone. Oct 4, 2004.

Laurence, Leo E., J.D. Interviewed by Author. Phone. Sep 10, 2010.

LeGrand, Terry. Interviewed by Author. Phone. Apr 20, 2009.

Little, Richard. Interview by Author. In person. Los Angeles, CA. Jun 6, 2012.

Mentley, Lee. Interviewed by Author. Phone. Nov 26, 2005.

Meyer, Mina. Interviewed by Author. Phone. Jan 27, 2009.

Perry, Troy D. Interview by Author. In person on tape. Los Angeles, Astro Diner. Mar 16, 2007.

Pearl, Ed. Interviewed by Author. Phone. Sep 15, 2009.

Platania, Jon. Interviewed by Author. Phone. Jan 26, 2010.

Rocco, Pat. Interviewed by Author. In person on tape. Los Angeles, Victor's Square. Aug 31, 2003.

Vezina, Gino. Interviewed by Author. Phone. Jan 12, Jan 13, Jan 22, 2009; Jun 10, 2010.

VonHamhorse Kaplan, Harry. Author. Phone. Jun 6, 2008.

Weathers, Carolyn. Interviewed by Author. Phone. Mar 13, 2005; Feb 12, 2006.

Weather, Carolyn. Interviewed by Author. In person on tape. Long Beach. Apr 9, 2005.

Yaroslavsky, Zev. Interview by Author. Phone. May 6, 2015.

Bradford, Fred. "Morris Kight." Email. Jul 14, 2005.

Effinger, John. "Morris Kight. Email. Oct 13, 14, 2009.

Platania, Jon. "Remembering Morris." Emails. Jan 30, 2010; Aug 22, 2010; Jun 26, 2015.

Stryker, Susan, PhD. "Angela Keyes Douglas." Email. Nov 15, 2007.

VonHamhorse Kaplan, Harry. "Morris." Email. Jun 4, 2008.

Weathers, Carolyn. "Morris_Brenda" Emails. Jan 28, 2009; Jan 29, 2009.

Whan, Del. "GLF." Emails. Jan 4, 2009; Jan 25, 2009; Jan 27, 2009; Jan 31, 2009; Jan 23, 2009; Jun 13, 2010.

Williams, Stanley. "Remembering Morris." Emails. Jan 28, 2010; Jan 30, 2010.

Whan, Del. "GLF." Email to Glenne McElhinney (Impact Stories) cc Author. May 8, 2008.

Foster Gunnison, Jr. Papers. Archives & Special Collections at the Thomas J. Dodd Research Center, University of Connecticut Library.

Harry Hay Papers. San Francisco Public Library. James C. Hormel LGBTQIA Center.

Harvey Milk Archives - Scott Smith Collection (GLC 35), Gay and Lesbian Center, San Francisco Public Library.

Morty Manford Papers, Manuscripts and Archives Division, The New York Public Library.

Morris Kight Papers and Photographs (Coll2010-008), ONE National Gay & Lesbian Archives, Los Angeles, California.

Randy Shilts Papers. San Francisco Public Library. James C. Hormel LGBTQIA Center.

CHAPTER 12: GAY-GENCIES

Clendinen, Dudley, and Adam Nagourney. *Out for Good: The Struggle to Build a Gay Rights Movement in America.* New York: Simon & Schuster, 2016.

Segal, Mark. *And Then I Danced: Traveling the Road to LGBT Equality.* OpenLens, 2015. ISBN-10: 1617753998

Wat, Eric C. *The Making of a Gay Asian Community.* Rowman & Littlefield Publishers, 2001. ISBN-10: 074251109X

Kepner, Jim. "Mort Sahl Stirs Gay Rage." *The Advocate.* Apr 23, 1975.

Timmons, Stuart. "Coors + Outfest = Outrage." *Frontiers.* Aug 22, 1997.

Hammond, Paul. "A Quarter Century of Liberation – Plus." *New York Native,* Feb 18, 1991.

"Sahl Show Stirs 'Gay' Protest.'" *Los Angeles Times.* Mar 25, 1975.

Bart, Everett. "Postscript: Alpine County Stays Serene and Straight; Mall Stands Tall; Freeway Reflections." *Los Angeles Times.* Apr 28, 1975.

"COORS." *The Advocate.* Liberation Publications, Inc. Nov 6, 2001.

Laird, Cynthia. "Coors donation stirs controversy." *Bay Area Reporter.* Jul 24, 1997.

Dallmeyer, Bob. "Being Alive." *Berkshire Sample.* Sep 13, 1987.

Solomon, Norman Solomon. "The Media's Favorite Think Tank; How the Heritage Foundation Turns Money into Media." *Extra!* Jul/Aug 1996.

Kearns, Michael. "Morris Kight Remembered." gaytoday.com, Feb 2003. www.gaytoday.com.

Holmberg, Timothy P. "An Open Letter to the Gay and Lesbian Times." *Gay and Lesbian Times Update.* Jul 1997.

"Center Accepts 5K from Coors Contribution." *Gay and Lesbian Times Update.* Aug 6, 1997.

"Gays Plan Rally to Back Job Bias Bill." *Los Angeles Times.* Dec 27, 1979.

Ciotti, Paul. "Morris Kight: Activist Statesman of L.A.'s Gay Community." *Los Angeles Times,* Dec 9, 1988.

Lisotta, Christopher. "Hail, Mary and why John Kerry has nothing to do with it." *LA Weekly.* Oct 22, 2004.

"Beer Chosen to Show Gay Buying Power." *Los Angeles Times.* Oct 31, 1970.

Goldsmith, Susan. "Beer Brawl." *New Times Los Angeles.* Jun 4, 1998.

Drew, Jim. "Coors wants end to boycott." *OutNOW!* Jul 11, 1995.

Hansen, Alison. "Former heir seeks faith over fortune." *OutNOW!* Nov 30, 1995.

Kingston, Tim. "Rocky Mountain Venom: Coors & Queers." *San Francisco Bay Times.* Part 1: Mar 24, 1994; Part 2: Apr 7, 1994.

UTLA Newsletter. Dec 18, 1998.

Public Access Video of WeHo City Council Meeting. Jun 1, 1998. MK Collection, ONE.

Kight, Morris. Interview by Paul D. Cain. Transcription. Los Angeles, Jun 6, 1994.

Bottini, Ivy. Interview by Paul D. Cain. Transcript. Los Angeles, Feb 1, 2005.

Bottini, Ivy. Interview by Author. In Person. Los Angeles. Jan 23, 2009.

Cordova, Jeanne. Interviewed by Author. Phone. Feb 18, 2014.

DeCrescenzo, Terry. Interviewed by Author. Phone. Jul 30, 2010.

Green, Jaime. Interviewed by Author. Phone. Oct 4, 2004.

Jackson, Miki. "LA Riots." Email. May 25, 2019.

Lachs, Steve. Interview by Author. Phone. Oct 15, 2010.

Rocco, Pat. Interviewed by Author. In person on tape. Los Angeles, Victor's Square. Aug 31, 2003.

Segal, Mark. Interview by Author. Phone. Jul 8, 2019.

Vezina, Gino. Interviewed by Author. Phone. Jan 12, Jan 13, Jan 22, 2009; Jun 10, 2010.

Yaroslavsky, Zev. Interview by Author. Phone. May 6, 2015.

Kilhefner, Don, PhD. "Coors Boycott – Now More Than Ever! A Call to Gay and Lesbian Conscience." Unpublished position paper for Boycott Distribution. Jul 4, 1997. ONE.

Morris Kight Papers and Photographs (Coll2010-008), ONE National Gay & Lesbian Archives, Los Angeles, California.

Morty Manford Papers, Manuscripts and Archives Division, The New York Public Library.

For more information:

AHF. (2019). *AHF. Cutting-Edge Medicine and Advocacy. AIDS Healthcare Foundation.* Online. Available at: www.aidshealth.org/

"Our History." Alliance for Housing and Healing, n.d. alliancehh.org/history/.

CHAPTER 13: DODDERING OLD MAN

Noxon, Christopher. "Gay center, founder wrangle over property." *Los Angeles Independent.* Sep 14, 1994. pp. 1, 3.

"53-year-old man found dead at club." *The Desert Sun.* Nov 9, 1996. A3.

"Coroner identifies body found at club." *The Desert Sun.* Nov 11, 1996. p. A3.

Haberman, Douglas and Jim Specht. "No clues revealed in activist's death." *The Desert Sun.* Nov 16, 1996, p. A1, A6.

Klein, Kenny. "AIDS figure died using inhalant." *The Desert Sun.* Jan 8, 1997. p. A1.

Anonymous #1. Interview by Author. Phone. Taped. Jul 26, 2008.

Bottini, Ivy. Interview by Author. In Person. Los Angeles. Jan 23, 2009.

Bottini, Ivy. Interview by Paul D. Cain. Transcript. Los Angeles, Feb 1, 2005.

Bradley, Ann. Interview by Author. Phone. Sep 14, 2007; Jun 3, 2008.

Dallmeyer, Bob. Interview by Author. Phone. Sep 5, 2008. In person. Los Angeles, Cat 'n Fiddle. Dec 3, 2008.

Frater, David Lee. Interview by Author. Phone. Sep 22, 2008.

Greene, Rose. Interview by Author. Phone. Jun 12, 2008.

Jackson, Miki. Interview by Author. Phone. Aug 8, 2008; In person. Los Angeles, Cat 'n Fiddle. Dec 3, 2008.

Jean, Lorri. Interview by Author. Phone. Feb 8, 2012.

Lam, Henry. Interview by Author. In person. Los Angeles, Charlie Chan Print Shop. Nov 1, 2008.

Little, Richard. Interview by Author. In Person. Los Angeles, Jun 6, 2012.

Perry, Reverend Troy D. Interview by Author. Los Angeles, Mar 16, 2006.

Vezina, Gino. Interview by Author. Phone. Jan 12, 13, 22, 2009, Jun 10, 2010.

Los Angeles Superior Court, public records.

Laglc.net Los Angeles Gay and Lesbian Center, Management Biographies. 2005.

"Real Estate, Apartments, Mortgages & Home Values." Zillow, n.d. www.zillow.com/.

Thank you:

Morris Kight Papers and Photographs (Coll2010-008), ONE National Gay & Lesbian Archives, Los Angeles, California.

Palm Springs Library.

CHAPTER 14 : THE VENERABLE

Adleman, Jeanne (et al.). *Lambda Gray: A Practical, Emotional, and Spiritual Guide for Gays and Lesbians.* North Hollywood, CA: Newcastle Publishing Company, Inc, 1993.

Hammond, Paul. "A Quarter Century of Liberation – Plus." *New York Native,* Feb 18, 1991.

Kearns, Michael. "Morris Kight Remembered." gaytoday.com, Feb 2003. www.gaytoday.com.

Mah, Roseanna. "Gay senior housing complex in the works." *Hollywood Independent,* Jul 21, 2005. Los Angeles.

Towarnicky, Carol. "Being Gay: The Second Generation." *Philadelphia Daily News,* Jul 1, 1987.

Wagner, Eugene. "LAMBDA GRAY reviewed." *Chiron Rising Magazine Review Issue.* Issue No. 67. Apr/May 1995.

"Locked Out, Left Behind, Lonely: When Does the Alienation Begin?" *NewsWest.* Jan 20–Feb 3, 1977.

Kight, Morris. Interviewed by Jack Nichols for *Gay Today.* 1997.

Kight, Morris. Interviewed by Paul D. Cain. Transcript. Los Angeles, Jun 6, 1994.

Sullivan, Tony and Richard Adams. Interview by Paul D. Cain. Transcription. Los Angeles, Nov 11, 2005.

Bottini, Ivy. Interview by Paul D. Cain. Transcript. Los Angeles, Feb 1, 2005.

Copilow, Barry. Interview by Author. Phone. Oct 14, 2010.

Dallmeyer, Bob. Interview by Author. Phone. Sep 5, 2008.

Jackson, Miki. Interview by Author. Phone. Aug 15, 2008.

Lachs, Steve. Interview by Author. Phone. Oct 15, 2010.

Perry, Troy D. Interview by Author. In person on tape. Los Angeles, Astro Diner. Mar 16, 2007.

Vezina, Gino. Interview by Author. Phone. Jan 12, 13, 22, 2009, Jun 10, 2010.

Yaroslavsky, Zev. Interview by Author. Phone. May 6, 2015.

Brass, Perry. "Morris Kight." Email. Aug 10, 2012.

Jackson, Miki. "What Morris said about Clyde Tolson and J. Edgar." Email. Nov. 9, 2011.

DeCrescenzo, Terry. *Notes on a conversation with Morris Kight 01/03/2003.* Los Angeles: Personal Note. Aug 7, 2010.

Grobson, Mitch. *Videotape of MK Memorial* (Feb 2003, Los Angeles: Personal Footage), VHS.

Acknowledgments

The following resource centers were essential to the research for this story:

- Albuquerque Public Library.
- The Albuquerque Museum.
- Archives & Special Collections at the Thomas J. Dodd Research Center, University of Connecticut Library.
- Center for Southwest Research, University of New Mexico General Library.
- Charles E. Young Research Library, University of California, Los Angeles.
- Collection of the Center for the Study of Political Graphics (CSPG).
- Gay and Lesbian Center, San Francisco Public Library.
- Manuscripts and Archives Division, The New York Public Library.
- ONE National Gay & Lesbian Archives, Los Angeles, California.
- San Francisco History Center, San Francisco Public Library.
- San Francisco Public Library. James C. Hormel LGBTQIA Center.
- 20th Century Organizational Files, Southern California Library for Social Studies and Research, Los Angeles, California.

Thank you to John Ferry, who introduced me to Morris Kight.

Many helped along the way:

- Angela Bailey (ALGA)
- Ryan Basilio
- Frederick Buccolini
- Joey Cain
- Robert Camino
- Jane Cantillon
- Dana Champion
- Margaret Chevian (Providence Public Library)
- Maureen Cotter
- Shamey Cramer
- Janet Cunningham
- Steve Finger (*Los Angeles Free Press*)
- Chris Freeman
- Craig Fries
- Phyllis Green
- Mary E. Holmes
- David Hunt
- Jonathan Ned Katz
- Michael Kearns
- Doreen Kovach
- Thomas Lannon (NYPL Manuscripts & Archives Division)
- Tina Mascara
- Steven J. McCarthy
- Glenne McElhinney
- James Moore (Albuquerque Museum)
- Peter M. Nardi
- Joy Novak (Center for the Study of Political Graphics)
- Karen Ocamb
- Michael Perri
- Linda Rapp, University of Michigan
- Al Regensberg (New Mexico State Archives)
- Robert Rickey
- Steven Reich
- Eric Seiferth (New Orleans Collection)
- Kenneth Silk
- Nicholas Snow
- Graham Stinnett (University of Connecticut)
- Susan Stryker, PhD (Vancouver, BC)
- Erika Suderburg (Somatography)
- Pat Thomas
- Suzanne Thompson
- Don Tinling (*Frontiers*)
- Jean Tretter
- Cate Uccel
- Melissa Watterworth-Batt (University of Connecticut)
- Carol Wells (Center for the Study of Political Graphics)
- Tim Wilson (SFPL)
- Thomas Wilsted (University of Connecticut)
- Melanie Yolles (NYPL Manuscripts and Archives Division)
- Roy Zucheran

A special thank you to Paul D. Cain for allowing me permission to use a two-day interview that he did with Morris in 1994. It proved to be a valuable resource. Also, for allowing me to use his interview with Ivy Bottini (2005) and Tony Sullivan and Richard Adams (2005).

MARY ANN CHERRY

A special acknowledgment of appreciation to:
Angela C. Chandler; Carol Kight-Fyfe; Cori MacNaughton; Stanlibeth Peters

Thank you to my patient and precise editors, you make me look well:
Diana Faust; Michael Kearns; Kari Pearson; Justin Tanner.

Special acknowledgment to the staff at ONE Archives:
Michael C. Oliveira; Loni Shibuyama; Bud Thomas.

Special gratitude to all my interviewees for your honesty, candor, and sometimes rancor. Each of you gave fresh perspective to the Morris Kight story:

Wallace Albertson
Jeanne Barney
Bill Beasley
Ivy Bottini
Malcolm Boyd
Fred Bradford
Ann Bradley
John Burnside
Rob Cole
Barry Copilow
Jeanne Cordova
Bob Dallmeyer
Terry DeCrescenzo
Ed Dilkes
Vic Dinnerstein
John Effinger
John Embry
Lillene Fifield
David Lee Frater
Billy Glover
Richard Gollance
Harold Gordon
Jaime Green
Rose Green
David Hunt
Miki Jackson
Lorri Jean
Harry Kaplan
Malcolm Kight
Carol Kight-Fyfe
Sheila Kuehl
Steve Lachs
Kight Lane
Leo Laurence
Terry LeGrand
Richard Little
Lee Mentley
Mina Meyer
Peter Nardi
Torie Osborn
Ed Pearl
Reverend Troy Perry
Stanlibeth Peters
Dr. Jon Platania
Sharon Raphael
Pat Rocco
Mark Segal
Bill Spaulding
Susan Stryker, PhD
Tom Swann
Mark Thompson
Andre Ting
Jean Tretter
Kay Tobin
Gino Vezina
Paul Waters
Carolyn Weathers
Michael Weinstein
Del Whan
Stanley Williams
James Windsor
Carol Wells
Zev Yaroslavsky

Thank you to Mitch Grobson for the generous use of his many videos of Morris. Thank you Stuart Timmons. Thank you to Miki Jackson for many things.

The photographer's contributions are crucial to this story. Thank you for your generosity and accessibility and for showing up with a camera:

Walt Blumoff
Harold Fairbanks
George Lear
Sydney Lee
Lee Mason
Richard Meade
Karen Ocamb
Stathis Orphanos
Pat Rocco
Don Saban
Stephen Stewart
William S. Tom
Henning von Berg
Jason Wittman

Thank you Don Bachardy.

A personal note of gratitude to:
Patrick and Kathleen Cherry; all my teachers; Jimmy Drinkovich; Ruth Drinkovich; Tony Lawless; Fr. Richard Russell; Arnie, Buzz, Tio, and Mike.

Index

F

G

H

I

J

K

L

M

N

O

P

R

S

T

U

V

W

Y

Z

Author MARY ANN CHERRY befriended Morris Kight during the last decade of his life. With Morris' permission, she began writing his biography. Cherry is a Los Angeles-based writer whose wide-ranging work includes television and film producing as well as creating and maintaining the historical archives for the AIDS Healthcare Foundation.